ScienceQuest
Junior Certificate Science

Randal Henly – Sinéad McNamara – Michael O'Callaghan

The Educational Company

The Educational Company of Ireland
Ballymount Road
Walkinstown
Dublin 12

A Trading Unit of Smurfit Services Limited

© Randal Henly   Sinéad McNamara   Michael O'Callaghan

Editor: Warren Yeates
Jacket Design: Andréa Sperle
Design: Andréa Sperle, Leonie Grehan
Book Layout : Natquest – Brenda Barrett, Enda Caulfield
Cartoon Illustrations: Rodger Horgan
Artwork: Daghda, Corel Corporation
Colour Separations: Impress Communications
Printed in the Republic of Ireland by Smurfit Print

0 1 2 3 4 5 6 7 8 9

ASC5201S

Acknowledgements
Acknowledgement is made to the following for supplying photographs, for permission to reproduce copyright photographs, or for allowing photographs to be taken on their premises. We would also like to acknowledge the help of Tommy Darcy of Fuji Centre, Artane Castle Shopping Centre, who spent many hours perfecting prints for reproduction.

Adelaide Hospital
Aer Lingus
ESB
Irish Times
Marie Leahy
National Concert Hall
National Museum
Oxford Scientific Films
Permutit Ltd
Rialto Garage
Science Photo Library
The Science Museum
The Slide File
Superquinn
Trinity College, Dublin
Trocaire
UKAEA
UNESCO

Other photographs in the book are by Dallas Camier and Randal Henly

Approved Quality System

The paper used in this book comes from Managed Forests in Northern Europe For every tree felled, at least one new tree is planted

FOREWORD

ScienceQuest is a textbook of science for the Junior Certificate syllabus. In writing this book, one of the main objectives has been to relate the syllabus material to everyday life. Many photographs of domestic and industrial applications of the scientific principles involved have been used in order to make the book relevant, interesting and readable. A style has been chosen and the reading age has been kept low in order to make the text suitable for the full ability range of those who will use it. Material which is necessary only for those doing the higher level course is marked by a grey bar alongside the text.

In order to cater for the different abilities of pupils and different styles of teaching, there is a large selection of questions. The questions are varied in order to develop pupils' skill in answering. At the end of each chapter, two main types of question are set: (i) multiple completion paragraphs, which the pupils have to rewrite and fill in the blanks; these correspond to the 'quickie' questions that appear on Junior Certificate examination papers, and when completed and corrected, should make useful revision material; (ii) questions involving longer written answers, for example, explanations about how things work and descriptions of experiments. Questions also appear within most of the chapters, relevant to the topic just described. To reinforce the various numerical topics in physics, there are plenty of calculation-type problems.

A certain amount of subject matter – terminology, laws and principles – has to be learned by heart in order to make progress in understanding. Such material is highlighted in 'boxes' in the text. Each of the chapters ends with a summary, highlighting the key aspects of that chapter. A glossary of scientific words appears at the end of the book.

About 150 experiments are presented, in an easy-to-follow format. Some of these are quick investigations, while others are more lengthy, requiring time, measurements and calculations. While all experiments are labelled as experiments, a number of them, for a variety of reasons, will have to be done as teacher demonstrations. Most of the experiments require only standard school-laboratory apparatus which should be readily available.

The order in which the chapters are arranged within each of the three main sections (Physics, Chemistry, Biology) is a suitable teaching order, which is tested and favoured by the authors. There are, of course, other possible and suitable orders.

In the Applied Science section (chapters 41 to 48), the six topics are Earth Science, Horticulture, Materials Science, Food, Electronics and Energy Conversions. All higher level exam candidates, and ordinary level candidates taking applied science, are required to study two of these units.

We are indebted to many people for help given in producing this book, especially: Frank Roden, Pauline Fay, Brian Smyth, Barry Kearns, Jonathan Shackleton, who read draft chapters and made many constructive suggestions, Anthony Murray, Senior Editor of The Educational Company of Ireland with whom it has been a pleasure to work, and those who supplied photographs, gave permission to reproduce copyright photographs and who allowed photographs to be taken on their premises. We would especially like to put on record the work of the book's editor, Warren Yeates of Bookworks, whose dedication and meticulousness has resulted in what we hope will be a practical and useful textbook.

The Teachers' Guide and Resource Book, published separately, consists of the following:

(i) lists of recommended apparatus and chemicals needed for the course,

(ii) details of how to prepare all of the reagents needed,

(iii) lists of the equipment and chemicals needed for each of the 150 experiments long with, in many cases, helpful hints for carrying out the experiments,

(iv) teaching hints for many of the course topics and answers to the numerical problems in relevant chapters,

(v) instruction sheets for many of the more-involved experiments; these give detailed practical instructions and include spaces for results and for answers to questions. Copyright is waived on these sheets so that teachers can make photocopies in bulk as required.

Randal Henly
Sinéad McNamara
Michael O'Callaghan

CONTENTS

Physics

1. Introducing Science 1
2. Measuring 7
3. Energy 15
4. Force, Weight and Gravity 23
5. Heat Travel 29
6. Magnetism 38
7. Density 42
8. Levers and Centre of Gravity 46
9. Electric Circuits and Electric Charges 53
10. Effects of Heat 63
11. Work, Motion, Energy 71
12. Pressure 77
13. Effects of Electric Current 87
14. Electricity in the Home 93
15. Light 101
16. Sound and Waves 109

Chemistry

17. Matter or Substances 117
18. Mixtures and Solutions 129
19. Chemical Reactions 136
20. The Air and Oxygen 140
21. Fuels and Fire 148
22. Water 152
23. Atomic Structure and the Periodic Table 159
24. Acids, Alkalis and Salts 168
25. Chemical Bonding 177
26. Hardness in Water 184
27. Metals 188
28. Chemistry and Electricity 194

Biology

29.	Introduction to Biology: Animals and Plants	199
30.	Cells, Tissues, Organs and Systems	207
31.	Nutrition and Digestion	212
32.	Breathing and Respiration	219
33.	Transport, Circulation and Excretion	226
34.	Support, Movement and Sensitivity	234
35.	Human Reproduction and Inheritance	241
36.	Photosynthesis and Transport in Plants	248
37.	Plant Responses	255
38.	Plant Reproduction	258
39.	Ecology 1	263
40.	Ecology 2	277

Applied science extensions

41.	Earth Science 1: Astronomy	285
42.	Earth Science 2: The Atmosphere	292
43.	Horticulture 1	300
44.	Horticulture 2	306
45.	Materials	318
46.	Food Types, Food Processing, Food Preservation	327
47.	Electronics	341
48.	Energy Conversions	348

Glossary . . . 354
Index . . . 360

1
INTRODUCING SCIENCE

(a) A silicon wafer on which is printed 160 computer 'chips', each containing thousands of electronic components

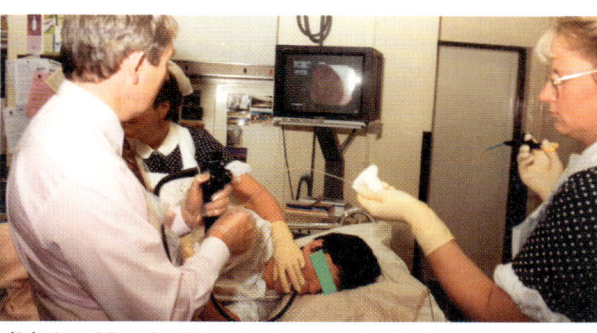

(b) Looking inside the human body by means of optic fibres.

(c) A radio telescope which can 'see' far into space.

(d) A picture of 'Earthrise', taken from the moon

(e) A firefighter's suit being tested.

(f) 'Handling' radioactive liquids by remote control from behind thick safety glass.

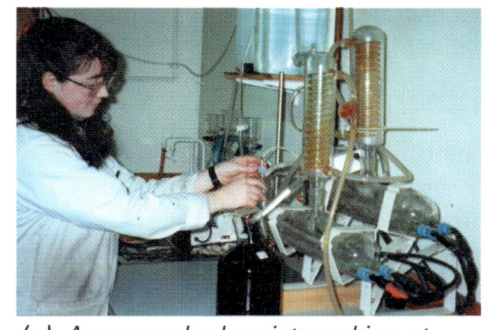

(g) A research chemist working at apparatus for chromatography.

fig. 1.1 Science at work

What is science all about and what does a scientist do? To answer these questions fully in a few lines would be difficult, but a short answer is that science is all about finding out how and why things happen. Figure 1.1 should give you an idea of some of the things that science has done for the modern world.

Some scientists set out to solve certain problems and therefore have definite aims; others spend their time searching for explanations about natural occurrences and do not know in advance what they are going to discover. Astronomers discover new stars, engineers design things such as spacecraft, or spare parts for the human body, chemists invent new drugs and medicines, doctors cure diseases, physicists find new sources of energy, and geologists find new minerals.

The history of science has many examples of important discoveries and inventions being made unexpectedly or by accident. For example, the familiar plastic polythene (which is used for supermarket bags) was discovered when an experiment went wrong and a white waxy solid was found in a container which should have just contained a gas. The electric motor was invented when an electric generator was wired up incorrectly at an exhibition in Vienna in the last century. The antibiotic penicillin, a chemical which has saved many lives, was also an accidental discovery.

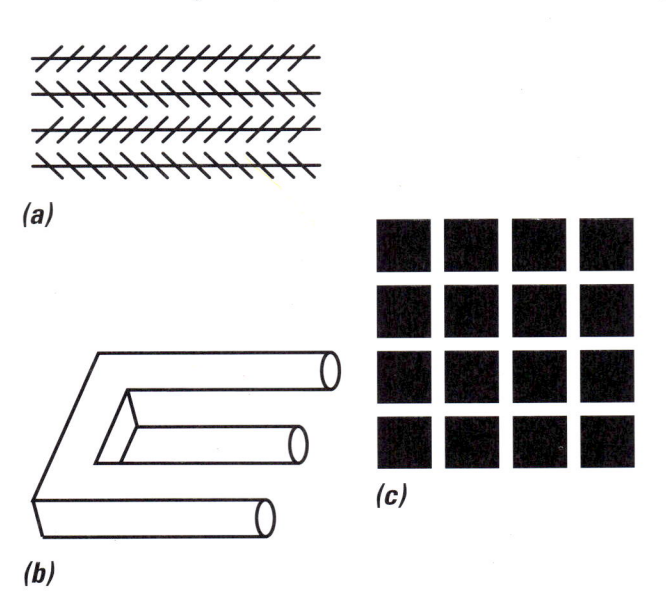

fig. 1.2 *You cannot always believe your eyes. They can deceive you. Scientists therefore do experiments to find out facts. Are the lines in (a) parallel? How many prongs has (b)? Are there really shadows at the corners of the squares in (c)?*

BRANCHES OF SCIENCE

There are many different branches of science, each dealing with the study of a different aspect of the subject. The three main branches are **biology**, **chemistry** and **physics**. **Biology** is the study of living things; that part of it which deals with plants is called **botany** and the study of animals is called **zoology**. **Chemistry** is about what substances and materials are made of and what changes they can undergo. **Physics** is the study of energy in all its different forms such as heat, light and electricity.

Other branches of science such as **geography** are about the Earth and its peoples and climate, and **geology** is to do with rocks and the Earth's crust. **Astronomy** deals with heavenly bodies such as stars and planets, while **mathematics** is the study of magnitude and numbers and their relationships. And the list could continue . . . . . .

Before you can study any of the advanced sciences, you have to acquire a basic knowledge of some biology, chemistry and physics, and this is what your course in Junior Certificate science is all about.

LABORATORY EQUIPMENT

A laboratory is a scientist's workshop, and is equipped with many specialised tools. Figure 1.5 shows many of the tools (pieces of 'apparatus') used in a simple laboratory such as your school laboratory. You have to learn the names of these pieces of apparatus and know what each looks like, and what it is used for.

DRAWING AND LABELLING DIAGRAMS

When drawing diagrams of apparatus, do not draw them 'in perspective' (this means as they look in reality), but draw simple line diagrams in cross section. For example, a tripod with a gauze and beaker on it looks like this in reality:

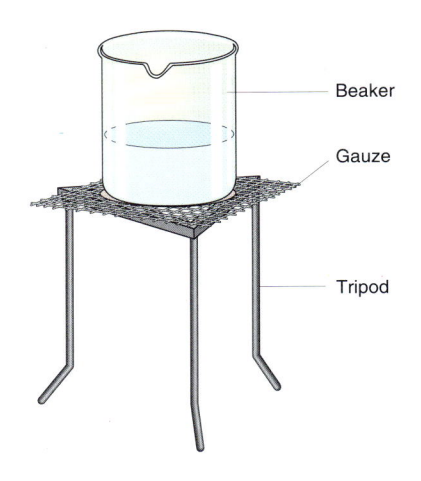

fig. 1.3 *Perspective view*

But when drawing them, always do so like this:

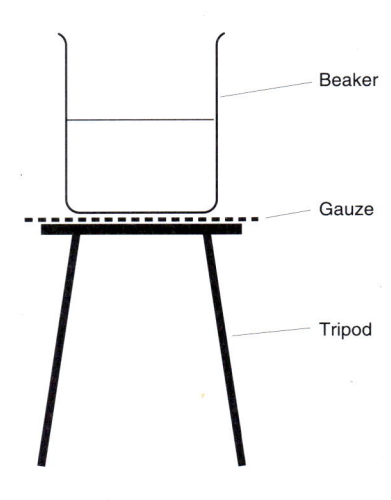

fig. 1.4 *Cross-section drawing*

Physics • 1

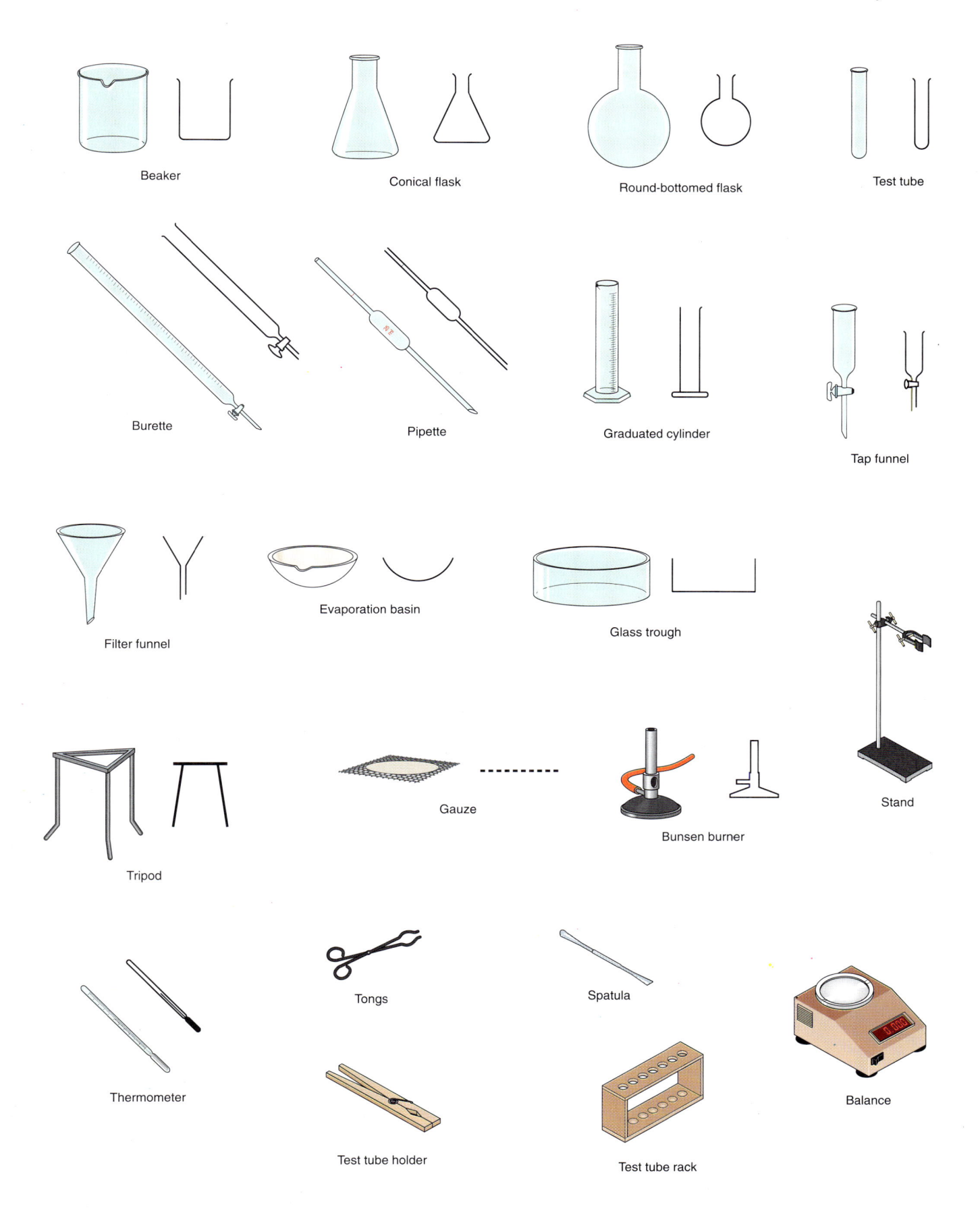

Beaker	Conical flask	Round-bottomed flask	Test tube
Burette	Pipette	Graduated cylinder	Tap funnel
Filter funnel	Evaporation basin	Glass trough	
Tripod	Gauze	Bunsen burner	Stand
Thermometer	Tongs / Test tube holder	Spatula / Test tube rack	Balance

fig. 1.5 Laboratory equipment

SAFETY AND LABORATORY RULES

A laboratory can be a dangerous place if common sense is not used and care is not taken when doing experiments. Study Figure 1.6 and see if you can pick out any situations which could lead to accidents.

In order to prevent accidents, there are rules which must be obeyed in laboratories. Your own school laboratory probably has its rules on a notice board in the room, but a typical set of sensible rules is given inside the front cover of this book.

THE BUNSEN BURNER

One of the most useful pieces of equipment which is to be found in practically every laboratory is the bunsen burner. This is a gas burner which has an adjustable air supply. By means of a 'collar' on the burner, the amount of air entering it can be controlled. The amount of air which is let in controls the type of flame and how hot the flame is. A flame which gives out light is described as **luminous** and one which doesn't is **non-luminous**.

fig. 1.6 *A badly run laboratory*

Experiment 1.1
The bunsen burner

The diagram shows the main parts of a bunsen burner.

1. Turn the collar of the bunsen. What does this do to the air hole?
2. Connect the bunsen to the gas tap. Close the air hole fully. Put on your safety glasses. Strike a match, turn on the gas supply fully and light the bunsen.
3. Observe the flame. Turn the collar to half open the air hole. How does the flame change? Now fully open the air hole. What happens to the flame?
4. In each case, describe the flame and make a drawing of its appearance.
5. You can test the hotness of each flame by using a nichrome wire. This type of wire glows red, orange, or white, according to how hot the flame is. Take a piece of nichrome wire and hold it by its glass handle or in a pair of tongs.
6. Place the wire in the flame with the air hole first fully closed, then half open, and finally fully open.
7. (a) Which flame is least hot? (b) Which flame is hottest? (c) Which part of the hottest flame is the hottest?

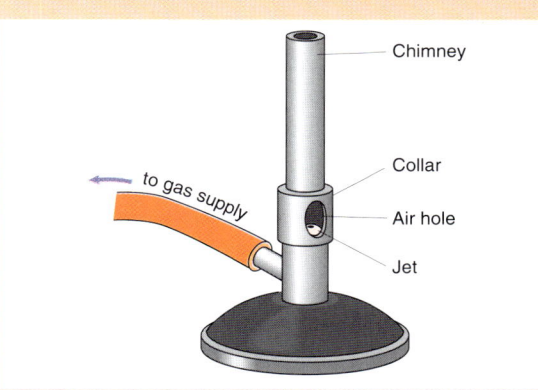

fig. 1.7

8. Make an accurate drawing of the hottest flame, marking the hottest part.
9. In this last part of the experiment, you will find out that one type of flame is clean and another is dirty. Using a pair of tongs, hold a piece of white porcelain at the top of a yellow flame for about half a minute. Then examine it carefully. What has happened to it?
10. Now put the piece of porcelain in a blue flame. What happens?

fig. 1.8

The bunsen burner is named after its inventor, Robert Bunsen (1811–1899), who was a very famous chemist, and also a professor of chemistry at Heidelberg University in Germany. While he was there, he also invented a new type of battery, a filter pump, and many other pieces of scientific apparatus.

QUESTIONS

Q. 1.1

This question is all about the bunsen burner.

(a) How do you control the hotness of the flame?
(b) How do you set the air hole to give a yellow coloured flame?
(c) How do you set the air hole to give a noisy blue flame?
(d) How do you set the air hole to give a quiet blue flame?
(e) How do you set the air hole to give a very hot flame?
(f) What is the effect on the flame of turning down the gas supply at the gas tap?
(g) Which flame is a dirty flame?
(h) How do you think the bunsen should be left if it is not being used for a few minutes? Explain why.

Q. 1.2
Name three branches of science and say what each one is the study of.

Q. 1.3
Draw a diagram of a tripod with a gauze on top of it and a conical flask on the gauze. Indicate some liquid in the flask. Then draw a bunsen burner underneath the tripod. Label the four items in your diagram.

Q. 1.4
Identify each of the pieces of laboratory equipment in Figure 1.9 and say what each is used for.

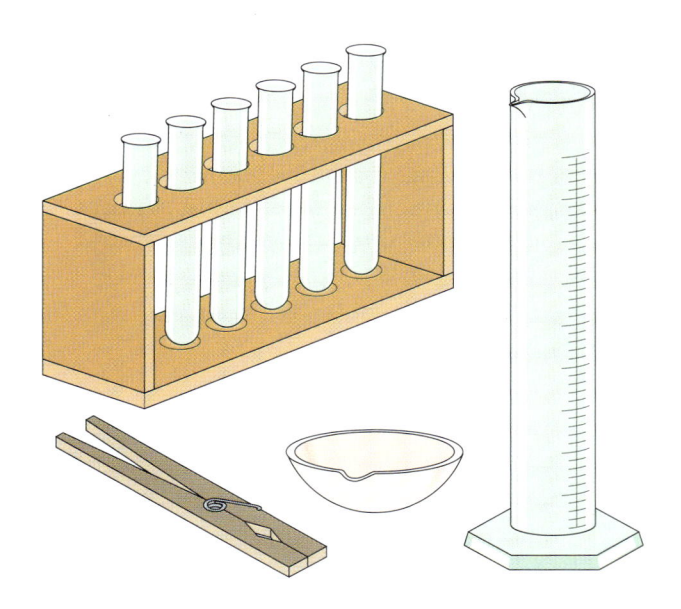

fig. 1.9

Q. 1.5
Why do you think each of the following is recommended when doing experiments in a laboratory?

(a) tying back long hair
(b) wearing eye protection
(c) following the instructions accurately
(d) washing your hands afterwards

Q. 1.6
Why do you think each of the following should not be done in a laboratory?

(a) trying out your own experiments
(b) tasting laboratory chemicals
(c) throwing a book or a piece of apparatus to a friend
(d) eating your lunch

Q. 1.7
Name the branch of science that is the study of each of the following:

(a) energy
(b) animals
(c) stars and planets
(d) rocks
(e) what substances are made of
(f) numbers
(g) the people and places on Earth
(h) living things
(i) heat, light and electricity
(j) plants

Q. 1.8
Name a piece of laboratory equipment that could be used for each of the following:

(a) holding a liquid
(b) heating a liquid
(c) measuring volume
(d) holding test tubes
(e) holding a hot object
(f) pouring a liquid into a bottle
(g) supporting a beaker over a bunsen
(h) measuring temperature

2 MEASURING

fig. 2.1 *The importance of measuring is shown in this picture of the flight deck of an aircraft. The various dials show the aircraft's altitude (height above sea level), direction, speed, engine performance, amount of fuel and many other pieces of information needed by the pilots in order to fly the aircraft.*

In daily life, people have to measure things, and even thousands of years ago, people were measuring things. Noah's Ark, as described in the bible (Genesis, Ch. 6), was 300 cubits long, 50 cubits wide and 30 cubits high. A cubit was the distance between the elbow and the tip of the middle finger with the arm outstretched.

Measurements are of great importance to scientists, as well as to everyone else. When you are cooking, you must measure out the various ingredients. Some are weighed on a scales and others are measured, by volume, in a measuring jug. When wallpapering a room or laying carpet, you need to know the measurements of the room. When travelling, you want to know the distances between places, and when buying and selling goods, you need to know the quantities of those goods.

There are many instruments for measuring. Some are very simple, like a measuring tape or the scales in your home, while others are more complicated, like those on the dashboard of a car – the speedometer, the fuel, oil pressure and temperature gauges. In the aircraft flight deck shown in Figure 2.1 there are a great many more, so that the pilot can take off, navigate, and land safely.

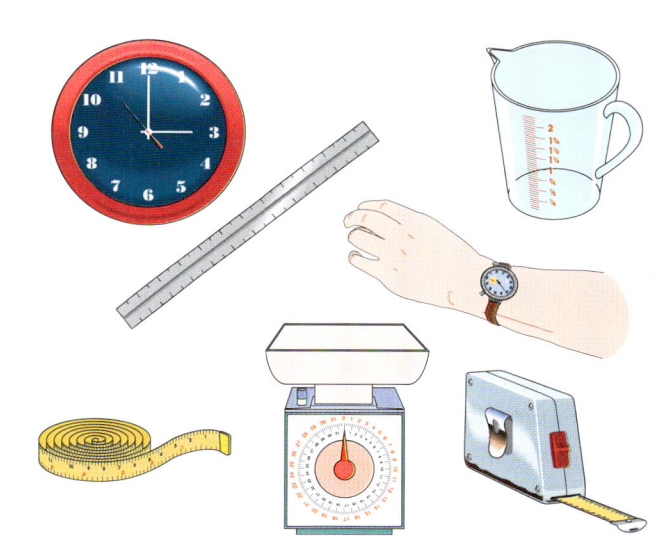

fig. 2.2 *Some common measuring instruments*

In order to measure accurately, there must be a set of definite units. The metre is the standard unit of length. You will see many 'metre sticks' in your school laboratory. For smaller measurements, the metre is divided into centimetres (1 cm = $1/100$ metre) and millimetres (1 mm = $1/1000$ metre), and for measuring large distances, the kilometre is used (1 km = 1000 metres).

These *prefixes* (milli-, kilo-, etc.) as they are called, always have the same meaning. **Centi** always means 1/100, **milli** always means 1/1000 and **kilo** always means one thousand times. You will meet these prefixes again with other units.

MEASURING LENGTH

It is reasonably easy to measure the length of a straight line such as the length of a room – you just use a metre stick or a measuring tape. Measuring the diameter of something circular is also quite easy, if you know how. Shown below are two methods for finding the diameter of a table tennis ball. To use the callipers, you adjust the size of the gap so that the ball will just fit into it. Then, without altering it, hold a ruler beside the gap and measure the distance across it.

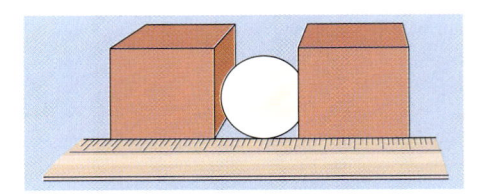

fig. 2.3 (a) Measuring the diameter of a table tennis ball

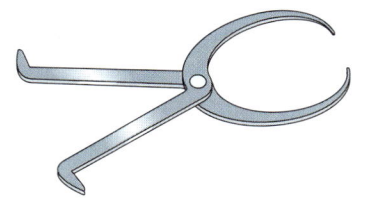

fig. 2.3 (b) Callipers

MEASURING CURVED LINES

There are two ways of measuring the length of curved lines. The simplest method is to use a piece of thread. A knot is tied at one end of the thread and this knot is placed at one end of the line to be measured. The thread is placed along the line and it is marked where it reaches the other end of the line. It is then stretched out along a metre stick and the length read.

The other way to measure curved lines is to use an instrument called an **opisometer**. This consists of a wheel on a screwed axle, with a handle attached. When the wheel is wheeled along the line, it also travels sideways along the axle. To use it, the wheel is started at one end of the line, and wheeled along the line until the other end of the line is reached. Then, starting at the zero mark of a metre stick, the wheel is wheeled backwards along the metre stick until the wheel reaches the start of the screwed axle. The distance travelled on the metre stick equals the length of the curved line, which is then read on the stick.

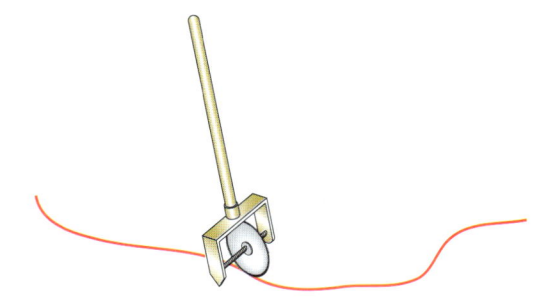

fig. 2.4 An opisometer

fig. 2.5 A **trundle wheel** is really a giant opisometer and is used for measuring distances along curved paths such as footpaths

Experiment 2.1
Measuring length

Measure each of the following and make a list of all your measurements. Be sure to give the unit for each measurement. Measure the diameter (part (f)) of the circular object by each of the two methods described above.

(a) the length of the laboratory (use a metre stick)
(b) the length and width of this textbook
(c) the height of the laboratory benches
(d) the length of your pencil or pen
(e) your own height (you will need a friend's help to do this)
(f) the diameter of something circular (e.g. a table tennis ball, a test tube, a beaker)

Experiment 2.2
Measuring curved lines

1. Using a pencil, draw a long curved line on a page of your science notebook. Do not make any part of the curve too sharp.
2. Mark a definite beginning and end to the line.
3. Now measure this line using both thread and an opisometer.
4. On the page, write in your measurement found by each method. If your two measurements are the same (or very close to each other) your work is accurate.

MEASURING AREAS

Area is a measure of the amount of surface on something. The area of a regular figure (shape) such as a rugby pitch, a laboratory bench or the cover of this book is easily found – by multiplying its length by its width. Area can be expressed in metres squared (m^2) or centimetres squared (cm^2).

QUESTIONS

Q. 2.1
Measure the length and the width of this textbook, and then calculate the area of its cover.

Q. 2.2
Measure the area of the laboratory bench or desk at which you are working.

Measuring areas of irregular figures

The easiest way to make this sort of measurement is to trace the outline of the irregular figure on to squared paper such as the graph paper in your science notebook, and then to count the number of squares inside the outline. Most science notebooks have their graph pages marked in centimetres which are further divided into either 5 divisions (0.2 cm or 2 mm each) or 10 divisions (0.1 cm or 1 mm).

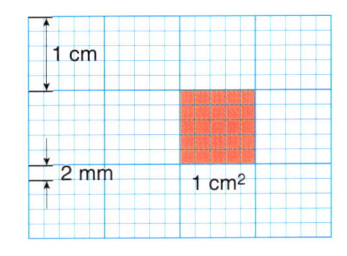

fig. 2.6 (a) One cm^2

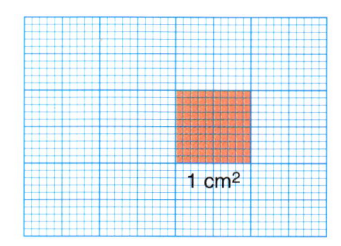

(b) One cm^2

Experiment 2.3
To measure the area of an irregular-shaped figure

1. Draw the outline of something irregular such as your hand (with closed fingers) on to one of the squared pages in your notebook.
2. Draw a line across the position of your wrist to show where your hand starts.
3. Count the number of complete centimetre squares inside the outline you have drawn. For the small squares that are cut by the outline, count them if half or more is included by the line, but ignore them if less than half falls inside the outline.
4. Work out how many small squares on your graph paper equal one complete centimetre squared and then add the two to get the total area. Be sure to give the units in which the area has been measured.

MEASURING VOLUME

The volume of an object is the amount of space which it occupies.

The standard unit of volume is the metre cubed (m^3), but this is so large that for most practical purposes the centimetre cubed (cm^3) is usually used.

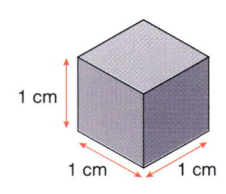

fig. 2.7 One cm^3

The litre is a larger unit of volume than the cm³ and is equal to 1000 cm³. The litre is the volume unit used for many purposes in everyday life. A millilitre (milli = $^1/_{1000}$) is one thousandth of a litre and is thus the same as a centimetre cubed.

$$1 \text{ cm}^3 = 1 \text{ mL}$$

Measuring volumes of regular-shaped objects

The volume of a rectangular solid is calculated by multiplying together the solid's length, width and height. Measure these three values for a regular shaped wooden block and then multiply the values together to obtain its volume.

fig. 2.9 (a) *Reading a graduated cylinder*

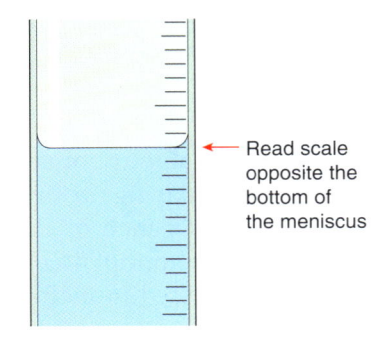

fig. 2.9 (b)

Beakers and flasks usually have volume measurements marked on them, but these are only approximate and cannot be used for accurate measurements.

You will notice that when you have water in a cylinder, its surface is not flat, but rises up slightly at the sides. This curved surface is called the **meniscus**, and the measurement reading should be made at the bottom of the meniscus.

Two other vessels for measuring volumes of liquids accurately are the pipette and the burette. These are not designed to hold a particular volume, but to measure out a particular volume into a flask or beaker.

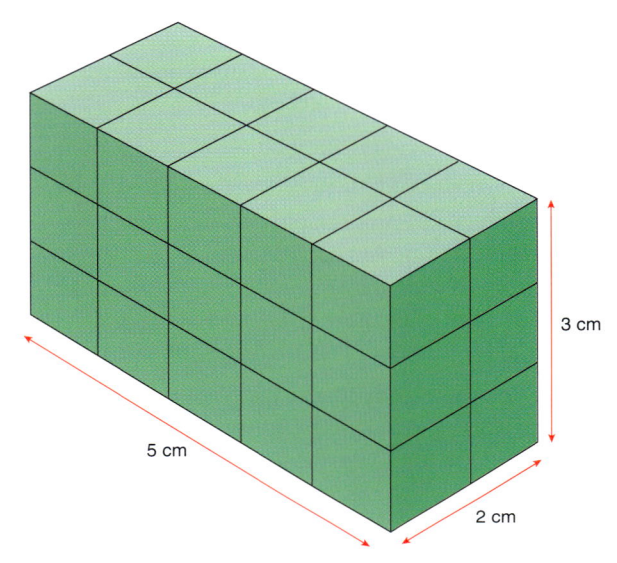

fig. 2.8

QUESTIONS

Q. 2.3
What is the volume of the pile of blocks shown above?

Measuring volumes of liquids

The volume of a liquid cannot be measured by multiplying its length, width and height since a liquid does not have a definite shape. The simplest way to measure liquid volume is to use a measuring or graduated cylinder. As its name suggests, it is a cylinder which is marked or graduated – usually in cm³ or millilitres (mL). When reading the volume of a liquid in a cylinder, the cylinder must be upright and read at eye level – to avoid what is called a parallax error. This is the error that arises from not looking 'straight on' at it.

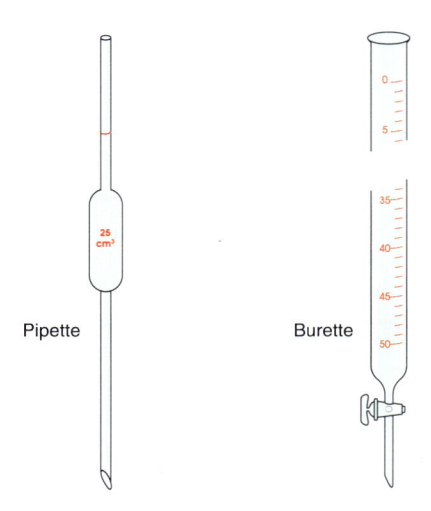

fig. 2.10 *Pipette (left) and burette*

Experiment 2.4
To measure the volume of a test tube

1. Fill a test tube with water and pour the water into a graduated cylinder.
2. Notice the meniscus on the top of the liquid in the cylinder.
3. Read the scale of the cylinder opposite the bottom of the meniscus. This is the volume of the water that was in the test tube.

Measuring volumes of irregular-shaped solids

The volume of an irregular-shaped object can be found in two ways:

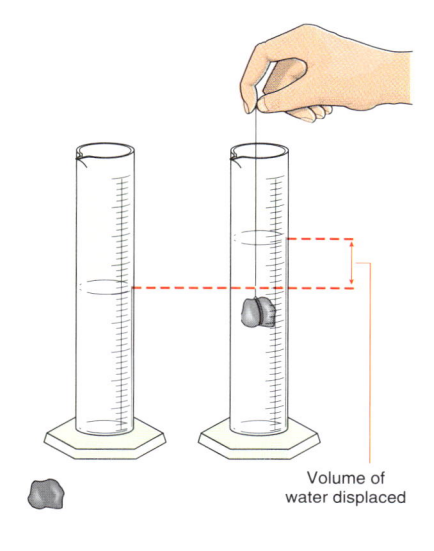

fig. 2.11 (i) By using a graduated cylinder. The amount by which the volume increases when the object is lowered into the cylinder is the volume of that object.

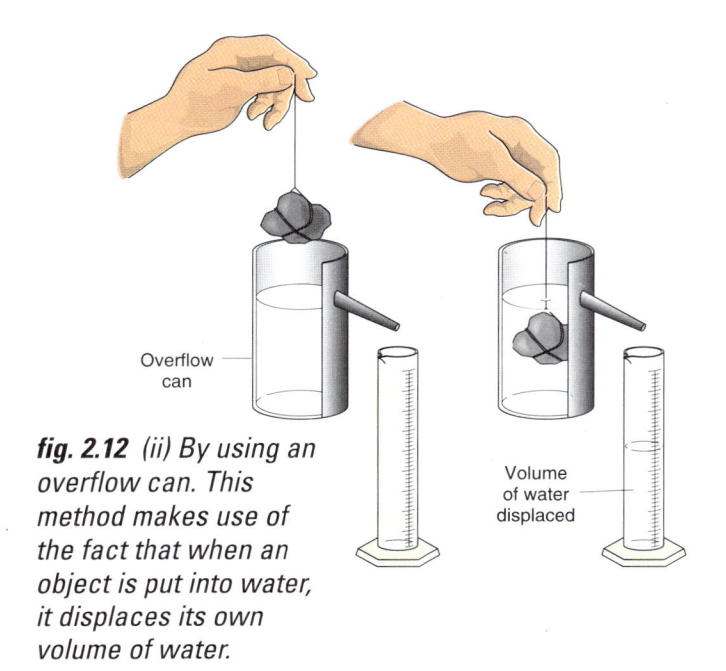

Volume of water displaced

fig. 2.12 (ii) By using an overflow can. This method makes use of the fact that when an object is put into water, it displaces its own volume of water.

Overflow can

Volume of water displaced

Experiment 2.5
To measure the volume of a stone

Method 1:
Using a graduated cylinder

1. Put enough water into the graduated cylinder so that when the stone is put in it will be covered.
2. Read the volume of the water in the cylinder.
3. Gently lower the stone into the cylinder, and again read the volume in the cylinder.
4. Subtract the first value from the second to find the volume of the stone.

Method 2:
Using an overflow can

1. Fill the can with water and wait until the water stops dripping from the spout of the can.
2. Place an empty graduated cylinder under the spout and then gently lower the object to be measured into the can.
3. The stone displaces its own volume of water into the graduated cylinder, which is read when the spout has stopped dripping.

If the object floats, it should be pushed beneath the surface of the liquid with a pin or needle.

MEASURING TEMPERATURE

You are probably familiar with the word *temperature* and with a *thermometer* which is used to measure temperature. **Temperature is a measure of how hot or how cold something is**. In your home a thermometer is used to measure the temperature of the oven, or the freezer, or to measure your own temperature if you are sick. When you hear the temperature for the following day announced on the weather forecast, you can tell whether the day will be hot or cold.

The temperature scale which is most commonly used is the **Celsius scale**, named after the Swedish astronomer who first proposed it in the eighteenth century. On this scale, the freezing point of pure water is zero degrees (written 0°C) and the boiling point of pure water is 100°C. Temperature is important in many laboratory experiments and you must learn to read a temperature scale accurately.

2 • Measuring

QUESTIONS

Q. 2.4
What are the values of the temperatures at points L, M, N and O?

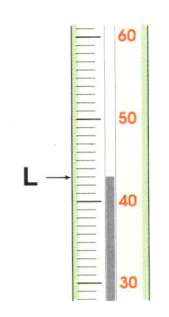

fig. 2.13

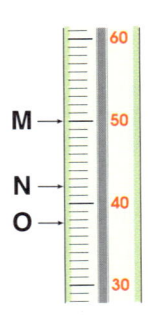

Experiment 2.6
Measuring temperature

In this experiment, you are going to use a thermometer to measure a number of different temperatures. A thermometer is a delicate and expensive piece of apparatus. When it is not being used, lay it carefully near the back of the bench so that it cannot roll or fall off. Never cool down a hot thermometer by putting it in cold water.

1. Figure 2.14 shows you what to do. Measure the temperature of: (a) the air inside the laboratory, and (b) the air outside the building. Make a note of your measurements.

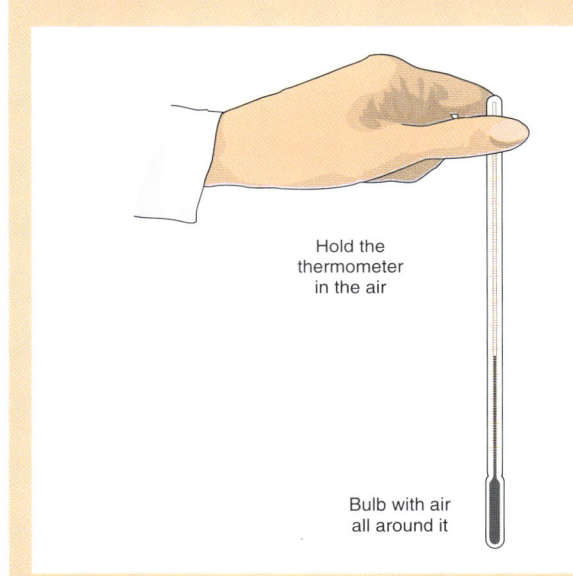

fig. 2.14

2. Measure the temperature of the water from the cold tap. Do this by putting some tap water into a beaker and measuring it there.

3. Place the beaker of water on a tripod and gauze. Put on your safety glasses. Light the bunsen burner (remember the rules). Place it underneath the tripod and let the water boil. When it is boiling, measure its temperature. Turn off the bunsen and leave the beaker of water to cool.

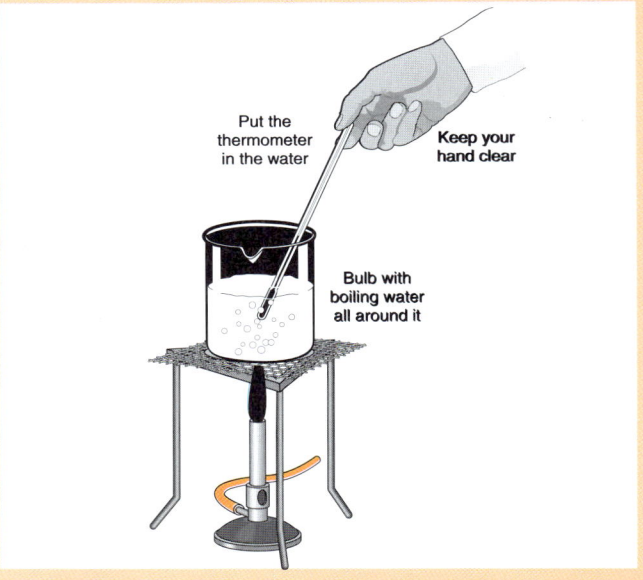

fig. 2.15

4. Half fill a beaker with water from the hot tap and measure its temperature.

5. Measure the temperature of your hand. Figure 2.16 shows you how to do this

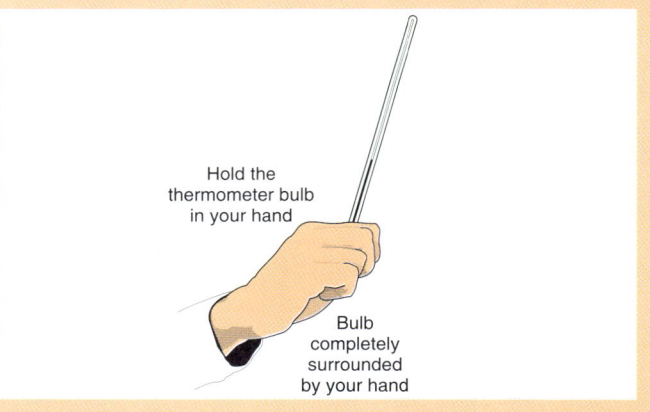

fig. 2.16

6. Measure the temperature inside a beaker containing ice cubes.

SUMMARY

- The unit of **length** is the **metre**; it is divided into 100 cm or 1000 millimetres. The length of curved lines can be measured using either thread or an opisometer. The area of a regular-shaped figure is found by multiplying its length by its breadth (width). The **area** of an irregular-shaped figure is found by tracing its outline on to squared paper and counting the squares inside the outline. Small areas are best expressed in cm^2.

- **Volume** is the amount of space taken up by something and is measured in litres or cm^3. 1 litre = 1000 cm^3 = 1000 mL. The volume of a liquid can be found using a graduated cylinder. The volume of an irregular-shaped solid can be found using either a graduated cylinder directly or an overflow can with a graduated cylinder.

- **Temperature** is a measure of the 'hotness' of something. It is measured with a thermometer and is expressed in degrees Celsius (°C).

QUESTIONS

Q. 2.5
Rewrite and complete the following sentences:

(a) 1 m = ____ cm
(b) 1 cm = ____ mm
(c) 1 m = ____ mm
(d) 1 L = ____ cm^3
(e) 1 L = ____ mL
(f) 1 km = ____ m
(g) 1 h = ____ min
(h) 1 h = ____ sec
(i) 1 kg = ____ g

Q. 2.6
Read the values shown on each of the following scales.

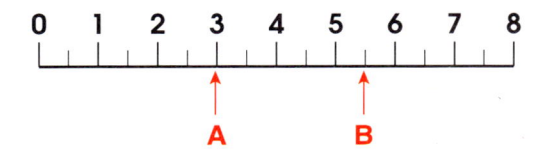

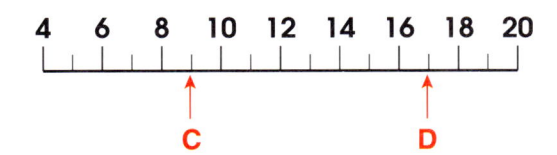

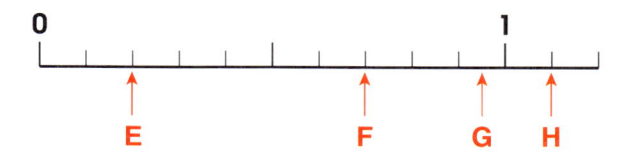

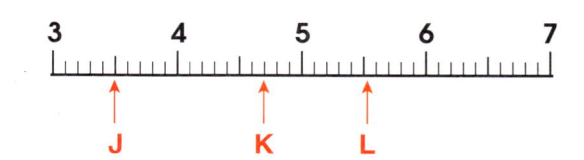

fig. 2.17

Q. 2.7
State the names and symbols of the units that are used to measure:

(a) length
(b) volume
(c) area
(d) temperature

Q. 2.8
State how many millimetres there are in:

(a) 1 cm
(b) 5 cm
(c) 0.5 cm
(d) 200 cm
(e) 1 metre

Q. 2.9
How many:

(a) cm in a metre?
(b) cm^3 in a litre?
(c) grams in a kilogram?
(d) seconds in an hour?
(e) metres in a kilometre?

Q. 2.10
Calculate each of the following:

(a) the area of a garden which measures 25 metres by 15 metres
(b) the area of a book measuring 20 cm by 12 cm
(c) the volume of a cube whose side is 4 cm
(d) the volume of a wooden block measuring 4 cm by 5 cm by 6 cm
(e) the volume of a block of ice cream measuring 5 cm by 10 cm by 20 cm
(f) the volume of milk in a carton measuring 7 cm by 7 cm by 21 cm

Q. 2.11
On graph paper, draw a circle of radius 5 cm. Find its area in the manner described on page 9.

Q. 2.12
Work out how you would find the volume of each of the following:

(a) a small ball bearing
(b) a drop of water
(c) an irregularly shaped sugar lump
(d) a cork

Q. 2.13
Name the instrument that would be most suitable to measure:

(a) the length of a curved line
(b) the length of the laboratory
(c) the volume of some liquid
(d) the volume of a chestnut
(e) the length of a pencil
(f) the diameter of a marble
(g) the volume of a marble
(h) the length of a railway line on a map
(i) the capacity of a mug

Q. 2.14
Five boys are each given a metre stick and told to measure the length of the school drive. They return with the following measurements:

Tom: 234 m 56 cm 2 mm
Dick: 225
Harry: 23 km
Peter: 223 m
Paul: 228.44 m

(a) What is wrong with Dick's value?
(b) Can you find any fault with the results of Tom and Paul?
(c) What mistake has Harry made?
(d) What would you say is the length of the drive?

Q. 2.15
What is the temperature of each of the following?

(a) boiling water
(b) melting ice
(c) freezing water
(d) a comfortable room
(e) the healthy human body (see page 68 if necessary)

Q. 2.16
(a) What was a cubit? Why are cubits no longer used?
(b) In metric measurements, what is the approximate size of a cubit?
(c) Work out, using modern measurements, what was the approximate size of Noah's Ark?

Q. 2.17
Draw labelled diagrams of the apparatus that you could use to measure each of:

(a) the length of a desk
(b) the length of a curved line
(c) the volume of some milk
(d) the volume of a piece of coal
(e) the temperature of a cup of tea
(f) the diameter of a golf ball

Q. 2.18
Name measuring instruments on which you would find the following units:

(a) centimetres
(b) centimetres cubed (or millilitres)
(c) kilometres (or miles) per hour
(d) litres
(e) degrees Celsius
(f) hours and minutes

Q. 2.19
Make a list of the words which are missing from the following paragraph.

The metre is a unit of __ and can be divided into __ centimetres. The prefix kilo always means __ times and so a kilometre is equal to __ metres. Centimetres cubed (also called milli-__) are units of __. There are 1000 centimetres cubed in one __. A measure of how hot or cold something is called its __ and its units are __. An instrument used to measure this is a __. Time can be expressed in __, __ or __. There are 60 __ in one __ and 60 __ in one __.

3 ENERGY

fig. 3.1 *Just before lift-off a fully laden Jumbo possesses about 1500 million joules of kinetic energy*

Energy is always in the news. Do you know what exactly is meant by energy? Anything which is able to do useful work is said to possess energy. You have energy and so you can do work – but only if you are fed with food to provide this energy. Machines can also do work and they too must be 'fed' with energy, in the form of electricity, oil or some other fuel.

fig. 3.2 *The steam engine experiment*

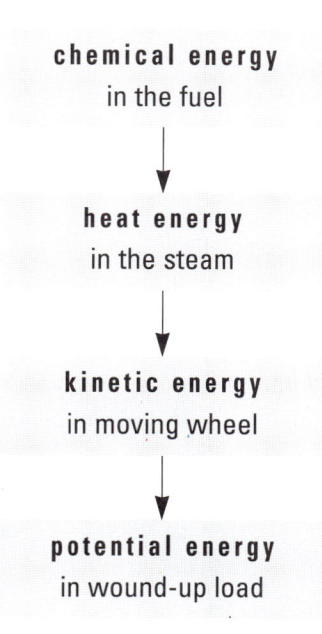

> **Energy is defined as the ability to do work.**

Foods and fuels consist of chemical compounds and these are stores of a form of energy called **chemical energy** – which can be used to enable people and machines to do useful work.

FORMS OF ENERGY

There are many other forms of energy. Heat, for example can do useful work such as driving engines to move people and things or to generate electricity. The experiment illustrated in Figure 3.2 shows heat driving a steam engine which is lifting up a load. In this experiment, the fuel (a source of **chemical energy**) burns and produces **heat energy** which boils the water and generates steam. This steam drives the pistons which make the wheels turn (energy of movement is called **kinetic energy**). The wheel is attached to a shaft around which is a line that raises the load. So, chemical energy produces heat energy which produces kinetic energy which raises the load or weight.

chemical energy in the fuel
↓
heat energy in the steam
↓
kinetic energy in moving wheel
↓
potential energy in wound-up load

The raised-up weight has now got what is called **potential energy** since it can do useful work on its return journey downwards. Some clocks make use of the potential energy of a raised-up weight to keep the clock going. A clock of this type is illustrated in Figure 3.3.

3 · Energy

fig. 3.3 The weights of this cuckoo clock are wound up once a day, and this keeps the clock going and 'cuckooing' for the next 24 hours

fig. 3.4 Winding up the spring of a clockwork dinosaur gives it a store of potential energy in the spring. When the spring is allowed to unwind, the potential energy in the spring changes to kinetic energy and the dinosaur 'walks' forwards.

Machines then, do not generate energy; they only convert it from one form to another. Energy conversions are basic to everyday life. In most ESB power stations (e.g. Ringsend in Dublin or Portarlington in Laois) a fuel such as oil, peat or coal is burned to produce heat – which changes water to steam, and the steam drives a turbine which works a generator and produces electricity.

In hydroelectric power stations such as Ardnacrusha on the Shannon or Poulaphuca on the Liffey, use is made of the potential energy of a very large mass of water stored at a height – usually behind an artificially constructed dam. This water is made to flow down through a turbine which drives a generator and produces electricity.

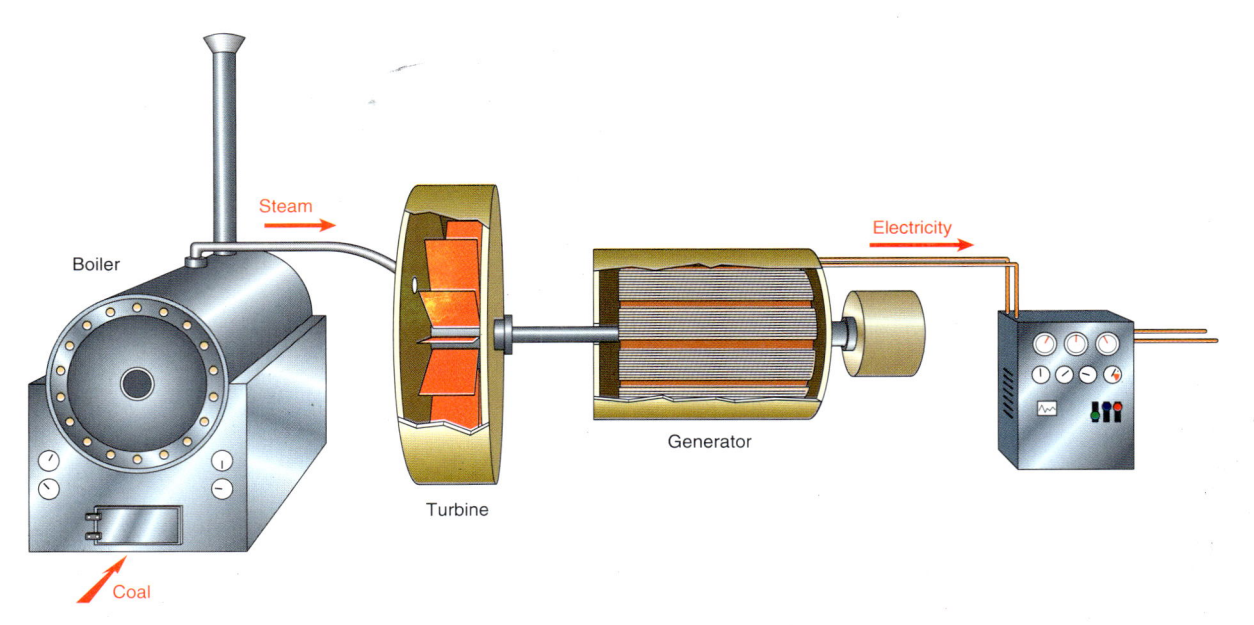

fig. 3.5 What happens in a coal-fired power station

fig. 3.6 *The ESB power station at Ardnacrusha, Co. Clare, which opened in 1929, was the first hydro-electric power station in Ireland. Its location is due to the fact that between Lough Derg and Limerick, the level of the Shannon falls by about 30 metres. The potential energy of this water is used to generate electricity.*

In homes and factories too, fuels are burned to produce heat. In your home, electrical energy is converted to **heat** in devices such as electric heaters, immersion heaters and hair dryers, to **light energy** in bulbs and to **sound energy** in radios and television sets. Electrical energy is converted to movement (**kinetic energy**) in washing machines, electric drills and cake mixers.

A battery contains a useful store of energy. If you have broken up an old torch battery you will find that it is full of chemicals. When a battery is in use, the **chemical energy** in it is converted to **electrical energy** which can be used to light bulbs, or to work your 'Walkman' or your calculator.

fig. 3.7 *There is no electricity in a battery; it is a collection of chemicals*

Some instances of energy changing from one form to another are very common. When you rub your hands together, you are converting kinetic energy ('movement' energy) into heat energy – which will be very noticeable if you rub your hands really hard. Other energy changes are less common; in a device called a radiometer, **light energy** is converted to **kinetic energy** and in a solar cell, **light energy** is converted to **electricity** (electrical energy).

In the living world, all organisms require energy for the activities of life. Green plants obtain this energy from the Sun, by a process called **photosynthesis**. This is a chemical reaction in which the Sun's **solar energy** is converted into chemical energy in plants. In the plant, the energy is stored as carbohydrates like

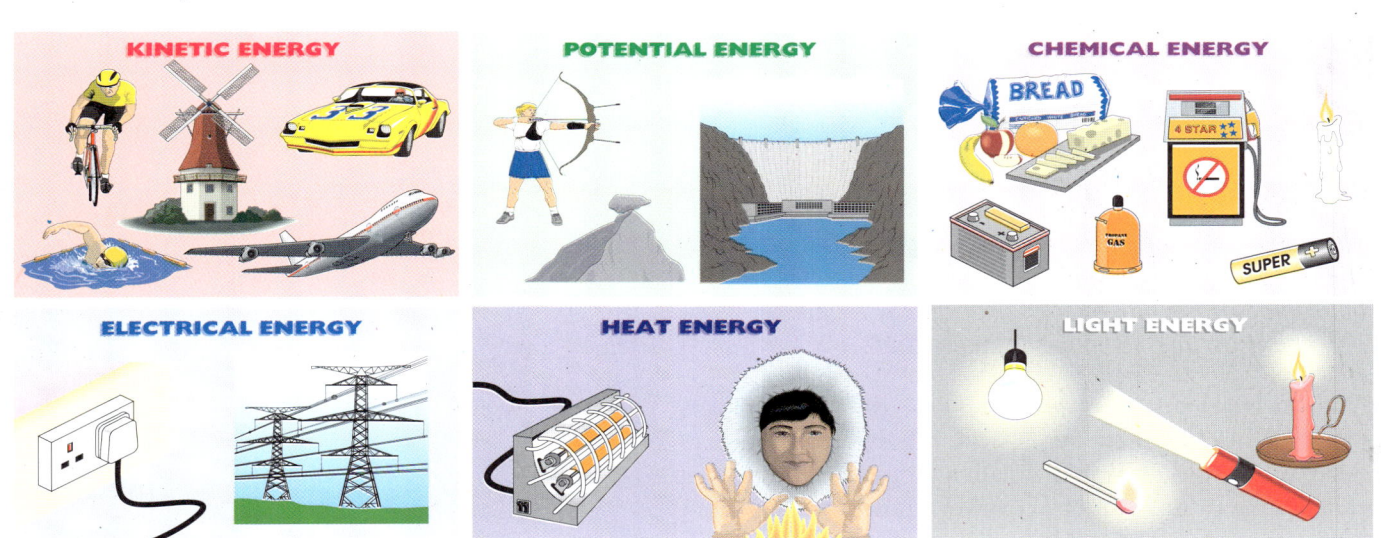

fig. 3.8 *Forms of energy*

sugar and starch, which are sources of food. When the plants are eaten by others, the chemical energy is passed on to the eater.

fig. 3.9 *A radiometer (left) converts light energy to kinetic energy; a solar cell (right) converts light energy to electrical energy*

fig. 3.10 *This food chain shows the transfer of energy. The Sun's energy causes the grass to grow. The grass is eaten by the cow, which provides milk, which is consumed by the girl, enabling her to play tennis. Her energy to do this comes from the Sun.*

Nuclear energy is energy which is stored in the nuclei of atoms of certain elements, which is released when these atoms are split into smaller atoms – a process called fission. In a nuclear power station, atoms of uranium, and sometimes plutonium, undergo fission. This process releases enormous amounts of energy, much in the form of heat, which is used to generate electricity in the usual way (i.e. to produce steam, which drives turbines, which power generators).

The Sun produces its heat and light by nuclear energy. More about nuclear energy will be found in Chapter 23, which is all about atoms and what they consist of.

CONSERVATION OF ENERGY

So, when a source of energy does work, the energy is not 'used up', but is converted to some other form. The law of conservation of energy expresses this and states:

> **Energy can neither be created nor destroyed, but can be converted from one form to another.**

Most people have some sort of idea of this law; few would believe in the invention of a motor car which ran without having any source of energy.

QUESTIONS

Q. 3.1

Copy the following diagram into your notebook. On each arrow write the name of a device which can convert the first form of energy to the next. To start you off, some answers are given. (You may find Figure 3.8 helpful in answering this question.)

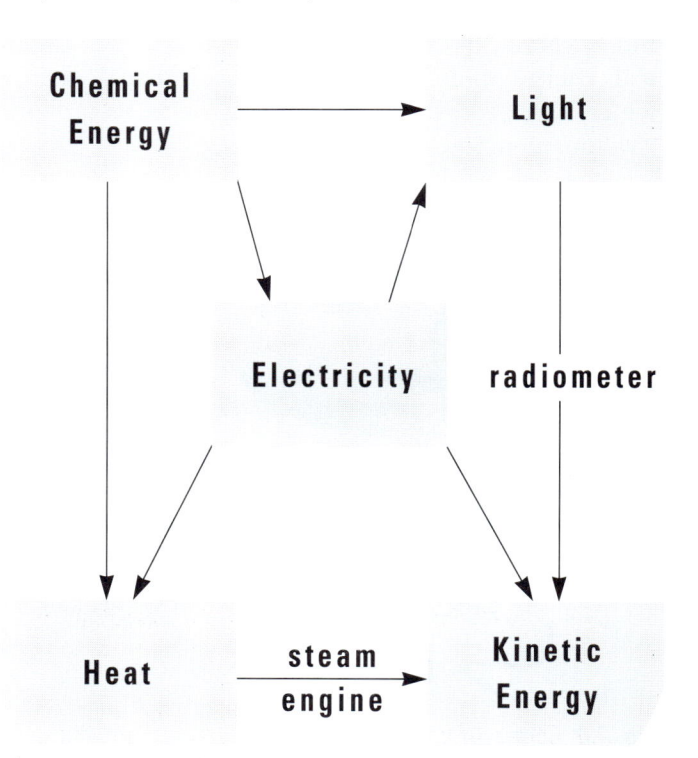

Q. 3.2

For each of the pictures shown in Figure 3.11, state what is the initial (starting) form of energy, and to what form it is being converted.

fig. 3.11

Q. 3.3

Name one form of energy possessed by each of the following:

(a) a can of petrol
(b) a stretched elastic band
(c) falling water
(d) a lump of uranium
(e) a moving train
(f) the air in a balloon
(g) cornflakes
(h) a wound-up clock weight
(i) a torch battery
(j) a switched-on torch bulb
(k) a kettle of boiling water
(l) a vibrating guitar string

SOURCES OF ENERGY

Have you ever wondered where all of the energy that is used on the Earth comes from? It all comes from, or came from, the Sun – either directly or indirectly. The radiometer and the solar cell (Figure 3.9) show that the Sun can do work directly, but indirectly the Sun provides energy in many other ways. Figure 3.10 shows a simple energy chain which started with the Sun, and ended up as energy being used by a girl to play tennis.

However, much of the world's energy comes from oil, gas, coal and turf. These fuels are called **fossil fuels** because they were formed millions of years ago; they cannot be reformed quickly. They are therefore **non-renewable** sources of energy. Supplies of these sources of energy are being quickly used up.

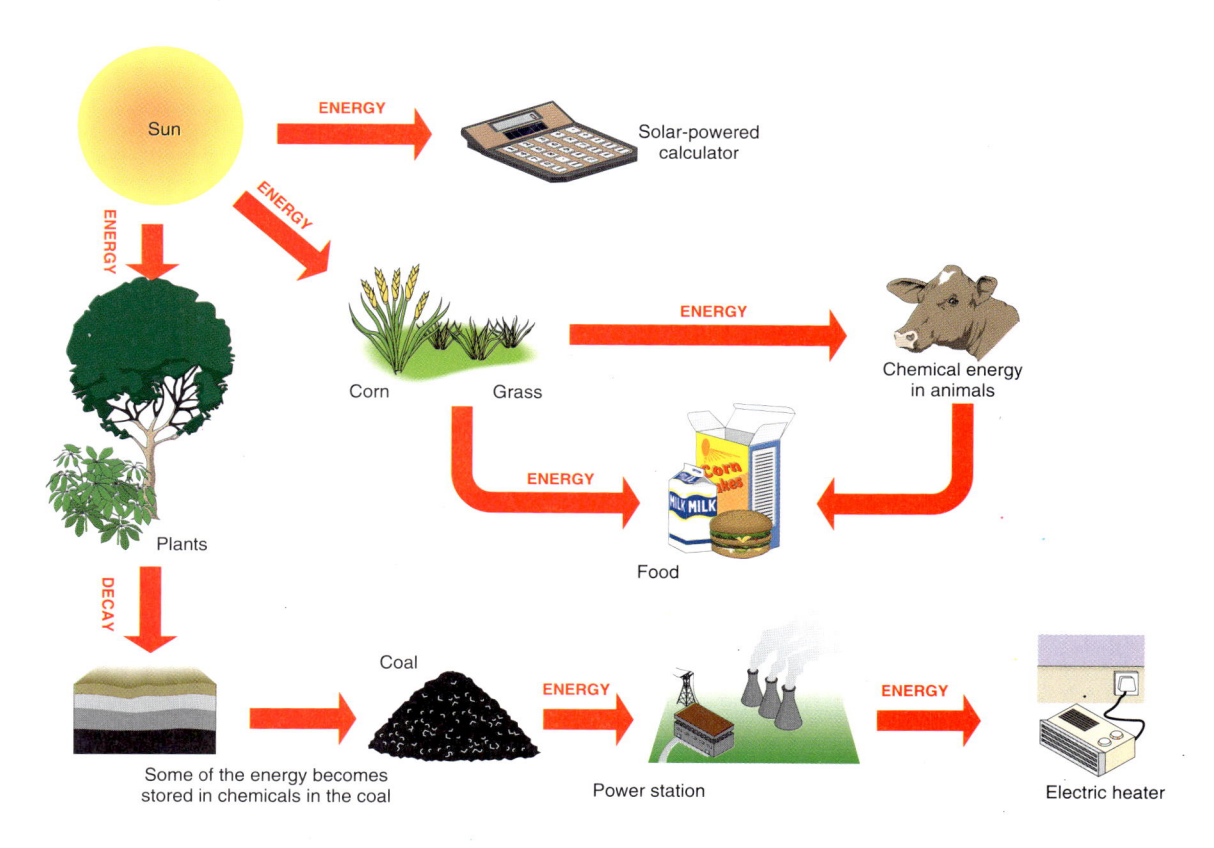

fig. 3.12 *The Sun is the source of all energy on Earth*

3 • Energy

The stored chemical energy in the fossil fuels came from the Sun – over 100 million years ago. At that time, there were large areas of dense forests on Earth – which grew because of the sunlight falling on them. In time, these forests died and decayed. Lakes and rivers covered them with mud and rocks, and eventually because of great heat and pressure, they changed into coal. Turf (peat) was formed in a similar way, but more recently, perhaps only about 100 000 years ago!

Petroleum ('crude oil') was formed from plants and tiny animals which lived in the seas hundreds of millions of years ago. When these died, they sank to the bottom and became sealed under layers of mud before they rotted. In time, they changed into oil under the great pressure of the layers of mud and the sea.

The fossil fuels consist mainly of chemical compounds called **hydrocarbons**. When they burn, they form carbon dioxide gas and water vapour.

THE COST OF ENERGY

Energy is expensive; it costs money to produce it and also to move it around. Most of the energy used in the home is to keep ourselves and our surroundings warm, and most of that energy comes from fossil fuels.

This includes electricity, which is not itself a fuel, but is a very good way of moving energy from place to place, such as from the power station to the home. The table below shows the cost of heating a typical home, using different kinds of heating.

energy source	cost per year
coal/solid fuel	£360
oil	£250
natural gas	£270
bottled gas	£455
electricity (day rate)	£1000
electricity (night rate)	£335

There are dangers involved in providing most forms of energy. Mining coal can be hazardous to miners' health, and explosions can occur in mines. In the extracting of oil and natural gas from the ground, there is a constant risk of fire and explosion. The burning of all fossil fuels leads to some pollution of the atmosphere. It is one of the major tasks of today's scientists to provide safe and clean forms of energy for the future.

RENEWABLE AND ALTERNATIVE SOURCES OF ENERGY

Hydroelectricity

The generation of hydroelectricity makes use of part of the water cycle (Figure 22.10, page 156) which is directly due to the Sun shining on the Earth. Have you ever wondered why the sea never 'fills up' when thousands of rivers are continuously pouring water into it? As this is happening, water from the sea is continually evaporating and changing into water vapour in the atmosphere – from which, on cooling, it falls back to Earth again, as rain. The rain finds its way into streams and rivers, and then back to the sea. Some rivers are dammed to provide a 'head' of water (a reservoir of water at a height) and from the potential energy of this, hydroelectricity is generated (See Figure 3.6, page 17).

There is a plentiful supply of energy available from other sources which are part of Nature e.g. the Sun, the wind, waves and plants. These forms of energy are not being used up, and are called renewable sources of energy. They cause little or no pollution, but compared to fossil fuels, they produce much smaller amounts of useful energy.

Solar energy

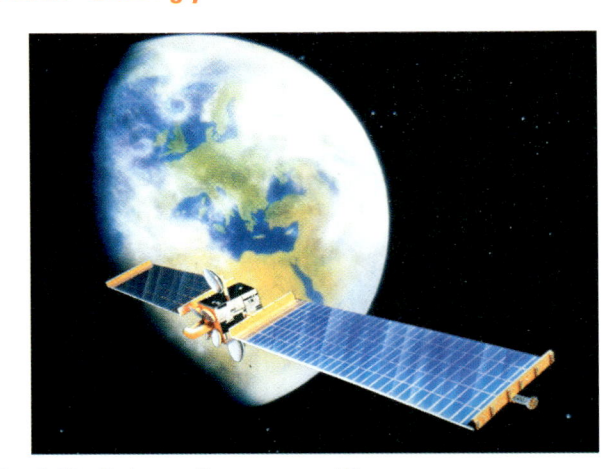

fig. 3.13 Solar cells on a satellite

The Sun's energy can be used directly to heat water or to generate electricity. Space ships and satellites use solar cells to convert sunlight into electricity, and, on a smaller scale, many calculators run on electricity produced by solar cells. For generating electricity for commercial use, huge areas of ground would have to be covered by solar panels. It has been estimated that to generate the same quantity of electricity as a modern power station, 40 square kilometres of ground would be needed.

Wind energy

fig. 3.14 Wind-powered generators at a 'windfarm' in Germany

The wind has been used as an energy source for hundreds of years – for grinding corn and for pumping water. But it is only in the last twenty years that serious thought has been given to building wind-powered electricity generators. Modern wind-powered generators are very efficient, but about 2000 of them would be needed to provide the same power as one of today's coal or oil-fired power stations. Winds are caused by the Sun heating different parts of the Earth unequally and air moving from cool to warm areas, so this wind energy really comes from the Sun.

Wave energy

Experiments are being carried out on using the energy in moving waves to generate electricity. One idea is to use large floats which move up and down with the wave movement, and then using this up-and-down motion to work a generator. However, a wave generator could be an obstacle to shipping and to fishing.

Biomass

When energy is extracted from any biological material (plant or animal), the energy is called biomass energy. Burning wood is the simplest example of using biomass energy and about 50% of the world's population rely on wood as their main energy source. Wood is a renewable source of energy because trees can be planted to replace those cut down. Unfortunately this is not being done in a number of parts of the world.

fig. 3.15 Transporting firewood in Somalia

Sugar cane is a fast growing plant, and in Brazil, which has very little oil, large areas of land are devoted to growing this crop. From sugar cane they make alcohol, which is used instead of petrol, in their cars.

Methane gas can also be produced from plants and animal waste. When these substances are allowed to decompose (decay) in closed containers, a gas called biogas (which is mainly methane) is formed. In India and China, there are millions of biogas generators, providing gas for heating and cooking. Plants grow because of energy obtained from the Sun, so biomass energy also comes from the Sun.

Some typical energy values

Energy needed to lift an apple from floor to desk	1 J
Potential energy possessed by a brick on the desk	30 J
Kinetic energy of brick having fallen 10 m	300 J
Energy you need to climb a flight of stairs	1500 J = 1.5 kJ
Energy needed to boil a kettleful of water	700 kJ
Energy stored in a fully charged car battery	2000 kJ
Energy contained in one litre of petrol	35 000 kJ
Kinetic energy of a Jumbo aircraft at lift-off	1 500 000 kJ

MEASURING ENERGY

Energy is measured in units called joules. One joule (1 J) is a very small amount of energy. If a match is allowed to burn completely away, it provides about 2000 J of heat energy. A 100 watt bulb uses about 6000 J of electrical energy every minute. Because a joule is such a small unit, kilojoules (kJ) are often used. A kilojoule is 1000 joules.

SUMMARY

- **Energy is the ability to do work.**
- There are different forms of energy, including **electrical** energy, **kinetic** and **potential** energy, **chemical** energy, **heat**, **light**, **sound**, and **nuclear** energy.
- Energy does not get 'used up'. When work is done, energy is converted to another form of energy. The law of conservation of energy states: "**Energy is neither created nor destroyed, but is converted from one form to another.**"
- All energy comes from, or originally came from, the Sun.
- Renewable sources of energy include hydroelectricity, solar energy, wind energy, wave energy, biomass energy.

QUESTIONS

Q. 3.4

Rewrite the following sentences and complete the spaces.

(a) A dynamo converts __ energy to __ energy.
(b) A light bulb converts __ energy to __ energy.
(c) A burning candle converts __ energy to __ energy.
(d) A falling brick converts __ energy to __ energy.
(e) A electric fire converts __ energy to __ energy.
(f) A loudspeaker converts __ energy to __ energy.
(g) A microphone converts __ energy to __ energy.
(h) A car engine converts __ energy to __ energy.
(i) A firework converts __ energy to __ energy.

Q. 3.5

Describe, using a diagram in each case, how you would show by experiment that the following are all forms of energy:

(a) electricity
(b) heat
(c) moving water
(d) a wound-up weight
(e) light

Q. 3.6

(a) Name two fossil fuels and explain why they are described as non-renewable.
(b) What is meant by a renewable source of energy?
(c) Name two such sources and explain why they can be renewed.

Q. 3.7

(a) Describe the energy changes involved when: (i) electricity is generated in a coal-burning generating station, (ii) hydroelectricity is generated.
(b) Which of the above methods of generating electricity is renewable and why?

Q. 3.8

(a) What is the law of conservation of energy?
(b) Describe how the law is illustrated when you are riding a bike at night with the dynamo powering the light.
(c) List the four forms of energy involved.

4

FORCE, WEIGHT AND GRAVITY

A force is not something that can be seen or touched, but it is something that everyone knows about.

A simple definition of a force is that it is a push or a pull.

fig. 4.1 *A force is a push or a pull*

Forces can have different effects on objects or bodies. A force can make an object move or speed up (you increase the speed of a ball when you throw it). Or, if the force acts in the opposite direction, it can make the object slow down or stop (you decrease the speed of a ball when you catch it).

A force can change the direction of a moving object (you change direction when you exert a force on the handlebars of your bike), or change the shape of an object (you can bend or break a ruler by exerting a force on it).

Force is measured in units called newtons, named after a very famous scientist, Sir Isaac Newton, who lived in the seventeenth century. Newton spent much of his life investigating forces. As he was sitting in his garden one day, an apple is supposed to have fallen on his head, and this set him wondering why the apple fell down and not up. He eventually put forward the idea that the Earth's force of gravity causes all bodies (objects) to be attracted towards the Earth, and is also responsible for keeping the Moon in orbit around the Earth.

A newton is a very small unit. You exert a force of about 1 N to lift an apple, 12 N to lift this book, 20 N to open a can of 'Coke', 50 N to squash an egg and 100 N or more to push a supermarket trolley. Car brakes can exert a force of about 5000 N.

fig. 4.2

Sir Isaac Newton was born on Christmas Day 1642 and lived until 1727. As a boy he was always making and studying small scientific items, such as water clocks, sundials and kites. Because he was not very good at school, he was taken away when he was 14 to help on his father's farm. However, his uncle saw that he was very interested in mathematics, and sent him back. Later on he went to college and in time became professor of physics at Cambridge University. His laws of motion became the foundation for all modern mechanics.

4 · Force, Weight and Gravity

Experiment 4.1
To investigate forces

1. Roll a lump of plasticine into a ball. Now press hard on it. Which of its properties changes?
2. Use a spiral spring or a rubber band for this experiment. Hold one end, and pull the other. Which of its properties changes? What change occurs?
3. Give a wooden block a push so that it slides along the bench. Does it keep moving or does it come to rest? A force called **friction** acts on all moving objects. What effect does friction have on the moving block?
4. Obtain a pair of magnets and hold one of them near the other. Does a magnet exert a force on another magnet? Is the force a push or a pull or can it be either?
5. Rub a plastic pen or biro vigorously on a woollen cloth or on the sleeve of your jumper, and then hold it near to some paper torn or cut up into very small pieces. Does the pen exert a force on the pieces of paper? The name given to the force here is **electrostatic** force.
6. Push a block of aeroboard down underneath the surface of water in a sink. Can you feel a force acting? In what direction is it acting? The force exerted by the water is called **upthrust**.
7. Get a rubber band. Hold one end and pull the other. At which end do you feel a force, or can you feel a force at each end?
8. Using a spring balance or newton meter, find out what force is needed to lift a mass of:
   (a) 100 g, (b) 1 kg (1000 g).
9. If two newton meters are available, connect them together as shown. Attach one of them to something like a gas tap, and pull the other. Then read the force acting on each. See Figure 4.3.
10. Answer the following questions. In which part of the experiment did a force:
    (a) change the length of something?
    (b) change the shape of something?
    (c) act upwards?
    (d) slow something down?

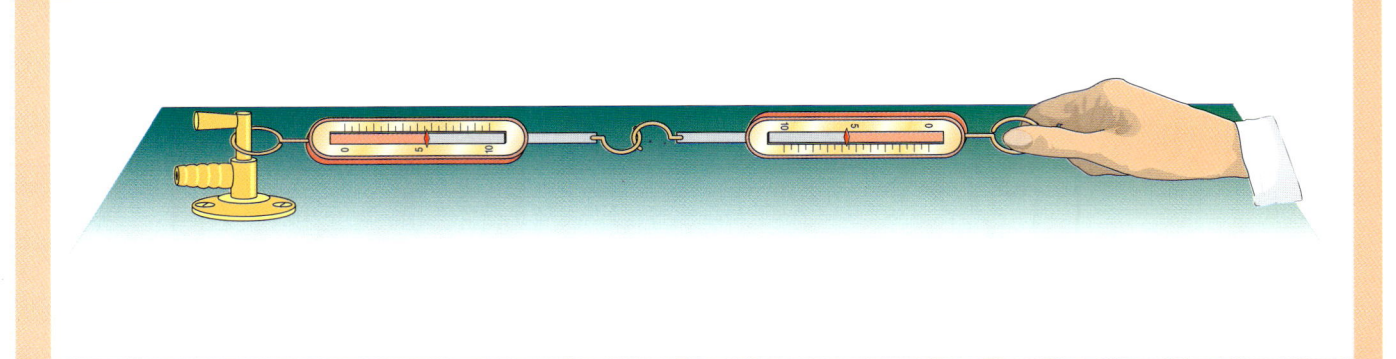

fig. 4.3 Equal and opposite forces

QUESTIONS

Q. 4.1
Write out the following sentences which are about Experiment 4.1, and complete the gaps.

(a) When a force was applied to ___ its shape was altered.
(b) When a force was applied to a ___ ___ its length was changed.
(c) A magnetic force was felt when ___ ___ were brought together.
(d) When a block of aeroboard was pushed into water, a force called ___ was felt. It acted in an ___ direction.
(e) The force that slows down moving objects is called ___ .
(f) Forces occur in pairs. This was shown by ___ .

Q. 4.2
What force is needed to lift:
(a) 100 g
(b) 500 g
(c) 1 kg
(d) 5 kg
(e) this book

Q. 4.3
List six different effects that a force can have when it acts on an object.

Q. 4.4

In Figure 4.4 is the man pulling the donkey, or the donkey pulling the man, or both? Explain your answer.

fig. 4.4

If you have carried out Experiment 4.1, you should have learned several things about forces. As well as forces due to gravity, there are forces due to friction, there are upward forces when objects are put in water, there are magnetic forces between the poles of a magnet and electrical or electrostatic forces between charged or electrified objects.

FRICTION

Friction is the force that exists between surfaces that are rubbing together, which tends to slow down their movement. No surface is absolutely flat; seen under a microscope, most 'flat' surfaces look as illustrated below. When two such surfaces rub together, the jagged edges catch in each other and so make movement difficult. This is what causes friction.

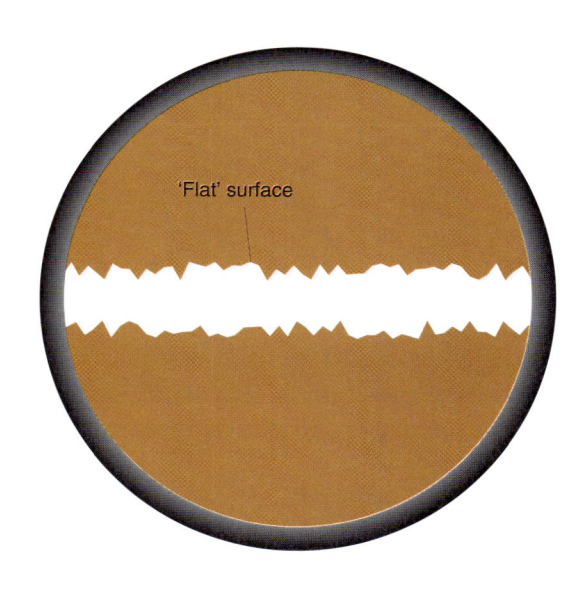

fig. 4.5 A 'flat' surface seen under a microscope

Experiment 4.2
To investigate friction

Set up the apparatus as shown.

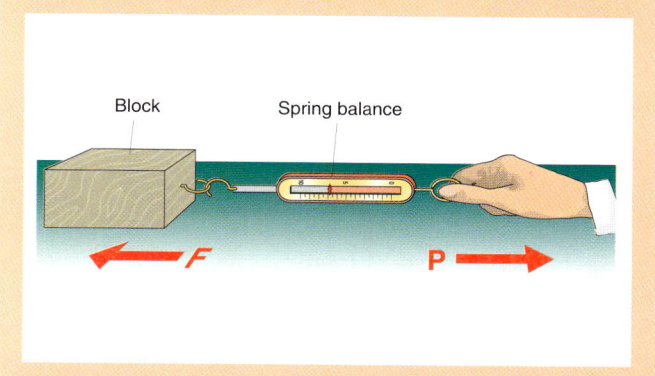

fig. 4.6

1. Pull on the spring balance (force meter) until the block of wood just starts to move. Note the reading on the scale. Do this several times and take the average value.
2. Now repeat the experiment but with the block of wood resting on a piece of sandpaper.
3. Finally, do it once again, but, instead of sandpaper under the block, lubricate the bottom of the block by rubbing soap on it.
4. Results: Force needed to move block:
   (a) on sandpaper ....
   (b) on the bench ....
   (c) on the bench but with lubrication ....

Advantages of friction

Sometimes friction is useful. Bicycle brakes work because of the friction between the brake blocks and the rim of the wheel. You can cycle on the road because the friction between the tyres and the road enables the tyres to grip. Friction enables you to walk uphill; without the friction between the soles of your shoes and the ground, you would slide backwards. You will be aware of how easy it is to slip on an icy road or pavement – when there is very little friction.

Friction is what holds nails into timber and therefore holds parts of your house together. Pieces of string which are tied together are held by friction, and a belt moving over a pulley is stopped from slipping by friction. When a ship is docking, the force of friction between a rope attached to the ship and a bollard on the quay is used to slow it down.

4 • Force, Weight and Gravity

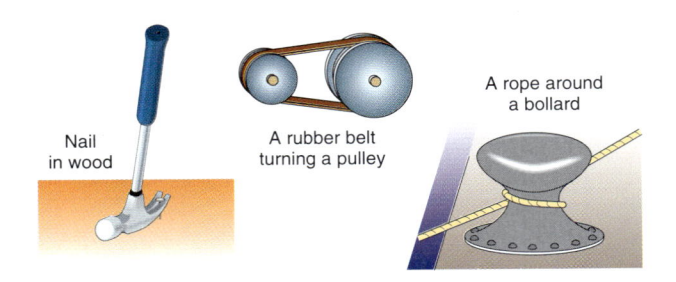

fig. 4.7 Uses of friction

Disadvantages of friction

However, friction is sometimes a disadvantage or hindrance and causes problems. Machines wear out because of friction between moving parts. Friction also converts useful energy into wasted heat energy. Where there are moving parts, it is always an advantage to reduce the friction between them as much as possible.

Reducing friction

Oiling machines reduces friction and makes movement easier. The moving parts of a car engine are automatically kept lubricated all the time that the engine is running. Door and gate hinges should be oiled occasionally to stop them from squeaking, and bicycles too should be oiled to make them run freely and to reduce wear. Sanding and polishing surfaces also helps to reduce friction.

Parts of the human body are lubricated too. To prevent bones rubbing together at joints such as shoulders and elbows, between the bones there is a layer of soft material called cartilage that is lubricated with a liquid called synovial fluid. This allows the bones to move freely with little friction.

A hovercraft rides on a cushion of air. This reduces the friction between it and the sea or the ground over which it is travelling.

fig. 4.8 A hovercraft

One of the world's most important inventions, made by the ancient Egyptians thousands of years ago, was a method of reducing friction. It was the wheel.

EQUAL AND OPPOSITE FORCES

Another thing that Newton discovered is that forces always occur in pairs. When a force acts in one direction, another force always acts in the opposite direction. Consider the picture of the donkey in Figure 4.4; is the man pulling the donkey, or the donkey pulling the man, or both? If you did the aeroboard experiment, you should have noticed that when you pushed the aeroboard down under water, you could feel the aeroboard pushing upwards. And when you held the stretched rubber band, you should have felt an inwards pull at both ends.

fig. 4.9 Forces acting in opposite directions

This principle of opposite forces is what makes rockets travel; the rocket engine drives hot gases out backwards, and this causes the rocket to travel forwards. You have probably often released a blown-up balloon whose neck is untied. Work out why it flies about.

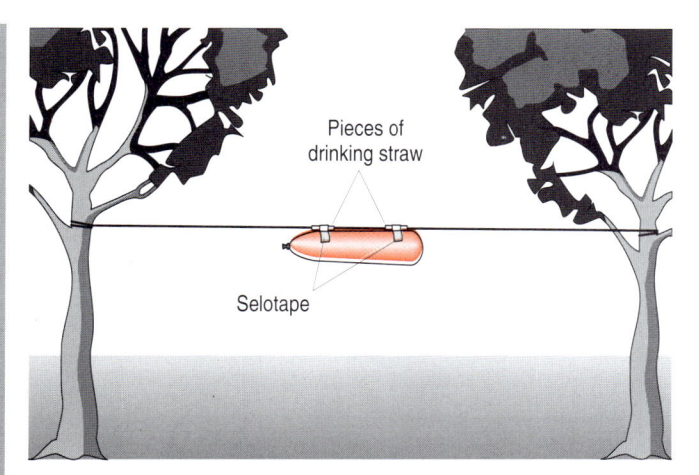

fig. 4.10 A homemade 'rocket'

MASS AND WEIGHT

Mass and weight are two quantities which are similar in ways but are not the same. People often refer to weight when they mean mass, but to a scientist, these are two different things.

> **The mass of an object is the quantity of matter in it, and it is measured in grams or in kilograms.**

The mass of an object is fixed and doesn't vary. A lump of lead for instance, will not gain or lose lead if it is taken to the Moon, or taken into space, or if it is put in water, but its weight changes in all of these cases.

In order to lift the lump of lead from the ground it is necessary to exert a force. This is because the Earth's gravity is pulling the lead downwards with a force – a force which is called weight.

> **The weight of an object is the downwards force exerted on it by the Earth (or by another body such as the Moon).**

The Moon's force of gravity is only about one sixth of the Earth's force of gravity, so objects on the Moon weigh only about one sixth of what they weigh on Earth. This is why astronauts can jump about so easily on the Moon. In space, the force of gravity is virtually zero, so spacemen can float about – they are 'weightless'. However, there is just as much astronaut in space as there is on Earth, i.e. the mass in unchanged.

(a) On Earth a spaceman weighs 600 N

(b) On the Moon his weight is only 100 N

(c) In space he is weightless

fig. 4.11 Weight changes with gravity

Because weight is a force, it is measured in force units, i.e. newtons. On Earth, a 1 kg mass has a weight of about 10 newtons.

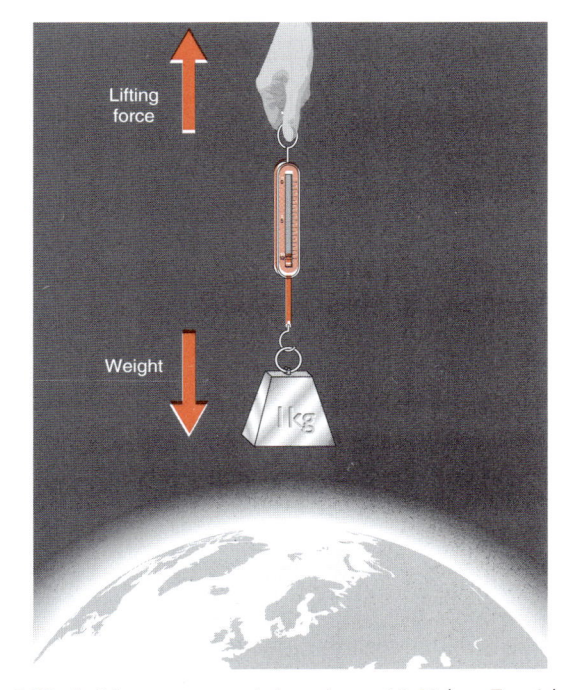

fig. 4.12 A 1 kg mass weighs about 10 N (on Earth)

If the 1 kg is taken to the Moon, it will weigh only about 1.6 newtons, even though the 1 kg is still all there. If the 1 kg were taken to the planet Jupiter (where the force of gravity is about 27 times that of Earth), it would weigh about 270 newtons.

■ 4 • Force, Weight and Gravity

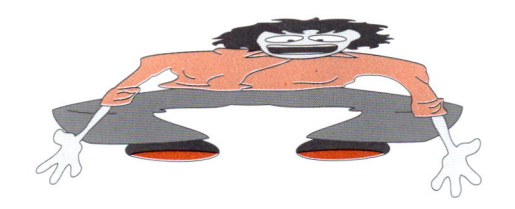

fig. 4.13 If you went to Jupiter, you would be unable to stand up because you would weigh so much

Weight is measured with a spring balance or newton meter. It is unfortunate that often in everyday life, you sometimes see markings such as *Cornflakes, net weight 500 g* which should correctly read *net mass 500 g*.

SUMMARY

- **A force is a push or a pull**. Forces always occur in pairs – equal and opposite. Force is measured in newtons. The different types of force include: gravitational, magnetic, electrostatic, weight, upthrust, friction, air resistance.

- The **mass** of an object or body is the quantity of matter in it and is measured in grams or kilograms. **Weight** is a force and is measured in newtons. The mass of an object or body is constant but its weight can and does vary. A mass of 1 kg has a weight (on Earth) of about 10 newtons.

QUESTIONS

Q. 4.5

Copy out the following paragraphs and fill in the spaces.

(a) A simple definition of a ___ is that it is a push or a ___. When a force acts on an object, it can change the object's ___, or its ___ or its ___. The first man to investigate the force of gravity was ___, and one of his many discoveries was that when a force acts on an object, there is always another force acting in the ___ direction. A rocket engine, for example, forces hot gases out ___, and the other force causes the rocket to move ___.

(b) Mass and weight are closely related to each other. The mass of a body (object) is the amount of ___ in it, and the weight of a body is the ___ force exerted on it by the force of ___. The units of mass are ___ but the correct units of weight are ___; this is because weight is a ___. The ___ of a given body is fixed, but the ___ is not and can change for example, if the body is put ___.

When a 1 kg mass of iron is hung from a newton balance, the reading on the balance is about 10 ___.

Q. 4.6

Look at the diagram.

fig. 4.14

(a) If both boy and girl push, who will move?
(b) If only the girl pushes, who will move?
(c) If only the boy pushes, who will move? If in doubt about the answer, try the experiment!

Q. 4.7

A piece of thread is tied around a brick which is then lifted by the thread. The thread breaks. The thread does not break if the brick is placed in a bucket of water and then lifted. Explain why this is so.

Q. 4.8

(a) What is meant by a force?
(b) Give an example of friction being useful.
(c) Give an example of friction being a hindrance.
(d) Describe how friction could be reduced.
(e) Name two surfaces between which there is (i) very little friction, (ii) a lot of friction.

Q. 4.9

A bag of breakfast cereal is marked 2 kg. What is its weight (i) on Earth, (ii) on the Moon, (iii) on Jupiter?

5
HEAT TRAVEL

Heat is a form of energy. It is fairly obvious to most that it must travel from place to place; heat from the Sun reaches the Earth, heat from a fire or a radiator warms the room, and heat from a cooker cooks food in a saucepan placed on it. Heat always travels from a place of higher temperature to a place of lower temperature, but the way in which it does so differs. In the three examples given above, the heat travels by different methods. From the Sun, heat reaches the Earth by **radiation**, the room is heated mainly by **convection**, and heat travels through the saucepan by **conduction**.

CONDUCTION OF HEAT

Experiment 5.1
To show conduction of heat

1. The apparatus consists of a metal bar with a row of pennies or small weights held on with wax.

2. When end A of the bar is heated with a bunsen burner, the pennies fall off one at a time, and in order from left to right, as the heat travels through the bar and melts the wax.

3. Heat travelling through solids like this is called **conduction**.

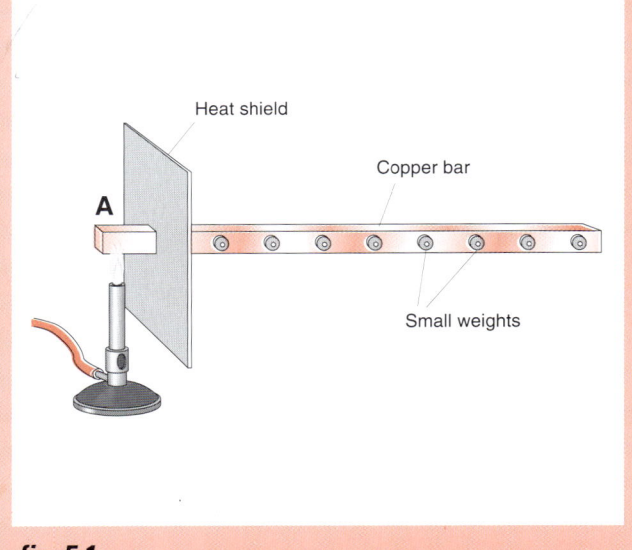

fig. 5.1

Experiment 5.2
To compare heat conductivities

1. Not all substances conduct heat equally well and in this experiment, the conducting powers of a number of metals are compared.

2. The apparatus consists of rods of different metals, with one end of each rod being heated in a bunsen flame.

3. At the other end of each is a 'heat detector' which consists of a small coin held on with wax.

4. When the heat reaches this end of the rod, the wax melts, and the coin falls off.

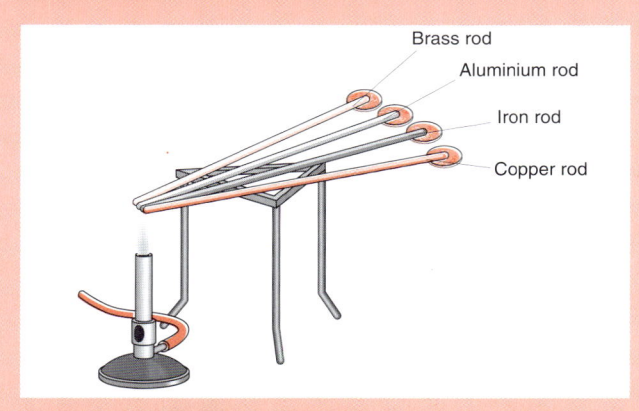

fig. 5.2 Coins held on with wax

5. In order for the comparison between the metal rods to be fair (for the results to be 'valid'), the rods must be of equal length and of equal thickness.

6. When the experiment is carried out, the coins fall off at different times, showing that not all metals conduct heat equally well.

USES OF CONDUCTORS

Good conductors of heat are used whenever heat is required to travel through something. For example, kettles, saucepans, boilers and radiators are made of metals such as aluminium, iron and copper. Conduction of heat is the reason why many materials feel cold to touch. A stone floor, for instance, feels much colder than a mat which is placed on it even though they are both at the same temperature. This is because stone is a better conductor of heat than the mat. The stone conducts heat from anything touching

5 • Heat Travel

Experiment 5.3
To compare the insulating properties of different materials

For this experiment you need several calorimeters (metal beakers) and lids, a thermometer, and equal lengths of the different materials to be compared.

1. Set up the apparatus as shown, with one of the material pieces wound around the outside of a calorimeter.
2. Use an elastic band or some sellotape to prevent it unwinding.
3. Pour 100 cm^3 of hot water into the calorimeter, put the lid in place.
4. Measure the temperature of the water and note the time or start a stop watch.
5. Repeat the experiment for each of the materials to be tested.
6. After 15 minutes, stir the water to make sure that the temperature is uniform, and then measure the temperature.
7. Calculate the temperature drop in each.
8. The calorimeter whose temperature has dropped the least is the one which has kept in the heat best and is therefore surrounded by the best insulator.

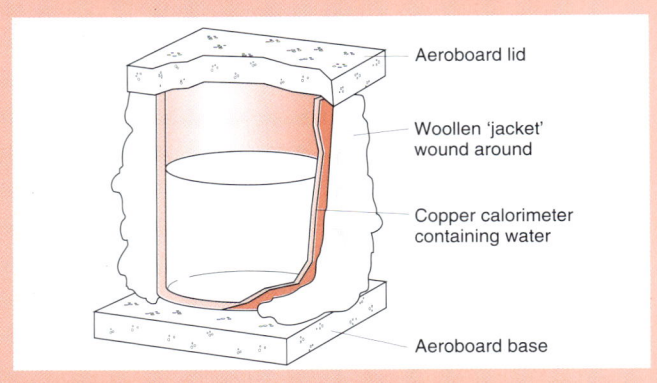

fig. 5.3

it – which is why it feels cold when you touch it with your hand. The mat does not feel cold because, being a poor conductor of heat, it does not conduct heat away from whatever is touching it.

Poor conductors of heat are **called insulators.** The handles of teapots, saucepans, electric irons are made of materials such as plastic or wood – because these are heat insulators. Cork is used for table mats. Air is one of the poorest heat conductors (i.e. one of the best heat insulators), and materials containing it (cotton, wool, straw, etc.) are used as heat insulators. Insulating houses is very important since the cost of heat can be very high and supplies of some fuels are limited. Figure 5.4(a) shows how heat escapes from an uninsulated house.

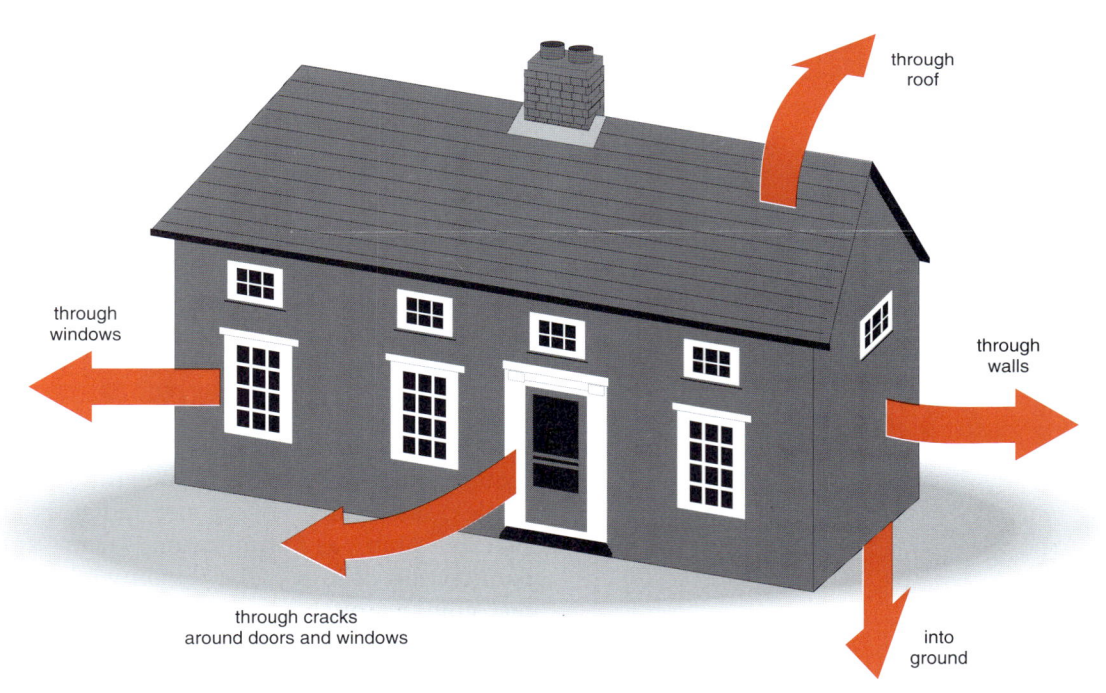

fig. 5.4 (a) *How an uninsulated house can lose heat*

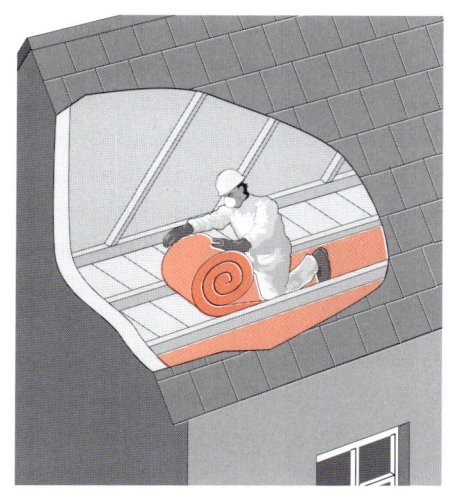

(b) Heat loss through the roof is reduced by putting insulating material such as 'Cosywrap' (loosely packed glass wool containing much air) between the joists above the ceiling

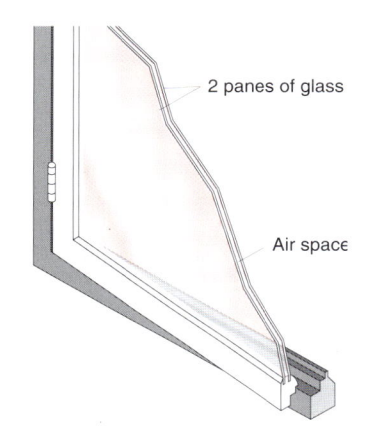

(c) Double glazing of windows consists of having two panes of glass with an air space between them

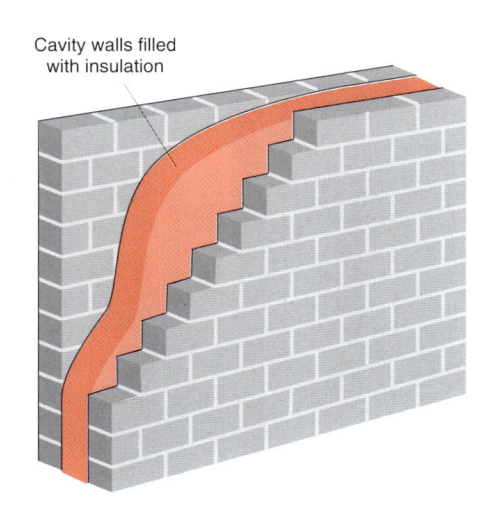

(d) Aeroboard is an excellent heat insulator and is placed between the double walls of buildings to keep the heat in

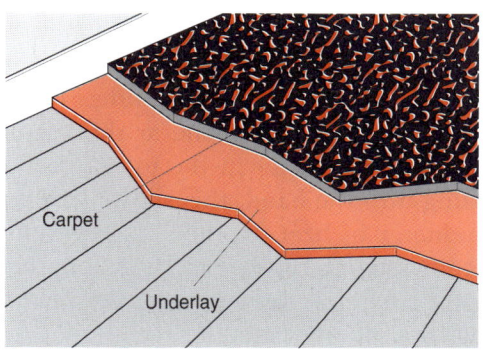

(e) Carpet with thick underlay reduces heat loss through the floor

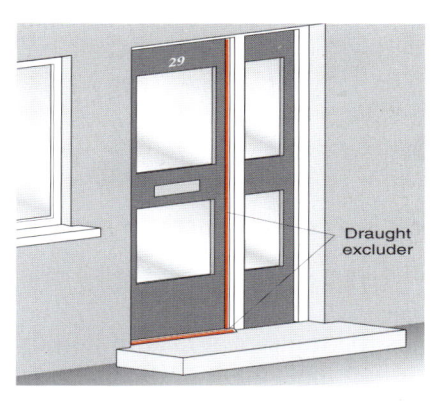

(f) Draught excluders on doors reduce heat loss and keep out cold air

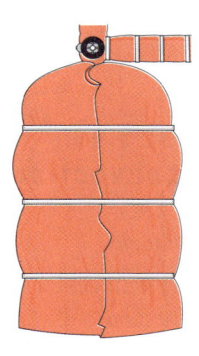

(g) Heat loss from a hot water tank can be reduced with a lagging jacket

Your clothes are insulators, and they keep you warm by preventing or reducing the amount of heat loss from your body. The insulating value of a material is indicated by its **tog value**. Articles like continental quilts (duvets) usually have their tog values on the labels. Tog values of duvets vary from about 7 (lightweight duvets) to about 13.

Insulators are also used to keep places cold. The walls of a refrigerator have glass wool or foam inside them to stop heat from outside passing through. Campers often use 'coolboxes' (these are insulated with aeroboard) for keeping their food supplies cool in warm weather.

5 • Heat Travel

Water is a poor conductor of heat, but it carries heat well by a different method. This can be demonstrated in a simple experiment. Two test tubes of water are heated, one at the top and one at the bottom. It is possible to boil the water in the top of tube A while still holding it in the hand; this shows that water is a poor conductor of heat. In tube B, however, the top soon becomes much too hot to hold, long before the water boils. Therefore in this tube, the heat must be travelling by a different method.

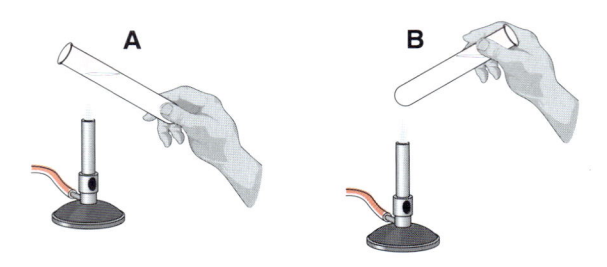

fig. 5.5 Water is a poor conductor of heat

CONVECTION

Convection is the transfer of heat in liquids and gases by the (upwards) movement of the liquid or gas itself. It happens because these substances expand on being heated, therefore become less dense than the cold substance, and so rise. This upwards movement is called a **convection current**.

Black marks often appear on walls or ceilings above lights or radiators. They are caused by dust being carried upwards in air convection currents produced by hot lights and radiators. The apparatus illustrated in Figure 5.8 is used to show air convection currents. The direction of the convection current created by the candle is made visible by the smoke from a smoldering piece of string or rope.

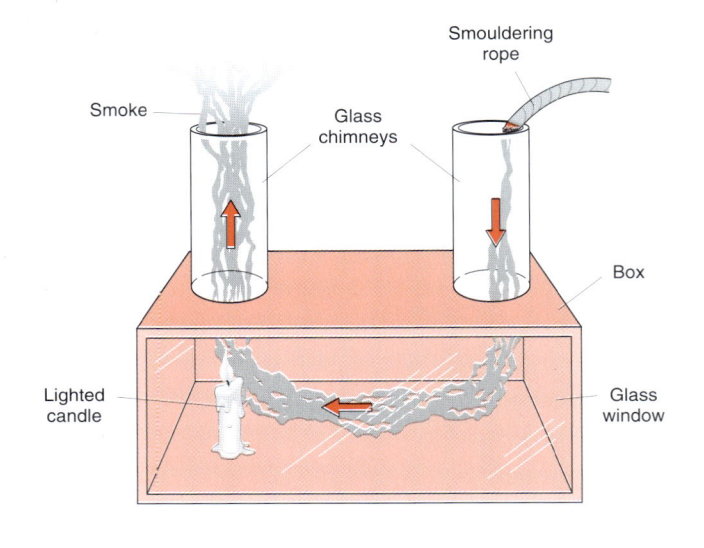

fig. 5.8 Apparatus for showing convection currents

Experiment 5.4
To show convection currents

Part 1: Convection in a liquid

1. Fill a flask or beaker with cold water and wait unti the water has become still.
2. Then, very carefully, drop a crystal of potassium permanganate down a glass tube so that it goes to the bottom of the flask. Slowly and very carefully, remove the tube.
3. Heat the flask, with a small bunsen flame and without using gauze, just below the point where the purple crystal is resting.
4. Watch the convection currents, which will be coloured by the permanganate crystal.

Part 2: Convection in a gas

5. Cut a paper spiral like that illustrated. Use fairly heavy paper and do not cut the spiral too wide.
6. Place a pin, or a length of thread with a knot at the end, through the centre hole of the spiral.
7. Hold it high above a bunsen flame and watch it being rotated by the convection current of air ascending from the burner.

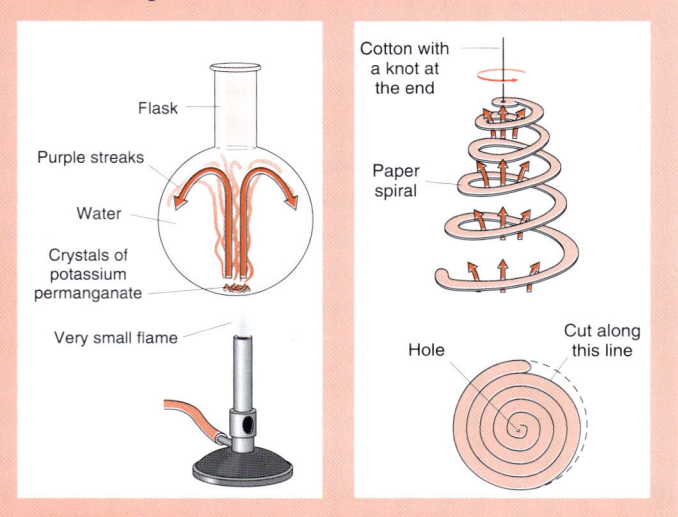

fig. 5.6

fig. 5.7

Convection currents set up by electric and gas heaters are used to heat our homes. Many so-called 'radiators' are really convector heaters. The hot water system of a house functions because of convection currents. Study Figure 5.9. The boiler (always the lowest part of the system) heats the water, which therefore rises up to the hot water cylinder for storage. The hot water outlet is always at the top of this cylinder. When a hot tap is turned on, the pressure caused by the cold water tank (usually in the roof space or attic) drives water out of the hot tank to the tap.

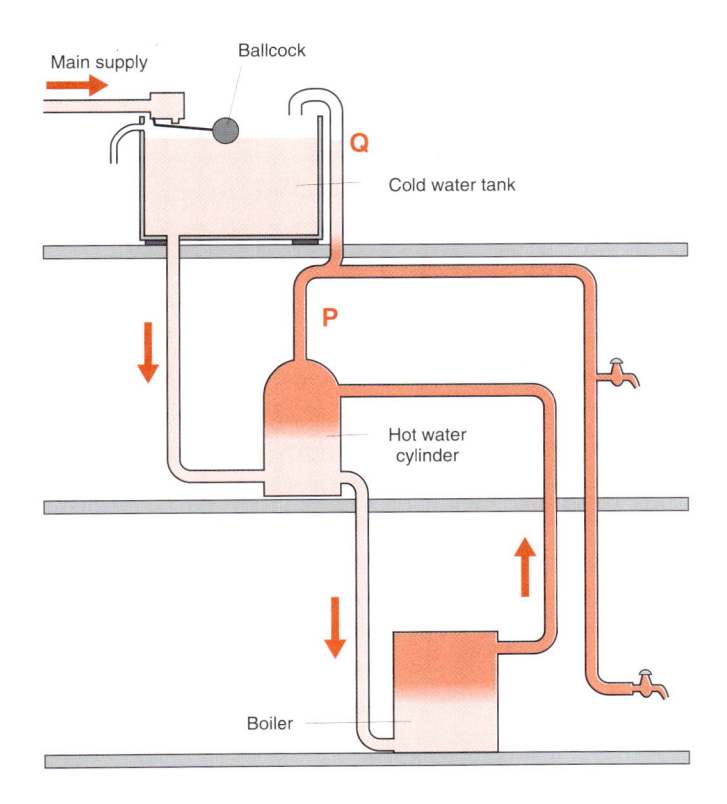

fig. 5.9 Hot water system in a house

Natural convection currents

Gliders and hang-gliders make use of natural convection currents (called thermals) to stay in the air. By flying from one thermal to another, gliders can stay in the air for hours. Hovering birds also make use of natural convection currents.

Balloons containing hot air rise because hot air is less dense than cold air. The first hot air balloon was made in 1783 by the Montgolfier brothers, who were French paper makers. The first 'passengers' to ascend in such a balloon were a sheep, a cock and a duck. They 'flew' for eight minutes during which time they ascended to a height of about 550 metres and travelled a distance of 3 km.

fig. 5.10 Modern hot air balloon

Land and sea breezes are also caused by natural convection currents. How these are caused is explained in Chapter 42.

QUESTIONS

Q. 5.1

(a) What is meant by conduction of heat?
(b) What sort of substances are conductors of heat?
(c) What name describes substances which do not conduct heat?
(d) List three conductors and three non-conductors found in the home.
(e) Say where each is used, and why.

Q. 5.2

Describe, with the aid of a diagram, an experiment that shows heat conduction. Explain what happens, and why, when the experiment is carried out.

Q. 5.3

(a) What is meant by convection of heat?
(b) In what sort of substances does convection take place?
(c) Describe, illustrating your answer with a diagram, an experiment to illustrate convection. Say what happens, and why, when the experiment is carried out.
(d) Name an everyday application of convection in your home.

Q. 5.4
Do your clothes make you warm or keep you warm? Explain the difference, and give the reason for your chosen answer.

Q. 5.5
Refer to Figure 5.9, which illustrates the hot water system of a house.

(a) Does water flow down or up through pipe P?
(b) Why is the boiler the lowest part of the system?
(c) Why is the supply pipe to the hot taps taken from the top of the hot water cylinder rather than from the middle or bottom?
(d) Why is the cold water storage tank in the roof space rather than in the kitchen, garage or shed?
(e) Suggest a reason for pipe Q.

Q. 5.6
(a) Describe an experiment in which you compared the insulating properties of some materials.
(b) Draw a diagram to show the apparatus used.
(c) State what you discovered in the experiment.

Q. 5.7
Name five ways in which houses can lose heat, and describe what can be done to reduce the heat loss by each of these ways. Why is it important to do so?

RADIATION

Consider the experiment shown in Figure 5.11. The beaker of water gets hot. The heat cannot reach it by conduction (since there is no conductor between the beaker and the heater); neither can heat reach it by convection (because heat by convection travels upwards). Therefore heat is travelling by a third method.

Radiation is the name of the third way in which heat travels from place to place. Radiation can take place in a vacuum (no substance need be present) whereas both conduction and convection need a substance to take place. It is by radiation that heat from the Sun reaches the Earth. It does this by means of invisible waves called electromagnetic waves; light and radio signals also travel by this method.

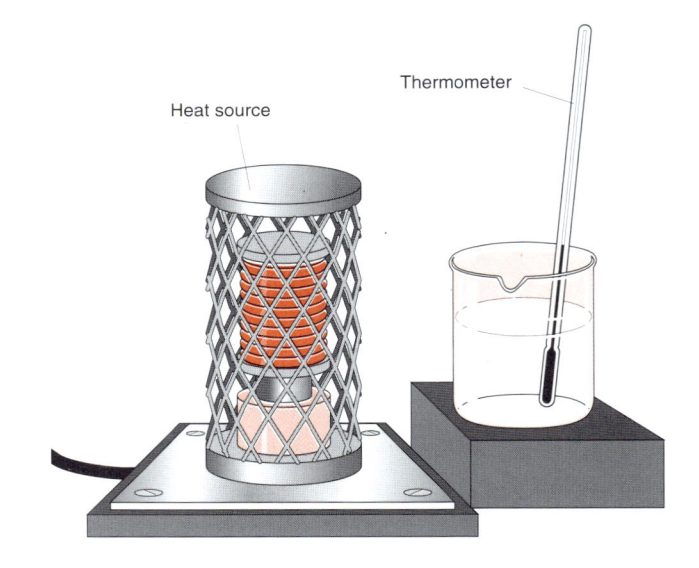

fig. 5.11 *Radiation of heat*

Experiment 5.5
To investigate absorption of heat radiation

1. Place 100 cm³ of water in each of two calorimeters (these are metal beakers). One calorimeter is polished on the outside and the other is blackened.

2. Place a thermometer in each and stand them both close to and at the same distance from a heat radiator. Measure the temperature of each.

fig. 5.12

3. Switch on the heater, and measure the temperature of the water in each calorimeter every minute.

4. You will find that one heats up much more quickly than the other. Black surfaces are good absorbers of radiated heat whereas polished surfaces reflect radiated heat – just as mirrors reflect light.

Experiment 5.6
Heat absorption by different surfaces

This experiment shows the same effect as Experiment 5.5, but in a slightly different way.

1. Two metal plates, one shiny and the other matt-black, are set up facing a heat radiator.

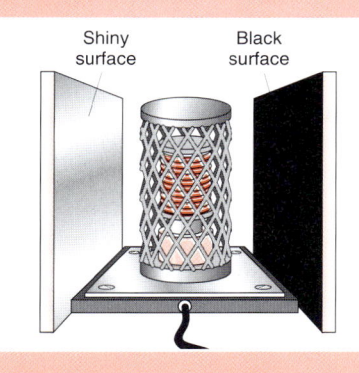

fig. 5.13

2. On the back of each, a small object such as a coin, has been stuck on with wax.
3. The heater is then switched on.
4. The coin behind the black surface falls off quickly but the one behind the shiny surface stays for much longer. This is because the black surface absorbs heat (and so the wax on that one melts first) but the shiny surface reflects most of the heat falling on it, and so it takes longer for the wax on that one to melt and release the coin.

Experiment 5.7
Heat emission by different surfaces

This experiment requires two calorimeters, one of which is shiny and the other matt black.

1. At a given time, pour equal volumes (e.g. 100 cm^3) of boiling water into each of them and then cover each with a lid.
2. After two minutes, measure the temperature of the water in each calorimeter.
3. Repeat this measurement every two minutes, for about twenty minutes.
4. Which calorimeter cools (loses heat) faster?
5. Do you find that the black one does?
6. As well as being the best absorbers of heat radiation, black sufaces are also the better radiators or emitters of heat, and this is why the black calorimeter cools faster.

The 'Thermos' flask

The 'Thermos' or vacuum flask was invented for keeping liquids very cold, and this it does very well. However, it is usually used nowadays for keeping liquids hot. Its design is such that heat loss by all three methods – conduction, convection and radiation – is reduced to a minimum. It consists of a double walled glass container with a vacuum between the two walls. The walls are silvered.

Little heat is lost by conduction because there are only insulators between the hot liquid and the outside. Convection cannot take place because there is a vacuum (i.e. nothing) between the walls of the vessel. Little heat is radiated from it because the walls are very highly silvered (like a mirror). So, hot liquids stay hot and cold liquids stay cold.

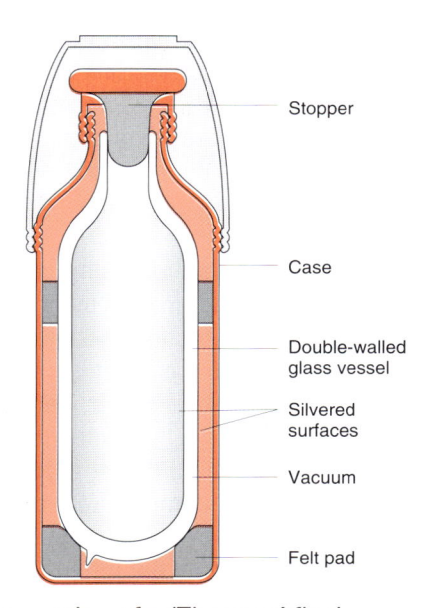

fig. 5.14 *Cross-section of a 'Thermos' flask*

SUMMARY

- Heat always travels from a high temperature area to a lower temperature area. **Conduction** is the process by which heat travels through solids. Metals are good conductors of heat with copper being one of the best. Non-metals are generally poor conductors of heat. Poor conductors are called **insulators** and many of them contain trapped air. The **tog value** is a measure of the insulating ability of insulators such as continental quilts.

- **Convection** is the transfer of heat through a fluid (liquid or gas) by means of the upwards movement of the fluid itself; this upwards movement is called a convection current. *(continued)*

> • **Radiation** is the transfer of heat by means of invisible rays which travel outwards from the hot source. These rays are one type of electromagnetic wave. Black surfaces are both good absorbers and also good emitters of heat radiation. Shiny surfaces reflect heat radiation. No medium is necessary for heat radiation to travel.

QUESTIONS

Q. 5.8

Rewrite the following paragraphs and complete the gaps.

(a) Heat travels from places at ___ temperature to places at ___ temperature and it does so by three different methods, ___, ___ and ___. It travels through solid materials by a process called ___, and three materials in which it travels well are ___, ___ and ___. Such materials are called good ___ of heat. The opposite sorts of material, in which it does not travel well, are called ___, and three examples of these are ___, ___ and ___.

(b) When a beaker of water is being heated, the heat travels through it mainly by ___. Heat travelling by this method is always in an ___ direction, and the flow of heat is called a ___ ___. When air is heated it travels ___ and this is the reason why ___ ___ balloons ___.

(c) Heat from the ___ reaches the Earth by a process called ___. In this method of heat travel, the heat is carried by ___, and it can travel through ___ while heat travelling by the other methods can not. If two calorimeters, one black and one shiny, are placed in front of an electric radiator, the ___ one heats up more quickly. This is because it ___ heat more than the other one, which ___ much of the heat falling on it.

Q. 5.9

(a) What is meant by radiation of heat?
(b) Name two sources of heat radiation.
(c) Describe an experiment to demonstrate heat radiation.
(d) Mention two examples of using heat radiation at home.

Q. 5.10

(a) In what way is heat transferred in (i) a liquid, (ii) empty space, (iii) metals?
(b) Describe, with a diagram, an experiment to show that heat travels through metals.
(c) Name two methods used to prevent heat loss in your home.
(d) Why is a central heating 'radiator' badly named?

Q. 5.11

State whether conduction, convection or radiation is involved in each of the following.

(a) making toast
(b) boiling water in a metal kettle
(c) frying sausages
(d) grilling sausages
(e) heating a room using the central heating 'radiator'
(f) using a soldering iron
(g) flying in a hot air balloon
(h) you can burn your hand if you are stirring a hot liquid with a metal spoon
(i) when you heat the bottom of a kettle of water, all of the water gets hot
(j) sunbathing

Q. 5.12

Suggest a reason for each of the following statements.

(a) a metal teapot often has a plastic or a wooden handle
(b) thick paper is often wrapped around a bag of chips
(c) a hot air balloon rises
(d) a string vest, which might be described as a collection of holes surrounded by string, keeps a person warm

fig. 5.15

(e) a central heating 'radiator' is inaccurately named
(f) bicycle handlebars always feel colder than the handlegrips
(g) the element of an electric kettle is at the bottom of the kettle
(h) houses in hot countries are often painted white (fig. 5.16)

fig. 5.16 Houses in Greece

(i) a glass rod is used in the laboratory for stirring
(j) the central heating boiler is placed in the basement of an office block

Q. 5.13
Explain a reason for each of the following:
(a) a hot water cylinder has an insulating jacket around it
(b) a hotpress has slotted shelves
(c) an igloo can be much warmer inside than outside
(d) there is often a dirty mark on the ceiling above a light
(e) an astronaut's suit is well padded
(f) gliders can ascend when they are above a town

fig. 5.17

(g) there is a layer of aeroboard between the outer and inner walls of a building (fig. 5.17)
(h) the icebox is at the top of a refrigerator rather than at the bottom
(i) people who live in hot countries usually wear white clothes
(j) a refrigerator has insulating material in its walls
(k) kettles and teapots are often highly polished (it is not only for good appearance)

Q. 5.14
(a) What is heat radiation?
(b) What sort of substances are good at radiating heat?
(c) What sort of substances are good at absorbing heat radiation?
(d) Describe an experiment to demonstrate your answer to (c). Draw a diagram, and say what happens when the experiment is carried out.

Q. 5.15
(a) Name the three methods by which heat is transferred.
(b) Describe an experiment to demonstrate each of these methods.

6 MAGNETISM

Magnetism has been known for thousands of years. The Chinese, as long ago as 2000 BC, are supposed to have known about a magnetic form of iron ore called magnetite, which is used to make simple compasses. In the *Arabian Nights*, the story of the Black Mountain tells the tale of a ship which sailed too close to the mountain. According to this story the ship fell to pieces because all the iron nails holding the ship together were pulled out by the attraction of the mountain. There can be little truth in this story, since magnetite is only weakly magnetic and could not account for the force needed to pull nails out of ships.

Today all magnets are artificial ones, and are usually manufactured from steel or an alloy such as 'Alnico' (**Al**, **Ni** and **Co**). Magnets have a great number of uses and are found in many everyday devices. Refrigerator doors and many cupboard doors have magnetic catches in them to keep them closed. Loudspeakers in radios, TV sets and the earpieces in 'Walkmans' and telephones all depend on magnets for their operation. Bicycle dynamos contain magnets and all electric motors work because of magnetism.

Experiment 6.1
To study permanent magnets

1. Place a bar magnet on top of a quantity of pins or paper clips spread out on the bench. Where on the magnet do most of the pins stick? Where does this suggest that the magnetism is strongest? These parts are called the **poles** of the magnet.

fig. 6.1

2. Hang a magnet up so that it is quite free to swing horizontally. Make sure that there are no other magnets or iron objects nearby. Wait for the magnet to come to rest. When it does so, it will be pointing in a north-south direction. The end which is pointing north is called the **north pole** of the magnet, and the end which is pointing south is the **south pole**. Put a mark on the north end.

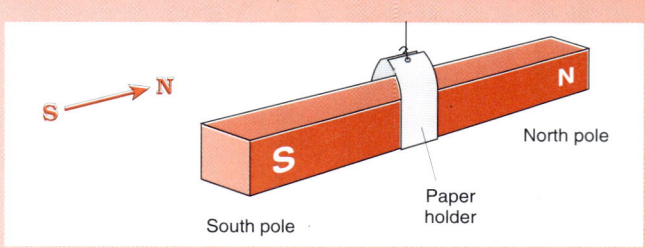

fig. 6.2

3. Find the north pole of a second magnet in a similar way. Now investigate the effect which two magnets have on each other. Bring the north pole of one magnet near the north pole of the second magnet. What happens? Now bring the north pole of one magnet near the south of the other. Finally bring the two south poles together.

fig. 6.3 Ring magnets

4. Find out what substances are attracted to a magnet. Test a selection of both metals and non-metals. Examples of suitable metals to try are iron, copper, zinc, brass, nickel, steel, tin, a 'tin' can, aluminium, and examples of non-metals are wood, paper, plastic, glass and cork. Make a list of those substances which are attracted to a magnet. Such substances are called magnetic substances.

Complete the sentence:

A force of attraction occurs between ...... magnetic poles and a force of repulsion occurs between ..... poles.

5. Support a magnet in a clamp and see how many paper clips or pins you can hang from it, in the manner shown. Pins, when placed near to or touching a permanent magnet, have magnetism induced into them and become magnets by induction.

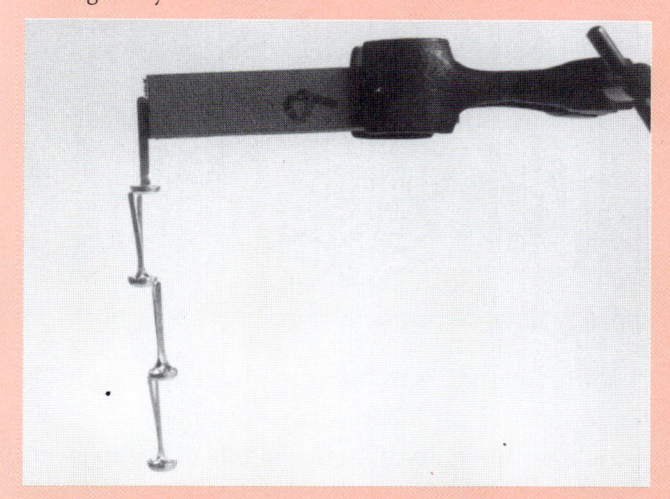

fig. 6.4

The magnetic compass

A compass consists of a magnet or a magnetised needle free to rotate. The sailors of old who explored the oceans and discovered new continents depended on the compass for navigation. Amongst items salvaged from the wrecks of the Spanish Armada are compasses, and these can be seen in the Ulster Museum in Belfast.

fig. 6.5 Magnetic compasses

STORING MAGNETS

If magnets are not stored properly, they become weak with age. This can be prevented by storing them in pairs, with unlike poles beside each other, and with pieces of soft iron called **keepers** across the ends.

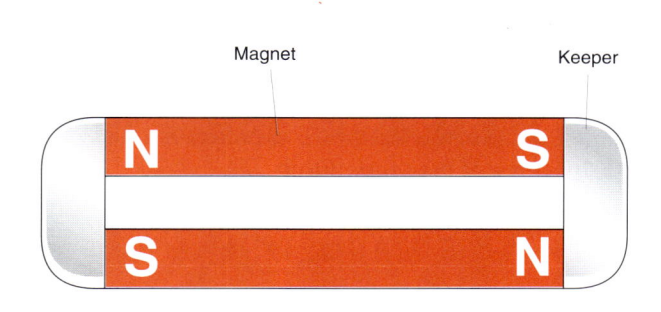

fig. 6.6 Magnets with keepers

PROPERTIES OF MAGNETS

1. A magnet has two poles, one at each end.

2. A magnet hung up free to swing, points in a north-south direction. The end pointing north is called the **north pole** of the magnet, and the end pointing south is the **south pole**.

3. Like poles repel each other; unlike poles attract.

4. A magnet attracts the metals iron and steel, nickel and cobalt. 'Tin' cans are attracted because they are made mainly of steel.

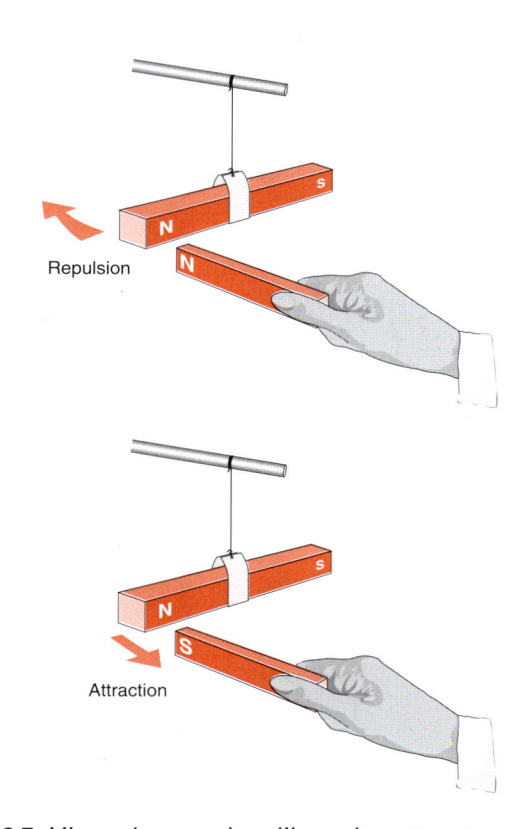

fig. 6.7 Like poles repel; unlike poles attract

MAGNETIC FIELDS

You have now discovered that magnets exert a force. In the next experiment, you will investigate this magnetic field.

6 • Magnetism

The region surrounding a magnet in which the magnetism can be detected is called the magnetic field of the magnet.

Experiment 6.2
To investigate a magnetic field

1. Lay a bar magnet in the middle of a large sheet of paper. Mark the position of the magnet by drawing its outline on the paper. Place a small plotting compass at the north pole of the magnet and, in pencil, place a dot on the paper in line with the north pole (the head of the arrow) of the compass. Then move the compass, placing the tail of the pointer exactly over the pencil dot. Mark another dot in line with the head of the arrow.

2. Continue in this way until you reach the south pole of the magnet (or until the dots approach the edge of the paper). Then join the dots, or better still, draw a smooth curve passing through the dots.

3. Make another series of dots, by starting with the plotting compass at a slightly different position (but still at the magnet's north pole). As before, draw a line through the dots. In this manner, draw about ten lines on each side of the magnet. Put arrow heads on each line, pointing from the north pole to the south pole. The lines which you have drawn are **lines of magnetic force**.

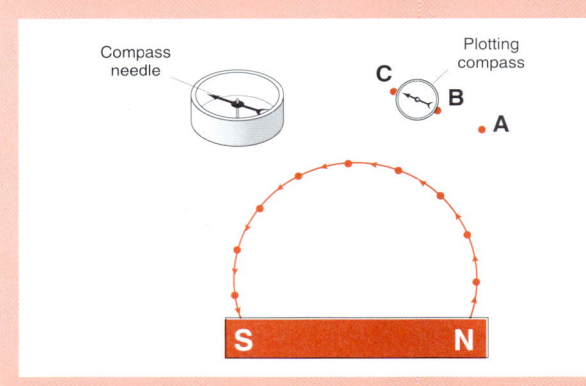

fig. 6.8

Lines of magnetic force are lines which go from the north pole of a magnet to the south pole, showing the direction in which a compass needle will point.

Magnetic fields, and also lines of magnetic force, can be shown in other ways. If a large number of plotting compasses is placed around a magnet, they show the pattern and the direction of the lines of force.

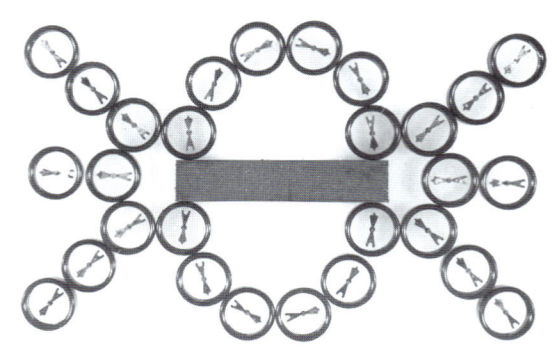

fig. 6.9 Lines of magnetic force

Another method is to use iron filings. To do this, lay a large sheet of cardboard over a magnet placed on the bench. Sprinkle iron filings lightly and evenly over the cardboard. Then tap the cardboard gently several times, when the filings will arrange themselves into the field pattern.

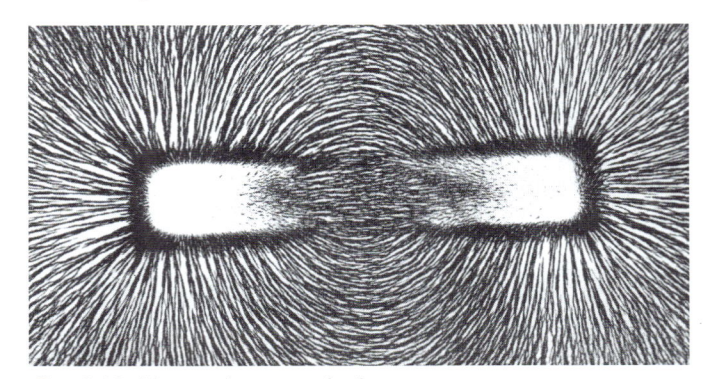

fig. 6.10 Lines of magnetic force

THE EARTH'S MAGNETISM

Everywhere on the Earth's surface, the compass needle points in a definite direction – towards magnetic north (which is not quite the same point as geographical north). This is why a compass is such a useful instrument in navigation, particularly where there are no roads, like on the sea and in the sky. All ships and aircraft carry compasses.

The Earth behaves like a huge magnet and has a magnetic field surrounding it. The first man who tried to explain this was Dr William Gilbert nearly 400 years ago. Gilbert was the doctor of Queen Elizabeth I of England, as well as being a scientist. In a book which Gilbert wrote in 1600, he suggested that the Earth acted as though it had an enormous magnet buried in it, with its south pole near the Earth's north and its north pole near the Earth's south. This explained why a compass needle points north. He had the right idea but his ideas cannot be completely true because the high temperature inside the Earth would destroy the magnetism of a natural magnet. There is still no fully satisfactory explanation of the Earth's magnetism.

fig. 6.11 Gilbert explaining the Earth's magnetism to Queen Elizabeth I

SUMMARY

- A magnet has two poles, one at each end. The end pointing north is called the **north pole** and that pointing south is the **south pole. Like poles repel** and **unlike poles attract**. Magnets attract **iron** and **steel**, **nickel** and **cobalt**. These are called magnetic metals.

- A **magnetic field** is the region surrounding a magnet in which the magnetism can be detected. A **line of magnetic force** is a line, going from the north pole to the south pole of a magnet, along which a compass needle points. Magnetic fields can be shown with a plotting compass or with iron filings.

- The Earth behaves like a huge magnet and has a magnetic field surrounding it; it is for this reason that one end of a compass needle points north (and the other end points south).

QUESTIONS

Q. 6.1
Rewrite and complete the spaces in the following paragraph:

A magnet has two ____, one at each end. When a magnet is hung up free to swing, it comes to rest pointing in a ____ ____ direction. The end of the ____ which points north is called the ____ ____ of the magnet. Like poles (e.g. ____ and ____) ____ each other and ____ poles ____ . Three metals attracted to a magnet are ____, ____ and ____ . 'Tin' cans are also attracted to a magnet; this is because they consist mainly of ____.

Q. 6.2
List three properties of magnets. Which of the following are magnetic metals: copper, iron, steel, tin, nickel, brass?

Q. 6.3
Explain the terms (i) magnetic field, (ii) line of magnetic force. Describe how you would plot the magnetic field around a bar magnet. Draw a diagram of the field pattern which would be produced.

Q. 6.4
The north pole of a magnet is brought near :
(a) the north pole of another magnet
(b) the south pole of another magnet
(c) a piece of steel
(d) a piece of copper

Describe what happens in each case.

Q. 6.5
Explain each of the following terms that are used in magnetism:
(a) pole of a magnet
(b) north pole
(c) magnetic metal
(d) keeper
(e) magnetic field
(f) line of magnetic force

Q. 6.6
(a) Name three magnetic metals.
(b) What is meant by the pole of a magnet?
(c) What names are given to a magnet's two poles?
(d) What happens when (i) like poles, (ii) unlike poles, are brought together?
(e) A magnet is hung up so it is free to swing. In what direction will it point?
(f) Name an instrument used to find direction.

7
DENSITY

fig. 7.1 Aeroboard has such a low density that even a 5 year old child can support a block of it measuring 100 cm by 60 cm by 20 cm

You know that iron is 'heavier' than wood, yet an iron nail is lighter than a wooden chair. Of course the reason is that there is more wood in the chair than there is iron in the nail. To make a fair comparison between the 'heaviness' of substances, you must compare the masses of equal volumes of those substances. This is what density is all about. In learning about density, remember the difference between weight and mass. Weight is the downwards force exerted by the Earth's gravity on an object, and so is not relevant to density.

The density of a substance is defined as the mass of unit volume of it.

The simplest units of mass and of volume are grams and cm^3, and so you can think of density as the mass (in grams) of each 1 cm^3 of the substance. For example, the mass of 1 cm^3 of iron is 7.8 g and the mass of 1 cm^3 of aluminium is 2.7 g.

To measure the density of a substance, you have to first find the mass and volume of a piece of the substance. Mass is easily measured – on a laboratory balance – and you should already know several ways of finding the volume of a substance. The formula which relates density, mass and volume is:

$$\text{density} = \frac{\text{mass}}{\text{volume}}$$

and the usual units are grams per cm^3 (g/cm^3).

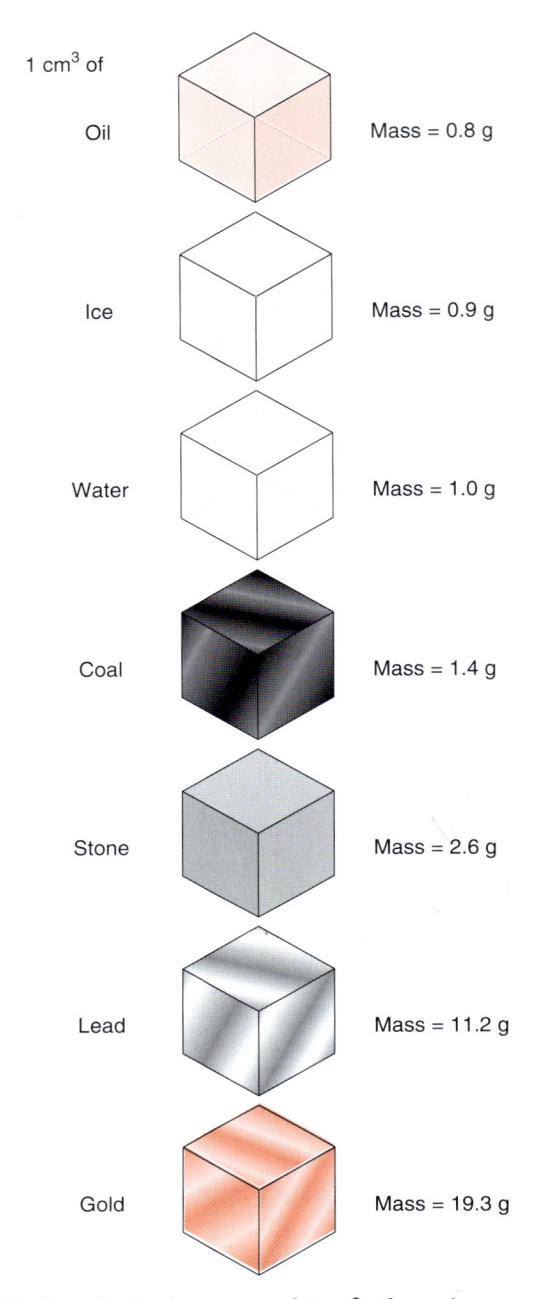

1 cm^3 of

Oil	Mass = 0.8 g
Ice	Mass = 0.9 g
Water	Mass = 1.0 g
Coal	Mass = 1.4 g
Stone	Mass = 2.6 g
Lead	Mass = 11.2 g
Gold	Mass = 19.3 g

fig. 7.2 Density is the mass of 1cm^3 of a substance

Worked example

A piece of coal whose mass is 48 g has a volume of 30 cm^3. Calculate its density.

$$\text{Density} = \frac{\text{mass}}{\text{volume}} = \frac{48}{30} = 1.6$$

1.6 what? 1.6 grams per cm^3, or, for short, 1.6 g/cm^3.

Experiment 7.1
To measure the density of a regular shaped solid

1. Find the dimensions (length, breadth and height) of the given object as accurately as you can measure them (to the nearest 0.1 cm).
2. Calculate the volume of the object to the nearest whole number. Be sure to give the correct unit for the volume.
3. Find the mass of the object by weighing it on the laboratory balance. Record its mass to the nearest gram. Be sure to put the correct unit after the value.
4. Using the formula which relates mass, volume and density, calculate the density of the object. Remember to put the correct unit after its value.
5. In the same way, find the density of several different materials.

Experiment 7.2
To measure the density of an irregular shaped solid

1. Select an irregular shaped solid, such as a stone or a piece of coal.
2. Find its mass by using the laboratory balance.
3. Find its volume; there are two ways of doing this; see page 11.
4. Calculate its density using the density formula.

Experiment 7.3
To measure the density of a liquid

1. Find the mass of a dry empty beaker (or conical flask).
2. Fill a second beaker with water. Now use a pipette (or small graduated cylinder) to transfer 25 cm³ of water to the beaker. Remember the rules about using a pipette, and use it as carefully and as accurately as possible.
3. Find the new mass of the beaker + water. Make sure that the beaker is not wet on the outside.
4. Subtract the mass of the empty beaker to find the mass of the liquid.
5. Calculate the density of water using the density formula.

Densities are of great practical importance to many people. Architects and engineers have to know about the densities of concrete and of steel in order to calculate the weight of a future bridge or building so that they can design foundations strong enough to support that weight. Designers of aircraft have to make use of the density of aluminium and of other metals in order to design wings large enough to provide sufficient 'lift'.

The density of a substance is a characteristic property of that substance, or, in other words, every substance has its own particular density, which is 'special' to that particular substance. The density of an iron nail is the same as the density of an iron girder.

Densities of substances vary from very high values to very low ones. The heaviest metal, osmium, has a density of 22.5 g/cm³. One of the lightest solids is expanded polystyrene or 'aeroboard', whose density is only about 0.02 g/cm³. Aeroboard is used in packing, in providing buoyancy for boats, and for heat insulation.

TABLE OF DENSITIES

Substance	Density (g/cm³)
Aeroboard	0.02
Aluminium	2.7
Brass	8.5
Brine	1.1
Candle wax	0.9
Coal	1.4
Copper	8.9
Cork	0.2
Glass	2.5
Gold	19.3
Ice	0.9
Iron	7.8
Lead	11.2
Mercury	13.6
Osmium	22.5
Paraffin oil	0.8
Sugar syrup	1.5
Stone (average)	2.6
Water	1.0
Wood	0.6 to 1.1

7 • Density

> The metal osmium is the densest substance known on Earth. Its density is about twice that of lead; if this book were made of osmium, it would weigh as much as a television set.

CALCULATIONS

This triangle may help you to do calculations on densities. Cover up the quantity you want, and you will be left with the terms for working it out. For example, if you want D, cover it up, and you are left with M/V, and that is how you calculate D.

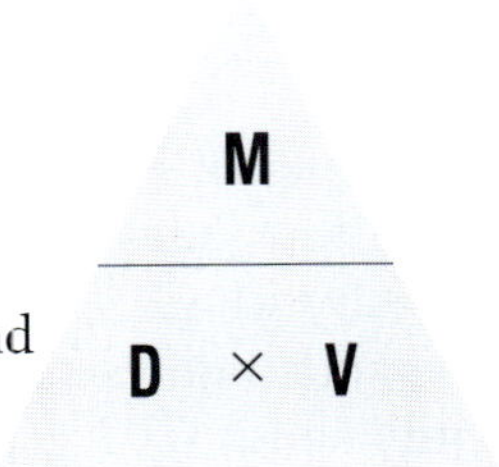

Worked Example

Q. Calculate the mass of 20 cm³ of lead.

A. Cover up the 'M' (the value that is needed) in the triangle; what remains is D × V.
So, mass = density × volume.
The density of lead is 11.2 g/cm³, and the volume needed is 20 cm³,
so the mass is 11.2 × 20, which is 224 grams.

QUESTIONS

Q. 7.1

Calculate the density of each the following items:
(a) a 200 cm³ block of aluminium which has a mass of 540 grams
(b) a metal block whose mass is 96 g and which measures 2 cm × 3 cm × 4 cm
(c) a brick which measures 20 × 10 × 6 cm, and has a mass of 3 kg
(d) a wooden cube whose side is 2 cm in length, and mass is 28 g
(e) a bar of soap, which has a volume of 200 cm³ and a mass of 220 g
(f) a 'pound' of butter, measuring 7 × 7 × 10 cm, and having a mass of 454 grams

Q. 7.2

Refer to the table of densities, and calculate the mass of each of the following:
(a) a stone whose volume is 20 cm³
(b) 500 cm³ of paraffin oil
(c) a pane of glass of thickness 0.4 cm and measuring 50 cm by 40 cm

Q. 7.3

Refer to the table of densities, and calculate the volume of each of:
(a) 100 g of glass
(b) 100 g of brass
(c) 100 g of softwood
(d) 100 g of aeroboard

FLOATING AND SINKING

Do coal and wood float? You will probably answer 'no' for the coal and 'yes' for the wood – but you could be wrong. The answer depends on what liquid they are put into.

> **Experiment 7.4**
> **Floating and sinking**
>
> 1. Into separate beakers put some (a) water, (b) paraffin oil, (c) brine, (d) sugar syrup.
>
> 2. Then into each, in turn, place a stone, a piece of coal, a piece of hardwood, a piece of softwood, and a cork.
>
> 3. Make a note of which materials float, and in which liquids. Now refer to the table of densities, and work out why a substance sometimes floats and other times it sinks.
>
> 4. An ice cube floats on water because ice is less dense than water.
>
> 5. An ice cube sinks in paraffin oil because ice is more dense than oil.

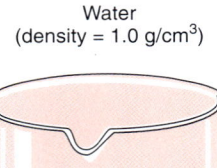

Water (density = 1.0 g/cm³)
Ice cube (density = 0.9 g/cm³) floats

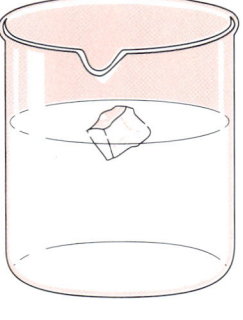

Paraffin oil (density = 0.8 g/cm³)
Ice cube (density = 0.9 g/cm³) sinks

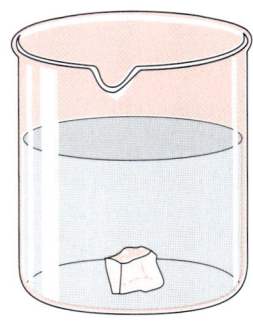

fig. 7.3 *An object floats on a liquid that is more dense than the object, but sinks in a liquid that is less dense*

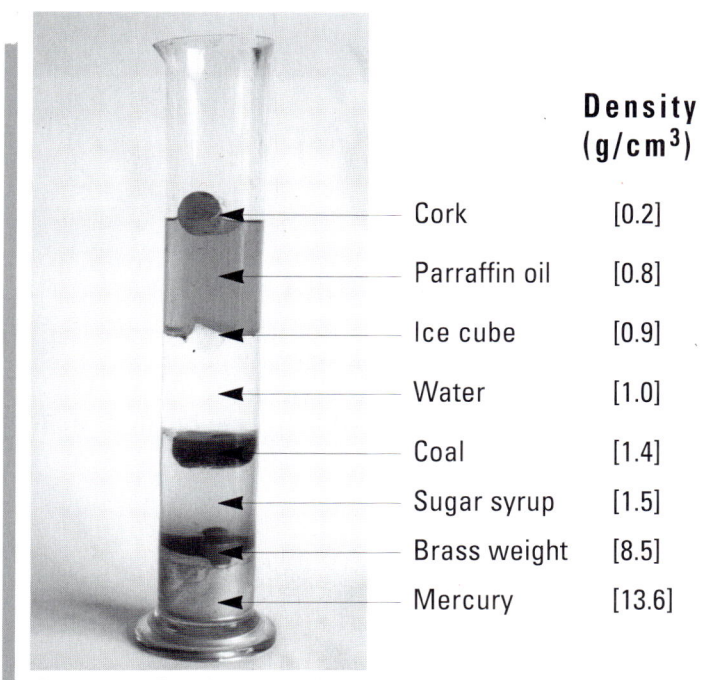

	Density (g/cm³)
Cork	[0.2]
Parraffin oil	[0.8]
Ice cube	[0.9]
Water	[1.0]
Coal	[1.4]
Sugar syrup	[1.5]
Brass weight	[8.5]
Mercury	[13.6]

fig. 7.4 A floating experiment

SUMMARY

- The **density** of a substance is its mass per unit volume, and it is usually expressed in g/cm³. To measure density, the mass and the volume of the substance is found, and the density then calculated. The formula which relates density, mass and volume is density = $^{mass}/_{volume}$. A solid floats on a liquid if the solid is less dense than the liquid, and it sinks if the solid is more dense than the liquid.

QUESTIONS

Q. 7.4
Write out the following paragraphs and complete the spaces:

(a) The density of a substance is the __ of __ cm³ of it. To find the density of, say a stone, both its __ and its __ must be measured. The density is calculated by dividing the __ of the stone by its __. Density is normally expressed in the units __.

(b) A solid which floats on a liquid means that the ___ of the solid is ___ than the ___ of the __. The density of candle wax is (consult the density table) __ and so it __ on water (density = 1 g/cm³) but __ in paraffin oil (density = __).

Q. 7.5
Which has the greater mass: 16 cm³ of iron or 10 cm³ of lead? (refer to the table of densities).

Q. 7.6
Consult the density table to answer this question. Which of the substances listed below float on (i) oil, (ii) sugar syrup (iii) mercury.

Gold, lead, ice, cork, rubber, candle wax, hardwood.

Q. 7.7
If you are a swimmer, you will know that it is much easier to float in the sea than in fresh water in a swimming pool. Explain why. It is easier still to float in the Dead Sea in Israel. Can you suggest the reason?

fig. 7.5 Floating on the Dead Sea

Q. 7.8
Explain each of the following:

(a) A bad egg floats on water, but a good egg sinks.
(b) A good egg can be made to float by dissolving salt in the water.
(c) When a ship passes from a river into the sea, it rises.
(d) Car oil floats on the tops of puddles of water.

Q. 7.9
Describe, using a diagram in each case, how you would measure the density of:

(a) a golf ball
(b) lemonade

Q. 7.10
A beaker weighs 37.3 g when empty, and 79.8 g when 50 cm³ of oil are added. What is the density of the oil?

Q. 7.11
Refer to the block of aeroboard shown in fig. 7.1, and to the density of aeroboard (on table of densities). Then calculate the mass of the block being carried by the child.

8 LEVERS AND CENTRE OF GRAVITY

TURNING FORCES – LEVERS

fig. 8.1 *Question: What is needed to do these jobs?*

A lever is a device or a simple machine which enables larger forces to be applied. Look at the diagrams above. Could these jobs be easily done without the lever?

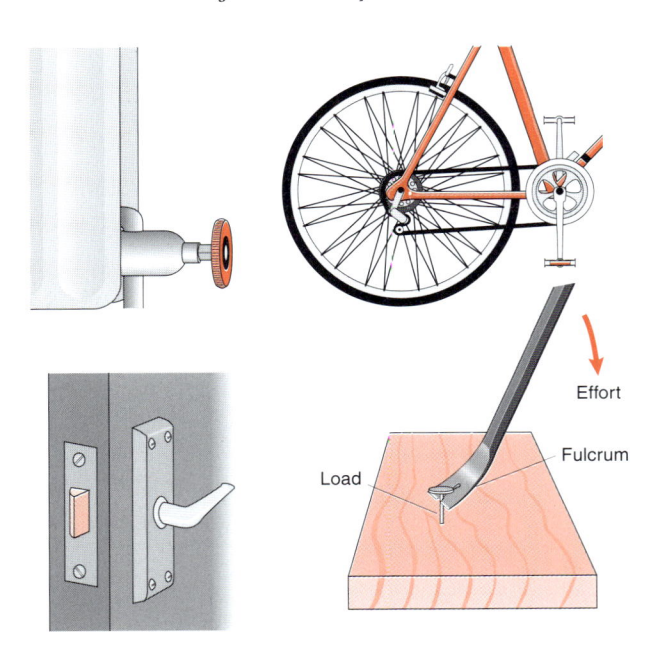

fig. 8.2 *Answer: Something that gives you a greater turning effect, i.e. a lever.*

If you think about a lever, it has several important points:

(i) it must be **rigid**, i.e. it must not bend;
(ii) there is a point about which it rotates, called the **fulcrum**;
(iii) a force or **effort** is applied to one end, and
(iv) there is a **load**, or work to be done, at the other end.

> **A lever is a rigid body which can rotate about a fixed point called the fulcrum.**

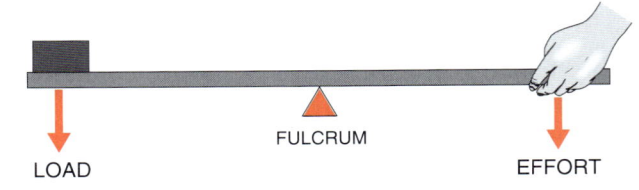

fig. 8.3 *Crowbar type lever*

There are other types of lever as well as the crowbar type. Can you spot the basic difference between the crowbar type and those shown in Figure 8.4?

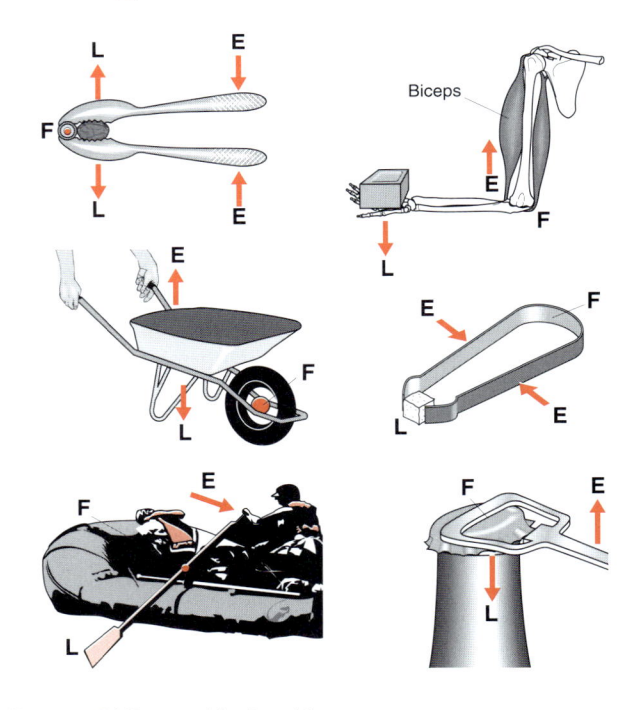

fig. 8.4 *Different kinds of lever*

Did you notice that the order of fulcrum, effort and load differs? In the crowbar type of lever, the fulcrum is in the middle, in the nutcracker, the load is in the middle, and in the forearm, the effort is in the middle. Another feature of levers is that double levers are quite common – fire tongs, nutcrackers, and a pair of scissors are all examples of double levers.

The turning effect of a force is called the moment of the force, and it depends on two things: (i) the size of the force, and (ii) how far the force is from the fulcrum.

> A moment is defined as the product of the force and the distance between the force and the fulcrum. (A product is the result of multiplying two numbers together.) Or in short,
> moment = force × distance

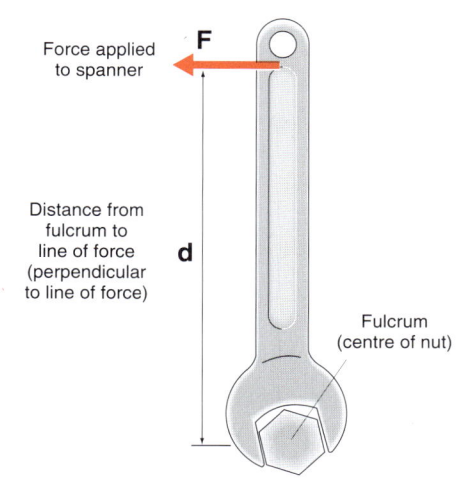

fig. 8.5 The moment is force × distance

Quote from Archimedes:
"Give me a lever long enough and a fulcrum strong enough and I will move the world."

Experiment 8.1
To investigate levers

1. Arrange the apparatus as shown in the diagram. If the metre stick does not balance, attach one or more rubber bands, or some sticky tape, to one end, until it does.

2. In this experiment, all distances are to be measured from the fulcrum, and readings are to be made to the nearest 0.1 cm.

3. Hang a 0.5 N weight (= 50 g) on the left hand side of the fulcrum, and at a distance of exactly 20 cm from it. *This weight is to remain there for the entire experiment*.

4. Hang a 1 N weight on the right hand side, in such a position that the metre stick balances. Note its position and work out its distance from the fulcrum. Draw out a results table such as shown below, and record the weight, and its distance from the fulcrum.

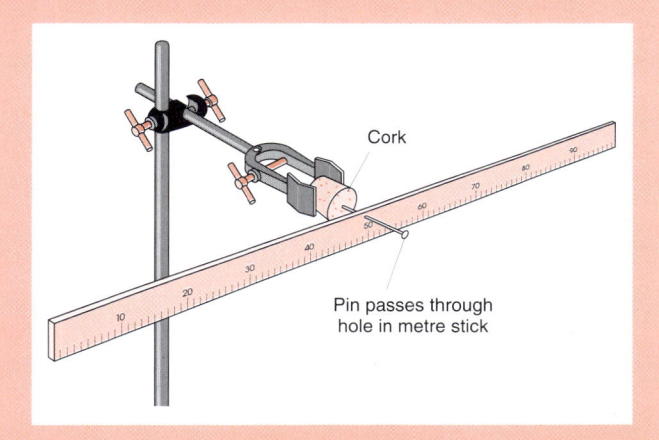

fig. 8.6

RESULTS

Left-hand side			Right-hand side		
Weight	Distance of weight from fulcrum	Moment	Weight	Distance of weight	Moment
0.5 N	20 cm	10	1 N 0.5 N etc.	? ?	? ?

(continued)

5. Now replace the 1 N weight with a 0.5 N weight – again placed in such a position that the metre stick balances. In the results table, make a note of the weight (0.5 N) and the distance between it and the fulcrum.

6. Repeat this procedure (as described in Step 5) but using weights of 0.4 N, and then 0.3 N. If you wish, you can also try other values, for example, any or all of 0.8 N, 0.7 N and 0.6 N. In each case, mark your findings in the results table.

7. Calculate the moment for each of the weights given in the table. What do you notice about their values?

8. What is the value of the moment on the left hand side? In order for the metre stick to balance, what must the moment on the right hand side be?

9. This information is given in the **law of the lever** which states:

When a lever is balanced, the total clockwise moment is equal to the total anticlockwise moment.

Worked examples

Remember: when doing calculations, it is the distance from the weight to the fulcrum that is needed.

Question 1

A metre stick hangs from its centre point. When a weight of 6 N is hung from the 10 cm mark, and a wooden block from the 80 cm mark, the stick balances. (i) Draw a diagram of the arrangement. (ii) Calculate the force exerted by the wooden block.

Answer 1

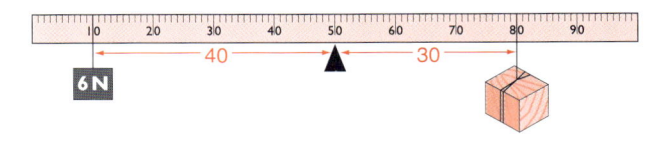

(i) **fig. 8.7**

(ii) Distance from wooden block (of weight x) to fulcrum = 30 cm
Clockwise moment = $30 \times x = 30x$

Distance from 6 N weight to fulcrum = 40 cm
Anticlockwise moment = $40 \times 6 = 240$

Metre stick balances,
∴ $30x = 240$, ∴ $x = {}^{240}/_{30} = 8$.

The wooden block weighs 8 N.

Question 2

A metre stick is hung from its centre point and a 2 N weight is hung from the left hand side, at a distance of 45 cm from the fulcrum. From where must a 5 N weight be hung so that the stick balances? Draw a diagram of the arrangement.

Answer 2

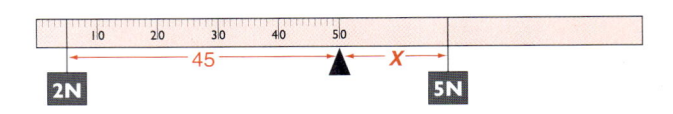

fig. 8.8

Distance from 5 N weight to fulcrum = x
Clockwise moment = $5x$

Distance from 2 N weight to fulcrum = 45 cm
Anticlockwise moment = $45 \times 2 = 90$

Metre stick balances, ∴ $5x = 90$, ∴ $x = {}^{90}/_{5} = 18$

The 5 N weight must be hung at the right-hand side of the fulcrum, at a distance of 18 cm from it. The point on the metre stick is therefore the 68 cm mark (i.e. 18 cm past the fulcrum).

Question 3

A metre stick is balanced with four weights hanging from it, as shown. Calculate the weight of the unknown one.

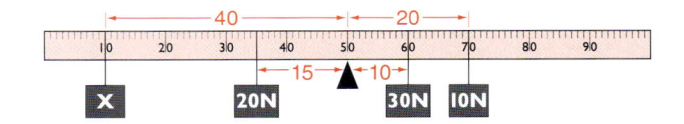

fig. 8.9

Answer 3

Anticlockwise moments
= $40x + (15 \times 20) = 40x + 300$.

Clockwise moments
= $(10 \times 30) + (20 \times 10) = 300 + 200 = 500$.

Since stick is balanced, moments are equal,
∴ $40x + 300 = 500$, $40x = 500 - 300 = 200$,
$x = {}^{200}/_{40} = 5$ N.

QUESTIONS

Q. 8.1
Draw diagrams of a wheelbarrow, a claw-hammer, tweezers, bicycle brake control, see-saw, and mark the fulcrum, the load, and the effort in each case.

Q. 8.2
A mechanic applies a force of 200 N at the end of a spanner of length 20 cm. What moment is applied to the nut?

Q. 8.3
Which of the levers in Figure 8.10 are balanced? For each of the unbalanced ones, state which end requires more weight to balance it.

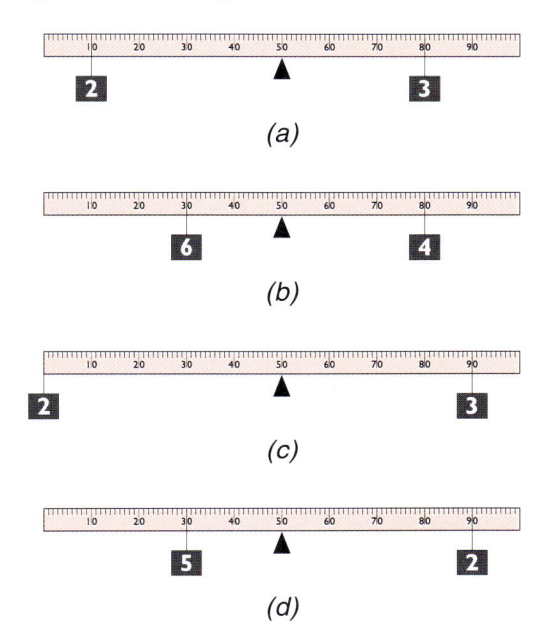

fig. 8.10

Q. 8.4
A uniform metre stick is hung from its centre. A 3 N weight hangs from the 88 cm mark and another weight from the 35 cm mark. Draw a diagram of the arrangement and calculate how heavy the other weight is.

Q. 8.5
A uniform metre stick is hung from its centre. A 30 N weight hangs from the 78 cm mark and another weight from the 38 cm mark. Draw a diagram of the arrangement, and calculate how heavy the other weight is.

Q. 8.6
A boy who weighs 400 N sits on a see-saw at a distance of 3 m from the fulcrum. Where must a girl who weighs 300 N sit, so that the see-saw balances?

Q. 8.7
A uniform metre stick hangs from the 50 cm mark, and a 2 N weight is attached at the 65 cm mark. Where must a 1 N weight be attached so that the metre stick balances? Draw a diagram of the arrangement.

Q. 8.8
A metre stick is suspended at its centre, and a 10 N weight is hung from the 30 cm mark. From what point must (i) another 10 N weight, (ii) a 5 N weight be hung so that the stick balances in each case?

Q. 8.9
Here are diagrams of four levers balanced under the action of different forces. Calculate the value of x in each case.

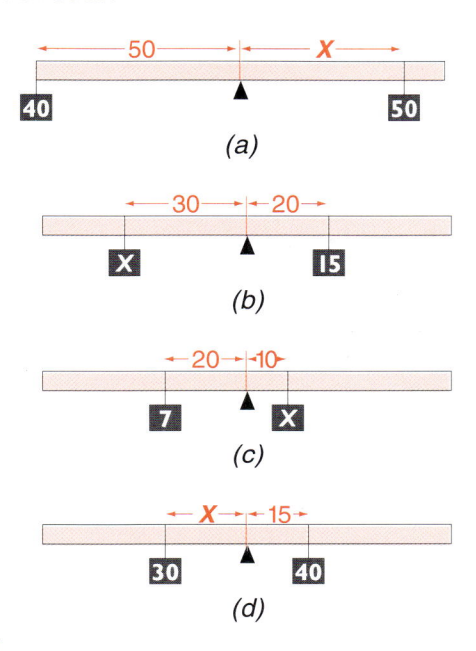

fig. 8.11

Q. 8.10
A metre stick is suspended from the 50 cm mark and a 5 N weight from the 20 cm mark. (i) What weight hanging from the 65 cm mark will balance the metre stick? (ii) Where must a 10 N weight be hung so that the stick balances?

Q. 8.11
A boy weighing 600 N sits on a see-saw at a distance of 2 m from the fulcrum. What force at a point 3 m from the fulcrum is necessary to balance him? (The see-saw is supported at its centre.)

Q. 8.12
A uniform metre stick hangs from the 50 cm mark and a 20 N weight is attached at the 65 cm mark. Where must a 10 N weight be attached so that the stick balances?

Q. 8.13

A metre stick hangs from the 50 cm mark and a 10 N weight from the 20 cm mark. Where must a 15 N weight be hung so that the stick balances? Draw a diagram of the arrangement.

Q. 8.14

A uniform metre stick is hung from its centre. The following weights are hung from it: 2 N from the 10 cm mark; 3 N from the 30 cm; 8 N from the 40 cm. What weight must be hung from the 72 cm mark to make the stick balance?

CENTRE OF GRAVITY

A metre stick can be balanced by supporting it at its centre. Although every part of the stick has weight, it behaves as if its whole weight is at the centre – where it balances. This point is called the **centre of gravity**.

> The centre of gravity of an object is the point where its whole weight acts, or appears to be concentrated.

The centre of gravity of a regular object such as a metre stick is at its centre, but for an irregular object, the centre of gravity must be found by experiment. When an object is freely suspended, its centre of gravity always lies directly below the point of suspension (the point from which it is hung) and if a vertical line is drawn down from the point of suspension, it must pass through the centre of gravity.

EQUILIBRIUM

> An object that is standing or suspended in such a way that it stays where it is put is said to be in *equilibrium*.

When all the forces acting on an object cancel out, it stays where it is put. It is then said to be in **equilibrium**.

There are three different states of equilibrium. Look at the bottle which is shown in Figure 8.13. In which of these positions do you think it is most stable, i.e. most likely to remain in that position? And in which position is it least likely to do so?

Experiment 8.2
To find the centre of gravity of a piece of cardboard

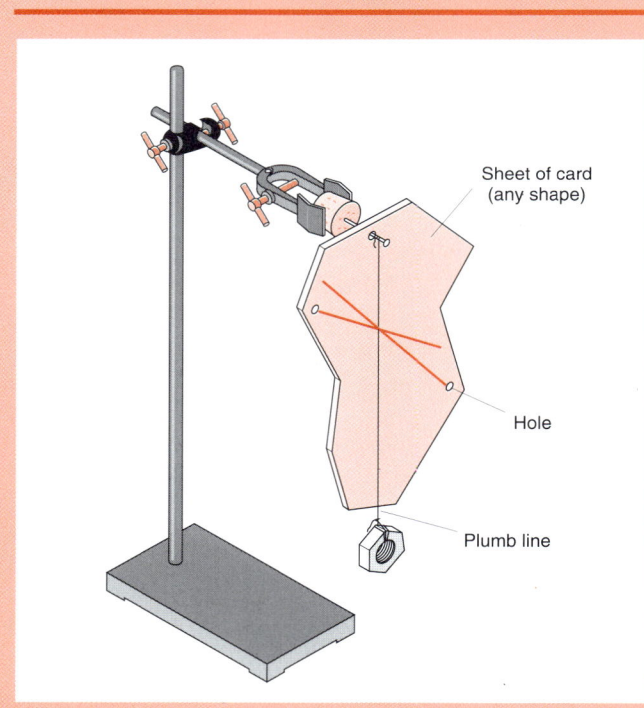

1. Set up the apparatus as shown.
2. **Carefully and accurately** put a few pencil marks on the cardboard directly behind the plumbline.
3. Remove the cardboard and draw a straight line (use a ruler) through the marks.
4. Hang the cardboard from a different point and repeat the procedure.
5. The centre of gravity is the point where the two lines cross.
6. You can check on the accuracy of your work in the following two ways: (i) Place the point you have found on the tip of your finger (pointing upwards); if your work was accurate, the cardboard will balance. (ii) Draw another line on the cardboard in the same manner as those already drawn; if your work is accurate, all three lines will cross at the same point.

fig. 8.12

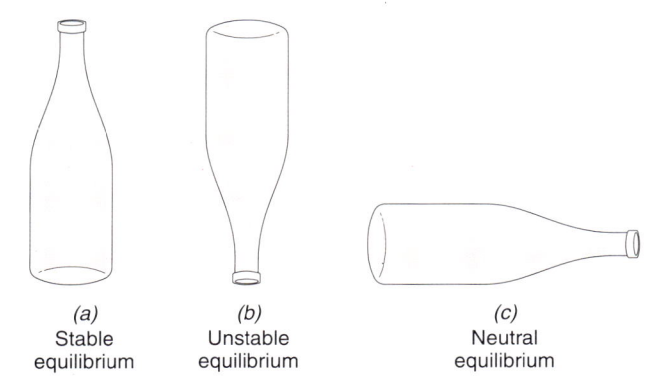

fig. 8.13 Stable, unstable and neutral equilibrium

(a) Stable equilibrium
(b) Unstable equilibrium
(c) Neutral equilibrium

fig. 8.14 The anglepoise is stable because of the wide base and low centre of gravity

In (a), the bottle is least likely to fall over and is said to be in **stable equilibrium**.

In (b), it if is given a small push, it will probably topple over; it is said to be in **unstable equilibrium**.

In (c), if it is given a small push, it will roll and just stay in its new position, and is described as being in **neutral equilibrium**.

For greatest stability, the centre of gravity of an object should be as low as possible, and the base of the object as large as possible. Can you explain the design of the anglepoise lamp shown in the diagram?

There are many amusing toys that look as if they are unstable, but are, in fact, stable. In the toys illustrated in Figure 8.15, the centre of gravity is low (below the point of suspension if the object is hanging), and so they stay balanced.

SUMMARY

- A **lever** is a rigid body which can rotate about a fixed point called the **fulcrum**. There are three parts to a lever: the **effort**, the **load** and the **fulcrum**.
- A **moment** is a measure of a turning effect. It is the product of a force and the distance between the force and the fulcrum.
- The **law of the lever** states that when a lever is balanced, the sum of the clockwise moments is equal to the sum of the anticlockwise moments.
- The **centre of gravity** of a body is the point at which its whole weight acts.
- There are three states of equilibrium. A body is in **stable equilibrium** if, when it is moved slightly, it returns to its original position; if it moves further away, it is in **unstable equilibrium**, and if it stays in its new position, it is in **neutral equilibrium**.

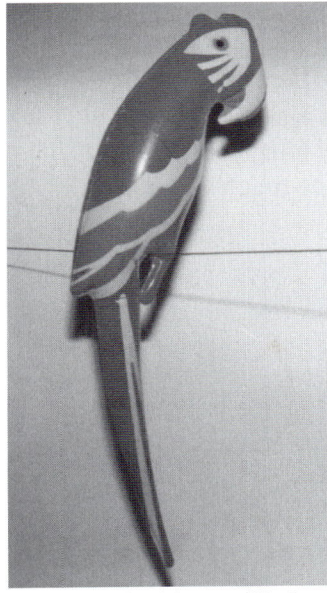

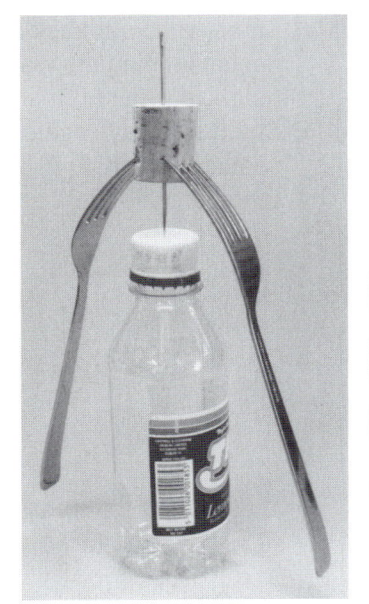

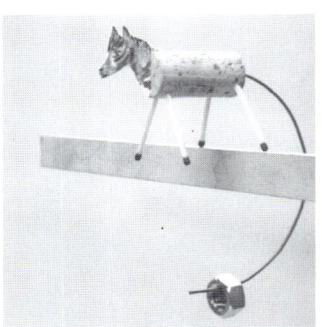

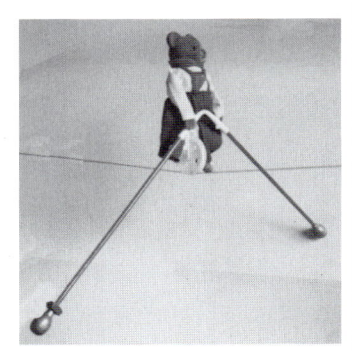

fig. 8.15 Stable equilibrium

8 • Levers and Centre of Gravity

QUESTIONS

Q. 8.15
Copy out and complete the following paragraphs:

(a) A lever is a ____ body which can ____ about a fixed point called the ____ . The turning effect of a force is called the ____ of the force. When an ___ is applied to a lever, the lever rotates about the ___ and makes the ___ move. The moment of a force is equal to the ___ multiplied by the ____ between the ___ and the ____. The law of the lever states that when a lever is ___, the sum of the ___ moments is ___ to the sum of the ___ ___.

(b) The ___ of ___ of an object is the point at which all its ___ acts, or appears to be concentrated. When an object stays where it is put, it is said to be in ___. There are three states of ___, stable, ___, and ___. The stability of an object can be increased by ____ its centre of ____ or by increasing the area of its ____ .

Q. 8.16
Write an account of an experiment in which you showed the law of the lever to be true. Do this under the headings:
(i) a diagram of the apparatus used
(ii) a description of how you carried out the experiment
(iii) measurements taken
(iv) conclusion

Q. 8.17
Write an account of an experiment in which you found the centre of gravity of an irregularly shaped piece of material. Include:
(i) a diagram of the apparatus used
(ii) a description of how you carried out the experiment
(iii) how you showed that your conclusion was correct

Q. 8.18
Which of the objects in Figure 8.16 is in:
(a) neutral equilibrium?
(b) stable equilibrium?
(c) unstable equilibrium?

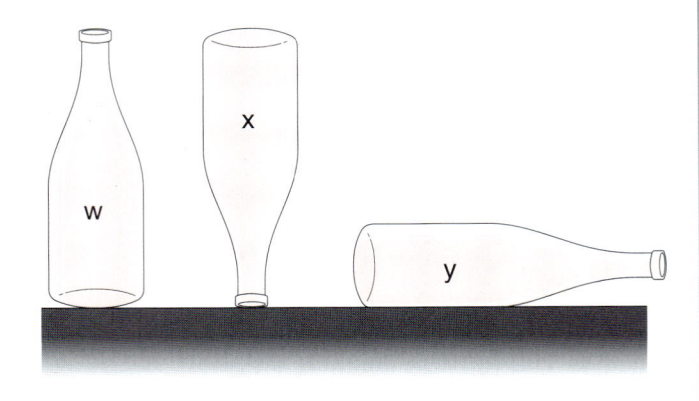

fig. 8.16

Q. 8.19
What is meant by each of the following terms?
(a) force
(b) lever
(c) the law of the lever
(d) equilibrium
(e) centre of gravity
(f) fulcrum

Q. 8.20
Carry out the following two experiments and explain the results in terms of centre of gravity and equilibrium. Draw diagrams to illustrate your answers.
(a) Stand with your back to the wall, put your heels touching the wall, and bend over and touch your toes.
(b) Stand sideways against a wall with your shoulder touching it. Now bring your two feet together, with the inner one touching the wall.

9
ELECTRIC CIRCUITS AND ELECTRIC CHARGES

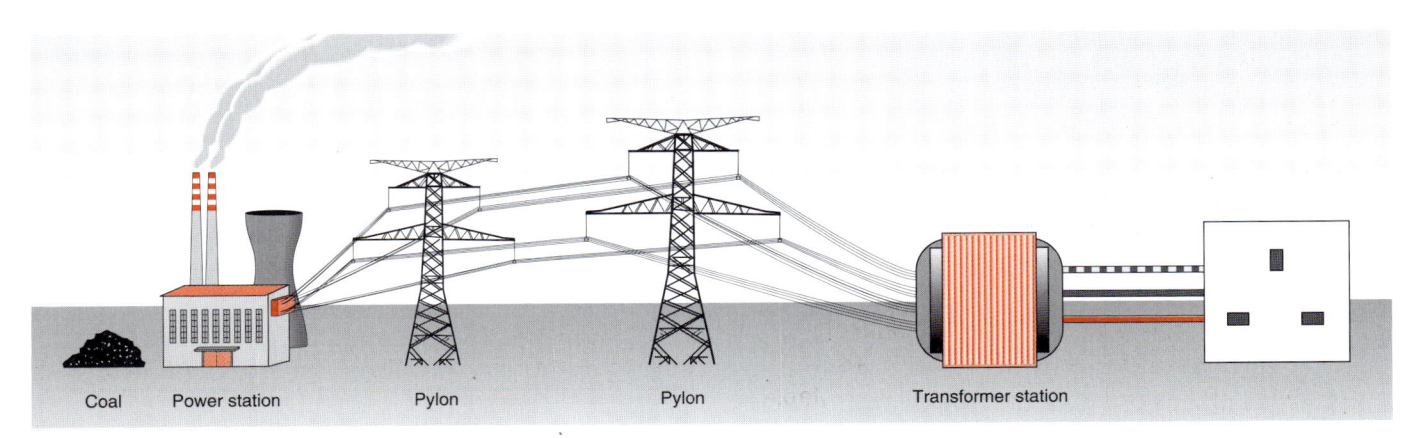

fig. 9.1 How electricity gets to the plug

Can you imagine life before the days of electricity? Think of how much you use electricity in your home and in your daily life. How many electrical devices did you make use of today – electric light, cooker, toaster, kettle? Something with an electric motor in it, such as a hair dryer, tape deck or 'Walkman'? And how did you travel to school – by car, bus or train? You see, you depend very much on electricity in your daily life. So, where does electricity come from?

Electricity comes from power stations where it is generated in huge quantities to satisfy the needs of the modern world. Electricity also comes from batteries. The strength of a battery or other source of electricity is measured in units called **volts**, after the Italian scientist, Alessandro Volta, who invented the battery.

A single cell battery, like one of those shown in fig. 9.2, produces about 1.5 volts and when, for example, four of these are connected together as in a torch, a 6 volt battery is produced. The battery in a car provides 12 volts. The strength of the mains electricity in your home is 230 volts and this high voltage can be dangerous if misused. People have been killed from shocks from mains electricity and so mains electricity must only be used with suitably designed equipment.

You can think of a battery as a pump for electricity. It produces what can be thought of as electrical 'pressure' which is what makes an electric current flow. The scientific word for electrical pressure is **potential difference**. **Electric current is a flow of electric charge**, and it is measured in units called **amperes** (which are usually called **amps** for short).

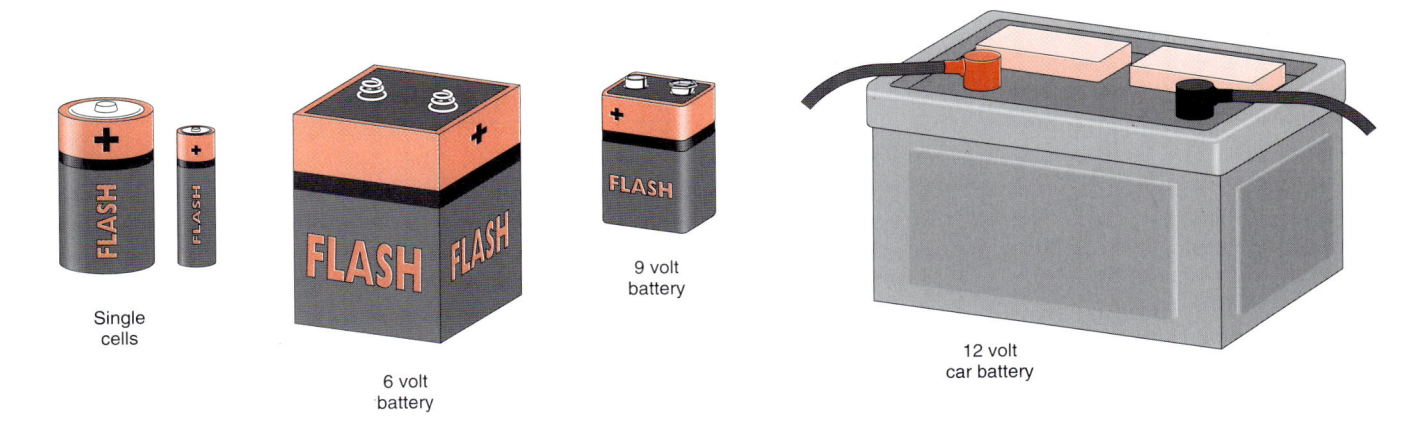

fig. 9.2 Single and multi-cell batteries

■ 9 • Electric Circuits and Electric Charges

fig. 9.3

Alessandro Volta, who lived from 1745 to 1827, was an Italian professor of physics. His great discovery was that when two different metals dipping into dilute acid were connected by a wire, an electric current flowed through the wire. This was the first means of getting a continuous flow of electricity. His discovery led to all of the batteries that are in use today.

ELECTRIC CIRCUITS

Just as water has to flow through a pipe or channel, electricity has to flow through wires – or other 'conducting' materials. The path taken by an electric current is called an **electric circuit**. A simple circuit is shown below.

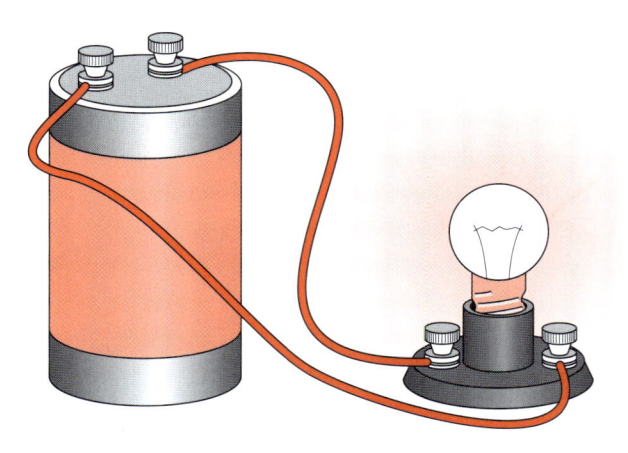

fig. 9.4 Note that the bulb is connected to the battery by two wires, one from each terminal. The two wires are necessary to provide a path for the electricity to the bulb, and then from the bulb back to the battery.

An electric circuit is a continuous path for an electric current, from one terminal of the battery, through wires and bulbs, etc. back to the other terminal of the battery. If the circuit is not complete, a current does not flow.

In electric circuit diagrams, symbols are used to represent items such as batteries, bulbs and switches, rather than life-like drawings. You need to remember the symbols shown in the diagram.

	SYMBOL	DEVICE
Ammeter	—(A)—	
Battery (The symbol for a battery denotes a positive and negative pole; the long stroke is the + terminal)	—|--|—	
Bulb	—(○)—	
Fuse	—[ ]—	
Motor	—(M)—	
Resistor	—[ ]—	
Single cell	—|⋅—	
Switch	—/ —	
Variable resistor	—[⌿]—	
Voltmeter	—(V)—	

fig. 9.5 Electrical symbols

Experiment 9.1
Investigating electric circuits

Part 1: Switches

Using two connecting wires, join a battery to a bulb so that the bulb lights. Now, using only three wires, connect a switch into the circuit so that it switches the bulb on and off (if necessary, see Figure 9.4).

Part 2: Conductors and Insulators

Wires used to connect circuits like that of the previous experiment are made of copper – which is a good **conductor** of electricity (i.e. it can carry current well). Not all substances conduct electricity; those that do not are called **insulators**. Use your circuit to find out which materials are conductors, and which are insulators. Remove the switch, and into the gap, insert pieces of different materials, e.g. iron, brass, wood, plastic, zinc, cardboard, aluminium, glass, steel, cloth, pencil 'lead'. List these in two columns, conductors and insulators.

Part 3: Resistance

Into your circuit, connect a length of wire such as 'nichrome' or 'constantan'. Find out if varying the length of the wire makes any difference to the brightness of the bulb.

Part 4: Rheostats (variable resistors)

Now in place of the wire, connect a rheostat. Find out the effect of moving the rheostat control.

Part 5: Series and Parallel Circuits

The diagrams show two ways of connecting electrical components together. Connect a battery to two bulbs in series with each other. What happens when one bulb is unscrewed? Can you explain why? Does the same happen when the other is unscrewed? Why?

Now connect a battery to two bulbs, this time in parallel with each other. Does the light from the bulbs differ from what it was like when they were in series? What happens when one bulb is unscrewed?

fig. 9.6 (a) Bulbs connected in series

fig. 9.6 (b) Bulbs connected in parallel

Part 6: Ammeters

Electric current is measured in units called **amperes** (or 'amps'). A bulb is not the best indicator of current. A much better indicator is an ammeter. Into the circuit of the previous experiment, connect a rheostat and an ammeter in series with the bulbs. Note the effect on the current of moving the rheostat. What happens to the current when the resistance is (i) increased, (ii) decreased?

CONDUCTORS AND INSULATORS

Electrical wire is made of copper because it is one of the best **conductors**; this means that electricity can flow through it. Wire is covered with plastic, because plastic is one of the best **insulators** (electricity cannot flow through it). Insulators are just as important as conductors in the construction of electrical equipment. Plugs and switches have plastic cases to insulate them, and electrician's pliers and screwdrivers have plastic handles for the same reason. Porcelain insulators are used on ESB poles for connecting the wire to the pole.

9 • Electric Circuits and Electric Charges

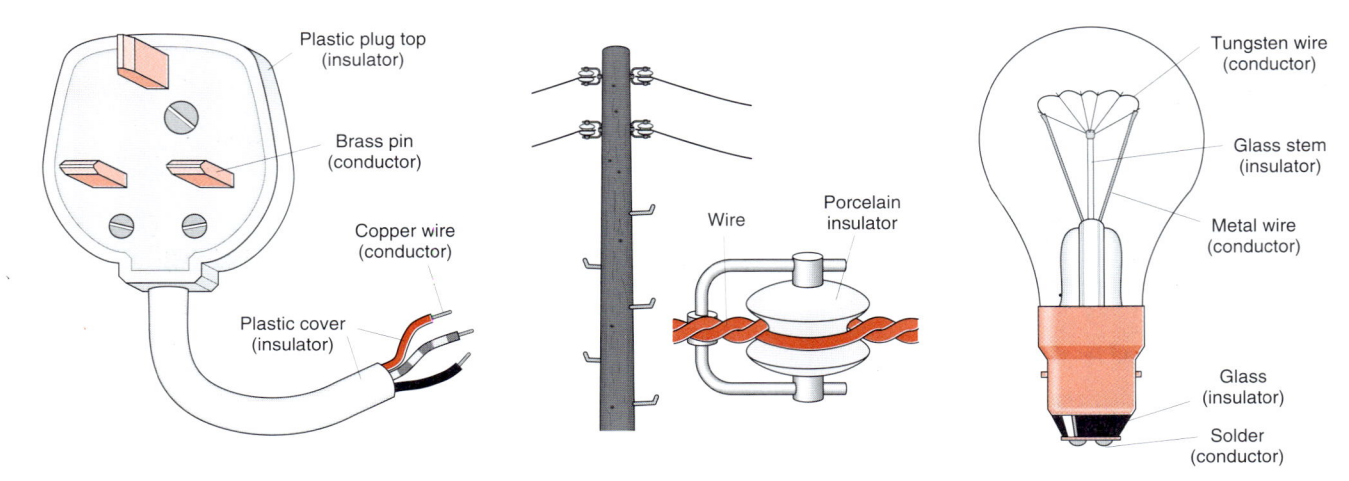

fig. 9.7 Conductors and insulators

SERIES AND PARALLEL CIRCUITS

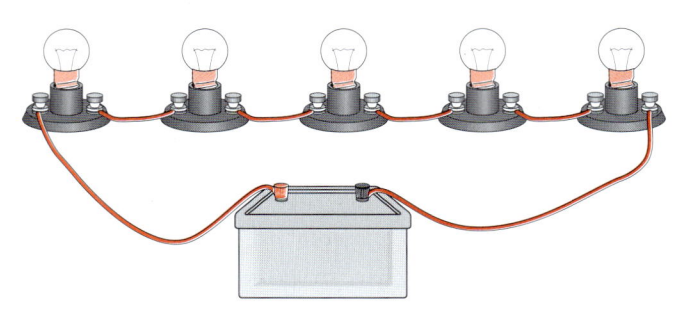

fig. 9.8 Bulbs in series

These bulbs are connected in series. They have to share the battery voltage, and so each gets only one fifth of the total voltage. They do not light fully. If one bulb is removed, the circuit is broken so the others also go out.

Batteries can also be connected in series in order to provide larger voltages. In most torches, 'Walkmans', and other battery-operated devices, there are several 1.5 V batteries, connected 'one after the other', in order to provide whatever voltage is required by the device.

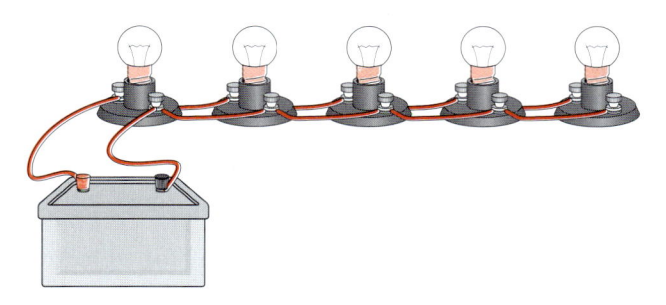

fig. 9.9 Bulbs in parallel

These bulbs are connected in parallel. Each has a direct connection to the battery and so each gets the full battery voltage. Each lights fully. If one bulb is removed, there is still an unbroken connection to the others and so they continue to light.

RESISTANCE AND RHEOSTATS

All wires offer some opposition to the flow of current, and this property is called **resistance**. Copper wire has a very small resistance which means it can conduct well. Some special types of wire (e.g. nichrome, constantan) offer resistance to current. The longer the length of such wire in a circuit, the greater is the resistance and the smaller is the current that flows.

If a sufficiently large current is passed through resistance wire, the wire gets hot. For this reason, resistance wire is used in appliances such as electric fires and hair dryers.

Resistance is measured in units called **ohms** (after a German scientist) and are denoted by the symbol Ω (this is a Greek letter called omega). A resistor is a component specially constructed to have resistance. Resistors are used in all radios and TV sets, tape recorders, calculators and computers, and they are made in values ranging from very low (e.g. 0.1 ohm) to very high (e.g. 10 million ohms).

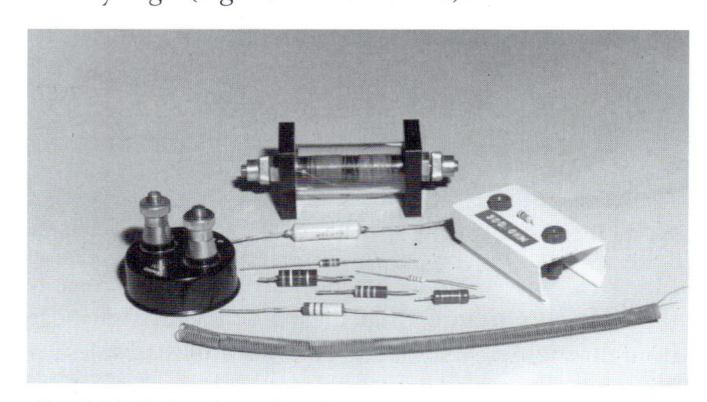

fig. 9.10 Selection of resistors

Some types of resistors are variable in value and these are called **rheostats** or **variable resistors**. The common laboratory rheostat like that illustrated, consists of a coil of resistance wire wound on an insulated frame. A metal contact slides over, and makes contact with the top of the coil. The amount of resistance depends on the position of the sliding contact. In some rheostats, the wire is wound on a circular frame and the resistance is varied by turning a knob attached to the sliding contact. Rheostats are used to dim lights, and to vary the volume of the sound in radios and TV sets.

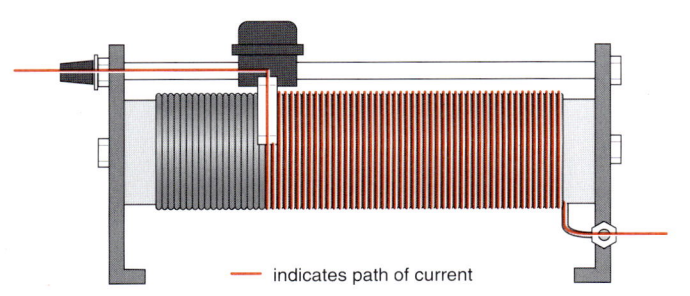

— indicates path of current

fig. 9.11 A variable resistor or rheostat

QUESTIONS

Q. 9.1

Rewrite the following paragraphs and complete the spaces in each:

(a) Some materials allow electricity to flow through them. Such materials are called ____, and three examples are ____, ____ and ____. A flow of electricity is called an electric ____ and it is measured in units called ____.

(b) The resistors shown in the diagram are connected in ____ and they have a combined resistance of ____ ohms. When they are connected to a ____, a ____ flows through them. The strength of a battery is measured in ____, and ____ is measured in amps.

fig. 9.12

(c) Electric wire is normally made of the metal ____ (because it is a ____ of electricity) and it is covered with ____ because this substance is an ____.

Q. 9.2

Name (i) three good conductors of electricity, (ii) three good insulators of electricity.

Q. 9.3

A light bulb contains both conductors and insulators. Draw a bulb (have a look at one to help) and label two parts that are conductors and two that are insulators.

Q. 9.4

What are the readings shown by the following instruments. Give the correct unit of each quantity.

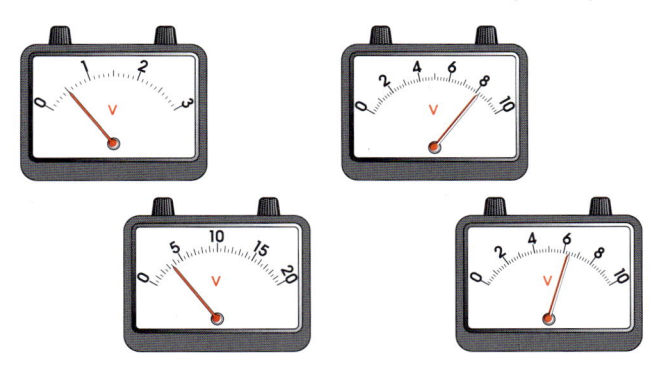

fig. 9.13

Q. 9.5

Describe an experiment to find out if a given material is a conductor or insulator. Draw a diagram of the electrical circuit you would use, and describe what you would do.

Q. 9.6

You have a supply of 1.5 volt batteries. Describe how you would use them to obtain:

(i) 6 volts, (ii) 9 volts, (iii) 4.5 volts.

Draw diagrams to illustrate your answers.

Q. 9.7

Draw circuit diagrams of a battery connected to

(a) two bulbs in series
(b) two bulbs in parallel
(c) two bulbs in parallel with a switch controlling both of them
(d) two bulbs in series with a switch controlling just one of them
(e) two bulbs in series with a rheostat controlling their brightness

Q. 9.8

How does the current in the following circuit change when:

(a) the resistance of the rheostat is increased
(b) the resistance of the rheostat is decreased
(c) the single cell is replaced by a two-cell battery
(d) another bulb is placed in series with the one that is there already

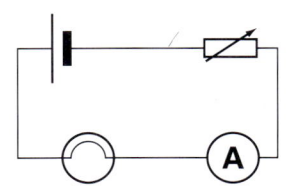

fig. 9.14

ELECTRIC CHARGES OR STATIC ELECTRICITY

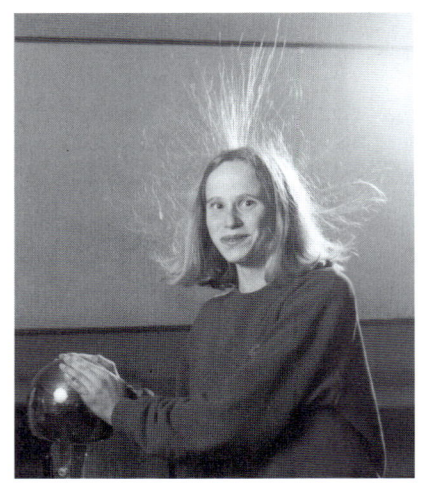

fig. 9.15 *Kate is charged up to about 50 000 volts from the van de Graaff generator. Like charges repel and so her hair is repelled from her head.*

You probably know something about static electricity already – without knowing that you do! Have you ever unrolled some 'clingwrap' and discovered that it sticks to itself, and to your hands and to anything else that it touches? Have you ever rubbed a balloon on your jumper and found that it can stick to the ceiling? (A sausage-shaped balloon is best for this.) Have you ever felt a shock when you have been walking on nylon carpets and then touched a metal object? Or have you noticed that when you take off an acrylic, nylon or polyester garment, particularly in warm dry weather, that you hear a crackling sound? If you do this in the dark you can sometimes see sparks!

Electric charges are produced when insulators are rubbed with a dry cloth, and the effects mentioned above are all caused by static electricity, which is sometimes referred to as just 'static'. The ancient Greeks of 2000 years ago knew about this type of electricity. In fact the word for electricity comes from the

Experiment 9.2
Investigating electrostatics

For these experiments to work properly, all apparatus must be absolutely dry. Use a hair dryer to dry the equipment if necessary.

1. Rub a polythene rod with a dry cloth until you can hear a slight crackling sound. Then bring the rod near some small pieces of paper or broken-up aeroboard. Are the pieces attracted? Bring the charged rod near to a thin stream of water from the tap (Fig. (a) below). Is the water attracted?

2. Charge the polythene rod again and hang it up in a stirrup, like that shown. Charge another polythene rod, and bring it near the hanging rod (Fig. (b)). Is it attracted or repelled?

3. Repeat the previous test, but with a charged acetate rod. Is the result the same or different?

4. Could the charge on the polythene rod be the same as the charge on the acetate rod?

5. Take two strips of polythene and charge them by pulling them through the folds of a cloth. Then hold the two strips together (Fig. (c)). Why are the strips repelled from each other?

6. Suspend a polystyrene sphere from a piece of thread, and bring a charged rod near (Fig. (d)). Can you explain what happens?

7. Hold a charged rod above the head of one of your friends who has dry fine hair.

(continued)

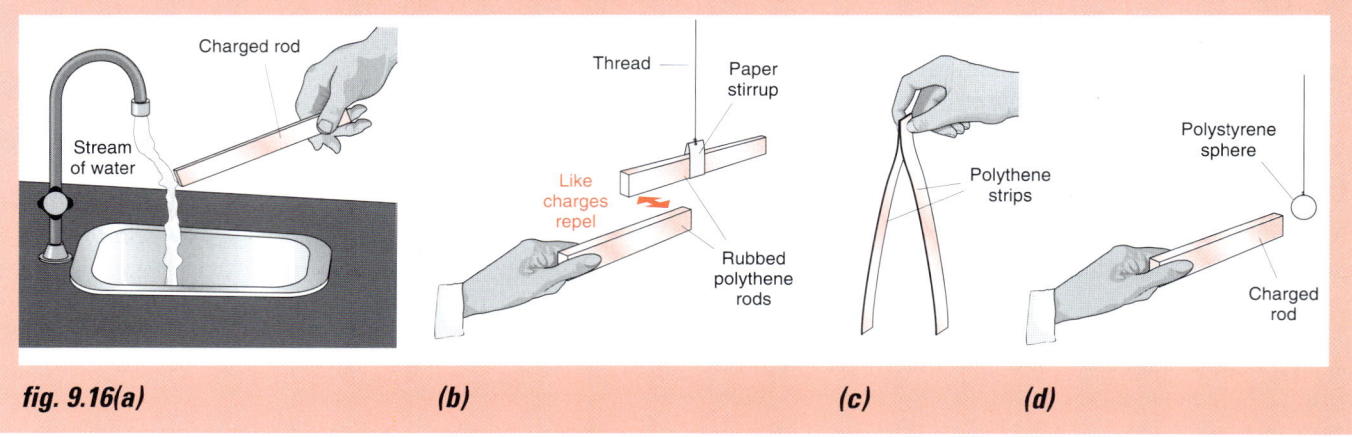

fig. 9.16(a)   **(b)**   **(c)**   **(d)**

Conclusions

- When insulators are rubbed, they become electrically charged or 'electrified'.
- There are two types of charge: positive and negative.
- Polythene becomes negatively charged, acetate positive.
- Like charges repel; unlike charges attract.
- Charged objects exert a force on other objects.

Greek word ηλεκτρον which means 'amber' – a substance which they used to make necklaces. When this substance was rubbed, it was able to attract and pick up small objects.

Modern plastics and other synthetic (man-made) materials are much more easily charged than the amber which the Greeks used, and in your experiments on static electricity you will use two different types of plastic, polythene and acetate. Polythene is the familiar material of which supermarket bags are made and acetate (cellulose acetate) is the plastic which is made into films. Alternatively, perspex could be used for these experiments.

Static electricity can build up on moving vehicles and aircraft – generated by the friction between the air and the sides of the moving body. Precautions have to be taken that no sparks will be produced at the wrong moment. For instance, static electricity on petrol tankers must be discharged before any petrol is emptied, as a spark could ignite the petrol vapour. For the same reason, aircraft are always earthed before being fuelled.

THE VAN DE GRAAFF GENERATOR

A van de Graaff generator is a machine that produces electric charges at very high voltages. It works by rubbing. A rubber belt rubs against a plastic drum as it rolls around it. The belt becomes charged and the charges are carried up on the belt to collect on a large metal dome at the top of the machine. The dome is supported on an insulator and so the charges cannot escape. They accumulate on the dome and the electrical pressure (voltage) builds up. When the charge becomes too great, the air ceases to be an insulator, and the charge jumps to the nearest object, in the form of a large spark, like a miniature flash of lightning.

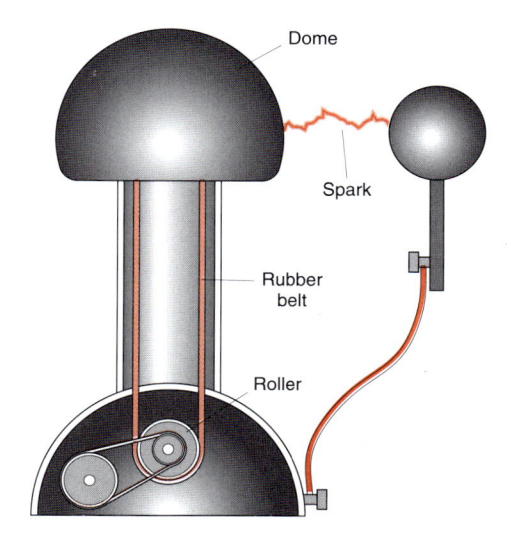

fig. 9.17 *Van de Graaff generator*

FRANKLIN AND LIGHTNING

The most powerful and spectacular effect of static electricity is a flash of lightning. A high electrostatic charge builds up in the clouds, and when it is large enough it jumps to earth as a massive spark.

While the effects of static electricity were known from early times, it was only in the 18th century that people began to wonder about it. An American scientist, Benjamin Franklin, built an electrical machine that generated electric charges by rubbing, and from it he could produce big sparks.

fig. 9.18 *A machine for producing electricity made by Benjamin Franklin over 200 years ago. The glass cylinder at the top was turned by the big wheel and rubbed against the pad of cloth underneath it.*

From the sparks from his electrical machine, Franklin suspected that lightning might also be just a large electric spark. In order to test his theory, he sent a kite up into a cloud during a thunderstorm. When the string was wetted by the rain (and hence became a conductor), Franklin was able to draw off sparks from the lower end of the string, and so he proved his theory.

fig. 9.19 *Franklin's kite experiment*

The experiment was a dangerous one and several people who repeated it were killed. Before this time, large buildings had often been destroyed on being struck by lightning. After his discovery, Franklin hit on the idea of the lightning conductor. This is a thick metal rod which is fixed to the top of a tall building, with the lower end buried in the earth. When a charged thunder cloud passes overhead, lightning can discharge harmlessly and silently to earth through the rod, and so the building is protected.

fig. 9.20 *Lightning is a discharge of electricity from clouds to earth*

fig. 9.21 *A lightning conductor on a church spire. It ends in a metal rod buried in the ground.*

fig. 9.22

Benjamin Franklin (1706–1790) was a statesman, inventor and scientist. As statesman, he helped draft the American Declaration of Independence. However, he is better remembered for his work on electricity. He discovered that there are two types of electric charge, positive and negative, and also that they could be attracted by pointed objects. This led him to the famous kite experiment, and gave him the idea for the lightning conductor, used all over the world today.

ELECTRIC CHARGES AND ELECTRONS

Where do electric charges come from? Rubbing does not create positive and negative charges – they are there to start with; the rubbing just separates them from each other.

An atom consists of a positively charged nucleus, with negative electrons revolving around it. Normally the amount of positive charge is the same as the amount of negative charge; so the charges cancel each other out and the atom is neutral. However, electrons can easily be removed from some atoms, and there are other atoms which can easily take on extra electrons. When this happens, the atoms become charged – either positively or negatively.

When polythene is rubbed with cloth, electrons are rubbed off some of the atoms of the cloth and on to atoms of the polythene. Since electrons are negatively charged, the **polythene gets a negative change** (and also, the cloth becomes positive).

When perspex is rubbed with cloth, some of the electrons of the **perspex** are rubbed off it (and on to the cloth). Since the perspex has lost electrons (negative charges), it **is then positively charged** (and the cloth negative).

STATIC ELECTRICITY
→ CURRENT ELECTRICITY

There is no fundamental difference between static electricity and current electricity. In static electricity, electric charge is not moving; in current electricity, it is. If static electric charges are made to move, it becomes current electricity.

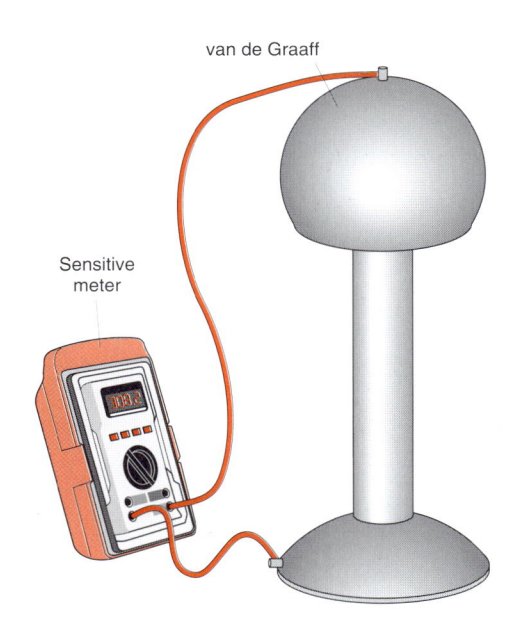

fig. 9.23 In this experiment, a sensitive ammeter is connected between the dome of a van de Graaff generator and its base. When the generator is operated, the meter shows a current. (A 'sensitive' ammeter is one which is able to detect very small currents.)

SUMMARY

- A battery or cell produces a **potential difference** or **voltage**, and this is what makes a current flow around a circuit. The strength of a battery (or other source of electricity) is measured in **volts**, and current is measured in **amps**.

- **An electric circuit is a continuous path for current**, from one terminal of a battery, through wires, bulbs, etc., back to the other terminal of the battery. A circuit must be continuous for current to flow.

- Most metals are good conductors of electricity, and non-metals are usually non-conductors or insulators. Resistance is opposition to current and it is measured in ohms. A variable resistor is called a rheostat.

- When insulators are rubbed, they become electrically charged, or electrified. There are **two types of electric charge: positive and negative**. Like charges repel each other, unlike charges attract. An object which is negatively charged has gained extra electrons; one which is positively charged has lost electrons.

- The van de Graaff generator is a machine that produces electric charges and very high voltages. Lightning is the discharge of static electricity from a charged cloud to earth.

QUESTIONS

Q. 9.9

Rewrite the following paragraph and complete the spaces:

When ____ are rubbed together, they become electrically ____. There are two types of charge, ____ and ____. Polythene, on being rubbed, becomes ____ charged, and it happens because the rubbing causes it to ____ electrons. Rubbing causes acetate to ____ electrons and so it becomes ____ charged. When two pieces of charged polythene are brought together, they ____ each other, but when charged polythene is brought near to some charged ____, there is a force of ____ between them.

Q. 9.10

What happens to a charged and hanging polythene strip when each of the following is brought near: (i) a charged polythene rod, (ii) an uncharged polythene rod, (iii) a charged acetate rod, (iv) your hand?

Q. 9.11

Explain why:

(a) A rubbed balloon can stick to the ceiling.
(b) Nylon clothes often crackle on taking them off, but cotton ones do not.
(c) Cleaning dust off the TV screen can cause still more dust be attracted to it.
(d) Aircraft tyres have a high proportion of carbon in them.
(e) Some lorries have a chain hanging from the chassis, trailing on the ground.

Q. 9.12

Describe what a lightning conductor is, say where you would find one, and explain what it does, and when.

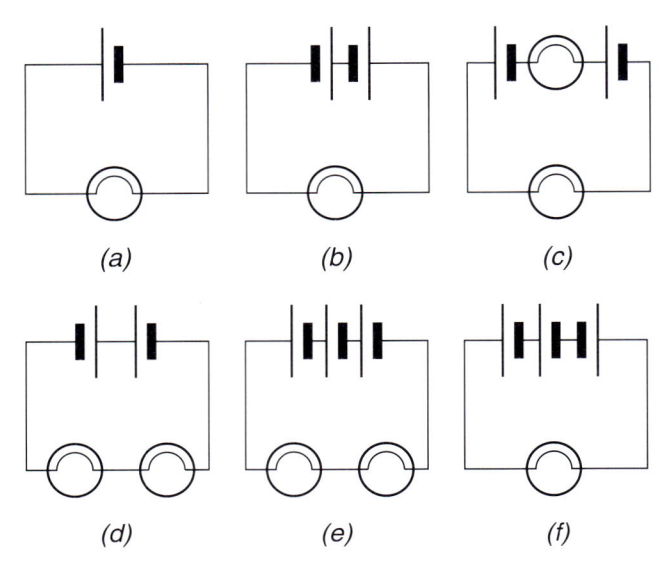

fig. 9.24

Q. 9.13

The bulbs and batteries in all of the circuits shown below are the same. One battery lights one bulb to full brightness. State about each bulb whether it is not lighting, partially bright, fully bright, or extra bright.

10
EFFECTS OF HEAT

Heat can have a number of different effects on a substance or an object. The obvious effect is that the object can get hot – or put scientifically, its temperature rises. However, this does not always happen; an ice cube for instance does not get hot when heated, nor does boiling water get any hotter when it is heated. Other changes too can happen when a substance is heated, and that is what this chapter is all about.

EXPANSION OF SOLIDS

If you have ever looked at railway lines closely, you will see that at the joins, the rails are not touching end to end; there are either small gaps between them, or else there is a tapered overlap, as shown in Figure 10.1.

fig. 10.1 *Allowances made for expansion*

This arrangement is to allow for the expansion of the rails in warm weather; if no allowance were made, the rails could buckle and bend outwards. Two simple experiments show that solids expand when heated.

Experiment 10.1
To show that solids expand when heated

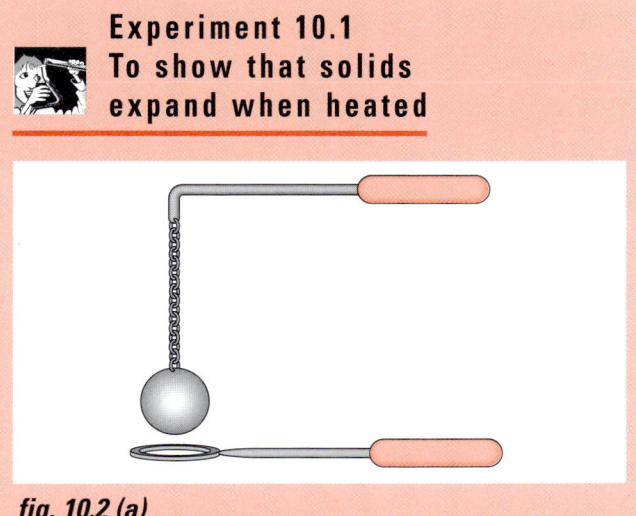

fig. 10.2 (a)

In the 'ball and ring' apparatus, the ball fits through the ring when it is cold, but when it is heated it does not – because it has expanded. The opposite of expansion is called *contraction*, and when the ball cools, it contracts, and fits through the ring once more.

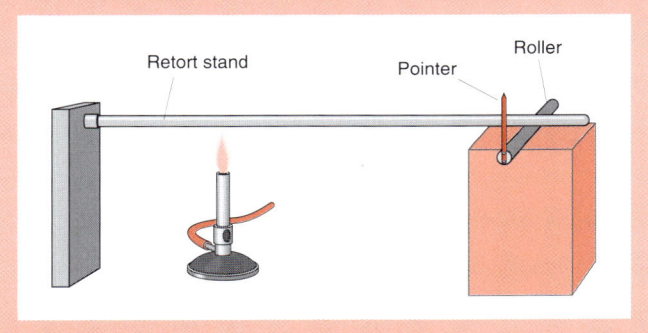

fig. 10.2 (b)

In the second method for showing expansion, the retort stand is heated; the rod expands, turns the roller clockwise, and moves the pointer. This arrangement is necessary because solids expand by only a very small amount when they are heated.

The bimetallic strip

Not all metals expand by the same amount; brass, for example, expands more than iron. A bimetallic strip is a strip consisting of two different metals welded together. When such a strip is heated, it is forced into a curved shape with the brass on the outside since the brass expands more than the iron.

10 • Effects of Heat

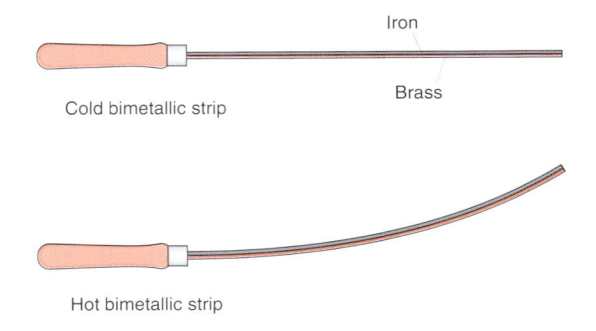

fig. 10.3

Bimetallic strips have many practical applications, for example, in thermostats and fire alarms. The operation of a fire alarm is illustrated.

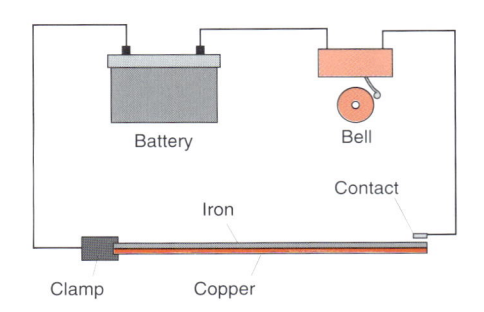

fig. 10.4 Fire alarm circuit

The strip is placed where it would not normally be subjected to heat. If a fire occurs, the strip becomes heated and bends upwards, completing an electrical circuit, which causes an alarm bell to ring.

Expansion in everyday life

fig. 10.5 Allowance made for expansion

Apart from the bimetallic strip, there are many everyday examples of expansion. The photograph shows heating pipes in a school gymnasium. The bends are there so that when the pipes are heated, there is room for them to expand; if there were not, they would be forced outwards and in time might themselves crack or perhaps crack the gym wall.

fig. 10.6 Allowance made for expansion

Where there are long metal bridges, one end must be put on rollers to allow for the expansion of the bridge. If this were not done, the bridge would buckle (bend outwards) in hot weather.

When the Victorian glasshouse in the National Botanic Gardens, Dublin was being restored, allowance had to be made for the expansion of the glass when it becomes warm in summer.

fig. 10.7 Victorian glasshouses

EXPANSION OF LIQUIDS AND GASES

In Experiments 10.2 and 10.3, you can investigate how liquids and gases behave when they are heated. The same apparatus is used for both investigations. Water is used in the first experiment, and air in the second.

Experiment 10.2
To investigate how water behaves when it is heated

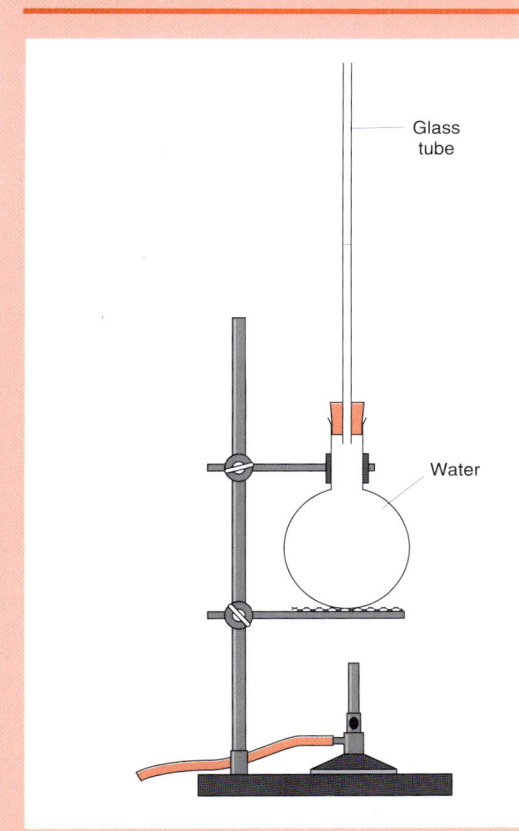

fig. 10.8

1. Set up the apparatus as shown. Make sure that the flask is **completely** full of water and that the top of the water is about half way up the glass tube. (If you add some colouring to the water it is easier to see.)
2. Mark the water level in the tube with a sticky label or a rubber band.
3. Heat the flask with a bunsen burner for about five minutes. Has anything changed? What change occurred?
4. Turn off the bunsen burner. Place the stand either in or beside the sink, and pour cold water over the flask until another change occurs. What is the change, and why did it happen? (Now wipe up all the splashed water.)
5. Write out and complete the sentence: When water is heated it __ and when it is cooled it __.

Experiment 10.3
To investigate how air behaves when it is heated

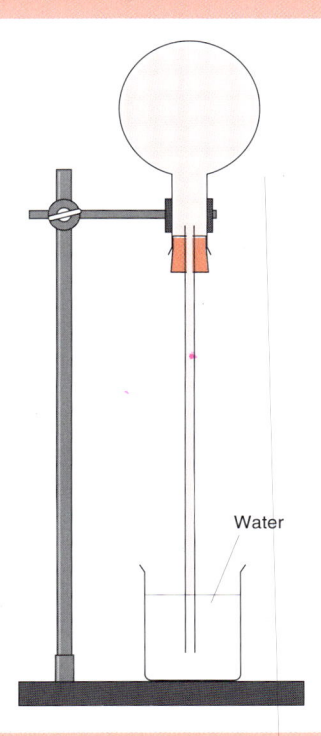

fig. 10.9

1. Set up the apparatus as shown. Note that the flask is now 'empty' (i.e. full of air).
2. Place your hands around the flask for about half a minute. What do you see happening?
3. Put the stand either in or near the sink. Now pour a beakerful of hot water over the flask and observe the *bottom* of the glass tube *carefully*. What do you see happening. Can you explain why it happens?
4. Now pour a beaker of cold water over the flask. What happens this time, and why? (Again, wipe up all splashed water.)
5. Write out and complete the sentence: When air is heated it __ and when it is cooled it __ .

Experiments 10.2 and 10.3 show that both liquids and gases expand when they are heated. When the water in the flask is heated, it expands and moves up the glass tube attached to the flask. The narrow tube is necessary because the amount of expansion is small and would not be seen otherwise.

When the air in the flask is heated, bubbles come out the end of the glass tube. This happens because the air in the flask expands. When the flask is cooled (by pouring cold water over it), the air contracts, and water is 'sucked in' (forced in by atmospheric pressure) to the flask. Gases expand much more than either solids or liquids and even hand warmth on the flask will cause bubbles of air to be forced out.

Not all liquids expand by the same amount. This can be shown by the experiment illustrated below.

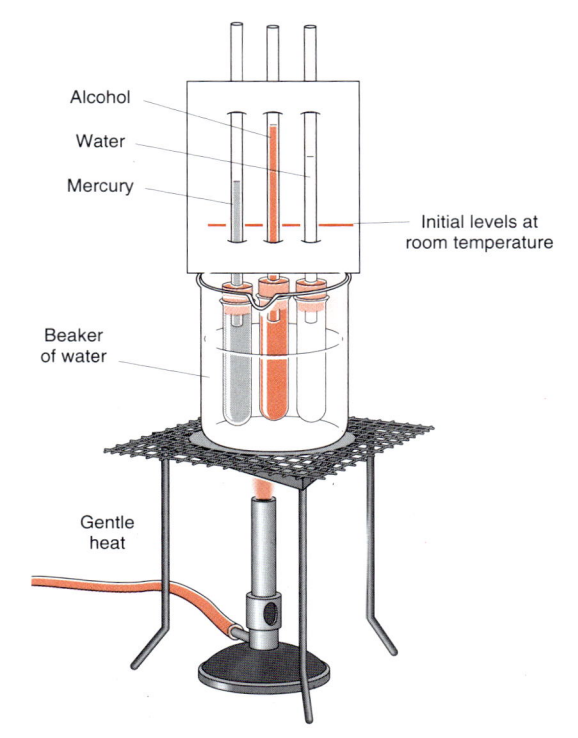

fig. 10.10 *Different liquids expand by different amounts*

Three tubes, one containing alcohol, another water, and a third containing mercury are placed in a beaker of hot water. The liquids expand, but the amount by which the alcohol level rises up the tube is much greater than the rise of the others. This happens because the alcohol expands more than the water or mercury (for the same increase in temperature). Use is made of this property in the alcohol thermometer (next page).

Unusual expansion of water

As water is cooled to 4°C, it contracts as would be expected. However, as it is cooled further, from 4°C down to 0°C, it expands again. Its density is therefore maximum at 4°C. As it changes to ice at 0°C, it expands considerably, every 100 cm³ of water becoming about 110 cm³ of ice. The expansion of water as it changes to ice is the cause of burst water pipes in freezing weather.

The unusual expansion of water as it falls in temperature from 4°C to 0°C results in water freezing from the surface downwards. Water at the top of a pond cools first, becomes more dense and sinks to the bottom (behaving normally). When the temperature of the water reaches 4°C, it has reached its maximum density and convection stops. When the temperature falls further (below 4°C), it expands again, becomes less dense, and remains on the top, eventually forming a layer of ice at 0°C. Fish and other aquatic life in the warmer water below the ice can therefore survive beneath the ice.

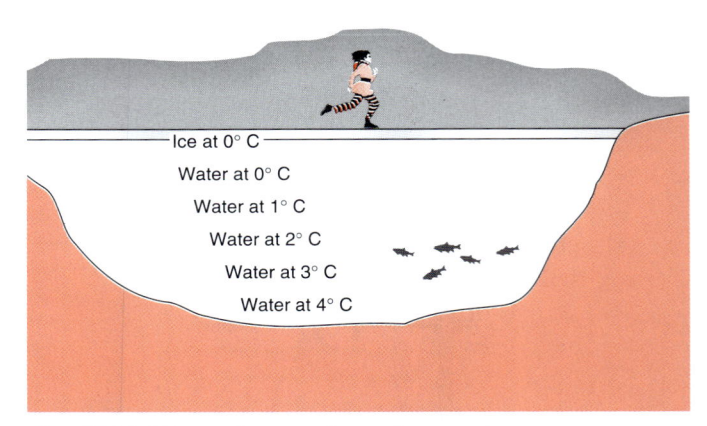

fig. 10.11 *Water freezes from the top down*

QUESTIONS

Q. 10.1

Refer to Experiments 10.2 and 10.3

(a) What happened to the water when it was heated?
(b) Why is a **narrow** tube attached to the flask?
(c) What happened to the air when it was
   (i) heated, and (ii) cooled?
(d) Why is the bunsen necessary to heat the water whereas warm hands showed the same result for air?
(e) Which expands more: water or air?

Q. 10.2

Describe, with the aid of a diagram in each case, how you would show the expansion of
(i) a solid, (ii) a liquid, (iii) a gas.

Q. 10.3

Rewrite the following paragraph with the missing words filled in.

When water is heated it ___, and therefore occupies a ___ volume than when it is ___. This means that hot water is ___ dense than ___ water, and so ___ water rises. This ___ movement of hot water is called a ___ current. For the same reason, hot air is ___ dense than ___ air, and this is why hot-air balloons can rise. When the balloonist wants to descend (come down), he allows the air in the balloon to ___. The force of ___ then brings the balloon ___ to the ground.

TEMPERATURE AND THERMOMETERS

It is important not to confuse the temperature of a body with the amount of heat energy in it.

Temperature is a measure of 'hotness' i.e. how hot (or cold) something is. It is measured with a thermometer and its units are degrees. The most common type of thermometer makes use of the fact that liquids expand when heated (and contract when cooled). The apparatus in Figure 10.8 could be used as a thermometer but it would not be very convenient.

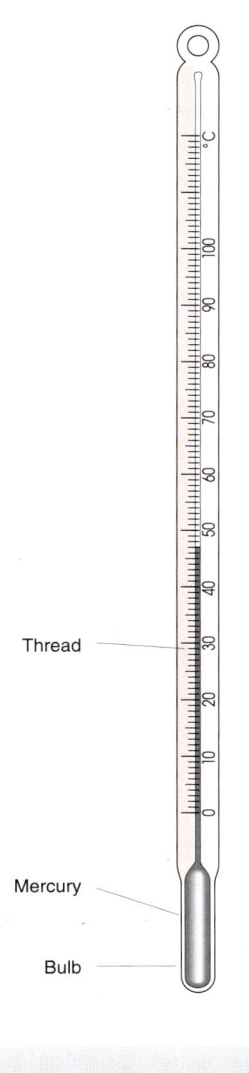

fig. 10.12
A Celsius thermometer such as used in laboratories

The thermometer illustrated in Figure 10.12 consists of a bulb containing a liquid, with a long graduated capillary (fine bore) tube coming out of it. When the temperature of the bulb increases, the liquid in it expands and is pushed along the tube, where it shows the temperature on the scale. The two liquids commonly used are mercury and alcohol. Each has its own advantages and disadvantages – listed in the table below.

THERMOMETER SCALES

The scale is put on a thermometer by marking two 'fixed points' (definite temperatures) and then dividing the distance between these points into degrees. The most commonly used scale of temperature is the **Celsius scale** (named after a Swedish scientist) and its two fixed points are the **boiling point** and **freezing point** of water. On this scale, boiling point (the temperature at which pure water boils at normal atmospheric pressure) is 100°C and freezing point (the temperature at which pure water freezes) is 0°C.

The 0°C mark is put on the thermometer by placing the bulb of the thermometer in a funnel of melting ice and marking the mercury level on the thermometer when it has become steady. For the 100°C mark, the thermometer is placed in the steam from boiling water and the mercury level marked when it has stopped rising. The distance between the two marks is then divided into 100 equal divisions.

THERMOMETER LIQUIDS COMPARED

MERCURY	ALCOHOL
Advantages	
High boiling point (therefore suitable for ovens, etc.)	Low freezing point (therefore suitable for very low temperatures)
Conducts heat well (therefore responds quickly)	Expands much more than mercury (therefore degree markings further spaced out)
Doesn't stick to the glass	Cheap
Disadvantages	
Freezes at −39°C (not suitable for very low temperatures)	Boils at 78°C (not suitable for high temperatures)
Poisonous (therefore danger from broken thermometers)	Clings to side of glass
	Poor conductor of heat (therefore slow to respond)
Expensive	Liquid thread has tendency to break

10 • Effects of Heat

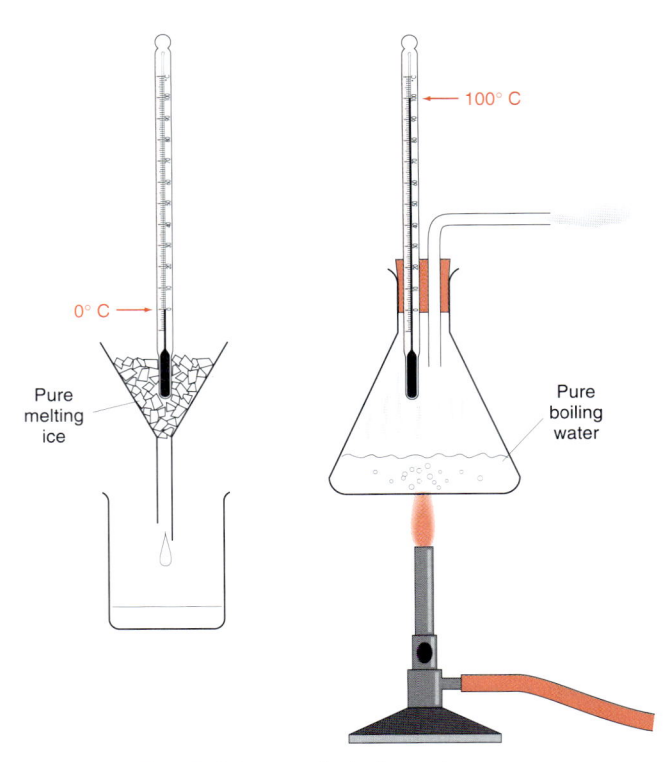

fig. 10.13 *The Celsius scale is based on the freezing and boiling points of water*

The clinical thermometer

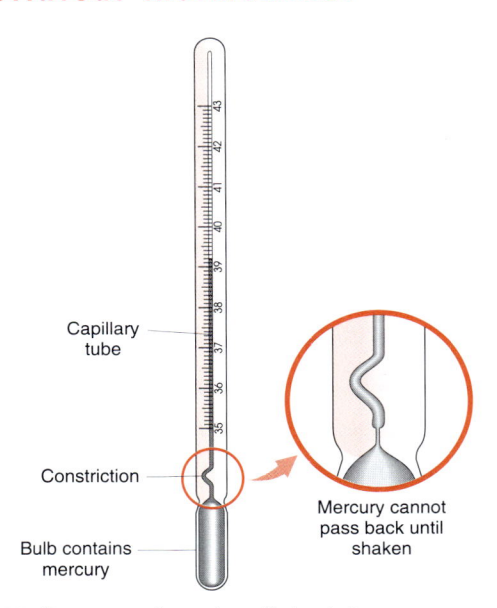

fig. 10.14 *Construction of a clinical thermometer*

A clinical thermometer is used for measuring body temperature. It is a mercury thermometer with a very short scale, usually only from 34°C to 42°C. However, it is made so that the mercury does not move back down the tube when the thermometer is removed from the body, i.e. it records the highest temperature reached. This is done by having a small constriction (a very narrow part) at the start of the capillary tube.

When the thermometer is removed from the body, the mercury in the bulb cools and contracts (as usual), but the thread of mercury breaks at the constriction and the part of it further up the tube remains where it was. The highest temperature reached is therefore recorded so that there is no need to read the thermometer while it is still in contact with the patient's body. Before the thermometer is next used, the mercury is shaken back into the bulb.

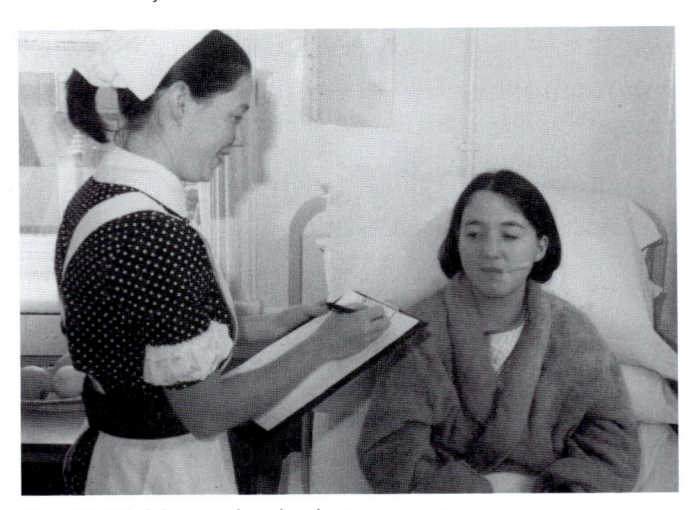

fig. 10.15 *Measuring body temperature*

Body temperature is an indication of the state of one's health and this is why doctors and nurses measure their patients' temperatures. The temperature of the healthy human body is 37°C. An abnormal increase in temperature means that something is wrong and if it stays high, medical help is needed.

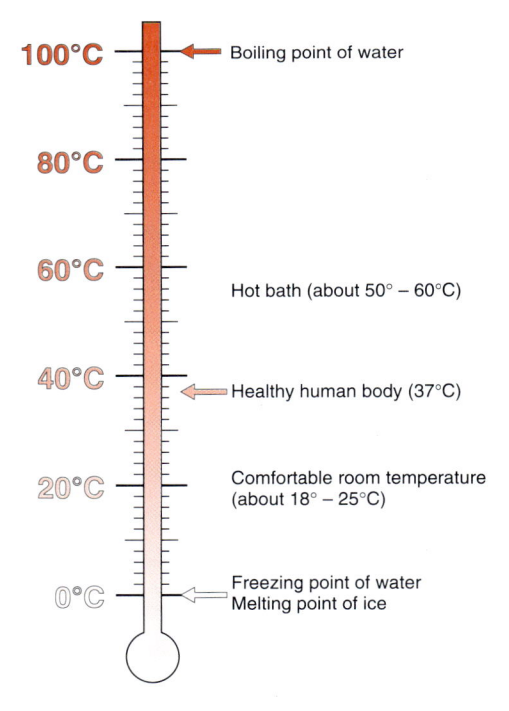

fig. 10.16 *Celsius temperatures*

QUESTIONS

Q. 10.4
What is a clinical thermometer? How does it differ from the ordinary laboratory thermometer. Give two reasons why it is more suitable for its purpose than a laboratory thermometer.

Q. 10.5
If you consider water as a liquid for use in thermometers, you will find that its only advantage is that it is cheap. List reasons why water would be a most unsuitable liquid for use in a thermometer.

Q. 10.6
What are the two liquids commonly used in thermometers? List the advantages and the disadvantages of each.

Q. 10.7
Why does a clinical thermometer:

(a) have a constriction above the bulb?
(b) cover only a small range of temperature?
(c) have an extremely fine bore?
(d) have to be shaken before it is used?

Q. 10.8
What is the Celsius scale of temperature? What are its 'fixed points'? How are these fixed points put onto a thermometer?

LATENT HEAT

Heat normally causes the temperature of a substance to rise, but there are two main exceptions. Do ice cubes become hotter when they are heated, or does boiling water get any hotter if you continue heating it? The answer to both of these questions is "no". The ice cubes melt and become water (at 0°C), and the boiling water stays at a temperature of 100°C as it changes to steam. When a substance is changing its state (solid to liquid, or liquid to vapour), the temperature remains the same during the change.

The heat needed to change the state of a substance is called latent heat.

Experiments show that 2257 J are needed to change 1 g of boiling water to 1 g of steam; this value is called the **latent heat of steam**. Conversely, when 1 g of steam changes back to 1 g of water, 2257 J of heat are released. This high value is the reason why a burn from steam can be much more serious than a burn from boiling water.

Heat is also needed to change a solid to a liquid, e.g ice to water. The heat needed to change 1 g of ice to 1 g of water is called the **latent heat of ice**, and its value is 330 J. This high value is the reason why ice cubes are much better at cooling a drink than an equal amount of iced water.

> **Experiment 10.4**
> **To show that evaporation causes cooling**
>
> This experiment uses a compound called ether, which is a liquid that evaporates at a very low temperature (it is described as being *volatile*). Put a little ether (or alcohol) on the back of your hand and let it evaporate. Notice that your hand feels cold as evaporation occurs.

Like all liquids, ether needs heat to evaporate. When heat is not supplied, it takes the heat needed from its surroundings (your hand in the experiment) and the temperature falls. The workings of a domestic refrigerator makes use of this fact. In pipes in the walls of the ice box, a liquid is evaporating, and this causes the cooling. In pipes at the back of the refrigerator, the vapour is changing back to a liquid. Since this change releases heat, the back of a refrigerator gets hot while it is working.

There are many other everyday applications of cooling by evaporation. Sweating – the body's way of keeping itself cool – is an example. Sweat, which consists mainly of water, is secreted by the sweat glands just under the skin. In hot weather, more than the usual amount is secreted, and the evaporation of this causes cooling.

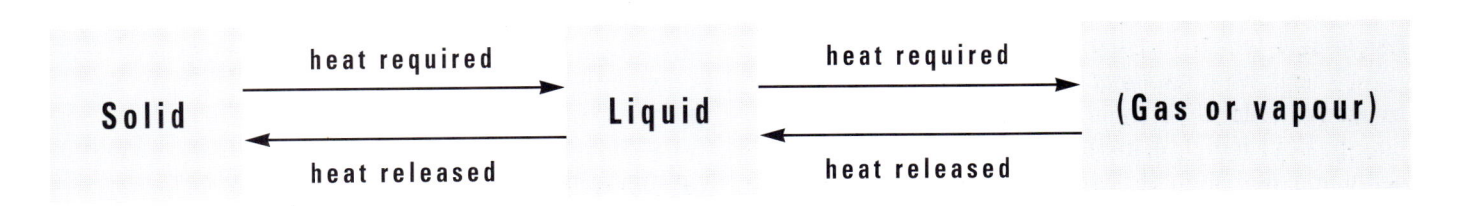

| Solid | heat required → / ← heat released | Liquid | heat required → / ← heat released | (Gas or vapour) |

SUMMARY

- Solids, liquids and gases expand when heated and contract when cooled. Solids and liquids expand by only a small amount, but gases expand quite a lot. Large forces are produced when solids and liquids expand and allowances must be made for these in buildings, bridges, and pipes which become heated.

- A **bimetallic strip** consists of two different metals welded together and when it is heated, it bends into a curved shape. Fire alarms and other heat-sensitive devices use bimetallic strips.

- As water is cooled, it contracts until its temperature reaches 4°C. Then it starts to expand again as it approaches its freezing point. As it changes to ice, it expands a lot and this expansion can cause pipes to burst in winter.

- **Thermometers** make use of the fact that liquids expand when they are heated. The two commonly used liquids in thermometers are **mercury** and **alcohol**.

- In the Celsius scale of temperature, the two fixed points are the temperatures of melting ice (which is given the value 0°C) and boiling water (whose value is taken to be 100°C).

- A **clinical thermometer** has a short scale, is divided into tenths of degrees and it records the maximum temperature reached. Normal healthy body temperature is 37°C.

- When a substance changes its state, there is a heat change which is called **latent heat**. The latent heat of steam is the heat needed to change water to steam, and the latent heat of ice is the heat needed to change ice to water. When a liquid evaporates and heat is not supplied, the liquid cools.

QUESTIONS

Q. 10.9

Copy out and complete the spaces in the following paragraphs.

When a substances changes its state (e.g. a solid changing to a ___) heat must be either supplied or ___. This heat is called ___ heat. When ice changes to ___ (this change is called ___), heat must be ___. Conversely, when ___ changes to ice, heat must be ___ . This is what happens when ___ is put into the freezer. In order for a liquid to change to a gas (this change is called ___), heat must be ___. If heat is not supplied, then the temperature will ___. A machine which makes use of this fact is the ___. For the same reason, you feel ___ if you stand around in a ___ swimsuit. This is because water is ___ from it, and the ___ needed for it to do so is taken from your ___.

Q. 10.10

Suggest a reason for each of the following:
(a) A jam jar cracks if boiling water is poured into it.
(b) Gaps are left between the concrete sections when a road or path is being laid.
(c) An over-tight metal cap on a bottle can often be loosened by pouring hot water over it.
(d) A bimetallic strip made of two strips of iron does not work.
(e) There can be hot water at the top of the hot water tank (in the hot press) but cold water at the bottom.
(f) House roofs and furniture can creak at night after a warm day.
(g) Overhead electric cables are left slack (slightly loose) when they are being hung in warm weather.

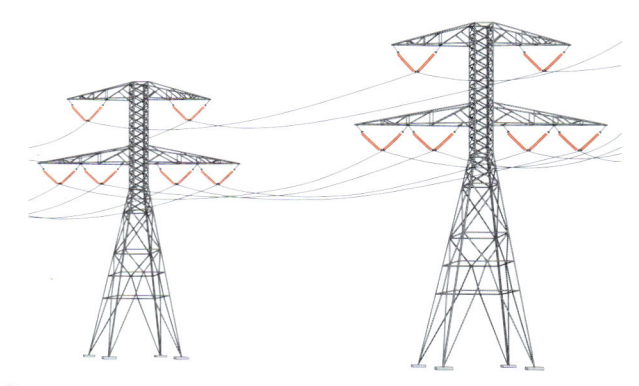

fig. 10.17

(h) Oven shelves are never a tight fit.
(i) A beach ball may burst if left in the sun for too long.
(j) Ice forms on the top of a pond and not on the bottom.

Q. 10.11

(a) What is meant by latent heat?
(b) Is heat needed or released when water changes to (i) water vapour? (ii) ice?
(c) The latent heat of ice is 330 J/g; what does this mean?

Q. 10.12

(a) Draw a large clear diagram of a mercury thermometer.
(b) Show the markings on it.
(c) Explain how it works.
(d) Name two of its applications at home.

11
WORK, MOTION, ENERGY

fig. 11.1 *The cheetah is the fastest land animal, and can accelerate faster than a racing car*

SPEED AND VELOCITY

Speed is something that most people know about. All cars, and some bicycles too, have a speedometer – which measures the speed at which they are travelling; the speedometer is normally marked in miles per hour or perhaps kilometres per hour. If, by car, you travel a distance of 80 kilometres in 2 hours, then your average speed is 40 kilometres per hour, i.e. distance/time. However, 40 kilometres per hour is only an average value; the speed of the car varies continually during a journey, and the actual speed at any moment may differ considerably from this value.

In scientific work distance is always measured in metres and time in seconds, so speed is expressed in metres per second (m/s).

Fig. 11.1 shows a running cheetah, who can cover a distance of 100 metres in 4 seconds. Its average speed is therefore $^{100}/_4$ which is 25 metres per second.

Velocity is similar to speed except that it means the speed in a certain direction.

Velocity is distance travelled per unit time (in a particular direction).

Like speed, it is also expressed in metres per second.

Velocity can be worked out from:
$$\text{velocity} = \frac{\text{distance}}{\text{time}}$$

ACCELERATION

What happens when the accelerator of a car is pressed? The car goes faster. This is what acceleration is all about.

Acceleration is the increase in velocity per unit time.

The unit for acceleration is **metres per second per second**, written as m/s^2.

Worked example 1

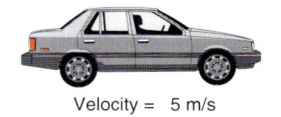

Velocity = 5 m/s   10 seconds later Velocity = 35 m/s

fig. 11.2 *Acceleration*

Imagine a car travelling at 5 metres per second. Now imagine that it speeds up, and 10 seconds later its velocity has increased to 35 m/s.

Its velocity increases from 5 m/s to 35 m/s, i.e. an increase of 30 m/s.

Since it increased its velocity by 30 m/s in 10 s, its increase in each one second is 3 m/s ($^{30}/_{10}$), and this is its acceleration: 3 m/s^2.

Worked example 2

Q. A bus travels 100 m in 5 seconds. What is its velocity? It then accelerates, and after 8 seconds has increased its velocity to 36 m/s. What is its acceleration?

A. The bus travels 100 m in 5 seconds; its velocity is $^{100}/_5$ = 20 m/s (metres per second).

After 8 seconds its velocity has increased to 36 m/s. The increase in velocity is 16 m/s (i.e. 36 – 20).

The increase in velocity **per second** is 2 m/s (16 m/s in 8 s = 2 m/s in 1 s).

The acceleration is thus 2 m/s each second, and this is written as 2 m/s^2.

11 • Work, Motion, Energy

Slowing down
Acceleration can have a negative value – it just means that a body is slowing down rather than speeding up, i.e. the velocity is decreasing. A negative acceleration is called a **deceleration**.

> **How fast do things move?**
>
> A snail travels at 0.005 m/s, a person walking at 2 m/s, a sprinter at 10 m/s, an express train at 60 m/s, sound in air at 340 m/s, Concorde at 600 m/s, the Earth around the Sun at 30 000 m/s, light and radio waves at 300 000 000 m/s.

QUESTIONS

Q.11.1
What is the velocity, in metres per second, of each of the following:
(a) a sprinter who runs 100 metres in 10 seconds
(b) a toy car which travels 2 metres in 5 seconds
(c) a cheetah which runs 200 m in 8 s
(d) Julie, who runs 60 m in 12 s
(e) Ann, who does a 25 m length of the swimming pool in 50 s
(f) a racing car which covers 3000 m in a minute
(g) a Jumbo aircraft which travels 14 km in a minute
(h) a tortoise who takes 25 s to crawl 100 cm

Q.11.2

fig.11.3 An electric train converts electrical energy to kinetic energy

Dublin's DART travels a distance of 1000 m in 50 s.
(a) What is its average speed?
(b) How far would it travel in (i) 10 s, (ii) 1 minute, (iii) half an hour? (continued)
(c) How many minutes of travel time (excluding stopping time) are there between Howth and Bray, which are 33 km apart?
(d) Given that it stops for one minute at each of the 25 intermediate stations, how long should the journey from Howth to Bray take?

Q.11.3
A car travels 500 m in 20 s.
(a) What is its average speed?
(b) Why might its actual speed be different from its average speed?
(c) How far will the car travel in (i) 6 seconds, (ii) 12 seconds, (iii) 60 seconds, (iv) 10 minutes, (v) 1 hour?
(d) How long will it take for the car to travel (i) 100 m, (ii) 1000 m, (iii) 10 km?

Q.11.4
Julie is cycling at 3 m/s on the top of a hill. She then cycles down it, accelerating at 2 m/s^2 as she does so. What is her velocity after (i) 1 s, (ii) 2 s, (iii) 4 s?

Q.11.5
This racing car can reach a speed of 30 m/s in 6 seconds. What is its acceleration as it does this?

fig. 11.4

MOTION GRAPHS
Graphs are useful ways of showing the motion of moving bodies. You can tell a lot from them. They can:

- show how far something has travelled in any given time
- show the time taken to travel any given distance
- be used to work out the speed of the moving body
- tell if the speed is constant, or if the body is accelerating

Distance/time graphs

In an experiment, Ann starts off cycling along a cycle track, and makes a note of her distance from the start every five seconds. She records the following values:

Time (s)	0	5	10	15	20	25	30	35	40
Distance (m)	0	12	24	36	48	60	72	84	96

Later her friend Julie carries out the same experiment and records the following results:

Time (s)	0	5	10	15	20	25	30	35	40
Distance (m)	0	6	14	24	36	50	66	84	104

Later, she plots graphs of the two sets of values, and these are shown below.

Information from the graphs

1. Graph 1 is a straight line; this means that Ann is travelling at a constant speed or velocity, i.e. she is not accelerating.

2. Suppose Ann wants to know the distance she had travelled in 8 seconds. Draw a line up from the 8 second position on the time (bottom) axis until it hits the graph, then draw another line across from that point until it hits the distance axis, and read off the distance where the line meets the axis. It works out to be 19.2 metres.

3. Ann also wants to know the time it took her to travel 90 metres. Draw a line across from the 90 m mark on the distance axis until the line meets the graph. Then from that point, draw another line down to meet the time axis. Read off the time at the point where the line meets that axis. It works out to be 37.5 seconds.

4. To work out Ann's speed, take any point on the graph, and use the formula velocity = $distance/time$ to calculate it.

    For example: velocity = $48/20$ = 2.4 m/s.

5. Graph 2 is not a straight line; this means that Julie is **not** travelling at a constant speed. The graph is getting steeper because she is accelerating. In the same way as in Graph 1, Julie could work out from Graph 2 the distance she travelled in 8 seconds or the time taken to travel 90 metres. Since her speed is changing all the time, she cannot work out her actual speed for the journey. She can only calculate the average speed for the 40 seconds during which she timed herself.

Velocity/time graphs

Don't confuse velocity/time graphs with distance/time graphs. They may look similar, but they have different meanings – they show how the **velocity** changes with time. Here are three velocity/time graphs.

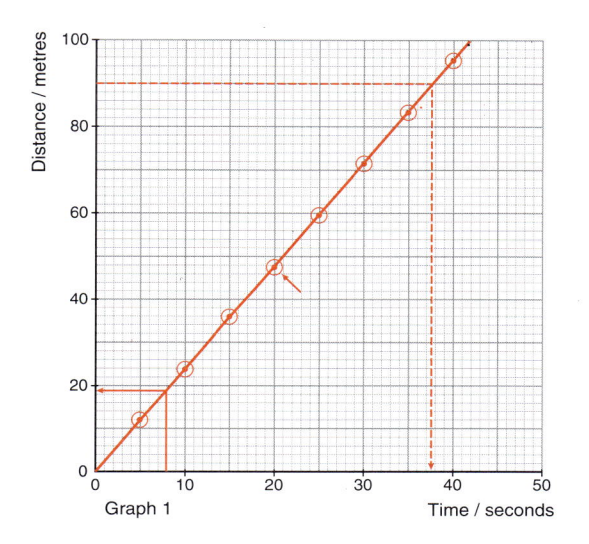

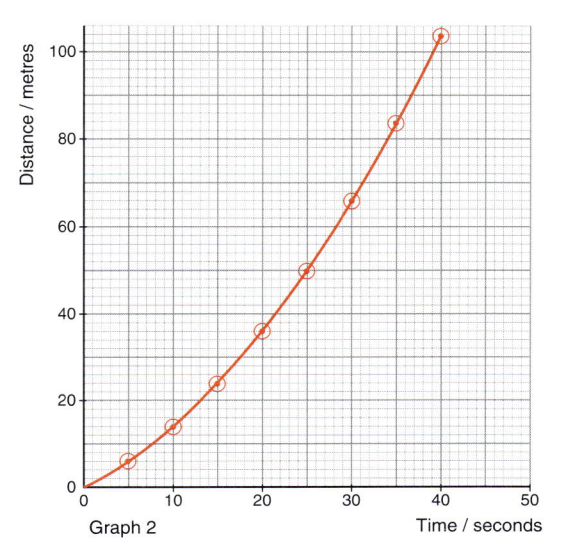

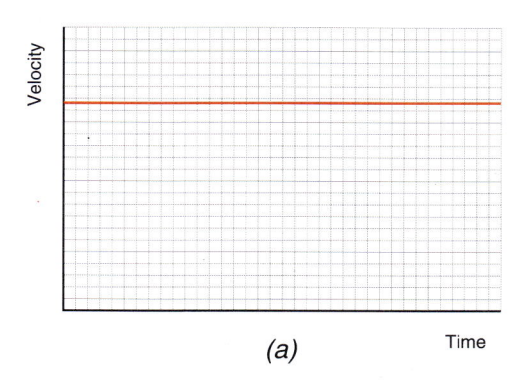

fig. 11.5 *Distance/time graphs*

11 • Work, Motion, Energy

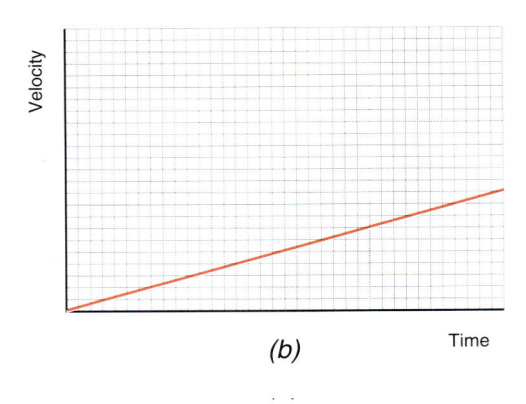

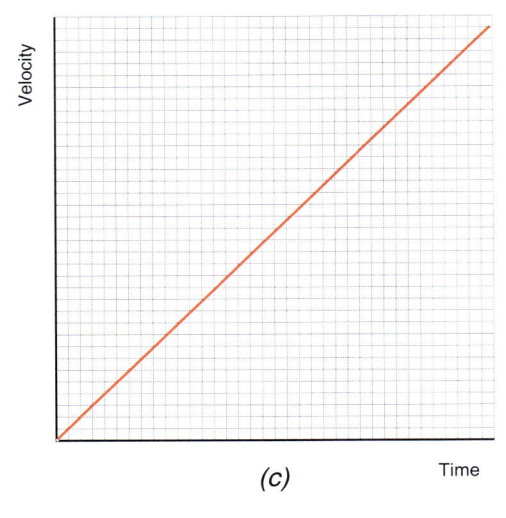

(b) Velocity vs Time

(c) Velocity vs Time

fig. 11.6 Velocity/time graphs

Graph (a) shows that the velocity is not changing, or, in other words, that the body is not accelerating (or decelerating). In graph (b), the velocity is increasing (the body is accelerating) and, since the graph is a straight line, the acceleration is constant (the body is getting faster at a steady rate). Graph (c) also shows a steady acceleration, but it is a greater acceleration than that shown in graph (b) (assuming that both graphs are on the same scale).

QUESTIONS

Q. 11.6
Refer to Graph 1 on page 73 of Ann's cycle trip.
(a) How far did she travel in 8 seconds?
(b) How long did it take her to travel 90 m?
(c) What was her average speed?

Q. 11.7
Liebig, the laboratory cat is resting under a tree. On seeing a mouse, he runs towards it at high speed and catches it. He stays in the same place while he eats the mouse. Then, with a full stomach, he wanders back to the tree. The accompanying graph illustrates his movements.

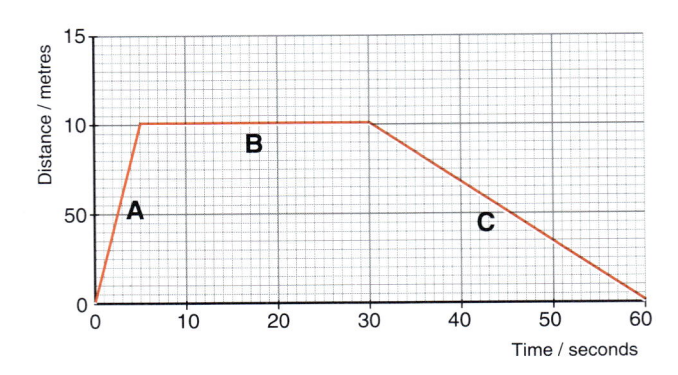

fig. 11.7

(a) How far was the mouse from the tree?
(b) How long did Liebig take to reach the mouse?
(c) At what speed did he run in order to catch the mouse?
(d) How long did he take to eat the mouse?
(e) Why is section B of the graph flat?
(f) Why is the slope of section C of the graph not as steep as that of section A?
(g) How long did Liebig take to get back to the tree?
(h) What was his speed as he wandered back?

Q. 11.8
Describe the motion of the objects whose distance/time graphs are shown.

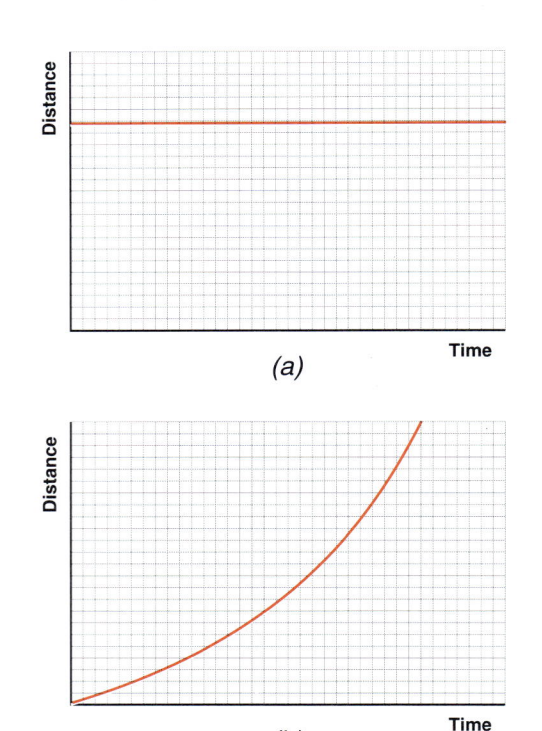

(a) Distance vs Time

(b) Distance vs Time

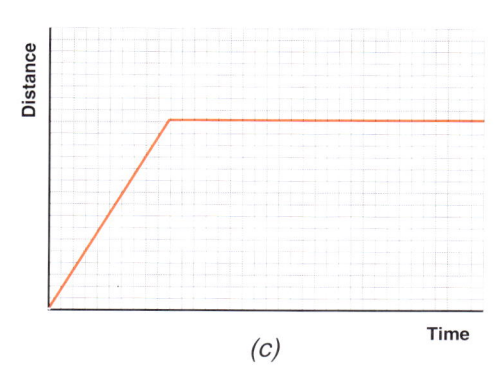

fig. 11.8

Q. 11.9
The table shows how the velocity of a jet aircraft changes as it accelerates before take-off:

Time (s)	0	2	4	6	8	10	12	14	16	18	20
Velocity (m/s)	0	5	10	15	20	25	30	35	40	45	50

(a) Draw a velocity/time graph for these values.
(b) What is the velocity at
 (i) 5 s, (ii) 15 s?
(c) At what time is the velocity
 (i) 22 m/s, (ii) 33 m/s?
(d) From the graph, find the acceleration.

WORK AND ENERGY

Like many words that are used in everyday conversation, there is a slight difference between the ordinary use of the word *work* and the scientific meaning of it. When you spend an hour or two sitting at the table doing your homework, you are doing no work – in the scientific sense anyway. In everyday language *work* can mean anything from writing an essay to digging the garden. To scientists and engineers however, work has a very definite meaning.

> **Work is done when a force moves something. The amount of work done is equal to the force multiplied by the distance moved.**

The unit of work is the joule (J), and one joule is the work that is done when a force of one newton moves something a distance of one metre.

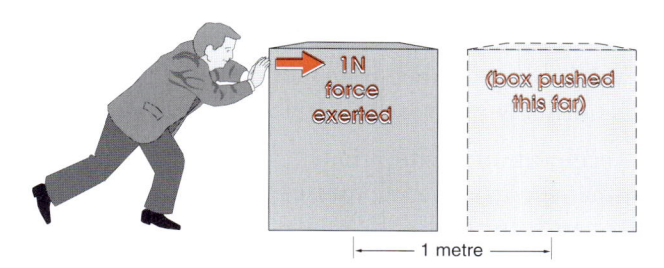

fig. 11.9 *1 joule of work done*

So, if you have to push with a force of 50 N to slide a box, and you move it a distance of 3 m, the work you do is 150 J (i.e. 50 × 3).

If you climb a 5 metre ladder carrying a weight of 60 N, then the work done in raising the weight is 300 J (i.e. 5 × 60). (In addition you will also have done more work in raising your own weight up the ladder.)

MOMENTUM

Momentum is a quantity which is useful when collisions between bodies are being considered. All moving bodies have **momentum**.

> **Momentum is defined as mass multiplied by velocity.**

The unit for momentum is **kilogram metre per second**. A 2 kg rock falling through the air at 4 m/s has a momentum of 8 kg m/s.

fig. 11.10 *A moving juggernaut has a lot of momentum because of its large mass*

Large moving objects, even moving slowly (trains, juggernauts, ships), have a lot of momentum because of their large masses. However, small objects (travelling bullets) can also have a lot of momentum because of their speed. Bodies with a lot of momentum are not stopped easily and they can do much damage if they hit something.

11 • Work, Motion, Energy

SUMMARY

- **Velocity** is distance travelled per unit time and it is normally expressed in **metres per second** (m/s).
- **Acceleration** is the change in velocity per unit time, and its units are **metres per second** (m/s²). A distance/time graph relates distance travelled with the time taken. A velocity/time graph shows how the velocity of a body changes with time. In these graphs, **time is plotted on the bottom axis**.
- **Work** is done when a force moves. The amount of work done (in joules) is equal to the force (in newtons), multiplied by the distance moved (in metres).
- The **momentum** of a body is the mass of the body multiplied by its velocity, and its units are kilogram metres per second (kg m/s).

QUESTIONS

Q. 11.10

Here is a list of jobs. In which ones are **you** doing mechanical work?

(a) pushing a garden roller
(b) walking up a hill
(c) stretching a rubber band
(d) holding a stretched rubber band
(e) swimming
(f) floating
(g) learning scientific definitions
(h) standing on a weighing scales
(i) blowing up a balloon
(j) ascending in a lift
(k) travelling in a car
(l) climbing a ladder

Q. 11.11

A man lifts a barrel of mass 30 kg on to a lorry 1 metre high.

fig. 11.11

(a) What is the weight of a mass of 30 kg?
(b) What force must the man exert to lift the barrel?
(c) What work does he do in lifting the barrel?

Q. 11.12

A crane lifts a steel girder up to a height of 40 m in 50 s.

(a) If the girder has a mass of 500 kg, what is its weight?
(b) What force does the crane have to exert to lift the girder?
(c) How much work is done by the crane?
(d) How much work is done by the crane each second?
(e) What energy change occurs as the girder is being lifted?
(f) What might be the starting source of energy for the crane to operate?

Q. 11.13

An electric motor raises a 50 kg load by 5 m.

(a) What is the weight of the load?
(b) What force must the motor exert to lift the load?
(c) How much work does the motor do in raising it?
(d) What energy conversion occurs in the motor as it is working?
(e) What kind of energy does the weight have afterwards?

Q. 11.14

Julie wrote in her notebook "My weight is 45 kg."

(a) What is wrong with her statement?
(b) What is really her weight?
(c) What does the 45 kg refer to?
(d) How much energy does she need to climb a ladder 5 m high?

Q. 11.15

Calculate the momentum of each of the following:

(a) a cannon ball of mass 5 kg travelling at 10 m/s
(b) a sprinter of mass 60 kg running at 8 m/s
(c) a bullet of mass 0.01 kg moving at 50 m/s
(d) a juggernaut of mass 10 000 kg travelling at 3 m/s
(e) a one tonne car travelling at 30 m/s (1 tonne = 1000 kg)
(f) a cyclist of mass 50 kg riding a bike of mass 20 kg moving at 10 m/s

12 PRESSURE

fig. 12.1

The girl shown in the picture is exerting a greater pressure on the ground than the digger. How can this be when the digger is obviously much heavier? Some people think of pressure as just an amount of 'push' or force, but this is not correct; it is something more specific than that.

Pressure is the force acting on unit area.

This means the number of newtons pressing on each square metre (or square centimetre) of surface. You can think of pressure as being a measure of how 'concentrated' a force is. When you want to cut meat or vegetables, you will know that it is easier to do so with a sharp knife than with a blunt one. A sharp knife has a very thin edge to the blade – which means that the force you apply is concentrated in a small area, i.e. the pressure you apply is greater.

Force is expressed in newtons and area in either metres squared, or centimetres squared. Therefore the units of pressure can be either N/m^2 or N/cm^2. When pressures are expressed in N/m^2 the values are very large and so N/cm^2 are often more convenient units to use.

To calculate the pressure exerted by an object, you need to know the force exerted by the object, and the area over which it is acting. The following diagram shows a block of mass 6 kg resting on the bench.

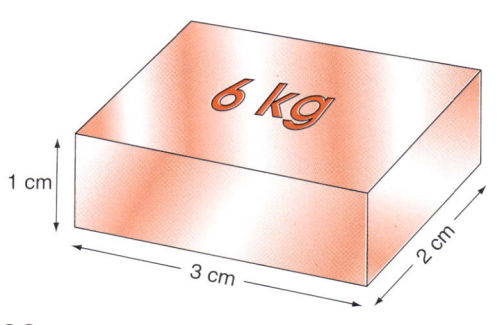

fig. 12.2

Remembering that a 1 kg mass (on Earth) exerts a force of about 10 N (see Chapter 4), the 6 kg mass exerts a force of 60 N. This force is acting (pressing on) on the base of the block, whose area is 6 cm² (3 cm × 2 cm). The force acting on each 1 cm² is thus 10 N (60 N divided by 6), and that is the pressure, 10 N/cm². So,

$$\text{Pressure} = \frac{\text{Force}}{\text{Area}}$$

From that formula, it follows that Force = Pressure × Area.

QUESTIONS

Q. 12.1

If the 6 kg mass is turned so that the front face rests on the bench, the pressure exerted by it will change (but not its weight). Calculate the new pressure.

Q. 12.2

The mass of the digger is 20 tonnes (20 000 kg), and the area of each of its caterpillar tracks is 10 000 cm². Calculate the pressure it exerts on the ground.

Q. 12.3

The girl on stilts has a mass of 50 kg, and the stilts are made of timber measuring 5 cm × 4 cm. Calculate the pressure she exerts when she is standing on:

(i) both stilts, (ii) one stilt.

Do you now realise why the digger has wide caterpillar tracks? When it is necessary to reduce the pressure exerted by something, the load is spread over a larger area. If the digger had four wheels like a car, it would exert a much larger pressure and would sink into soft ground. For the same reasons, camels and elephants have large feet, and skiers do not sink into soft snow. To rescue somebody who has fallen through ice on a frozen lake, a ladder is often laid across the ice to support the weight of rescuers, who would otherwise break through the ice.

fig. 12.3 (a) Elephants have large feet so that they don't sink into the ground

fig. 12.3 (b) Skis have a large area so that they don't sink into the snow

Conversely, if a high pressure is required, a force is made to act over a small area. A nail has a point so that when a hammer applies a force, the pressure which is produced is large enough for the nail to penetrate the wood.

PRESSURE IN LIQUIDS

A solid object only presses downwards on its base, but in a liquid, pressure is exerted in every direction, including upwards. Try the experiment which is illustrated in the diagram.

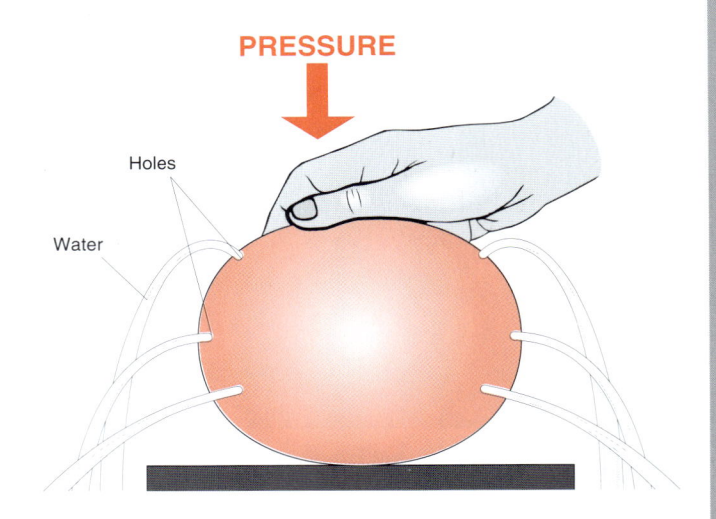

fig. 12.4 Pressure in a liquid acts in all directions

The pressure exerted by a liquid depends on two factors: the depth of the liquid and the density of the liquid. How pressure depends on depth is shown by the experiment which is illustrated below. A tall can with holes at different heights is filled with water. The water jet from the lowest hole travels furthest while the jet from the top hole only travels a short distance. Conclusion: pressure increases with depth. If you swim under water, you will know that the deeper you go, the greater is the pressure acting on your body. Deep sea divers have suits made of strong thick material which can withstand the high pressure in deep water.

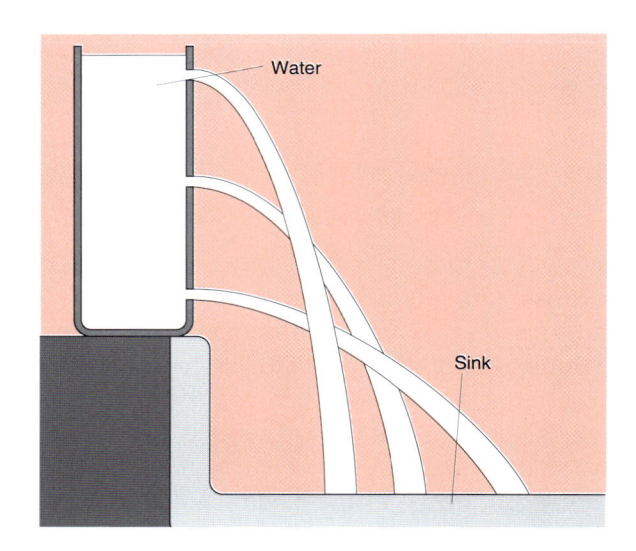

fig. 12.5 Pressure increases with depth

The pressure in a liquid also depends on the density of the liquid – the denser the liquid, the greater the pressure it exerts. However, the pressure does not depend on the volume of a liquid or on the area of the base of the container. If the latter were true, tea would flow up the spout of a teapot since the base has a larger area than the spout.

WATER SUPPLY SYSTEMS

'Water always finds its own level' is an old saying. In the 17th century, Blaise Pascal, a French scientist, designed the following apparatus in order to show how a liquid in connected vessels finds a common level.

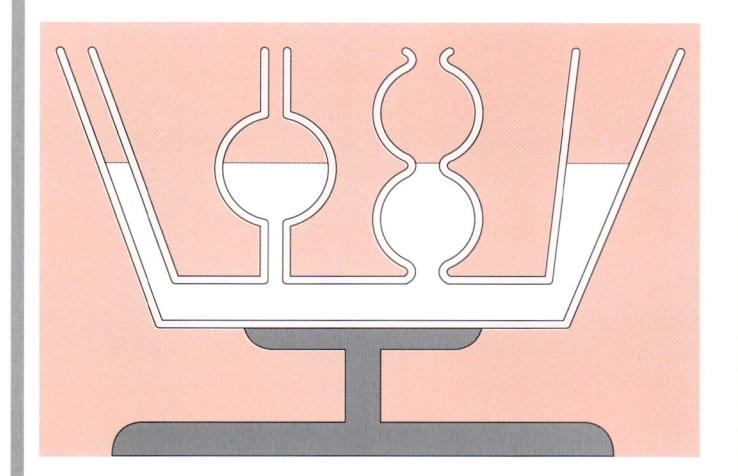

fig. 12.6 Pascal's vases

It is for this reason that water flows upwards from the supply pipes under the road to the storage tank in your attic. A water supply usually comes from a reservoir or a tank on a high level, so that when the water flows up to your tank, it is really flowing down (from where it had been) to the tank. (The way hot water circulates in a house due to convection is described in Chapter 5 on *Heat Travel*.)

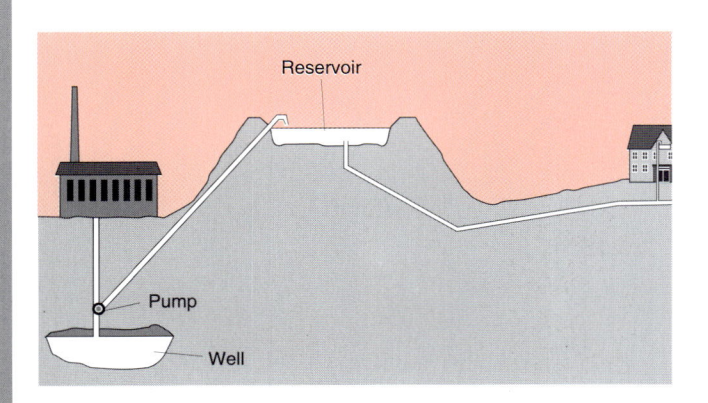

fig. 12.7 A reservoir at a high level

fig. 12.8 A water tower

USES OF PRESSURE

Liquids cannot be compressed, and because of this they are used to transmit pressure between different parts of machines. A hydraulic jack is a simple example using this effect. Remembering that **force = pressure × area**, a large force can be produced even when the pressure is small, but is acting on a large area.

fig. 12.9 A car hoist; how does it work?

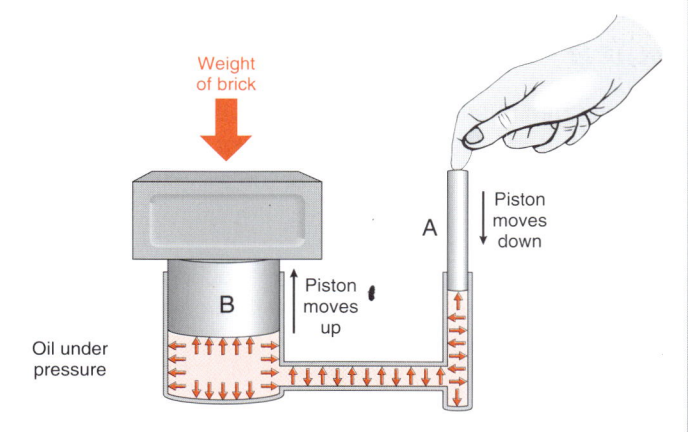

fig. 12.10 A small force can produce a large force

In the hoist shown in Figure 12.10, pressure is generated in the liquid when a force is applied to piston A. This pressure acts on the bottom of the very large piston B.

Because the area of B is much larger than the area of A, the force produced by B is much greater than the force which is applied to A.

Imagine a force of 50 N (equivalent to the weight of 5 kg) being applied to the small piston A whose area is 5 cm². Since pressure = force/area, the pressure generated will be 50/5 which is 10 N/cm².

This pressure is transmitted through the liquid to the bottom of the large piston, which has an area of 1000 cm² (corresponding to a diameter of 36 cm).

Since force = pressure × area, the force generated is 10 × 1000, which is 10 000 newtons. This is the weight exerted by a 1 tonne (1000 kg) mass, which is approximately the mass of an average sized car.

Other applications of pressure being transmitted through a liquid are in the braking system of a car, the controlling of the bucket movement in a digger such as a JCB, and the raising of a dentist's chair.

QUESTIONS

Q. 12.4
(a) A girl presses her finger on the table with a force of 8 N. If the area under her finger is 2 cm², what pressure does she exert?

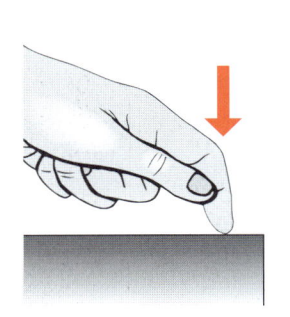

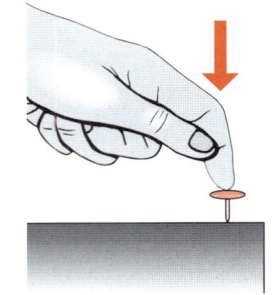

fig. 12.11

(b) She then pushes a drawing pin with the same force. If the area under the point of the pin is 0.01 cm², what pressure does the pin exert?

Q. 12.5
An elephant has a mass of 5 tonnes (5000 kg), and each of its feet has an area of 400 cm². What pressure does it exert when it is standing on (i) all four feet, (ii) two feet?

Q. 12.6
(a) What is the weight of a concrete block whose mass is 10 kg?
(b) What is the area of the base of a block which measures 50 cm by 10 cm?
(c) What is the pressure under one concrete block resting on the ground?
(d) Calculate the pressure on the foundations of a wall which is built of four rows of concrete blocks.

Q. 12.7
Refer to Fig. 12.3 (b)

(a) The skier weighs 540 N. Each of her skis measures 10 cm by 180 cm. Calculate the pressure which the skis exert on the snow. Why can she ski on soft snow without sinking in?

ATMOSPHERIC PRESSURE

At the bottom of the sea, there is great pressure – because of the weight of the water above. So also there is great pressure at the bottom of the 'sea of air' which could describe the Earth's atmosphere. Air is much less dense than water, but because the height of the atmosphere is greater than the depth of any known ocean, the pressure exerted by the atmosphere is very great. You do not normally notice this pressure, because inside your body, your blood is exerting a pressure slightly greater than that, and so the outside pressure is balanced. Several experiments can show that the atmosphere does exert a pressure, and that the pressure is very great. You can do the first two of these experiments at home.

> **Experiment 12.1**
> **To investigate atmospheric pressure**
>
> 1. Place a tissue at the bottom of a cup or beaker. Invert the cup and then push it straight down into a bucket or a sink full of water. Does the tissue get wet?
>
> 2. Fill a cup to the brim with water and then slide a flat piece of cardboard over the top. While holding the cardboard in place, invert the cup and then remove your hand from the cardboard. Why does the water not fall out? (N.B. Do the experiment over the sink!)

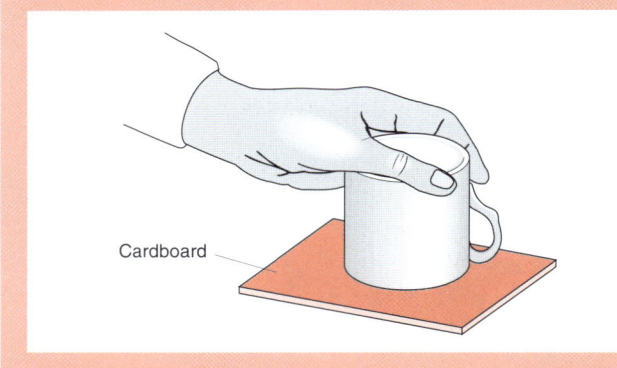

fig. 12.12

The explanation is that the atmospheric pressure pushing upwards on the cardboard is greater than the downwards pressure exerted by the water. So the cardboard stays in place.

Experiment 12.2
To demonstrate atmospheric pressure

Remove the air from inside a large 'tin' can (such as an oil can) and see what happens. This is most simply done by connecting the can to a vacuum pump for a few minutes.

If a pump is not available, it can be done as follows.

Some water is boiled in the can for a minute or two (until all of the air has been driven out), the source of heat then removed and the cap immediately screwed on. The steam condenses, and leaves a vacuum inside the can. The atmospheric pressure which is pressing on the outside of the can then squashes the can quite dramatically.

fig. 12.13 *The can, before and after the experiment*

The Magdeburg hemispheres

Over three hundred years ago, in 1651, a very famous experiment was carried out at Magdeburg in Germany by Otto von Guericke, who was the mayor of Magdeburg at the time. Guericke, who was an engineer, did much experimenting in his spare time and he invented, amongst other things, the vacuum pump.

In his famous experiment, which he did in order to show that the atmosphere exerts pressure, he pumped out the air from between two large copper hemispheres, each 55 cm in diameter. The hemispheres were then held together by the atmospheric pressure pushing on their outsides. He found that two teams of eight horses each were then needed to separate the hemispheres from each other.

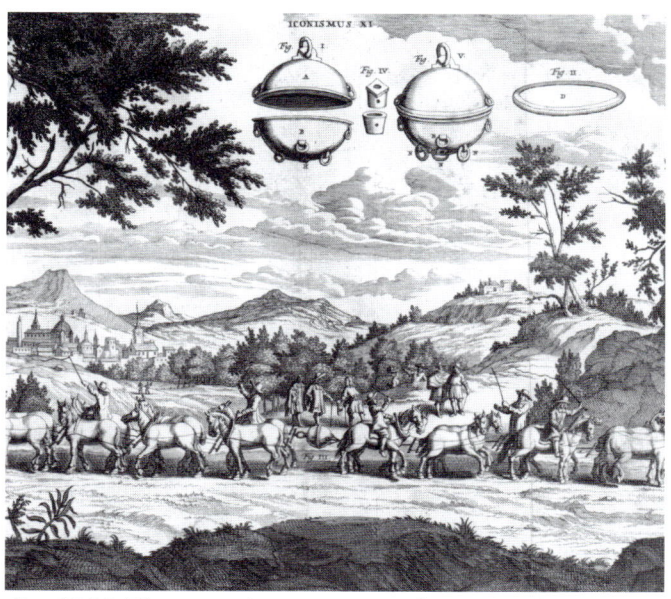

fig. 12.14 *The experiment was performed before the Emperor Ferdinand III and his Imperial Court*

As it is rather difficult to fit 16 horses into a school laboratory, a smaller version of the experiment can be done using hemispheres of about 8 cm diameter, which are available for the purpose.

fig. 12.15 *Only atmospheric pressure holds the hemispheres together*

THE MERCURY BAROMETER

The barometer is an instrument for measuring atmospheric pressure. The simplest kind is the mercury barometer, and it works rather like a see-saw. The pressure caused by a column of mercury inside a glass tube is balanced by the pressure of the atmosphere outside the tube. When the atmospheric pressure increases, the mercury is pushed higher up the tube, and so the height of the mercury in the tube is a measure of the atmospheric pressure. Normal atmospheric pressure is about the same as that exerted by a column of mercury 760 mm high.

12 • Pressure

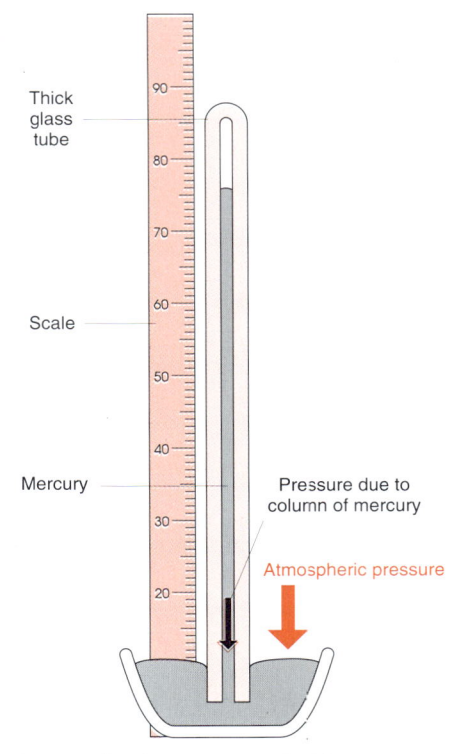

fig. 12.16 Atmospheric pressure holds the column of mercury up

THE ANEROID BAROMETER

The mercury barometer is large, fragile and not convenient to carry around. A much more convenient type is the aneroid barometer. The essential part of this instrument is a corrugated box out of which some of the air has been removed. The corrugations make the centre of the box flexible (able to move in and out). When the atmospheric pressure increases, the centre of the box is pushed slightly inwards, and this inwards movement makes a pointer move over a scale. Study the diagram and work out how the movement of the box is transmitted using levers.

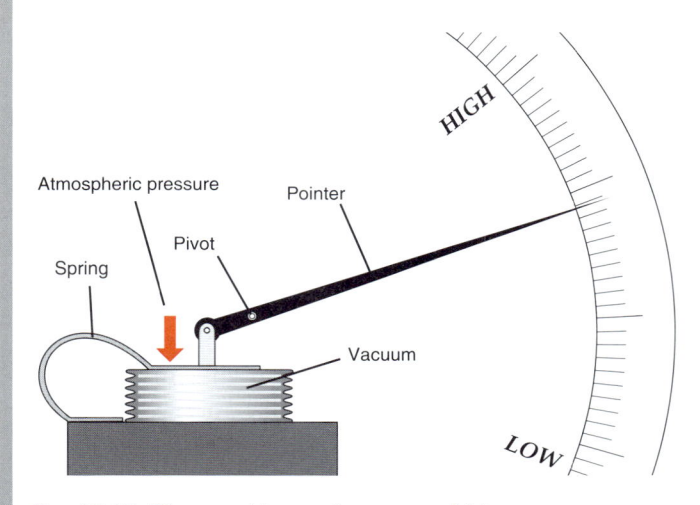

fig. 12.17 The workings of an aneroid barometer

fig. 12.18 Aneroid barometer

ALTITUDE AND PRESSURE

As one ascends into the atmosphere, the pressure decreases (because as you go upwards, there is less and less air above you). So the value of the atmospheric pressure can be used as a measurement of height. An altimeter is essentially an aneroid barometer, but has its scale marked in height units rather than pressure units.

fig. 12.19 An altimeter in an aircraft

Large commercial airliners usually fly at a height of about 10 km and upwards, and at this height the pressure of the atmosphere is only about one quarter of its pressure at sea level. This also means that there is only one quarter of the normal amount of oxygen present and so one cannot breathe properly at this height. Such aircraft are *pressurised* or 'pumped up' so that the air pressure inside them is similar to that at sea level; one can then breathe normally. In unpressurised aircraft flying above about 3 km, pilot and crew must wear oxygen masks to enable them to breathe at these high altitudes where the air is 'thin'.

ATMOSPHERIC PRESSURE AND THE WEATHER

Atmospheric pressure is related to the weather, and in particular to the amount of water vapour in the atmosphere. Water vapour is less dense than air, so as the fraction of it which is present increases, the density of the air, and hence the pressure which it exerts, decreases. The barometer then 'falls' and this indicates that rain is expected. A region of low atmospheric pressure is described as a trough of low pressure, and one of these is shown on the weather map in Fig. 12.20.

Conversely, when there is little water vapour present in the atmosphere, the pressure is high; this indicates dry weather. A region of high pressure is also shown on the weather map.

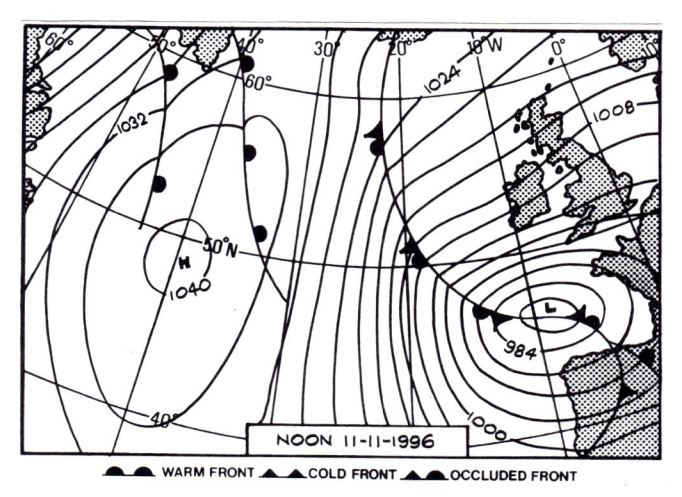

fig. 12.20 The lines on the map are drawn through places of equal atmospheric pressure. Such lines are called isobars.

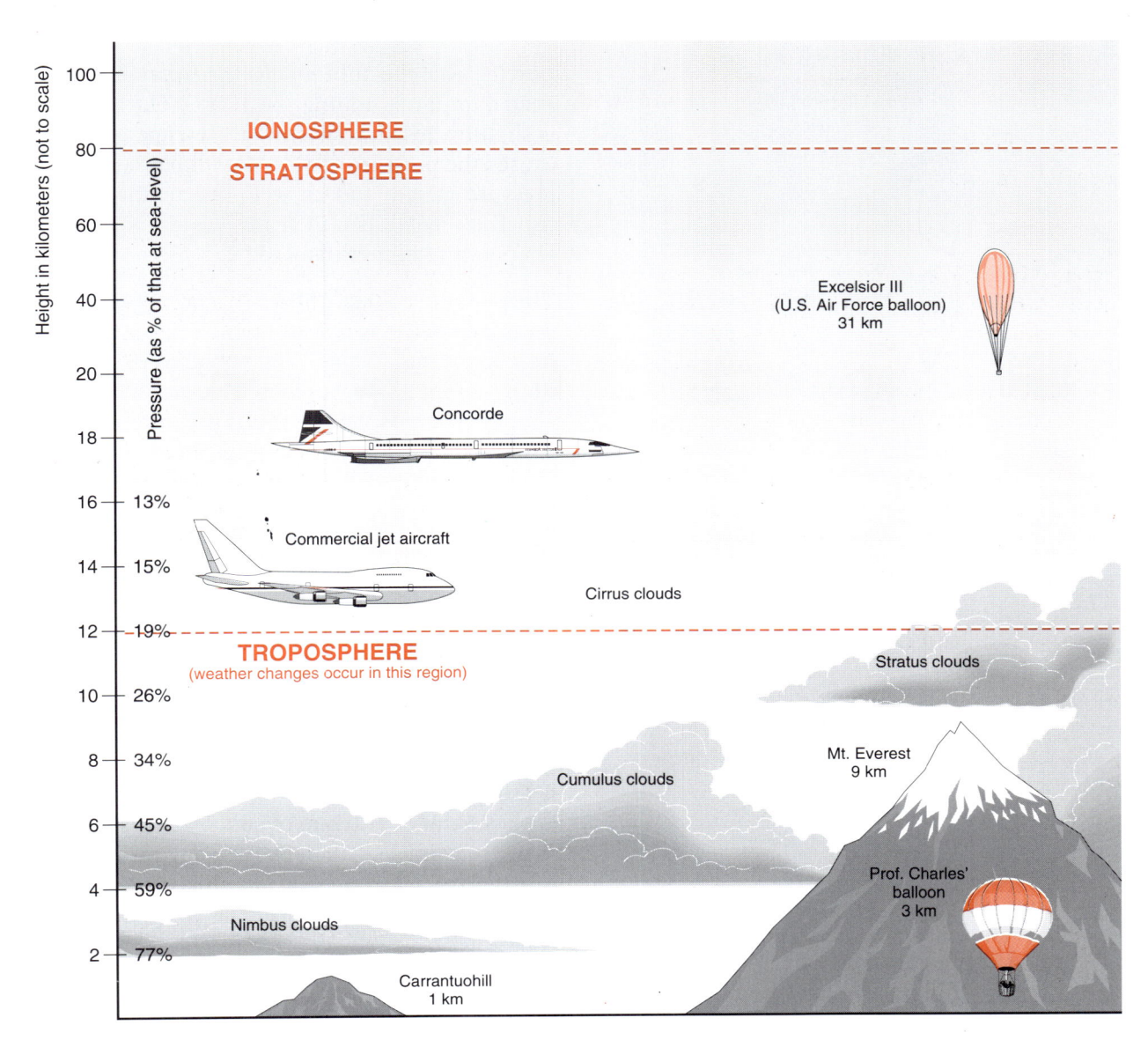

fig. 12.21 Pressure decreases with height

So a knowledge of atmospheric pressure, particularly the **changes** occurring, and how it is **changing** at any particular time, is very important in forecasting the weather. In this part of the world, atmospheric pressure varies between about 975 and 1030 millibars, or, in terms of the height of the barometer, between about 740 and 780 millimetres of mercury (mmHg).

PRESSURE AND MELTING POINT

The normal melting point of ice (and the freezing point of water) is 0°C. However this value depends on the pressure. **Increased pressure lowers the melting point of ice** and this is demonstrated in the following experiment. In it a copper wire travels through a block of ice without cutting the ice into two!

Experiment 12.3
To show the effect of pressure on melting point

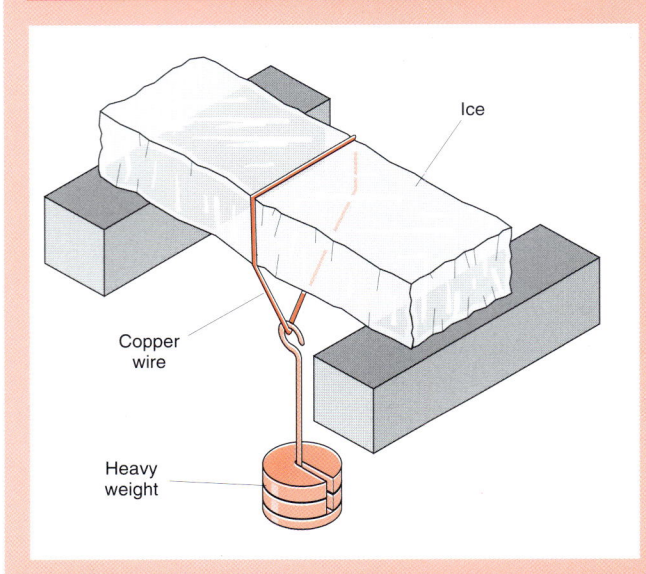

fig. 21.22

The apparatus is set up as shown. A large pressure is exerted on the ice below the wire. The melting point is lowered. The ice (being at 0°C) melts, since its temperature is now above its new melting point. The wire sinks through the water and the water above the wire then refreezes, since it is no longer under pressure.

PRESSURE AND BOILING POINT

Just as pressure affects melting point, it also affects boiling point. The normal boiling point of water is 100°C, but this only applies at standard atmospheric pressure. **Increased pressure raises the boiling point of water**. The following demonstration illustrates this effect.

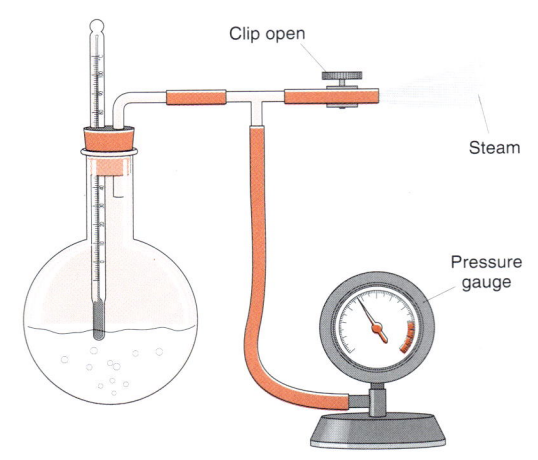

fig. 12.23 Showing that increased pressure raises boiling point

The apparatus is set up as shown. The temperature inside the apparatus is read on the thermometer and the pressure on the Bourdon gauge.

Leaving the clip fully open, the water in the flask is heated until it is boiling – at 100°C. The tap or the clip is slightly closed, restricting the escape of steam. This causes the pressure to rise, as will be indicated by the pressure gauge, and as well, the temperature inside the flask will also increase: water is boiling at a temperature higher than 100°C.

The pressure cooker utilises this principle. A domestic pressure cooker is a vessel which has a tightly-fitting lid containing a valve. The valve keeps the steam in until the pressure reaches a certain value, usually about two atmospheres. At this pressure, water boils at 120°C, and at this temperature, food cooks in much less time that it would in an open saucepan with water boiling at 100°C

Water can be boiled by cooling it!

Conversely, decreased pressure lowers the boiling point of water, and water can be made to boil at temperatures much lower than 100°C. The water is heated to boiling point and the steam is allowed to escape from the flask. After a minute or so (when all the air has been driven out) the clip is closed and the heating stopped. After another minute or so, the flask is placed under a stream of cold water. This causes the steam to condense, thereby reducing the pressure, and causing the water to boil. In this way, water can be made to boil at as low as 50°C.

At low atmospheric pressure, it is difficult to cook food properly. On the top of Mount Everest, for example, atmospheric pressure is in the region of 250 mmHg, and at this pressure, water boils at about

70°C. At this temperature, many foods will not cook. Climbers of high mountains must cook their food in pressure cookers.

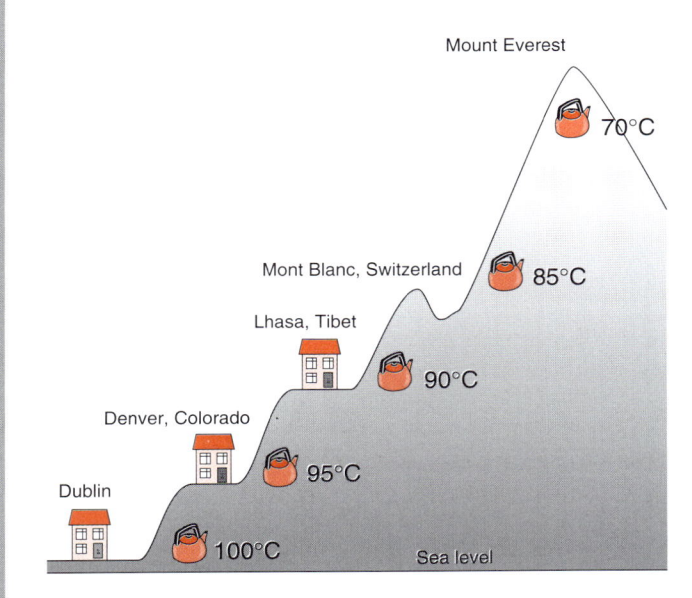

fig. 12.24 Boiling point decreases with altitude

SUMMARY

- Pressure is force acting on unit area, and is expressed in either N/m² or N/cm². The pressure exerted by an object is small if it is pressing on a large area, and is large if the object is pressing on a small area.

- Pressure in a liquid acts in all directions and depends on both the depth of the liquid and its density. Pascal's vases show that a liquid always finds a common level in vessels which are connected together. Liquids cannot be compressed and are used to transmit forces in many devices.

- The Earth's atmosphere exerts pressure – about the same as that exerted by a column of mercury 760 mm high. A barometer measures atmospheric pressure; there are two types, the mercury barometer and the aneroid barometer. Atmospheric pressure decreases with increasing height, and an altimeter is essentially a barometer marked in height units.

- The boiling point of a liquid depends on pressure. As pressure increases, boiling point also increases, and this is the principle used in the pressure cooker. Conversely, as pressure decreases, boiling point decreases. It is not possible to cook food properly in open saucepans on the tops of high mountains.

QUESTIONS

Q. 12.8
Copy out and complete the following paragraphs.
(a) Pressure is defined as ___ acting on ___ area. Its units are ___. Pressure can be calculated by dividing the ___ by the ___.
(b) Pressure in a liquid depends on both the ___ and the ___ of the liquid. The liquid in a barometer is ___. It is used because it has a high ___. A barometer can be likened to a see-saw. In a barometer, the pressure of the ___ is balanced by the pressure exerted by a column of ___. The normal height of the ___ column in a barometer is ___ millimetres. When atmospheric pressure increases, the level of the ___ goes ___.
(c) The lines on a weather map are called ___, and they are drawn through places at equal ___. Weather depends on various factors such as ___ and ___. On a fine sunny day, the pressure is ___ and therefore the level of the liquid in the barometer is ___. When rain is forecast, the level ___.

Q.12.9
A barometer tube is normally about 80 cm long.
(a) Why is this?
(b) What would happen if it were (i) 70 cm, (ii) 90 cm?
(c) What would happen if a small hole were made in the top of the barometer tube?
(d) What would you expect to happen if a barometer were taken up a mountain?
(e) Given that the density of water is 13.6 times less than the density of mercury, calculate the height which a water-filled barometer would have to be in order to work.

Q. 12.10
Suggest a reason for each of the following:
(a) Alpine walkers wear snow shoes in winter.

fig. 12.25

(b) The foundations of a house cover a large area.
(c) A deep-sea diver wears a strong suit, often made of steel.
(d) A rubber suction cup stays attached to the wall.

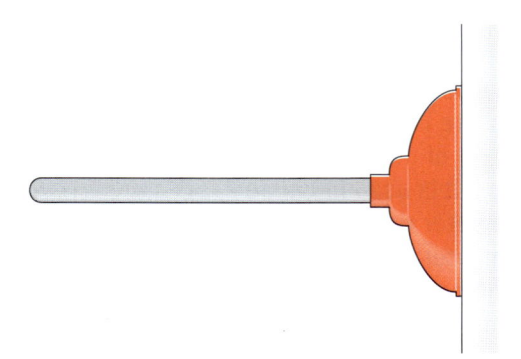

fig. 12.26

(e) A tin can collapses when the air is removed from it.
(f) It hurts to carry a heavy parcel by the string.
(g) An air pressure gauge does not read zero when not connected to anything.

fig 12.27

(h) It is easier to cut with a sharp knife than with a blunt knife.
(i) An aneroid barometer can be used to measure the height of a mountain.
(j) The thickness of a dam is greater at the base than at the top.

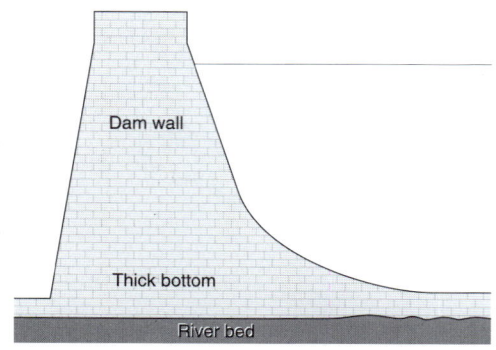

fig. 12.28

(k) It is difficult to cook eggs properly on top of Mount Everest.
(l) When you pump air into your bicycle tyre, it doesn't come out when you disconnect the pump.
(m) The mountaineer does not burn himself with the boiling water.

fig. 12.29

(n) The man does not get hurt when lying on the bed of nails.

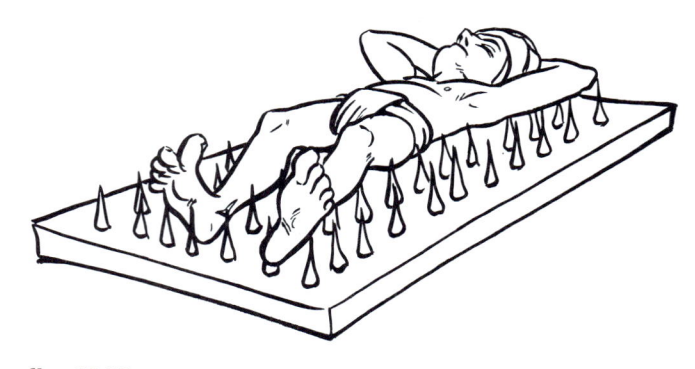

fig. 12.30

Q. 12.11

Describe, using a diagram in each case, three experiments which show that the atmosphere exerts pressure.

Q. 12.12

A man weighs 800 N. Calculate the pressure he exerts when he is wearing:

(a) shoes, with an area of 400 cm² in contact with the ground
(b) ice skating boots, whose blades have an area of 2 cm² in contact with the ice
(c) snow shoes, which make contact with the snow over an area of 2000 cm²

13
EFFECTS OF ELECTRIC CURRENT

Electricity as such is of little use to you – unless you like giving yourself electric shocks! Its great value lies in the fact that because it is a form of energy, it can be converted to most other forms of energy – such as heat, light, sound, chemical, kinetic and potential – by devices which can be operated by just moving a switch. There are three main effects of an electric current, and practically all of the electrical devices used in homes, schools and industries produce one (or more) of these effects. These three effects are **heating**, **magnetic**, and causing **chemical changes**. (The latter effect is described in Chapter 28.)

THE HEATING EFFECT

Every home contains appliances that produce heat from electricity: electric kettles, cookers, electric fires and immersion heaters.

Experiment 13.1
To demonstrate the heating effect of an electric current

A simple experiment which shows that electricity can produce heat consists of connecting a coil of fine resistance wire across a battery or other voltage supply; the coil of wire becomes hot and may even glow red or white hot if the current is high enough.

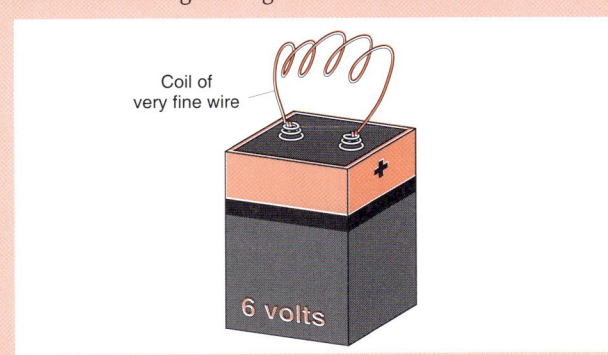

fig. 13.1 *Wire connected across a 6 volt battery glows red hot*

An electric light bulb contains a filament of very fine tungsten wire inside a glass bulb from which the air has been removed and replaced by argon or nitrogen. When a current is passed through the filament, the wire glows white hot, and gives out light.

fig. 13.2 *Inside a light bulb*

If air were present, the tungsten would combine with the oxygen of the air (to form tungsten oxide) and 'burn out'. Tungsten is used because it has a very high melting point. There is a drawing on page 56 showing the construction of an electric light bulb.

If a coil is placed in a beaker of water, it is illustrating the principle of the electric kettle or the immersion heater. The heater in an electric kettle is known as *the element*. The heating wire is contained inside (but insulated from) a metal cover. An element is the essential part of all heating appliances.

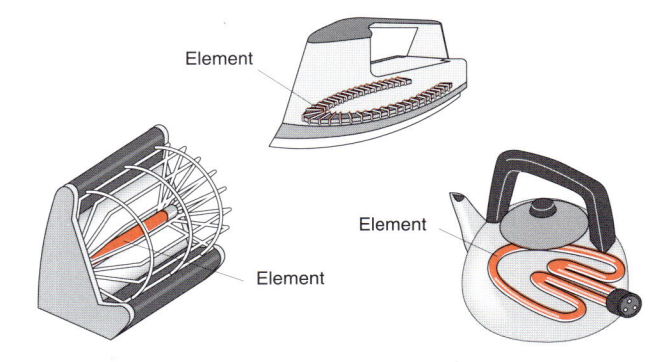

fig. 13.3 *The element is the part of an electric appliance in which heat is generated*

13 · Effects of Electric Current

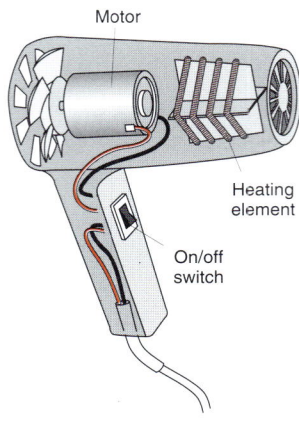

fig. 13.4 Air, blown by the fan, is heated by the element

Energy efficient bulbs

fig. 13.5 Energy saving bulbs

Ordinary filament bulbs convert most of the electrical energy that they consume into heat rather than into light. Approximately 80% of it ends up as heat, and therefore 80% of the cost of lighting these bulbs is wasted. The modern energy-efficient bulbs use a different principle to produce light (they don't have a white-hot filament) but they only waste about 20% of the electricity as heat – and therefore 80% of the electrical energy appears as light. They are more costly to purchase but in the long term are better value for money.

FUSES AND CIRCUIT BREAKERS

A fuse is a safety device in an electrical circuit. It consists of a short piece of low-melting-point wire in a porcelain case, and it is connected in series in a circuit. If, due to a fault in an appliance or in the wiring, the current becomes too great, the wire melts (*fuses* or *blows*), the circuit is broken and the current is cut off. This arrangement prevents the danger of something overheating and perhaps causing a fire.

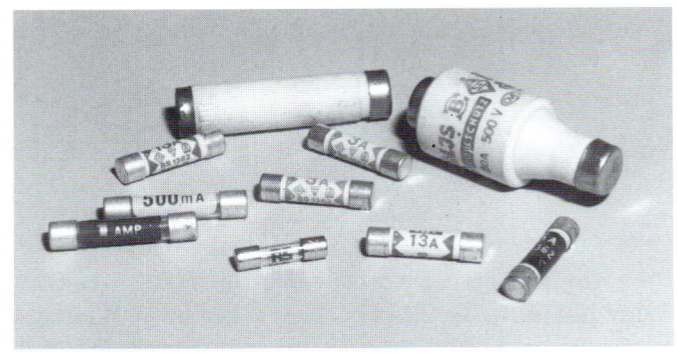

fig. 13.6 A selection of fuses

Demonstration of fuse action

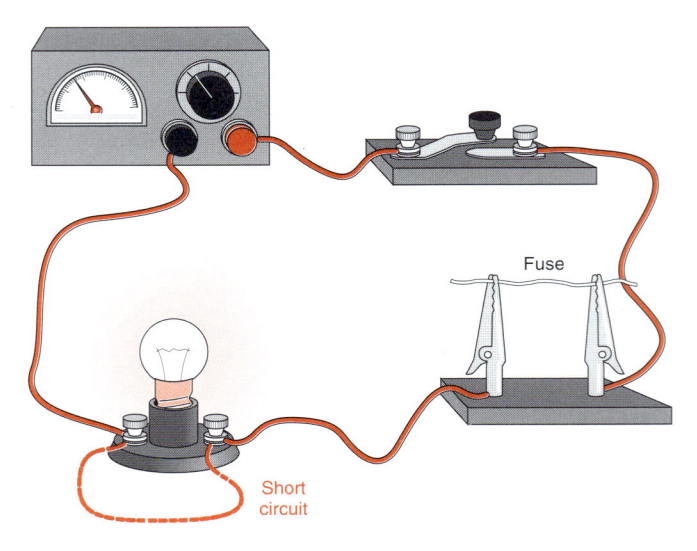

fig. 13.7 When the 'short circuit' is connected across the bulb, the resistance of the circuit becomes very small, so the current becomes very large. This causes the fuse wire to melt (it 'fuses'), breaking the circuit and so stopping the current.

The fuse (and also the switch) for a device is put into the live (dangerous) wire of the circuit. Then when the fuse blows, it is the live wire that is disconnected and the device is 'dead'. If the fuse were wrongly placed in the neutral wire, the device could still be live even though the fuse had blown.

Choosing the right fuse

Fuses of different sizes are available (1 A, 3 A, 5 A, 10 A, 13 A, 25 A) to suit different uses. The correct fuse to use for an appliance is the one whose value is just above the normal current taken by the appliance. For example, a toaster uses about 3 amps; the correct fuse to have in the circuit is a 5 A one. When a plug is purchased, it normally contains a 13 A fuse, but this should always be replaced by the right fuse for the appliance to which it is being connected.

If the fuse for an appliance blows more than once, it usually indicates a fault in the appliance or the circuit, and an electrician should then be called on to check for a fault. It can be dangerous to replace the correct fuse with one of higher value, or worse still, by a piece of heavy wire or a nail.

Circuit breakers

fig. 13.8 *Circuit breakers are modern devices that are often used on a fuseboard in place of fuses. They do the same job but by a different method. When they break the circuit, they can be reset. Like fuses, the circuit breaker should be the right size for the circuit which it is protecting.*

EARTHING

Most mains plugs have three pins. Two of these are for carrying the current to and from whatever appliance is connected to the plug. The third pin (the large one) is the earth pin and is a safety device. It connects the metal frame of the appliance to earth.

If a fault occurs in an appliance and a live wire touches the metal frame, a large current flows from the live wire to earth (through the earth wire) and blows a fuse – cutting off the current and preventing the frame from becoming live. This makes it safe until the fault has been repaired. In the absence of an earth wire, the frame would become live and dangerous; anyone touching it could get an electric shock or be injured.

Earthed kettle   Unearthed kettle

fig. 13.9 *Mains appliances should be earthed for safety*

THE MAGNETIC EFFECT OR ELECTROMAGNETISM

Electricity produces magnetism. This discovery was made in the early nineteenth century by a Danish scientist, Hans Christian Oersted. He was experimenting with a wire carrying an electric current and he noticed that a compass needle nearby moved when the current was switched on. Oersted's experiment can be repeated to show that it still works today:

Experiment 13.2
To show that electricity produces magnetism

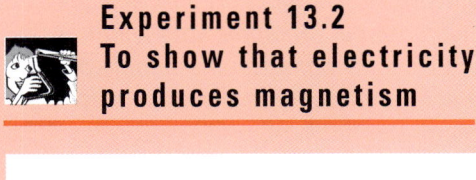

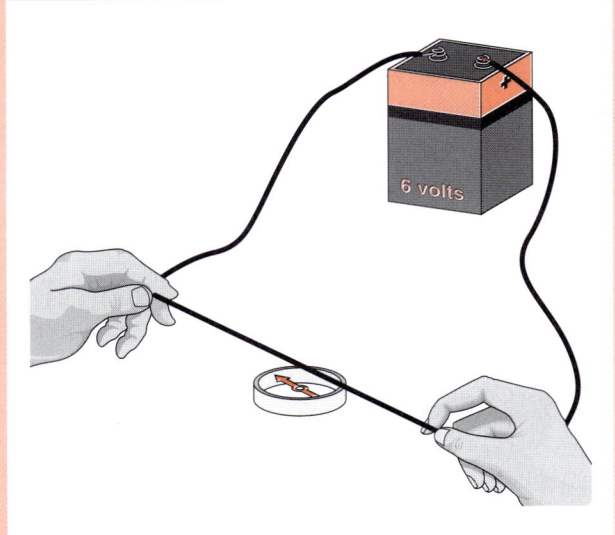

fig. 13.10

(a) The wire is held above and parallel to the compass needle and the current is switched on; the compass needle deflects. If the current then is reversed (by changing around the connections to the battery), the needle deflects the other way.

(b) If now the wire is held above but at right angles to the compass needle and the current switched on, the needle is unaffected. This is because the lines of magnetic force are at right angles to the wire and the compass needle is already pointing in the direction of the lines of magnetic force.

The lines of magnetic force surround the wire and are always at right angles to it. This can be shown using the apparatus illustrated in Figure 13.11. A large current is passed through the wire, and either iron filings or plotting compasses (or both) can be used to see the lines of force.

13 • Effects of Electric Current

fig. 13.11 Apparatus for showing the flux around a straight wire. Note that in the apparatus which is shown, the wire actually consists of a bundle of wires; this increases the magnetic effect, making it strong enough to move the iron filings.

The magnetic field of a solenoid can be shown in a similar way. A current is passed through the solenoid, and again either iron filings or plotting compasses are used to see the lines of force.

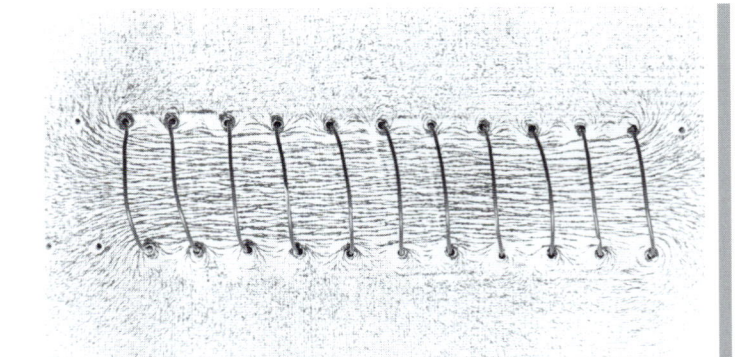

fig. 13.12 Lines of magnetic force around a solenoid

SOLENOIDS AND ELECTROMAGNETS

A solenoid is an open coil of wire. When a current flows through the wire, the coil behaves like a magnet. If there is an iron core inside the solenoid, the device is an electromagnet. This type of magnet behaves like an ordinary bar magnet, but can be switched on and off as required.

Experiment 13.3
Making a solenoid and converting it to an electromagnet

Part 1: Soleniod

Wind, in a single layer around a pencil, about 30 turns of fine insulated wire. The turns should be wound close to each other. Cover the wire with Sellotape to prevent it unwinding, and then slide it off the pencil. Lay it on the bench and place two plotting compasses, one at each end of the solenoid. Connect the solenoid to a battery. Do the compasses detect any magnetism? In what direction do they point? Reverse the connections to the battery; what is the effect of doing this?

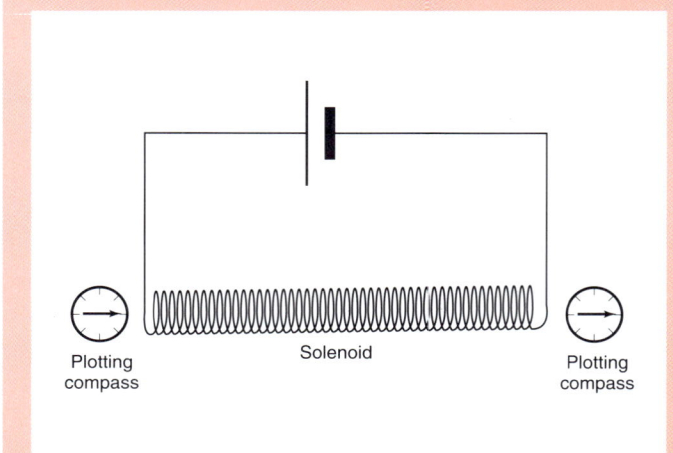

fig. 13.13

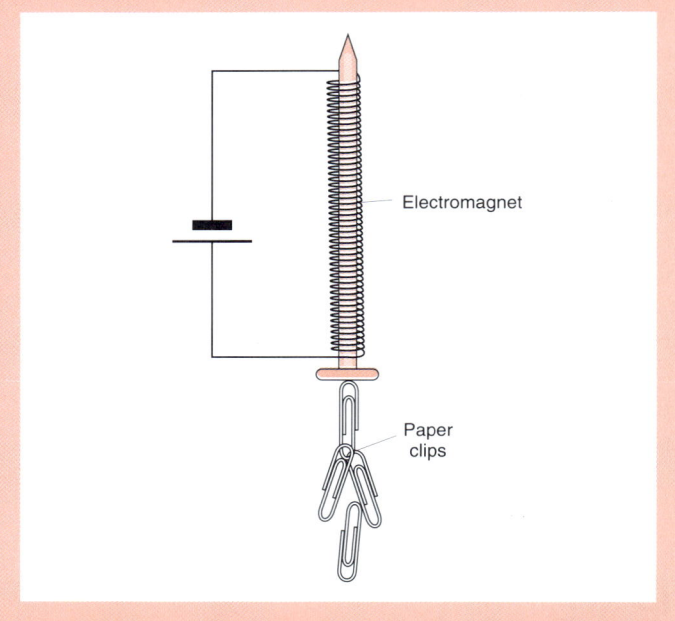

fig. 13.14

Part 2: Electromagnet

Place a large nail or several nails inside the solenoid and repeat the experiments. You should find that the magnetic field is now stronger. Dip the electromagnet into a pile of pins or paperclips. What happens? Switch off the current; what happens now?

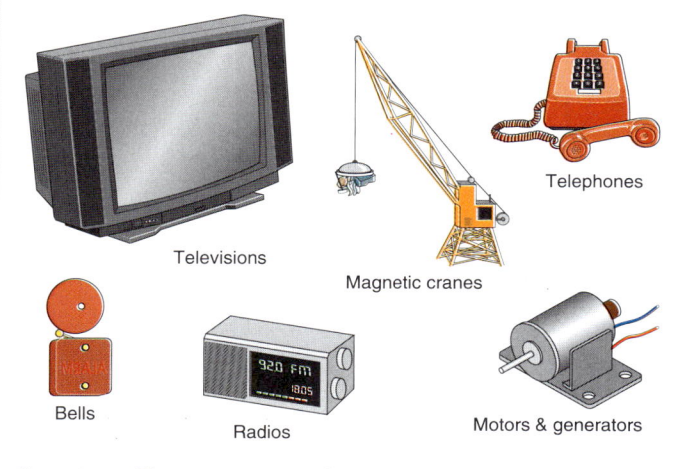

fig. 13.15 Electromagnets have many uses; small ones are used in telephones and door bells, and large ones are used in scrapyards for carrying scrap iron about.

fig. 13.16 An electromagnet in use in a scrapyard

SUMMARY

- The three main effects of an electric current are (i) **heating** (including lighting), (ii) **magnetic**, and (iii) **chemical**. The heating effect is utilised in electric cookers, immersion heaters, light bulbs and many other household devices.

- **A fuse is a safety device** in an electric circuit and consists of a piece of thin wire which melts if the current flowing through it becomes too great.

- The magnetic effect of an electric curent can be shown by placing a magnet on a wire carrying a current. The magnetic flux surrounding a wire carrying a current is a series of concentric circles.

- A **solenoid** is a long open coil of wire. An **electromagnet** consists of a solenoid with a soft-iron core; it has a magnetic field similar to that of a bar magnet. All electric motors work because of the magnetic effect of an eletric current.

QUESTIONS

Q. 13.1

Rewrite the following paragraphs and complete the gaps.

(a) There are ___ main effects of an electric current. These are the ___ effect, ___ effect and the magnetic effect. The circuit which is shown in Fig. 13.17 can be used to demonstrate the ___ effect. When the switch is closed, ___ flows around the circuit, and in the coil of wire, ___ energy is converted to ___ energy. The ___ of the water therefore rises. This effect is used in many household devices such as the ___ and the ___.

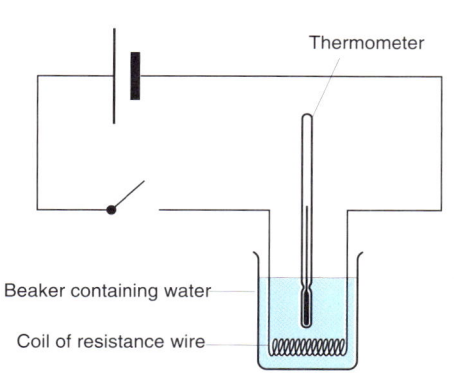

fig. 13.17

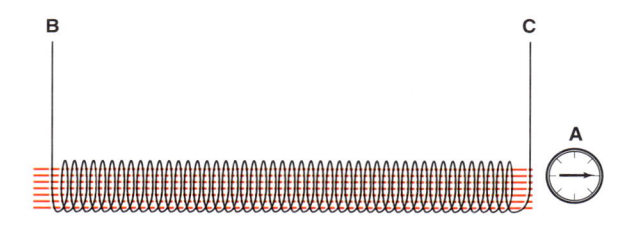

fig. 13.18

(b) In Fig. 13.18, the ___ effect is being demonstrated. When the ends of the wire B and C are connected to a battery, a ___ flows through the wire, and item A (which is a ___) detects ___. This effect of an electric current is used in a ___.

(c) A safety device in an electric circuit is the ___. This item consists of a short piece of low melting-point ___, and when the current flowing through it becomes too great, it ___ and therefore makes a break in the ___. The current therefore ___. These items come in various sizes. When a new plug is purchased, it contains a ____ amp ___. For things such as table lamps, this size is too large, and it should be replaced by a smaller value one, such as a ___ amp ___.

Q. 13.2

(a) In the electric kettle, why is the heating wire insulated from the kettle?
(b) Why is the cover of the heating element made of metal?
(c) Give two reasons why the heating element is at the bottom of the kettle rather than the top?
(d) Why does the kettle have a plastic handle?
(e) Why is the filament of an electric bulb made of tungsten?
(f) Why is the air removed from inside an electric bulb?

Q. 13.3

List six items in your home that convert electrical energy to heat energy.

Q. 13.4

Describe with the aid of a diagram, an experiment which showed that electricity can produce heat. Name one household appliance that makes use of this effect.

Q. 13.5

Describe with the aid of a diagram, an experiment which showed that electricity can produce magnetism. Name one household appliance which makes use of this effect.

Q. 13.6

Name three domestic devices that contain electromagnets. Draw a diagram of one of them and label the parts.

Q. 13.7

Describe an experiment in which you constructed an electromagnet. Draw a diagram of the magnet and label the parts. Describe two experiments which you did with the electromagnet.

Q. 13.8

Describe an experiment which showed (a) that there is a magnetic field around a straight wire carrying a current, and (b) that a solenoid has a similar magnetic field to a bar magnet.

14
ELECTRICITY IN THE HOME

Many different units of measurement are used in electricity. There are amps, volts, watts, ohms, kilowatt-hours and others. Why so many units? What do they all measure? Just as athletes for instance must know about distance, time and speed, people who design and repair electrical equipment must know about electrical units.

In Chapter 9, which introduced electrical circuits, you should have learned that:

- a flow of electricity is called an **electric current**
- a battery produces a **potential difference** or '**voltage**' which drives electricity around a circuit
- a circuit always offers some opposition (called **resistance**) to current
- voltage is measured in **volts** (symbol V)
- current is measured in **amps** (symbol A)
- resistance is measured in **ohms** (symbol Ω)

The current flowing in a circuit depends on the potential difference or voltage of the battery which is driving it, and it also depends on the resistance of the circuit.

Experiment 14.1
To investigate the relationship between current and voltage

In this experiment, different voltages are connected to a length of resistance wire, and for each voltage, the current flowing through the wire is measured. The different voltages are most conveniently obtained from a low-voltage power supply, but batteries can be used also.

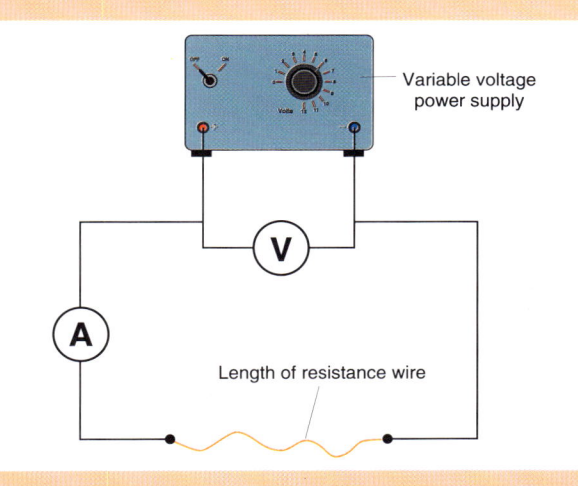

fig. 14.1

fig. 14.2

Connect up the circuit as shown. Set the voltage at 1 volt. On the ammeter, read the current flowing through the wire. Increase the voltage to 2 V, and again read the current. Continue in this way to about 12 volts. Record the results (the voltage and the current) in the form of a table, such as shown.

RESULTS

Voltage/V	1	2	3	4	etc.
Current/A					

To find the relationship between the two sets of values, plot a graph of the current against voltage. When this is done, the graph turns out to be a straight line. A straight line graph means that the two quantities are proportional to one another (or are in the same ratio). So, in this case, the current is proportional to the voltage or potential difference.

The first scientist to discover this was a German scientist, Professor Ohm, who lived in the last century, so the relationship is called **Ohm's law**. In full it states:

> The current flowing through a conductor is proportional to the potential difference applied to it.

Expressed as a formula, Ohm's law is:

$$V = IR$$

$$\text{or } R = \frac{V}{I}, \text{ or } I = \frac{V}{R}$$

This triangle method may be used again for Ohm's law calculations. Cover up the quantity you want, and you will be left with the terms for working it out. For example, if you want R, cover it up, and you are left with V/I, and that is how you calculate R.

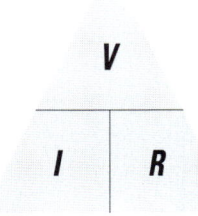

Measuring resistance

The resistance of a device is measured by connecting a known voltage to it and then measuring the current which flows through it. The resistance is then calculated using Ohm's law. For example, what is the resistance of a 6 volt bicycle bulb which takes a current of 2 amps?

$$R = \frac{V}{I} = \frac{6}{2} = 3 \text{ ohms}$$

QUESTIONS

Q. 14.1
A car has a 12 volt battery. Calculate the resistance of:
(a) a headlamp bulb which takes a current of 8 amps, and
(b) a sidelamp bulb which takes 2 amps

Q. 14.2
A torch bulb takes 0.3 amps when it is connected to a 6 volt battery. What is its resistance? What current would the bulb take if connected to a 12 volt battery?

Q. 14.3
An electric fire has a resistance of 60 ohms and takes a current of 4 amps from the electricity supply. What is the voltage of the supply?

Q. 14.4
A 'Walkman' takes a current of 100 milliamps from a 3 volt battery. Express 100 milliamps in amps. What is the resistance of the 'Walkman'?

Q. 14.5
Household electricity is supplied in this country at a voltage of 230 volts. Calculate the current that flows through a device with a resistance of:
(a) 100 ohms, (b) 200 ohms?

ELECTRICAL POWER OR WHAT IS A WATT?

The power of an electrical device is measured in units called **watts**, and it indicates the rate at which it uses electricity (i.e. converts electricity to other forms of energy). One watt is one joule per second, so that a 60 watt bulb, for example, uses 60 joules of electricity each second (or 360 joules per minute). One watt is a very small amount of power and kilowatts are usually used for high-power items (1 kW = 1000 W).

The power (in watts) of an appliance is easily calculated, by just multiplying the voltage connected to it by the current flowing through it, i.e.

> power = voltage × current,
> or $P = VI$

Worked examples

Q. What is the power of a 12 volt car bulb which takes a current of 5 amps?

A. Power = voltage × current = 12 × 5 = 60 watts.

Q. An electric fire is marked 230 V, 2 kW. What current flows through it?

A. Current = $\frac{\text{power}}{\text{voltage}} = \frac{2000}{230} = 8.7$ amps
(2 kW = 2000 W)

POWER RATINGS OF HOUSEHOLD APPLIANCES

The power rating of an electrical appliance means the amount of power it uses. Such values vary considerably for similar items, but the table below shows typical power ratings for various household appliances.

Computer	110 W
Dishwasher	1.5 kW
Electric blanket	400 W
Electric cooker	11 kW
Electric fire (2 bar)	2 kW
Electric hob	6 kW
Electric iron	960 W
Electric kettle	1.5 kW
Hair dryer	600 W
Immersion heater	3 kW
Microwave oven	1.6 kW
Power drill	300 W
Refrigerator	180 W
Stereo system	140 W
Table lamp	100 W
Toaster	700 W
TV set	110 W
Vacuum cleaner	900 W
Video recorder	50 W
Washing machine	2 kW

QUESTIONS

Q. 14.6
A torch bulb is marked 3.5 V, 0.3 A. What is its power?

Q. 14.7
An electric motor has a resistance of 12 ohms.
(a) What current flows through it when it is connected to a 6 volt battery?
(b) What is its power?

Q. 14.8
What is the power of each of the items in questions 14.1, 14.2 and 14.3?

Q. 14.9
Refer to the table of household appliances which are designed for the 230 volt ESB mains. For each of the following items, calculate the current which flows through it, and select the most suitable fuse (from the following list) to use in its plug:
1 A, 3 A, 5 A, 13 A.
(a) electric iron
(b) computer
(c) microwave oven
(d) hair dryer
(e) kettle
(f) toaster

BUYING ELECTRICITY

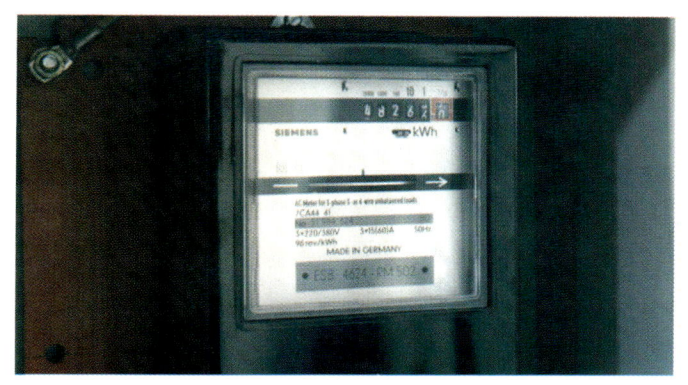

fig. 14.3 An ESB meter

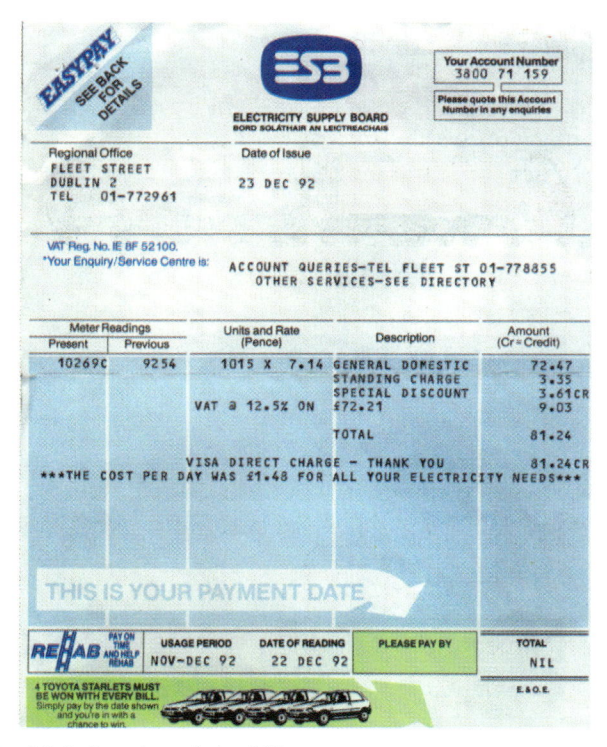

fig. 14.4 An electricity bill

When you pay an electricity bill, you are paying for energy. Since a joule is a very tiny unit of energy, the ESB (Electricity Supply Board) uses a very much larger unit, called a **kilowatt hour** – which is known as a '**unit**' of electricity.

14 • Electricity in the Home

> A kilowatt hour is the amount of energy supplied when 1 kilowatt is used for 1 hour.

Worked example

Q. How many units of electricity are used by a 2 kilowatt electric fire in 6 hours? What is the cost of using it when electricity costs 8p per unit?

A. The total number of units used by an electrical device is found by multiplying the number of kilowatts by the number of hours.

Number of units used = 2 × 6 = 12 units.
Cost = 12 × 8 = 96p.

The more powerful an appliance is, the greater the rate at which it uses electricity, and the more costly it is to use. Notice that the appliances in the previous table that produce heat are the ones which use electricity at the greatest rate. Figure 14.5 shows what one unit of electricity can do.

QUESTIONS

Use the table of power ratings (page 95) to answer these questions.

Q.14.10

Calculate how much energy is used by:

(a) an immersion heater for 2 hours
(b) an electric blanket for 2 hours
(c) two table lamps for half an hour
(d) a hair dryer for 10 minutes

Q. 14.11

If electricity costs 8p per unit, calculate the cost of using each of the following items for the times given (use the table of power ratings):

(a) an electric fire (both bars) for 2 hours
(b) a stereo system for 4 hours
(c) a TV set and video, for half an hour
(d) a hair dryer for 30 minutes
(e) a computer for 6 hours
(f) an electric kettle for 10 minutes

fig. 14.5 What one unit of electricity can do

- operates a TV set for 8 hours
- heats all 4 rings on an electric hob for 10 minutes
- toasts 70 slices of bread
- boils 10 litres of water
- runs a hairdryer for 4 hours
- powers a vacuum cleaner for 1½ hours
- drives an electric drill for 3 hours
- washes 1 load of dishes
- runs a stereo system for 8 hours
- keeps a refrigerator going for 1 day
- runs an electric fire (2 bar) for ½ hour
- lights a 100 W bulb for 10 hours
- heats an electric blanket for 4 hours

Q. 14.12

To heat enough water for a hot bath, an immersion heater needs to be on for one hour. An 'instant' shower (6 kW) heats the water as it passes through it, and a shower takes five minutes. Calculate the cost of having (i) a hot bath, and (ii) a hot shower.

Q. 14.13

A football stadium is floodlit by six lighting towers, each of which carries twenty-four 2 kW floodlights. Calculate the cost of lighting a football match for 2 hours when electricity costs 8p per unit.

ALTERNATING CURRENT

A battery has two terminals, a positive and a negative. When it is in use, current flows from the positive terminal of the battery, around the circuit in one direction, and then back to the negative terminal of the battery. Such a current is called **direct current** (denoted by d.c.)

Mains electricity is different. As well as being at a much higher voltage, the current is **alternating current** (a.c.). This means that it is constantly changing its direction. One hundred times every second, its direction reverses; fifty times per second it is flowing in one direction, and fifty times in the other.

The two terminals of a mains supply cannot be labelled positive and negative because they are changing all the time. One terminal is at the same voltage as earth, and is called the **neutral**; the other is the **live** (and is the very dangerous one). In an electrical socket, the neutral is on the left-hand side and the live on the right (assuming that the socket is correctly wired). The **earth** is in the large opening at the top.

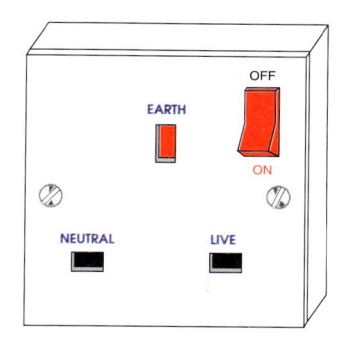

fig. 14.6 Earth, neutral and live terminals

Rectifying alternating current: use of the diode

Why this is done, and how, is described in Chapter 47.

DOMESTIC WIRING

Here is a simplified diagram of a household wiring circuit. The 230 volt mains supply comes in at A. It goes through a main switch B and the ESB's electricity meter C, and then to the fuse board (or circuit-breaker board), D. From the fuse board there are several outlets. One outlet, E, goes to supply the lights, and will probably be protected by a 5 A fuse. Another outlet, F, supplies the plugs and is likely to have a 25 A fuse. (As well, every appliance has a separate fuse in its own plug.) There are also separate outlets from the fuse board for high-power items like the electric cooker and the immersion heater.

The wiring for the plug supply is generally by means of a ring main. The cable carrying this supply contains three wires, the **live**, the **neutral** and the **earth**, and it

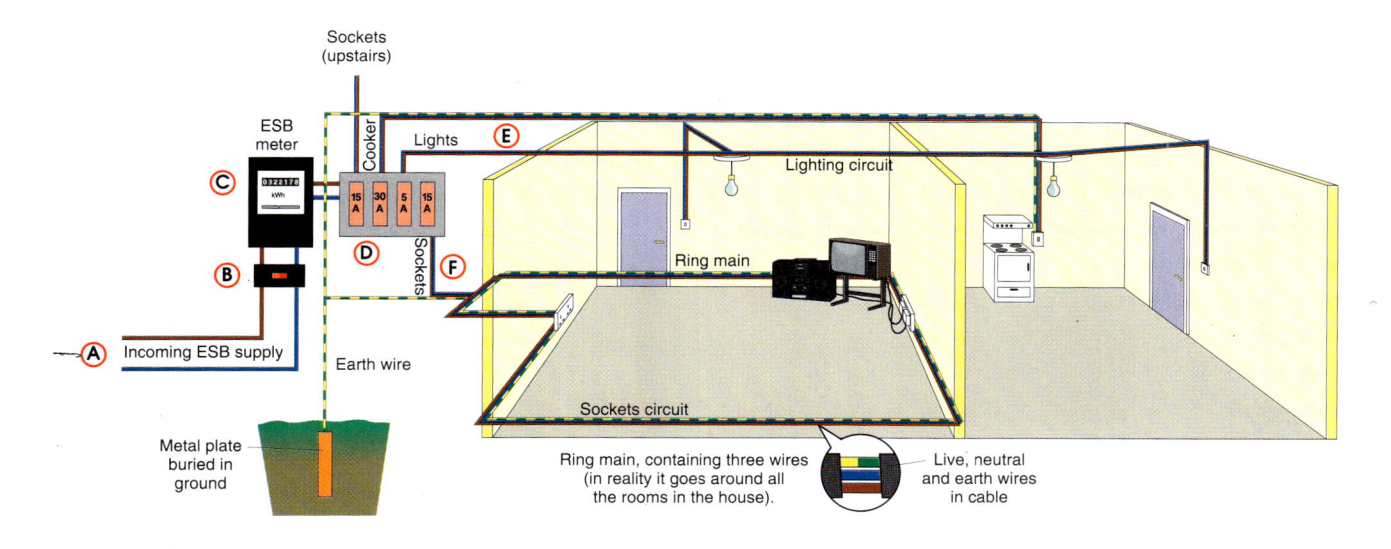

fig. 14.7 A domestic ring circuit

14 • Electricity in the Home

both starts and ends at the fuseboard. The advantage is that current can reach any socket by two routes, each route carrying only half the load.

The operation of lights and heaters is described on page 87.

USING ELECTRICITY SAFELY

Every year thousands of people are killed or injured by electric shocks and thousands of fires are caused by faults in electrical appliances. The most common dangers consist of plugs which are fitted with the wrong fuses, are incorrectly wired or cracked, or have poor earth connections. Cables on items like vacuum cleaners and hair dryers often become twisted, and this can weaken the insulation inside the outer cable. Regular checks need to be made on all electrical devices to diagnose weaknesses before accidents occur.

Fuses and Earthing

This has been described in Chapter 13. Refer back to page 88 to revise what fuses are and why appliances are earthed. It is important to use the right fuse in the plug of an electrical appliance. Low-power items (lamps, radios, TVs) should have 3 or 5 A fuses and only heating appliances should be left with the 13 A fuse which is supplied in plugs when purchased. Having too high a fuse in the plug of a lower-power item means that, in the event of a fault, it could overheat without the fuse blowing.

Some modern appliances have double insulation and the plugs on these often have two pins, live and neutral. Because of the double insulation, an earth wire is not used.

How to wire a plug correctly

1. Using a screwdriver, remove the cover from the plug.
2. Remove one (or both) of the screws holding the cord grip and also loosen the screws of each pin (Figure 14.8 (a)). Removing the fuse usually gives more space to work.
3. Cut back about 4 cm of the outer covering of the flex to be connected (if this is not already done) (Figure (b)).
4. Identify the three wires from their colours, and cut the live and neutral wires about 1 cm shorter than the earth wire (Figure (c)).
5. For each of the three wires, strip back about 15 mm of the insulation and then twist the thin strands of wire around each other so that the end of each wire becomes a single unit rather than a loose collection of strands (Figure (d)). It is also a good idea to double back the wire on itself as this will ensure a very firm connection in the plug terminal (Figure (e)).
6. Connect the brown wire into the live pin, the blue wire into the neutral pin, and the green/yellow wire into the earth pin. **Tighten the screws well** (Figure (f)).
7. Secure the outer covering of the flex into the cord grip. **Tighten the screws well. Make sure that it is the outer covering that is secured**, and not just individual wires, as the grip will not hold individual wires securely (Figure (g)).
8. While plugs are normally supplied with 13 A fuses, this is not the safest value for most items. Obtain a fuse of the correct value and insert it into the fuse holder.
9. **Check that there are no small strands of wire hanging loose.** Screw back the cover on to the plug. Make sure that the holding screw is tight.

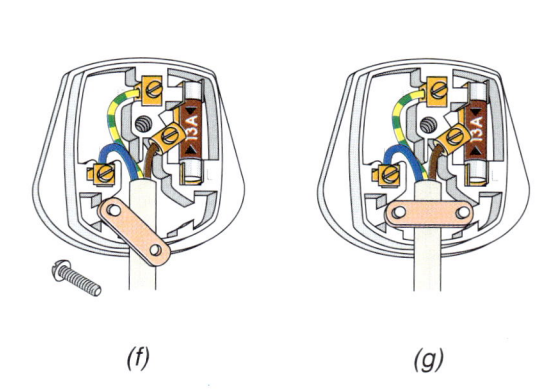

fig. 14.8 *Stages in wiring a plug*

SUMMARY

- The **current** flowing through a circuit depends on the resistance of the circuit and the voltage of the battery (or other power supply) which is driving it. **Ohm's law**, which relates the three quantities, is $V = IR$.

- **Power** is the rate at which energy is converted from one form to another and is measured in watts. One watt = one joule per second. The power of an electrical device can be calculated from $P = VI$.

- Electricity is bought by the **kilowatt hour**, which is known as a 'unit' of electricity. This is the amount of electricity supplied in one hour when one kilowatt is being used. The number of **units used = kilowatts × hours**.

- **Mains electricity** is supplied in the form of **alternating current**. The two wires are the live and the neutral. The wiring in most houses is by means of a **ring main**. Each separate circuit is protected by its own fuse or circuit breaker, and plug outlets have three terminals, the live, the neutral and the earth. **It is very important to know how to use mains electricity safely.**

QUESTIONS

Q. 14.14

(a) Calculate the number of units of electricity (kilowatt hours) used by each of the following (refer to the table of power ratings on page 95): (i) an electric kettle for two hours (ii) a toaster for half an hour (iii) 40 hours television viewing (iv) a 2-bar electric fire for 1 hour each evening for a week (v) 5 table lamps for 3 hours each evening (for a week).

(b) Calculate also (i) the **total** number of units consumed in the house where the above appliances are used and (ii) the cost of the week's electricity (electricity at 8p per unit).

Q. 14.15

This diagram shows a plug.

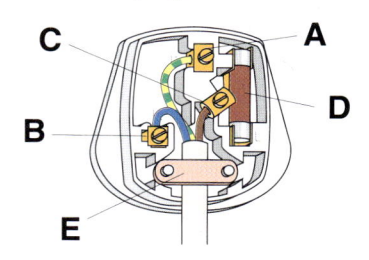

fig. 14.10

fig. 14.9 Electrical 'do nots'

14 • Electricity in the Home

(a) Which is the (i) live pin, (ii) the neutral pin, (iii) the earth pin?
(b) What colour wires should be connected to B and to D?
(c) What colour is the earth wire?
(d) What are D and E, and what is the function of each?

Q. 14.16
(a) State Ohm's law.
(b) Draw a labelled diagram of a circuit which you could use to verify Ohm's law.
(c) List the measurements that you would make in carrying out the experiment.
(d) How could the measurements be used to verify the law?

Q. 14.17
(a) What is each of the following units a measure of: (i) volt, (ii) amp, (iii) ohm, (iv) watt, (v) joule, (vi) kilowatt hour?
(b) What voltage electricity does the ESB supply to homes?
(c) What is the unit of energy used by the ESB? Why is the standard unit of energy not used?

Q. 14.18
Copy out the following table, and into the spaces, write the missing values.

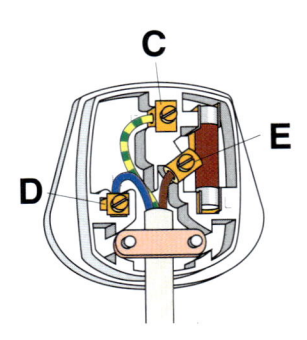

fig. 14.11

Q. 14.20
List six sources of possible electrical accidents in the home.

Q. 14.21
What is meant by each of the following terms?
(a) a fuse
(b) an earth wire
(c) a ring main

Q. 14.22
(a) Why is the earth wire connected to the body of a kettle?
(b) Why is the fuse connected into the live wire?

Device	Correct voltage	Current taken	Resistance	Power	Best fuse to use (1, 3, 5, 10 or 13 A)
Units					
Electric fire	200		40		
TV set	250			125	
Microwave		1		200	
Walkman	3	0.03			
Torch	6		12		
Car starter motor	12			1200	

Q. 14.19
(a) What do a.c. and d.c. stand for?
(b) What is the difference between a.c. and d.c.?
(c) Name a source of each.
(d) Identify the terminals A, B, C, D and E, on the items in the diagram.

15 LIGHT

fig. 15.1 Laser beams show that light travels in straight lines

LIGHT IS A FORM OF ENERGY

Light is a form of energy and therefore can do work or be converted into other forms of energy. This can be shown in several different ways. In the radiometer (shown below), light that falls on it makes the vanes rotate, as the light energy is converted into kinetic energy. In a solar-powered calculator, light energy is converted into electricity to power the calculator. Most cameras contain an exposure meter, which measures the intensity of the light. This works in a similar way to a solar cell. In photosynthesis, light energy from the Sun is converted into the chemical energy in green plants as they grow.

An object can only be seen if light from it reaches the eye. Some objects are **luminous**, which means that they give out their own light. Examples of these are the Sun, electric lamps and glow worms.

Most objects however, do not give out light, but only reflect the light that falls on them, and only when this happens can they be seen (why can you not see objects in a dark room?).

fig. 15.2 Light-powered devices

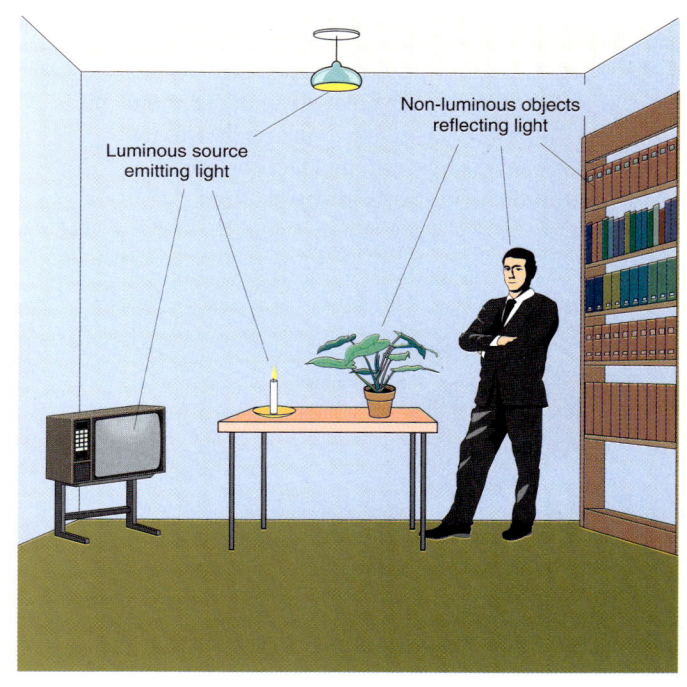

fig. 15.3 Luminous and non-luminous objects

LIGHT TRAVELS IN STRAIGHT LINES

Have you ever seen rays of sunlight in a wood or forest? Or the beam of a car headlight on a foggy night, or a laser beam at a rock concert? If you have, you will have noticed that light travels in straight lines. There are several laboratory experiments which also show that this is true.

Experiment 15.1
To show that light travels in straight lines

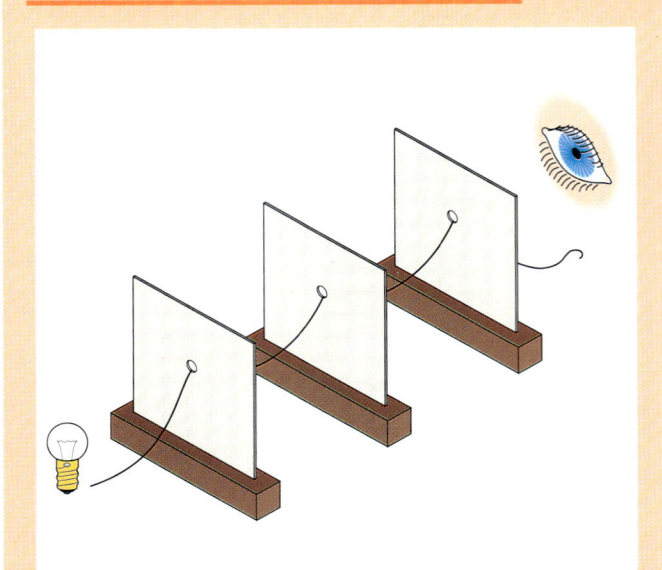

fig. 15.4 (a)

1. Set up the apparatus shown in (a). Position the cardboards so that the light can be seen through the holes. Carefully pull the thread taut (tight). You will find that all of the holes are in the same straight line. If you now move one of the cardboards out of position, the light will no longer be visible. Conclusion: light travels in straight lines.

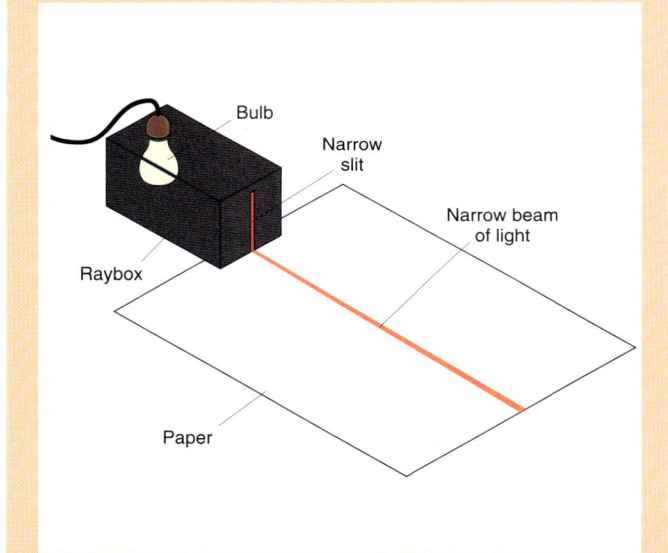

fig. 15.4 (b)

2. Set up a raybox as shown in (b). Hold a ruler along the ray of light. You will discover that the ray of light is quite straight.

SHADOWS

fig. 15.5 The sundial shows that it is 1 o'clock

The formation of shadows results from light travelling in straight lines and something getting in the way. A sundial makes use of this fact. The gnomen (the upright part of the sundial) casts a shadow on the scale – which is marked with the various hours of the day.

Eclipses also result from the formation of shadows. Eclipses occur because the Moon and the Earth can cast large shadows. In a **solar eclipse** (an eclipse of the Sun), the shadow of the Moon falls on the Earth, and darkness can occur in the middle of the day! The stars can be seen, the temperature falls and the birds stop singing.

In a **lunar eclipse** (an eclipse of the Moon), the shadow of the Earth falls on the Moon, and the curved shape of the Earth is seen.

There are diagrams in Chapter 40 showing how eclipses occur.

REFLECTION OF LIGHT

Light travels in straight lines, but it can be made to bend – by means of mirrors; the name given to this property of light is **reflection**.

When a ray of light hits something, it 'bounces back' or is reflected from it.

Experiment 15.2
To show reflection of light

1. Arrange the apparatus as shown, so that a ray of light strikes the mirror.

2. Rotate the mirror (about a vertical axis). What happens to the ray of light that is reflected from the mirror?

3. On the paper, mark the position of the mirror and the position of the rays of light. Shade the back of the mirror, label the rays of light and put arrows on them to show their direction.

4. Replace the slit in the raybox with a slit giving three rays and observe the reflection of the rays of light as before.

5. Place a second mirror in position parallel to the first, so that the rays are reflected again (see Figure 15.7). This is the principle of the periscope.

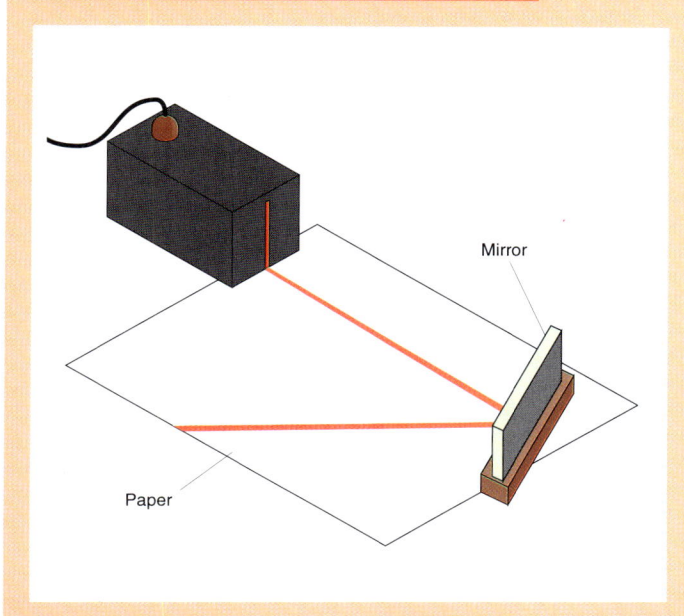

fig. 15.6

fig. 15.7 Ray diagram for periscope

fig. 15.8 (a) Refraction

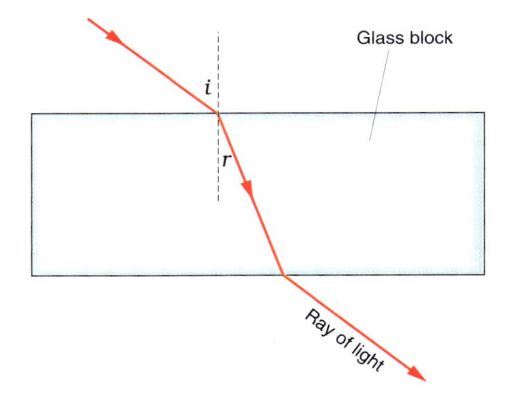

fig. 15.8 (b) Note that when a ray of light goes into the block, the angle in the block (r) is smaller than the angle (i) at which it enters. Conversely, when the ray of light comes out of the block, the angle outside the block is larger than the angle inside it.

REFRACTION OF LIGHT

Why does a swimming pool look shallower than it really is? Why does the pencil in Figure 15.10 appear to be bent? The reason for both of these is **refraction**. This is the name given to the bending of rays of light when they pass from one substance into another.

15 • Light

Experiment 15.3
To show refraction of light

Method 1.

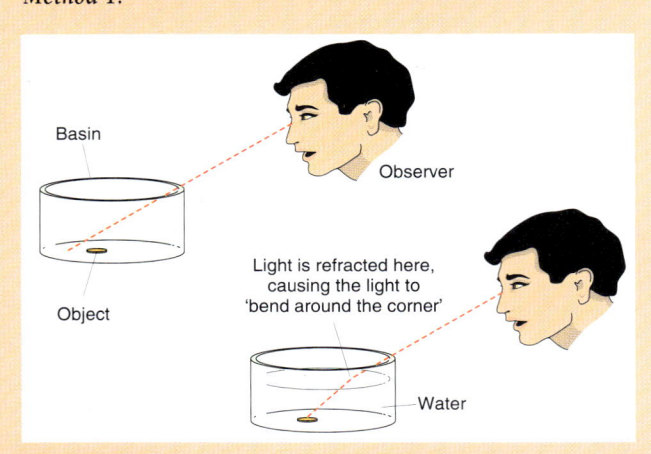

fig. 15.9 (a)

Arrange the apparatus as shown in diagram (a). You can use the laboratory sink, or a trough, or, if you do the experiment at home, you can use a mug. Place yourself in such a position that the object is just out of view, and do not move from this position. Now get someone to pour water into the container. As it is filled with water, the object comes into view. This is because the ray of light bends (is refracted) at the water surface – as in diagram (b).

Method 2.

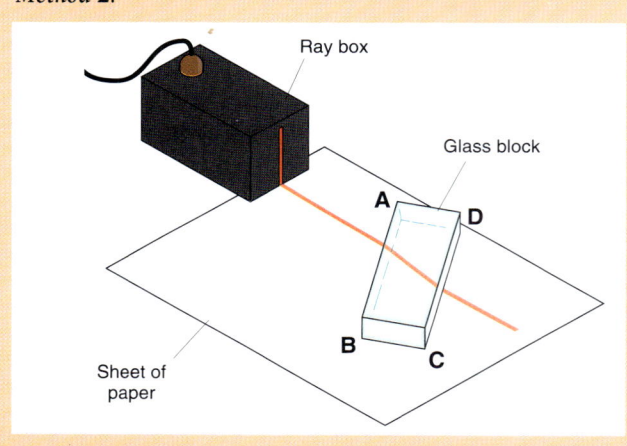

fig. 15.9 (b)

1. Arrange the apparatus as shown, so that a ray of light strikes the glass block at an angle, enters it, and comes out the far side.

2. On the paper, mark the position of the glass block, and draw the positions of the light rays which enter and which leave the block.

3. Remove the glass block, and draw a line showing the direction of the light as it went through the block. Put arrows on all rays of light to show their direction.

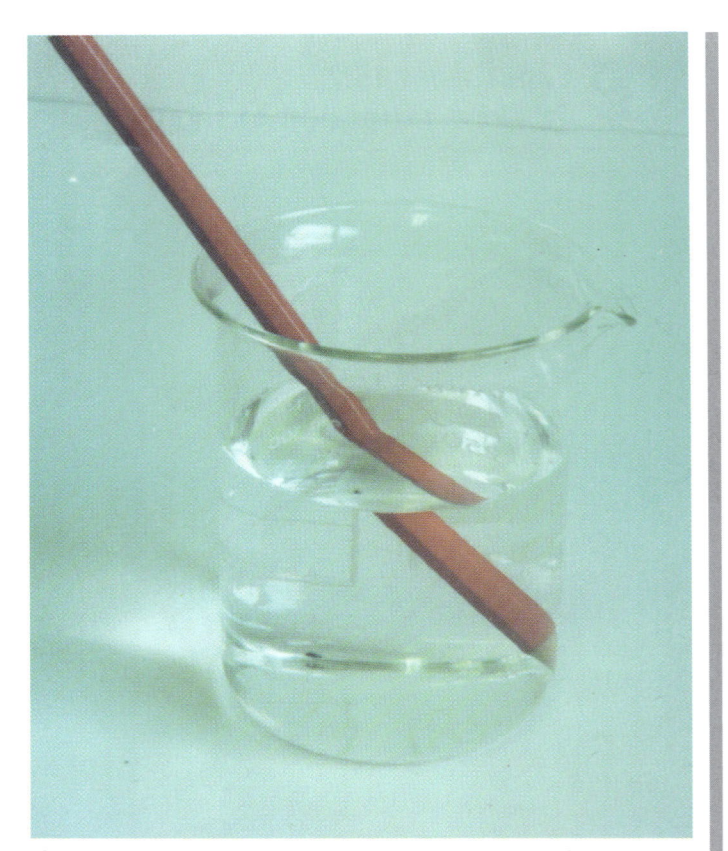

fig. 15.10 *Refraction of light at the water surface makes the pencil appear broken*

LENSES

The most important application of refraction is in lenses. Lenses are an essential part of practically every optical device that exists – spectacles, telescopes, binoculars, 'peep-holes' in doors, cameras and spotlights. There are two main lens types – ones that can make things look larger and ones that make things look smaller.

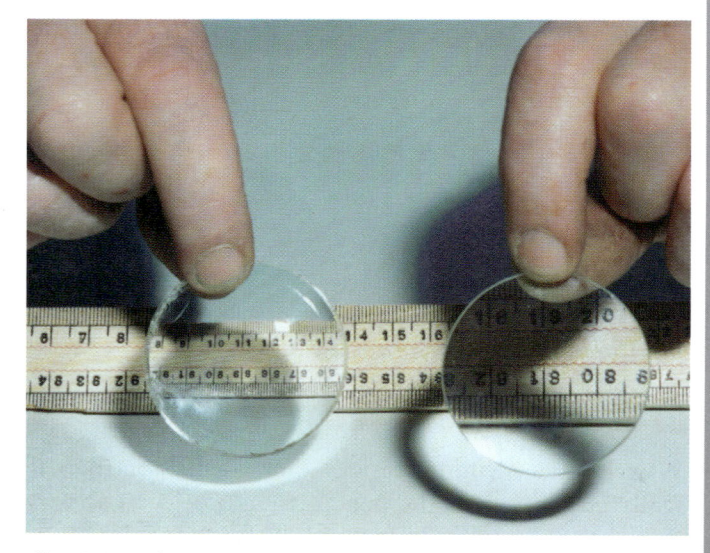

fig. 15.11 *A concave lens makes things appear smaller; a convex lens makes things appear larger*

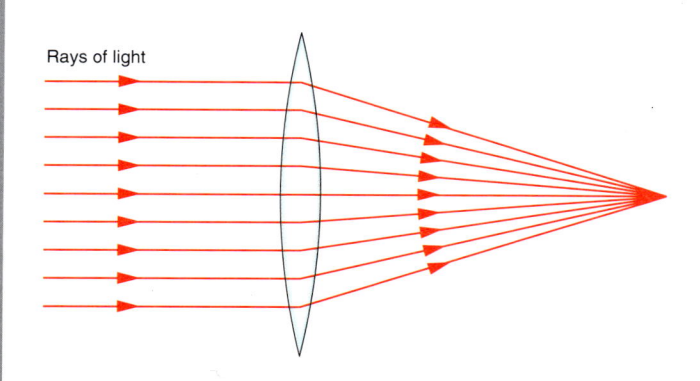

fig. 15.12 (a) A lens that is 'fat' in the middle is called a **convex lens**. When parallel rays of light strike it, the rays converge, or come to a focus. Hence, such a lens is also called a converging lens. A magnifying glass is simply a convex lens.

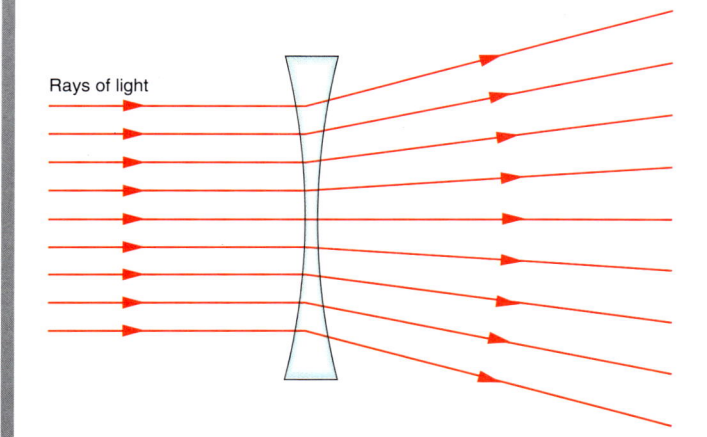

fig. 15.12 (b) A lens that is thin in the middle is a **concave lens**. When parallel rays of light strike this type of lens, they spread out or diverge. Such a lens is also called a diverging lens.

DISPERSION OF LIGHT

Where do all the colours of the rainbow come from? Do they come from the sunlight or from the rain? Sir Isaac Newton was the first scientist to explain this. The story goes that one day a ray of sunlight entered his darkened laboratory through a hole in the shutters and fell on a prism (a triangular-shaped piece of glass) on his bench. A band of colours was produced on the far side of the room. Newton then discovered that if he recombined all of the different colours, he got white. So, white light is made up of different colours.

fig. 15.13 Newton discovered that white light is made up of different colours

This band of colours he called the **spectrum**, and he named the individual colours **red**, **orange**, **yellow**, **green**, **blue**, **indigo** and **violet**. The name given to the splitting up of white light into its separate colours is **dispersion**.

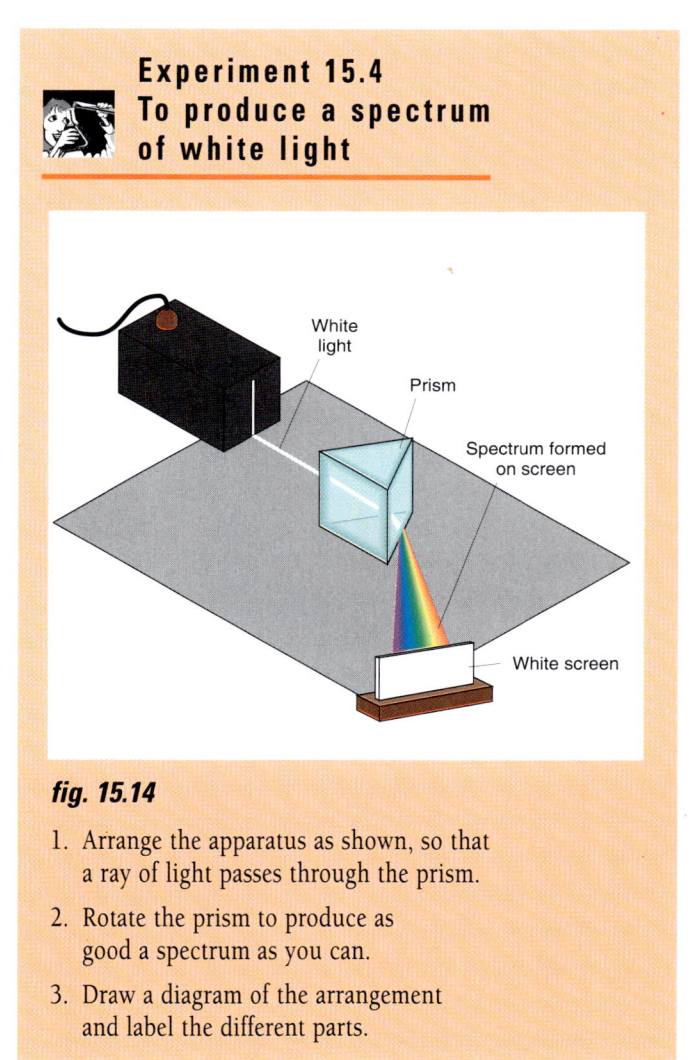

Experiment 15.4
To produce a spectrum of white light

fig. 15.14

1. Arrange the apparatus as shown, so that a ray of light passes through the prism.
2. Rotate the prism to produce as good a spectrum as you can.
3. Draw a diagram of the arrangement and label the different parts.

15 • Light

fig. 15.15 Newton's disc is a piece of apparatus designed to show that when the colours of the spectrum are recombined, white is again formed. When the disc is rotated so quickly that the individual colours can no longer be seen, it appears to be white, as the colours have blended into each other.

COLOUR

When the seven colours of the spectrum are mixed together, white is obtained. However, all seven colours are not needed. White can be produced by just mixing three of them. These three colours of light are red, green and blue, and they are called the **primary colours**. When lights of these three colours are mixed, white light is produced. Mixing any two of these colours produces another colour called a **secondary colour**. When, for example, red and green are mixed, yellow is produced. The three secondary colours of light are **yellow**, **cyan**, and **magenta**.

Note: Mixing coloured paints is a different and more-involved process than mixing coloured lights, and the primary colours used by artists are not the same as the primary colours of light.

Complementary colours are two colours which when mixed produce white. Examples of complementary colours are yellow and blue, and magenta and green.

fig. 15.16 Primary colours overlapping produce secondary colours

---

Experiment 15.5
To show the effect of mixing different coloured lights

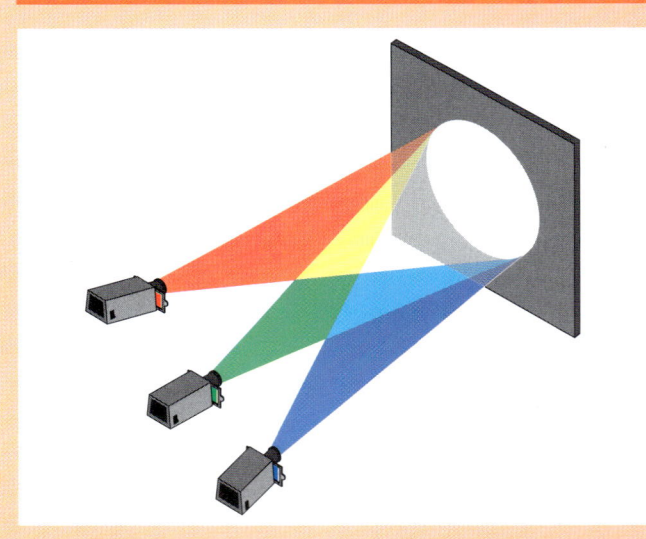

fig. 15.17

Method 1.

The most effective way to mix the three colours is to use three projectors, each giving a beam of one of the three primary colours. When all three projectors illuminate the same screen, white is the colour of the light on the screen.

If now, for example, the projector giving the green light is switched off, the light on the screen is magenta, as the red and blue mix.

This experiment can also be done with ray boxes containing filters of the three different primary colours.

Method 2.

Some computer programs have the facility of being able to mix the three primary colours in any required ratio, to produce any colour that is desired. If you have access to this, you will discover that 100% red + 100% green + 100% blue produces pure white. Similarly, you can show, for example, that 100% red and 100% green gives yellow, and you can make that yellow become paler and paler as you add blue to it, it eventually becoming white as the percentage of blue reaches 100%. All the colours which you see on a TV screen are formed in this way – by mixing the three primary colours in different ratios.

ELECTROMAGNETIC SPECTRUM

Outside the visible spectrum (the band of colours which can be detected by the eye), there are other types of radiation that are invisible, or that cannot be detected by the eye. Immediately beyond the violet end of the spectrum, there are invisible rays called **ultra-violet** rays, and just beyond the red, there are rays called **infra-red**.

This large band of rays or waves is called the **electromagnetic spectrum**. Each of the different types of electromagnetic rays has important uses.

Infra-red rays are heat rays and so make things hot. They are absorbed by black surfaces and reflected by shiny surfaces (just as visible light is). They are used to send remote control signals from, for example, your TV control unit to the TV receiver. Infra-red cameras are used by rescue workers when a building has collapsed. These cameras can detect the infra-red (heat) radiation given off by bodies of people trapped in the wreckage, who can then be rescued. Automatic lights are switched on by the infra-red radiation that is given off by people who approach the light's detector.

Ultra-violet rays are the rays that cause suntan. They are produced by the Sun and by some electric lamps. Ultra-violet rays cause some substances to *fluoresce*; this means to give off visible light even though the substances are only being illuminated with invisible (ultra-violet) rays. Ultra-violet light and fluorescent materials are often used for special stage effects.

Both infra-red and ultra-violet rays are similar to light in many ways. They all travel at the same speed (300 million metres per second) and they all can travel through empty space.

SUMMARY

- Light is a form of **energy** and it travels in straight lines. **Eclipses** are the results of shadows of the Earth and the Moon. Light can be made to bend in two ways, by reflection and by refraction. **Reflection** is the 'bouncing off' of light from something. **Refraction** is the bending of light when it passes from one substance to another.

- There are two main lens types. **Convex** lenses are fat in the middle and they converge rays of light falling on them. **Concave** lenses are thin in the middle and they diverge rays of light falling on them.

- When white light is passed through a **prism**, it is split up (**dispersed**) into its component colours: **red**, **orange**, **yellow**, **green**, **blue**, **indigo** and **violet**. When these colours are recombined, white light is formed. The **primary colours** of light are **red**, **green** and **blue**. When these colours are combined, white light is formed. Mixing any two of the primary colours produces a **secondary colour**. Red and blue produce **magenta**, red and green give **yellow**, and blue and green form **cyan**.

- Outside the visible spectrum there are bands of invisible rays; **ultra-violet** is beyond the violet and just before the red is the **infra-red**.

QUESTIONS

Q. 15.1

Rewrite the following paragraphs and fill in the spaces.

(a) Light is a form of ___. In a piece of apparatus called a___, ___ energy is converted to ___ energy, and in the process of photosynthesis it is

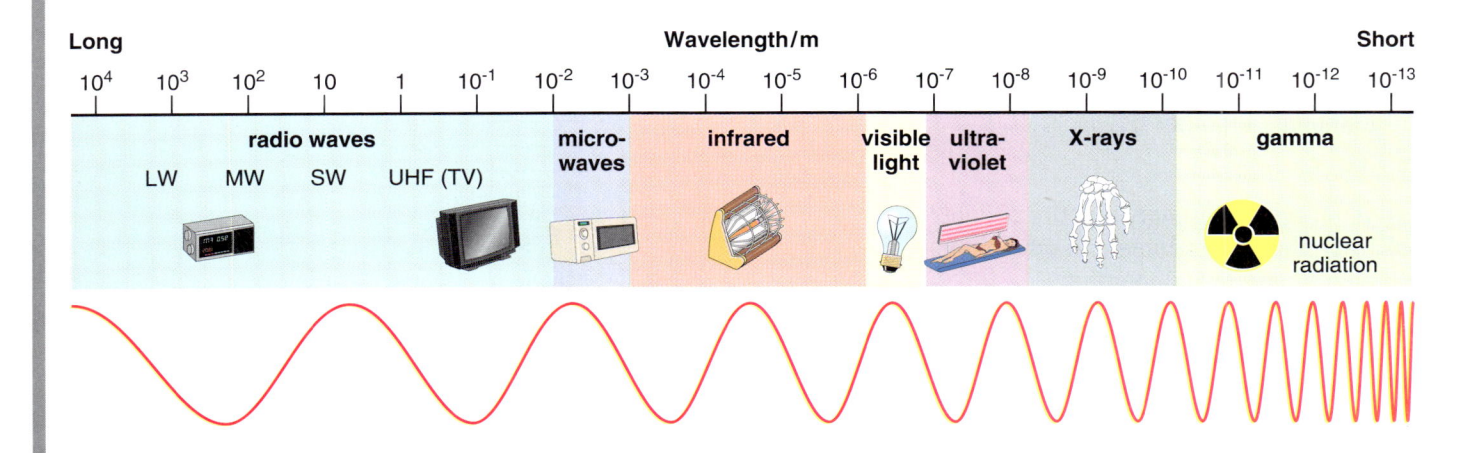

fig. 15.18 The electromagnetic spectrum

15 • Light

converted to ___ energy. Light travels in ___ lines, but it can be made to change direction is two ways, by ___ and ___ . When light strikes a mirror it is ___ and when it enters a glass block it is ___.

(b) Eclipses result from the fact that light travels in ___ ___. In a lunar eclipse (i.e. an eclipse of the ___), the ___ comes between the ___ and the ___, and a shadow of the ___ is cast on the ___.

(c) Experiment 15.4 shows how light, on being passed through a ___, is split up into its component colours. This process is called ___ and the band of colours that is formed is called a ___. The colours are, in order, red, ___, ___, ___, ___, ___, and ___. When all of these colours are recombined, ___ light is produced. This property of light was discovered by the scientist ___.

(d) The three primary colours of light are ___, ___ and ___. When these colours are mixed, ___ light is formed. Mixing any two primary colours produces a ___ colour. The three secondary colours of light are ___, ___ and ___. Two colours which when mixed produce white light are called ___ colours.

Q. 15.2

List three ways in which you can tell that light is a form of energy. To what kind of energy is the light changed in each case?

Q. 15.3

Explain each of the following terms:
(a) reflection, **(b)** refraction,
(c) dispersion, **(d)** visible spectrum.
(e) In each case, use a diagram to illustrate your answer.

Q. 15.4

(a) Using a diagram, show how white light can be split up into different colours.
(b) What is the name of the band of colours? Name the colours present.
(c) What happens when the colours are combined together again?

Q. 15.5

(a) What are the primary colours of light?
(b) Describe an experiment in which these colours are mixed together.
(c) What is a secondary colour?
(d) Name the secondary colours and state how each is formed.
(e) What are complementary colours? Give an example.

Q. 15.6

What are (i) infra-red rays, and (ii) ultra-violet rays? Name a source of each, and give three properties of each.

Q. 15.7

Describe an experiment to show that light travels in straight lines. Use a diagram to illustrate your answer.

Q. 15.8

Describe with the aid of a diagram, an experiment that showed light being reflected.

Q. 15.9

Describe with the aid of a diagram, an experiment that showed light being refracted.

Q. 15.10

Describe with the aid of a diagram, an experiment that showed light being dispersed.

Q. 15.11

Copy out and complete the following ray diagrams.

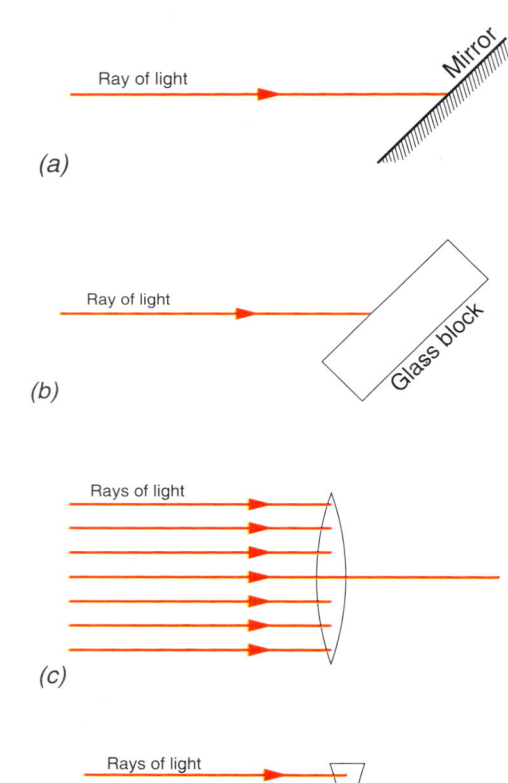

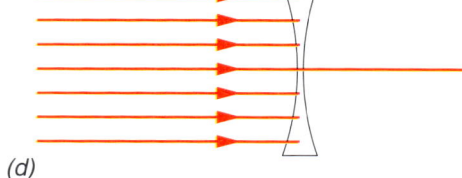

fig. 15.19

16
SOUND AND WAVES

fig. 16.1 In an organ, sound is produced by air vibrating in pipes. The organ of the National Concert Hall, Dublin contains 4045 separate pipes, ranging in length from 5 m to 2 cm. The longest pipe produces a note of frequency 16 Hz and the shortest about 9 kHz. Inset: Concert Hall organist Peter Sweeney at the console.

SOUND AND VIBRATIONS

What is sound and how is it produced? What is the difference between a guitar string that is sounding a note and one that isn't, or how does a sounding trumpet differ from a silent one? You should be able to answer the question about the guitar string, because what a sounding string is doing is easy to see. Its hazy appearance shows that it is vibrating – and that is what all sounding bodies are doing – they are vibrating, or moving back and forth, very rapidly or many times per second.

A stretched string such as in a guitar, a column of air such as in a trumpet, the stretched skin of a drum, the cone of a loudspeaker and the vocal cords in your own larynx, all vibrate as they produce sound.

fig. 16.2 (a)

fig. 16.2 (b)

A tuning fork is a useful source of sound, because every tuning fork has the number of vibrations which it makes per second marked on it. A tuning fork marked 256 means that its prongs vibrate (move in and out) 256 times per second. It is easy to show that a tuning fork is vibrating by holding it against either your fingers or a suspended polystyrene ball – which is knocked sharply aside. Alternatively, if it is placed on the surface of water, ripples will be observed.

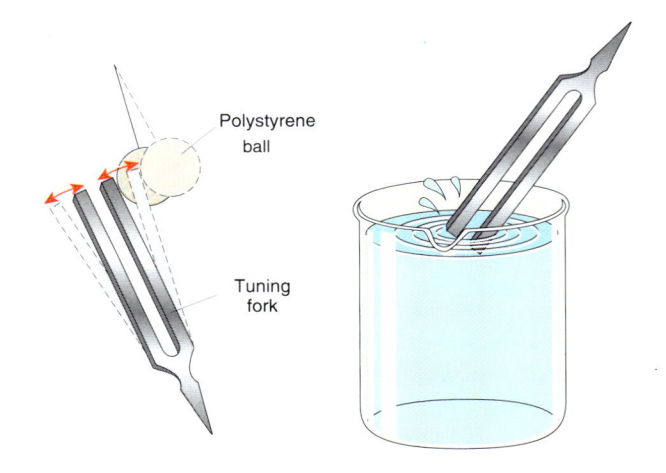

fig. 16.3 Showing that a tuning fork vibrates

HOW SOUND TRAVELS

You know from your own experience that sound travels through air, and if you can swim underwater, you will know that sound can also travel through water. But what about solids? In a quiet room, place your ear to the table, and then get a friend to very gently scratch or tap the other end of the table. You should be able to hear the sound quite clearly. And if you lift your ear away from the table, you will either not hear the sound or hear it much less clearly. So, sound also travels through solids.

Does sound travel through a vacuum?

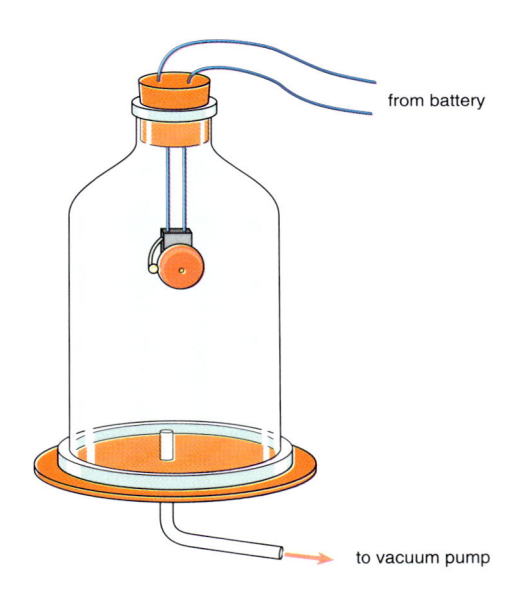

fig. 16.4 Showing that sound does not travel through a vacuum

A vacuum is a space containing nothing, not even air. The apparatus for this investigation consists of an electric bell inside a glass bell jar which is connected to a vacuum pump. When the bell is connected to a battery, it can be heard ringing. The pump is then switched on and the air removed from inside the bell jar. As this happens, the sound dies away until, when all of the air has gone, it can no longer be heard – although the bell can still be seen ringing inside the jar. When the air is let back in to the jar, the sound can be heard once more. So, unlike light, sound does not travel through a vacuum. It needs a material medium (the medium is the name given to a substance through which waves travel).

HOW FAST DOES SOUND TRAVEL?

If you think about it, you know that sound travels more slowly than light. During a thunderstorm for example, a flash of lightning is seen, and is followed some seconds later by the sound of the thunder – even though both the flash and the sound occurred up in the clouds at the same instant.

Or, if you have watched a cricket, baseball or football match from a distance, you may have noticed that there is a slight delay after seeing a player hitting the ball before you hear the sound. Light travels extremely quickly, but sound much more slowly.

An echo, which is a reflection of sound, is another observation that shows that sound takes a little time to travel. If you shout some distance from a large hard surface such as a high wall or a cliff face, there is a slight delay before the sound comes back to you.

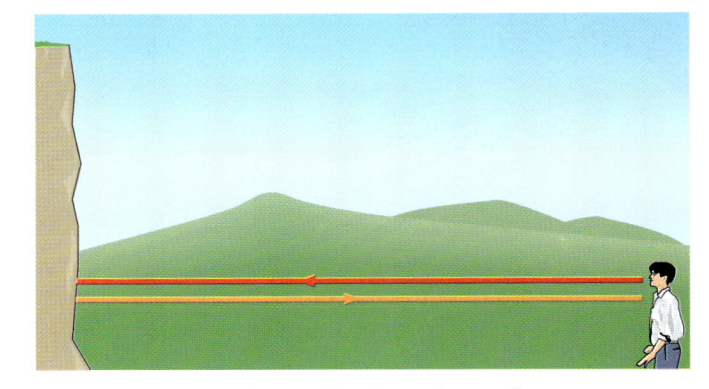

fig. 16.5 An echo is a reflection of sound

The speed of sound in air is about 340 metres per second – which is about 760 miles per hour. (The actual value depends on the temperature). This means that it takes sound about 3 seconds to travel a kilometre, or 5 seconds to travel a mile.

If, during a thunderstorm, there is an interval of 5 seconds between seeing the flash of lightning and hearing the thunder, then the thunder cloud is about a mile distant – or, if the delay is 10 seconds, then it is about 2 miles away.

Uses of echoes

Echoes have important uses. They are used by ships for measuring the distance from other ships and from obstacles, for detecting shoals of fish, and for measuring the depth of the sea beneath them. This is done by sending a sharp sound down into the seabed and timing how long it takes for the sound to return.

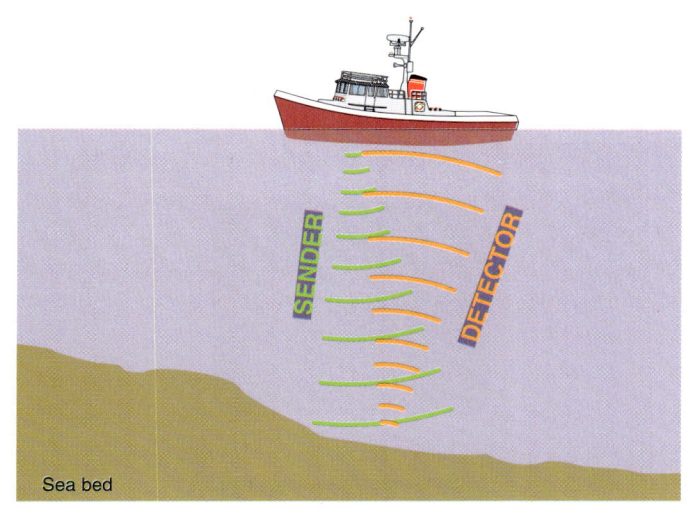

fig. 16.6 *A use of echoes*

WAVES

fig. 16.7 *Water waves*

fig. 16.8 *Waves travelling through a spring*

If a stone is thrown into the middle of a pond, a series of ripples or waves travels outwards from the middle of the pond. The waves reach the edge of the pond, but there is no gap left in the middle where the waves came from, that is, the water hasn't travelled. Sound energy travels just like that – by means of waves, which spread out from the sounding body.

Slinky spring

The sort of motion shown by air molecules as they carry sound waves can be illustrated using a 'Slinky' spring. If this is extended (someone needs to hold the other end), and a couple of coils of it pinched together or compressed, then on releasing the spring, the compression travels to the other end, from which it may be reflected back and forth a few times. The spring itself doesn't travel; it is just the waves that travel through it.

Waves carry energy. It is not only sound (energy) that travels by waves, but all of the different kinds of electromagnetic radiation (described in Chapter 15). Light, ultra-violet and infra-red radiation, and microwaves, radio waves and X-rays all travel by waves.

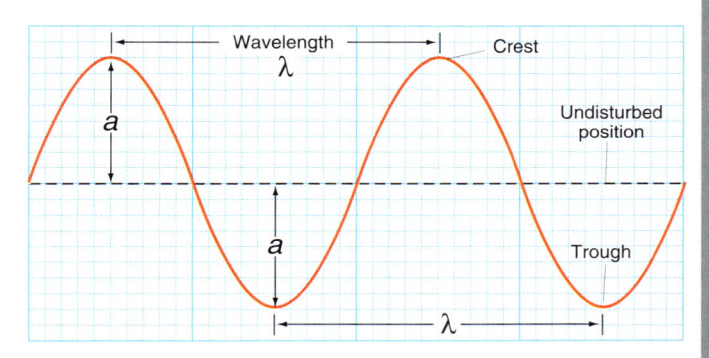

fig. 16.9 *Describing waves*

The above diagram shows a wave. The tops of the waves are known as **crests** and the bottoms are called **troughs**. The distance between any two successive crests (or troughs) is the **wavelength** (denoted by the Greek letter lambda, symbol λ) of the wave. Like all

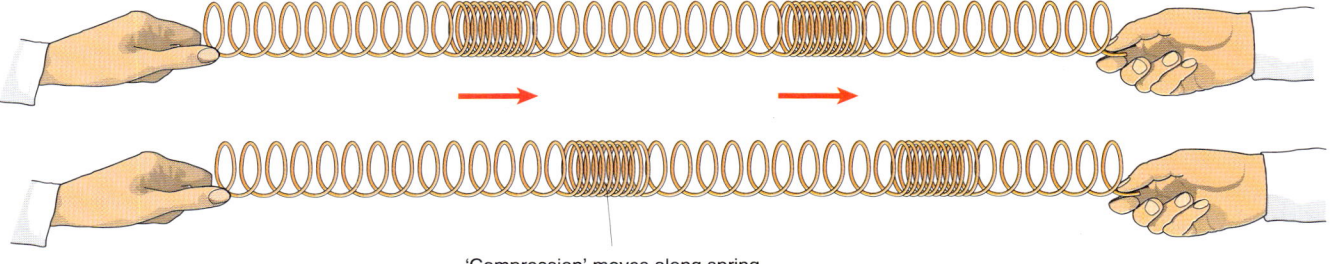

16 • Sound and Waves

lengths, wavelengths are measured in metres. The **amplitude** of a wave is the height of a crest of the wave above the average position, and this is denoted by 'a' in the diagram.

The number of waves per second is called the **frequency** (symbol f). It is measured in units called hertz. One hertz is one wave per second. For high frequency waves such as radio waves, kilohertz (kHz) and megahertz (MHz) are used.

The **velocity** of a wave is the distance it travels per second (just like the velocity of a car or anything else).

TO SHOW THE WAVE NATURE OF SOUND OR 'SEEING SOUNDS'

An oscilloscope is an instrument which can be used for observing sound waves. It works a bit like a television set. When a sound signal is fed into it, the screen displays a picture of the signal. In order to display sound waves, the experiment illustrated below is set up.

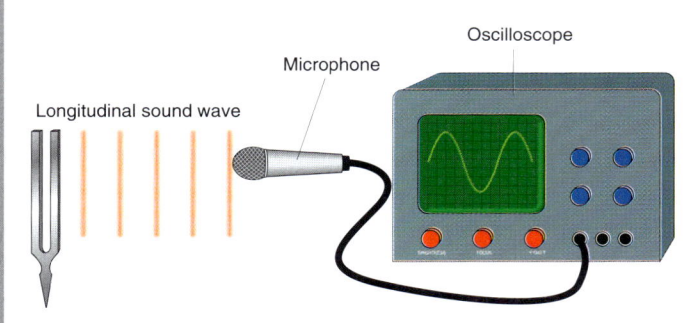

fig. 16.10 *A 'picture' of a soundwave*

In the microphone, the sound produced by the tuning fork is converted into electrical energy (sound is a form of energy). The electric current is fed into the oscilloscope, which then shows a picture of the sound waves. If you talk into, or play a tune beside the microphone, you will be able to see how the sound wave pattern changes with the different sounds.

When an instrument plays the note called middle C, the frequency of the vibrating body is 256 Hz. As higher notes are played, the sounds produced are of higher frequencies, and you will notice that a greater number of waves get packed on to the screen of the oscilloscope.

Alternatively, an instrument called a signal generator can be used to make the sound. This instrument can generate a note of any required frequency (the principle is used in a music keyboard). When a signal generator is connected to the oscilloscope, you can see the shape of the sound waves which it generates, and you can see how, as the frequency is increased, the number of waves on the screen increases.

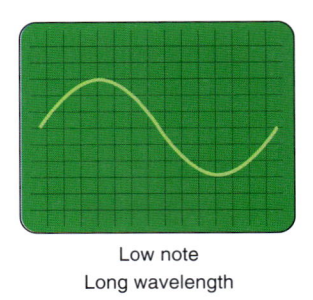

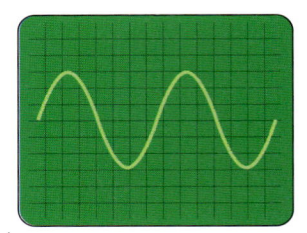

Low note
Long wavelength

Middle note

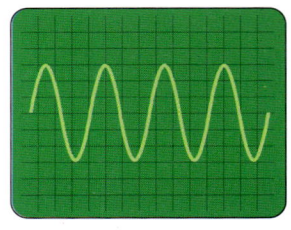

High note
Short wavelength

fig. 16.11 *Waveforms of different notes*

Velocity = Frequency 3 Wavelength OR, $v = f\lambda$

An important relationship exists between velocity, frequency and wavelength. Suppose 20 waves are being produced each second (i.e. 20 waves are moving outwards each second), and the length of each of these waves is 5 metres. Then the distance moved by each wave in one second (velocity) will be 100 m (i.e. 20 × 5). In other words, velocity = frequency × wavelength.

> **Velocity = Frequency × Wavelength,**
> **or, $v = f\lambda$**

This means that high frequency sounds have small wavelengths, and low frequencies have large wavelengths. It also means that if the frequency of a sound is doubled, then its wavelength is halved.

Worked examples

(velocity of sound in air is 340 m/s)

Q. What is the wavelength of middle C, whose frequency is 256 Hz.

A. $v = f\lambda$, $\Rightarrow \lambda = \dfrac{v}{f} = \dfrac{340}{256} = 1.33$ m

Q. What is the frequency of a note whose wavelength is 50 cm?

A. 50 cm = 0.5 m.
$v = f\lambda \Rightarrow f = \dfrac{v}{\lambda} = \dfrac{340}{0.5} = 680$ Hz.

QUESTIONS

(Velocity of sound in air is 340 m/s; all sounds have this same value)

Q.16.1
A guitar string vibrates 100 times per second. What is the wavelength of the note which is heard?

Q. 16.2
A tuning fork vibrates 1000 times in 5 seconds. What is its frequency? What is the wavelength of the note which sounds?

Q. 16.3
A piano note has a wavelength of 5 metres. What is the frequency of the note?

Q. 16.4
If a note of frequency 20 Hz has a wavelength of 16 metres, what value do these measurements give for the velocity of sound?

Q. 16.5
A guitar string sounds a note of wavelength 1.7 metres. What is the frequency of the note? What is the wavelength of the note with double that frequency?

Q. 16.6
If a gun is fired 34 metres from a cliff, how long does the sound take to reach the cliff? How long after firing the gun is the echo heard?

Q. 16.7
A bat flying towards a wall emits a sound and receives its echo back after 1 second. How far away is the wall?

Q. 16.8
Radio FM104 broadcasts on a frequency of 104 MHz. Given that radio waves travel at the same speed as light (see page 114), calculate the wavelength of the signal coming from FM104. (MHz = megahertz; mega = 1 000 000)

PITCH, LOUDNESS AND TONE

Sounds from musical instruments differ from each other in three main ways, pitch, loudness, and tone. These three things depend on frequency, amplitude and waveform.

Frequency and pitch

The pitch of a note means how high or how low it is. The frequency (f) is the number of vibrations per second. The pitch of a note depends on the frequency of the vibration which is causing it. The higher the frequency the higher the note, and the lower the frequency, the lower the note (see Figure 16.11).

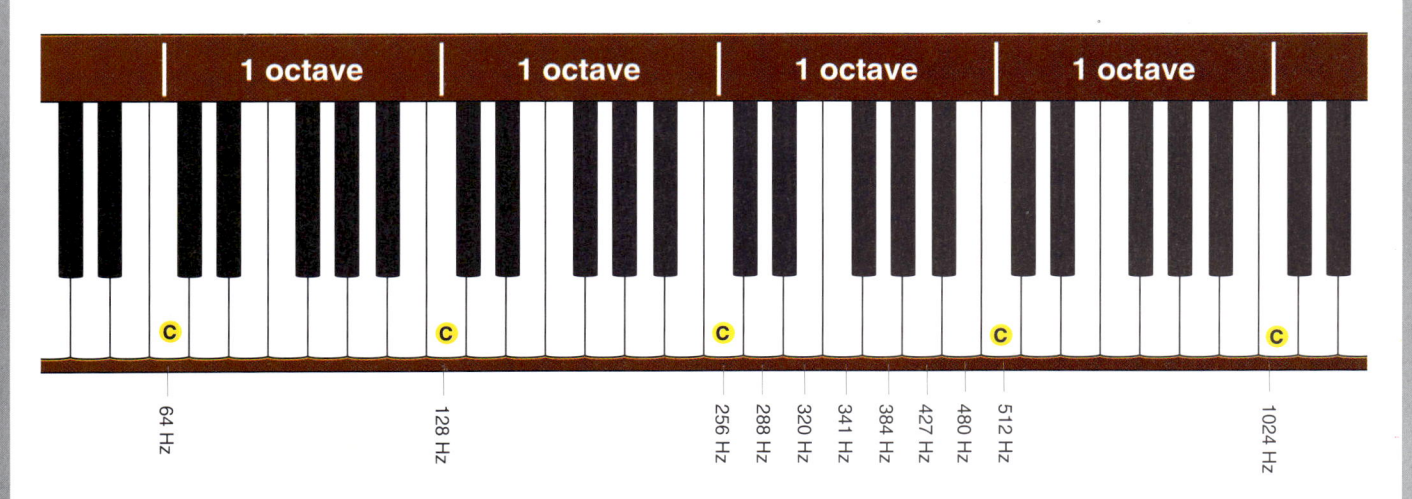

fig. 16.12 Frequencies of different musical notes in the octave up from middle C. Note: the scientific scale of frequencies is slightly different from the scale used by musicians.

16 • Sound and Waves

Audio frequencies are those that can be heard by the human ear. In young children, they range from about 20 hertz to 20 kilohertz (20 000 Hz). The upper limit decreases with increasing age.

Amplitude and loudness

The loudness of a note depends on the amplitude of the vibration causing it. If the vibration is of large amplitude, a loud sound is produced, and if the amplitude is small, the sound is much quieter.

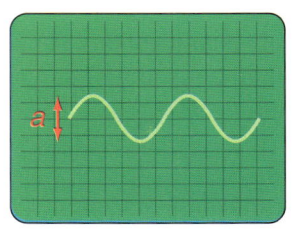

Soft note

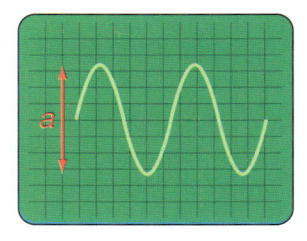

Same note but louder

fig. 16.13 *Amplitude causes loudness*

Waveform and tone

Different musical instruments sound different (their tones are different) because the sounds they generate have different waveforms. The diagrams below show the shape of middle C when played by a tuning fork, a violin, a piano and flute. Can you work out why a violin sounds 'richer' than a tuning fork?

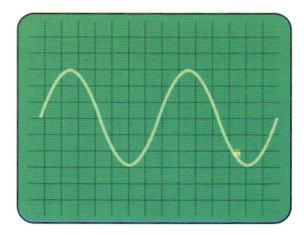

Tuning fork

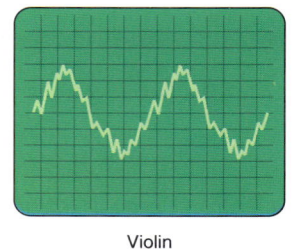

Violin

Piano

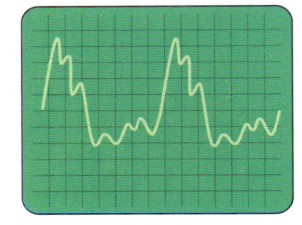

Clarinet

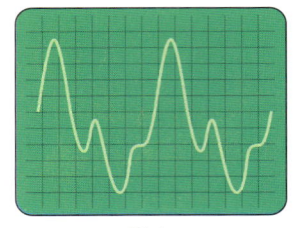

Flute

fig. 16.14 *Waveform causes tone*

You can now do further investigations with the oscilloscope. If you make sounds of different pitch (sing or play up a scale), you will see that the higher the note, the shorter the wavelength becomes. And since velocity = frequency × wavelength, the shorter the wavelength, the higher the frequency. When the frequency of a note is doubled, a note one octave higher is sounded. High notes have high frequencies and low notes have low frequencies.

You can also see that when the sound is loud, the wave is of large amplitude, and as the sound gets quieter, the amplitude gets smaller.

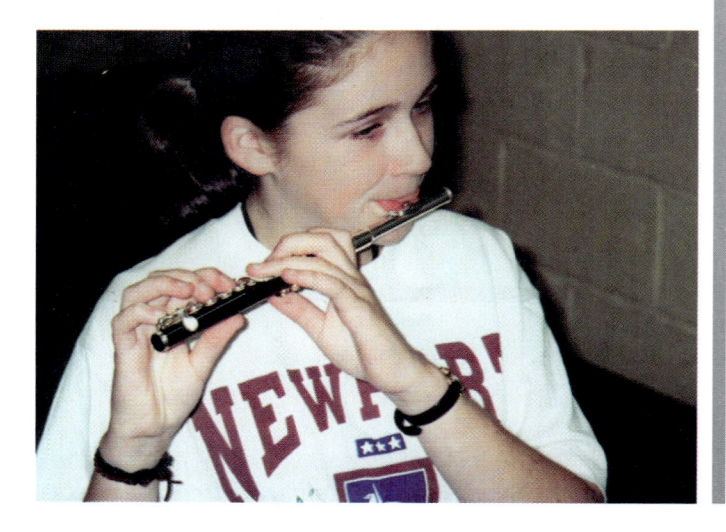

fig. 16.15 High notes are produced by small instruments and have high frequencies, and low notes are produced by large instruments and have low frequencies

SUMMARY

- All sounds are produced by vibrating bodies.
- Sound can travel through solids, liquids and gases, but not through a vacuum. The velocity of sound in air is about 340 m/s. An **echo** is a reflection of sound.
- Sound travels by means of waves. The **wavelength** of a wave is the distance between any two successive crests, and the **frequency** is the number of waves per second. The **velocity** of a wave is the distance travelled per second.
- **Velocity = frequency × wavelength**.
- The **pitch** of a sound depends on the frequency of the sound, the **loudness** depends on the amplitude and the **tone** depends on the waveform.

QUESTIONS

Q. 16.9
Rewrite the following paragraphs, completing the gaps in each.

(a) In order to produce sound, something must be _____ . Sound is a form of ___. In a microphone, sound ___ is converted to ___ energy.

(b) Sound can travel through solids, ___ and ___, but it cannot travel through a ___. The velocity of sound in air is about ___ m/s. An echo is a ___ of sound.

(c) Sound travels by means of ___. The tops of the waves are called ___ and the bottoms are ___. The distance between successive crests is called the ___ of the ___ and is denoted by the Greek letter ___. The height of a crest is known as the ___ of the wave. Frequency is the number of ___ per ___ and is measured in units called ___. The ___ is the distance travelled per ___. Velocity = _____ multiplied by _____. The pitch of a note depends on the ___ of the wave and the loudness depends on the ___.

Q. 16.10
Say what is vibrating when you hear
(a) a guitar string
(b) a piano
(c) a trumpet
(d) a violin
(e) a drum
(f) a radio
(g) a flute
(h) a cymbal
(i) a bell
(j) your own voice

Q. 16.11
Describe, with the aid of a diagram, an experiment that shows that sound is a wave motion.

SOUND AND LIGHT

	Light	Sound
Nature	electromagnetic waves	longitudinal waves
Medium for transmission	none needed; can travel through a vacuum	travel through solid, liquid and gas; cannot travel through a vacuum
Speed	300 000 000 m/s	340 m/s (about 760 miles/hour)

Q. 16.12
Refer to the drawings of waves.

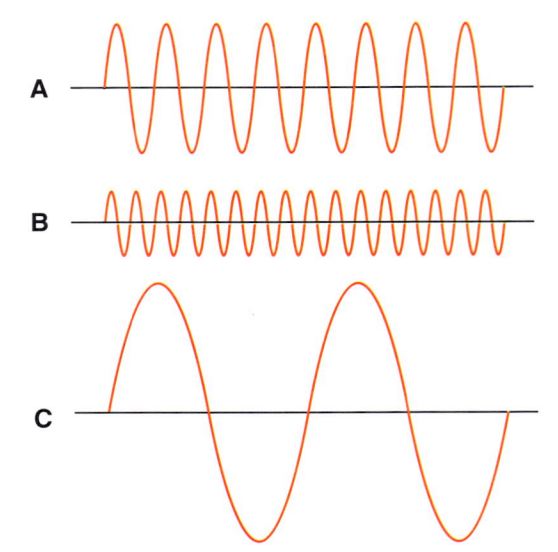

fig. 16.16

(a) Which of the above waves has the (i) highest frequency, (ii) greatest amplitude, (iii) longest wavelength?
(b) Which wave will result from the (i) loudest sound, (ii) the softest sound, (iii) the highest note, (iv) the lowest note?
(c) Use a millimetre ruler to measure (i) the wavelength, and (ii) the amplitude of wave C.

Q. 16.13
Describe, with the aid of a diagram, an experiment that shows that sound can be reflected.

Q. 16.14
Describe, with the aid of a diagram, an experiment which shows that sound cannot travel through a vacuum.

Q. 16.15
(a) What do sound and light have in common?
(b) Name one property in which sound and light differ.

Q. 16.16
Draw a diagram of a wave. Indicate on it
(a) a crest
(b) a trough
(c) the wavelength
(d) the amplitude

17
MATTER OR SUBSTANCES

fig. 17.1 Solids have fixed volumes and shapes, and stay where they are put. The Pyramids in Egypt haven't changed their shape, volume or position since they were built over 4000 years ago.

The world is made up of many different materials. Some of these materials occur naturally – rocks, minerals, trees, oil and water; others are artificial or man-made – glass, plastics, fibres and paint. Look around you and count the number of different materials you can see. If you are in the laboratory you may be able to see hundreds of different substances. The scientific name for materials or substances is **matter**. Anything that takes up space and has weight is called matter.

Think of the various ways in which matter differs. Some materials feel hard, others soft; some feel cold and some warm; some are heavy and others light. Materials differ in their colour, and in whether they stay where they are put or not, and some substances are even invisible. The name given to all these features or characteristics which vary from substance to substance is **properties** (of matter). The word **volume** means the amount of space taken up by a substance.

STATES OF MATTER

Substances can be classified or divided into groups in many different ways. They can be divided into metals and non-metals, or into hard substances and soft ones, or into groups of different colours. One of the most useful ways of classifying materials is to divide them into **solids**, **liquids** and **gases**. These are known as the **states of matter**.

You see plenty of solids and liquids every day, but probably not quite so many gases. A gas is just as much a real substance as a solid or a liquid is. You might think of an empty bottle as having nothing in it, but of course it is full of air – which is a gas.

fig. 17.2 The glass is solid, the lemonade is liquid, and the bubbles consist of gas

Gases can be poured or moved from place to place quite easily. The diagram shows how you can 'pour' air from one beaker to another. You must do it under water, and the beakers must be upside down to start with; one is full of water and the other full of air. Try the experiment in a sink or in a bucket full of water.

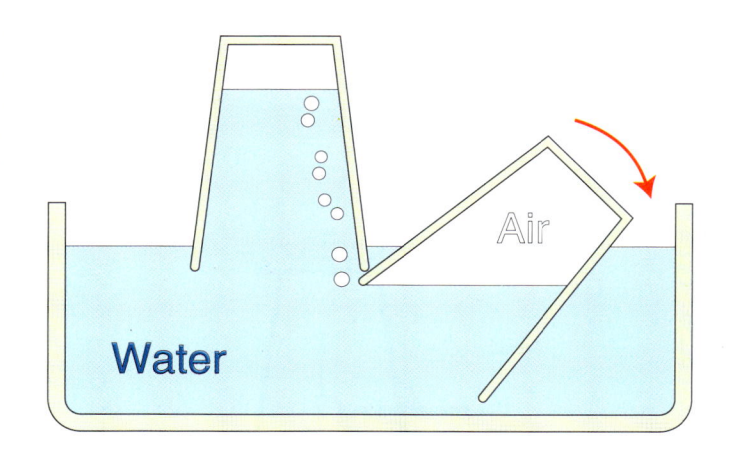

fig. 17.3 Pouring air from one beaker to another

■ 17 • Matter or Substances

Experiment 17.1
To investigate properties of solids, liquids and gases

Part 1

Start off by investigating water. Measure out 100 cm^3 of water in a graduated cylinder, and then pour it (every drop of it) into a beaker (or conical flask). Read the volume of water in the beaker. Does water flow? Does the water change its shape? Does the water change its volume?

Part 2

You investigate air here. Gases are more difficult than liquids to investigate because you can't see most of them. However, you can use water to show where they are and what they are doing.

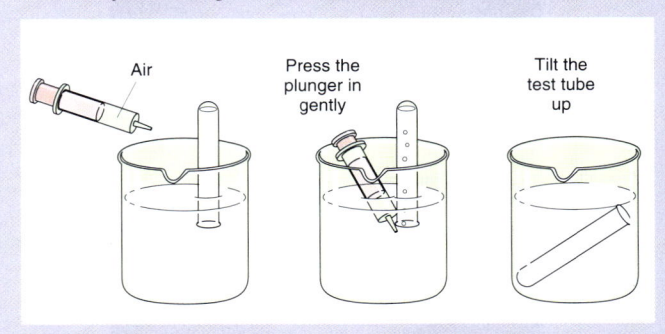

Air   Press the plunger in gently   Tilt the test tube up

Arrange the apparatus as shown. Note that the syringe has no needle. You can use the sink, a trough or other large container for the water. The test tube is upside down and full of water to start with, and the syringe is full of air. Gently push in the plunger of the syringe. What happens? You could also try the experiment which is illustrated in Figure 17.3. Can gases be poured and moved about?

Part 3

In this experiment you are going to find out if you can change the volume of a substance. Take a block of wood and try squashing it or stretching it. Can you compress it (make it smaller) or expand it?

Part 4

In order to try the same experiment with liquids and gases, you need a container. A syringe is suitable for this. Fill the syringe with water. Put your finger over the nozzle and firmly hold it there. Push on the plunger. Can you compress the liquid? Repeat the experiment with the syringe full of air. Can you compress the air?

fig. 17.4

SOLIDS, LIQUIDS AND GASES

A solid has a definite volume and a definite shape.

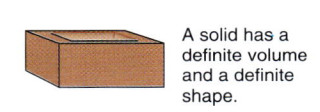

A liquid has a definite volume (it cannot be compressed) but has no fixed shape (it can be poured and takes the shape of its container).

A gas has neither definite volume nor definite shape. It completely fills its container. A gas is very much lighter than the same volume of a solid or a liquid.

fig. 17.5

Experiment 17.2
To investigate changes of state

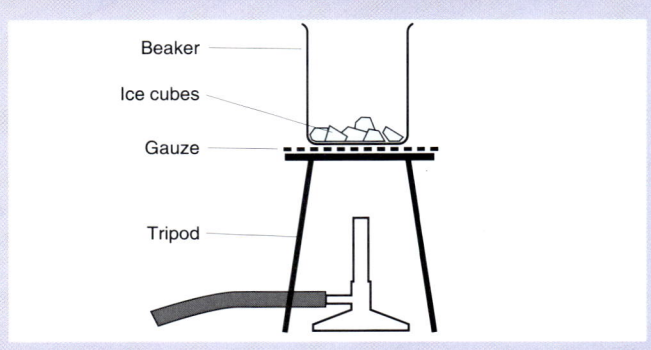

Beaker
Ice cubes
Gauze
Tripod

fig. 17.6

Part 1

Arrange the apparatus as shown. Put on your safety glasses and light the bunsen burner. Heat the ice cubes until they change to something else. What do the ice cubes turn into? What name is given to this change?

Continue heating until the water is bubbling. What is the water changing to? What name is given to this change?

Now hold a dry test tube above the beaker. Observe the outside of it after about 20 seconds. What has formed on the outside of the test tube? What name describes this change?

You will need the boiling water for the next two parts of the experiment.

Part 2

In this part of the experiment, you use the boiling water in the beaker. Turn down the bunsen so that the water is boiling gently. Do not let the beaker boil dry. Into the beaker of boiling water place a test tube containing some wax. Leave it there until it changes to something else. What change occurs? To what state (solid, liquid or gas) does it change?

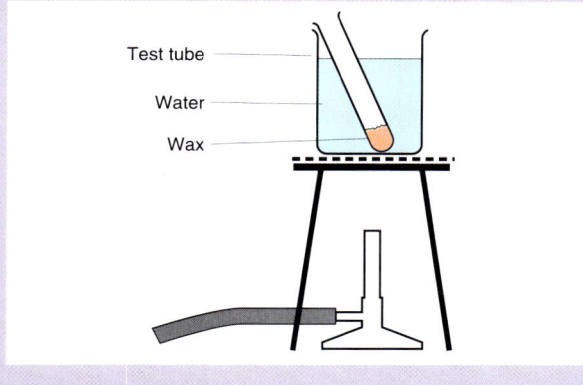

fig. 17.7

Using a test tube holder, lift the test tube out of the beaker and place it where it cannot fall over (e.g. standing in an empty conical flask). Wait until a change occurs in it. What does it change to?

Part 3

Turn off the bunsen burner. Into a dry test tube, place about 1 cm^3 of nail varnish remover. Use a dropper to do this. Place the test tube in the beaker of hot water and watch what happens. What happens to the nail varnish remover?

Part 4

Place about 1 cm^3 of a liquid called ether on the back of your hand. Use a dropper to do this. Does anything happen to it? What name describes the change?

Rewrite and complete the spaces in the following paragraph:

Ice is a _____ . When ice is heated, it ____ and changes to a _____ called _____ . When this substance is heated further, it _____ at a temperature of _____ °C and changes to _____ . When steam is cooled it changes back to _____ ; this change is called _____ .

CHANGES OF STATE

Heating and cooling can change solids, liquids and gases. In these experiments you will investigate some of the changes that occur.

If you did Experiment 17.2, you will have seen that water, which usually exists as a liquid, can be changed to a gas – by evaporating or boiling it, or can change to a solid – by freezing it. Most substances are like that – you can change their state by heating them or cooling them.

The changing of a solid to a liquid is called **melting**, and the changing of a liquid to a gas is known as **evaporation or boiling**. **Condensing** is the turning of a gas into a liquid, and **freezing** is the changing of a liquid to a solid.

There are a few solid substances which do not melt when they are heated, but change directly into a gas. This change (solid → gas) is called **sublimation**. The temperature at which a solid melts is known as its **melting point**, and the temperature at which a liquid boils is called its **boiling point**.

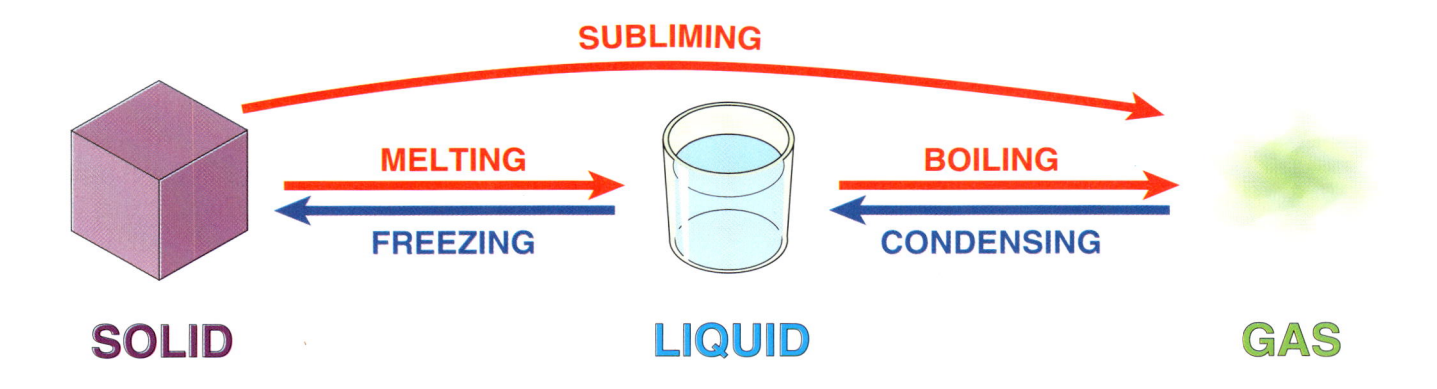

fig. 17.8

17 • Matter or Substances

Experiment 17.3
To find the melting point of candle wax

In this experiment, solid candle wax is heated, and the temperature at which it melts is measured with a thermometer.

1. Set up the apparatus as shown. The clamp should be tight enough to hold the test tube securely, but not so tight that it might crack the test tube.
2. Put on your safety glasses. Light the bunsen burner and adjust it to give a blue flame of medium height.
3. Start heating the water in the beaker and look at the wax in the tube. When the wax starts to melt, remove the burner from underneath the beaker, and then read the temperature on the thermometer. This temperature is the melting point of the wax.

fig. 17.9

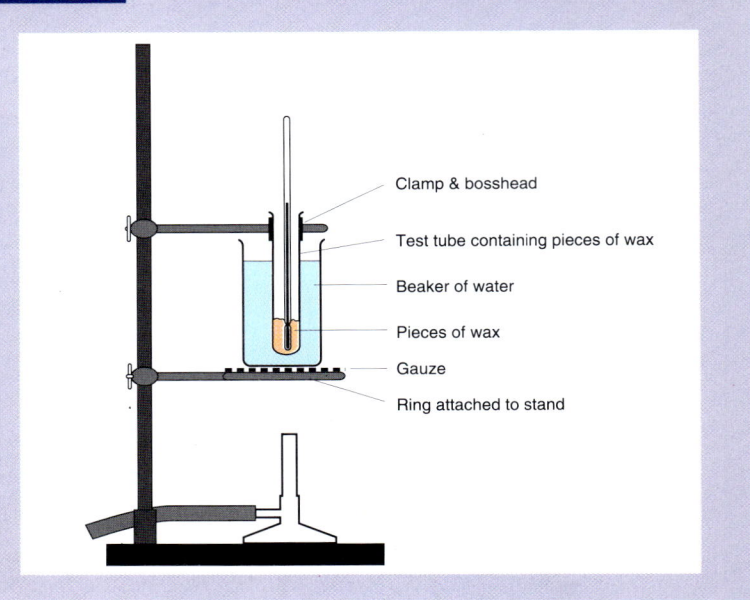

QUESTIONS

Q. 17.1
Divide a page of your homework copy into three columns. Label these columns **solids**, **liquids** and **gases**. Then list each of the following substances in its correct column. Leave out any that you have not heard of.

Substances: salt, chalk, petrol, iron, golden syrup, paraffin oil, soap, wood, steam, aeroboard, sugar, hydrogen, butane, air, coal, lead, chlorine, vinegar, paint, candle wax, bleach, copper, mercury, glass, carbon dioxide, aluminium, nail varnish, foam rubber.

Q. 17.2
What happens to water in a saucepan when it is put on the cooker and boiled – or to rain on the pavement after a shower? Does it disappear? Explain what you think happens.

Q. 17.3
(a) What does water change to when it is put into the freezer?
(b) What name is given to this change?

Q. 17.4
What is meant by the melting point of a substance? Describe how you would find the melting point of margarine. Use a diagram as part of your answer.

Q. 17.5
What word describes each of the following?
(a) a substance which has a fixed volume but no fixed shape
(b) the changing of a solid to a liquid
(c) the temperature at which a solid changes to a liquid
(d) the changing of a gas to a liquid
(e) the changing of a solid directly to a gas
(f) the amount of space taken up by a substance
(g) a space from which all matter has been removed

WHAT IS MATTER MADE OF?

Is matter continuous like cheese appears to be or is it made up of particles like sand? People have wondered about these questions for thousands of years and eventually found the answers. All matter, you and everything around you, both living and non-living, is made up of tiny, tiny particles. You have often seen a beach from a distance. The sand looks like a continuous layer, but you know from experience, that the layer of sand consists of millions and millions of grains or particles. All matter is just like that, except the particles are very, very much smaller, so small in fact that even with the most powerful microscope, a single particle cannot be seen. How big, or rather how small, are these particles? Do they move or do they stay still – or does it depend? Experiment 17.4 should provide some answers.

DIFFUSION

You have now seen that the particles in both gases and liquids move. The particles of a solid do not. **Diffusion** is the name given to the way in which gases and liquids spread themselves throughout any space into which they are put. Diffusion is a common occurrence. A smell is a substance in the form of a gas and so smells move about of their own accord. The smell of flowers such as roses can be noticed throughout a whole room, and cooking smells from the kitchen are quickly detected in other rooms. A sealed balloon gradually 'goes down' because the rapidly moving gas particles escape or diffuse out through tiny holes in the rubber.

SOLIDS, LIQUIDS AND GASES – THE EXPLANATION

You already discovered that solids have a fixed shape and fixed volume, liquids have no fixed shape but have a fixed volume, and gases have neither fixed shape nor fixed volume. Now you have seen that particles of liquids and gases move about, but particles of a solid do not. The kinetic theory is a way of explaining all of these observations. This suggests that the particles are arranged differently in solids, in liquids and in gases.

Experiment 17.4
To investigate properties of particles

Part 1

A layer of potassium permanganate solution (this is a highly coloured purple substance and is easily seen) is gently poured into the bottom of a graduated cylinder full of water and left undisturbed. After a few hours it is seen that the purple solution has started to spread upwards into the water. The next day it will be seen that the purple colour has spread throughout the entire cylinder. Do particles in a liquid move?

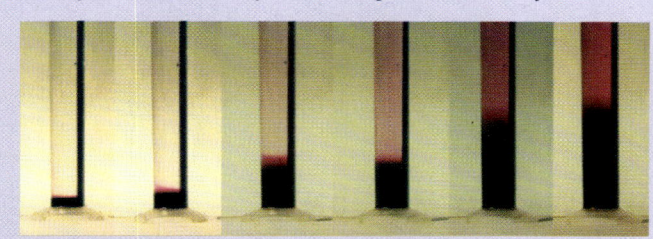

fig. 17.10 Potassium permanganate in water. The 6 pictures were taken at intervals during a 2 day period.

Part 2

Into three beakers of water, one cold, one warm and one hot, are placed a few crystals of potassium permanganate. The beakers are left undisturbed. After 10 minutes or so, it is seen that the colour has started to spread, slightly in the beaker of cold water, more in the warm water, and very much in the hot water. Do particles in a liquid move? Does the temperature affect the amount of movement? If so, how?

Part 3

Nitrogen dioxide is a brown gas and so can easily be seen. It is also heavy – much heavier than air. In this experiment, a gas jar of nitrogen dioxide is placed underneath a gas jar containing air and left undisturbed. After 10 minutes it is noticed that the brown gas has started to travel upwards into the jar of air and after about half an hour, it has spread out

fig. 17.11

to fill it completely. Do particles of a gas move about? See Figure 17.13 for explanation

Part 4

Take exactly 100 cm^3 of water in one graduated cylinder and exactly 100 cm^3 of alcohol or methylated spirits in another. Now pour one into the other and read the new volume. Are you surprised to see that it is only about 190 cm^3? The next experiment should provide an explanation for this strange result.

Part 5

Take 100 cm^3 of rice or barley or sugar in one graduated cylinder and exactly 100 cm^3 of dried peas in another. Now pour the two into a larger cylinder and read off the new volume. Can you see why the new volume is less than 200 cm^3? It is because the particles of one substance fit into the spaces between the particles of the other. This same explanation also applies to the water and alcohol of the previous experiment. There are spaces between the particles of a substance.

17 • Matter or Substances

SOLID → MELTING → LIQUID → BOILING → GAS

Molecules are packed tightly together in an orderly arrangement and are not free to move about.

Molecules are in contact with each other but are free to move about.

Molecules are widely separated and completely free. They are in constant motion at high speed.

fig. 17.12 In **solids**, the particles are packed tightly together and are arranged in a regular manner and are not free to move about. This structure explains the fact that solids have both fixed volume and fixed shape.

In **liquids**, the particles are also close together but are not arranged in any pattern. They are continuously moving about. So liquids can diffuse and they can flow and take the shape of their containers. Because the particles are touching, liquids cannot be compressed.

In a **gas**, the particles have complete freedom from each other. They are widely separated and are moving about in all directions at high speeds. This explains diffusion of gases. For the same reason, a gas fills any space into which it is put and it can always be compressed into a smaller space.

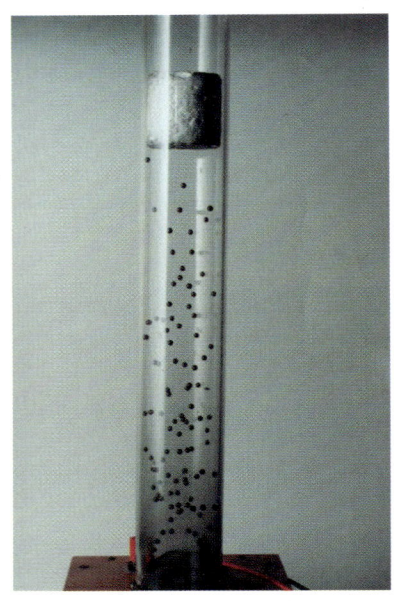

fig. 17.14 A model that illustrates the movement of the particles of a gas

BROWNIAN MOTION

By now you have learned that particles of liquids and gases are continuously moving about. You cannot of course see the actual particles doing this because they are much too small but there is an experiment in which you can see something being moved about by these tiny particles.

Brownian motion is named after a Scottish botanist called Robert Brown who, nearly 200 years ago, was looking through a microscope at pollen grains.

(Pollen is a substance produced by plants; if you rub a buttercup between your fingers, the yellow dust which rubs on to your fingers is pollen.) Brown was observing pollen grains under a microscope, and he noticed this constant, erratic motion. He thought the motion was due to the pollen being alive, so he boiled the pollen in water, tried the experiment again, and saw the same movement as before. He never was able to explain why it happened. It just didn't occur to him that molecules might have anything to do with it.

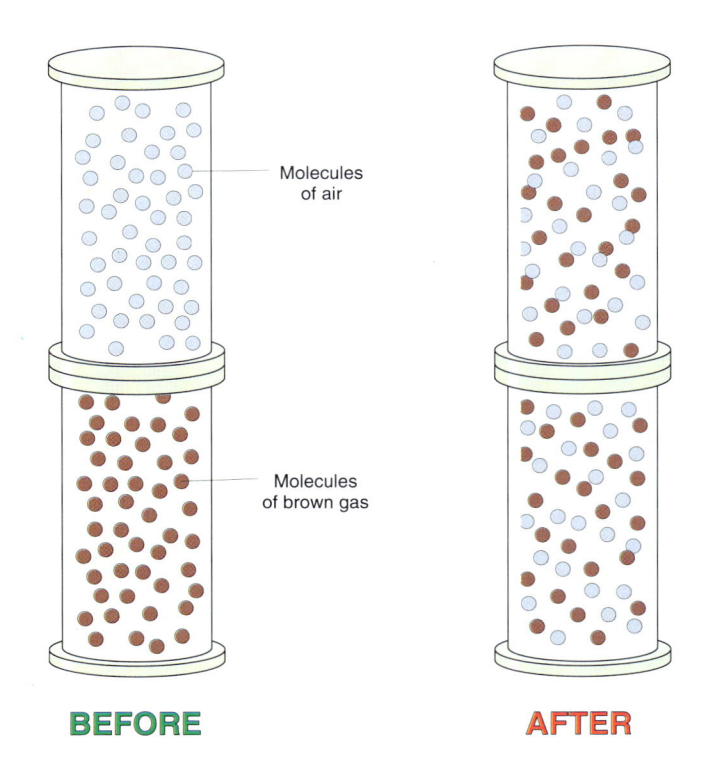

BEFORE — **AFTER**

fig. 17.13 What happens when nitrogen dioxide gas diffuses into air

Experiment 17.5
To observe Brownian Motion

The apparatus consists of a small transparent box or tube containing smoke and placed under a microscope. Smoke consists of tiny particles or specks of soot floating about in hot air. When the smoke particles are viewed through the microscope, they are seen to be constantly moving about or vibrating, in a random way, just like this:

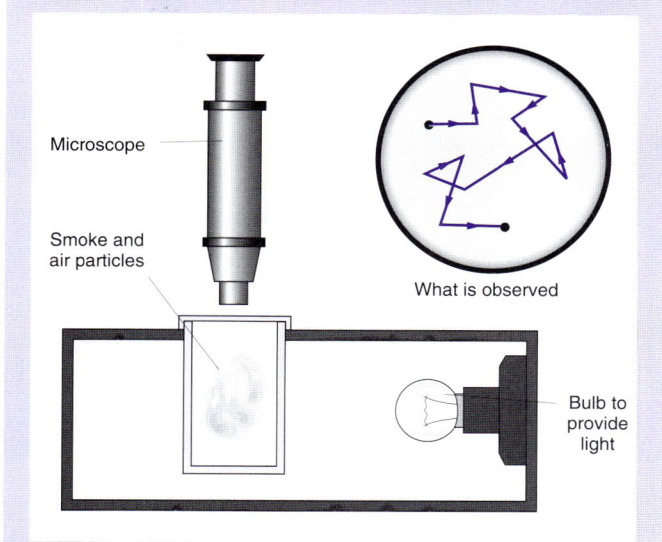

Microscope
Smoke and air particles
What is observed
Bulb to provide light

fig. 17.15

The explanation is that the particles of smoke are being bombarded or knocked about by the molecules of the air. Since the motion of the smoke particles is very erratic, it supports the idea of air molecules constantly and irregularly moving about in all directions. Looking at smoke particles under a microscope could be compared with looking at a hockey match from a height and being able to see the ball but not the players.

The smoke particle is much larger than the air molecules

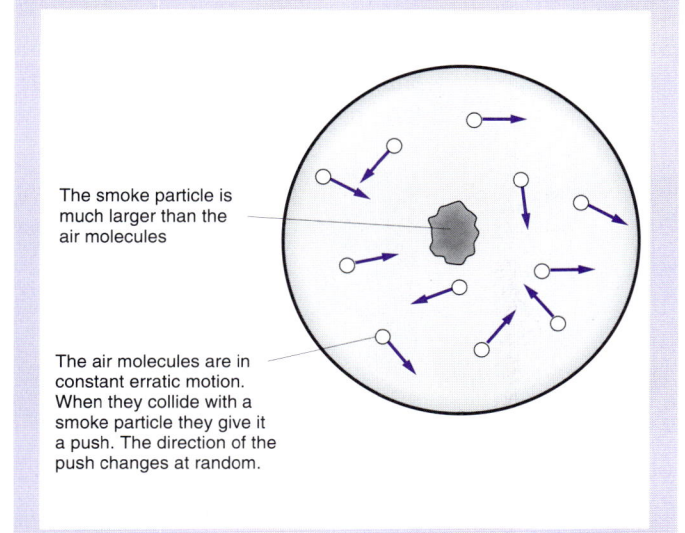

The air molecules are in constant erratic motion. When they collide with a smoke particle they give it a push. The direction of the push changes at random.

fig. 17.16

ATOMS AND MOLECULES

Atoms are very, very small, so small in fact, that inside an empty matchbox there are about one thousand million, million, million atoms of oxygen and nitrogen. If you could imagine a drop of water magnified to the size of the Earth, then the atoms present would be about the size of golf balls. A pin contains about 400 000 000 000 000 000 000 atoms of iron and a single drop of water has about 5 000 000 000 000 000 000 000 atoms of hydrogen and oxygen in it.

In this · dot of printer's ink, there are more atoms than there are people in the world.

There are just over one hundred different types of atom. Ninety two of these are naturally occurring, i.e. they are found on Earth, and the remainder have been artificially formed in nuclear reactions.

ELEMENTS AND COMPOUNDS

Some substances consist of only one kind of atom; these substances are called **elements**. Because there are about 100 different kinds of atoms, there are about 100 different elements. All elements are different – each has its own special properties such as melting and boiling points, colour, hardness, and so on. Many elements are common in everyday life.

Other substances, called **compounds**, consist of two or more kinds of atom chemically joined together ('combined'). Water is the most abundant of all compounds, and it consists of the gases hydrogen and oxygen combined together.

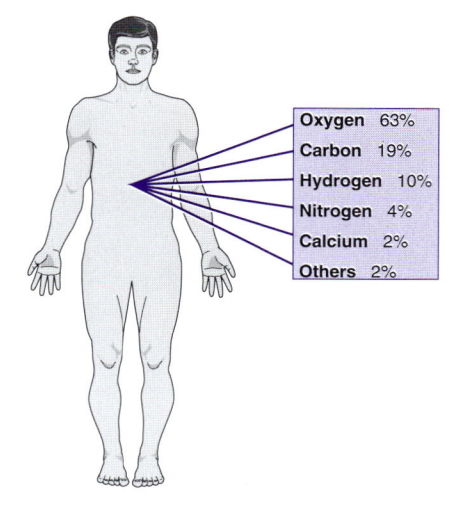

Oxygen	63%
Carbon	19%
Hydrogen	10%
Nitrogen	4%
Calcium	2%
Others	2%

fig. 17.18 *Elements in the human body*

17 • Matter or Substances

(a) **Tin** is used to cover steel cans to stop them rusting

(b) **Aluminium** is used to make cooking foil, drink cans, window frames and greenhouses

(c) **Chromium** is a shiny element and doesn't easily correode. It is used to cover such things as car radiator grills and bicycle handle bars for both protection and good appearence

(d) Street lights containing **sodium** are used in towns and cities everywhere

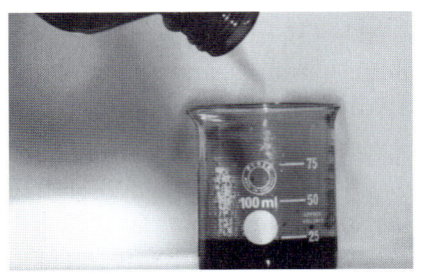

(e) **Bromine** is a brown, volatile liquid element (volatile means that it vaporises very easily)

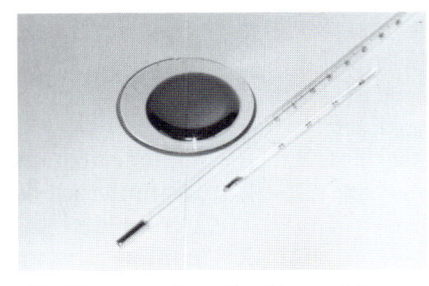

(f) **Mercury** is a liquid used in thermometers

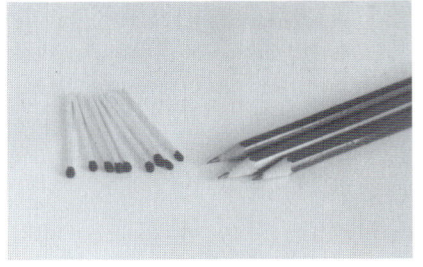

(g) Match heads contain phosphorus, and pencil 'lead' is a form of **carbon**

(h) Barbecues use **charcoal**, another form of carbon

(i) **Zinc** is used to cover items like iron bicycle racks and dustbins to stop them rusting

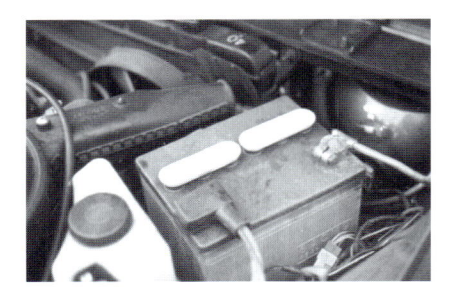

(j) **Lead** is an essential element in car batteries

fig. 17.17

Thousands of compounds too, are in common use in everyday life. The compound which is sold in the largest quantity in Irish shops is sucrose. Known to all by its common name 'sugar', it consists of carbon, hydrogen and oxygen all combined together. Salt is another common compound, and it is made up of the metal sodium and the gas chlorine. Other compounds found in the home are sodium bicarbonate, acetyl salicylic acid, sodium palmitate, acetone. These may appear to be very strange substances, but give them their common names (bread soda, aspirin, soap, nail varnish remover) and they become very familiar.

Each of the elements has its own chemical symbol and most laboratories have a chart, called the Periodic Table, listing all the elements. There is a Periodic Table on the inside back cover of this book.

Symbols for elements

argon	Ar	lead	Pb
aluminium	Al	magnesium	Mg
calcium	Ca	mercury	Hg
carbon	C	neon	Ne
chlorine	Cl	nitrogen	N
copper	Cu	oxygen	O
helium	He	silicon	Si
hydrogen	H	silver	Ag
iodine	I	sulphur	S
iron	Fe	zinc	Zn

Many of the symbols are the initial letters of the elements; other have a second letter where there are more than one starting with the same letter. Some of the symbols are derived from the Latin names for the elements (ferrum = iron, cuprum = copper) since a number of the elements were known in Roman times.

MOLECULES

As a general rule, atoms do not exist singly; they join together to form molecules. A molecule can be described as a group or a cluster of atoms either the same or different, joined together chemically. If the atoms in the molecules of a substance are all the same, the substance is an element, but if the atoms in the molecules are different, the substance is a compound.

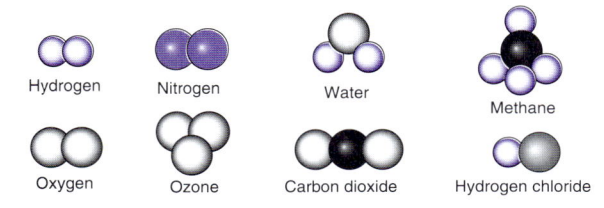

fig.17.19 Molecules consist of atoms joined together

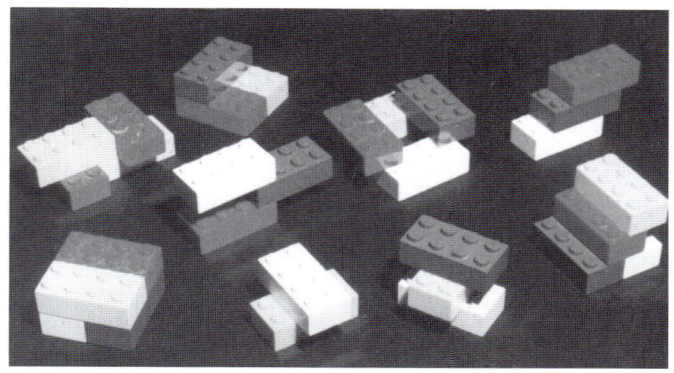

fig. 17.20 These 'Lego' models are made up of different numbers of bricks of different colours. In a similar way, molecules of compounds are made up of different numbers of atoms of different elements, all joined together.

MIXTURES AND COMPOUNDS

Apart from elements and compound, there is another kind of substance called a **mixture**. In elements and compounds, the molecules are all alike, but in a mixture, there are different kinds of molecules present.

A mixture contains two or more different substances, not chemically joined together, but just blended or mixed together. Mixtures occur everywhere; the air you breathe is a mixture of several gases, the food you eat contains many different substances – protein, carbohydrate, fat, water, salt, and others. The soil in your garden is a mixture, as are many other everyday substances such as toothpaste, petrol, paint, and concrete.

An **alloy** is a very important kind of mixture. It consists of two or more metals mixed together. Some common alloys (and what they consist of) are brass (copper and zinc), 'silver' coinage (copper and nickel), stainless steel (iron, chromium and nickel) and solder (lead and tin).

fig. 17.21 (a) James Joyce's statue is made of bronze, an alloy of copper and tin

17 • Matter or Substances

fig. 17.21 (b) Coinage metal is an alloy of copper and nickel

fig. 17.21 (c) Brass is an alloy of copper and zinc

Experiment 17.6
To make a mixture and to change it to a compound

This experiment will show the difference between a mixture and a compound. Iron filings and sulphur are used. Iron filings are very small particles of the metal iron; they are grey in colour and are attracted by a magnet. Sulphur is a non-metallic element; it is yellow and it is not attracted by a magnet.

Take some iron filings in a basin or on a sheet of paper and add about twice its bulk of powdered sulphur. Notice the colour of each element.

Now mix the two elements *very well* together so that the mixture looks uniform (the same colour and appearance throughout). If you bring a magnet near, you will see that the iron can be pulled out of the mixture (if you do this, remix the substances well before continuing).

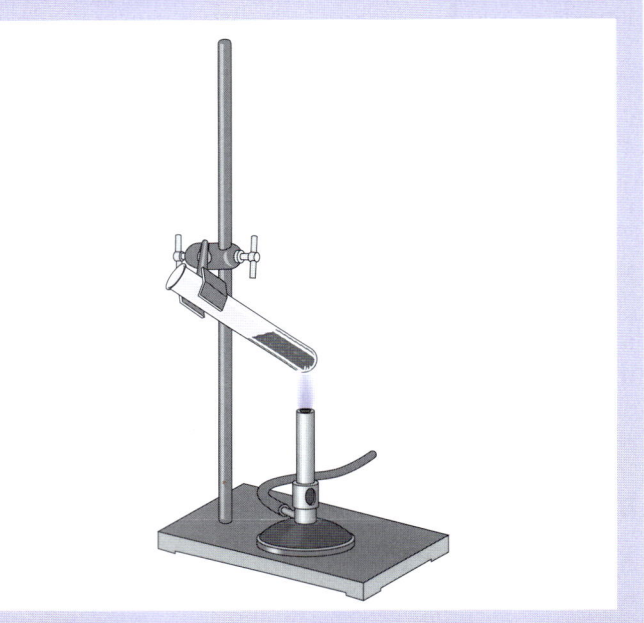

fig. 17.23

Place the mixture in a test tube like that shown and heat the end of the tube, gently at first and then more strongly. Watch carefully. When the mixture starts to glow, remove the burner. The two elements are then combining together to form a compound. When the reaction has finished and the tube has cooled, examine the product.

You should see that it is brownish grey in colour and if you bring a magnet near, it will not be attracted. The iron and sulphur are no longer present, but they have formed a new substance called iron sulphide – which is a compound.

fig. 17.22

Another difference between a mixture and a compound is that a compound always has a fixed composition (e.g. iron sulphide always contains 64% of iron and 36% of sulphur), but a mixture can have any composition. You can make a mixture of iron and sulphur containing whatever amount of iron you put into it. More about compound formation will be found in Chapter 25.

SUMMARY

- Matter exists in three different states: **solid**, **liquid** and **gas**. A solid has both a fixed volume and fixed shape; a liquid has a fixed volume but no fixed shape, and a gas has neither fixed volume nor fixed shape.

- The state of most substances can be changed by either heating or cooling them. On heating a solid, it **melts** to become a liquid, which, on further heating **boils or evaporates** to become a gas or vapour. A gas when cooled, **condenses** to become a liquid, which, on further cooling, **freezes** into a solid. **Sublimation** is the changing of a solid directly into a gas.

- All matter is made up of particles, which may be either atoms or molecules.

- Particles of liquids and gases are always in motion. **Diffusion** is the name given to the way in which they spread themselves throughout any space into which they are put. In **solids**, the particles are packed tightly together and are arranged in a regular manner and they are not free to move about. In **liquids**, the particles are also close together but they are not arranged in any pattern. They are continuously moving about. In **gases**, the particles have complete freedom from each other; they are widely separated and are moving about in all directions at high speeds.

- **Brownian motion** is the movement of very small particles in a gas or liquid, caused by their being bombarded by the molecules of the gas or liquid.

- All substances are made up of atoms. An **element** is a substance which consists of only one type of atom, or which cannot be split up into simpler substances by chemical means. There are just over 100 different elements. A **compound** is a substance composed of two or more elements chemically joined together. An **atom** is the smallest part of an element which can exist. A **molecule** consists of two or more atoms chemically joined together. A **mixture** contains two or more different substances not chemically joined together.

QUESTIONS

Q. 17.6
Rewrite the following paragraphs and fill in the missing words.

(a) The scientific name for substances is __ and there are __ different states in which it exists. These states are __, __ and __. A __ is a substance which has a fixed shape and a fixed __, a __ has a fixed __ but no fixed __ and a __ has neither fixed __ nor fixed __.

(b) It is usually possible to convert a substance from one state to another by either __ or __, and there are names for the various changes which occur. Melting is the change from the __ to the __ state and boiling is the change from __ to __ . The name given to the change from liquid to solid is __ and from gas to liquid is __. Some substances change directly from solid to __ and this unusual change is called __.

(c) All substances are made of very, very tiny particles called __ and there are about __ different types of these. As a general rule, these particles do not exist singly, but in groups called __. If a substance is made up of __ containing only one type of __, the substance is called an __, but if the __ contain two or more types of __, then the substance is known as a __

(d) __ motion was first noticed by Robert __ He was looking through a __ at __ grains in water. He saw that the grains were in constant erratic __. We __ this motion by saying that the water __ are moving about in the liquid and that they __ the grains, causing them to __ . It is __ for the movement of particles in the __ and __ states.

Q. 17.7
What element is used for each of the following purposes:
(a) in breathing apparatus
(b) to make railway lines
(c) in greenhouses and window frames
(d) in swimming pool water
(e) in thermometers
(f) coating steel food cans
(g) in 'Coke' and lemonade cans
(h) for filling balloons
(i) in advertising lights
(j) making electrical wires
(k) cooking foil
(l) match heads

Q. 17.8

The chart below shows the melting points and boiling points of various substances. What is the state (solid, liquid or gas) of each of these substances at room temperature (20°C)?

Substance	Melting point/°C	Boiling point/°C
water	0	100
iron	1540	2900
acetone	−95	56
butane	−158	−1
sodium	98	890
oxygen	−219	−183
ethanol	−115	78
sulphur	119	445

Q. 17.9

(a) What is the state (solid, liquid, or gas) of each of the substances listed in the table?
(b) Which substance could be
 (i) water
 (ii) air
 (iii) iron

Substance	m.p./°C	b.p./°C
A	1040	2330
B	120	444
C	−39	357
D	0	100
E	−217	−183
F	−30	170

Q. 17.10

(a) What are the names of the elements which have the following symbols: C, H, I, N, S, Cu, Fe, He, Ne, Ag.
(b) What is the symbol for each of the following elements: aluminium, argon, calcium, chlorine, lead, magnesium, mercury, oxygen, silicon, zinc.

Q. 17.11

What name describes each of the following:
(a) the spreading out of a liquid or a gas
(b) a mixture of two or more metals
(c) the smallest part of an element that can exist
(d) a substance made up of only one kind of atom
(e) a particle made up of two or more atoms joined together
(f) a substance made up of two or more elements joined together

Q. 17.12

State two differences between a mixture and a compound. Name one mixture that can very easily be changed into a compound and describe how you would do this. Use a diagram to illustrate your answer.

Q. 17.13

(a) A large crystal of potassium permanganate is put at the bottom of a beaker of water and left. Describe what would be seen after (i) five minutes, (ii) five days.
(b) Explain your answers using the idea of particles.
(c) Name the two processes that occurred during the experiment.

Q. 17.14

Use the idea of particles to explain each of the following observations:
(a) Cooking smells can be noticed throughout the house.
(b) A balloon gets smaller after a few days.
(c) When smoke is viewed under a microscope particles are seen jigging around.
(d) Dye can spread through a load of white washing.

18
MIXTURES AND SOLUTIONS

SOLUTIONS

Have you ever thought about what happens to the sugar that you put into your tea or coffee? Can you see it in the drink or feel it at the bottom of the cup? If you have tried this, you will know that it cannot be seen or felt – but it is obviously still there because the drink tastes sweet. Some people might say that the sugar has melted in the drink, but this is incorrect. What happens is that the sugar has **dissolved** in the liquid and formed a solution.

A **solution** can be described as a mixture of (usually) a solid in a liquid. In a solution, the molecules of one substance are evenly distributed amongst the molecules of the other substance.

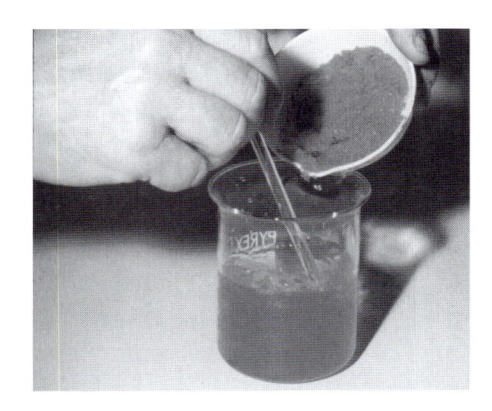

fig. 18.1 (a) Making a solution

Molecules of bluestone evenly distributed throughout the water

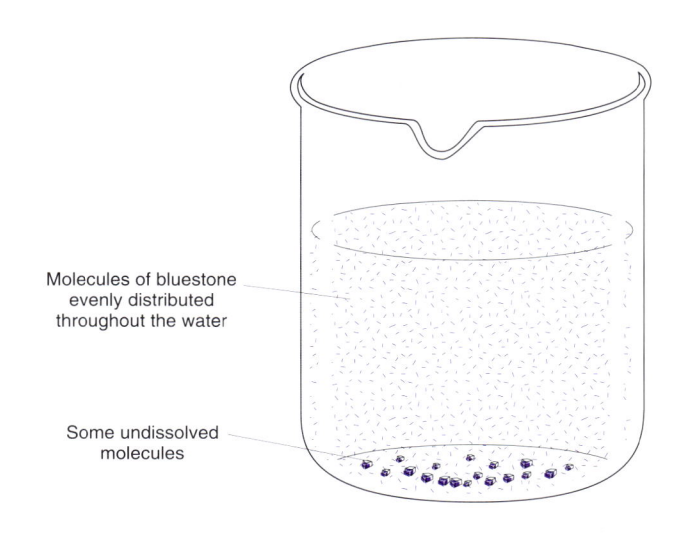

Some undissolved molecules

fig. 18.1 (b) Molecules in a solution

Solutions are very common in everyday life. Fizzy drinks contain the gas carbon dioxide dissolved in them; sea water contains salt and other substances dissolved in it; swimming pool water contains the gas chlorine; perfumes contain plant extracts dissolved in alcohol; glues contains an adhesive dissolved in some kind of solvent.

Experiment 18.1
To discover substances which are soluble and ones which are insoluble

In this experiment you are going to test a number of different substances to find out whether they are soluble in water or not. Suitable substances to try are sugar, oatmeal, powdered milk, sand, iron filings, bluestone, Rochelle salts, sulphur, candle wax, salt, washing soda, washing-up liquid, glucose, citric acid, benzoic acid.

1. Take a small amount (as much as will fit on the tip of a spatula) of one of the substances and put it in a test tube.
2. About half fill the test tube with water.
3. Put a cork in the test tube and shake for about half a minute.
4. Examine the contents of the test tube and decide whether the substance has dissolved (does it seem to have 'disappeared'?), or has not dissolved (you can still see it).
5. Rinse out the test tube and test the next substance in the same way.
6. Make two lists of substances, one containing those that are soluble (do dissolve), and the other containing those that are insoluble (do not dissolve).
7. Repeat the experiment, but this time test the solubility of the substances in alcohol (methylated spirits) instead of water.

18 • Mixtures and Solutions

fig. 18.2 Some solutions found in the home

In a solution, the solid which dissolves is called the **solute**, and the liquid in which it dissolves is the **solvent**. When you dissolve sugar in tea, sugar is the solute and the hot water is the solvent. A substance which dissolves in a liquid is said to be **soluble**, and one which does not dissolve is **insoluble**. Sugar, for example, is soluble in water but sand is not.

Concentrated and dilute solutions

When a small amount of salt is dissolved in water, the solution is said to be **dilute**. When a lot of salt is dissolved in the water, the solution becomes **concentrated**. If you continue adding salt to the water, a stage is reached when the salt will no longer dissolve because the water then holds as much salt as it can; the solution is then described as being **saturated**.

The orange squash which you buy in the supermarket is concentrated. It must be diluted by adding water before it is nice to drink.

fig. 18.3 Concentrated orange squash and dilute orange squash

OTHER SOLVENTS

The solutions mentioned so far have been solutions of substances in water. However, water is not the only solvent. You probably know that turpentine or white spirit is used for thinning oil paint and for cleaning brushes. This is because turpentine is a solvent for paint. Water cannot be used because oil paint is insoluble in water.

Nail varnish remover is a liquid called acetone. Nail varnish is insoluble in water but is soluble in acetone and so can be 'washed off' by using acetone. Paint stripper contains a liquid called dichloromethane and paint is soluble in this liquid. Chewing gum is soluble in a liquid called xylene, and so this liquid can be used to remove chewing gum stains. The antiseptic tincture of iodine is a solution of iodine in alcohol. Biologists often use alcohol to dissolve the chlorophyll in leaves.

fig. 18.4 Some non-aqueous ('non-watery') solvents

QUESTIONS

Q. 18.1

Rewrite the following paragraph, filling in the missing words.

A solution is made by __ a solid (known as the __) in a liquid (which is called the __). Substances which dissolve are said to be __ and ones which do not dissolve are described as being __ . When sugar dissolves in tea, the sugar is the __ and the tea is the __ . Two substances which dissolve in water are __ and __ . When a solution contains as much solid as it can hold, it is described as being a __ solution.

Q. 18.2

Name substances which are:

(a) soluble in both water and alcohol
(b) insoluble in both water and alcohol
(c) soluble in water but insoluble in alcohol
(d) insoluble in water but soluble in alcohol

Q. 18.3
Name five substances which are soluble in water and five which are not. What name describes substances which are not soluble?

Q. 18.4
Describe an experiment in which you tested substances to find out if they were soluble or insoluble in water. Make out a table showing the results of your experiment.

SEPARATING MIXTURES

Having to separate mixtures is a necessity of everyday life. After vegetables are cooked, they must be separated from the boiling water in which they have been cooked; this is done by using a sieve or colander. In a dairy, cream is separated from milk, in a machine called a centrifuge. In a car engine, the air filter separates any dust or dirt in the incoming air, as the engine will not function properly with dirty air. In a scrapyard, scrap iron is separated from other metals using an electromagnet (see figure 13.16, page 91).

To separate substances which are mixed, you must find some difference between them. There are many different ways of separating mixtures, and some of these are described below.

FILTRATION

Filtration is a method of separating a solid and a liquid. Just as the sieve is used at home for separating vegetables and water, filter paper is used in the laboratory for separating a solid and a liquid. The 'holes' in filter paper though, are very much smaller than the holes in a sieve.

Experiment 18.2
To separate a mixture of sand and salt

This experiment makes use of the fact that salt is soluble in water whereas sand is not. Water is added to the mixture and stirred. The salt dissolves but the sand does not. The mixture is then filtered. The salt solution passes through the filter paper but the sand does not and is held in the filter paper. When the salt solution is evaporated, the solid salt is formed.

Note: Safety glasses should be worn for this experiment

1. Put a 'spoonful' of the mixture into a beaker and then add about 100 cm^3 of water.
2. Stir the mixture until the salt has dissolved.
3. Fold a piece of filter paper into a cone-shape and place it in a filter funnel.
4. Support the funnel in an upright position. An easy way to do this is to rest it in a tripod. Place the evaporating basin underneath the filter to catch the filtered liquid.
5. Carefully pour the mixture from the beaker into the filter. If it will not all fit, wait until some of the solution has passed through the filter and then add more of the mixture to the funnel until it has all been filtered.
6. When the evaporating basin is about half full, lift the filter funnel out of the tripod and rest it in a conical flask to catch the rest of the filtered liquid.
7. Place the evaporating basin on a gauze resting on the tripod. Boil the solution until most of the water has evaporated away. At this stage, the salt will start to separate from the water. It is likely to 'spit' and jump out of the basin. When this happens, cover the basin with a piece of cardboard with a hole cut in it.
8. When all of the water has evaporated away, the salt will remain in the basin.
9. The sand remains in the filter funnel. It can be dried by placing the filter paper in a warm oven or by heating it gently over a bunsen burner.

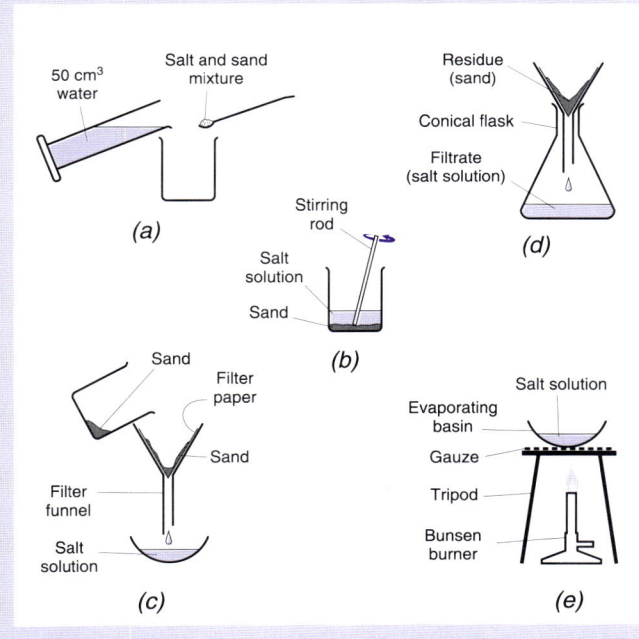

fig. 18.5

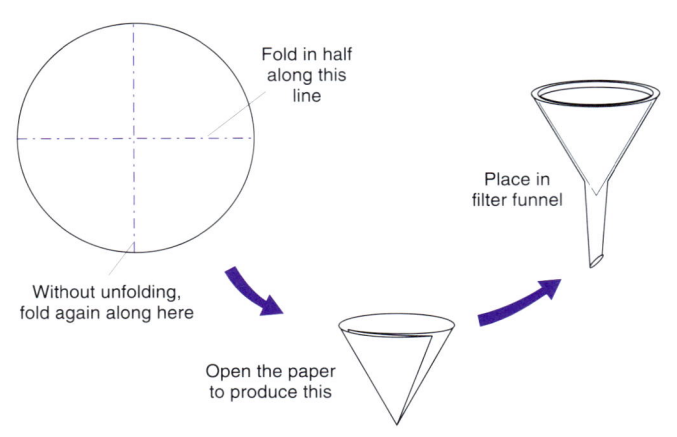

fig. 18.5 Folding a filter paper

There are many everyday examples of filtration. A coffee filter allows coffee through while holding back the coffee grounds. At water purification plants, water supplies are filtered through beds of sand. In car engines, both the air and oil are filtered. If old paint has some paint skin mixed with it, the skin can be filtered out using an old stocking. A tea pot has a strainer in it to filter out the tea leaves from the tea, and a tea bag allows hot water to dissolve solutes from the tea but it holds back the tea leaves.

DECANTING

Decanting is the name given to a very simple means of separating a liquid from a solid which does not dissolve in it. The solid is allowed to settle to the bottom of the container and the liquid then just poured off. If you carefully pour off the water from a beaker containing sand and water, you are decanting the water.

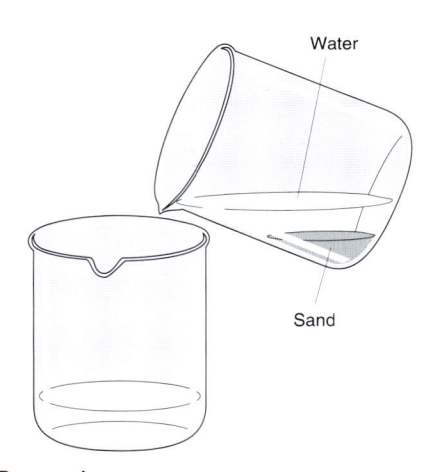

fig. 18.7 Decanting

DISTILLATION

Distillation is a process in which a liquid is boiled and the vapour from it is then passed through a vessel called a liebig condenser (named after its inventor). A liebig condenser consists of a pipe or tube inside another tube. Water circulates through the outer tube, and the vapour to be cooled is passed through the inner tube. As it does so, it is cooled and it changes back to a liquid. If there are any impurities in the original liquid, they are left behind in the distillation flask. Distillation can be used to purify a liquid, for example, to obtain pure water from dirty water or from sea water. It can also be used to separate two liquids from each other if the liquids boil at different temperatures.

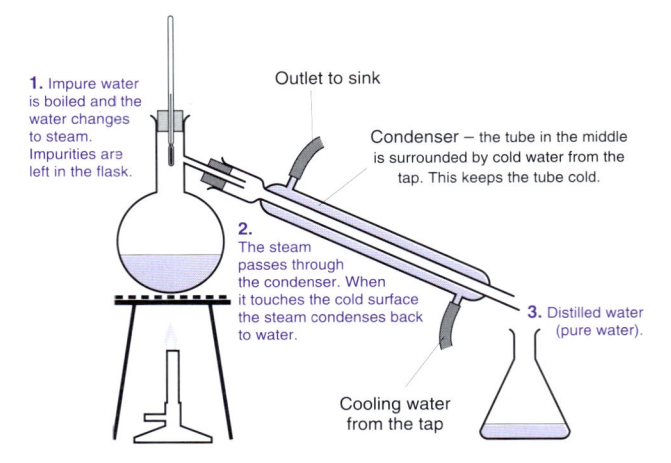

fig. 18.8 Distillation apparatus

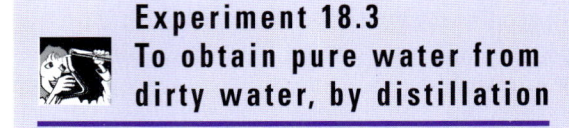

Experiment 18.3
To obtain pure water from dirty water, by distillation

A distillation apparatus is set up as shown in Figure 18.8. The flask contains dirty water. This water is heated with the bunsen burner until it is boiling. The water vapour which is formed is driven into and down the condenser. There, it is cooled and changes back to liquid water, which flows out the end of the condenser and is collected in a flask.

Distillation in daily life

Distillation is a process that has many important uses. In Middle East countries where there is no natural supply of fresh water, distillation is used to desalinate sea water (to remove the salt from it) to provide drinking water. Laboratories require a supply of distilled water and many laboratories have a water still to provide this (see figure 18.9). Distilled water is needed for medical preparations and also for car batteries. Steam irons are best filled with distilled water, as tap water can leave a deposit after a time and make the iron work less efficiently.

Chemistry • 18

fig. 18.9 In this laboratory water still, the water is heated by an electric immersion heater. The water vapour rises up out of the large flask and is pushed down through the condenser (on the left) where it is cooled by cold water passing through the inner coil. Distilled water runs out of the bottom of the condenser.

Liquids which mix with each other can be separated by distillation. For example, if a mixture of alcohol and water is distilled, the alcohol distils first (when the temperature of the mixture reaches 80°C (the boiling point of alcohol), and when all of the alcohol has distilled, the temperature rises to 100°C and the water distils. Separation of liquids by this method is called **fractional distillation**.

Distillation is an essential process in many industries. In the making of whiskey and other spirits, the fermented liquor is distilled in order to extract the alcohol out of it. In oil refining, it is also an essential process for extracting the petrol, kerosene, paraffin oil and fuel oil from the petroleum (crude oil).

SEPARATING IMMISCIBLE LIQUIDS

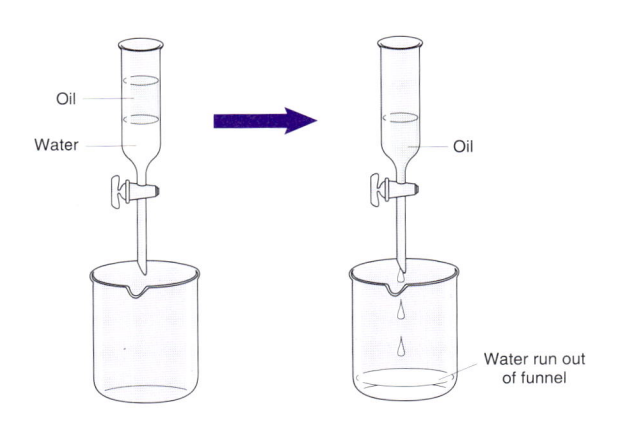

fig. 18.10 Separating oil and water

Liquids which do not mix with each other are described as **immiscible**. Separation of such liquids is very easily done – with a special kind of funnel called a **separating funnel**. The mixture is just poured into the funnel, and after a short time, the denser liquid goes to the bottom while the less-dense liquid floats on top. The denser liquid at the bottom is then run off into one beaker, the tap is closed, and the beaker is then replaced by a second beaker. The less-dense liquid is then run into the second beaker. Oil and water can quickly be separated by this method.

SUSPENSIONS

Some substances which do not dissolve in water can form suspensions, which mean that they stay distributed throughout water rather than settling to the bottom. Such a mixture is called a **suspension**. It is a mixture of a liquid and a finely divided insoluble solid.

Calamine Lotion and *Milk of Magnesia* are both suspensions. If you look at bottles of these, you will see the instruction "shake well". This is to make sure that the solid becomes evenly distributed throughout the liquid before use.

If chalk powder is mixed with water and stirred, it does not dissolve and neither does it settle to the bottom. It becomes distributed throughout the water and stays there: it forms a suspension.

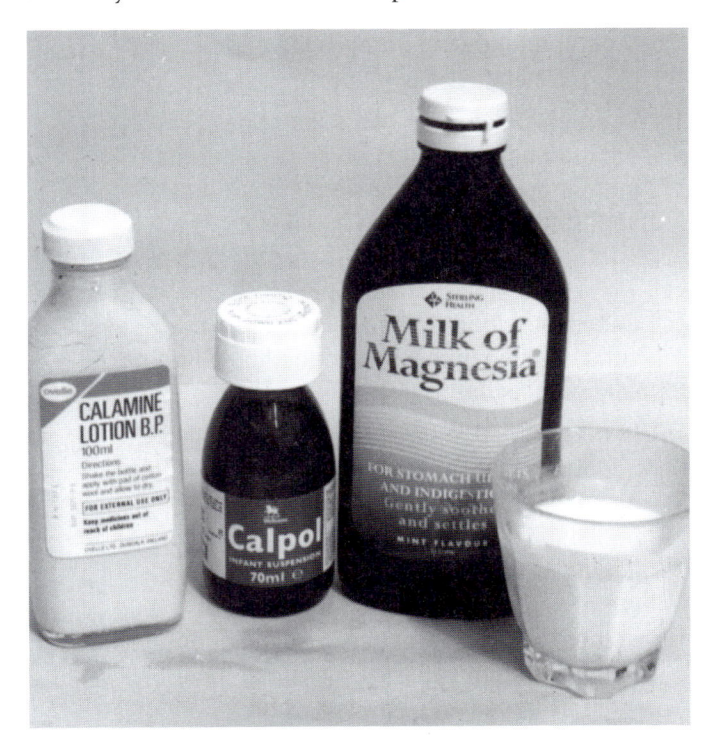

fig. 18.11 Some suspensions found in the home

18 • Mixtures and Solutions

SUMMARY

- A **solution** consists of a solid (the **solute**) dissolved in a liquid (the **solvent**). Substances which dissolve are soluble and ones which do not dissolve are **insoluble**. When there is a lot of solute present, the solution is **concentrated**, and when there is only a small amount, the solution is **dilute**. A solution which contains as much solute as it can hold is **saturated**.

- A solid can be separated from a liquid by **decanting** (pouring off the liquid) or by **filtration** (pouring the mixture into filter paper).

- **Evaporation** is used to recover the solute from a solution.

- **Distillation** is a double process – a liquid (or a mixture containing a liquid) is boiled, and the vapour which is formed is condensed (by passing it through a condenser).

- Liquids which do not mix with each other are described as being **immiscible**. They are separated from each other by using a **separating funnel**. A **suspension** is a mixture of a solid distributed throughout a liquid (but not dissolved in it).

QUESTIONS

Q. 18.5

Copy out the following paragraphs and fill in the missing words.

(a) In order to separate two substances from each other, there must be some difference in their properties. The simplest method of separating a solid and a liquid is to __ it. This is done by pouring the mixture into a __ __ held in a __ funnel, with a __ placed under the funnel. When this is done, the solid ends up in the __ and the liquid (which is known as the __) in the __.

(b) In the distillation process, a liquid is __ and the __ which is formed is then ____ by passing it through a __ in order to cool it. This process can be used to __ liquids. If a mixture of sand, salt, dye and water is distilled, pure __ is obtained at the end of the process. __ distillation can be used to separate __ which have __ boiling points, such as __ and __.

Q. 18.6

The diagrams illustrate an experiment in which sand and salt are being separated, but the diagrams are not in the order in which the experiment is carried out.

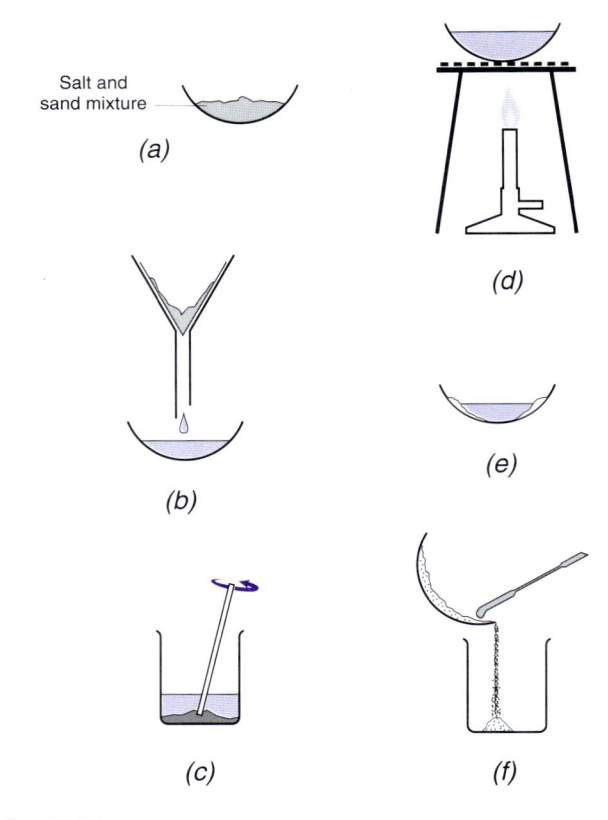

fig. 18.12

List the correct order for carrying out the experiment, and explain what is being done in each diagram.

Q. 18.7

Draw a labelled diagram of a distillation apparatus. Describe how it could be used to obtain some pure water from sea water.

Q. 18.8

Which method of separation would be best to:
(a) obtain pure water from sea water
(b) obtain salt from sea water
(c) remove mud from lake water
(d) separate oil and water
(e) separate peas from boiling water
(f) obtain petrol from crude oil
(g) separate methylated spirits and water
(h) separate sand and salt
(i) separate sugar and salt
(j) separate stones and sand

Q. 18.9

Name:

(a) a liquid which evaporates easily
(b) a mixture which can be separated by filtration
(c) a mixture which cannot be separated by filtration
(d) an everyday substance made by distillation
(e) a substance which does not dissolve in water but which dissolves in white spirit
(f) a liquid which will remove chewing gum

Q. 18.10

What is meant by each of the following words: dissolving, solute, solvent, soluble, insoluble, concentrated, dilute, suspension, immiscible, filtration, filtrate, residue, decanting, evaporation, distilling?

Q. 18.11

A solid was dissolved in water in a beaker to make a solution. The solution was then heated until all of the water had evaporated away. Given the following masses, calculate (i) the mass of the solute and the mass of water in the solution, (ii) the percentage of solute in the solution.

Mass of beaker = 54.5 g
Mass of beaker + solution = 99.6 g
Mass of beaker + solid = 64.5 g

Q. 18.12

Describe, using diagrams to illustrate your answer, how you would separate a mixture of cooking oil, water and salt.

19

CHEMICAL REACTIONS

fig. 19.1 (a) A fireworks display is the result of a chemical change

fig. 19.1 (b) Chemical changes occur as fruit rots

CHEMICAL AND PHYSICAL CHANGES

The word *chemical* is often misunderstood, and taken to mean something harmful. This is far from the truth. Everything in the world is made from chemicals – including yourself! In ancient times before chemical reactions had been discovered, people used substances just as they found them – plants and animals for food, animal skins for clothing, wood for burning, rocks for tools and caves for shelters.

fig. 19.2

Today, most of the things that you use have been changed from the way in which they occur in nature. Foods are processed to make them better for you and to make them keep longer. Many clothes are made from artificial fibres – that is, fibres which have been made by chemical processes. Many things are made from plastics and other man-made substances. Metals are made from substances that occur in rocks. Some medicines, cleaning agents and cosmetics are made from substances that occur in crude oil. Fertilisers are made from substances that occur in natural gas and in the air.

Chemistry is about changing what the world has into what the world needs.

fig. 19.3 Modern life would not exist without chemicals

In daily life, changes are happening all the time. The water in the sea evaporates and then returns to earth as rain. Plants grow, and many of them are then used as food. Fuels are burned in homes, factories, cars and aircraft to provide heat and transport. Minerals are taken from the earth and changed into useful substances.

Scientists classify changes into two groups, physical changes and chemical changes. When a lump of fat is placed on a pan and heated, it melts to become a liquid; when the pan is allowed to cool, the fat changes back to a solid. No new substance is formed when the fat is heated. Changes like this are called **physical changes**.

However, if a raw egg is broken on to the hot pan and left for a few minutes, the runny liquid becomes white and the yolk become solid. If the egg is left to cool, it does not become runny again; some new substances are formed when the egg is cooked. Changes like this in which something new is formed are called **chemical changes**.

A physical change is one in which no new substance is formed.

Physical changes are often only temporary and involve a change in the state (solid, liquid, gas) of, or the appearance of, a substance – like the fat being melted. The melting of ice and the evaporation of water are other examples of physical changes.

A chemical change (or a chemical *reaction*) is one in which a new substance is formed, i.e. a substance whose properties differ from those of the original substance.

A chemical change involves the breaking up of molecules and the rearranging of their atoms to form different molecules. As well, a chemical change often involves a heat change, like the egg being cooked. The burning of coal and the baking of bread are other examples of chemical changes, and the two photographs in Figure 19.1 also show chemical reactions.

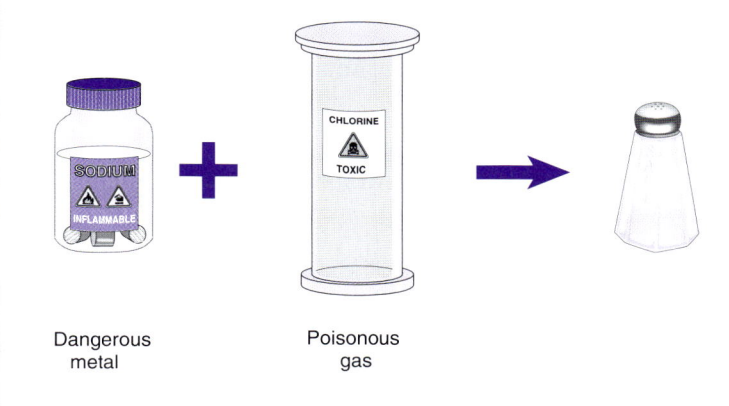

Dangerous metal   Poisonous gas

fig. 19.4 *Sodium chloride (salt) is completely different from the elements of which it is composed*

Experiment 19.1
To investigate some chemical and some physical changes

safety glasses needed

In this experiment you are going to investigate the effect of heat on a number of different substances, and then try to work out whether each change is a chemical or physical one.

1. Select one of the given substances. Observe it carefully, and make a note of its appearance.

2. If the substance is a powder, put about 1 cm depth of it in a **dry** test tube. If the substance is a hard solid, (i) hold it in a pair of tongs, and (ii) put the bunsen on a slight tilt so that none of the substance can drop into it

3. Heat the substance in a bunsen flame, gently at first and then more strongly, until a change occurs. Then stop heating.

4. Carefully observe the substance as it is being heated. Describe what happens. Describe also, the appearance of the substance after it has been allowed to cool.

5. Decide whether the change was chemical or physical, and record your conclusion.

6. Repeat the experiment with another substance, doing exactly the same as already described. Make a note of your findings.

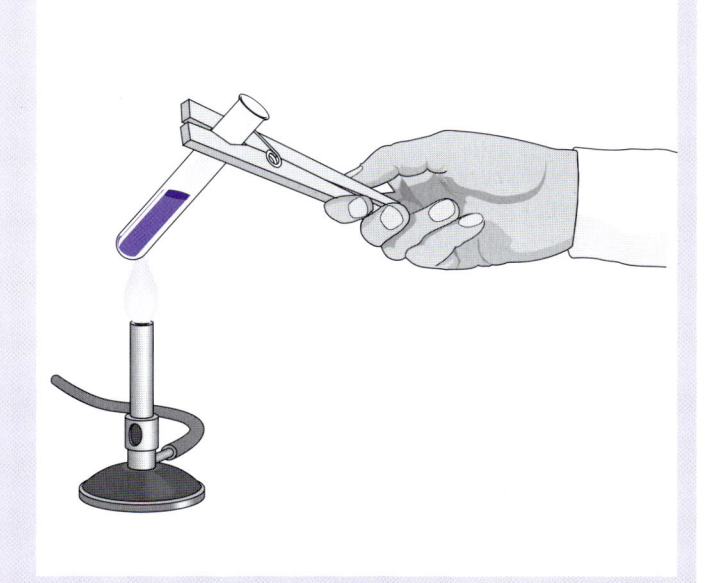

fig. 19.5 *How to heat a test tube*

7. Test six difference substances, and for each, record what you discovered.

19 • Chemical Reactions

HEAT CHANGES IN CHEMICAL REACTIONS

Some chemical reactions give out heat when they take place, whereas others need heat to make them happen. A fuel burning is an obvious example of a reaction which gives out heat, and cooking food is a good example of a reaction which needs heat.

> A reaction in which heat is given out is called an exothermic reaction.

Exo- always means out, as in exit, and *thermo* (which comes from the Greek word for heat) always means to do with heat.

> A reaction which requires heat to make it happen is called an endothermic reaction.

SUMMARY

- A **chemical change** is one in which a new substance is formed. Such a change is often permanent or difficult to reverse. A **physical change** is one in which no new substance is formed; it often only involves a change of state.
- A reaction which gives out heat is called an **exothermic** reaction; one which takes in or needs heat is called an **endothermic** reaction.

QUESTIONS

Q. 19.1

Rewrite the following paragraph, and complete the spaces in it.

A __ change is one in which a new substance is is formed, whereas in a __ change, no __ __ is formed. There is usually a heat change when a __ change occurs. The melting of candle wax is a __ change, but when it burns, the change is __.

Experiment 19.2
More chemical reactions

safety glasses needed

1. Put some bluestone (copper sulphate crystals) in a test tube to a depth of about 1 cm. Heat them in a bunsen flame, gently at first, and then more strongly, until all of the blue colour has gone. Is this a physical or a chemical change? Set the tube aside and allow it to cool (continue with part 2 of the experiment).
2. Take some more bluestone crystals (a '**spatulaful**') and dissolve them in about half a test tube of water.
3. To the test tube, add a few cm³ of aqueous ammonia (ammonia dissolved in water). Describe what happens. Is the change physical or chemical?
4. To about 1 cm depth of washing soda crystals in a test tube, add a few cm³ of vinegar. Describe what happens. Is this change chemical or physical?
5. Take the test tube containing the powder from part 1 (it should have cooled by now), and add one or two cm³ of water from a dropper (see Figure 19.6). Place your hand around the tube. What do you notice? Did the reaction produce heat or require heat? What word describes this type of reaction?
6. Put some ammonium chloride in a test tube to a depth of about 2 cm. Place a thermometer in it and read its temperature. From a dropper, add about 1 cm³ of water and read the temperature again. Did the reaction give out heat or take in (use up) heat? What word describes this type of reaction?

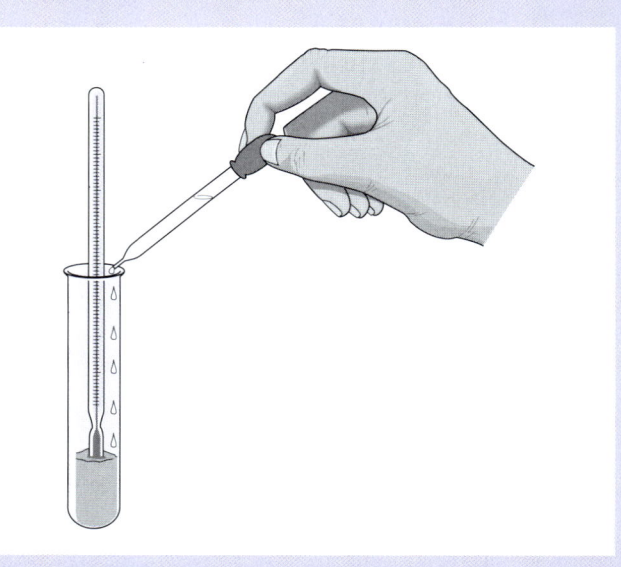

fig. 19.6 *Water being added to powder*

7. Rewrite the sentence and complete the spaces:

   an _____ reaction is one which produces or gives out heat, whereas one that uses up or takes in heat is called an _____ reaction.

Q. 19.2

Describe an experiment in which you caused (i) a chemical change, (ii) a physical change. For each experiment, describe the substance you started with, what you did to it, what happened, and what you had at the end. Explain how you decided whether the change was physical or chemical.

Q. 19.3

(i) Explain each of the following: chemical change, physical change, exothermic reaction, endothermic reaction.

(ii) Give an example to illustrate each explanation.

Q. 19.4

Consider each of the following changes and decide whether it is chemical or physical:

(a) dissolving sugar in water
(b) switching on an electric light
(c) blowing up a balloon
(d) burning toast
(e) boiling an egg
(f) an apple rotting
(g) freezing food
(h) making orange juice from oranges
(i) burning a match
(j) burning magnesium

fig. 19.7 Magnesium burning in oxygen is a chemical change. The light for the photograph comes only from the reaction.

Q. 19.5

State whether each of the following changes is physical or chemical:

(a) burning coal
(b) dissolving sugar in tea
(c) heating bluestone crystals
(d) melting lead
(e) baking bread
(f) milk turning sour
(g) drying clothes
(h) iron rusting
(i) perfume evaporating
(j) candle wax burning
(k) candle wax melting
(l) ripening a tomato

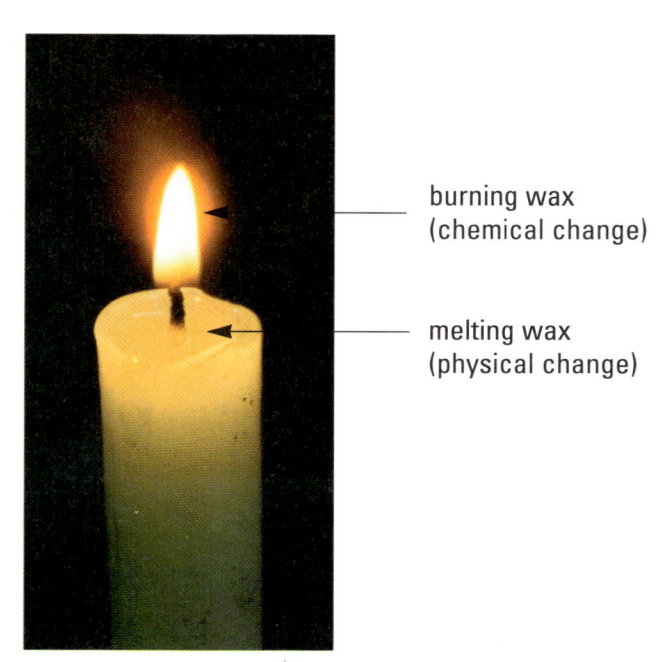

burning wax (chemical change)

melting wax (physical change)

fig. 19.8 A burning candle involves both a physical change (the melting of the wax) and a chemical change (the burning of the wax)

20
THE AIR AND OXYGEN

fig. 20.1 *The space shuttle leaving its launchpad at Cape Canaveral, Florida*

In Chapter 17 you learned that air is a substance which takes up space and has weight. In this chapter you are going to find out what air contains or what it consists of. The layer or 'ocean' of air which covers the Earth is called the **atmosphere**, but unlike the ocean of sea – which has a definite depth at any place, the atmosphere has no fixed height. It gradually becomes less dense or 'thinner' as one ascends. On the top of Mount Everest – the highest mountain in the world – the air is only one third as dense as it is at sea level. In the following few experiments, you can find out more about the composition of the air.

Experiment 20.1
To investigate burning

Part 1
Place a small lighted candle on a glass plate, and then cover it with a jar such as a bell jar. The candle soon goes out. Can you think why? Has all the air been used up? The next experiment will provide further information.

Part 2
Place a small candle either in a floating dish or supported above the level of the water in a trough or basin. Alternatively, a floating 'night light' is very suitable for the purpose. The water should not be too deep. Light the candle, place a bell jar over it, and put a stopper in the mouth of the bell jar.

As before, the candle soon goes out. If you now look at the water in the bell jar, you will see that it has risen. This is because some of the air has been used up. If a burning taper is now put into the space above the water in the jar, it is immediately extinguished (put out). The portion of the air which allows substances to burn in it is called **oxygen**.

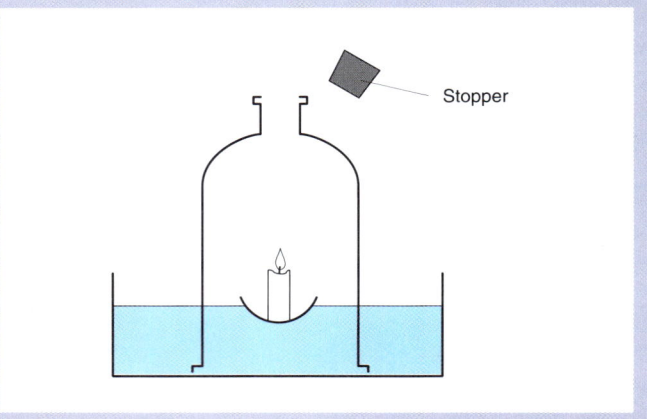

fig. 20.2

(Such a gas is said to **support combustion**). The gas left after the candle has gone out is mainly **nitrogen**, and this gas does not support combustion (i.e. substances will not burn in it). This experiment shows that air is a mixture, because it contains two substances with different properties.

Part 3

In this experiment you will learn that there is yet another gas in the air. Fill a large test tube with crushed ice, insert a stopper into its mouth, and then thoroughly dry the outside of the tube. If you examine it carefully after about two minutes, you will see that water has formed on the outside of the tube. There is **water vapour** in the air, and it condenses when it comes in contact with the cold surface of the outside of the tube. (Can you say why it cannot be coming from inside the tube?)Dew, which you find on the ground after a cold night, is formed the same way.

Part 4

This experiment shows that there is also a gas called **carbon dioxide** in the air. This is done by bubbling air through a liquid called **limewater** for a few minutes. Limewater is a clear liquid, and when carbon dioxide is bubbled through it, the limewater becomes 'milky'. The diagram shows a suitable apparatus for the experiment.

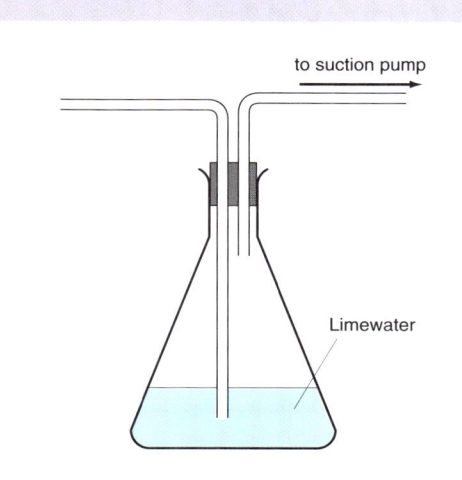

fig. 20.3

Finally, air contains a gas called argon, and tiny amounts of others which are very similar to it. They are helium, neon, krypton and xenon.

Experiment 20.2
To prepare and examine oxygen

safety glasses needed

Oxygen can be produced in the laboratory in several ways. The simplest is to react a black solid called **manganese dioxide** with a colourless liquid called **hydrogen peroxide**. The oxygen comes from the hydrogen peroxide and the purpose of the manganese dioxide is to speed up the reaction. The manganese dioxide is not used up in the reaction and it remains there at the end. This type of substance is called a **catalyst**.

A catalyst is a substance that speeds up a reaction without being consumed.

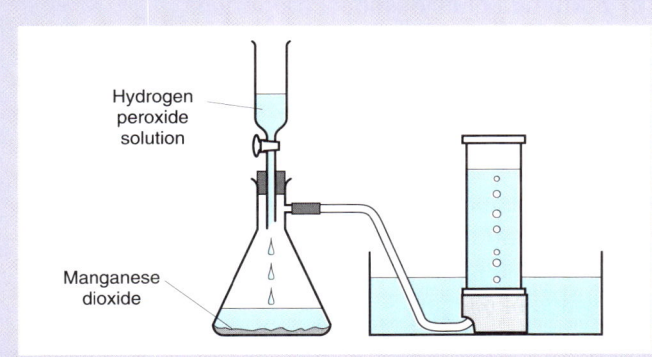

fig. 20.4

Set up an apparatus like that in Figure 20.4. Allow a few cm³ of hydrogen peroxide into the manganese dioxide; this will produce oxygen which will bubble up through the water in the trough. Place one of the collecting tubes (full of water and inverted) over the beehive shelf and let it fill with oxygen. When it is full, place a cork in it and remove it from the water. Collect three or four tubes of oxygen in the same way. Carry out the following tests:

(i) Note the colour and the smell of oxygen.
(ii) Apply a lighted match or splint to the gas; does it burn?
(iii) Light a wooden splint and then blow out the flame, leaving the splint 'glowing'. Insert this glowing splint into a tube of oxygen. Describe what happens.
(iv) Heat a piece of charcoal in a bunsen flame until it is glowing. Now insert it into a tube of oxygen. What happens? When the flame goes out, remove the charcoal and quickly pour in a few cm³ of lime water. Place a cork in the top of the tube and shake. What happens to the limewater?
(v) Place a piece of blue litmus paper in a tube of the gas. (Litmus is a dye which turns red in an acid.) Is oxygen acidic? Repeat the test with a piece of red litmus (Red litmus tells if an alkali – the opposite of an acid – is present.) Is oxygen alkaline?
(vi) Your teacher can show you what happens when burning magnesium is put into a jar of oxygen. It burns with a dazzling white flame, and changes to a white powder.

20 • The Air and Oxygen

Experiment 20.3
To measure the percentage of oxygen in the air

There are several different methods for measuring this value. The method described here makes use of an element called phosphorus. This element has a very high *affinity* (attraction) for oxygen and combines very fully with it when it burns. In this way it can take all of the oxygen out of a sample of air. **Phosphorus is a dangerous element** and this experiment must be done by your teacher.

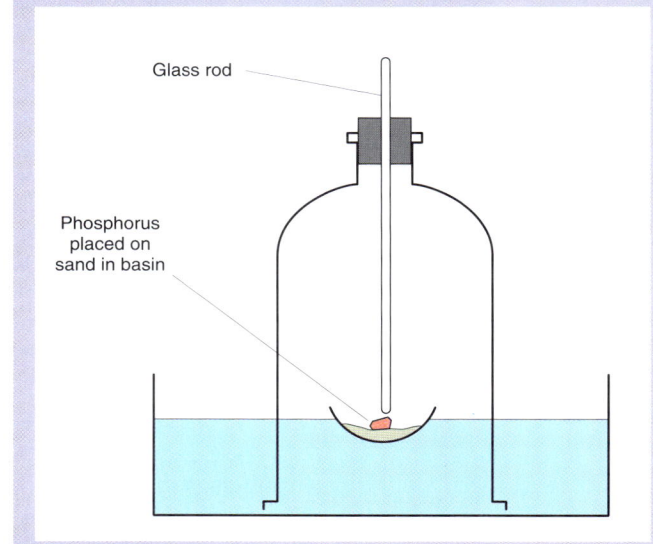

fig. 20.5

The apparatus is similar to that used for the burning candle, but instead of a candle, there is a piece of phosphorus placed on some sand in a dish, and there is a glass rod inserted through the stopper in the flask. Before the experiment, the water level is marked by stretching a rubber band around the outside of the jar. The phosphorus is then ignited by touching it with the end of the glass rod, which has been heated. The phosphorus burns and combines with the oxygen present. The white 'smoke' which is produced is the compound phosphorus oxide, formed when the oxygen combines with the phosphorus.

When all the burning has finished and the apparatus has cooled down, the new water level is marked with another rubber band. The apparatus is then dismantled (taken apart), and the bell jar turned upside down. Water is used to find the volume of the jar marked by the rubber bands. The jar is filled, in turn, to the level of each rubber band and each time the water is poured into a large graduated cylinder in order to find its volume. The volume of the air used up (the volume of the oxygen) is then worked out as a percentage of the total volume that was there at the start of the experiment.

Properties of oxygen

1. It is a colourless, odourless gas.
2. It is slightly soluble in water (fish breathe the dissolved oxygen in water).
3. It does not burn.
4. It supports combustion very well (this means that substances burn in it very well).
5. It relights a glowing splint (this is how you test for oxygen).
6. Elements burn well in oxygen forming compounds called **oxides**, e.g. magnesium burns to form magnesium oxide and carbon forms carbon dioxide.
7. Oxygen is essential for both burning and breathing.

QUESTIONS

Q. 20.1
In Experiment 20.3, the volume of air in the bell jar at the start was 1500 cm^3, and at the end it was 1200 cm^3.

(a) Calculate the actual volume of air used.
(b) Calculate the percentage of the starting volume of air which was used.
(c) What did the remaining 1200 cm^3 consist of?

Q. 20.2
Describe, using a diagram in each case, how you would show that air contains (i) a gas which does support combustion, and (ii) a gas which doesn't.

Q. 20.3
(a) What is a catalyst?
(b) Give an example of one.
(c) State two of its essential properties.
(d) Is oxygen a catalyst in the burning of magnesium?
(e) Explain your answer.

Q. 20.4
Describe, with the aid of a labelled diagram, an experiment in which oxygen is prepared and collected in the laboratory. List the properties of oxygen.

Composition of air

Very approximately, air is made up of one-fifth oxygen and four-fifths nitrogen. More exactly, the gases present, and their amounts, are:

Gas	Percentage
Nitrogen	78
Oxygen	21
Argon	1
Carbon dioxide	0.03
Other gases	0.002
Water vapour	very variable 0–4%

BURNING OR 'COMBUSTION'

You should now have learned that burning is the chemical combination (joining together of elements) of oxygen with the burning substance, and that if there is no oxygen present, a substance will not burn. Pure oxygen makes substances burn much better than they do in air, and where substances have to be burned where there is no air, a supply must be provided. The scientific name for burning is **combustion**; this is a chemical reaction in which a fuel combines with oxygen to produce heat and/or light energy. Look at the picture of the American Space Shuttle on page 140 which is about to send astronauts into space. At 'lift-off', it carries 1.5 million litres of liquid hydrogen fuel and over half a million litres of liquid oxygen to enable the fuel to burn.

In daily life, combustion of fuels in homes, factories and cars provide heat, electricity and transport. In the body, food undergoes a similar process; it combines with oxygen to release heat and other forms of energy.

BREATHING

Humans and other animals depend on oxygen for their existence, and in the absence of oxygen they die. When people go to places where there is little or no air, they must take a supply of oxygen with them. Cylinders of oxygen are an essential part of the equipment of teams of people who set out to climb high mountains or to go into space. Can you think of any other places where oxygen is required?

Exhaled (breathed out) air contains less oxygen and more carbon dioxide than inhaled (breathed in) air.

The composition of air before and after breathing is approximately:

Gas	Before	After*
Oxygen	21%	17%
Carbon dioxide	0.03%	4%
Nitrogen	79%	79%

Water vapour is also present in exhaled air.

USES OF OXYGEN

All the gases of the air, particularly oxygen, are very important in modern life, and they are produced in great quantities by firms such as BOC Gases which have factories in both Dublin and Cork.

The largest industrial use of oxygen is in the manufacture of steel, although this process is not

Experiment 20.4
To show that exhaled air contains more carbon dioxide than inhaled air

The apparatus is set up as shown. It contains limewater which is a clear liquid that turns 'milky' when carbon dioxide is added to it. When air is blown into tube T, it passes out through the limewater in flask B. But when T is sucked, air is taken in through flask A, which also contains limewater. In use, a person blows and sucks air through this apparatus. After about half a minute, the limewater in B has become milky, but the limewater in A only turns milky after about five minutes. Thus, there is much more carbon dioxide in exhaled air than in inhaled air.

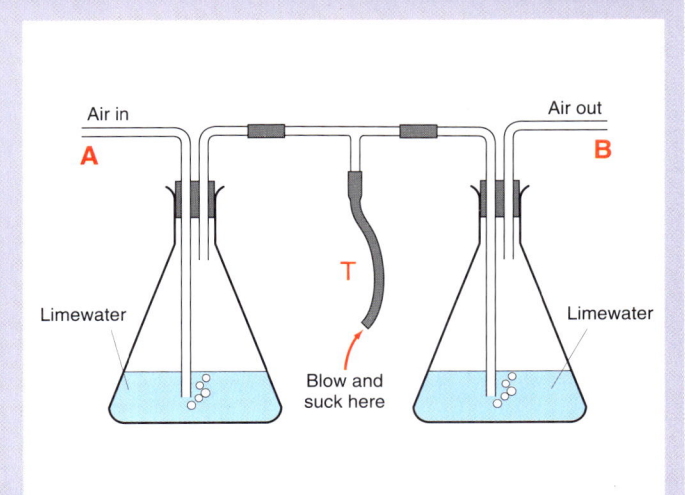

fig. 20.6

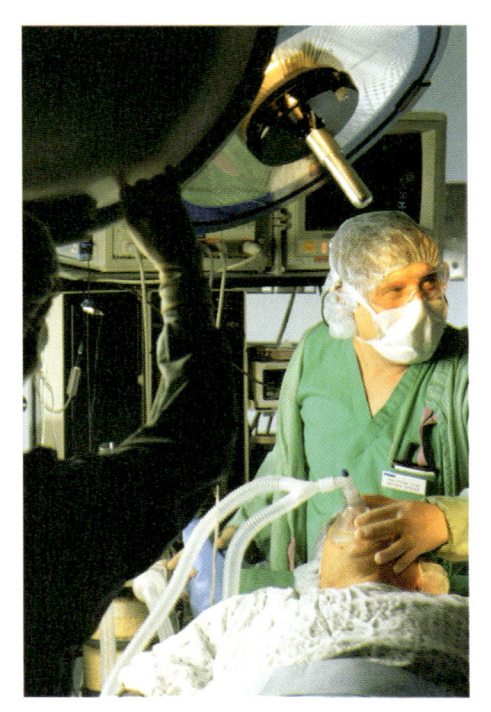

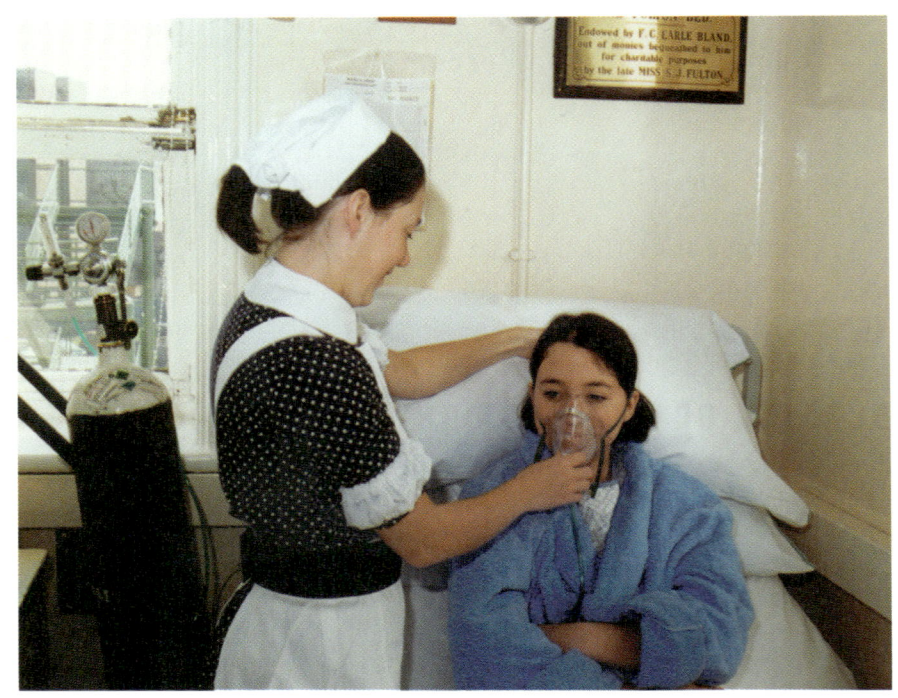

20 • The Air and Oxygen

Oxygen being used in hospital

A welder at work. To his right are cylinders of oxygen and acetylene.

Crew in an unpressurised high-flying aircraft wearing oxygen masks

Pouring molten steel during its manufacture. Oxygen is an essential element in steel production.

fig. 20.7 Uses of Oxygen

carried out in Ireland. A photograph in fig. 20.7 shows molten iron being poured into a steel making furnace. Oxygen will then be blown in to remove impurities.

Many of the uses of oxygen are connected with breathing. In hospitals, oxygen is given to babies and other patients who have breathing difficulties. Astronauts and underwater explorers require oxygen so it must be carried in spacecraft and submarines.

Where there is not enough air to breathe comfortably, such as on the tops of high mountains, oxygen must be carried by those who go there. Firefighters often carry oxygen too, when working in smoke-filled buildings. Jet aircraft always carry oxygen, so that if the cabin air system fails, it can be supplied to passengers and crew.

Oxygen is used to make flames hotter. Acetylene gas burning in oxygen (oxy-acetylene) can produce a flame as hot as 3000°C, and this is used for cutting and welding (joining by melting together) steel. Mixtures of oxygen with propane or butane are used for the same purpose.

The main use of nitrogen is in the manufacture of ammonia (a compound of nitrogen and hydrogen) which is used to make fertilisers and other nitrogen compounds. A number of uses of nitrogen depend on the fact that it is rather inert (chemically unreactive). It is used for filling light bulbs, and to provide an inert atmosphere during welding and also while filling aircraft fuel tanks. Liquid nitrogen was used to extinguish burning oil wells in Kuwait after the Gulf War. Liquid nitrogen is also used as a **coolant** (to provide very low temperatures) in the freezing of meat and other foods, and during the manufacture of some medical preparations.

The other gases too have their uses. Neon is used in advertising signs and also, along with argon and krypton, in special lights. Helium is a very light gas and is used in balloons. A mixture of helium and oxygen is used by deep-sea divers. Helium is used in preference to nitrogen because, at great depths, nitrogen can dissolve in the blood, causing a very unpleasant condition called the bends.

USES OF THE OTHER GASES OF THE AIR

(a) An airship rises because it is filled with **helium**, a gas which is lighter than air

(b) **Neon** is a gas, and is the essential element in advertising lights

(c) Liquid nitrogen being poured

(d) A 2000 watt cinema projection bulb contains xenon gas. The concave mirror behind the bulb reflects the light onto the film.

fig. 20.8

Experiment 20.5
To prepare and examine carbon dioxide

1. Set up the apparatus as shown.

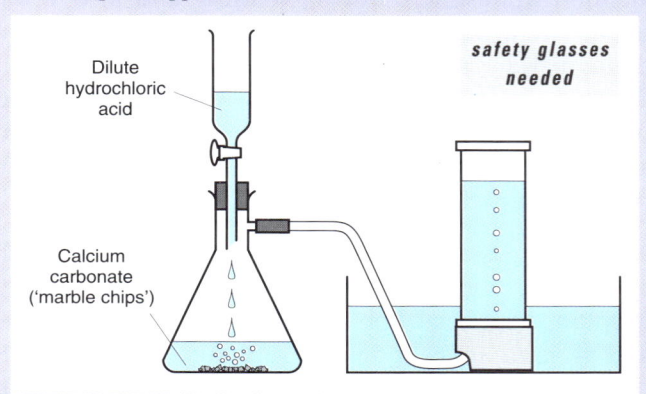

fig. 20.9

2. Add some acid to the test tube containing the sodium carbonate. This produces carbon dioxide, which bubbles up through the water in the trough.
3. Place one of the collecting tubes (full of water and inverted) over the beehive and let it fill with carbon dioxide.
4. When it is full, place a cork in it and remove it from the water. Collect three more tubes of gas in the same way.

Carry out the following tests.

(i) Note the colour and smell of the gas.
(ii) Apply a lighted match or splint to the gas; does it burn?
(iii) Light a wooden splint and then insert the burning splint into a tube of carbon dioxide. What happens?
(iv) Pour a few cm³ of limewater into a tube of the gas, cork the tube and shake. What happens?
(v) Place a piece of blue litmus paper into a tube of the gas (litmus is a dye which turns red in an acid). Is carbon dioxide acidic?
(vi) Repeat the test with a piece of red litmus (red litmus turns blue in an alkali which is the opposite of an acid). Is carbon dioxide alkaline?

CARBON AND CARBON DIOXIDE

Carbon is a very important element in life. Nearly all fuels contain carbon, and all living things are made of compounds of carbon. Carbon dioxide is formed whenever carbon, or any compound containing it, is burned. In the laboratory, carbon dioxide is prepared by reacting dilute **hydrochloric acid** with **sodium carbonate** (or calcium carbonate, which is often called marble chips).

Properties of carbon dioxide

1. It is a colourless, odourless gas.
2. It is slightly soluble in water.
3. It is heavier or more dense than air.
4. It does not burn.
5. It does not support combustion (i.e. substances do not burn in it.)
6. It turns limewater milky.
7. It forms an acid when it is dissolved in water.

Uses of carbon dioxide

fig. 20.10 *'Smoke' from dry ice being poured*

Carbon dioxide has several important uses:

- **Fizzy Drinks.** The sharp 'tingling' taste of drinks like coke and lemonade is due to dissolved carbon dioxide. The gas is dissolved under pressure, as this increases its solubility (and is also the reason why, when a can or bottle of drink is opened, that bubbles of gas start to escape (see Figure 17.2).

- **Fire Extinguishers.** Carbon dioxide is suitable for this purpose for two reasons: (i) it does not support combustion, and (ii) it is denser than air. It forms a layer around the burning material and this keeps out oxygen (see Figure 21.10).

- **Special Stage Effects.** It is used to create mist or smoke effects. When solid carbon dioxide (*dry ice*) is put into hot water, the solid sublimes and produces thick clouds of harmless 'smoke'. Because it is denser than air, it stays close to the floor.

- **Refrigerants.** It is used for cooling, and keeping cool, ice cream, meat and soft fruits. It is used for this purpose because it is colder than ice, and as it warms up, it sublimes rather than forming a liquid which might damage the material being cooled.

SUMMARY

- Air is a mixture, and consists of approximately one fifth oxygen and four fifths nitrogen. Oxygen is the element which supports burning and breathing, whereas nitrogen is a rather inactive element. Also contained in air are small amounts of carbon dioxide, water vapour and argon. The percentage of oxygen in the air can be found by burning phosphorus in an enclosed volume of air and measuring the volume used up.

- Oxygen is prepared by reacting **hydrogen peroxide** with **manganese dioxide**. The oxygen comes from the hydrogen peroxide and the function of the manganese dioxide is to speed up the reaction; such a substance is called a catalyst.

- Oxygen is a colourless, odourless, gas, and is slightly soluble in water. It does not burn, but readily supports combustion (allows things to burn in it). The simple test for oxygen is that it relights a glowing splint. Most uses of oxygen are associated with breathing and making things burn better.

- **Burning** (or **combustion**) is the combining of a substance with oxygen. When an element burns, an oxide of the element is formed. An oxide is a compound of an element with oxygen.

- **Carbon dioxide** is prepared by reacting dilute **hydrochloric acid** with **sodium carbonate** or calcium carbonate. Carbon dioxide is a colourless, odourless gas, and is slightly soluble in water. It does not burn and does not support combustion. The simple test for carbon dioxide is that it turns limewater milky. It is used in fizzy drinks and in fire extinguishers.

QUESTIONS

Q. 20.6
It is possible to make zinc oxide from zinc. Suggest how you could do this. Is zinc oxide an element, a compound or a mixture? Is it composed of atoms or of molecules?

Q. 20.7
What reaction is used to test for the gas carbon dioxide? Describe how you would show that air contains carbon dioxide.

Q. 20.8
A solid element X, when burned in a jar of gas Y, formed a gas Z which turned limewater milky. Identify X, Y and Z, and describe the appearance of each.

Q. 20.9
Why must space rockets carry a supply of oxygen? Why is it always liquid oxygen?

Q. 20.10
A solid substance, A, reacts with an acid, B, to produce a gas, C, which turns the liquid D milky. The gas C is a compound which contains the elements E and F.
Identify substances A to F.

fig. 20.11 Joseph Priestly

The Rev. Joseph Priestly (1733–1804) is regarded as the discoverer of oxygen. Although trained for the church, he had a great interest in science from an early age. There was a brewery next door to his home in Leeds, and there he had access to chemical apparatus and supplies of carbon dioxide. He discovered that a solution of carbon dioxide in water was pleasant to drink, and so discovered soda water. He was the first to prepare many common gases including ammonia, nitrous oxide (laughing gas), and sulphur dioxide. His most famous experiment was that in which he heated 'red calx of mercury' (mercury oxide) using a burning glass (a convex lens), and he discovered that a gas was given off which made a candle burn with a 'remarkable vigorous flame', and which made a mouse very lively when placed in it. He had discovered oxygen, although he gave it the name 'pure air'. Priestly travelled around Europe and was friendly with other scientists such as Lavoisier, Watt and Franklin.

21

FUELS AND FIRE

fig. 21.1 A fire-eater

A fuel is a substance that burns easily in air to produce heat energy.

The commonest and most abundant fuels are the fossil fuels. These are the ones that have been produced by the decay of plants and animals that lived millions of years ago, and they include coal, oil (and oil products like petrol), and natural gas (see page 19).

Fossil fuels contain carbon and hydrogen. When they burn, the carbon present forms carbon dioxide and the hydrogen present forms water (vapour). Nearly all fuels cause some pollution when they are burnt. Owing to tiny amounts of sulphur in both coal and oil, these fuels produce some sulphur dioxide when they burn, and sulphur dioxide is one of the causes of acid rain.

A good fuel must be easy to ignite, but not so flammable that there would be a high risk of fire or explosions. There are solid fuels (coal, peat, charcoal), liquid fuels (oil, petrol, alcohol) and gaseous fuels (natural gas, bottled gas, hydrogen). There is no 'best fuel'. Different fuels are best for different jobs; one is very suitable for one job but not for another.

- **Coal** is the most plentiful of the fossil fuels. It is relatively cheap and is suitable for burning in power stations and in home fireplaces. However, it is bulky to store and would not be convenient for use in a central heating boiler or for powering a car or an aircraft. As well, it produces some undesirable pollutants. There is very little coal mined in Ireland.

fig. 21.2 The peat burning power station at Rhode, Co. Offaly. The peat bogs are to the left hand side of the picture

- **Peat** comes from peat bogs. In Ireland there are about 80 000 hectares of bogland, much of which is worked for the peat. 'Milled' peat is the fuel that is used in power stations in the Midlands for generating electricity. For domestic use, peat briquettes are available. These are made from compressed peat; they are light and burn easily but do not give out as much heat as coal.

- **Natural gas** (methane, CH_4) is convenient for industrial and home central-heating boilers but could not easily be stored in cars. It is one of the cleanest fuels because it is almost completely converted to carbon dioxide and water when it burns. The Kinsale gas field off the south coast is one of the important sources of energy in this country.

- **Bottled gas** is mainly propane (C_3H_8) or butane (C_4H_{10}). It is useful where there are no supplies of natural gas, and as well, large quantities of it can be compressed and stored in steel cylinders.

- **Petroleum** or *crude oil* comes from oil fields in places such as the North Sea, USA and the Middle East. It is the source of many fuels such as petrol (for cars), heating oils (for homes and factories), kerosene (for aircraft), and fuel oil (for trains and ships).

fig. 21.3 *This is an oil production platform, which takes oil out of the ground under the sea. On the right is a helicopter landing pad. The high structure near the left is the drilling tower. The platform's legs stand on the sea bed.*

- **Petrol** is suitable for use in cars because it is volatile (it evaporates easily) and a small volume of it contains a lot of energy. However, it would be too dangerous for use in home heating systems.
- **Heating oil** is suitable for burning in homes and factories because it is relatively cheap and it burns well in small boilers, but is not as dangerous as petrol.
- **Charcoal** (mainly pure carbon) is suitable for barbecues because it smoulders slowly and doesn't produce smoke. It would be useless on an open fire.
- **Food as a 'fuel'** Animals, like machines, need energy to keep them working. 'Animal fuel' or food, releases its energy when it is consumed in the body. Respiration is the name of the process in which food combines with oxygen in the body, releasing energy as it does so (see Chapter 32).

FIRE AND THE FIRE TRIANGLE

Burning or *combustion* is a rapid chemical reaction. During combustion, something burnable (a fuel), reacts with oxygen from the air, and gives out heat. Three things are required for burning to take place: fuel, oxygen (air) and heat. The **fire triangle** is a way of illustrating this.

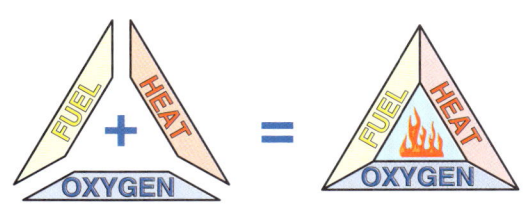

fig. 21.4 *The fire triangle*

Combustion reactions are an essential part of our world; the combustion or burning of coal, gas, petrol and oil produces the heat necessary to cook food, run factories, heat homes and provide transport. However, accidents can cause combustion to get out of control and this can be dangerous as buildings, cars and forests can be totally destroyed in this way.

fig. 21.5 *A burning building*

Every year property is destroyed and people are killed as a result of fire – many of which occur in homes. Fires in homes have been caused by matches, cigarettes, candles, Christmas tree lights, open fires, oil heaters, electric devices with damaged or frayed flexes, chip pans and deep fat fryers.

Fires can be extinguished (put out) by removing any one of the three things in the fire triangle, and there are different ways of doing this. So, to put out a fire, you can:

- remove the fuel, by turning off the gas or electricity, or by covering puddles of oil with sand or soil;
- remove the heat, by cooling the burning item with water (however, **water should not be used on electrical fires** since water can conduct electricity, nor should it be used on oil fires since oil floats on water and could spread the fire even further);
- remove the air supply, by covering the burning item with foam, carbon dioxide or a fire-blanket.

21 • Fuels and Fire

In a burning building it is not practical to remove either the fuel (the building itself) or the air. The only method is therefore to remove the heat. This is done by spraying water from high-pressure hoses onto the fire so that heat is taken away, and the fire is unable to continue.

In a forest fire, fuel (trees) is removed by creating a fire break; this means cutting down trees from a strip of ground ahead of the path of the fire so that the fire cannot spread further.

fig. 21.6 *A fire break in a state forest*

A burning chip-pan is best extinguished by covering it with a tightly-fitting lid or a wet towel or a heavy breadboard; this cuts off the air supply so that the fire will go out. It is important to leave the cover there long enough so that it will cool sufficiently and the fire will not start again when it is removed.

FIRE EXTINGUISHERS

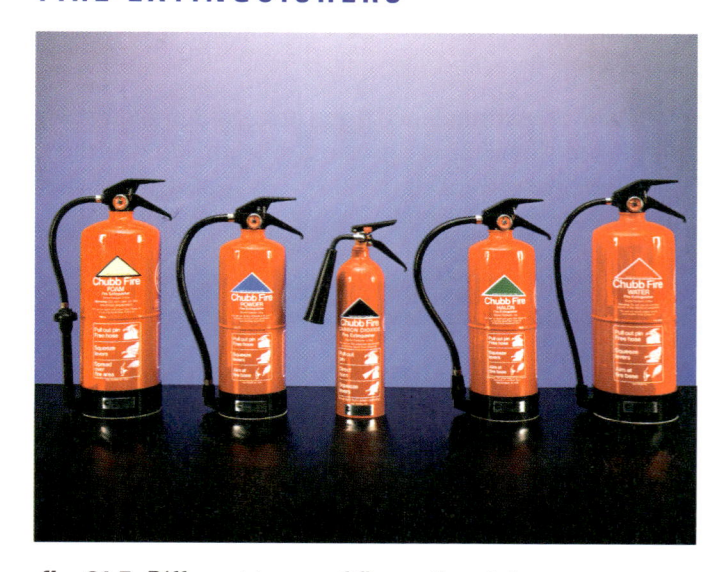

fig. 21.7 *Different types of fire extinguisher*

There are different types of fire extinguisher. A common type contains water that is forced out by pressurised gas when the extinguisher is operated. Figure 21.8 shows the inside of one of these, while fig. 21.9 shows a laboratory model of a water-filled extinguisher which illustrates how the real thing works. This type is suitable for extinguishing ordinary domestic material like curtains and carpets, furniture, waste paper baskets and plastics.

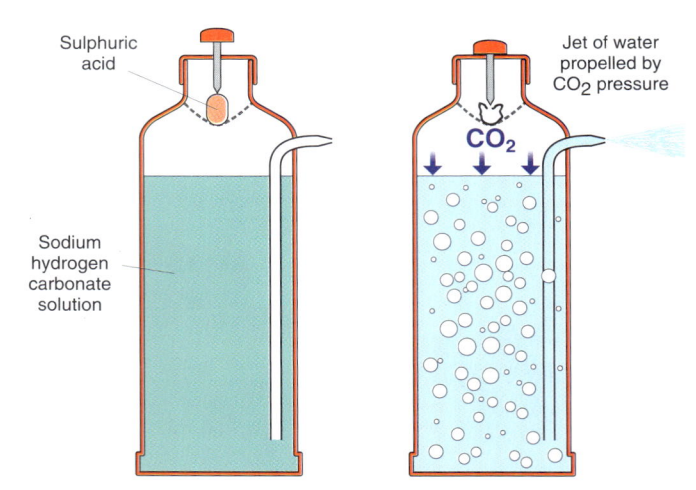

fig. 21.8 *When the plunger at the top of the extinguisher is pressed, the bottle of acid is broken. This reacts with the carbonate solution, producing carbon dioxide gas, which forces the water out of the container.*

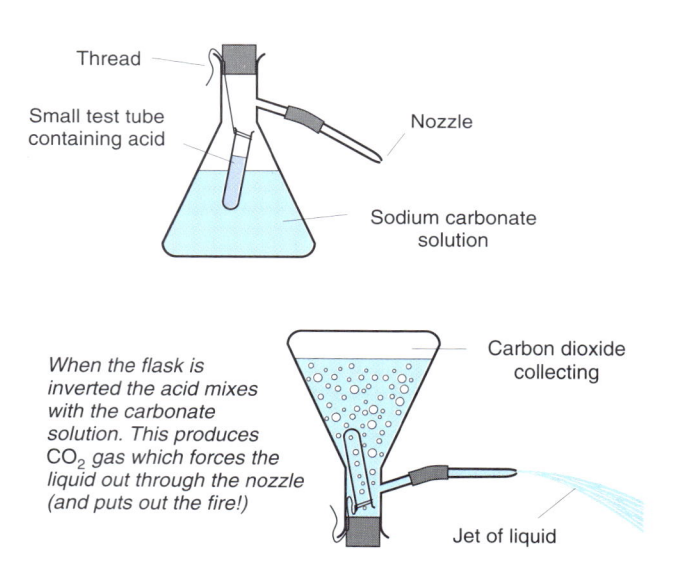

fig. 21.9 *Laboratory model of a fire extinguisher*

Another common type of extinguisher is the CO_2 (carbon dioxide) type. This contains carbon dioxide gas under high pressure. When the handle is pressed, the outlet value is opened, and the gas is forced out. CO_2 extinguishers are very suitable for electrical fires.

fig. 21.10 A carbon dioxide extinguisher in use

Another of the extinguishers illustrated in Figure 21.7 is a foam extinguisher. This contains carbon dioxide and a foaming agent like washing-up liquid. When the extinguisher is operated, it shoots out carbon dioxide foam, which blankets the fire, cutting off the oxygen supply. This type is very suitable for oil and petrol fires.

Never try to put out a petrol fire, a chip-pan fire or an electrical fire with water.

SUMMARY

A **fuel** is a substance which burns easily in air to produce heat energy. Most of the common fuels are the fossil fuels and include, coal, oil, gas. Three things are needed for burning ('combustion') or for fire to occur: fuel, oxygen and heat. Extinguishing a fire involves removing one of these things. There are different types of fire extinguisher, for the different types of fire.

QUESTIONS

Q. 21.1

Rewrite and complete the spaces in the following paragraph.

A fuel is a substance that __ in air to produce __. Fossil fuels contain the elements __ and __. When they burn they form __ __ gas and __ vapour. Fossil fuels are __ renewable forms of energy because it took them __ of years to form. An example of a solid fossil fuel is __, a liquid one is __ and one that is gaseous is __.

Q. 21.2

(a) What is a fossil fuel?
(b) Name two solid fuels, two liquid fuels and two gaseous ones.
(c) Why does the burning of fossil fuels cause pollution?

Q. 21.3

Suggest, using the fire triangle, the best method of putting out the following fires:

(a) a person with a burning coat
(b) a fire in a waste bin
(c) a car engine on fire
(d) a smouldering television set
(e) a chip pan fire
(f) a child whose pyjamas are on fire

Q. 21.4

What type of fire extinguisher is suitable for putting out each of the following:

(a) burning oil
(b) a bonfire that has got out of control
(c) a smouldering television set

Q. 21.5

(a) What is a fuel?
(b) What fuel consists of methane?
(c) What compounds are contained in bottled gas?
(d) What fuels are made from petroleum?
(e) What element present in fossil fuels is a main cause of atmospheric pollution?
(f) What compound is formed when the element mentioned in (e) is burned?

Q. 21.6

List four precautions that can be taken in homes to prevent accidental fires.

22
WATER

fig. 22.1 Every second, six million litres of water flow over the Niagara Falls in North America

Water is the most common and most essential chemical compound on Earth. Because it is such a common chemical, few people think much about it. For most, it is a substance that comes out of the tap as it is needed, for drinking, cleaning, washing or cooking, or for swimming or fishing in, or for sailing on. About 80% of the Earth's surface is covered with water and about two-thirds of the human body consists of water.

USES OF WATER

Water is essential for life. The availability of a supply of clean water has, from ancient times, decided which parts of the Earth were suitable for human habitation. As well as the water which is used for drinking, washing and cooking, an enormous quantity of it is used in the manufacture of most of the things which you use. Much water is used in factories for washing and cooling purposes.

- LAVATORY
- WASHING & BATHS
- LAUNDRY
- DISHWASHING
- COOKING
- GARDENING
- WASTE

fig. 22.2 The water you use each day

WHAT IS WATER?

Water is a compound of hydrogen and oxygen. This can be shown in several ways. If you burn hydrogen (burning = combining with oxygen), water is formed. Alternatively, water can be split up (separated) into its elements, and when this is done, hydrogen and oxygen are formed.

For thousands of years however, it was thought that water was an element and it was only in the 18th century that a famous scientist, Henry Cavendish, carried out an experiment which showed that it is a compound containing hydrogen and oxygen.

ELECTROLYSIS

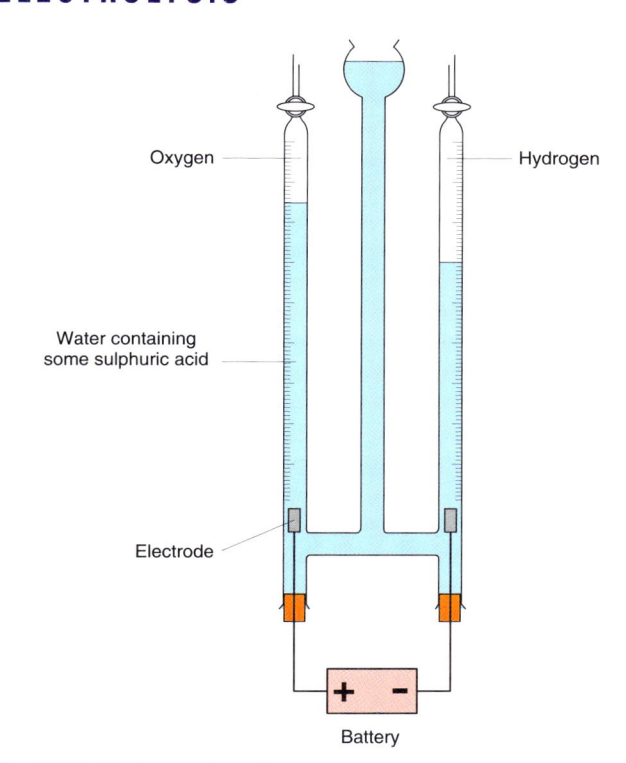

fig. 22.3 Hofmann's voltameter

An easy way to separate water into its elements is to pass an electric current through it. Figure 22.3 shows a piece of apparatus called **Hofmann's voltameter** that was designed for the purpose by a German chemist called Hofmann. It is filled with water and there are wires going into and out of it. These wires which carry the electricity into the water and out of it are called **electrodes**. The positive electrode (that connected to the + terminal of the battery) is called the **anode**, and the negative electrode is called the **cathode**. Water does not conduct electricity very well on its own and when the apparatus is used, a small amount of either sodium sulphate or dilute acid is added to the water as a catalyst. The splitting up of a compound by means of electricity is called **electrolysis**.

Experiment 22.1
Electrolysis of water

1. Set up the apparatus as shown. Add a few grams (a level 'teaspoonful') of sodium sulphate (or potassium nitrate) or 5 to 10 cm^3 of dilute sulphuric acid.

2. Note that the test tubes are full of water at the start, and that they are not resting on the bottom; there must be a gap between the bottom of the test tube and the electrode, so that electric current can flow.

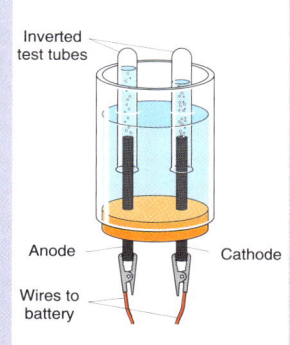

fig. 22.4

3. Connect the electrodes to a battery or to a power supply. Bubbles of gas should be produced at each electrode. Hydrogen is released at the negative electrode (or cathode) and oxygen appears at the positive electrode (or anode). Are equal volumes of hydrogen and oxygen produced? Try and estimate the ratio in which the gases are formed.

4. Collect a test tube of each gas. Put a cork in each of the tubes before removing it from the water.

5. **Testing for hydrogen**
   The test for hydrogen is that it burns with a 'pop'. Hold the tube of hydrogen upside down, remove the cork, and apply a lighted match or splint to the mouth of the tube. What happens?

6. **Testing for oxygen**
   The test for oxygen is that it relights a glowing splint. Light a wooden splint, blow out the flame, remove the cork from the tube of oxygen and insert the glowing splint into the tube. What happens?

This question is about the electrolysis of water.

(a) What colour is hydrogen?
(b) What colour is oxygen?
(c) In what ratio (by volume) are the hydrogen and oxygen produced?
(d) Explain why this is so.
(e) Why are you told to hold the tube of hydrogen upside down before lighting it?
(f) Why is this not necessary for oxygen?
(g) What name describes the splitting of a compound into its elements by passing electricity through it?
(h) What is meant by the term anode?
(i) What term has the opposite meaning?
(j) What is the characteristic test for oxygen?

SURFACE TENSION

Water has an unusual property called **surface tension** that is not shown by other liquids.

Experiment 22.2
To investigate surface tension

Part 1

Dip an inverted filter funnel into strong soap or detergent (washing up liquid) solution so that a film of liquid forms across its opening. Lift the funnel out of the solution and watch the film rising upwards. How is the **area** of the soap film changing as it does this?

Part 2

Into the same strong soap or detergent solution, dip a wire frame like that shown. When you remove it, there should be a soap film inside it. If there is not, try again. Very gently, lay a small loop of thread on this soap film (this requires a lot of patience and you may have to try several times).

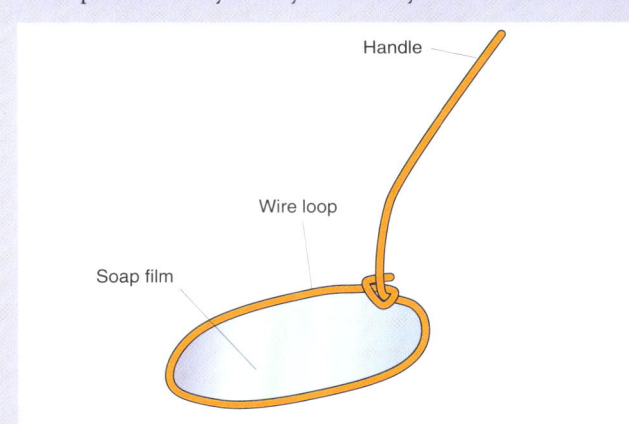

fig. 22.5

Now puncture the film inside the thread loop. What shape does the thread loop become? How does the area **inside** the loop change when you puncture the film? How does the area of the soap film (**outside** the loop) change when you puncture the film?

Think about the results of experiments 1 and 2, and answer the question: how does the area of a liquid surface try to change if it is allowed to?

Part 3

Drop a razor blade or an aluminium disc very carefully on to the surface of water in a trough or basin so that it floats. If you cannot make it float, place it on a small piece of filter paper floating on the water, and then **very gently** sink the paper using a pencil point. A razor blade is made of steel, and both steel and aluminium are more dense than water. Would you expect steel or aluminium to float or to sink in water?

In experiments 22.1 and 22.2, did you discover that the surface area of the water film tries to become as small as possible? If you did, you were correct. This is because there is a force pulling surface molecules inwards. The force is called **surface tension** and it causes water to behave as if it had a sort of an invisible 'skin' on its surface. For this reason, a razor blade can be made to float on water, and insects called pond skaters can walk on water.

fig. 22.6 Surface tension

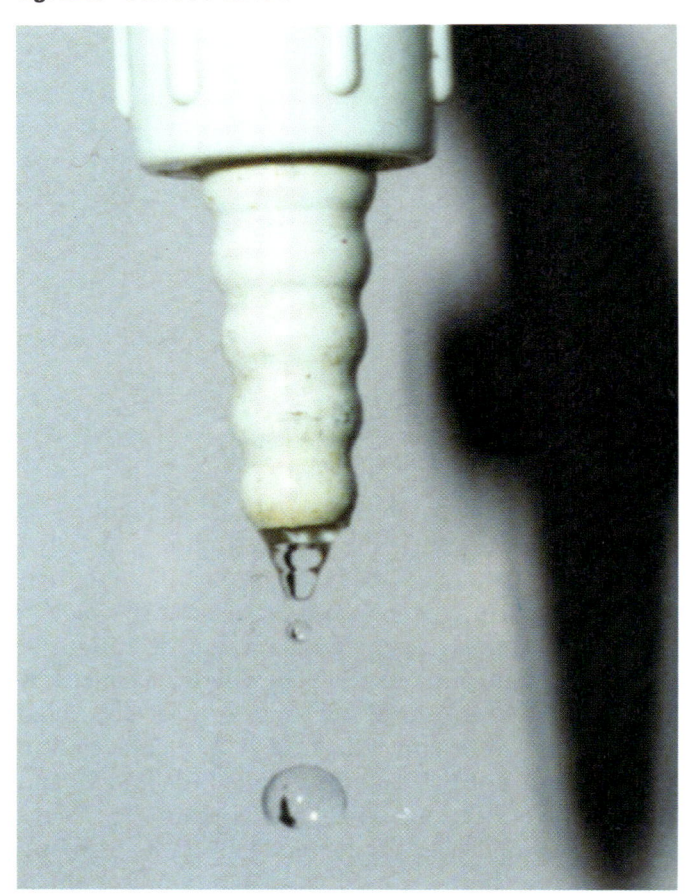

fig. 22.7 A drop of water that has just left the tap. It is spherical because this is the shape that has the smallest surface area for a given volume.

CAPILLARITY OR CAPILLARY ACTION

The word *capillary* means hair-like. A capillary tube is a tube with a very fine hole (called the *bore*) through it.

Experiment 22.3
To investigate capillarity

1. Place one end of a piece of narrow glass tubing in coloured water. Notice that the water rises a small distance up the tube. The water rises because of attraction between water molecules and glass. This effect is called capillarity or capillary action.
2. Repeat with other glass tubes of different diameters. Notice that the narrower the bore of the tube, the higher the water rises.
3. Carry out the experiment that is illustrated in the diagram. Explain why the water rises more at one end that at the other.

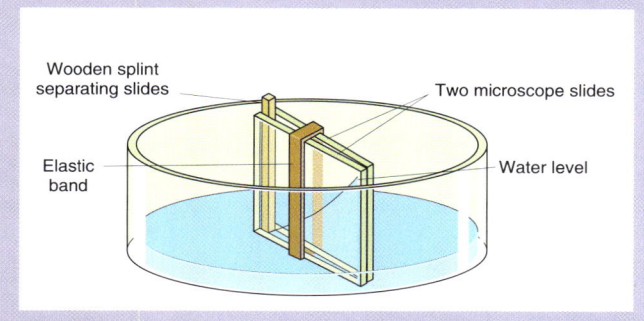

fig. 22.8

4. Hold a strip of filter paper or blotting paper with its end just dipping into the water. Observe what happens.

The action of blotting paper, wiping-up cloths, the rising of water up plant stems, and oil up the wicks in oil lamps, is due to capillary action. Water can also travel through bricks and concrete by capillary action and cause dampness to rise up through the walls of a house. Because of this, builders insert a layer of plastic (called a damp course) between the walls and the foundations of a house.

QUESTIONS

Q. 22.1
(a) What is a meniscus?
(b) From what you discovered in the experiment, explain why a meniscus is the shape that it is.
(c) What happens when a narrow glass tube is dipped in water? What would be the effect of using an even narrower tube?
(d) Mention two practical effects of capillary attraction.

PROPERTIES OF WATER

1. **Freezing point**
   When water is cooled to 0°C, it begins to freeze and form ice. 0°C is the freezing point of water. When ice melts, the reverse happens: when the cold ice reaches a temperature of 0°C, it starts to melt and form water. 0°C is thus also the melting point of ice.

2. **Boiling point**
   When water is heated to 100°C, it forms water vapour or steam. 100°C is thus the boiling point of water. Steam occupies very much more space than the water from which it came, and this is why steam can push up the lid of a kettle or saucepan, and why a steam engine works. A model steam engine is shown on page 15 in Chapter 3.

   ice ⇌ 0°C water ⇌ 100°C steam

3. **Water is a good solvent**
   Water is very good at dissolving substances and is described as being a good solvent (see Chapter 18). Many drinks (coffee, tea, orange squash, cola, beer, etc.) are solutions of substances in water. The sea is salty because the water from rivers carry into it different salts from the rocks and earth they pass through. The manufacturing industry depends on the solvent powers of water for making up solutions and for washing equipment. A solution of a substance in water is called an **aqueous** solution (aqua = water).

4. **The density of water is 1 g per cm^3** (Chapter 7).

5. **Water expands as it freezes** – which means that ice is less dense than water – which is why ice floats on water (see Chapter 10, page 66)

6. **Water is transparent**, so sunlight can pass into the water of rivers and allow plankton and water plants to photosynthesise and grow.

7. **Water has a high surface tension**.

8. **Water shows capillary action**

TESTING FOR WATER

When white anhydrous copper sulphate has water added to it, it turns blue. Another method of testing for water is to add some (dry) cobalt chloride paper. This paper is blue and it turns pink when water is added.

fig. 22.9

However, any liquid which contains water (e.g. milk) will make these tests work. In order to test for pure water (water with nothing else present), it is necessary to measure its freezing and boiling points – which should be 0°C and 100°C respectively.

THE WATER CYCLE

Where does water come from, and where does it go? Why does the atmosphere never run out of water? Where do clouds come from? How can rivers constantly pour water into the sea and yet the sea does not 'fill up'? The answers to all of these questions are explained by the water cycle.

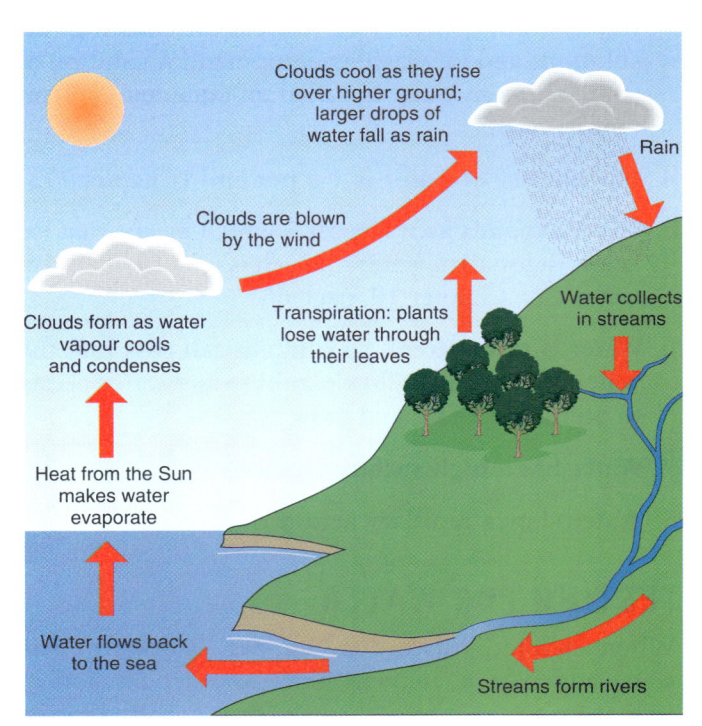

fig. 22.10 *The water cycle, showing evaporation, cloud formation, precipitation and run-off*

From the oceans, lakes and rivers, water evaporates. The water vapour rises into the atmosphere and when it cools, clouds are formed. Clouds consist of very tiny droplets of water – too small to fall. When clouds are cooled, larger drops are formed, which then fall to earth as rain (or snow). Rain water trickles through soil and porous rocks and forms rivers, which form lakes or run into the sea. This chain of water movement is called the **water cycle**.

WATER PURIFICATION

The availability of clean and safe drinking water is one of the necessities for a healthy life. It is a sad fact that in many countries of the world, people have to drink unclean water. Providing safe water is one of the tasks of the various county councils around the country.

fig. 22.11 *In many countries of the world, people have to walk long distances to collect water for use in their homes*

Most Irish water supplies come from rivers and lakes. Before it can be used for drinking, it has to be purified, and this is what happens at water treatment plants. Before being treated the water is often collected and stored in a reservoir. There are a number of stages in the treatment process, and they are usually as follows:

1. The water first passes through **screens** to remove floating and loose material such as leaves, twigs and gravel.

2. The water is then left in settling tanks for some time; in these, most of the solid matter in the water settles to the bottom. This process is called **sedimentation**.

3. The water is **filtered** through large filter beds of sand. Filtration removes any remaining solid matter from the water and leaves it clean looking. However, even though it now looks clean, it may still contain bacteria which could cause disease.

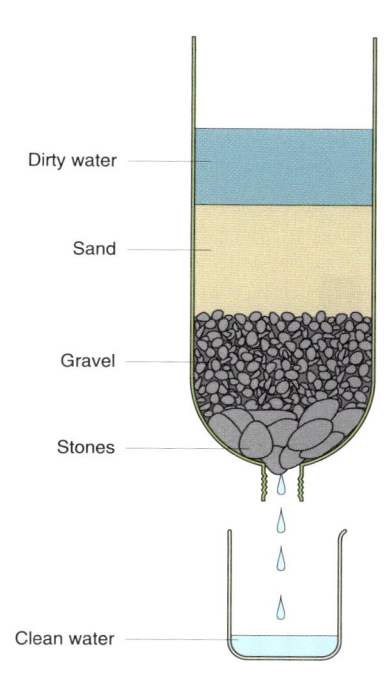

fig. 22.12 A model sand filter in a lemonade bottle

fig. 22.13 Sand filters at a water treatment plant

4. The clean water from the filters is then sterilised (made safe to drink) by adding **chlorine**. In the last century, horrible water-borne diseases such as cholera and typhoid were quite common, because water supplies were not purified. Chlorine kills the bacteria that cause such diseases. These diseases are still common in some under-developed countries of the world.

5. A **fluorine** compound is then added. The presence of a fluorine compound reduces tooth decay in growing teeth. Some toothpastes contain fluoride for the same reason.

6. The water then flows or is pumped through a network of underground pipes to homes, schools and factories.

SUMMARY

- Water is a compound of hydrogen and oxygen. This can be shown by the electrolysis of water, in which the water is decomposed into hydrogen and oxygen, in a ratio of 2:1 (by volume), because the formula of water is H_2O.

- The freezing and boiling points of water are 0°C and 100°C. Water has a high surface tension, and can behave as if it has a skin on its surface. Water shows capillary attraction. Water is a very good solvent.

- Water can be tested for by using either anhydrous copper sulphate or cobalt chloride paper.

- In the water cycle, water evaporates and forms clouds, which become cooled and condense, and then falls back to earth as rain.

- Water purification involves removal of loose debris, then settlement to remove suspended matter, filtration, chlorination and fluoridation.

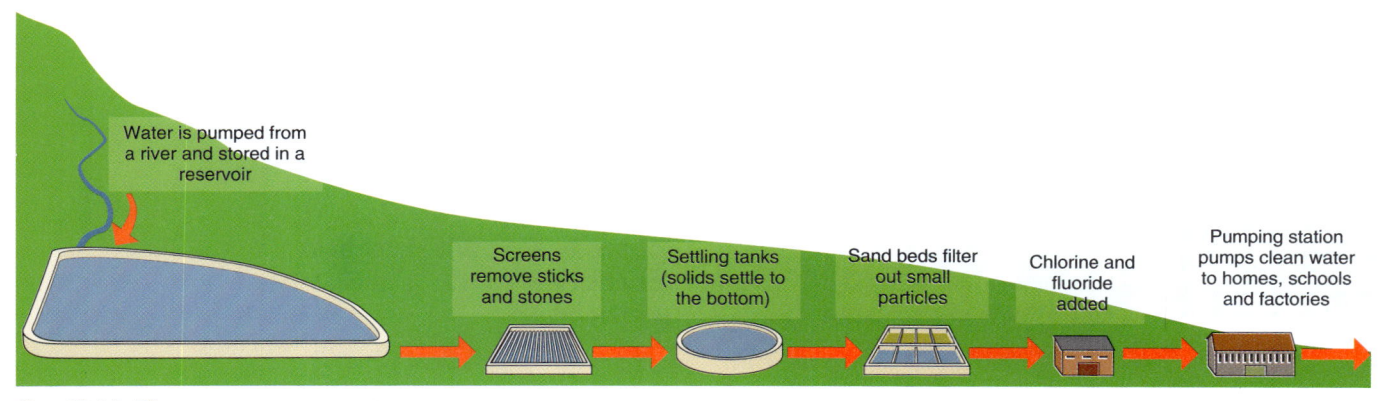

fig. 22.14 The water treatment process

QUESTIONS

Q. 22.2
Copy out and complete the spaces in the following paragraphs.

(a) Water is a compound of ___ and ___. This can be shown by passing a current of ___ through water contained in a vessel called a ___. This process is called ___, and when it is done, the water is ___ into ___ and ___.

(b) A compound can be split up into its elements by passing a current of ___ through it. This process is called ___. When water is ___, the elements ___ and ___ are formed. Water is therefore a ___ which contains these two elements. Water does not conduct electricity very well, and in the experiment some ___ is added to help ___.

Q. 22.3
In a water treatment plant, what is the purpose of (i) the screens, (ii) the filter beds, (iii) the reservoir? Why are (iv) chlorine and (v) a fluorine compound added?

Q. 22.4
What property of water is responsible for each of the following:

(a) salt 'disappearing' when stirred into water
(b) water being separated into hydrogen and oxygen
(c) small insects being able to walk on water
(d) the soaking up of water into filter paper or blotting paper
(e) an aluminium disc floating on water
(f) moisture rising up a plant stem
(g) ice being formed when water is cooled below 0°C
(h) steam being formed when water is heated to 100°C
(i) 100 grams of water occupies 100 cm^3
(j) water pipes can burst in winter

Q. 22.5
Describe an experiment in which water was electrolysed. Include a labelled diagram, and state what the experiment showed.

Q. 22.6
(a) What is meant by capillarity?
(b) Describe an experiment in which this property of water was illustrated.
(c) Mention two everyday effects of capillarity.

Q. 22.7
(a) What is meant by surface tension?
(b) Describe an experiment which illustrated this property of water.
(c) Explain why the hairs of the paint brush shown in Figure 22.15 stick together when the brush is taken out of water.

fig. 22.15

Q. 22.8
(a) What is meant by the water cycle?
(b) Describe two practical uses of this natural cycle.
(c) What source of energy makes it happen?

Q. 22.9
(a) What are the boiling and the freezing points of water?
(b) What word describes a solution in which water is the solvent?
(c) What is the density of water?
(d) What observation shows that ice is less dense than water?
(e) Describe how you would test a liquid to verify that it was water.

Q. 22.10
What use is made of each of the following during water purification?

(a) screens   (b) filter beds
(c) chlorine   (d) settling tanks
(e) fluoride

23
ATOMIC STRUCTURE AND THE PERIODIC TABLE

fig. 23.1 *Potassium reacting with water. Because of the structure of its atoms, potassium is a very reactive element.*

In Chapter 16 you learned that all matter is composed of elements, and that elements are composed of atoms. You might now ask what atoms are composed of. No one has ever seen an atom, because atoms are much too small, but there is little doubt about what they are composed of. The reactions of elements and the patterns in properties, such as those shown by the alkali metals, support the idea that atoms are composed of other, smaller particles.

PATTERNS IN CHEMISTRY

There are over one hundred elements, but there are many cases of a number of elements being very similar to each other in properties and reactions (what they look like and what they do). The **alkali metals** is a

Experiment 23.1
Investigating the alkali metals

safety glasses needed

(i) Lithium

Look at the colour of the pure metal after the crust which forms on its surface has been cut away; it is shiny and silvery in colour. Observe how easily it can be cut. Note the red colour of the flame as it burns. Its effect on water can be observed by putting a piece, about the size of a pea, in water, and covering the container with glass. Two ways of doing this are illustrated.

Notice the following about what happens when a small piece of lithium is dropped on to the water surface. The metal floats – which means that it is less dense than water; the metal melts – which means that it has a very low melting point, and the metal runs around the surface of the water and gradually becomes smaller – which means that it reacts with the water. When some litmus is added to the water afterwards, the litmus turns blue; this means that the reaction has produced an alkaline solution.

(ii) Sodium

As with lithium, observe the colour of the metal, and note how easily it can be cut. (Is it harder or softer than lithium?) Note the yellow colour of the flame when it is burned. Observe the effect when it is added to water (taking the safety precautions described in Fig 23.2). Notice that it is more reactive than lithium.

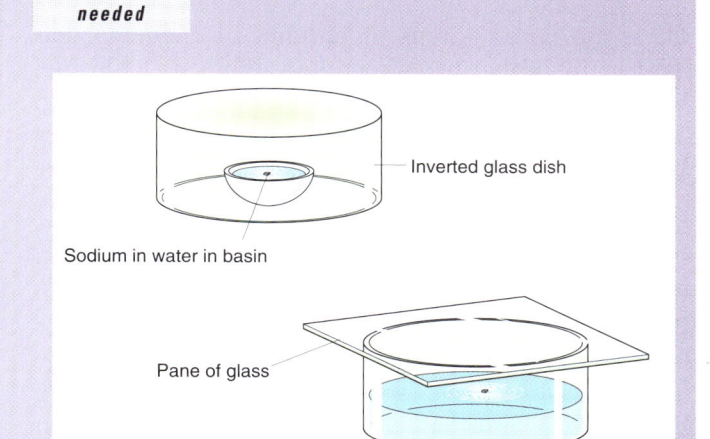

fig. 23.2 Safe methods of observing reaction of lithium with water

fig. 23.3 Cutting lithium and burning lithium

good example of a group of elements having very similar properties. The names of these metals are lithium, sodium, potassium, rubidium and caesium. These metals have very different properties from the ordinary metals of everyday life such as iron, copper and zinc. Rubidium and caesium are rare and will not be described.

If potassium is investigated, it too will be seen to have a shiny surface but which tarnishes rapidly, it is soft like the other two metals, and gives a characteristic purple colour to a flame when it is burned. When added to water, it floats, and immediately decomposes the water (splits it up into its elements). Figure 23.1 shows a photograph of this reaction.

Properties of the alkali metals

If you have seen all three metals, you should have noticed that they:
- are all soft and can be cut with a knife
- tarnish rapidly in air
- burn in a bunsen flame and give definite colours to the flame
- float on water
- react with water and produce alkaline solutions

There are other groups or families of elements that have many properties in common. Fluorine, chlorine, bromine and iodine, known as the **halogens** (see fig. 23.13), are good examples, as are magnesium, calcium and strontium. Atomic structure (what atoms are composed of) explains all this, as well as many more facts about chemical reactions.

Early in the nineteenth century, a scientist called John Dalton had said that atoms are small, indivisible (cannot be divided) and indestructible (cannot be destroyed) particles, and that there was nothing smaller than an atom; there was nothing to suggest otherwise – until the beginning of this century. However, in 1895, a very famous scientist, J. J. Thomson, discovered that there are particles of negative electricity in all atoms, and he called these particles **electrons**.

Then in 1911, another very famous scientist, Ernest Rutherford, discovered a most amazing fact – that atoms consist mainly of space! In the middle of that space is a hard dense core, now called the **nucleus**, which contains practically all the mass of the atom. The nucleus contains particles of positive electricity, which he named **protons**.

Finally in 1923, another scientist, James Chadwick, discovered a second kind of particle in the nucleus – this time with no electrical charge. These particles are called **neutrons**. How all of these discoveries were made is a complicated story, well beyond the scope of Junior Certificate science. You will learn more about it later in your physics or chemistry studies.

Experiment 23.2
The cathode ray tube

In this experiment, you can see the effect of streams of particles of negative electricity or electrons, in an apparatus called a cathode ray tube; this piece of apparatus is similar in ways to the tube inside a television set.

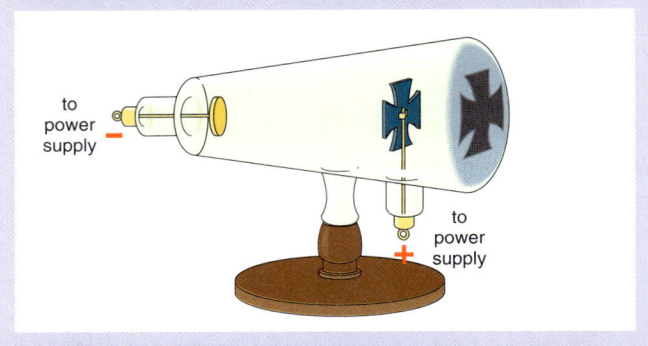

fig. 23.4 *The Maltese cross tube*

When the tube is connected to a suitable source of electricity, cathode rays, which are streams of electrons, travel outwards in straight lines from one end of the tube to the other. They cause a glow when they strike the glass at the end of the tube but cast a shadow where they are blocked by the cross in the tube. Streams of electrons are like light in this respect.

If a magnet is now brought near the tube, the shadow is moved, because a magnet exerts a force on an electron beam. In this way, streams of electrons are not like light.

SUB-ATOMIC PARTICLES

(Sub-atomic means smaller than atoms)

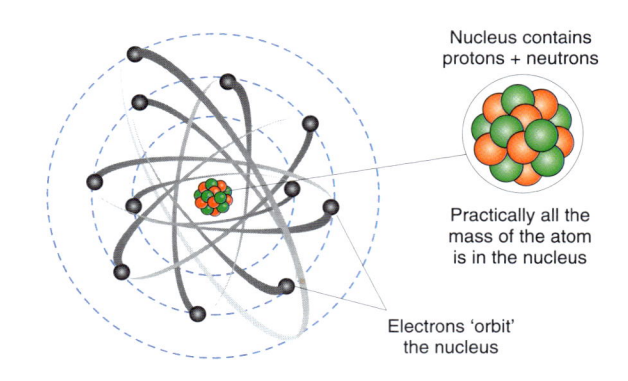

fig. 23.5 *If a sodium atom could be magnified about 300 million times, it might look like this*

So, atoms are made up of three different types of particle – and they differ in their mass, their electric charge, and where they occur in the atom. These particles, of which atoms are composed, are described as being **sub-atomic particles**. Masses of atoms are so small that if they were expressed in grams, a heavy one such as a uranium atom, would have a mass of about 0.000 000 000 000 000 000 000 4 grams! Masses of atoms are therefore expressed in units called **atomic mass units**. On this scale, the mass of the lightest atom (an atom of hydrogen) is about 1 unit. The following table summarises facts about atoms.

Particle	Mass (a.m.u.)	Charge	Location
proton	1	+1	in the nucleus
neutron	1	0	in the nucleus
electron	$1/1840$	–1	orbiting the nucleus in a series of 'shells'

It was a Danish scientist, Niels Bohr, who first discovered something about the way that electrons are arranged. He compared an atom to a miniature solar system with the nucleus at the centre, and around which are rotating the electrons in various orbits.

The smallest and simplest of all atoms is that of hydrogen; it consists of a proton with a single electron orbiting around it. The next element is helium, and its atoms consist of two protons, two neutrons, and two electrons. (In reality, the electron orbit is not circular, as the diagram suggests, but is spherical, so that an atom occupies a certain amount of volume.)

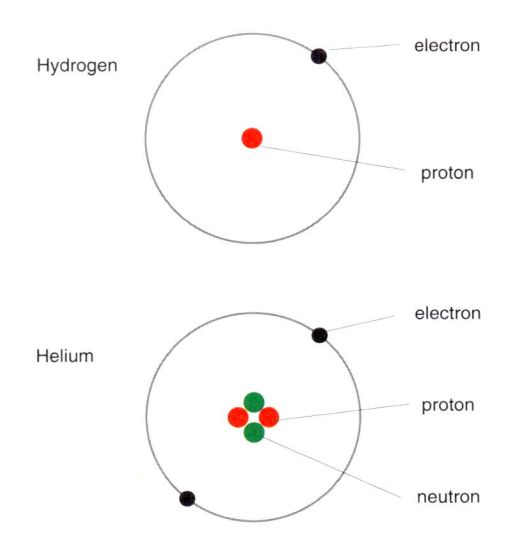

fig. 23.6 Atoms of hydrogen and helium

> The atomic number of an element is defined as the number of protons in an atom of that element.

This important number indicates a particular element. Thus, the element of atomic number 1 is hydrogen and atomic number 2 is helium.

ELECTRON STRUCTURES (ARRANGEMENT)

For the moment, the number of neutrons in atoms will not be considered. Helium, as shown, has two electrons in its shell, and its shell is then full. **The maximum number of electrons that this first shell can hold is two.**

In element number 3, lithium, whose atoms have three electrons, the extra electron occupies another shell, outside the first shell. The capacity of this second electron shell is eight. In elements numbers 3 to 10, there are different numbers of electrons in this second shell. The table gives the atomic numbers of these elements. Atoms of some of them are shown in Figure 23.8.

fig. 23.7 Filling electron shells is like filling a rack. You fill the lowest shells first.

Atomic Number	Element	Electrons in Shells	
		1st shell	2nd shell
1	hydrogen	1	0
2	helium	2	0
3	lithium	2	1
4	beryllium	2	2
5	boron	2	3
6	carbon	2	4
7	nitrogen	2	5
8	oxygen	2	6
9	fluorine	2	7
10	neon	2	8

23 • Atomic Structure and the Periodic Table

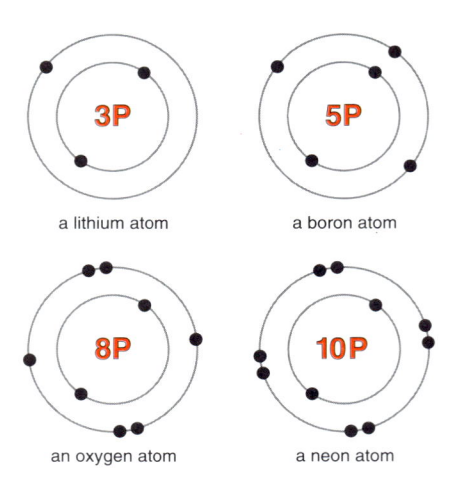

fig. 23.8

- a lithium atom (3P)
- a boron atom (5P)
- an oxygen atom (8P)
- a neon atom (10P)

In element number 10 (neon), the second electron shell is full, so for element number 11 (sodium), the extra electron enters a new shell (the third). Thus sodium has the electron arrangement (structure) 2, 8, 1. Two other examples of elements with three electron shells are aluminium and argon. Their electron structures are:

- sodium (11P)
- aluminium (13P)
- argon (18P)

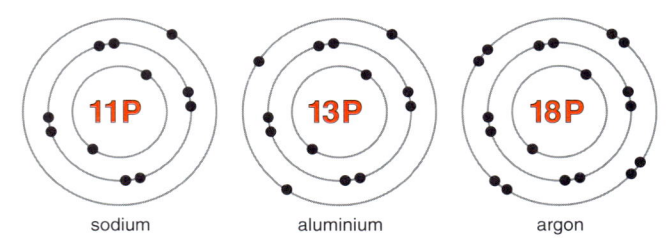

fig. 23.9

QUESTIONS

Q. 23.1
Copy out the following table and write in the numbers of electrons in each shell.

Atomic Number	Element	Electrons in shells		
		1st	2nd	3rd
11	sodium			
12	magnesium			
13	aluminium			
14	silicon			
15	nitrogen			
16	sulphur			
17	chlorine			
18	argon			
19	potassium			
20	calcium			

Q. 23.2
Using information given on page 161, draw diagrams of atoms of beryllium, carbon, nitrogen, fluorine. Show the number of protons in the nucleus of each, and the arrangement of the electrons.

Q. 23.3
Using atomic numbers from the table in Question 23.1, draw diagrams of atoms of magnesium, silicon, sulphur and chlorine. Show the number of protons in the nucleus of each, and the arrangement of the electrons.

Q. 23.4
The atomic numbers of lithium, sodium and potassium are 3, 11 and 19.

(a) What is the electron structure (arrangement) of atoms of each of these elements?

(b) Suggest a reason why these elements have similar properties.

THE NOBLE GASES

Eight electrons in the outer shell of an atom is a very important and a very stable electron structure. In fact, it is the most stable electron structure of all, the elements which have this structure are called the **noble gases**. These gases are very inert or unreactive and most of them form no compounds. Helium, which has two electrons in its outer (and only) shell is also included in this group, because its shell is full, and like the others, is inert or unreactive.

Element	Atomic Number	Electron Structure
helium	2	2
neon	10	2, 8
argon	18	2, 8, 8
krypton	38	2, 8, 18, 8
xenon	54	2, 8, 18, 18, 8

NEUTRONS

Practically all the mass of an atom is concentrated at its centre (see Figure 23.5), and is due to the protons and neutrons – each of which has a mass of 1 a.m.u. The mass of the atoms is therefore the same as the number of protons and neutrons in it.

> The mass number of an element is the number of protons and neutrons in an atom of that element.

In, for example, an oxygen atom, there are 8 protons and 8 neutrons, so its mass number is 16. (The mass of the electrons is so small ($1/1840$ each) that it can be ignored.)

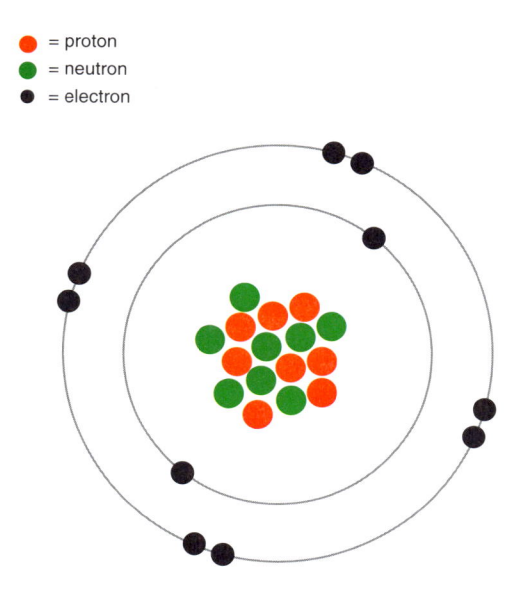

fig. 23.10 *An oxygen atom*

Since the **atomic number** of an element is the number of **protons** in each atom, and the **mass number** is the number of **protons + neutrons**, knowing these two numbers enables you to tell the number of neutrons (mass no. minus atomic no.) and the number of electrons (the same as the number of protons).

Example: An element has an atomic number of 13 and a mass number of 27. It has therefore 13 protons, 14 neutrons and 13 electrons.

When one wants to indicate the atomic number and mass number of an element, its symbol is written like:

mass number $\longrightarrow$ $^{40}_{18}Ar$
atomic number $\longrightarrow$

This is the symbol for argon, and it shows that its mass number is 40, and that its atomic number of 18. (Question: how many neutrons does this atom contain?)

Q. 23.5

(a) How many protons, neutrons and electrons are in atoms of each of:

$^{11}_{5}B$ $^{14}_{7}N$ $^{28}_{14}Si$ $^{19}_{9}F$ $^{39}_{19}K$ $^{24}_{12}Mg$

(b) How are the electrons arranged in each?

Q. 23.6

Copy out the following table and fill in the gaps.

Element	Mass	Protons	Neutrons	Electrons
Na		11	12	
	40			20
P		31		
	56	26		
			10	10
Cl			18	

THE PERIODIC TABLE

Whenever there exists a large number or collection of similar objects, it is sensible and helpful to arrange them in some sort of order. In your school library for instance, the books are likely to be arranged according to their different subjects and if you collects stamps or coins, they are probably classified according to the different countries. So it is also sensible to arrange the 100 or so elements which are known today.

fig. 23.11

Dimitri Mendeleev, who lived from 1834 to 1907, was the youngest of a large family in Siberia in Russia. He studied at the University of St Petersburg, and after that spent the next 11 years in France and Germany, where he studied with Bunsen. He returned to Russia to become professor of chemistry at the University of St Petersburg, a post which he held for 25 years. It was during that time that he devised the Periodic Table, which put order into all of the elements which were known at the time.

23 • Atomic Structure and the Periodic Table

In Mendeleev's Periodic Table, the elements are listed in order of increasing atomic number and arranged in groups according to the numbers of electrons in the outer shells of their atoms.

Atoms which have the same number of electrons in the outer shells of their atoms are listed in columns (vertical 'rows') called **groups**, and such elements have similar chemical properties (because of their similar electron structures). For example, lithium, sodium, potassium, rubidium and caesium all have one electron in the outer shell of their atoms, and this is why they are in the same periodic group – Group 1.

> **The group number of an element is the number of electrons in the outer shell of an atom of that element.**

Several of the groups have special names: the Group 1 elements are called the **alkali metals**; Group 7 are called the **halogens**, and Group 0 are the **noble gases**.

The horizontal rows of elements are called **periods**, and in any given period, the electrons are filling up one electron shell. **The period number is the number of the outermost shell.** For example, phosphorus has its outermost electrons in the third shell and so it is in Period 3.

The Periodic Table shown in Figure 23.12 is a simplified version of the full table. A section containing what is called the transition elements has been omitted (as the electron structure of these is somewhat irregular). The 'steps of stairs' is the approximate division between metal elements and non-metal elements. The metal elements are to the left-hand side of this line and the non-metals to the right. A complete Periodic Table appears inside the back cover of this book.

fig. 23.12 A simplified periodic table

fig. 23.13 The halogens are the elements of Group 7 of the Periodic Table. (This is because they have 7 electrons in the outer shell of their atoms.) Chemically they are all very similar; for example, they all combine with metals to give similar crystalline salts.

Fluorine (electron structure = 2, 7) is a yellowish gas and its compounds are used in 'fluoride' toothpaste.

Chlorine (structure = 2, 8, 7) is a greenish-yellow poisonous gas, and is used to sterilise swimming pool water, water for domestic use, and in the manufacture of hundreds of everyday substances such as plastics and bleach.

Bromine (structure = 2, 8, 18, 7) is a dark red volatile (evaporates easily) liquid. It is used to manufacture photographic films and medical preparations.

Iodine (structure = 2, 8, 18, 18, 7) is a dark grey crystalline solid. It is used dissolved in alcohol as the antiseptic tincture of iodine and also as a test for starch.

RADIOACTIVITY AND NUCLEAR ENERGY

An atomic nucleus is usually very stable; the atoms in your body have existed in their present form for millions of years. However, atoms of some elements have unstable nuclei, and they throw out particles spontaneously (this means all by themselves – without doing anything to them), and in doing so they become more stable. Elements which do this are described as being **radioactive**. Radioactive elements occur both naturally (e.g. uranium, radium and radon) and some are manufactured (e.g. plutonium).

Uses of radioactive substances

There are hundreds of uses of radioactive substances and today they are of extreme importance in industry and in medicine. In medical investigations, radioactive tracers are used to check the workings of, and to diagnose problems in, the brain, kidneys, lungs and bones. Radiation kills cancer cells and can often be successful in curing the disease.

The radiation which comes from some atoms can be used to kill bacteria. Hospital equipment (e.g. plastic syringes and surgeons' instruments) is often sterilised in this way. Many foods have their storage life extended by exposing them to suitable radiation (of the type which cannot be absorbed by the food).

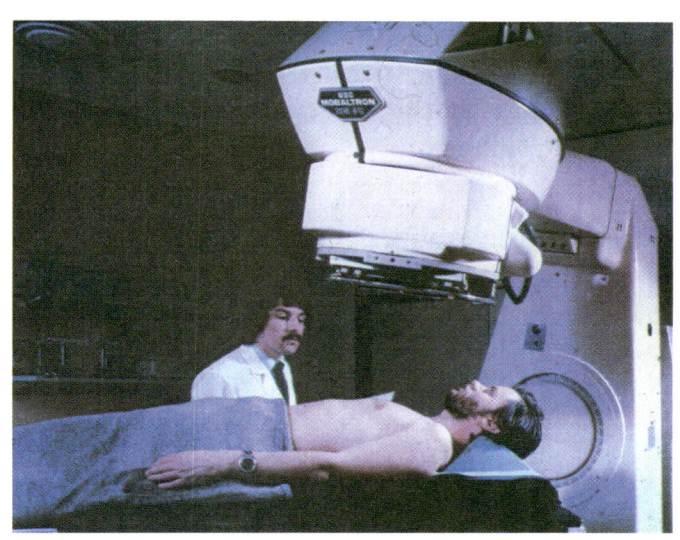

fig. 23.14 A patient undergoing radiation treatment for cancer

In industry, radioactive substances can be used to find cracks in underground pipelines, to check welds, and to control the thickness of aluminium foil as it is being rolled out. Smoke alarms, which are installed in most homes, make use of the radiation given off by a radioactive element.

Nuclear 'fission' or 'splitting the atom'

Nuclear fission is the process in which atoms of some elements (ones of high atomic number) are split into two or more smaller atoms, with the release of enormous quantities of energy – much of it in the form of heat. The heat is then used to generate steam in the usual way, and the steam works a turbine, which drives a generator, which produces electricity. Many countries produce much of their electricity by means of nuclear energy. One of the problems associated with this form of energy is disposing of the waste products; some of them can remain radioactive for hundreds of years, so they cannot just be dumped or used as landfill material.

fig. 23.15 A nuclear power station in Wales. Such power stations lack the tall chimney that is necessary in coal or oil-fired power stations

There are also dangers associated with nuclear energy and despite very strict safety precautions taken in power stations, there have been accidents. In 1986 there was a serious accident at a nuclear power station at Chernobyl in the Soviet Union which resulted in a lot of radioactive substances discharged into the atmosphere. Many people were killed as a result and many others got cancer from overdoses of radiation.

SUMMARY

- Atoms are composed of three types of particle. In the **nucleus** are **protons** (which have a mass of 1 a.m.u. and a positive charge) and **neutrons** (mass = 1 and uncharged). Orbiting the nucleus are the **electrons** (of mass $1/1840$ and negatively charged) arranged in various 'shells'. The first shell (the one nearest the nucleus) can hold 2 electrons, the second can hold 8 and the maximum capacity of the third is 18. Atoms that have 8 electrons in the outer shells of their atoms are very stable and unreactive. The elements that have this structure are called the **noble gases**.

- The **atomic number** of an element is the number of protons in an atom of it; this number is also the same as the number of electrons. The **mass number** is the combined number of protons and neutrons. Mendeleev's **Periodic Table** is a means of classifying the elements. On it, the elements are listed in order of increasing atomic number, and arranged in rows and columns. The columns, called **groups**, contain elements whose atoms have the same number of electrons in their outer shells. The horizontal rows, called **periods**, contain elements whose atoms have the same number of shells.

23 • Atomic Structure and the Periodic Table

- The **alkali metals** are the elements of Group 1. They have similar properties because their atoms all contain one electrons in their outer shells. Because of this similar structure, the elements have similar properties. All three elements are soft and can be cut with a knife, they float on, and decompose water, releasing hydrogen and forming alkaline solutions.

- **Radioactivity** is the spontaneous breaking apart of unstable atomic nuclei, with the release of radiation, some of which can be harmful. Radioactive elements have hundreds of uses in medicine and industry. **Nuclear fission** is the splitting up of unstable atomic nuclei with the release of enormous quantities of energy, and use is made of this in generating electricity in nuclear power stations.

QUESTIONS

Q. 23.7

Copy out the following paragraph and fill in the gaps:

(a) The three types of particle of which atoms are composed are called __, __, and __. The name given to the part of the atom which is at the centre is the __. This part contains two types of particles, one which is electrically charged, and one which is uncharged. The charged particle is the __, and it carries a __ charge. The uncharged particle is the __ and these particles have a mass of about __ atomic mass unit each. The particles which occur at the outside of the atom are called __; they carry a __ electric charge and they have a mass of about __ unit each.

(b) In the 19th century, a Russian scientist called __ devised the __ Table, which is a means of classifying the __. The columns in the table are called __ of elements and the horizontal rows are known as __ of elements. All the elements in any given group have the same number of __ in the __ shells of their atoms, and the group number of an element is the same as this number. All the elements in any given period have the same number of electron __, and this is denoted by the period number.

(c) For example, the element of atomic number 12 (which is called __) is in Group __ (which means that it has __ electrons in its __ shell), and it is in Period number __ (which means that it has __ shells of __). Some groups of the Periodic Table have special names; the elements of Group 1 are called the __ __, the elements of Group __ are known as the halogens, and the __ __ is the name given to the elements of the extreme right-hand group, which is Group number __.

Q. 23.8

From the following list of elements, Na, Al, Pb, I, Ne, O, N, write down the name of the one which has:

(a) the largest number of electrons
(b) the smallest number of electrons
(c) the greatest number of shells
(d) 3 electrons in the outer shell
(e) 3 electron shells
(f) space for 3 more electrons in the outer shell
(g) has the greatest density
(h) reacts with water
(i) is used in advertising lights
(j) is in Group 7

Q. 23.9

Explain each of:

(a) atomic number
(b) mass number
(c) group of elements
(d) alkali metal
(e) nucleus
(f) noble gas
(g) halogen

Q. 23.10

Two of the following atoms have similar properties. Which are they, and why?

Atom W has 9 protons and 10 neutrons;
X has 13 protons and 14 neutrons,
Y has 11 protons and 12 neutrons;
Z has 17 protons and 18 neutrons.

Q. 23.11

Sodium has a mass number of 23 and its electron structure 2,8,1.

(a) Draw a labelled diagram of an atom of sodium showing the protons, neutrons and electrons.
(b) Explain why a sodium atom is electrically uncharged.
(c) Rubidium is in the same group as sodium. Would you expect rubidium to be a metal or a non-metal?
(d) Suggest how rubidium should be stored.
(e) What would you expect to happen when rubidium is put into cold water?

Q. 23.12

(a) What is meant by a sub-atomic particle?
(b) Name the sub-atomic particle which:
   (i) has a positive charge
   (ii) has no charge
   (iii) is found orbiting the nucleus
   (iv) has almost no mass
   (v) has a mass of 1 a.m.u.
   (vi) is negatively charged

Q. 23.13

(a) What name is given to Group 0 of the Periodic Table?
(b) Give the names of the elements which occur in the group.
(c) What is common to the electron structures of these elements?
(d) What effect has this structure on the properties of these elements?

Q. 23.14

Give the exact symbols (including mass number and atomic number) for the atoms which contain

(a) 2 protons and 2 neutrons
(b) 6 protons and 6 neutrons
(c) 6 protons and 8 neutrons
(d) 15 protons and 16 neutrons
(e) 17 protons and 19 neutrons

Q. 23.15

(a) What is radioactivity?
(b) Name a radioactive element.
(c) What is nuclear fission?
(d) How can this process be used for electricity generation?
(e) State one problem associated with this source of energy.
(f) Mention two uses of radioactive elements.

Q. 23.16

For each of the following elements, give its:

(a) atomic number
(b) mass number
(c) electron structure
(d) periodic group number
(e) period number.

lithium, oxygen, aluminium, sulphur, calcium, bromine.

24

ACIDS, ALKALIS AND SALTS

fig. 24.1 (a) *These substances contain acids*

(b) *and these contain alkalis*

This chapter is all about acids and the opposite type of compound, called bases or alkalis. Some people think of acids as highly dangerous and damaging substances which should always be avoided, but this is far from true. A few acids are indeed dangerous, but many acids occur in everyday household substances, including foodstuffs. The word *acid* comes from the Latin word for sour, because acids and substances containing them have a sour taste. The sour taste of lemons, vinegar and sour milk are all due to acids present.

Experiment 24.1
To test various substances with litmus

safety glasses needed

In this experiment, a selection of both laboratory and household chemicals are tested with red litmus and with blue litmus. In order to test, the substance must be dissolved in water. So, in the case of the solid substances on the list, dissolve what will fit on the tip of a spatula in about half a test tube of water. Shake the mixture well to dissolve the substance. Some of the substances to be tested are corrosive and these are marked as being so; take particular care when using these substances.

To carry out the test, take two pieces of litmus paper, one red, and one blue.

1. Dip a clean glass rod into the liquid being tested and place a drop on each of the two pieces of litmus paper.
2. Observe and make a note, in a results table, of what happens.
3. Thoroughly rinse the glass rod by holding it under a stream of running water.
4. In the same way, test as many substances as are available.
5. Make out a chart listing: (i) acidic substances; (ii) neutral substances; (iii) alkaline substances.

(a) What is the colour of litmus in acidic solution?
(b) What is the colour of litmus in alkaline solution?
(c) What type of litmus is used to test for an acid?
(d) What is the effect of water on red litmus?
(e) Why is it important to rinse the glass rod after each test?
(f) What name is given to a substance such as litmus which is used to distinguish between acids and alkalis?
(h) Name three acidic substances found in the home.

Acids are a group of compounds with special properties, and a quick and easy test for an acid is to add a purple substance called **litmus**. This turns red in an acid solution. Litmus is described as an **indicator**. The opposite of an acid is a **base** or **alkali**. Red litmus turns blue in an alkali. A substance which is neither acidic nor alkaline is described as **neutral**.

COMPARING THE STRENGTHS OF ACIDS AND BASES: THE pH SCALE

So far, substances have been classified as either acids or alkalis – which is all that litmus can indicate about them. However, there are different strengths of both acids and alkalis, and their strength is measured on a scale of numbers called the pH scale. **The pH scale runs from 0 to 14.** The mid point, 7, of this scale indicates a neutral substance; numbers less than 7 indicate acids, and numbers greater than 7, bases or alkalis. The further away from 7 that a pH value is, the stronger is that substance. Thus, a substance with a pH of 1 or 2 is a strong acid, while one with a pH of 5 or 6 is a weak acid.

The simplest way to measure the pH of a substance is to use an indicator called universal indicator (or pH paper, which is just the indicator soaked up into paper). This indicator tells more than litmus does, and it shows, by means of different colours, the strength of the acid or base into which it is put. A special colour chart relates its colour to the corresponding pH.

fig. 24.2 A pH colour chart

Experiment 24.2
To determine the pH of various substances

As in the previous experiment, the substance must be liquid in order for it to be tested. In the case of the solid substances in the list, dissolve what will fit on the tip of a spatula in about half a test tube of water. Shake the mixture to dissolve the substance. Note that some of the substances on the list are corrosive; take particular care when using these.

To carry out the test, dip a clean glass rod into the liquid being tested, and then place a drop of the liquid on a piece of pH paper. Observe the colour to which it changes, and then use a colour chart to find its pH. Make out a 'results' table, and write in what you discover.

Thoroughly rinse the glass rod by holding it under a stream of running water, and then test the next substance in the same way.

(a) Which substances are acidic?
(b) Which are alkaline?
(c) Do all the acids have the same pH?
(d) Which is the strongest acid?
(e) Which is the strongest alkali?
(f) Name a weakly acidic foodstuff.
(g) Name an alkaline substance used in the home.
(h) How many neutral substances are there?

safety glasses needed

fig. 24.3

24 • Acids, Alkalis and Salts

Experiment 24.3
To prepare and use red cabbage indicator

safety glasses needed

Indicators can often be extracted from plant material. One of the chemicals in red cabbage is a very good indicator, and in this experiment, it is extracted from the leaves of the cabbage. A colour chart for this indicator is then prepared using chemicals of known pH.

1. Take a few leaves of red cabbage and tear them into small pieces.
2. Place the pieces in a beaker and add about 100 cm^3 of water.
3. Heat the water until it starts to boil and then allow it to **simmer** for about five minutes. Stir occasionally.
4. Decant (pour off, leaving the solid behind) the clear liquid into another container. This liquid is a universal indicator.
5. Into separate test tubes, pour about 5 cm^3 of each of the given solutions. These are solutions of known pH.
6. Using a dropper, add about five drops of the red cabbage indicator to each of the liquids, and mix well.
7. Observe the colour to which the indicator turns, and make a note of this colour. List the results in a table.
8. With the aid of markers or coloured pencils, make out a colour chart for red cabbage indicator.

Experiment 24.4
To investigate reactions of acids

safety glasses needed

Warning: Sulphuric acid is a corrosive substance; be extra careful when using it. Wear safety glasses.

1. Take about 5 cm^3 of dilute sulphuric acid in a test tube. As a safety precaution, hold the tube at a slight slant and pointing away from anyone nearby.
2. Add a few pieces of magnesium (or zinc) metal. Observe carefully; what happens to the metal? Is a gas liberated (set free)? Put your thumb over the top of the test tube, and when you feel pressure, remove your thumb and *immediately* apply a lighted match or splint at the top of the tube. What gas is it?
3. Feel the outside of the test tube. Is the reaction exothermic or endothermic? How do you know?
4. Repeat the experiment, but use dilute hydrochloric acid instead of sulphuric acid. What happens to the metal this time? Is a gas liberated? Apply a lighted splint to the gas. What happens? What gas is it?
5. This time use dilute hydrochloric acid and some small pieces of calcium carbonate (marble). What happens to the marble?
6. Using the apparatus shown in Figure 24.4, pass the gas through limewater. What happens to the limewater? What is the gas that does this?
7. Repeat step 5, but using dilute sulphuric acid and sodium carbonate. Is a gas formed? Test the gas and find out whether it is hydrogen or carbon dioxide.

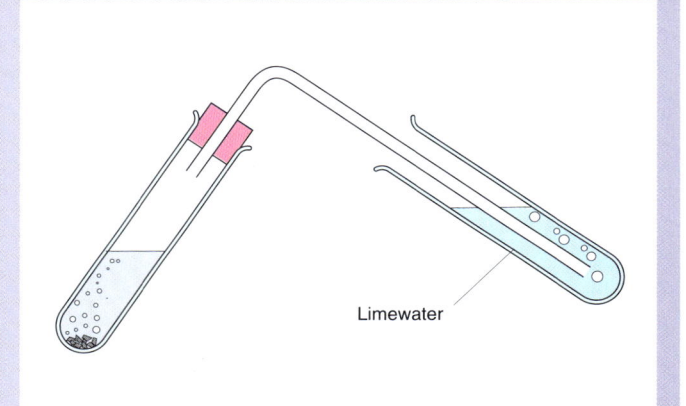

fig. 24.4

8. To about 5 cm^3 of dilute hydrochloric acid in a test tube, add a few drops of litmus solution. Add dilute sodium hydroxide (an alkali) in small portions at a time (use a dropper), and shake after each addition, until a change occurs. What change occurs? What has happened to the acid? What does the colour of the litmus tell about the solution which is now in the test tube?
9. Rinse the dropper well with water (or take a clean dropper). Now add dilute hydrochloric acid, drop by drop and shake after each addition, until another change occurs. What sort of solution is now in the test tube? The reaction occurring in this part of the experiment is called a **neutralisation**.

ACIDS AND SALTS

Experiment 24.4 showed that when a metal reacts with an acid, the metal seemingly disappears, and that a gas is produced; these two observations mean that a chemical change (or chemical reaction) must have taken place. A metal cannot of course 'disappear'. In the reaction it is converted to another kind of compound, called a **salt** (which remains dissolved in the solution). **This is one of the most important properties of an acid: it forms a substance called a salt.**

All acids contain hydrogen. When, for example, magnesium is reacted with sulphuric acid, the hydrogen is replaced by the magnesium, and the salt, magnesium sulphate, is formed. The hydrogen gas is released. The reaction can be summarised by the equation:

magnesium + sulphuric acid →
magnesium sulphate + hydrogen

or, in chemical symbols:

$$Mg + H_2SO_4 \rightarrow MgSO_4 + H_2$$

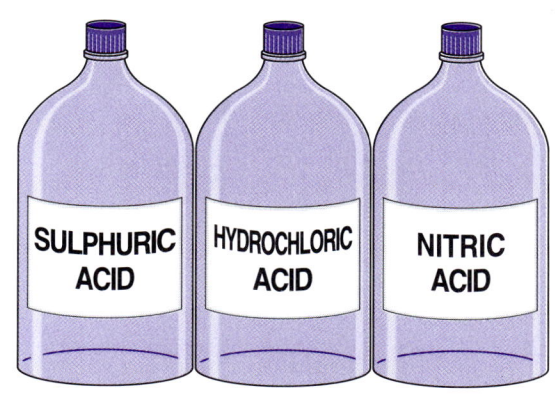

fig. 24.5 *The three common laboratory acids are* **sulphuric acid** *(formula* H_2SO_4*),* **hydrochloric acid** *(HCl), and* **nitric acid** *(*HNO_3*).*

You have seen that sulphuric acid when reacted with magnesium forms the salt magnesium sulphate. **Sulphuric acid always forms salts called sulphates.**

Likewise, **nitric acid forms salts called nitrates** and **hydrochloric acid forms salts called chlorides**. A salt has a double name, the metal name and the name derived from the acid, e.g. copper sulphate, sodium chloride.

Experiment 24.5
To prepare a salt by neutralisation

safety glasses needed

In this experiment, you are going to neutralise sodium hydroxide solution (the alkali) with hydrochloric acid. The salt sodium chloride will be produced. There are two parts to the experiment. In the first part, you have to find out what volume of the acid is necessary to neutralise 25 cm³ of the alkali. This is done by adding the acid from a burette, to the alkali in a conical flask which also contains some indicator. This process is called a **titration**.

In part 2 of the experiment, the alkali is mixed with the volume of acid which was found to neutralise it. This produces a solution of the salt, which when evaporated to dryness, leaves crystals of the solid salt.

Part 1

1. Set up a burette as in the diagram, and fill it with the hydrochloric acid (fig. 24.6 (a)).

2. With the aid of a pipette filler, pipette exactly 25 cm³ of the alkali into a conical flask, and add a few drops of litmus indicator (fig. 24.6 (b) and (c)). Place the conical flask on a white tile or piece of white paper underneath the burette.

3. Make a note of the reading on the burette to the nearest 0.1 cm³.

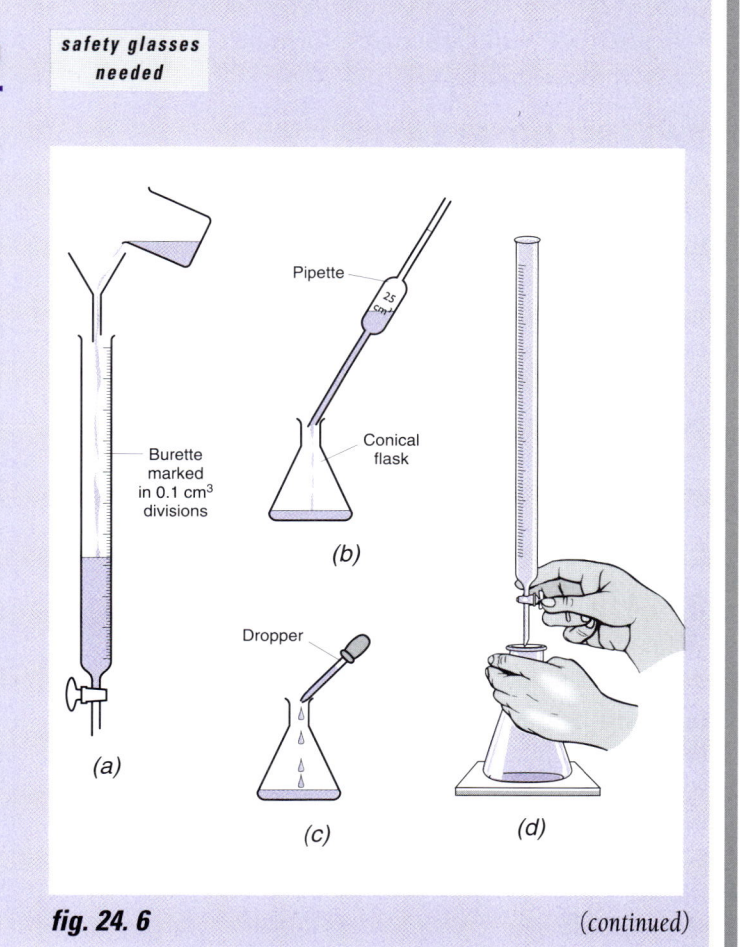

fig. 24.6

(continued)

4. While continuously shaking or swirling the flask, slowly add the acid from the burette, until the indicator changes colour (fig. 24.6 (d)).
5. Note the final reading on the burette, again to the nearest 0.1 cm³, and record this figure. Subtract the two readings to find the volume of acid used.
6. Pour away the solution, and rinse the flask several times with water.
7. Carry out two more titrations in the same way, and note these values in a results table. Do these titrations more carefully.
8. Calculate the average value of the volume of acid needed.

Part 2

Into a clean conical flask, pipette 25 cm³ of the sodium hydroxide solution (the **same** solution as was used in part 1, but do not add indicator). Then add, from the burette, the exact volume of acid which was needed to neutralise it. They react to form a solution of sodium chloride. Pour this solution into an evaporating basin and, using a tripod and gauze, evaporate the solution to dryness. The substance which remains is common salt – sodium chloride, formed by the neutralisation of the two starting substances.

PROPERTIES OF ACIDS

- Acids have a sour taste.
- Acids turn litmus red.
- Acids have a pH of less than 7.
- Acids react with many metals, forming hydrogen and a salt.
- Acids react with bases forming salts and water.
- Acids react with carbonates, forming a salt, water and CO_2.

BASES AND ALKALIS

A base can be defined as a substance which reacts with an acid to produce a salt and water. If the base is soluble in water, it is called an **alkali**. Most bases are metal oxides or metal hydroxides. The most common alkali is **sodium hydroxide**, which is commonly called **caustic soda**. Other bases found in the laboratory are **limewater** (calcium hydroxide solution) and **ammonia**. The reaction between an acid and a base is called a **neutralisation**. In such a reaction, each substance loses its characteristic properties and the product is usually neutral.

QUESTIONS

Q. 24.1

What is the name of the salt which is formed when each of the following reactions occurs?

(a) zinc + hydrochloric acid
(b) copper + nitric acid
(c) iron + sulphuric acid
(d) magnesium + hydrochloric acid
(e) calcium + nitric acid
(f) aluminium + sulphuric acid

Q. 24.2

Refer to the Experiment 24.5.

(a) Why is a white tile placed under the flask while titrating?
(b) Why are three titrations carried out?
(c) Why was no indicator used in part 2?
(d) If you had taken 100 cm³ of the sodium hydroxide, how much acid would be needed to neutralise it?
(e) What is the name of the salt which is produced in this reaction?

Q. 24.3

Write an account of the experiment in which you prepared sodium chloride by neutralising an alkali with an acid. Name the acid and alkali used, draw diagrams to illustrate your answers, describe what you did, and include the measurements you took in the experiment.

Q. 24.4

What is the name of the salt formed when each of the following pairs of substances react together?

(a) sodium hydroxide and hydrochloric acid
(b) sodium hydroxide and sulphuric acid
(c) sodium hydroxide and nitric acid
(d) potassium hydroxide and hydrochloric acid
(e) potassium hydroxide and sulphuric acid
(f) magnesium hydroxide and nitric acid
(g) calcium oxide and hydrochloric acid
(h) calcium oxide and nitric acid
(i) iron oxide and sulphuric acid
(j) copper oxide and sulphuric acid

ACIDS, ALKALIS AND SALTS IN EVERYDAY LIFE

Acids and substances containing them usually have a sour taste. Many acids occur in everyday substances. Acetic acid (also called ethanoic acid) is found in vinegar, and lactic acid in sour milk. Both lemons and grapefruit contain citric acid, and tartaric acid is found in grapes. Phosphoric acid is contained in rust remover and tannic acid is found in tea.

Perhaps you know that if you get a nettle sting, you should rub a dock leaf on it. A nettle sting is the result of an acid being injected into your skin. Dock leaves contain an alkali, and when you crush a dock leaf and rub it on the nettle sting, it neutralises the acid, reduces the pain and helps the swelling to go down. Dock leaves help bee stings and ant bites for the same reason.

A bee sting is also the result of an acid, so the remedy is to treat the sting with a mild alkali such as bread soda (*sodium bicarbonate*). On the other hand, a wasp sting is an alkaline sting and should be treated with a weak acid such as lemon juice or vinegar.

Your stomach contains hydrochloric acid and when you have indigestion, too much of it is present. The remedy is to neutralise some of the acid by taking an alkaline substance such as sodium bicarbonate or a preparation like '*Milk of Magnesia*' or '*Rennies*'.

fig. 24.7

Sodium hydroxide or *caustic soda* is a very strong and dangerous alkali. It is used in the home for cleaning greasy ovens because strong alkalis are good grease solvents. Ammonia, a mild alkali, is also used in the home for cleaning. Toothpaste is mildly alkaline and can neutralise the acids that attack teeth. Such acids are formed when the bacteria in saliva react with the sugar in foods.

Many salts too are in daily use. By far the most common is sodium chloride or common salt. In your home it is used for flavouring and preserving, and in industry, for the manufacture of other chemicals.

Sodium carbonate is a salt which can be found in some soap powders and bath salts; it softens hard water (see Chapter 26). Copper sulphate is used to spray potatoes, apple trees and other crops to prevent disease. *Plaster of Paris*, used to encase broken bones is a salt called calcium sulphate. Ammonium sulphate and potassium chloride are common fertilisers used in the garden and on the farm.

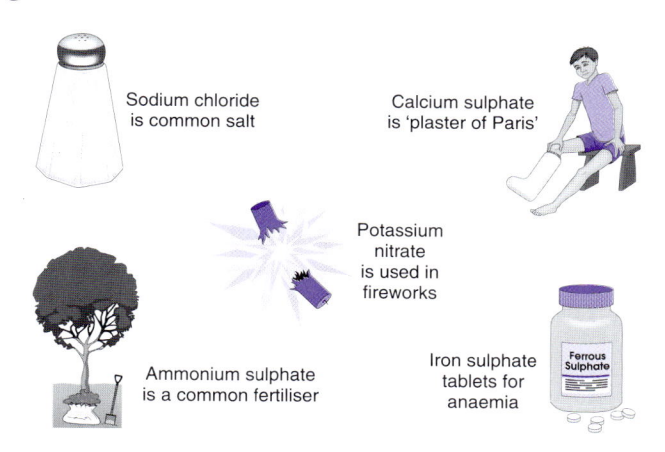

fig. 24.8

ACID RAIN AND POLLUTION

fig. 24.9 *The limestone in this headstone has reacted with the acid in rain over the years. The trees have been killed by acid rain.*

It is an unfortunate fact of life that the common fuels – coal and peat, oil and petrol, all contain a small amount of the element sulphur. When these fuels are burnt, the sulphur present also burns and forms the compound sulphur dioxide (SO_2). Sulphur dioxide is a colourless, choking and poisonous gas which irritates and can damage one's respiratory system. When it dissolves in rain, it produces sulphurous acid (H_2SO_3) and sulphuric acid (H_2SO_4) – two of the acids present in **acid rain**.

Another cause of acid rain is dissolved nitrogen dioxide (NO_2). Car exhausts contain, as well as sulphur dioxide, some nitrogen dioxide – resulting from oxygen and nitrogen combining together at the high temperature produced by the sparking plug. When nitrogen dioxide dissolves in rain, it produces nitrous (HNO_2) and nitric acid (HNO_3).

Acid rain does much damage; it attacks iron structures such as bridges, cars and machinery. It attacks limestone buildings and statues. It damages crops, it harms trees and other plants. It washes aluminium salts out of the soil into lakes and rivers where both the acidity and the presence of the aluminium salts kill fish and other aquatic life. In Scandinavia, thousands of lakes which used to contain fish no longer do so, and in Germany's Black Forest, thousands of trees have been damaged or killed. The acid rain is thought to have come from industrial areas of Great Britain and Germany. Many lakes have been treated by adding lime to them; lime is alkaline and neutralises the acidity in the lakes.

So the burning of oil, coal and turf necessary to heat buildings, to generate electricity, to power factories, and to drive cars and lorries, ships and aircraft, produces undesirable products. It is one of the challenges of today's scientists to find ways to reduce this atmospheric pollution which does so much damage.

fig. 24.10 *Tall chimneys send acid gases high into the atmosphere*

Various methods are in use to reduce the amounts of acid gases which are being put into the environment. Many factories and power stations have 'scrubbers' which remove sulphur dioxide from the chimney gases; one way of doing this is to neutralise it with lime. Very tall chimneys put any remaining gas high into the atmosphere where it becomes diluted and less harmful. Many modern cars have catalytic converters which remove the nitrogen dioxide from the exhaust gases. As well, most modern cars use lead-free petrol; this reduces the amount of lead which is released into the environment.

Experiment 24.6
To investigate the effect of acids on building materials

1. Collect a sample of several different building materials such as limestone, slate, concrete, marble, granite.
2. Place them in separate petri dishes. Note which is which.
3. Using a dropper, put about five drops of dilute hydrochloric acid on each material.
4. Observe what happens to each. Make a note of your observations.

(a) What does the fizzing of some materials with acid mean?
(b) What gas is released?
(c) Which materials react with acid?
(d) Which material(s) would react with acid rain?
(e) Which material(s) would be best to build with in an environment which received a lot of acid rain?

SUMMARY

- **Acids** are compounds containing hydrogen which can be replaced by metals forming salts. The three common laboratory acids are sulphuric (H_2SO_4), hydrochloric (HCl) and nitric (HNO_3). Acids react with metals forming salts and hydrogen, they turn litmus red and they have a sour taste.

- **Alkalis** are substances that react with acids forming salts and water (acid + alkali → salt + water); this type of reaction is called a **neutralisation**.

- An **indicator** is a substance which shows, by means of a colour change, whether a substance is acidic or alkaline.

- The **pH scale** is a scale on which the strengths of acid and alkalis are expressed and it runs from 0 to 14. The mid-point, 7, is the pH of neutral substances. Acids have a pH of less than 7 and alkalis more than 7. Universal Indicator (or pH paper) is used to find the pH values of substances.

- **Acid rain** is caused by the gases sulphur dioxide (from the burning of fossil fuels) and nitrogen dioxide (from motor engines) dissolving in rain. Acid rain kills trees, destroys lakes and kills fish, corrodes metals and causes health problems in humans.

QUESTIONS

Q. 24.5
Copy out and complete the spaces in the following paragraphs.

(a) An acid is a ___ that contains the element ___, and this element can be replaced by a ___ to form another compound called a ___. For example, when sulphuric acid reacts with the metal ___, the compound zinc ___ is formed, and the gas ___ is released.

(b) When an acid reacts with an alkali, two compounds are formed, a ___ and ___. When ___ acid reacts with the alkali sodium ___, the salt ___ chloride is formed as well as the liquid ___. This type of reaction is described as a ___.

(c) The substance ___ is an example of an indicator. In acidic solution, the colour of this substance is ___ and in alkaline solution it is ___. The pH scale is a scale of number from ___ to ___, and a number of this scale is a measure of the ___ of a substance. A pH of 7 means that the substance is ___; if it is ___, the pH is above 7 and if it is ___ the pH is less than ___.

Q. 24.6
In an experiment, a pupil put exactly 25 cm³ of an alkali into a flask and added a few drops of litmus solution. He then titrated it with sulphuric acid until the solution was neutral. This required 20 cm³ of acid.

(a) With what piece of apparatus could the alkali have been measured out?
(b) Draw a labelled diagram of the titration apparatus which was used.
(c) What was the colour of the solution in the flask at the start of the experiment?
(d) How did the pupil know when the alkali was neutralised?
(e) Was the alkali more concentrated or less concentrated than the acid? Give the reason for your answer.
(f) If the alkali was sodium hydroxide, what salt was formed in the experiment?
(g) How could a pure sample of the salt be obtained?
(h) Write a word equation for the reaction.

Q. 24.7
(a) What is an indicator?
(b) When is litmus indicator blue and when is it red?
(c) Why is universal indicator more useful than litmus indicator?
(d) What colour is universal indicator in (i) sulphuric acid, (ii) lemon juice, (iii) water, (iv) ammonia solution, (v) sodium hydroxide solution?

Q. 24.8
From the following pH values, 2, 5, 7, 9, 13, select the one which is most likely to apply to each of the following:

(a) pure water
(b) indigestion powder
(c) lemon juice
(d) hydrochloric acid
(e) vinegar
(f) oven cleaner
(g) car battery acid
(h) ammonia solution
(i) stomach acid
(j) sulphuric acid

Q. 24.9
(a) What kind of a compound is sodium nitrate?
(b) Name the acid and the alkali which would be needed to prepare it.
(c) What other substance would be needed in the experiment to prepare it?
(d) What other substance would be formed in the experiment?
(e) What word describes the reaction in which an acid reacts with an alkali?

Q. 24.10
What name is given to:

(a) a reaction in which an acid and a base react with each other
(b) a substance which reacts with an acid
(c) a base which is soluble in water
(d) a substance which has a different colour in acid and alkali
(e) the type of substance formed when an acid reacts with a base

Q. 24.11
Give an example of each of the following:

(a) a strong acid
(b) a weak acid
(c) a strong alkali
(d) a neutral substance
(e) an indicator
(f) a substance which turns blue litmus red

(g) a substance which has a pH of about 9
(h) a substance which reacts with hydrochloric acid

Q. 24.12

(a) Name two gases which dissolve in rainwater to produce acid rain.
(b) Name a source of each of these gases.
(c) Name two acids present in acid rain.
(d) State two ways in which acid rain affects the environment.
(e) State two ways in which the formation of acid rain can be reduced.
(f) Walking, cycling and using public transport can reduce acid rain. Explain why.

Q. 24.13

Decide about each of the following statements whether it is true or false.

(a) All acids contain hydrogen.
(b) Litmus turns red in acids.
(c) Litmus paper can be used to tell the pH of a substance.
(d) If a base dissolves in water, it is called an alkali.
(e) Alkalis turn litmus blue.
(f) All acids are dangerous substances.
(g) The pH scale goes from 0 to 7.
(h) The pH of sulphuric acid is about 7.
(i) Acids react with carbonates to give carbon dioxide.
(j) Lemon juice is a good remedy for bee stings.
(k) The equation: $Mg + HCl \rightarrow MgCl_2 + H_2$ is 'balanced'.
(l) Sodium hydroxide is a stronger base than ammonia.
(m) When magnesium dissolves in acid, it can be recovered by evaporating the solution.
(n) Give the equation for the reaction of any metal with hydrochloric acid.

25
CHEMICAL BONDING

Elements combine together to form compounds (e.g. magnesium and oxygen form magnesium oxide; hydrogen and oxygen form water), or, put another way, atoms combine together to form molecules. The atoms of the 100 or so elements that are known today combine in different ways to form millions of different compounds. The forces of attraction which holds atoms together are called chemical bonds.

THE OCTET RULE

Bonding between atoms involves electrons, particularly those in the outer shells of the atoms. The structure of the noble gases is very relevant to understanding bonding. These gases are different from other elements; they do not form compounds, which means that their atoms are unreactive and therefore very stable. It is also a fact that these elements (with the exception of helium) have eight electrons in the outer shells of their atoms. Putting these two facts together indicates that the structure of eight electrons in the outer shell of an atom is a very stable structure. An arrangement of eight electrons in the outer shell of an atom is called an **octet**.

When atoms bond together, they try to achieve (obtain) a structure of having eight electrons in their outer shells. They do this in two ways:

(i) by losing or gaining electrons (in ionic bonding) or

(ii) by sharing electrons (in covalent bonding).

IONIC BONDING

Ionic bonding occurs between metal atoms and non metal atoms, e.g. between sodium and chlorine or between magnesium and oxygen. Metals occur near the left-hand side of the Periodic Table, and so have a small number of electrons in the outer shells of their atoms. Non-metals, on the other hand, are near the right-hand side of the Table so the number of electrons in the outer shells of their atoms is approaching eight.

Sodium has the electron structure 2,8,1; it can become stable by losing its single outer electron – to become 2,8. Chlorine has the structure 2,8,7 and for it to become stable, it must gain one electron to become 2,8,8. When sodium and chlorine combine together, the single outer electron of the sodium atom is transferred to the chlorine atom – so making each stable.

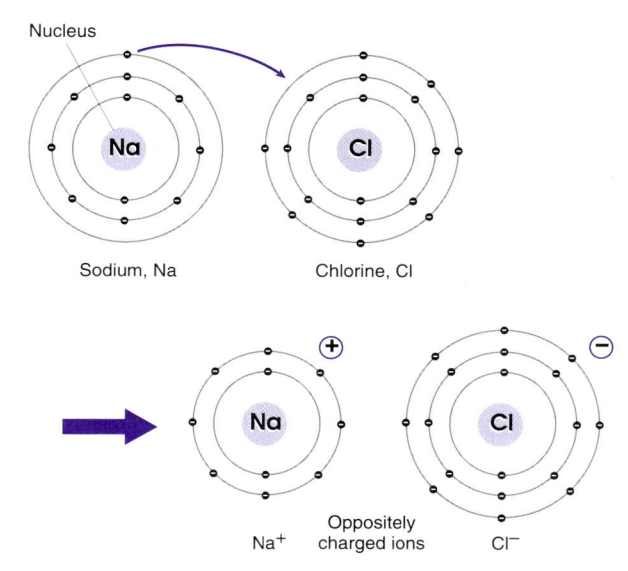

fig. 25.1

It is important to note that when atoms combine together, it is only electrons that are involved. The protons in the nucleus are unaffected. The particles that are formed in the above change are then no longer neutral atoms, since each chlorine atom has gained an electron (and therefore has become negatively charged) and each sodium atom has lost one (and become positively charged).

> **Atoms which have either gained or lost electrons to become negatively or positively charged are called ions.**

The chlorine ion is denoted as Cl^- and the sodium by Na^+.

The force of electrical attraction between these oppositely charged ions holds them together and is called an ionic bond.

> **An ionic bond is the electrical force of attraction between oppositely charged ions.**

This force of attraction occurs in all directions around an ion, so that a compound such as sodium chloride consists of, not just a single pair of ions held together, but an enormous number of ions of each kind held together in a three-dimensional and repeating pattern – called a lattice. Compounds containing ionic bonds are therefore normally crystalline.

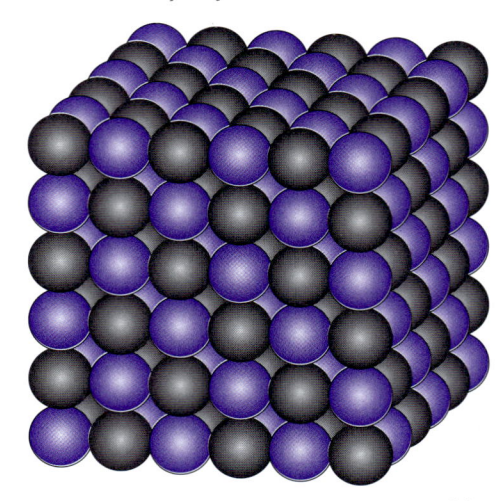

fig. 25.2 Arrangement of ions in sodium chloride

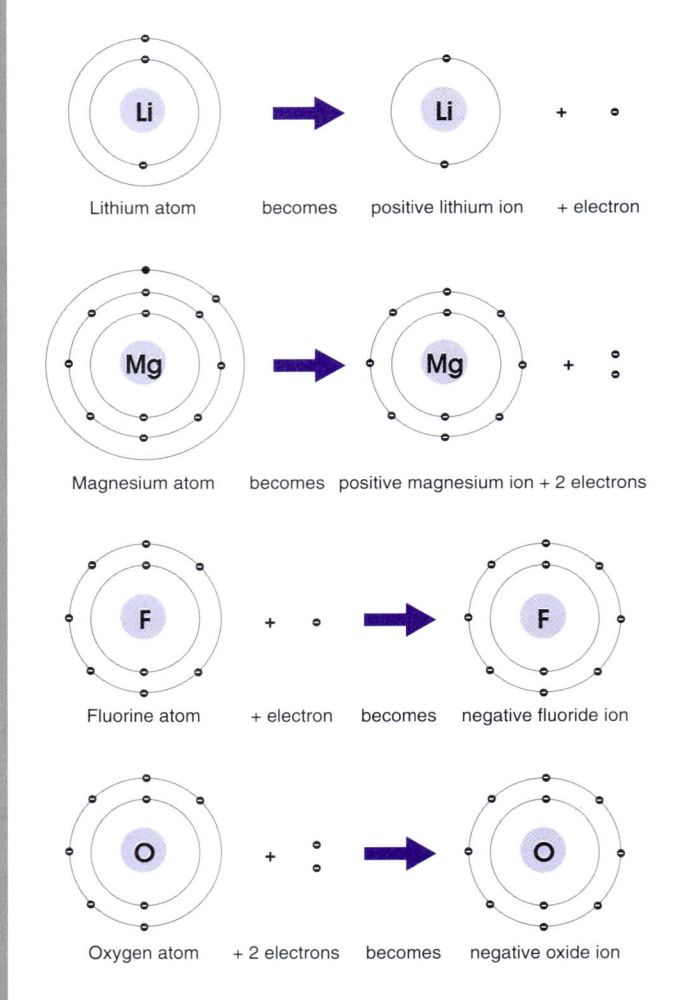

fig. 25.3 Formation of ions

Now consider the compound formed when magnesium combines with chlorine. Magnesium has the electron structure 2,8,2 and it must lose two electrons to become stable, i.e. to attain an octet structure. Since chlorine requires only one extra electron to become stable, each magnesium atom loses its two electrons to two chlorine atoms, to form the compound magnesium chloride – which must have the formula $MgCl_2$. The magnesium ion, since it was formed by the loss of **two** electrons, has the symbol Mg^{2+}.

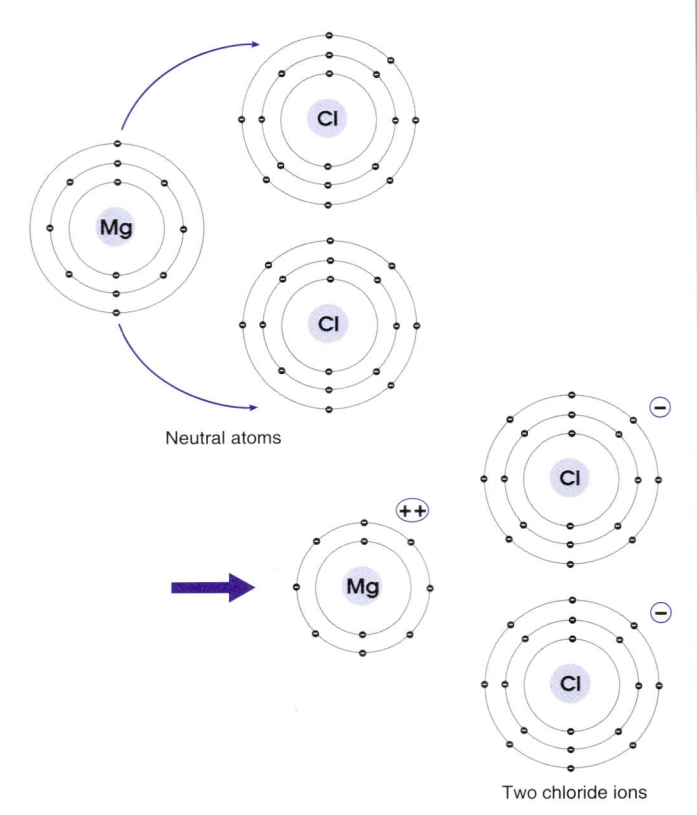

fig. 25.4

QUESTIONS

Q. 25.1

The compound magnesium oxide is formed in a similar way to sodium chloride. Answer the following questions about its formation:

(a) Draw the electron structure of a (neutral) magnesium atom.
(b) How does a magnesium atom most easily become stable?
(c) Draw the electron structure of an oxygen atom.
(d) How do oxygen atoms most easily become stable?
(e) Use your answers to (b) and (d) to predict what happens when a magnesium atom combines with an oxygen atom.
(f) Give the symbols for the ions which are formed.
(g) What is the formula for magnesium oxide?

Q.25.2

Draw diagrams showing the electron structures (arrangements) of ions of potassium, fluorine, magnesium, sodium, oxygen, aluminium, chlorine, calcium. Indicate the charge on each ion.

Q.25.3

Using the Periodic Table, work out what ions are formed, and the formulae of the compounds produced, when the following pairs of elements combine together:

(a) potassium and fluorine
(b) magnesium and fluorine
(c) sodium and oxygen
(d) aluminium and chlorine
(e) calcium and oxygen

Suggest names for each of the compounds that have been formed.

COVALENT BONDING

Covalent bonding is the type of bonding involved when atoms of non-metals combine with other non-metal atoms, for example, in forming water, ammonia, or chlorine gas. In this case, **each** atom needs to gain electrons to achieve the octet structure, and to do this, the atoms share their electrons with each other – as they form molecules.

It is a fact that chlorine does not exist as single atoms, but as molecules containing two atoms combined together. Chlorine atoms have the electron structure 2,8,7, so each requires one more electron to become stable. Two chlorine atoms can each do that by combining and sharing a pair of electrons, each of the atoms supplying one of that shared pair. The shared pair of electrons is called a covalent bond.

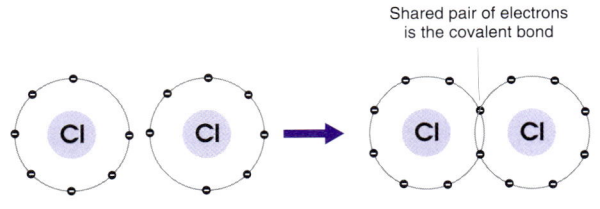

fig. 25.5

(Note: only outer shell electrons are shown)

A covalent bond consists of a pair of electrons shared by two atoms.

Atoms that require two extra electrons to become stable (i.e. atoms in Group 6) must share two pairs of electrons when combining and forming molecules. In a water molecule for example (see Figure 25.6), two hydrogen atoms must combine with each oxygen atom to provide the two shared pairs of electrons. And in the ammonia molecule, three hydrogen atoms combine with each single nitrogen atom for all to acquire the noble gas structure.

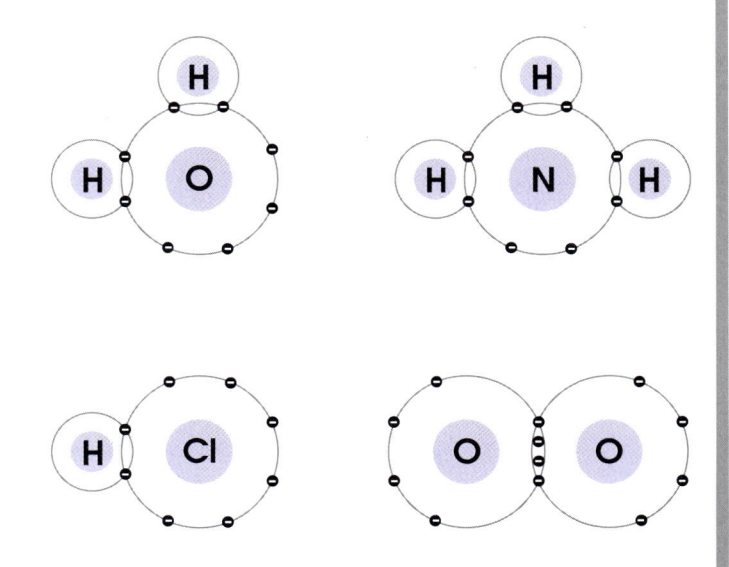

fig. 25.6

Molecules formed by covalent bonding usually contain a small number of atoms joined to each other. No electrons are lost or gained so there are no ions. There is therefore little force of attraction between molecules so they do not form a lattice or crystalline structure such as sodium chloride does. Covalent compounds usually exist as small separate molecules and are therefore either liquids or gases (whereas ionic compounds are usually solids).

QUESTIONS

Q.25.4

The formula for hydrogen is H_2 and for fluorine it is F_2. These two elements combine together to form the compound hydrogen fluoride, HF. Draw diagrams showing the arrangement of the electrons in the molecules of these three substances.

Q.25.5

The atoms in the following compounds are held together by covalent bonds. For each, draw diagrams showing how the electrons are arranged in their molecules: H_2S, PH_3, CH_4, CF_4 and CO_2.

ELECTROCHEMISTRY

In Chapter 9, *Electric Circuits and Charges*, you learned that of solid substances, only metals (and carbon) conduct electricity. Non-metals do not conduct electricity. In this experiment, you can investigate which liquids conduct electricity.

25 • Chemical Bonding

Experiment 25.1
Investigating liquids that conduct electricity

safety glasses needed

1. Arrange a circuit as shown. Check that the circuit is working by placing a piece of metal across the electrodes – when the bulb should light. If it does not, it is likely that there is a poor connection somewhere, or that the bulb or the battery is faulty.

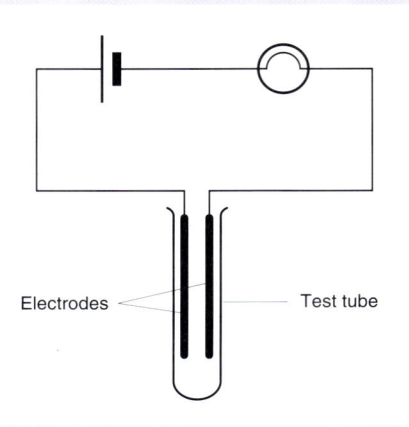

fig. 25.7

2. Place some pure (distilled) water (a covalent compound) in the beaker. Does it conduct electricity? (i.e. Does the bulb light?)
3. Replace the pure water with some sodium chloride (common salt) solution (an ionic compound). The easiest way to do this is to just add some salt to the water that is already there, and then stir to dissolve it. Does the salt solution conduct electricity?
4. Which type of compound conducts electricity?
5. Now using what you have discovered, test each of the following liquids (or as many as are available) to find out whether it is ionic or covalent. Rinse the electrodes with water after testing each substance.
6. Substances: copper sulphate, paraffin oil, methylated spirits, dilute hydrochloric acid, sugar solution, sodium hydroxide solution (care needed).

PROPERTIES OF COVALENT COMPOUNDS

- Covalent compounds consist of molecules.
- The molecules have a definite shape.
- The compounds have low melting and boiling points.
- They are usually insoluble in water.
- They do not conduct electricity.

PROPERTIES OF IONIC COMPOUNDS

- Ionic compounds are composed of oppositely charged ions.
- The ions form rigid crystalline lattice structures.
- The compounds have high melting and boiling points.
- They are usually soluble in water.
- Both the solution, and the molten (melted) compound, conduct electricity; this is because the ions are free to move about.

VALENCY

Atoms combine together in different ratios, depending on what the atoms are. For example, sodium chloride is NaCl, magnesium chloride is $MgCl_2$ and aluminium chloride is $AlCl_3$. Valency is a means of expressing the 'combining power' of an element and is a measure of the number of bonds that an atom of that element can form.

The valency of each element can be found from the Periodic Table. **It is the same as the number of electrons that atoms need to lose or to gain to become stable.** For instance, the elements of Group 1 need to lose one electron each to become stable so their valency is 1. Similarly the elements of Group 2 have a valency of 2. The halogens (Group 7) need to **gain** one electron each to become stable so their valency is 1. The accompanying chart shows the valency of some common elements.

Radicals

The chart also shows the valency of a few common **radicals**. These are groups of atoms which behave like single atoms in most chemical reactions.

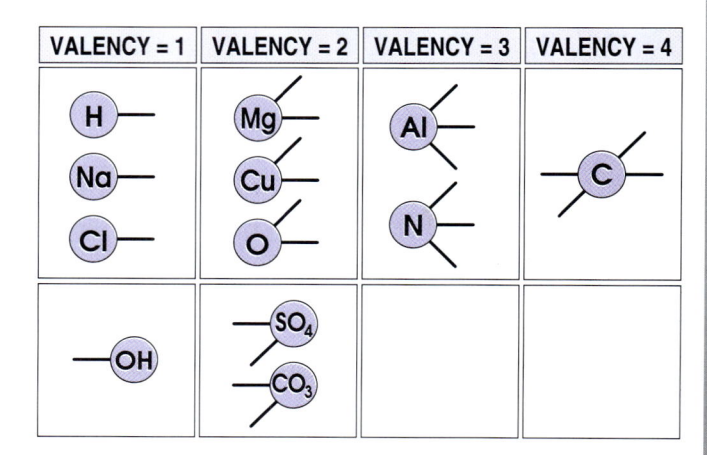

VALENCY = 1	VALENCY = 2	VALENCY = 3	VALENCY = 4
H, Na, Cl	Mg, Cu, O	Al, N	C
OH	SO_4, CO_3		

fig. 25.8

CHEMICAL FORMULAE

Hydrogen chloride contains the elements hydrogen and chlorine. Each of these has a valancy of 1. So, when they combine together, one atom of each element joins together, giving a molecule of formula HCl.

In the case of aluminium and chlorine, the aluminium has a valency of 3 (it can form three bonds), the chlorine has a valancy of 1 (one bond), so when they combine, each aluminium atom joins with three chlorine atoms, giving the molecule $AlCl_3$.

Hydrogen chloride, HCl

Water ('hydrogen oxide'), H_2O

Ammonia, NH_3

Magnesium oxide, MgO

Magnesium sulphate, $MgSO_4$

Copper carbonate, $CuCO_3$

Aluminium chloride, $AlCl_3$

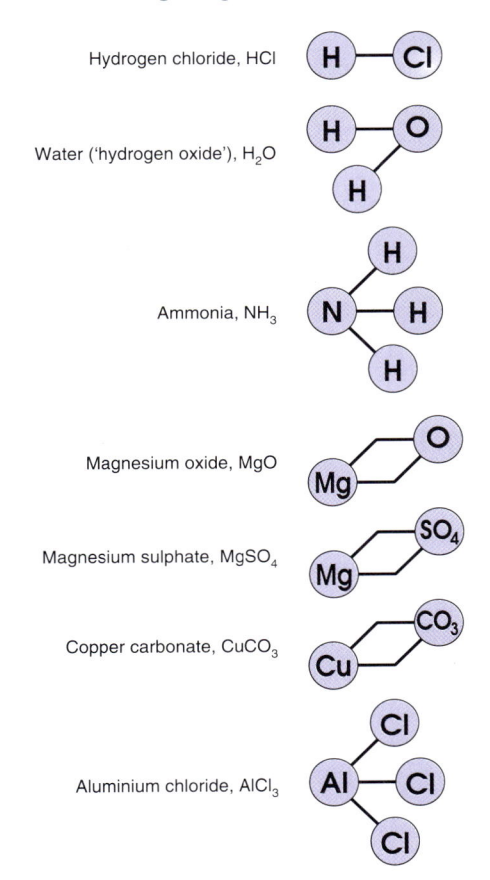

fig. 25.9

CHEMICAL EQUATIONS

A chemical equation is a way of summarising what happens in a chemical reaction. Think of what happens when shiny magnesium ribbon burns. There is a bright flame, the magnesium 'disappears' and all that remains is some white ash. In chemical language what happens is that the magnesium combines with oxygen (from the air) to form a new substance called magnesium oxide (the white solid), i.e.

magnesium + oxygen → magnesium oxide

This statement is called a **word equation**. The plus sign in the equation means *combines with* and the arrow means *to form*.

The same information can be shortened by using the chemical formula of each substance instead of its name. Remembering that the formula for oxygen is O_2, magnesium is Mg, and the formula for magnesium oxide is MgO, the equation can be written as:

$$Mg + O_2 \rightarrow MgO$$

However, the equation is not quite correct as the numbers of atoms do not match; an oxygen atom seems to have disappeared. There are two oxygen atoms on the left but only one on the right.

Remember that in a chemical reaction, all that happens is that the atoms are rearranged. They emerge at the end linked together differently than they were at the start; but no atoms are lost (or gained) in the process. The equation must therefore be balanced, i.e. it must end up with the same numbers of atoms of each kind on both sides.

The equation is balanced by writing two atoms of magnesium on the left-hand side, and two molecules of magnesium oxide on the right-hand side:

$$2Mg + O_2 \rightarrow 2MgO$$

There are now two atoms of magnesium and two atoms of oxygen on the left-hand side, and two molecules of magnesium oxide (each containing a magnesium atom and an oxygen atom) on the right-hand side, i.e. the equation is balanced.

The substances which react together are called the **reactants**. The substances which are produced in a reaction are called the **products** of the reaction. In the reaction described above, magnesium and oxygen are the reactants, and magnesium oxide is the product.

reactants → products

SUMMARY

- The **noble gases** have the most stable electron structures of all elements. The outer shells of their atoms contains eight electrons, and this is known as an octet. Atoms combine together in order to attain this structure and they can do so in two different ways.

- **Ionic bonding** occurs between metals and non-metals, and in it, **electrons are transferred** from the metal atoms to the non-metal atoms. This produces oppositely charged ions (with stable structures) which are held together by electrical attraction, and the attraction is called an ionic bond.

(continued)

25 • Chemical Bonding

- Ionic compounds are usually crystalline, have high melting and boiling points, are soluble in water forming solutions which conduct electricity.
- **Covalent bonding** occurs between atoms of non-metals, which **share electrons** with each other to become stable. Each atom donates electrons to the shared pair, which is known as a covalent bond.
- Covalent compounds are made up of molecules; they are usually liquids or gases, are insoluble in water and do not conduct electricity.
- The **valency** of an element is a measure of combining power, and is equal to the number of electrons or the number of spaces in the outer shell of an atom of the element.
- A correct chemical equation must have the same atoms on each side, i.e. it must be 'balanced'.

QUESTIONS

Q. 25.6
Rewrite the following sentence, and fill in the gaps.

(a) There are __ main types of chemical bonds. In __ bonding, __ are transferred from one atom to another, forming __ charged ___, which are then held together by __ attraction. This attraction is called an ___ bond. Bonds of this type are formed between metal __ and __ - __ atoms.

(b) Potassium is a metal and bromine is a __ - __. When these two elements combine together, each __ atom gives an __ to each __ atom. The potassium atom becomes __ charged and the bromine atom becomes __. These charged atoms are called __. The reason for the bromine ion being __ charged, is that the number of electrons (circling the __) is now __ than the number of protons (which are __ the nucleus).

(c) Bonds which consist of shared pairs of __ are called __ bonds. and they are formed when atoms of __ - __ combine with each other. When this happens, the __ structure of each atom becomes like the structure of a __ gas.

Q. 25.7
Rewrite and complete the following sentences:
(a) An ion is an ____ which has either ____ or ____ electrons.
(b) A negative ion is an ____ which has ____ ____.
(c) A covalent bond consists of a ____ pair of ____.
(d) The atoms in potassium iodide (KI) are held together by ____ bonds but in water (H_2O) the ____ are joined by ____ bonds.
(e) In a positively charged ____ , the number of electrons is ____ than the number of ____ .
(f) An ionic bond is formed by the ____ of electrons from one ____ to another ____.

Q. 25.8
(a) How would you use an electrical circuit to distinguish between pure water, and sodium chloride solution.
(b) Draw a diagram of the circuit, and describe what you would do.
(c) Which substance is ionic and which is covalent?

Q. 25.9
Make out a table showing the properties of
(a) ionic compounds, and (b) covalent compounds.

Q. 25.10
(a) What is the formula for molecules of: water, hydrogen, chlorine, ammonia, hydrogen chloride, sodium fluoride, magnesium oxide, magnesium fluoride, carbon dioxide.
(b) What kind of bonding is present in each?
(c) For each of the covalent molecules, draw diagrams showing how the electrons are arranged.

Q. 25.11
Use the valencies (page 180) to work out the formula for each of the following substances:
(a) copper oxide
(b) copper chloride
(c) nitrogen chloride
(d) aluminium chloride
(e) sodium hydroxide
(f) magnesium hydroxide
(g) aluminium hydroxide
(h) sodium oxide
(i) sodium sulphate
(j) sodium carbonate

Q. 25.12
In each of the following incomplete equations, work out the formula for the missing substance.

(a) $Mg + Cl_2 \rightarrow$ _____
(b) $CuCO_3 \rightarrow CuO +$ _____
(c) $Zn + H_2SO_4 \rightarrow ZnSO_4 +$ _____
(d) $Mg + H_2SO_4 \rightarrow H_2 +$ _____
(e) $H_2SO_4 + CuO \rightarrow H_2O +$ _____
(f) $Ca + 2H_2O \rightarrow Ca(OH)_2 +$ _____
(g) $N_2 + 3H_2 \rightarrow 2$_____
(h) $2Zn + O_2 \rightarrow 2$_____
(i) $HCl + NaOH \rightarrow NaCl +$ _____

(j) $Na_2CO_3 + H_2SO_4 \rightarrow Na_2SO_4 + CO_2 +$ _____
(k) $H_2O_2 \rightarrow H_2O + O_2$

Q. 25.13

Balance each of the following equations, all of which are complete, but unbalanced.

(a) $Mg + O_2 \rightarrow MgO$
(b) $Zn + O_2 \rightarrow ZnO$
(c) $H_2 + Cl_2 \rightarrow HCl$
(d) $Na + Cl_2 \rightarrow NaCl$
(e) $H_2 + O_2 \rightarrow H_2O$
(f) $Na + O_2 \rightarrow Na_2O$
(g) $Al + Cl_2 \rightarrow AlCl_3$
(h) $N_2 + H_2 \rightarrow NH_3$
(i) $CH_4 + O_2 \rightarrow CO_2 + H_2O$
(j) $H_2SO_4 + NaOH \rightarrow Na_2SO_4 + H_2O$

Q. 25.14

(a) What is another word for unreactive?
(b) Why are the noble gases atoms unreactive?
(c) Draw a diagram to show how a sodium atom becomes stable.
(d) Why has a sodium ion a charge of +1 but a chloride ion has a charge of –1?
(e) Why has a potassium ion a charge of +1 but a calcium ion has a charge of +2?
(f) Why is the formula for sodium chloride NaCl?
(g) Why is the formula for magnesium chloride $MgCl_2$?
(h) What is the name for the type of bond in which atoms share electrons?

Q. 25.15

The symbol for a sodium atom is ^{25}Na. The number of protons present is ____ and the number of electrons is ____ . The charge on a sodium atom is therefore ____ . The symbol for a sodium ion is $^{25}Na^+$. The number of protons present is ____ ; the charge is ____ and therefore the number of electrons is ____ . The word equation for the formation of a sodium ion is: sodium atom __ electron ____ sodium ion. The symbol equation is: ____ __ ____ ____ Na^+. A sodium atom differs from a sodium ion in two ways, (i) _____ and (ii) _____ .

Q. 25.16

Copy and complete the following sentence.

Lithium and fluorine combine to produce ___ fluoride. When this happens, each lithium atom gives ___ to each fluorine atom. Lithium ions and fluoride ___ are formed; each lithium ion has a ___ charge, and each fluoride ion a ___ charge. The ___ ions and the __ ions are held together by a strong ___ attraction. This attraction is called an ___ bond.

Q. 25.17

Give the names of the compounds whose formulae are:

NaCl, $MgCl_2$, MgF_2, KF, $AlCl_3$, CaO, $CaCl_2$, ZnO, $ZnSO_4$, $ZnCO_3$.

26

HARDNESS IN WATER

fig. 26.1 It is difficult to form a lather with hard water; it is easy to do so with soft water

DIFFERENT TYPES OF TAP WATER

If you have stayed away from home, you may have noticed that the tap water elsewhere seems different from the tap water in your home. It may 'feel' different or you may have noticed that the amount of soap you need for washing is much greater, or perhaps much less.

> Water which needs a lot of soap to produce a lather (suds) is described as being hard.

Water from chalk or limestone districts is generally quite hard and therefore much of Ireland's water supply is hard.

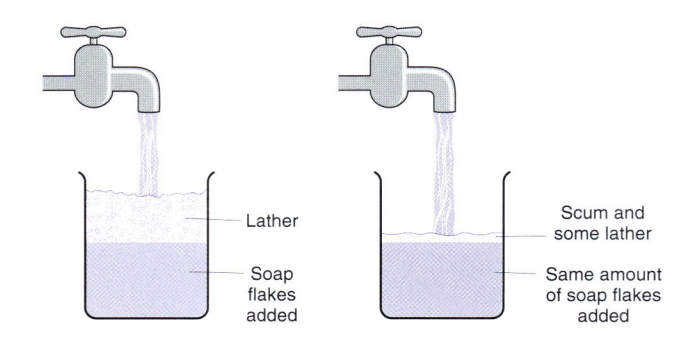

fig. 26.2 The effect of soap on soft water (left), and hard water (right)

Water which lathers easily or which forms plenty of lather is called **soft water**. The difference between hard and soft water is demonstrated in Experiment 26.1.

HARDNESS: WHERE IT COMES FROM

Water is a very good solvent. It dissolves many substance with which it comes in contact and as a result, water supplies from natural sources often contain dissolved salts. Hardness in water is caused by dissolved calcium and/or magnesium salts. In Ireland both calcium hydrogencarbonate and calcium sulphate are quite common in natural water supplies.

Calcium and magnesium ions react with soap to form an insoluble scum. You notice this scum on the sides of the wash basin after you empty out the water you have washed in.

Ca^{2+} ions + sodium stearate
         (soap)
                      $\rightarrow$ calcium stearate + Na^+ ions
                                  (scum)

A proper lather cannot form until the soap has reacted with all of the dissolved calcium or magnesium ions in the water. That means hardness in water wastes soap, so more soap is needed than with soft water.

fig. 26.3 The scum formed when soap reacts with very hard water (nothing has been washed in the water yet)

TEMPORARY AND PERMANENT HARDNESS

There are two kinds of hardness: temporary hardness and permanent hardness.

One kind of hardness is caused by dissolved calcium hydrogencarbonate. The water in this kettle contains dissolved calcium hydrogencarbonate, so it is hard.

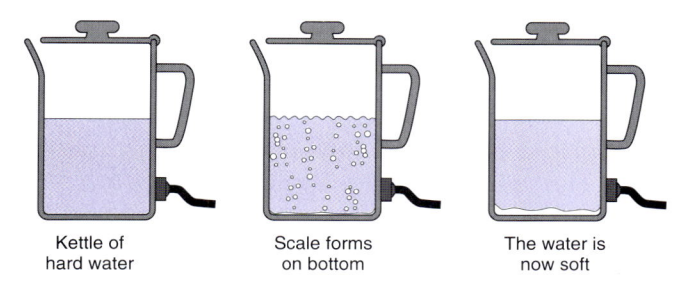

Kettle of hard water | Scale forms on bottom | The water is now soft

fig. 26.4

When it is boiled, the calcium hydrogencarbonate decomposes to form calcium carbonate:

$$Ca(HCO_3)_2 \rightarrow CaCO_3(\downarrow) + CO_2(\uparrow) + H_2O$$
calcium hydrogen-carbonate   calcium carbonate

Calcium carbonate is insoluble and it collects on the sides and the bottom of the kettle. It is called 'fur' or 'scale'.

The result is that all the calcium hydrogencarbonate gets removed from the water, and so that water is now soft. This kind of hardness is called **temporary hardness** since it is easily removed – by boiling the water containing it.

Hardness caused by other calcium and magnesium compounds is called **permanent hardness** because boiling does not affect it. Calcium sulphate is the compound most often found in water supplies.

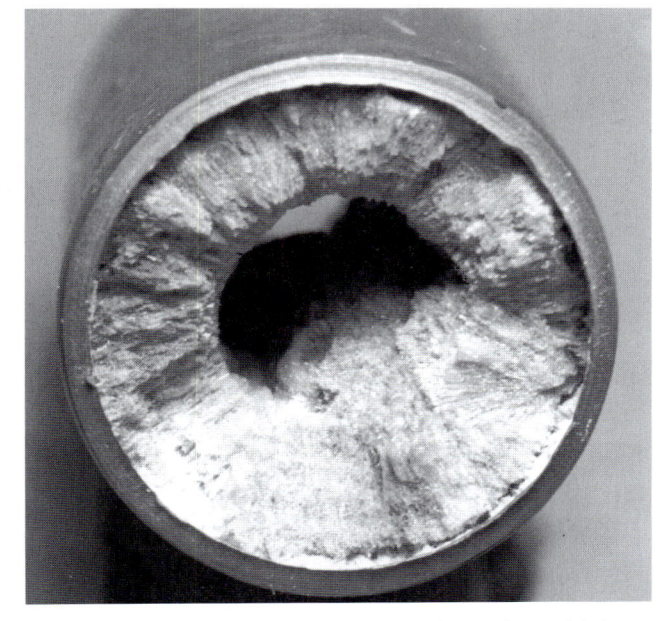

fig. 26.5 A serious build up of scale in a pipe which carried hot water containing temporary hardness

Experiment 26.1
Investigating hardness in water

In this experiment, the amount of hardness in samples of water from different sources is compared – by finding out how much soap solution each needs to give a permanent lather. The more hardness in the water, the greater is the quantity of soap needed to form the lather.

1. Set up a burette and fill it with the given soap solution. Alternatively, a syringe can be used to measure out the soap solution.
2. Using a graduated cylinder, measure out 50 cm³ of one of the water samples into a bottle.
3. From the burette, add 2 cm³ of soap solution into the bottle. Put on the cap and shake hard for 15 seconds; then leave it to stand.
4. If a permanent lather forms, on the water surface, record the volume of soap solution used.

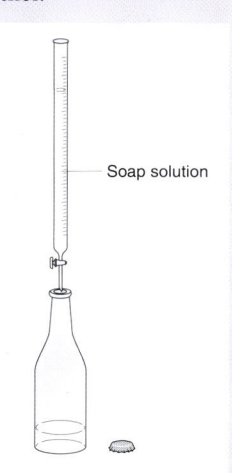

fig. 26.6

5. If no permanent lather is formed, add another 2 cm³ of soap solution, and repeat the procedure. Continue doing this until a permanent lather is formed on the water surface. Note the volume of soap solution used.
6. Carry out this same procedure on each of the other samples of water.
7. Heat a 100 cm³ sample of the tap water until it boils. Then turn down the gas so that it is just **gently** boiling. Leave it like this for about 5 minutes and then let it cool.
8. Pour 50 cm³ of this cool boiled water into a bottle and test it for hardness in the manner already described.
9. Again take some of the tap water and this time pour it through an ion-exchange column. Collect the water from the bottom of the column and test a 50 cm³ portion in the manner already described.
10. Answer the questions:
    (a) Which of your samples is the softest?
    (b) Which sample is the hardest?
    (c) What substance might this hard sample contain?
    (d) How does the amount of hardness in the original tap water compare with the hardness in it after it had been boiled?
    (e) Is the hardness in the tap water temporary or permanent?
    (f) How does the amount of hardness in the original tap water compare with the hardness in it after it was passed through the ion exchanger?

Specimen results

Shown below are the volumes of soap solution needed to form a permanent lather with 100 cm³ portions of different water samples.

Distilled water	2 cm³
Rain water	2 cm³
Dublin tap water	10 cm³
Wicklow tap water	4 cm³
Well water from Co. Clare	16 cm³
Dublin tap water after being boiled	4 cm³
Dublin tap water after being put through ion exchanger	2 cm³

HARD WATER: GOOD OR BAD?

Hard water has disadvantages, but it also has its good points.

Disadvantages of hard water

1. It leaves 'scale' in kettles, hot water pipes and boilers. This makes them less efficient and can also lead to blockage, see Fig. 26.5
2. It wastes soap and leaves a scum that can be difficult to clean.
3. It can leave clothes with a 'hard' feel after being washed.

Advantages of hard water

1. It generally tastes better than soft water.
2. It provides calcium for bones and teeth.
3. Some doctors think that it helps to prevent heart disease.

SOFTENING WATER (REMOVAL OF HARDNESS)

Because of the problems which it can cause, particularly in factories, hard water is often softened before use. This means removing from it the compounds which cause the hardness, i.e. the calcium and magnesium compounds.

Boiling

Boiling removes temporary hardness, by converting the calcium hydrogencarbonate to calcium carbonate which precipitates (but it does not affect the permanent hardness).

Distilling

Distilling removes both kinds of hardness, but on a large scale it is too expensive on account of the energy needed to boil the water, and so water is not softened in this way.

Ion exchangers

An ion exchanger is a device that does what it says, it exchanges ions. It is a container full of an ion exchange resin – which is a source of sodium ions. The calcium (and magnesium) ions in the hard water are replaced by sodium ions from the ion exchange resin. The sodium ions dissolve in the water but these ions do not cause hardness.

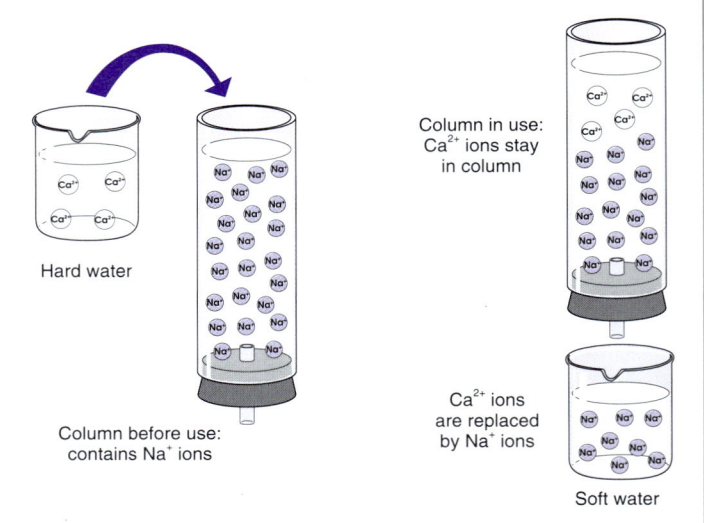

fig. 26.7 *How an ion exchanger works*

After a time, all of the sodium ions from the resin have gone and so no more hardness can be removed. Some resins can be regenerated by soaking them in a solution of sodium ions (e.g. common salt: sodium chloride), so that they can be used over and over again. Other types of ion exchangers need to have the resin replaced.

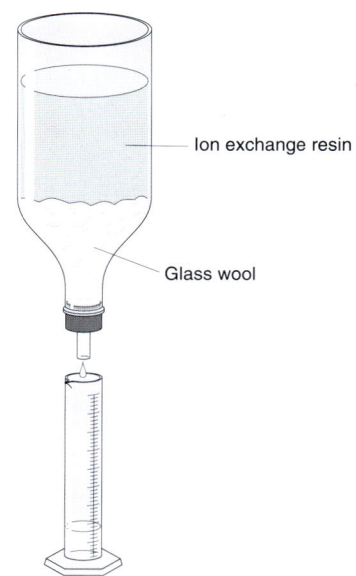

fig. 26.8 *A laboratory model of an ion exchanger*

SUMMARY

- Water which needs a lot of soap to form a lather is described as being **hard**. There are two types of hardness, temporary and permanent.
- **Temporary hardness** is caused by dissolved calcium (or magnesium) hydrogencarbonate, and it can be removed by boiling the water containing it. When this is done, a deposit of calcium carbonate (sometimes known as 'fur' or 'scale') remains.
- **Permanent hardness** is caused by calcium (or magnesium) sulphate and it cannot be removed by boiling. Both types of hardness can be removed by passing the water through an ion exchanger. In this, the calcium ions are replaced by sodium ions (which do not cause hardness).
- Hard water has both advantages and disadvantages.

QUESTIONS

Q. 26.1
Copy out and complete the following paragraphs.

(a) Calcium and ___ compounds dissolved in water make it ___. Soap does not ___ easily in ___ water. When these compounds react with ___ an insoluble scum is formed. There are two types of hardness, ___ and ___.

(b) The type of hardness that can be removed from water by boiling the water is called ___ and is caused by the compound calcium ___. Boiling turns this compound into calcium ___, which is ___ in water. Therefore when water with this kind of hardness in it is heated, deposit called ___ is left in the container. The type of hardness that is not removed by boiling is called ___ hardness, and it can be caused by the compound calcium ___. ___ has no effect on this compound.

(c) Both kinds of hardness are removed by passing the water through an ___ ___. In this, the ___ ions in the hard water are replaced by ___ ions, which do not cause hardness.

Q. 26.2
Describe an experiment in which you tested various samples of water for hardness. Draw a diagram of the apparatus used, and include a table of your results.

Q. 26.3
(a) Describe how you would find out whether your tap water supply is hard or soft?
(b) If your supply is hard, how would you decide whether the hardness is temporary or permanent?

Q. 26.4
(a) What are the advantages and the disadvantages of hard water?
(b) Name a compound that causes (i) temporary hardness, (ii) permanent hardness.

Q. 26.5
50 cm^3 samples of water from four different areas were tested with soap solution. The volumes of soap solution needed to give a permanent lather are shown in the results table. The experiment was repeated a second time, using samples that had been boiled and then a third time using samples that had been put through an ion exchanger.

(a) Which sample is the hardest? Give the reason for your answer.

Sample	Volume of soap solution needed/cm^3		
	Untreated	Boiled	Passed through ion exchanger
A	14	2	2
B	16	16	2
C	26	20	2
D	2	2	2

(b) Which sample could be distilled water? Explain why.
(c) Decide whether the hardness is temporary, permanent, or both, in:
(i) sample A, (ii) sample B, (iii) sample C.
(d) Name a compound that could be the cause of the hardness in (i) A, (ii) B.

27
METALS

fig. 27.1 *The metal steel is at the heart of many modern buildings*

Metals have been known for thousands of years. About eight were known in Roman times and now about eighty different *pure* or *elemental* metals are known. Metals are probably the most important construction materials of today's world.

Iron and steel are used in all modern buildings and machinery on account of their strength and relatively low cost. Copper is used for boilers because it is a good conductor of heat, and it is used for electric wire because it is a good conductor of electricity. Aluminium has a low density, so it is used in aircraft construction. Aluminium also doesn't corrode quickly, so it is used for window frames and greenhouses. Silver and gold are used for jewellery and valuable ornaments because they keep their shine and do not corrode, and zinc is used for galvanising iron (coating it with zinc) because it prevents the iron from rusting. The metal mercury is used in thermometers because it is a liquid at room temperature, and the filaments of electric light bulbs are made from tungsten because it has a very high melting point.

Apart from these familiar uses of metals, hundreds of compounds of metals are in everyday use. Such common substances as soap, salt, chalk and glass all contain metals. A simple definition of a metal is that it is a material which is usually hard and strong, shiny and dense, and conducts both heat and electricity.

The properties shown in Figure 27.2 apply to the ordinary metals of everyday life, such as iron, copper, and zinc. However, there is a group of unusual metals which

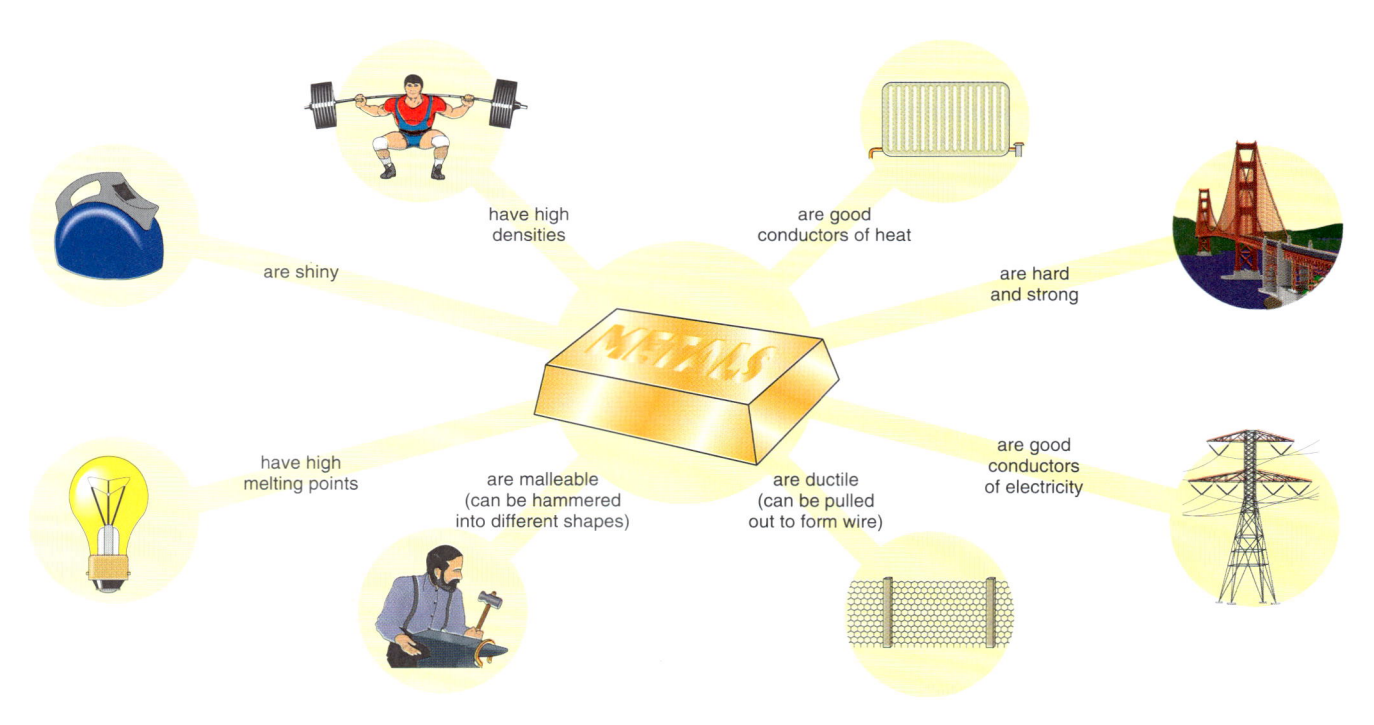

METALS
- are shiny
- have high densities
- are good conductors of heat
- are hard and strong
- are good conductors of electricity
- are ductile (can be pulled out to form wire)
- are malleable (can be hammered into different shapes)
- have high melting points

fig. 27.2

have some very different properties from these ordinary everyday metals. Do you remember them from Chapter 23 – the **alkali metals** which make up Group 1 of the Periodic Table? Your teacher may show you the reactions of these metals once more.

THE GROUP ONE METALS

The important elements in Group 1 are lithium, sodium and potassium. They are very reactive metals and quickly react with oxygen so they cannot be stored in air. Neither can they be stored in water because they react with that too; they are stored immersed in oil. They have similar, but not identical, properties. Sodium is perhaps the most important metal of the group.

Properties of sodium

- It is a soft, silvery metal.
- It tarnishes quickly in air (it does this because it combines with oxygen to form sodium oxide).
- It burns with a bright orange flame, forming sodium oxide.
- It reacts quickly with water, giving off hydrogen and forming sodium hydroxide solution:
  $2Na + 2H_2O \rightarrow H_2 + 2NaOH$
- It has a low density and floats on water.
- It is stored under oil to prevent it reacting with the air.

The properties of lithium and potassium are similar, but lithium is harder than sodium and potassium softer. Lithium is less reactive but potassium is more reactive than sodium. So the order of reactivity is potassium > sodium > lithium. Like sodium, lithium and potassium also form alkaline solutions when they react with water.

fig. 27.3 *Sodium is stored in oil to prevent it oxidising*

Uses of the alkali metals

The only important use of lithium metal is in the lithium batteries which are used in some watches and cameras. Sodium is the essential element in the familiar yellow street lights, and sodium compounds are important too. Potassium metal has few uses, but its compounds are very important and widely used.

QUESTIONS

Q. 27.1

Given that the symbols of lithium, sodium and potassium are $^{7}_{3}Li$ $^{23}_{11}Na$ $^{39}_{19}K$

(i) calculate the number of protons, neutrons and electrons in each,
(ii) draw diagrams showing the arrangement of their electrons.

Q. 27.2

List three properties of the alkali metals
(i) in which they resemble the 'ordinary' everyday metals, and
(ii) three properties in which they are very different from them.

Q. 27.3

How are the alkali metals stored?
Why is it necessary to store them in this way?

Q. 27.4

(a) Draw a diagram showing a piece of sodium reacting with water.
(b) Describe how you would show that the water has become alkaline after the reaction.
(c) Explain why this happens.

ALLOYS

Many metals in common use are not pure elements but are mixtures of two or more different metals (or sometimes of a metal and a non-metal); these mixtures are called **alloys**. An alloy usually has different properties than the metals of which it is composed and can be much more useful. For example, pure iron is not much use for the construction of buildings or machinery because it is too soft, it stretches, and it rusts very easily. When, however, some carbon is mixed with it, it becomes mild steel, which is much stronger and harder than the iron itself. If some nickel and chromium are included as well, it becomes stainless steel, which is harder still and does not rust.

27 • Metals

This table lists some alloys in everyday use.

Alloy	Composition	Uses
mild steel	iron, carbon	buildings, machinery
stainless steel	iron, Cr, Ni	kitchen implements, sinks and cutlery
brass	copper, tin	ornaments, musical instruments
bronze	copper, zinc	bearings, machine parts, statues
cupro-nickel	copper, nickel	'silver' coins
solder	lead, tin	joining pipes and wires
alnico	Al, Ni, Co	making magnets

fig. 27.4 Drill bits are made of steel (an alloy of iron and carbon), solder is an alloy of lead and tin, brass is an alloy of copper and zinc, and magnets are made of an alloy called 'Alnico' – an alloy of Al, Ni and Co

THE ACTIVITY SERIES

Do all metals react similarly? You have seen the reactions of some metals with water – reacting extremely quickly. Do they all react like that? What about iron and copper? Your everyday experience should tell you that these either don't react with water, or, if they do, they do so very slowly. The Ardagh Chalice which is made of silver and is in the National Museum of Ireland, was made is the eighth century and is still in perfect condition 1200 years later. So, different metals have different degrees of reactivity.

fig. 27.5

Experiment 27.1
To investigate reactivities of some metals

safety glasses needed

1. Take small but approximately equal sized amounts of magnesium, zinc and copper.
2. Set up three test tubes in a test-tube rack, and into each of them put dilute hydrochloric acid to a depth of about 3 cm.
3. At the same instant, place the three metal samples in the three test tubes of acid, and observe what happens.
4. Which metal reacts (i) fastest, (ii) slowest? List the three metals in **decreasing** order of reactivity.
5. Empty the three test tubes, and rinse them several times with water.
6. Set up the three test tubes again, but this time put about 3 cm depth of water in each.
7. Take small but approximately equal sizes amounts of calcium, magnesium and copper.
8. Sandpaper the magnesium until the shiny metal is clearly exposed.
9. At the same time, put the three metal samples into the three test tubes.
10. Observe what happens. Look **very closely** at the magnesium. Is anything happening? Which of the three metals reacts (i) fastest, (ii) slowest? List the three metals in decreasing order of reactivity.
11. From the results of the two experiments, list all four metals in decreasing order of reactivity.

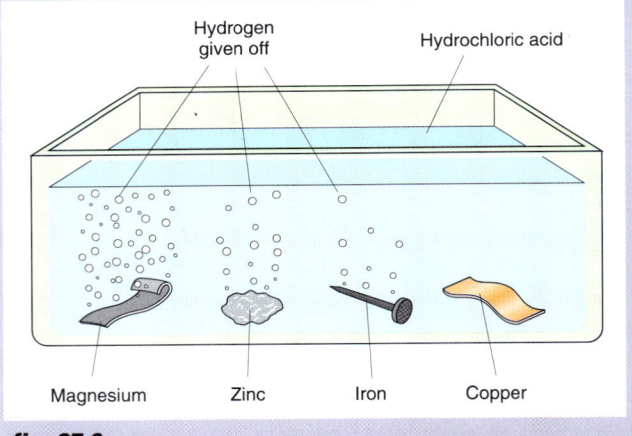

fig. 27.6

A list of the metals arranged in decreasing order of reactivity is called the activity series.

The following list contains some important metals, in their order in the activity series.

> potassium
> sodium
> lithium
> calcium
> magnesium
> zinc
> iron
> hydrogen (*)
> copper
> silver
> gold

(*) Although hydrogen is not a metal, it can often react like a metal and therefore it has a position in the activity series. Metals which are above hydrogen in the activity series will displace hydrogen from acid (e.g. zinc and hydrochloric acid yield hydrogen), but metals which are below hydrogen will not (e.g. copper and hydrochloric acid do not react with each other).

OXIDATION AND REDUCTION

The simple meaning of oxidation is that it is a reaction in which a substance combines with oxygen. While that definition is perfectly correct, it applies to only one type of oxidation, and a better definition of the term is that:

> **Oxidation is a reaction in which a substance loses electrons.**

Reduction is the reverse – it is a reaction in which oxygen is removed from a substance, but again, a better definition of it is that:

> **Reduction is a reaction in which a substance gains electrons.**

To understand how this definition applies to a reaction in which an element combines with oxygen, consider the oxidation of magnesium to magnesium oxide. Magnesium oxide is an ionic compound and is composed of Mg^{2+} ions and O^{2-} ions. So two things happen as the magnesium burns: (i) magnesium atoms lose two electrons to become Mg^{2+} ions (that is, the magnesium is oxidised), and oxygen atoms gain two electrons (i.e. it is reduced) to become O^{2-} ions.

$$\text{Mg atom} + \text{O atom} \rightarrow \underset{\text{oxidised}}{\overset{\text{reduced}}{Mg^{2+} \text{ion} + O^{2-} \text{ion}}}$$

Oxidation and reduction can and do occur without any oxygen being present at all. The combining of sodium and chlorine is an oxidation–reduction reaction.

$Na + Cl \rightarrow NaCl$ (which is made up of $Na^+ + Cl^-$).

So, what happens is that each sodium atom loses an electron (oxidation) and each chlorine atoms gains an electron (reduction) as they combine together to form sodium chloride.

RUSTING AND CORROSION

Many metals corrode or decay over a period of time. Iron acquires a brown flaky surface called rust which soon crumbles away; copper exposed to the atmosphere becomes covered with a layer of a green-coloured substance; and the zinc of batteries turns to a white powdery substance.

Corrosion can be described as an undesirable process in which a metal slowly changes to an oxide or some other compound. Corrosion often returns metals to their natural state – the state in which they existed in their ores.

Experiment 27.2
To investigate rusting

In this experiment, some iron nails are left in different conditions for a few days and then examined to see what conditions cause them to rust. The nail in (a) is exposed to moist air while that in (b) is in dry air. The nail in (c) is immersed in ordinary tap water while that in (d) is in cold boiled water (boiling water removes the dissolved air from it).

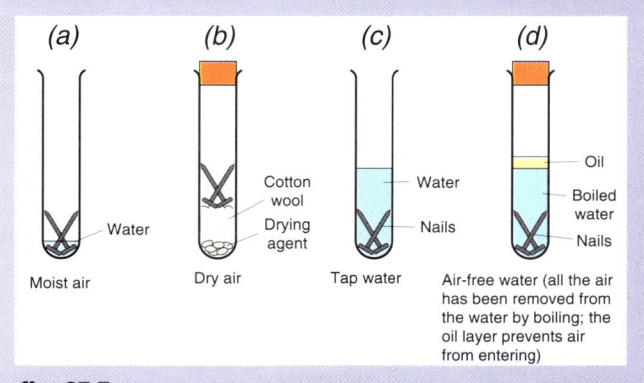

(a) Water — Moist air
(b) Cotton wool / Drying agent — Dry air
(c) Water / Nails — Tap water
(d) Oil / Boiled water / Nails — Air-free water (all the air has been removed from the water by boiling; the oil layer prevents air from entering)

fig. 27.7

1. Arrange four test tubes as shown. There are different conditions in each.
2. Into each, place a sandpapered, shiny iron or steel nail.
3. Place a cork in test tube (b), to keep the moisture from entering.

4. Leave the rack of test tubes where they will not be disturbed.
5. Examine the nails a week later.
6. Which nail(s) have rusted? What conditions cause iron to rust?

Did you discover that the nails in test tubes (a) and (c) had rusted? In these test tubes both air and moisture were present, so these conditions are necessary for rusting.

Rusting is the combining of iron and oxygen, and rust is mainly iron oxide (there is some water combined in it as well). Rusting is therefore similar to burning but takes place much more slowly. Steel rusts because it is an alloy containing iron. Rusting does great damage to objects made of iron and steel, and many methods are used to prevent it or to slow it down.

Preventing corrosion

Many different methods are in use to prevent or slow down the corrosion of metal objects, and these are illustrated below.

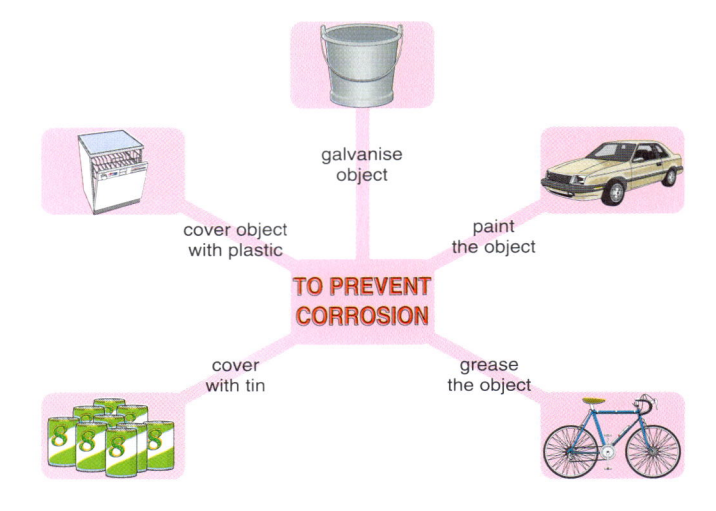

fig. 27.8 Preventing corrosion

The extraction of a metal from its ore, and the corrosion of the metal, are opposite processes:

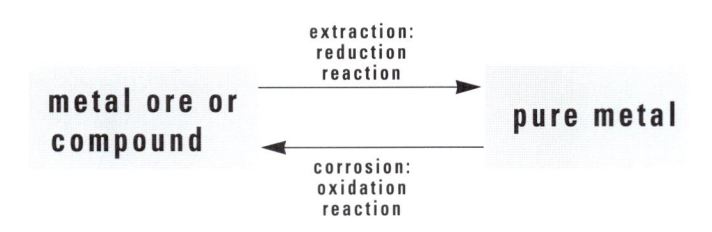

SUMMARY

- **Metals** are materials which are usually: hard and strong, have high densities, are shiny, have high melting points, are good conductors of heat, are good conductors of electricity, are malleable and ductile and can lose electrons to form positive ions.
- The metals of Group 1 of the Periodic Table (called the **alkali metals**) show a number of differences. They are very soft, float on water, and react with water liberating hydrogen from it.
- **Alloys** are mixtures of metals. Hundreds of alloys are in everyday use.
- **Metals** have different degrees of reactivity. The **activity series** is a list of metals in decreasing order of reactivity.
- **Oxidation** is a reaction in which a substance loses electrons, and **reduction** is a reaction in which it gains electrons.
- **Corrosion** is a reaction in which a metal slowly oxidises to an oxide or other compound. Rusting is the corrosion of iron (and steel). Various methods in use to hinder corrosion are painting, greasing, covering with plastic, galvanising, plating with tin or with chromium.

QUESTIONS

Q. 27.5

Copy out and complete the spaces in the following paragraph.

__, sodium and __ are three members of a family of elements called the __ __. These elements are in Group __ of the Periodic Table. When a piece of sodium is dropped into water, it __ on the surface of the water. It __ into a little sphere that __ around on the __ of the water. As it moves around, it makes a hissing sound as the gas __ is released. If, after the reaction has finished, the solution is tested with red and blue litmus paper, it is found that __ litmus stays __, but the __ litmus turns __. The water, which was __ before the reaction, has now become __.

Q. 27.6

Give the name and symbol for a metal which:
(a) is the main element in steel
(b) reacts with cold water
(c) is used for making electrical wires
(d) is a liquid at room temperature
(e) is used to cover cans to prevent them from rusting

(continued)

(f) floats on water
(g) is used for making jewellery
(h) is more reactive than sodium
(i) is more reactive than zinc but less reactive than calcium
(j) reacts with dilute acid to produce hydrogen
(k) is the main component of 'tin' cans
(l) is used to make drinks cans
(m) is in the yellow street lights
(n) burns with a bright white flame
(o) is used to make bulb filaments
(p) is used to make electric wire
(q) has a high density and is used for weights

Q. 27.7
List five metals that are found in your home and explain why each is used for its purpose.

Q. 27.8
What is meant by an oxidation reaction in terms of (i) oxygen, (ii) electrons. What is the opposite of oxidation? Give an example of each type of reaction.

Q. 27.9
Which of the following are oxidation reactions, and which are reductions? Explain why in each case.
(a) magnesium combining with oxygen
(b) magnesium burning
(c) iron rusting
(d) copper oxide being converted to copper
(e) hydrogen being converted to water
(f) magnesium forming magnesium ions
(g) chlorine forming Cl^- ions
(h) aluminium ore (aluminium oxide) being converted to aluminium

Q. 27.10
A metal X is dropped into water, and it reacts to form a gas Y and a compound Z which dissolves in the water. Identify X, Y and Z. What will happen to litmus paper when put into the water? Explain why?

Q. 27.11
Describe an experiment in which you investigated the conditions needed for iron to rust. Draw a diagram to illustrate your answer, and state what conclusions were reached.

Q. 27.12
Describe an experiment in which the relative reactivities of some metals were investigated. Draw a diagram showing how this was done, and state what conclusions were reached.

Q. 27.13
Suggest reasons for each of the following:
(a) Tent poles are made from aluminium and not iron.
(b) The chain of a padlock is made from iron, not aluminium.
(c) 'Silver' coins are not made from silver.
(d) 'Tin' cans are not made from tin.
(e) Dustbins are made from iron coated with zinc, but not from either iron or zinc.
(f) Electric light bulb filaments are made from tungsten but not copper.
(g) Aluminium is used to carry the current in overhead cables rather than copper.
(h) Mercury is the only metal that is used in thermometers.

28
CHEMISTRY AND ELECTRICITY

fig. 28.1 *Volta demonstrating his battery*

GETTING ELECTRICITY FROM CHEMICALS

How many devices do you use each day that depend on electricity? You probably do not think about this when using them – you take them all for granted. But two hundred years ago there was no electricity. At that time the only way known to make electricity was to rub various substances such as glass with cloth or fur, when it would become charged with 'static' electricity. People built machines for this purpose and while the machines could produce great sparks, they could not give a current of electricity, so this type of electricity was not very useful. There is picture of an early electrical machine on page 59.

It was therefore a great discovery in 1800, when Professor Alessandro Volta of Italy made the first electric battery, which he did by dipping two different metals into a salt solution.

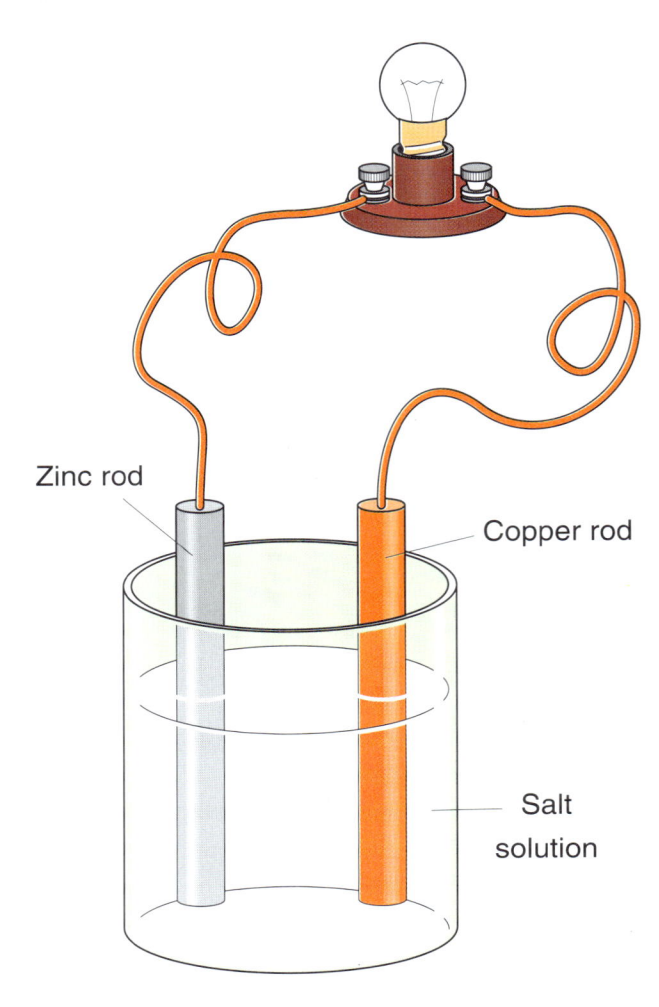

fig. 28.2 *Volta's simple cell*

When a cell like this is connected to a voltmeter, it reads about one volt. One volt will not light a bulb very brightly, but if a number of such cells are connected together, they will light the bulb more brightly.

Today's batteries are greatly improved on Volta's cells, but they work in exactly the same way. If you cut open a single cell, you will find a zinc case and a carbon rod (this acts as the second metal) along with a liquid, which in modern cells is made into a paste so that it cannot spill.

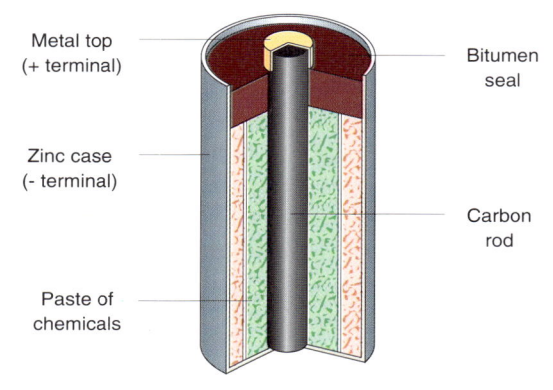

fig. 28.3 (a) Inside a 'dry' cell

The strength (voltage) of a cell depends on what the two metals are, and in the next experiment, the effect of using different pairs of metals is investigated.

Experiment 28.1
To investigate the effect of different metals on the strength of a cell

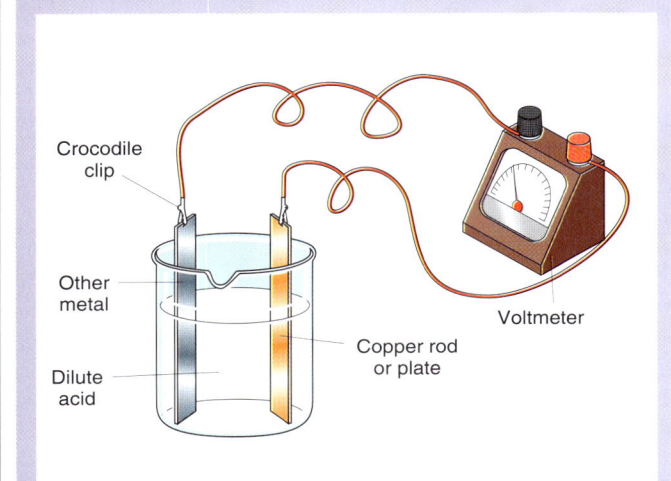

fig. 28.4

1. Set up the apparatus as shown. Insert one of the metals to be tested into the crocodile clip and dip the metal (but not the clip) into the acid.
2. Read and record the voltage produced.
3. Leaving the copper metal in position, replace the metal being tested with a second metal.
4. Read and record the new voltage.
5. Repeat this process with as many metals as are available.

Conclusion:
Different pairs of metals produce different voltages.

Explanation

Metals are elements which can lose electrons easily, to become positive ions, e.g. zinc atoms lose their two outer electrons to form zinc ions:

$$Zn - 2e^- \rightarrow Zn^{2+}. \quad (e^- = \text{an electron})$$

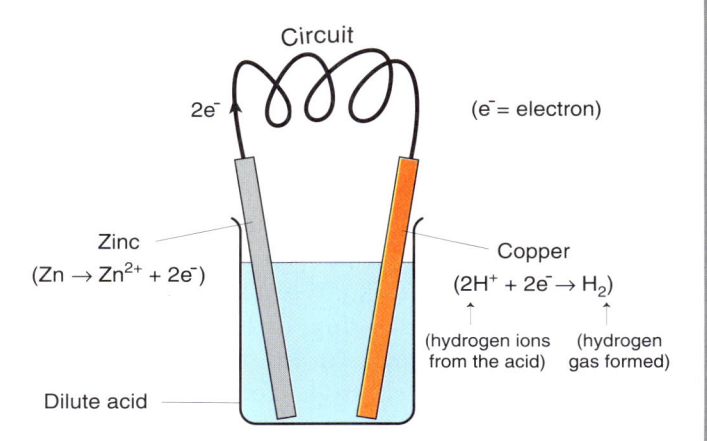

fig. 28.5

Zinc releases its two outer-shell electrons more easily than copper does, and when the cell is working (supplying a current), these two electrons are 'pushed' by the zinc atoms into the connecting wire and then around the circuit, to arrive back at the cell, at the other plate. (There, the electrons react with hydrogen ions from the acid, and form hydrogen gas.). The flow of electrons around the circuit is an electric current. As the current flows, the zinc metal is being converted to zinc ions, that is, it is being 'used up'. Therefore the cell eventually ceases giving an electron flow, or, it becomes 'dead'.

ELECTROLYSIS

You learned in Chapter 13 about two of the three main effects of an electric current, which are that it can cause heat, and that it can cause magnetism. The third main effect is that it can cause chemical changes, and this is what electrochemistry is all about — chemistry being caused by electricity. It is therefore the reverse of what happens in an electric cell, which is electricity being caused by chemistry.

> **Electrolysis is the decomposing (breaking down) of a compound by passing electricity through it.**

Can you recall an experiment in Chapter 22, *Water*, in which water was separated into its two elements by passing electricity through it? This was an example of an electrolysis reaction. Liquids containing ions (metal compounds and acids) conduct electricity and when they do so, various chemical changes occur. Such liquids are called **electrolytes**.

The German chemist Hofmann invented a piece of apparatus, called Hofmann's voltameter, for the electrolysis of water. There is an illustration of a Hofmann's **voltameter** on page 153. Note that a voltameter is a vessel in which electrolysis takes place. Do not confuse the term with **voltmeter**, which is an instrument for measuring voltage.

Water on its own does not conduct electricity very well, and in this experiment, some acid is added to it as a catalyst to make it do so. When an electric current is passed through this solution, hydrogen is produced at the negative electrode (called the cathode) and oxygen at the positive electrode (the anode). The two gases are produced in a 2:1 ratio by volume, because that is the ratio in which they are present in water (the formula for water is H_2O).

ELECTROPLATING

One very important use of **electrolysis** is electroplating. This is a process in which a layer of one metal is put on top of another by means of electricity. Its purpose is generally twofold: (i) to give protection to the metal underneath, and (ii) to produce a more attractive finish. Chromium plating is a familiar example of electroplating. It is found on bath taps, car bumpers, bicycle handlebars, towel rails and other household articles. Chromium does not corrode (it is quite low in the activity series); it can be polished to give a bright attractive appearance, and it is a hard metal which resists scratches and wear.

fig. 28.6 *A silver-plated tray, spoon and a pair of salt cellars*

Experiment 28.2
To electroplate a key with copper

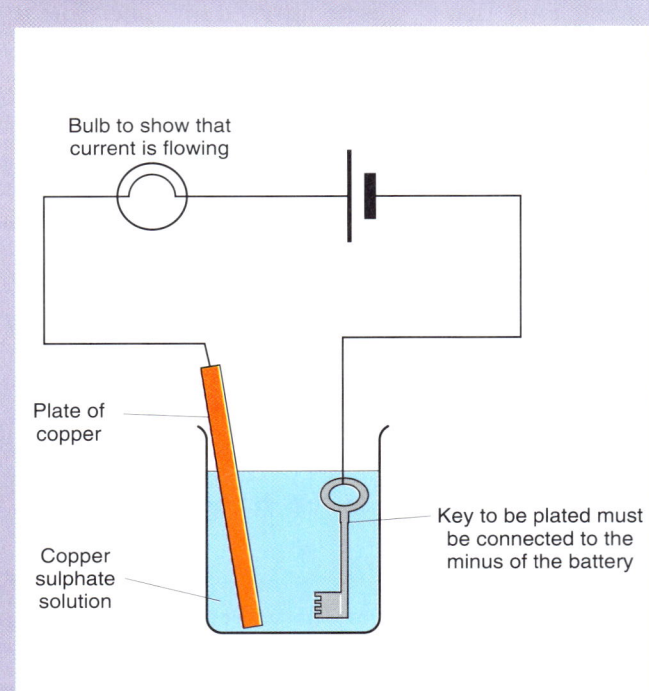

safety glasses needed

fig. 28.7

To electroplate an object, that object is used as the cathode (negative electrode) in an electrolysis. The anode (positive electrode) consists of a plate of the metal to be put on to it, and the electrolyte (the liquid in the container) must contain ions of that metal. For example, to electroplate a key with copper, the key is the cathode, a plate of copper is the anode, and the electrolyte is a solution of copper sulphate.

1. Lightly sandpaper the surface of the object to be electroplated. (If it is not clean, the copper plate will be 'patchy'.)

2. Set up the apparatus as shown. Make sure that the key is the cathode (connected to the negative terminal of the power supply) and that the copper plate is the anode.

3. Switch on the current and adjust it to no more than 0.5 A. (If too high a current is used, the covering metal will not stick properly.)

4. Allow the current to flow for about five minutes and then switch off or disconnect the power supply.

5. Wash the key under the tap and then dry it.

Silver plating is also quite common, for the same reasons. Silver plated items often have 'EPNS' stamped on them; this stands for 'electro plated nickel silver' Cutlery and cheaper jewellery items are often silver plated. These have the appearance of silver but are much less expensive.

The explanation

Copper sulphate is an ionic compound. When dissolved in water, it breaks up into Cu^{2+} and SO_4^{2-} ions. Remembering that a battery acts as an electron pump, it pushes electrons into the vessel at the cathode (the key).

At the cathode, the Cu^{2+} ions (from the solution) gain two electrons each, and become copper metal ($Cu^{2+} + 2e^- \rightarrow Cu$), which is plated on to the cathode (i.e. the key). At the anode, each copper atom loses two electrons to become copper ions ($Cu - 2e^- \rightarrow Cu^{2+}$).

The electrons are then pumped around the circuit by the battery. The net change is that copper is transferred from the anode to the cathode. The anode therefore gets 'used up' as copper is transferred from it to the cathode.

SUMMARY

- A simple **battery** consists of two different metals dipping into salt or acid solution. The strength (voltage) of the battery depends on the two metals used.
- **Electrolysis** is the decomposing of a compound by passing an electric current through it. When water is electrolysed, hydrogen and oxygen are formed.
- **Electroplating** is an important application of electrolysis. This consists of putting a thin layer of one metal on top of another, for appearance and protection.

QUESTIONS

Q. 28.1

Rewrite the following paragraphs, and complete the spaces in it.

(a) The first electric battery was made by the scientist ___ . It consisted of two different ___ dipping into a solution of ___. The strength of a battery (correctly called ___) is measured in ___, and this depends on what the two ___ are.

(b) An electric current has ___ main effects; these are the ___ effect (which is used in an electric kettle), the ___ effect (which is shown by the solenoid) and the ___ effect which is illustrated in Hofmann's Voltameter. In use, this piece of apparatus is filled with ___ to which some ___ has been added in order to make the ___ conduct. When an electric current is passed through it, the ___ is decomposed into its two elements ___ and ___. At the negative eletrode (called the ___) the gas ___ is released, and at the positive electrode (called the ___), ___ is released. The gases are released in a ___ ratio, because the atoms are present in this ratio in ___. The process of decomposing a substance using electricity is called ___.

Q. 28.2

Describe, with the aid of a diagram, an experiment to compare the voltages produced by different combinations of metals in a suitable electrolyte.

Q. 28.3

Draw a diagram of a dry cell and label the different parts. What advantage has the dry cell over the simple cell such as that which Volta invented?

Q. 28.4

Explain the terms: electrolysis, electroplating, electrode, anode, cathode, voltameter,

Q. 28.5

(a) What is meant by the term electrolysis?
(b) Draw a diagram of an apparatus which could be used for the electrolysis of water.
(c) Name a suitable material for the electrodes.
(d) What information does the experiment give about the composition of water?
(e) What substance must be added to the water so that current will flow?
(f) What is the reason for the answer to (e)?

Q. 28.6

What is meant by the term electroplating? Describe, with the aid of a diagram, how spoons could be electroplated with nickel. Why might one want to do this to the spoons?

Q. 28.7

Sugar and salt both dissolve in water but only the salt solution conducts electricity. Why is this? Name another substance which would conduct electricity when dissolved in water, and also one which wouldn't.

Q. 28.8

Describe with the aid of a diagram which shows the circuit used, a laboratory experiment in which you electroplated an object. Mention what the object was and what metal you plated it with.

fig 28.8 A 'fruit clock'. The 'battery' to power the clock consists of copper and zinc stuck into the orange (which contains citric acid).

29

INTRODUCTION TO BIOLOGY ANIMALS AND PLANTS

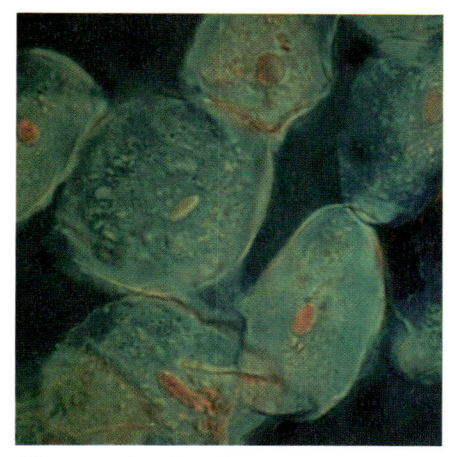

Human cheek cells (× 200 magnification)

Electron micrograph of a cockroach

Giant Sequoia trees. These can grow to a height of 80 metres and live for 3000–4000 years.

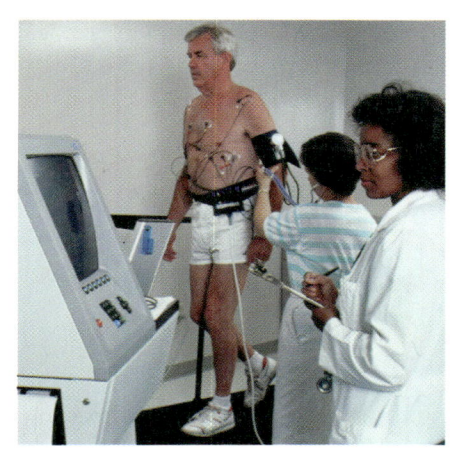

A man exercising as his heart rate is monitored

Ash seedling

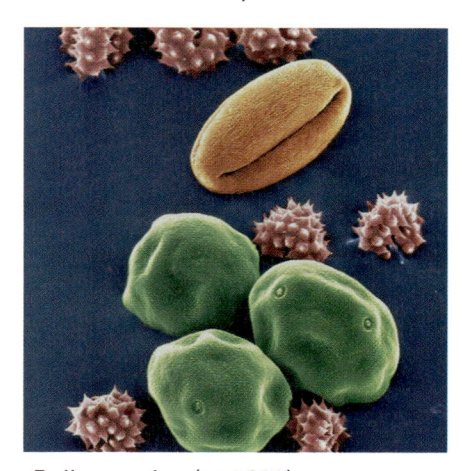

Pollen grains (× 1000)

Sunflowers

Ladybirds feeding on aphids

fig. 29.1

29 • Introduction to Biology: Animals and Plants

WHAT IS BIOLOGY?

Biology is the study of living things or **organisms**. The word organism is used by biologists to refer to any living thing. There are over one million different kinds of living organisms on Earth and human beings are just one of these. Biologists study organisms in order to find out how and where they live, what kind of food they eat, and how they reproduce. Areas where plants and animals live are called **habitats**. Biologists study habitats to learn about the organisms that live in them, how they depend on each other, and how humans are affecting these areas.

Living organisms are divided into two main groups or **kingdoms**, the plant kingdom and the animal kingdom. Within each kingdom there are smaller groups with common features – for example, animals which have backbones, or plants that produce seeds. The smallest natural group of organisms is called a **species**. Dandelions, daisies and roses are examples of plant species, and robins, sparrows and thrushes are three different bird species. In biology, the word animal is used to describe a huge variety of organisms, from the smallest of insects, up to humans, elephants and killer whales.

CHARACTERISTICS OF LIVING THINGS

All living things have seven common characteristics: feeding, growth, reproduction, movement, sensitivity, excretion and respiration.

- **Feeding**: All living organisms feed, to provide them with energy and to enable them to grow. Plants have a special ability to make their own food in a process called photosynthesis which you will learn about later (Chapter 36). Animals cannot make their own food so they must feed on plants or other animals.

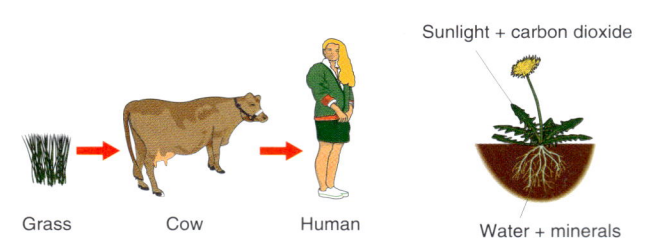

fig. 29.2 (a) Feeding

- **Growth**: All living things grow. Plants and animals increase in size, some at a different rate than others. After a certain time, animals cease to grow larger, but their cells, (the basic 'building blocks' of organisms) are being replaced all the time. You will learn more about cells in the next chapter.

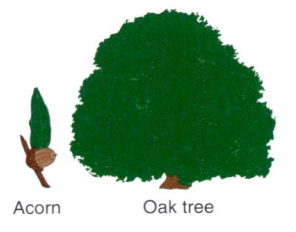

fig. 29.2 (b) Growth

- **Reproduction**: All living things produce offspring, which means that life is passed on to new individuals and the species survives. If organisms did not reproduce, the species would eventually become extinct (die out).

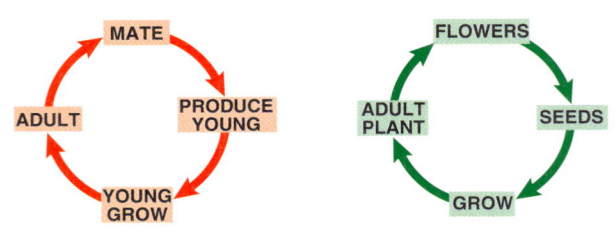

fig. 29.2 (c) Reproduction

- **Movement**: All living things move. Plants move in a gradual way – the buds of flowers open and close, and their roots move though the soil in search of water. Movement in animals is usually easy to see, as they walk, run, crawl, swim or fly, to avoid danger, and to search for food.

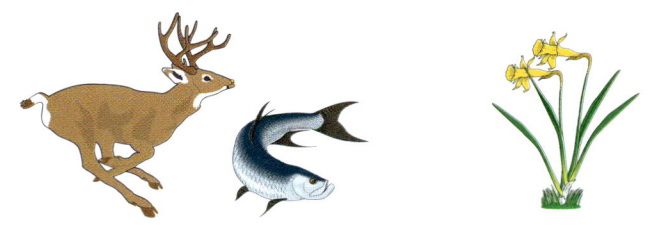

fig. 29.2 (d) Movement

- **Sensitivity**: All living things react to what is happening around them. Most animals react quickly to even slight changes in light, sound, heat or touch, but plants react much more slowly. You may have noticed that an indoor plant in a room grows toward the light. This is an example of a plant reacting to something. Humans get information about their surroundings using their sense organs – eyes, ears, skin, nose and tongue.

fig. 29.2 (e) Sensitivity

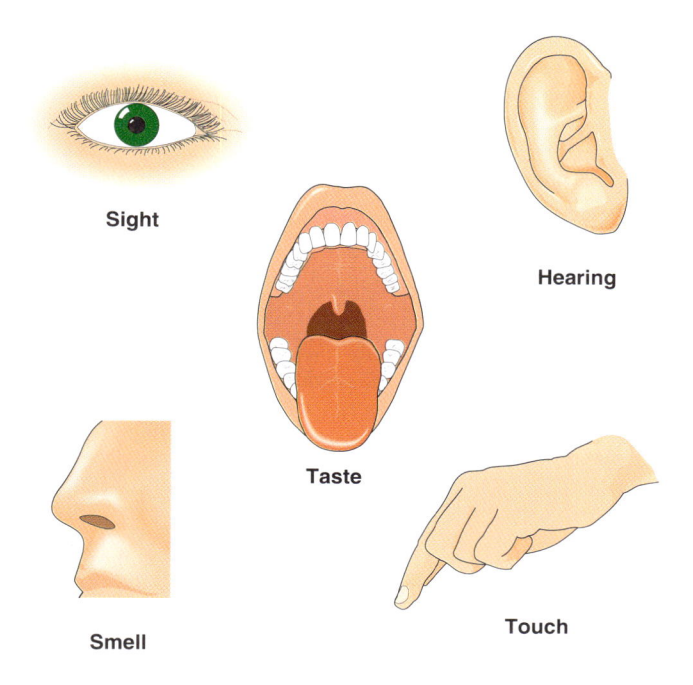

fig. 29.2 (e) Sensitivity

- **Excretion**: All living things produce waste products. If this waste were allowed to build up, it could be poisonous to the organism. Excretion is the name given to the way in which organisms get rid of waste.

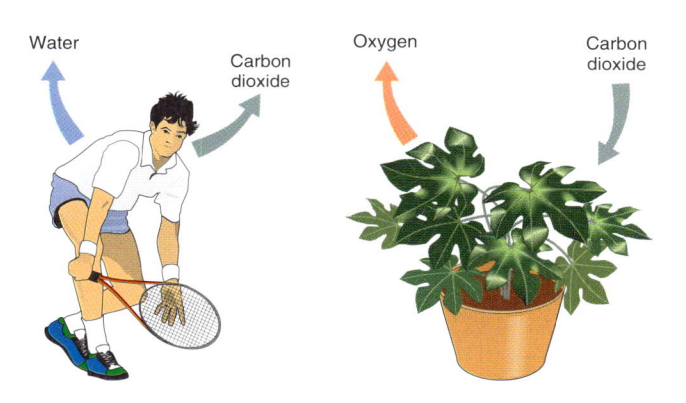

fig. 29.2 (f) Excretion

- **Respiration**: All living things respire. This is the name given to the process in which food combines with oxygen, releasing the energy from the food as it does so. The energy is then used by the organism for all its activities, such as moving, digesting food and breathing.

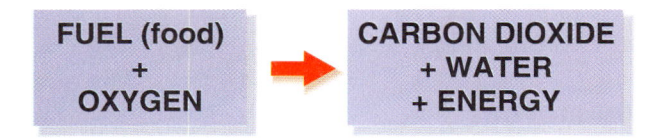

FUEL (food) + OXYGEN → CARBON DIOXIDE + WATER + ENERGY

fig. 29.2 (g) Respiration

In nature, living organisms depend on each other, and animals and plants play important roles in the habitats in which they live. Humans depend on plants and animals for many purposes, and some of these are explained in the next section.

IMPORTANCE OF ANIMALS

Agriculture

Humans rely on animals such as cows, pigs, sheep and poultry as sources of food and clothing. Agriculture means the rearing of animals and the growing of plants to provide this food and clothing. However, some animals cause damage and can make life more difficult. Examples are rats and mice which eat grain, insects which eat crops and can spread diseases, and thread worms which can infect the digestive systems of dogs and humans. Animals such as these are called pests.

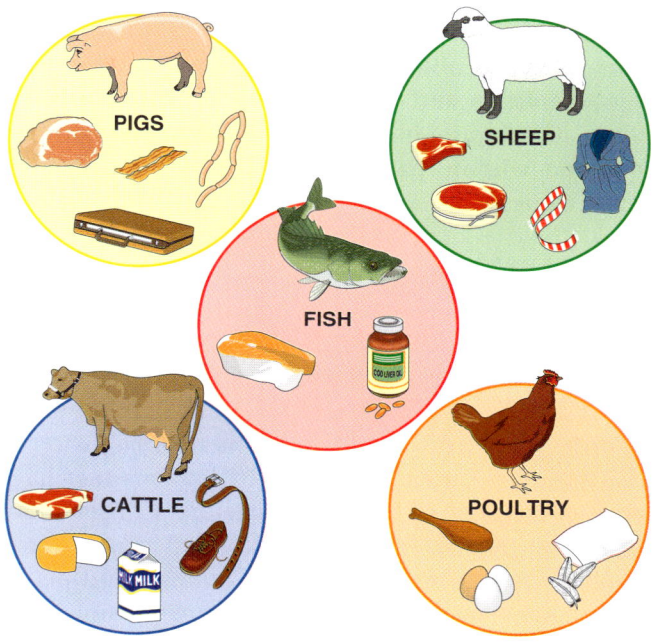

fig. 29.3 Animals have many uses

Mariculture

Mariculture is the growing and harvesting for human consumption of organisms that live in water. The fishing industry harvests cod, mackerel, and many other species of fish for food The regional fisheries boards have fish nurseries where thousands of trout and salmon are hatched. When these have developed, they are released into lakes and rivers. Shellfish such as mussels and oysters are harvested along the coasts of various parts of Ireland.

A balance needs to be achieved between making use of the resources available and destroying them by

29 • Introduction to Biology: Animals and Plants

overuse. Over-fishing causes problems, as it can dramatically reduce the numbers of particular species. If immature fish are harvested before they have a chance to reproduce, the fish population will drop.

Water pollution is a threat to fish, particularly shellfish which can be killed by coastal pollution. Some substances entering rivers and lakes from farmland, for example, can kill freshwater fish and other organisms.

Medicine

In medicine, animals such as mice, rats, monkeys and rabbits are used to test new drugs before they are used by humans. There are some animals however, which cause medical problems by spreading diseases. For example, mosquitoes spread malaria, cows can transfer brucellosis and dogs can transfer rabies.

Leisure

Humans have kept animals as pets for thousands of years. Many people enjoy the company of pet cats, dogs, hamsters and rabbits, while others like horse riding, show jumping and dog racing. We can visit zoos and wildlife parks to see animals that are not native to Ireland.

Conservation

Because of the importance of animals, it is important that animal habitats are not destroyed. Even the smallest of animals play an important part in the habitat in which they live. Unfortunately many of today's human activities are destroying animal habitats. In a matter of days or hours humans can destroy habitats that have taken thousands of years to develop. Conservation means the protection, preservation and management of natural resources and allowing animals and plants to exist in as natural an environment as possible.

fig. 29.4 (b) A salmon farm

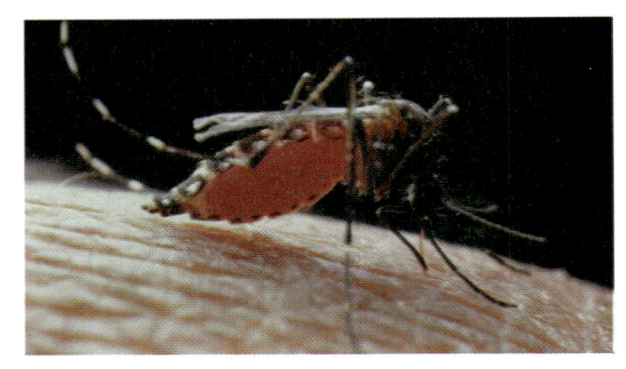

fig. 29.4 (c) Some animals, such as the mosquito, transfer diseases

IMPORTANCE OF PLANTS

Agriculture

Humans grow plants to provide food. Many plant species are used as food and different parts of these plants are eaten. We eat the roots, stems, leaves, fruits, and seeds of plants.

Plant part	Examples
roots	carrots, parsnips
stems	celery, rhubarb
leaves	lettuce, cabbage
fruits	apples, strawberries
seeds	nuts, beans

While most food plants are grown for humans to eat directly, some are grown mainly as feed for animals. For example, grass and mangolds are grown to feed cattle, sheep and pigs.

Commerce

Plants such as cotton and flax are grown in order to make cloth. Timber is produced to make houses,

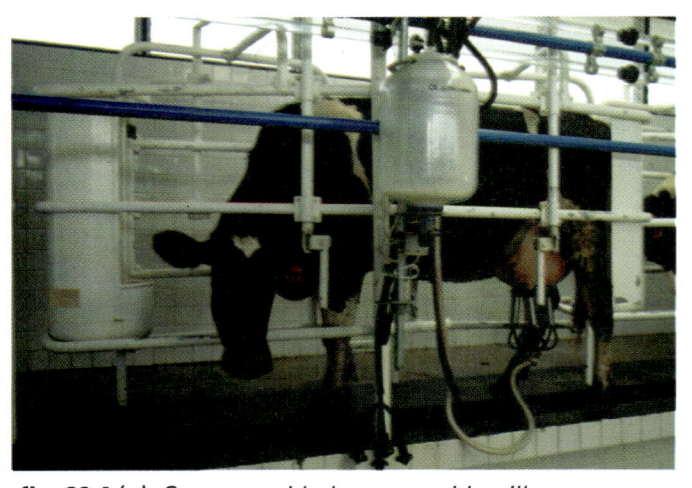

fig. 29.4 (a) Cows provide humans with milk

furniture, and tools. Some timber is processed to make paper or wood products such as chipboard.

Medicine

Humans have used plants to treat illnesses for thousands of years. In South America, tribes living in the rain forests rely almost totally on plants for effective natural remedies. Scientists are still discovering chemicals in plants that can be used to produce drugs for medical use. Some examples of commonly used drugs which are extracted from plants are shown in the following table. If plant species are destroyed, the diversity of organisms on the Earth will be reduced, and possible sources of new medical drugs will be lost.

Drug	Extracted from	Medical use
Quinine	Cinchona plant	Treatment of malaria
Digitalin	Foxglove plant	Treatment of heart disease
Morphine	Poppies	Relief of pain

Leisure

Many people enjoy looking at plants, and gardening is a very popular hobby with all age groups. Freshly cut flowers and plants add colour and scent to rooms, and they brighten up a house. Forests and woodlands are pleasant places where we can enjoy natural surroundings.

fig. 29.6 *Plants have many uses*

The bark of the Cinchona tree is a source of the drug quinine

Digitalin is extracted from foxgloves

Poppy flowers

fig. 29.5

29 • Introduction to Biology: Animals and Plants

PLANTS AND ANIMALS

Plants differ from animals in that plants are able to make their own food. They do this by using carbon dioxide from the air, water from the ground, light from the Sun, and chlorophyll which is contained in the leaves of the plant. The process by which plants make their food is known as **photosynthesis**.

Animals are not able to make their own food and so must eat plants or other animals, or both. Some animals eat only plants, and these are known as **herbivores**. Examples of these are cows, rabbits, and snails. Other animals, known as **carnivores**, eat only meat, and examples of this group are hawks, lions and killer whales. Animals which eat both plants and animals are called **omnivores** and examples are humans, badgers and starlings.

A **food chain** is a way of showing the feeding links between organisms – what they eat and what eats them. All food chains begin with green plants, which are called **producers**. Animals eat 'ready made' food when they eat other organisms, so animals are called **consumers**. For example, grass is eaten by rabbits, which are in turn eaten by foxes. Food chains are described in greater detail in Chapter 39.

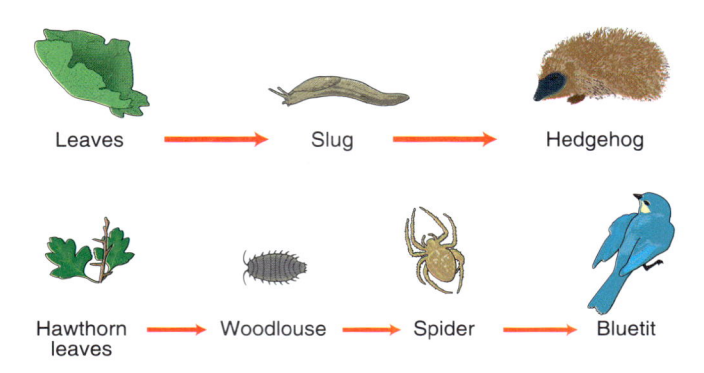

fig. 29.7 *Food chains show feeding links*

Oxygen is essential for all living things. Plants release this gas into the atmosphere when they are making their own food. Animals release the gas carbon dioxide when they breath out and plants use this gas in photosynthesis. Plants also provide habitats for many animals, from birds living in trees, to caterpillars living on and eating a cabbage plant in a garden. As animals are so dependent on plants, care must be taken to conserve plants and their habitats.

RECOGNISING PLANTS

There are many species of plants, some of which grow in forests, some in fields and others indoors as house plants. Plants can be identified by their leaves, flowers and fruits.

fig. 29.8 *Common trees found in Ireland*

The common buttercup

The dandelion seed head

Yellow rose flower

Daffodil flower

fig. 29.9 There are many types of flower

RECOGNISING ANIMALS

There are lots of different animals on Earth. Scientists classify animals into two main groups: those that have back bones, called **vertebrates**, and those which do not have backbones, known as **invertebrates**. Animals are identified by looking in detail at their structure and comparing them to other groups of animals to find similarities. Examples of features used to identify animals are the number of body parts they have, the number of legs, and whether they are covered by fur, scales or skin.

SUMMARY

- Biology is the study of living things or organisms All living organisms have seven characteristics in common: growth, respiration, feeding, sensitivity, movement, reproduction and excretion.

- Living organisms are divided into two main kingdoms, the plant kingdom and the animal kingdom. Plants are useful to humans for agriculture, medicine, commerce and leisure. Humans rely on animals for food, medicine and leisure.

- Plants are able to make their own food and are called producers. Animals are not able to make their own food and are called consumers. Food chains show the feeding links between organisms.

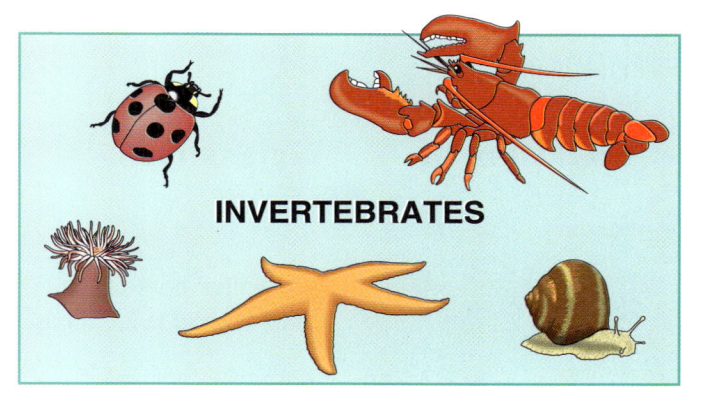

VERTEBRATES

INVERTEBRATES

FLOWERING PLANTS

NON-FLOWERING PLANTS

fig. 29.10

29 • Introduction to Biology: Animals and Plants

QUESTIONS

Q 29.1
Make a list of five different animal species and five plant species.

Q. 29.2
(a) What are organisms?
(b) What seven characteristics do all living organisms have?
(c) Name three ways in which animals are important to plants.
(d) Name three ways in which plants are important to animals.

Q. 29.3
The following statements describe animals and plants. Divide these statements into two lists, one of which applies to animals, and the other to plants:

do not make food
do not walk around
have leaves
make their own food
are used for transport
have no roots
grow towards light
have flowers

Q. 29. 4
Copy the following table and fill in the blanks.

Characteristic	Explanation
Feeding	
	Producing more of the same type of living thing
	Increasing in size
Movement	
	Getting rid of waste products
Sensitivity	

Q. 29.5
Copy the following paragraph and fill in the blanks.

(a) Biology is the study of __ things, or __ . The two main groups of living organisms are animals and __. All living things have seven characteristics in common; these are, ___, ____, ___, ___, ___, ___, and ___. Plants are important to humans for agriculture, __ __, and __. Animals are important to humans for ___, __ and __ . It is important to protect the habitats of plants and animals; this is called ___ . There are many different types of living ___ on earth. Animals are not able to make their own food but __ can.

Q. 29.6
(a) List two ways in which animals are used by humans.
(b) List two uses of plants.
(c) Why are plants called producers?
(d) Give an example of a simple food chain.
(e) Explain why a stone cannot be classified as a living organism.

Q. 29.7
(a) Give two examples of animals which cause problems for humans.
(b) Sensitivity is one of the characteristics of all living things. What does this mean?
(c) What senses do humans use to get information about what is going on around them?

Q. 29.8
(a) What does the term *mariculture* mean.
(b) Give two examples of animals that are cultured in this way.
(c) Many people enjoy fishing as a hobby. Give two examples of other leisure activities that rely on plants or animals.

Q. 29.9
Write a paragraph explaining how plants and animals depend on each other.

Q. 29.10
Humans eat many types of plants. Which part of the plant is eaten in each of the following: cabbage, carrot, celery, apple, peanut, turnip, lettuce, orange, spinach and parsnip?

30
CELLS, TISSUES, ORGANS AND SYSTEMS

All living things are made up of cells. Cells are extremely small and can only be seen using a microscope. Within most plants and animals, there are many types of cell, which vary in size, shape, appearance and what they do.

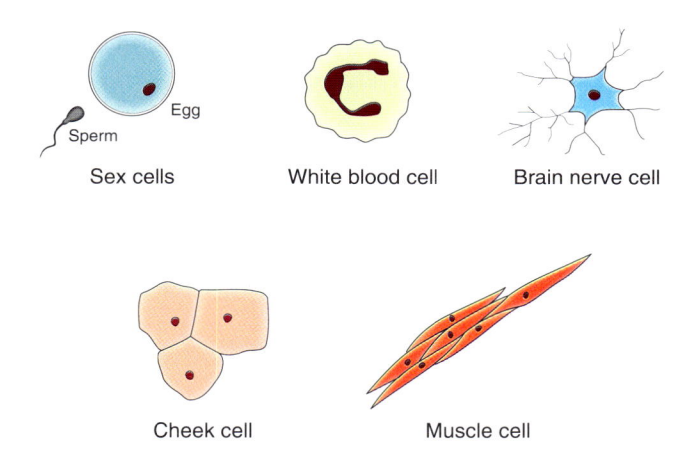

fig. 30.1 Each type of cell has a special job to do

Cells have three main parts. They have a **nucleus**, which controls everything that happens in the cell. The outer layer of the cell is called the **cell membrane**. This allows some substances to move in and out of the cell, while at the same time keeping others inside. Inside the cell membrane is a jelly-like fluid called **cytoplasm**, in which many substances, including food, salts, wastes and minerals, are dissolved. The cytoplasm is the name given to everything inside the cell membrane except the nucleus. Many cells have fluid-filled spaces called **vacuoles** which form part of the cytoplasm; plant cells have large vacuoles which help the cells to keep their shape.

PLANT AND ANIMAL CELLS

Plant and animal cells are not exactly the same. You have already learned that plants make their own food, but animals cannot do this. Plant cells have special structures called **chloroplasts** containing a green chemical called **chlorophyll**, which enable the plants to make their own food. This process, called **photosynthesis**, is described in Chapter 36. Plant cells have **cell walls** as well as cell membranes. The cell wall gives strength to the plant cells. The following table compares plant and animal cells.

Plant Cells	Animal cells
contain chloroplasts	do not contain chloroplasts
contain chlorophyll	do not contain chlorophyll
have a cell wall	do not have a cell wall
have large vacuoles	have small vacuoles

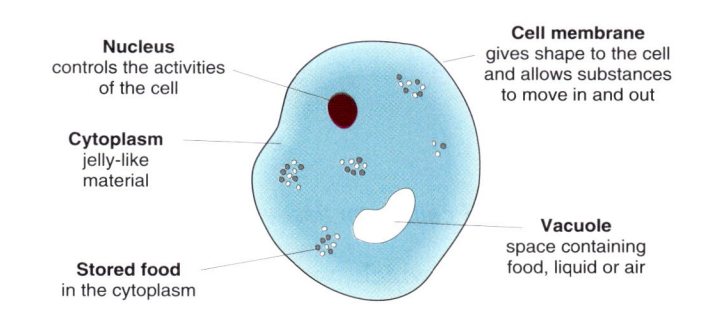

fig. 30.2 An animal cell

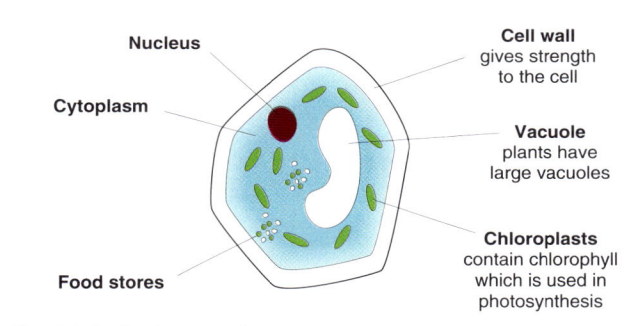

fig. 30.3 A plant cell

CELLS, TISSUES, ORGANS AND SYSTEMS

Living things are made up of different types of cell. Each type of cell has a particular task to carry out. Animals begin life as one cell, which then divides many times to form the millions of cells that make up the adult animal. The millions of cells do not act on their own, but are arranged in groups in order to carry out their tasks efficiently. When many of the same type of cell occur together, the group of cells is known as a **tissue**. For example, groups of skin cells make up skin tissue and transport tissue in plants is made up of xylem and phloem.

30 • Cells, Tissues, Organs and Systems

A tissue is a group of cells of the same type.

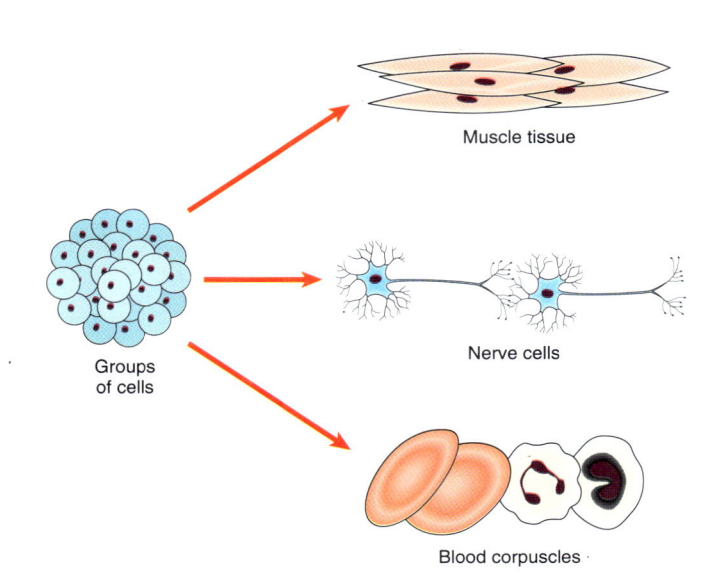

fig. 30.4 Groups of cells form tissues

Groups of tissues which work together to do a particular job are called **organs**. In animals, examples of organs are the heart, lungs, stomach, eyes and brain, and examples of plant organs are the flowers, leaves and roots.

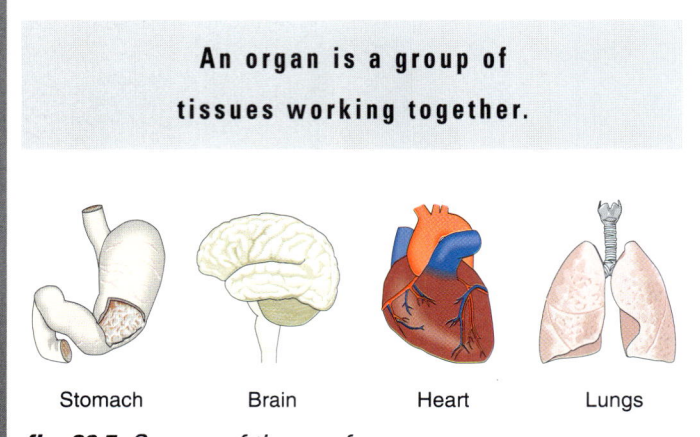

An organ is a group of tissues working together.

fig. 30.5 Groups of tissues form organs

A group of organs working together forms a **system**. Examples of systems in the human body are the digestive system, the breathing system, the transport system and the reproductive system.

A system is a group of organs working together.

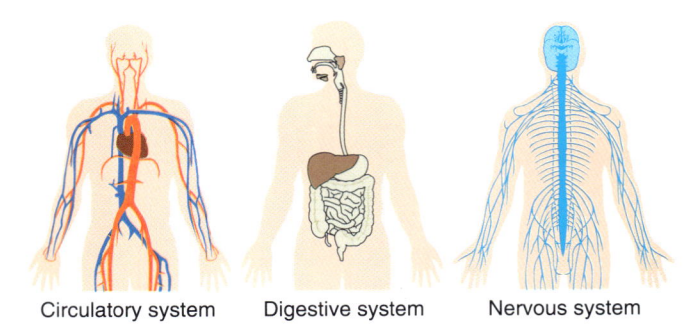

fig. 30.6 Groups of organs form systems

In summary, organisms are made up of systems, which are made up of organs, which are made up of tissues, which are made up of cells.

CELLS → TISSUES → ORGANS → SYSTEMS → ORGANISMS

fig. 30.7 Cells are the building blocks of living organisms

Studying small objects

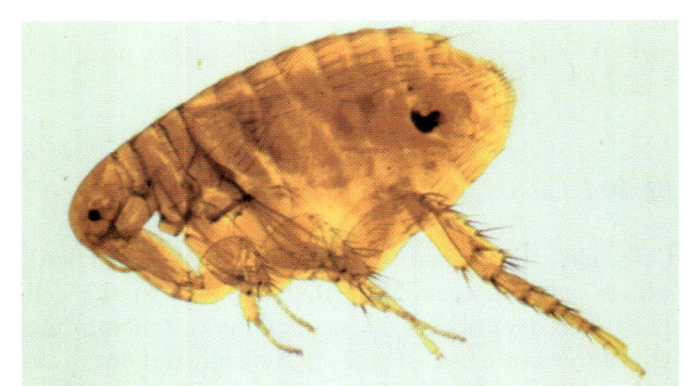

fig. 30.8 Dog flea as seen through a light microscope

fig. 30.9 Fruit fly as seen under an electron microscope

In order to look at, and study small objects in the laboratory, they must be made to appear bigger. For items like leaves and small insects, a hand lens is satisfactory as it can make things appear two or three times larger. But when something as small as cells have to be studied, magnification of much greater power is needed and for this purpose a microscope is used.

208

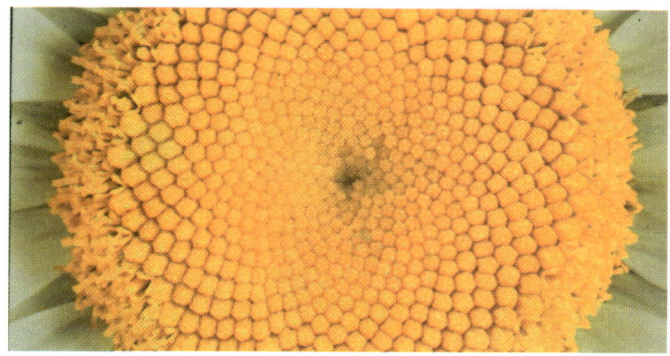

fig. 30.10 Daisy flower viewed using a hand lens

The word **magnification** means the number of times larger that an object appears to be, when viewed through a lens or microscope. Microscopes have different lenses that give different magnifications. The microscopes used in a school laboratory can magnify an object up to several hundred times, but more powerful microscopes called **electron microscopes** can magnify up to about 250 000 times. When an object is being observed under a microscope, light is passed through a very thin slice of the object, and when viewed through the eyepiece, a magnified image is observed.

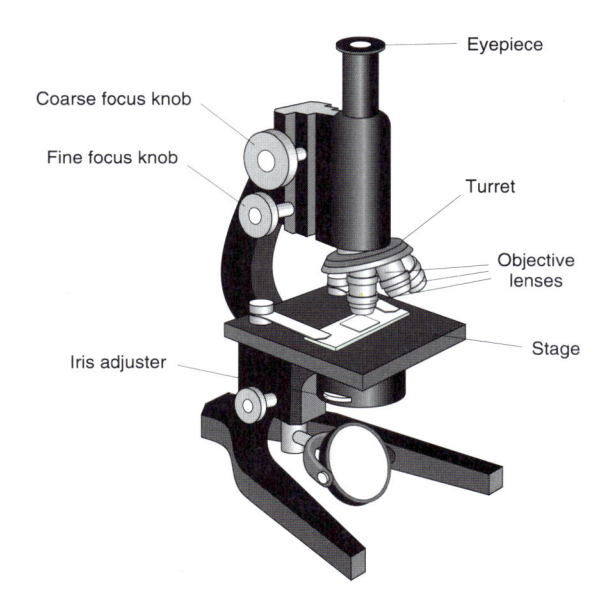

fig. 30.11 A light microscope

PARTS OF A MICROSCOPE

Eyepiece: This is the lens nearest the eye. It normally has its magnification stamped on it; for example, an eyepiece marked '× 10' means that it magnifies the object 10 times.

Objective lenses: There are generally several of these on the microscope, each with a different magnifying power. The shortest lens has the lowest power and the longest lens has the highest.

Turret: The objective lenses are mounted on this, and it can rotate to allow each of the different lenses to be used.

Stage: This is the 'table' on which the object to be examined is put. The object is first placed on a thin piece of glass, called a **slide**, which is then placed on the stage of the microscope. The slide is held in place by clips.

Light source: In some microscopes the object is illuminated by a bulb built into the base of the microscope, while in others, light from an external lamp, or from the sun, is reflected on to the object with the aid of a mirror.

Coarse focus knob: This allows the image to be brought roughly into focus.

Fine focus knob: This allows the image to be sharply focused.

Iris adjuster: This controls the amount of light reaching the object.

To work out the total magnification produced by the microscope, multiply the magnification marked on the eyepiece by the magnification marked on the objective lens being used. For example, an eyepiece magnifying four times used with an objective lens magnifying ten times will give a total magnification of forty, i.e. the object being examined appears forty times larger than it would appear to the naked eye.

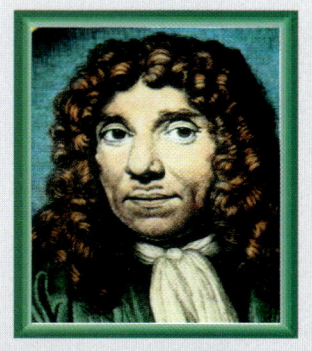

fig. 30.12 Anton van Leeuwenhoek

Anton van Leeuwenhoek, a Dutchman, had little schooling and no formal training in science. He developed an interest in microscopes, constructed his own instruments and experimented with different types of lens. He was one of the first people to observe blood capillaries, red blood cells and single-cell animals under the microscope.

30 • Cells, Tissues, Organs and Systems

Experiment 30.1
Using the microscope

Before you begin this exercise, study a microscope in the laboratory and identify the different parts listed above. If you have to carry a microscope, take great care as microscopes are fragile and expensive and can be heavy.

1. Clean microscope lenses only with lens tissue.
2. Switch on the microscope light, or, if there is no built-in light, adjust the mirror and lamp until the stage is illuminated.
3. Make sure the low power objective lens (the shortest one) is in position; if not, rotate the turret until it is.
4. Clip a prepared slide into position on the stage.
5. Focus the object using the coarse focus knob, and then adjust the fine focus knob until the image is sharp.
6. Move the iris adjuster to make the object appear as clear as possible.
7. Calculate the total magnification, from the two lenses used.
8. Move the slide around while you are looking through the eyepiece; only very small movements are needed to do this.
9. Repeat steps 5 to 8 using the medium power lens instead of the low power one.
10. Now try the high power lens. When using this, lower the lens **slowly** until it is almost touching the slide. Then using the fine focus knob, move the lens **upwards** until the image is sharply in focus.
11. To give practice at focusing, examine some or all of the following, first on low power and then on medium power: (i) a piece of newspaper, (ii) a thread, (iii) a hair, (iv) table salt (v) a butterfly wing, (vi) a feather.
12. Draw sketches of what you see, and in each case, make a note of the magnification used.

Experiment 30.2
Examining plant cells under the microscope

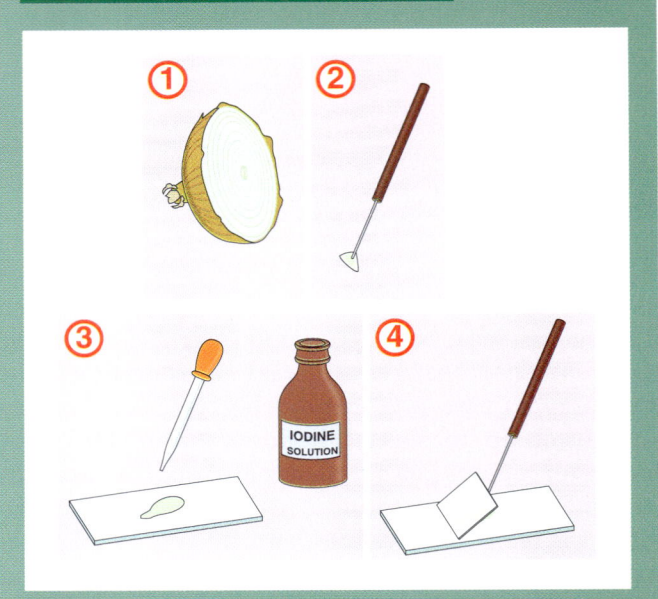

fig. 30.13

1. Tear away a tiny piece of skin from one of the inner layers of an onion.
2. Place the onion skin on a glass slide and add a drop of **iodine solution** (this is a stain and it enables you to see the cells more clearly).
3. Gently lower a **cover slip** on to the slide (your teacher will demonstrate this).
4. Soak up the excess iodine solution using a small piece of filter paper.
5. Prepare a second slide, but this time use a drop of water instead of iodine solution.
6. Look at both slides under the microscope and note any differences between them.
7. In each case, draw a sketch of what you see.

Experiment 30.3
To examine animal cells

1. Place a prepared slide of human cheek cells on the microscope stage.
2. Examine it under (i) low power, (ii) medium power and (iii) high power (remember to only use the fine focus knob when using high power).
3. In each case, draw a diagram of what you see.
4. Examine some other prepared animal cell slides.

In the mid seventeenth century, the English scientist Robert Hooke observed cork under the microscope. He noticed that the cork was made up of regular shaped boxes, which he called cells. Since then, the word has been used to describe the basic units of plant and animal life.

SUMMARY

- All living organisms are made up of **cells**. All cells have a **cell membrane**, **cytoplasm**, **nucleus** and many have **vacuoles**. Plant cells differ from animal cells in the following ways: plant cells have chloroplasts which contain the chemical chlorophyll, they have cell walls as well as a cell membrane, and they have large vacuoles.
- Groups of the same type of cell form a **tissue**. Groups of tissues working together form an **organ**. Groups of organs form a **system**. Groups of systems form an **organism**.
- To study small objects in detail a microscope is used. The important parts of the **microscope** are the eyepiece, objective lenses, stage, turret, iris adjuster, light source and focusing knobs. Plant cells are stained to allow them to be seen more clearly under a microscope.

QUESTIONS

Q. 30.1
Rewrite the following sentences and complete the spaces.

Plant cells have a __ __and ___. The green chemical ___ enables plants to make their food, and it is found in the ___ of plant cells. The part of the cell which controls the activities of the cell is the ___ . Plant cells have a __ wall and a cell membrane while animal cells have only a ___ ___ . The scientist ___ ___ was the person to give cells their name.

Q. 30.2
Rewrite the following paragraph and complete the spaces.

In living organisms, groups of cells working together form ___ . Groups of ___ working together form organs. Groups of organs working together form ___ . The __ is an example of an organ in humans. __ and ___ are organs found in plants. One of the systems found in humans is the ___ system.

Q. 30.3
(a) What is the function of the cell membrane?
(b) Describe the function of each of the following cell parts: nucleus, vacuole, and cytoplasm.
(c) Draw and label a diagram of (a) a plant cell, (b) an animal cell.

Q. 30.4
(a) Make a list of five different kinds of cell in your body.
(b) Which part of the cell controls all the activities in the cell?
(c) List three differences between plant cells and animal cells.

Q. 30.5
Describe how onion cells can be examined using a microscope.

Q. 30.6

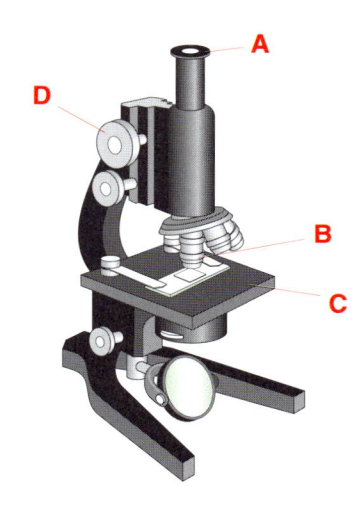

fig. 30.14

Name the microscope parts labelled A, B, C, D in Figure 30.14.

Q. 30.6
Copy out the following table and complete the spaces.

Part of microscope	Function
Stage	
Eye piece	
Low power objective lens	
High power objective lens	
Glass slide	
Cover slip	
Mirror	
Coarse focus knob	
Fine focus knob	

31
NUTRITION AND DIGESTION

FOOD

The need for food is one of the characteristics of living things. Food is necessary to supply energy and to enable the formation of new cells and structures required for growth and repair of tissues. Plants can make their own food by a process called photosynthesis. Animals must take in food by eating plants or other animals.

Energy is needed for functions such as heartbeat, muscular action (which allows for activities like walking, running and writing) and for the production of new body parts like blood cells, muscles, hair and skin. In addition to energy, food must supply the raw materials needed to make these new structures. There are five major types of food. These are called constituents or nutrients. Each constituent has a special function. Water is also needed to keep the body healthy.

fig. 31.1 *A selection of food types*

Constituent	Common Sources	Function
Carbohydrates		
- sugars	Fruits, honey, soft drinks chocolate	Fast supply of energy
- starch	Bread, potatoes, rice	Slower supply of energy
- fibre	Cereals, brown bread, fruit, vegetables	Helps to moves food through the intestines by a process called peristalsis (i.e. prevents constipation)
Proteins	Meat, fish, eggs, milk, cheese, nuts	Make muscle, hair, hormones, enzymes
Fat	Butter, cream, milk, oil margarine	Store energy in the body
Vitamins		
- Vitamin C	Fruit, green vegetables, potatoes	Keeps skin and gums healthy
- Vitamin D	Milk, butter, cheese, eggs fish-liver oil	Forms strong bones
Minerals		
- Iron (Fe)	Green vegetables, red meat, egg yolk	Part of red blood (forms haemoglobin which carries oxygen)
- Calcium (Ca)	Milk, cheese	Forms strong bones

FOOD AND ENERGY

The food types that contain energy are carbohydrates, fats and protein. Energy is measured in units called joules (J), but kilojoules (kJ) are used in practice because the joule is a very tiny unit. The release of energy from food in the body is called respiration.

Carbohydrates and proteins contain about the same amount of energy (i.e. 17 kJ in each gram). Carbohydrate is regularly used to supply energy needs. Protein is only used for energy if the body is on the point of starvation. Fats contain twice as much energy as carbohydrates (i.e. 38 kJ per gram). In general, the body only gets energy from fat if there is no carbohydrate present.

Different food sources have different energy contents. Sometimes the energy content can be seen on a nutritional contents panel on the packaging.

Beans

Approximate nutritional value per 100g	
Energy	326 kJ
Carbohydrate	13.8 g
Protein	4.3 g
Fat	0.5 g
Fibre	2.9 g

Biscuits

Typical composition per 100g	
Energy	1616 kJ
Carbohydrate	66.2 g
Protein	2.8 g
Fat	13.6 g
Fibre	0.4 g

fig. 31.2 *The biscuits shown are high in fat, carbohydrate and energy, but low in protein and fibre. The beans are high in protein and fibre, and low in fat, carbohydrate and energy.*

Energy requirements

A person's energy needs depend on age, gender and activity levels. For example:

The table at the bottom of the page gives examples of the energy needed for different activities.

Age	Sex	Energy required per day (kJ)
8	Male	9000
8	Female	8000
15	Male	11 400
15	Female	9400
40	Male	13 000 (15 000 if active)
40	Female	10 000 (11 000 if active)

Balanced diet

A balanced diet contains the correct amounts of each of the five food types. The actual amounts of food required vary according to the age, sex and activity levels. It is best to eat a little of everything. In this way you ensure a varied diet and good health.

Failure to eat a balanced diet (malnutrition) can result in a shortage (deficiency) of one or more nutrients. For example, a lack of vitamin C causes bleeding skin and gums (a disease called scurvy). A shortage of calcium causes weak and brittle bones (rickets).

Human nutrition

Nutrition (or feeding) involves five main steps.

1. Taking food into the mouth.
2. Breaking down the food so it is small enough to pass from the intestines into the bloodstream.
3. The small particles of food are then carried by the bloodstream to all parts of the body.
4. The food is then used by the body for different functions (as outlined in the table on page 212).
5. The waste material not taken into the body is released from the intestines.

Activity	Energy (kJ per hour)	Sample food with this energy
Sleeping	350	Six teaspoons of sugar
Sitting	400	One slice of bread
Walking slowly	600	One glass of milk
Running	3500	Small portion of chips

The stages in nutrition

1. **Ingestion** is the taking of food into the mouth.
2. **Digestion** is the breakdown of food.
3. **Absorption** occurs when the digested food passes from the intestine into the blood.
4. **Assimilation** takes place when the foods are absorbed and used by body cells.
5. **Egestion** is the getting rid of unabsorbed waste from the intestines.

TEETH

There are four types of teeth.

- **Incisors**. These are at the front of the mouth. They have sharp edges (like chisels) to cut and slice through food.
- **Canines**. These are long, fang-like teeth. They are used to grip and tear food.
- **Premolars**. These have flat surfaces to chew and grind food.
- **Molars**. These are the large teeth found at the back of the jaws. They also chew and grind food.

Structure of teeth

All four types of teeth have similar structures.

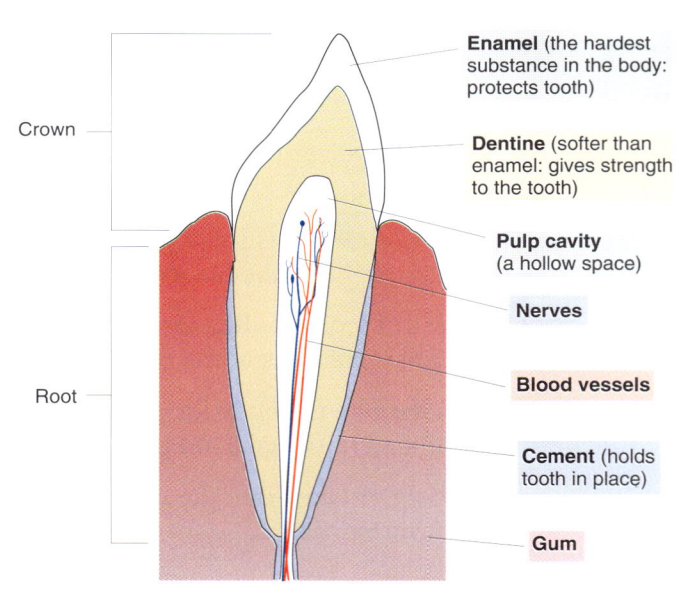

fig. 31.3 Structure of a tooth

Tooth decay (dental *caries*) is caused when bacteria in the mouth convert sugar to acid. These bacteria live in a layer of food that coats the teeth. This mixture of food and bacteria is called plaque. The acid dissolves the enamel on the teeth. Once the enamel is dissolved the next layer below the enamel, called dentine, is quickly broken down and bacteria are free to enter the pulp cavity. These bacteria can cause toothache (when the nerves are stimulated) or gum disease.

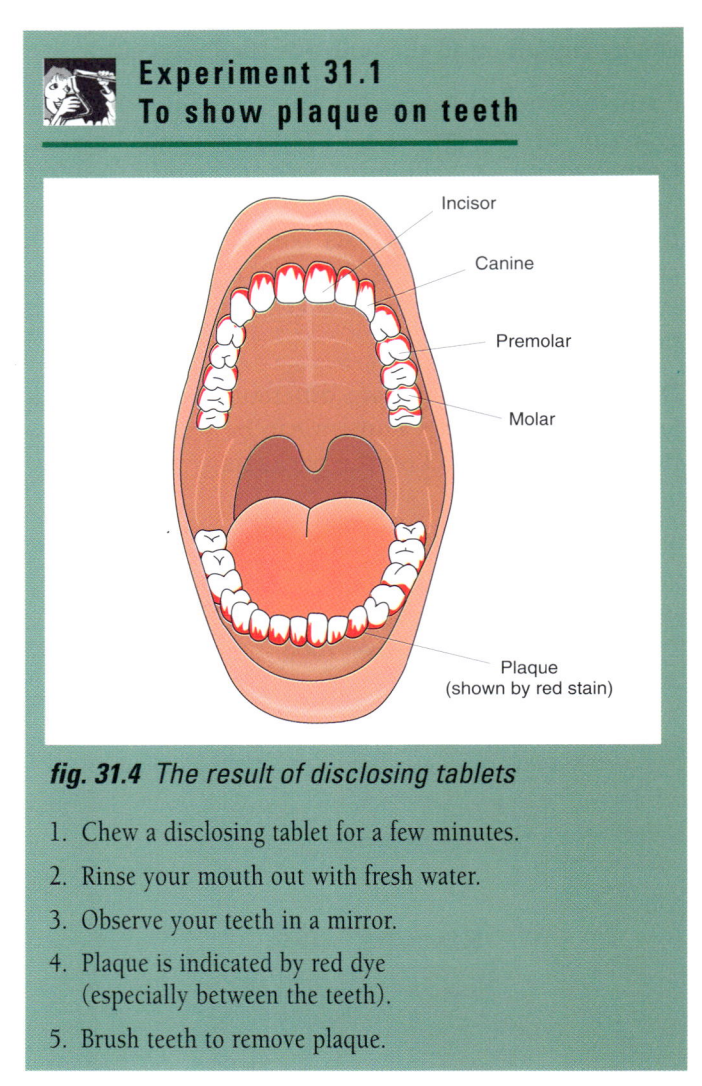

Experiment 31.1
To show plaque on teeth

fig. 31.4 The result of disclosing tablets

1. Chew a disclosing tablet for a few minutes.
2. Rinse your mouth out with fresh water.
3. Observe your teeth in a mirror.
4. Plaque is indicated by red dye (especially between the teeth).
5. Brush teeth to remove plaque.

Prevention of tooth decay

- Wash your teeth after each meal, or at least twice a day. Use a circular motion of the brush and do not forget to clean the backs of the teeth.
- Use a toothpaste containing fluoride. This helps to strengthen teeth. Irish water supplies have fluoride added.
- Dental floss can help remove plaque from between the teeth.
- Rinsing with a fluoride mouthwash can also help.
- Eat a proper diet. Avoid eating sweets or sugary foods unless you can wash your teeth soon afterwards.
- Visit a dentist regularly.

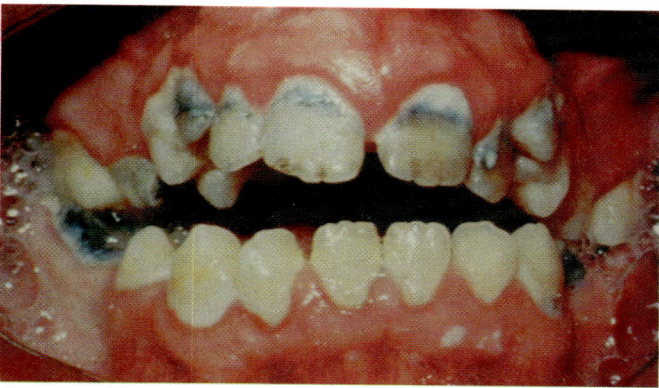

fig. 31.5 Tooth decay

THE DIGESTIVE SYSTEM

There are two types of digestion:

(a) Mechanical (physical) digestion involves food being chewed by the teeth. This breaks the food down so that the second type of digestion can work better.

(b) Chemical digestion takes place when food is broken down by enzymes. Enzymes are chemicals produced by the body that cause reactions to take place very rapidly. In this way enzymes are like catalysts.

The body produces many enzymes to speed up different processes. In the digestive system enzymes are produced by the mouth, stomach, small intestine and pancreas in order to speed up the breakdown of food.

Amylase

This enzyme is produced by the salivary glands in the mouth. It is released into the mouth with water (as saliva). It speeds up the digestion of starch to the simple sugar maltose. In the small intestine, maltose is then digested to glucose by another enzyme called maltase. Starch and maltose are called substrates. A substrate is the substance that an enzyme works on. These reactions can be summarised as:

Substrate	Enzyme	Product
Starch	Amylase →	Maltose
Maltose	Maltase →	Glucose

End products of digestion

Carbohydrates are broken down to simple sugars such as glucose.

Proteins are digested to sub-units called amino acids.

Fats are broken down to compounds called fatty acids and glycerol.

All these products are small enough to pass out of the intestine into the bloodstream.

Experiment 31.2
To show the action of amylase on starch

1. Add equal amounts of starch solution to two test tubes.
2. Add saliva (which contains the enzyme amylase) to tube A only.
3. Leave both test tubes for 20 minutes in a water bath as shown.

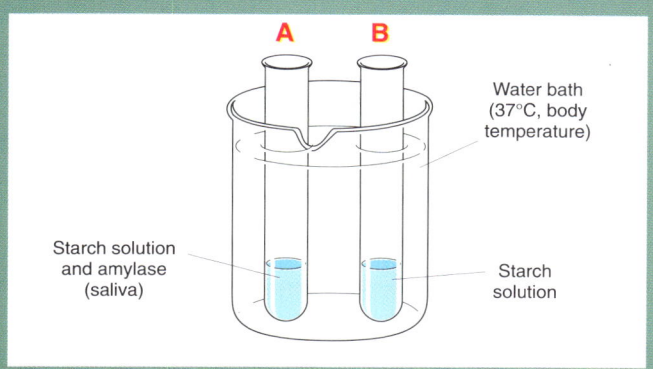

fig. 31.6

4. Test a few drops of each test tube with iodine solution on a dropping tile. Iodine turns from a red/yellow colour to blue/black if starch is present.

Result:

Tube A does not turn the iodine blue/black. This shows that starch is not present (it has been digested to maltose).

Tube B turns the iodine blue/black. In the absence of amylase the starch does not break down.

This shows that amylase digests starch.

Note

- At the end of the experiment the two tubes could be tested with Benedict's solution. If simple sugar is present the Benedict's solution turns from blue to orange/red when heated in a boiling water bath.
- The results in this case would be:
  - Tube A turns orange/red. This indicates a simple sugar such as maltose is present.
  - Tube B stays blue. This indicates there is no simple sugar (no maltose).
- This shows that starch was digested to simple sugar by the amylase in Tube A.

31 • Nutrition and Digestion

The digestive system

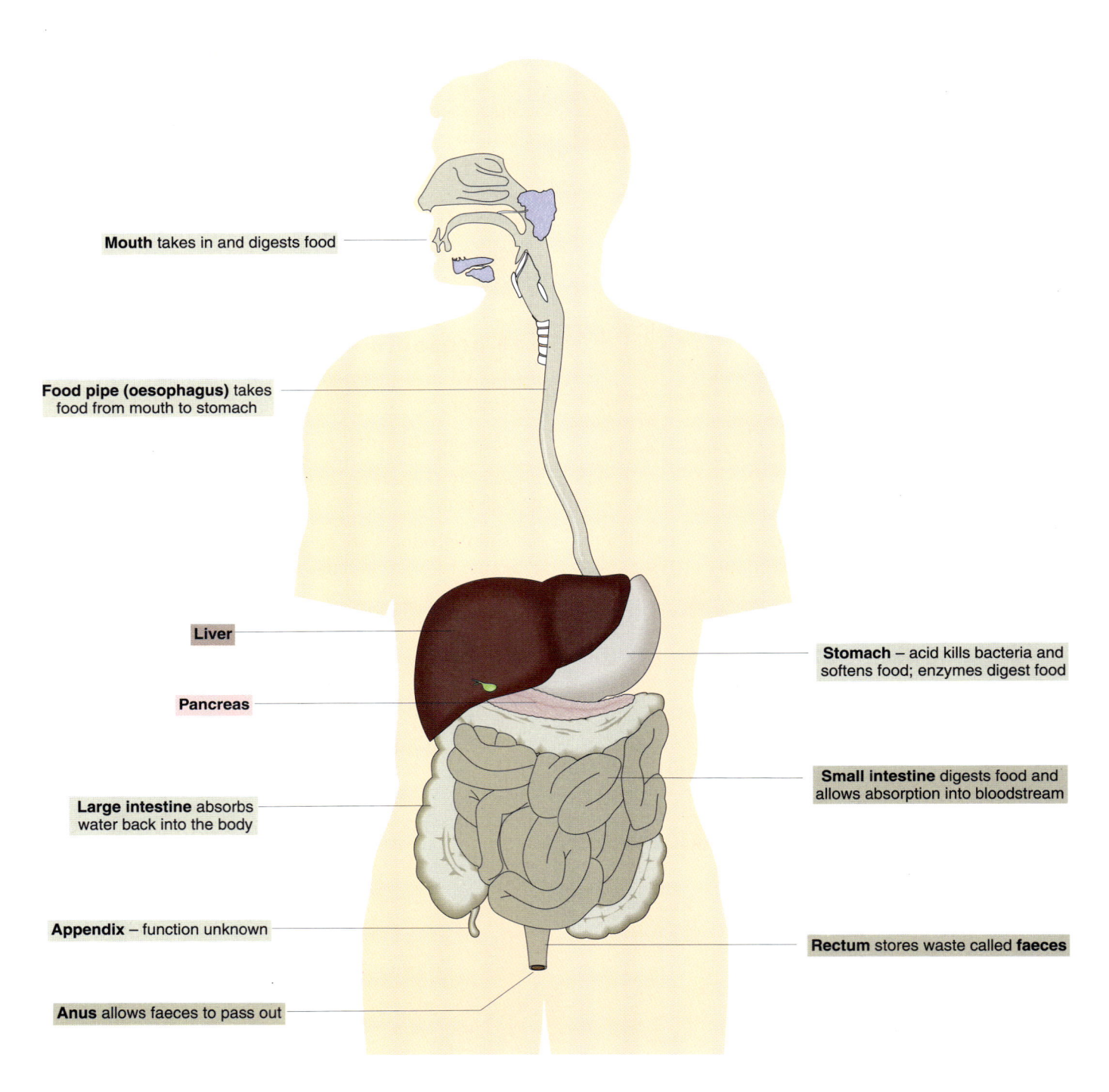

Mouth takes in and digests food

Food pipe (oesophagus) takes food from mouth to stomach

Liver

Pancreas

Stomach – acid kills bacteria and softens food; enzymes digest food

Small intestine digests food and allows absorption into bloodstream

Large intestine absorbs water back into the body

Appendix – function unknown

Rectum stores waste called **faeces**

Anus allows faeces to pass out

The **liver** and **pancreas** are organs attached to the digestive system.
The **liver** makes **bile** which helps to digest fats.
The **pancreas** makes **enzymes** to digest food.
Food does not enter these organs; instead their products pass out into the intestines.

fig. 31.7

SUMMARY

- Food is needed for energy, growth and repair.
- The five food types and their functions are:
  - **carbohydrates** (supply energy, and fibre, which is needed to move food through the intestines)
  - **proteins** (to make and repair body parts)
  - **fats** (store or supply energy)
  - **vitamins** (vitamin C ensures healthy skin, vitamin D forms strong bones)
  - **minerals** (iron forms part of red blood, calcium helps to form bones)
- Energy is supplied by carbohydrates and fats.
- Fats have twice the energy of carbohydrates.
- Energy needs depend on age, sex and activity levels.
- A balanced diet contains the correct amounts of each food type.
- Nutrition involves:
  - **ingestion** (taking in food)
  - **digestion** (breaking down food)
  - **absorption** (taking food into the bloodstream)
  - **assimilation** (changing food into body structures)
  - **egestion** (getting rid of waste from the intestines)
- The four types of teeth are: incisors (cutting), canines (gripping), premolars and molars (chewing).
- The main parts of a tooth are enamel (protection), dentine (strength), pulp cavity (contains nerves and blood vessels).
- Tooth decay is caused by acid, mostly produced by bacteria in plaque.
- Digestion can be mechanical (chewing) or chemical (enzymes).
- Amylase (in saliva) digests starch to maltose.
- Maltase (in small intestine) digests maltose to glucose.
- The final products of digestion are glucose (carbohydrates), amino acids (proteins) and fatty acids and glycerol (fats).

QUESTIONS

Q. 31.1
(a) Give two reasons why living things need food.
(b) Explain how (i) plants and (ii) animals get their food.

Q. 31.2
(a) Name the main food types and state two common sources of each type named.
(b) Name the three food types that are not used for energy.

Q. 31.3
Suggest a reason for each of the following:
(a) Weightlifters eat lots of protein.
(b) A lack of iron causes paleness.
(c) Sportspeople need large supplies of carbohydrate.
(d) Young people require lots of calcium.
(e) A person suffering from constipation is told to eat fruit and cereal.
(f) Fluoride is added to some water supplies.
(g) Sheep have few (and small) canine teeth.
(h) Grilled food is healthier than fried food.

Q. 31.4
Name the main food type in each of the following: bread, chicken, sausage, apple, pasta, cooking oil, nuts, oranges, cream, fish, chips.

Q. 31.5
Write out and complete the following:
(a) The units of energy are ____ . The food type with the greatest energy content is ____. Active people need ____ energy than inactive people. They normally get this energy from ____.
(b) There are ____ types of teeth. The teeth used for chewing food are the ____ and the ____. Teeth are covered with a layer of ____. This is a very ____ material, but it can be dissolved by ____. Plaque is a layer of ____ and ____ found on the teeth. It is harmful because the ____ convert sugar to ____, which causes tooth ____.
(c) Food is digested in order to allow it to be ____. It is then ____ into the ____ and carried to all parts of the body. Digestion occurs in the ____, ____ and ____ ____. Unabsorbed waste, called ____, is stored in the ____ and ____ through the ____.

Q. 31.6
(a) What are enzymes?
(b) Why are they similar to catalysts?
(c) Name two enzymes made by the body.
(d) For each enzyme named, state where it is produced, what it acts on and what it produces.

31 • Nutrition and Digestion

Q. 31.7

(a) Name the substance used to test for starch.
(b) State its colour, (i) in starch solution,
    (ii) in the absence of starch.
(c) State the result of a starch test on each
    of the test tubes A, B and C shown below.
(d) What do these results show?

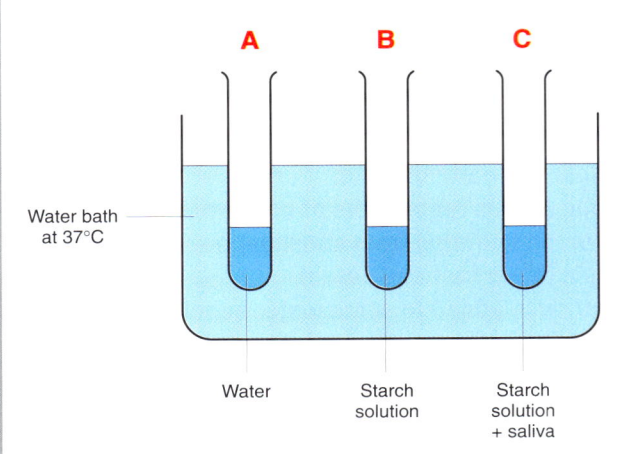

fig. 31.8

Q. 31.8

In an experiment to show enzyme action:

(a) Name a suitable enzyme.
(b) Why should the reaction be
    carried out at 37°C?
(c) Why would the result be tested with (i) iodine
    solution and (ii) Benedict's solution?
(d) What colour would you expect in each of
    the following: (i) iodine in tap water, (ii) iodine
    in starch, (iii) Benedict's solution (heated) in
    tap water, (iv) Benedict's solution (heated)
    in a soft drink?

Q. 31.9

(a) Record the nutritional information from
    one type of food (for example a box of
    cereal or a tin of soup).
(b) Which food type is your sample rich in?
(c) Name a nutrient not found in your sample.

Q. 31.10

(a) Name the parts of the diagrams
    shown (A to G).
(b) Give one main function for
    each labelled part.
(c) Which part (i) contains acid and
    (ii) is damaged by acid?

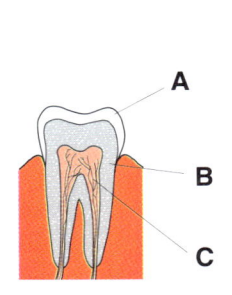

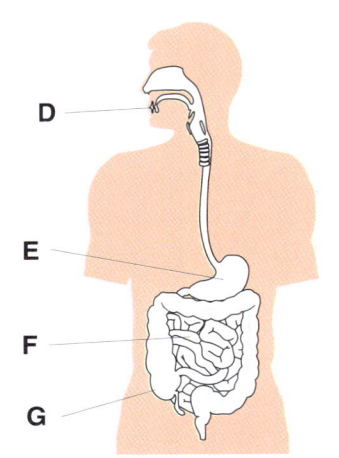

fig. 31.9

Q. 30.11

(a) Name one food in each case which is
    a good source of fibre, vitamin C, energy,
    calcium, protein, iron, fat, and vitamin D.
(b) What results would you expect in each
    case for a person who was short of
    vitamin C, calcium, fibre, carbohydrate,
    iron, vitamin D?

BREATHING AND RESPIRATION

A living organism such as a human is similar in ways to a machine like a car. Both the car and the human take in fuel (petrol or food) and oxygen. During the burning of the petrol in the car engine, or the digestion of the food in the human, these substances are converted to waste products (one of which is carbon dioxide) and energy is released, mainly as heat and kinetic energy ('movement' energy).

The release of energy from food involves two processes – breathing and respiration. **Breathing** is the process in which air (containing oxygen) is taken into the body, and carbon dioxide expelled. **Respiration** is the process in which the energy is released from food. The two process occur at the same time.

BREATHING

All animals need a good gas exchange system to provide oxygen for their cells and to remove waste carbon dioxide and water vapour. In humans, the lungs carry out this task in a process called **breathing**. As a person **inhales** (breathes in), air containing oxygen enters the body, and as he or she **exhales** (breathes out), air containing less oxygen but more carbon dioxide (and also water vapour) is released. The approximate composition of inhaled air and exhaled air is shown below, and is investigated in the following experiments.

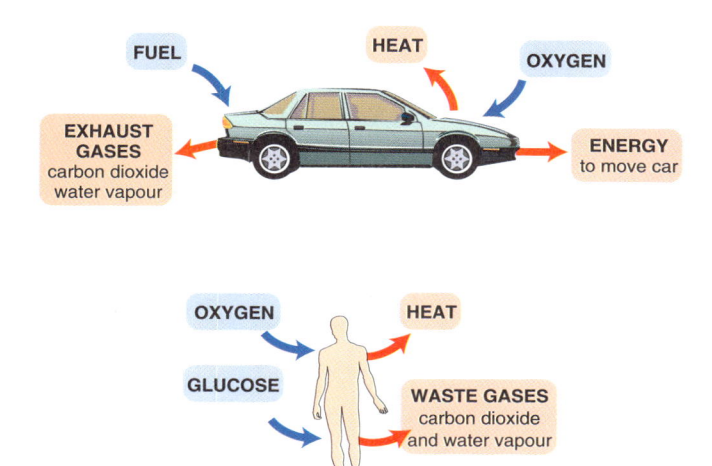

fig. 32.1

	Oxygen	Carbon dioxide
Inhaled air	21%	0.03%
Exhaled air	17%	4%

Experiment 32.1
To test exhaled air for the presence of water vapour

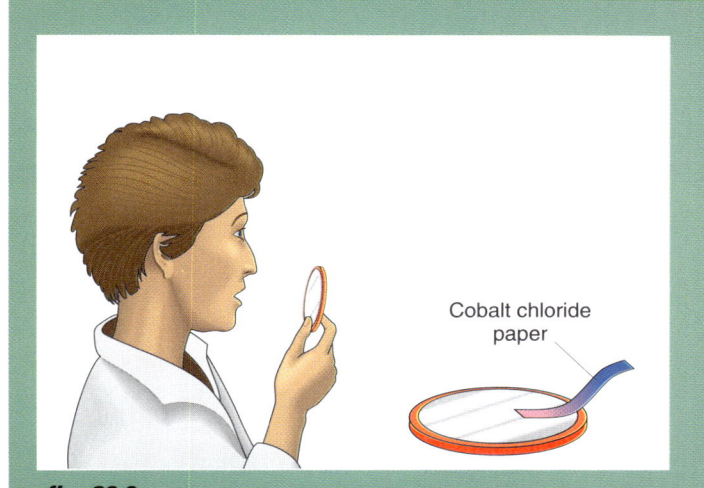

Cobalt chloride paper reacts to the presence of water or water vapour, by changing from blue to pink.

1. Breathe out onto the surface of a mirror or sheet of glass.
2. Test the substance that has formed with blue cobalt chloride paper.
3. What happens?
4. Record the result.

Did you find that the cobalt chloride paper turned pink? What does this tell about the substance which formed on the mirror?

fig. 32.2

32 • Breathing and Respiration

Experiment 32.2
To compare the differences in the carbon dioxide content of inhaled air and exhaled air

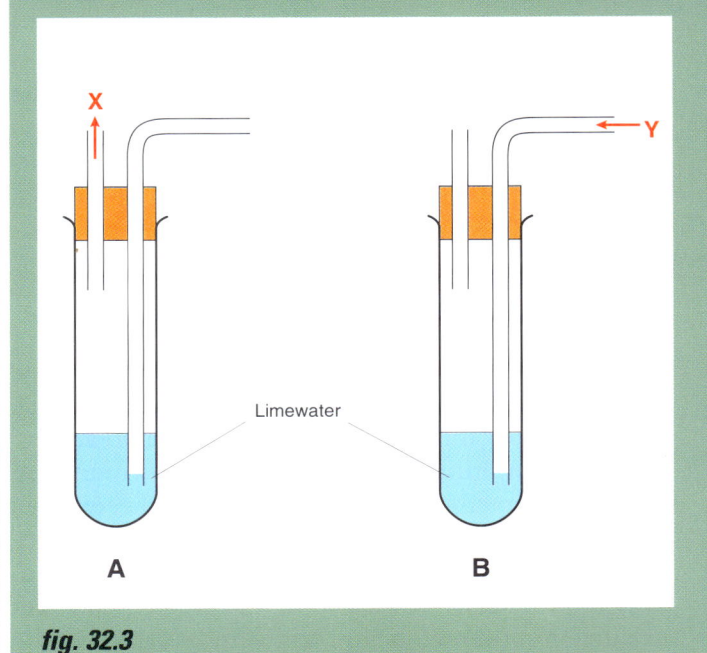

Limewater (which is colourless) turns milky when carbon dioxide is passed through it.

1. Set up the equipment as shown in Figure 32.3.
2. Place limewater in both tubes.
3. Suck air in through tube X and blow it out through tube Y.
4. Repeat the procedure until a change is observed in one of the tubes.
5. Record the result.

Did you find that the limewater in B turned milky? What does this tell about the exhaled air which was blown out through Y?

fig. 32.3

Structure of the breathing system

Experiment 32.3
What happens during breathing?

1. Sit quietly for one minute. Observe how the chest area moves when you are breathing.
2. Take a couple of large breaths. What parts of the body moved?
3. Try to predict how exercise might affect breathing rates.

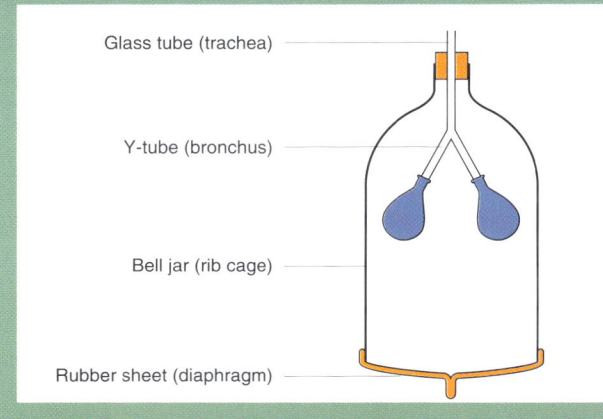

fig. 32.4

A model like that shown in Figure 32.4 can be used to illustrate what happens when the body inhales and exhales. When the rubber sheet is pulled down, the cavity above it increases in volume. This causes the balloons (the 'lungs') to expand and draw in air. When the rubber sheet is released, the cavity above it is reduced in size and the balloons deflate as they release air. The sides of the bell jar represent the ribs. The ribs are important in protecting the soft lung tissue from damage. The rubber sheet represents the muscle under the lungs, called the diaphragm.

A similar action occurs in the human body. When you inhale, the diaphragm contracts and moves down, the rib cage moves up and out, and air is drawn in through the nose and mouth. As the air passes through the nasal passage, it is warmed and some of the dirt and dust particles from the air are trapped by the hairs in the nose. For this reason, it is better to breathe through the nose than through the mouth. The air travels down the **trachea**, into each **bronchus**, and on to the **bronchioles**, reaching the air sacs or **alveoli** (singular: alveolus).

When you exhale, the action is reversed. The diaphragm relaxes and moves up, the rib cage moves down and in – reducing the space in the chest cavity, so that air is forced out of the lungs.

The **larynx** (voice box) contains the vocal cords, which create sound

The **trachea** (windpipe) is the tube that carries air to and from the lungs

The trachea divides to form two tubes, the **bronchi** (singular **bronchus**), one goes to each lung

The bronchi divide to form smaller tubes called **bronchioles**, which carry air into the lungs

The **alveoli** are tiny air sacs covered in many blood vessels called capillaries. The exchange of carbon dioxide and oxygen takes place in the alveoli

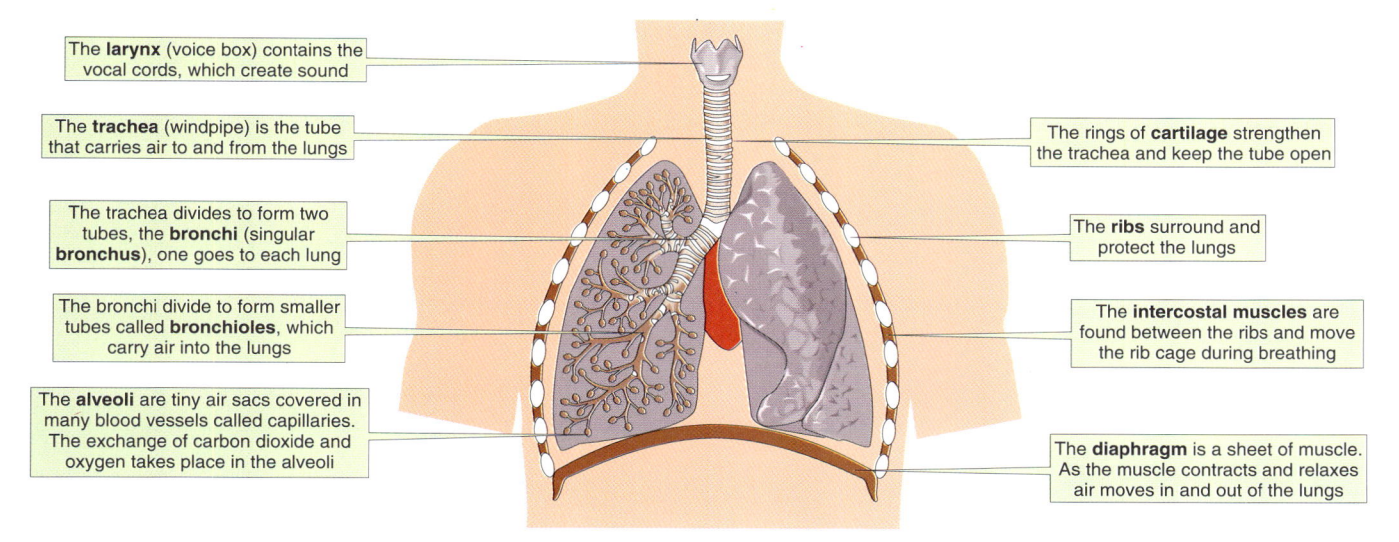

The rings of **cartilage** strengthen the trachea and keep the tube open

The **ribs** surround and protect the lungs

The **intercostal muscles** are found between the ribs and move the rib cage during breathing

The **diaphragm** is a sheet of muscle. As the muscle contracts and relaxes air moves in and out of the lungs

fig. 32.5 *The breathing system*

Gaseous exchange

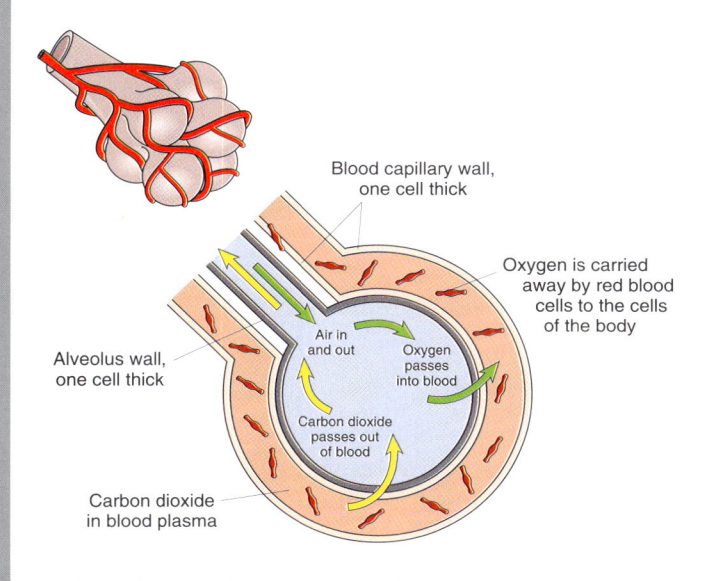

fig. 32.6 *Gas exchange in the alveoli*

The alveoli are the structures in the lungs in which the exchange of gases occurs. Each lung contains millions of alveoli. These are thin walled and surrounded by tiny blood vessels called **capillaries**. Oxygen passes from the alveoli into the blood in the capillaries, and waste carbon dioxide (from the body) passes from the capillaries into the alveoli. When you breathe out, the carbon dioxide is then forced out of the lungs into the atmosphere.

Healthy lungs

The breathing system is required to provide oxygen for every cell in the human body, and therefore it must be treated with care. Part of the breathing system is lined with tiny hairs and cells that produce a **mucus** (mucus is a sticky substance). These cells help to prevent unwanted dirt and micro-organisms from entering the lungs. If this process is not working, the lungs become irritated and infections can develop. In city areas, smog is often present, and can cause breathing difficulties for those with chest conditions such as asthma and bronchitis. **Aerobic exercise**, which makes one breathe more deeply, makes the breathing system more efficient.

fig. 32.7 *Students trampolining. Exercising regularly improves the efficiency of the heart and lungs.*

SMOKING

Every packet of cigarettes carries a government health warning because smoking poses dangers to health. The effects of smoking on the breathing system are listed on the next page.

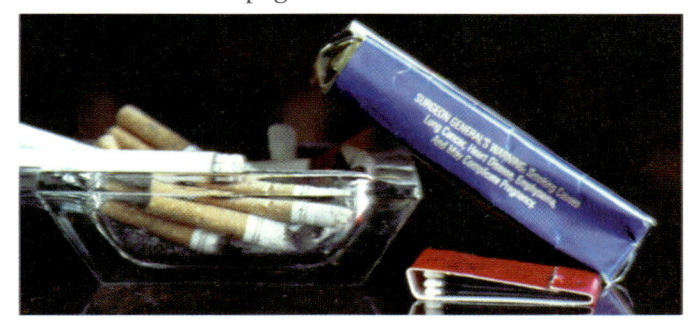

fig. 32.8 *Health warning on a cigarette packet*

32 • Breathing and Respiration

- Cigarette smoke prevents the tiny hairs in the air passages that trap dirt from moving. More particles of dust get into the lungs, causing irritation and clogging.
- Smoke irritates the lungs and causes increased risk of coughs.
- Smoking can cause lung cancer and heart disease.
- Smoking during pregnancy reduces the amount of oxygen getting to the baby, and this can result in smaller babies.
- Smokers often have bad breath.

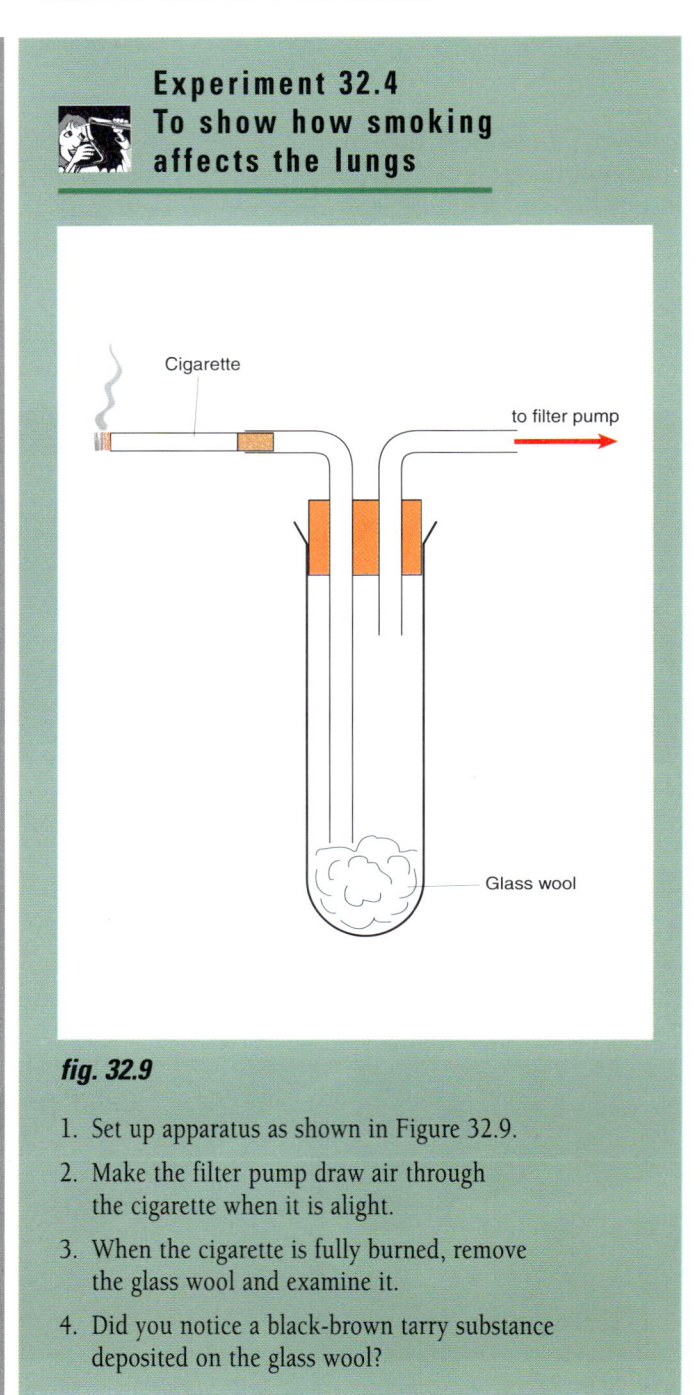

Experiment 32.4
To show how smoking affects the lungs

fig. 32.9

1. Set up apparatus as shown in Figure 32.9.
2. Make the filter pump draw air through the cigarette when it is alight.
3. When the cigarette is fully burned, remove the glass wool and examine it.
4. Did you notice a black-brown tarry substance deposited on the glass wool?

GAS EXCHANGE IN OTHER ORGANISMS

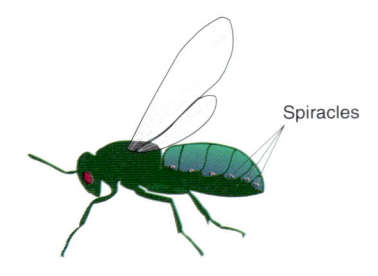

fig. 32.10 Instead of lungs, insects have holes called spiracles along the length of their bodies for gas exchange

fig. 32.11 Fish have gills, which allow them to absorb oxygen directly from water

fig. 32.12 Earthworms breathe through their skin

RESPIRATION

The breathing mechanism causes oxygen to be taken into the lungs, and waste gases to be removed. The oxygen which is inhaled is transported by the blood to every cell in the body. Blood also carries the food which has been absorbed during digestion (Chapter 31) and this too reaches every cell. To release the energy from food, a chemical process known as **respiration** takes place. Respiration and breathing are often confused. Respiration is the release of energy from food and it takes place in all living cells. Breathing is the exchange of gases between the air outside the organism and the lungs in humans (or the gills in fish). Breathing is necessary for respiration to occur.

Respiration is essentially the same reaction as if the food were burned in oxygen. The reaction is shown below, both as a word equation and as a balanced chemical equation.

Food (glucose) + oxygen →
    carbon dioxide + water + energy

$C_6H_{12}O_6 + 6O_2 \rightarrow 6CO_2 + 6H_2O +$ energy

In this process, food combines with oxygen to produce carbon dioxide, water and energy in cells. Plant and animal cells undergo respiration all the time. The parts of the plant exposed to light undergo photosynthesis as well as respiration. The process of photosynthesis is explained in Chapter 36.

Experiment 32.5
To show that living organisms produce carbon dioxide

fig. 32.13

1. Set up the apparatus which is shown in Figure 32.13.
2. Observe any change that occurs in the limewater.
3. Record and explain your results.
4. Did you notice that the limewater turns milky?

Living organisms give off carbon dioxide, which reacts with the limewater in the test tube, and turns it milky.

SUMMARY

- Cells require oxygen to allow energy to be released from food. The breathing system enables oxygen to reach the blood, which then transports it to all body cells. As a person breathes, oxygen is taken in, and carbon dioxide is released. This exchange happens in the lungs.

- Air enters the nose and mouth, and is transferred through the trachea, to each bronchus and then to bronchioles. It is in the alveoli at the ends of the bronchioles that the exchange of gases takes place. The alveoli are adapted to this task as they have thin walls and a rich supply of blood vessels around them.

- Smoking causes damage to the breathing system and general health. It also reduces the oxygen supply to babies whose mothers smoke while pregnant.

- Cobalt chloride paper is used to test for the presence of water; if it turns from blue to pink, water is present.

- Limewater is used to test for carbon dioxide; if the colourless solution becomes milky, carbon dioxide is present.

- Respiration is the release of energy from food and takes place in all animal and plant cells.

Food (glucose) + oxygen →
$$\text{carbon dioxide} + \text{water} + \text{energy}$$
$$C_6H_{12}O_6 + 6O_2 \rightarrow 6CO_2 + 6H_2O + \text{energy}$$

Experiment 32.6
To show that respiring peas release energy

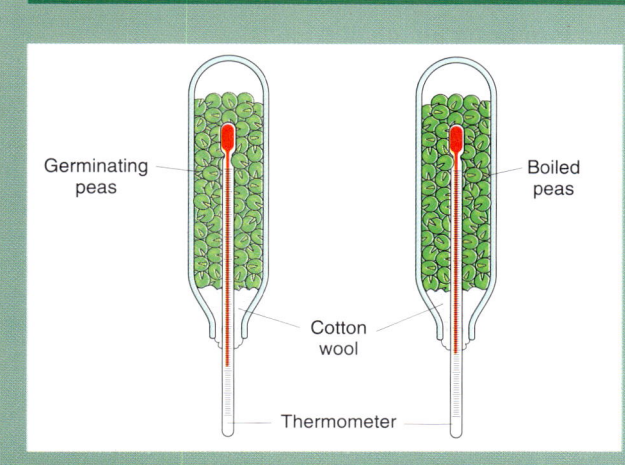

fig. 32.14

1. Set up the apparatus shown in Figure 32.14.
2. Read the temperature of the peas in each of the flasks.
3. Record the temperatures in the flasks once a day, for a period of about a week.
4. In which flask is there a rise in temperature? Explain why?

Did you notice that there is a rise in the temperature in the flask containing the germinating seeds? This means that germinating seeds are respiring, and so releasing energy.

32 • Breathing and Respiration

QUESTIONS

Q. 32.1
Rewrite the following, and fill in the blanks.

The part of the air that is essential for life to take place is __ . The process in which oxygen is used to help break down food is called __ . The air we breathe out contains __ and __. __ is the chemical used to show the presence of carbon dioxide in exhaled air. Cobalt chloride paper changes from __ to __ in the presence of water vapour. Breathing rate is __ by exercise.

Q. 32.2
Rewrite the following, filling in the blanks.

The main function of the rib cage is to __ the lungs. The main tube carrying air from the mouth to the lungs is the __ . Each bronchus branches to form smaller tubes called __. Exchange of gases takes place in the __ . These are suited to the task as their walls are very __ and they are surrounded by many __. When a person breathes in, the diaphragm __ and moves __, and the rib cage moves __ and __. Exhaling is caused by the diaphragm moving __ and the rib cage moving __ and __.

Q. 32.3
Rewrite the following paragraph and fill in the blanks.

Respiration is the release of __ from food; it occurs in all __ cells. The word equation for respiration is:
__ + oxygen —> carbon dioxide + __ + energy.
The chemical equation for the reaction is:
__ + $6O_2$ —> $6CO_2$ + __ + energy.

Q. 32.4
In the bell jar model (Figure 32.15) which parts of the body do each of the following represent?

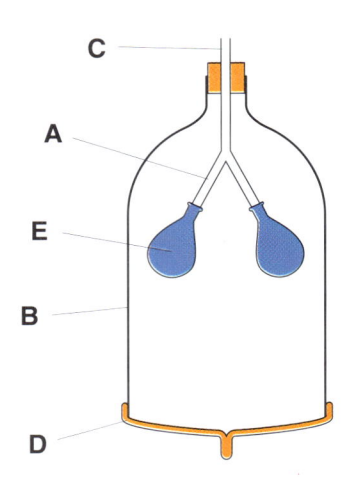

fig. 32.15

Q. 32.5
(a) Draw a labelled diagram of an alveolus and its blood supply.
(b) Copy and label the diagram of the alveoli (Figure 32.16).

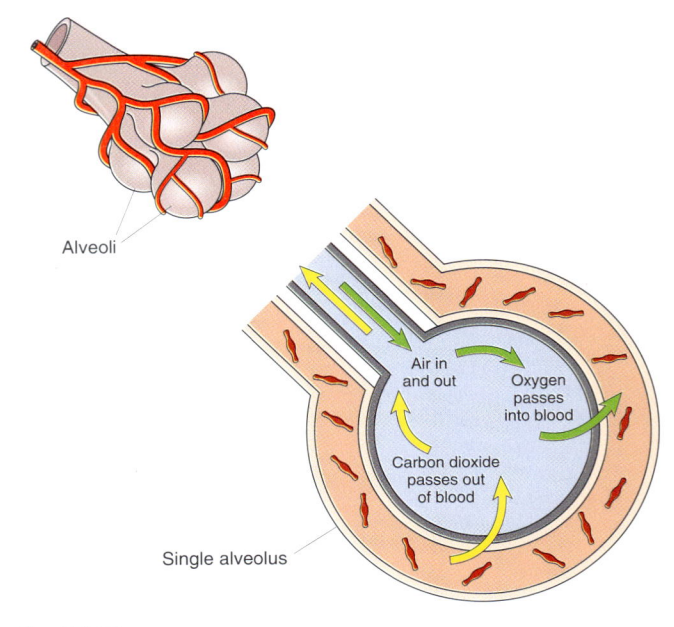

fig. 32.16

Q. 32.6
Suggest a reason for each of the following statements:

(a) The lungs are enclosed by the rib cage.
(b) Every person should be aware of air quality.
(c) Chest problems are more common in city areas.
(d) Each of the alveoli is surrounded by tiny blood vessels called capillaries.

Q. 32.7
(a) Write a paragraph explaining how smoking affects a person's health.
(b) Describe an experiment to show how smoking affects the lungs.
(c) What influences young people to start smoking, given the obvious dangers it poses to their health?

Q. 32.8
(a) What colour change occurs in cobalt chloride paper when it is placed in contact with water vapour?
(b) What name is given to the formation of water vapour on a cold surface?
(c) What substance is used to test for carbon dioxide?
(d) What change occurs to this substance when carbon dioxide is present?

Q. 32.9

(a) Why does an active person use more oxygen than a person at rest?
(b) How does exercise benefit the lungs?

Q. 32.10

(a) Describe an experiment to show that living organisms produce carbon dioxide.
(b) What is the purpose of the limewater in the experiment?

Q. 32.11

(a) Describe an experiment to show that respiration releases energy.
(b) Why does no increase in temperature occur in the flask containing the boiled peas?

Q. 32.12

Give three examples of how animals other than humans get oxygen into their bodies.

Q. 32.13

An experiment is carried out using wood lice to see whether they give off carbon dioxide during respiration. The apparatus is set up as shown in Figure 32.17. The test tubes are left in position for about half an hour.

(a) What indicates that carbon dioxide is produced?
(b) What is the purpose of test tube B?

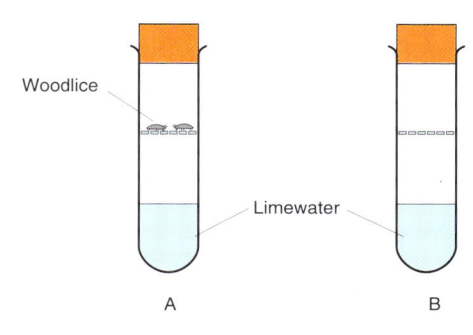

fig. 32.17

Q. 32.14

An experiment was carried out using the apparatus shown in Figure 32.18.

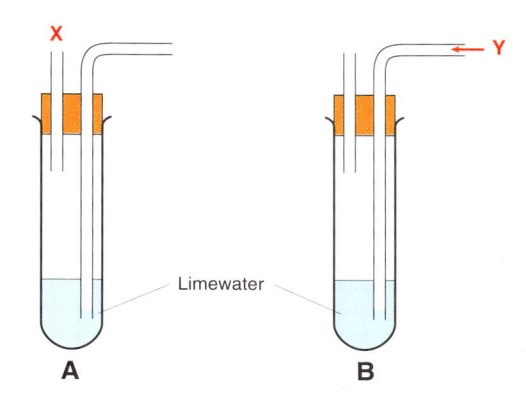

fig. 32.18

(a) What is the purpose of the experiment?
(b) Describe how this experiment is carried out.
(c) If the experiment is carried out before and after a person exercised, what effect would this have on the speed of the reaction?

TRANSPORT, CIRCULATION AND EXCRETION

The human body is like a city. All the people in the city need food, water, electricity and so on. All of these things have to be taken to where people need them, and the waste materials, like rubbish, have to be taken away. In order to move these things around a city, transport is needed. In the same way, all the cells in the human body need food and oxygen, and the waste materials such as carbon dioxide, have to be removed. Moving all these things around the human body also requires transport. Blood, moving through the circulation system, transports these substances around the body.

important chemicals such as hormones, around the body. It also carries carbon dioxide, salts and urea, which are the main waste products of the cells. Plasma contains three types of blood cell: red blood corpuscles, white blood cells and platelets.

fig. 33.2 William Harvey (1578–1637)

William Harvey, an English doctor, attended the most famous medical school of the time, in Padua, Italy. His patients included James I and Charles I. His interest in research led him to discover that the blood flows around the body and not to and fro, as was previously thought.

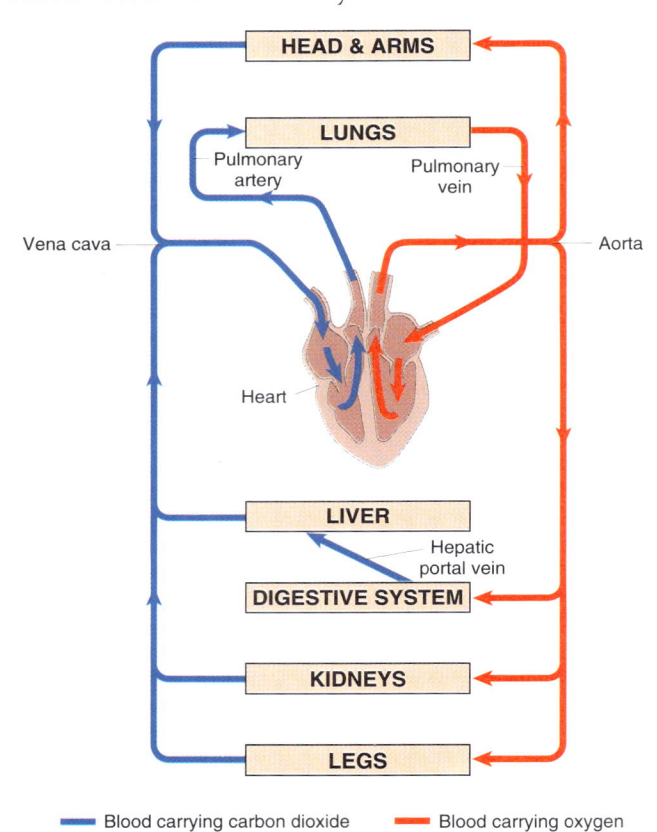

fig. 33.1 The circulation system

WHAT IS BLOOD MADE OF?

Blood consists of four main parts: plasma, red blood corpuscles, white blood cells and platelets.

Plasma

Plasma, the liquid part of the blood, is a pale yellowish colour. It is mostly water but has many substances dissolved in it. Plasma transports food, and other

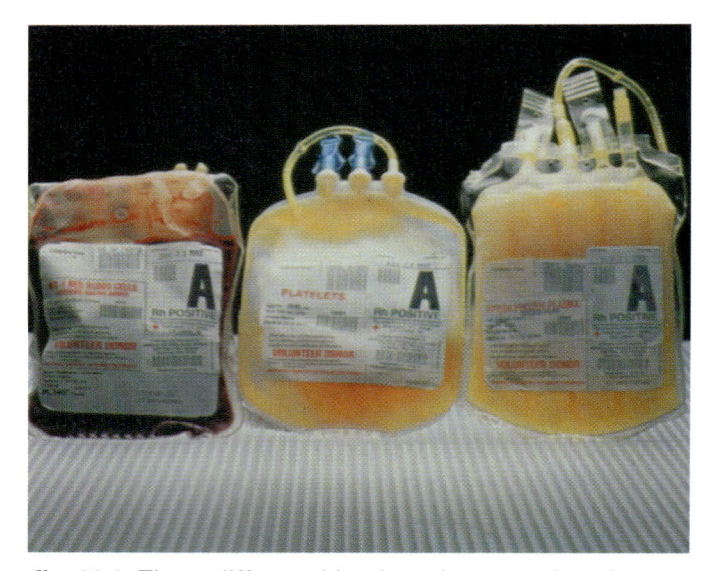

fig. 33.3 Three different blood products produced from donated blood. From left to right, concentrated red blood corpuscles, platelets and fresh plasma.

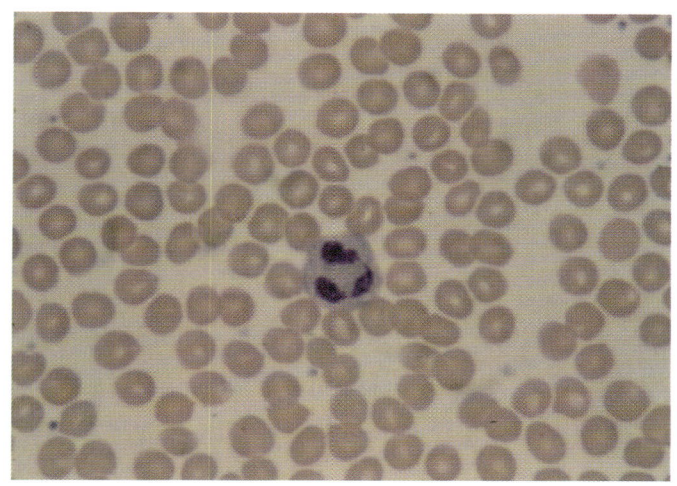

fig. 33.4 (a) Human blood cells as seen through a light microscope (magnification × 650)

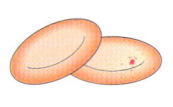

Red blood cells   White blood cells   Platelets

fig. 33.4 (b)

Red blood corpuscles

The red blood corpuscles give blood its red colour, due to a chemical called **haemoglobin**. It is because of this chemical that the corpuscles are able to carry oxygen around the body. Haemoglobin contains iron, so to make this substance, iron is needed in a person's diet. Red corpuscles are made in the bone marrow, and they have a life of about 120 days. After this time, they are broken down by the body, and are replaced by new ones.

White blood cells

White blood cells are used by the body to fight infection. Some of them 'eat' and digest micro-organisms. Others produce chemicals called **antibodies** which destroy micro-organisms trying to invade the body. There are fewer white blood cells than red corpuscles. White blood cells are also made in the bone marrow.

Platelets

Platelets are cell fragments and their main function is to clot the blood (to make it become solid). If the skin of the body is cut, the platelets combine with the red corpuscles to form a scab – which covers the wound. This process allows the damaged tissue underneath to heal. If clotting did not occur, severe blood loss would occur and as well, bacteria could enter the body causing infection.

Components of blood

- Red blood corpuscles carry oxygen
- White blood cells help fight disease
- Platelets help blood to clot
- Plasma transports food, carbon dioxide and waste

Experiment 33.1
To examine a prepared slide of human blood

1. Place the prepared slide on the stage of a microscope.
2. Examine it carefully, first using the low power lens, then the medium power and finally the high power lens.
3. Identify the different types of cell.
4. Draw a sketch of what can be seen.

FUNCTIONS OF BLOOD

Blood has many important functions:

- it transports oxygen and carbon dioxide around the body
- it transports waste from cells
- it protects the body against infection
- it transports nutrients to every cell in the body
- it helps maintain body temperature
- it transports hormones, which provide chemical messages, to various parts of the body (the function of hormones is explained in Chapter 34)

BLOOD VESSELS

In order for blood to flow around the body, it needs a route, and this is provided by the blood vessels – which are called **arteries**, **veins** and **capillaries**. The blood is kept circulating through these vessels by the **heart**, a large organ, which is essentially a pump.

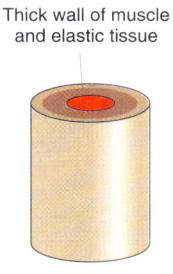

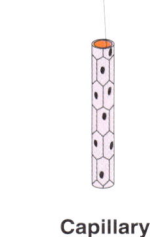

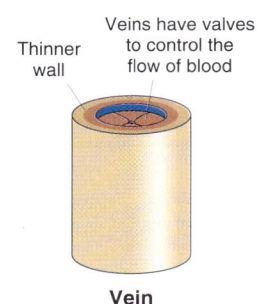

Thick wall of muscle and elastic tissue   Wall one cell thick   Thinner wall   Veins have valves to control the flow of blood

Artery   Capillary   Vein

fig. 33.5

Arteries

The arteries are the vessels that carry blood **away** from the heart. These vessels have thick walls as the blood is under high pressure. Blood carried in arteries is rich in oxygen, and is described as being **oxygenated**. There is one exception to this: the blood in the pulmonary artery (the artery that carries blood from the heart to the lungs) is low in oxygen, since it is on its way to the lungs where it will become enriched with oxygen. Blood which is low in oxygen content is described as **deoxygenated** blood. Arteries do not have valves as the blood is under high pressure and cannot flow backwards.

Veins

The veins are the vessels that carry blood **to** the heart. The walls of the veins are thinner than those of arteries since the blood is under lower pressure than it is in arteries. Along the length of the veins are valves, which prevent blood flowing the wrong way ('back flow') due to the action of gravity. Veins carry deoxygenated blood (low in oxygen content). Again there is one exception: the blood in the pulmonary vein, which carries oxygenated blood from the lungs to the heart.

Capillaries

Capillaries are the very thin vessels which link arteries and veins. The walls of capillaries are one cell thick and this allows substances to pass into, and out of cells. Oxygen enters cells from the capillaries, and carbon dioxide and waste from those cells pass into the capillaries. While these substances are transported around the body in the blood, it is from the capillaries that they actually reach the body cells.

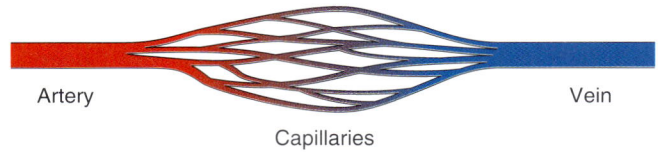

fig. 33.6

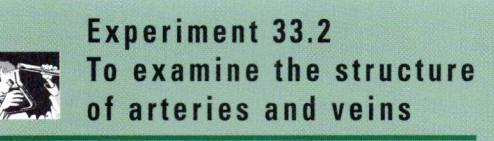

Experiment 33.2
To examine the structure of arteries and veins

1. Place a prepared slide on the stage of the microscope.
2. Examine it carefully, using the low power lens.
3. Identify the differences between arteries and veins.
4. Make sketches of what you see.

There are 2500 km of capillaries in the human body. The diameter of a capillary is about 0.009 mm. There are about 5 million white blood cells and 5000 million red blood corpuscles in every cm^3 of blood. About 5 million red cells are made every second in bone marrow. Blood with a high level of carbon dioxide is darker in colour than blood with a high level of oxygen in it.

THE HUMAN HEART

Blood is kept circulating around the body by the heart. The heart is a large muscular organ, situated in the chest and slightly to the left-hand side of the human body. The muscle tissue of the heart never stops and the heart is always active and always pumping blood. The faster the heart pumps, the faster the blood flows, and the faster the substances dissolved in the blood are transported around the body. The average human heart beats about 72 times per minute, but this rate varies according to the person's fitness, age and health.

fig. 33.7 A sheep's heart

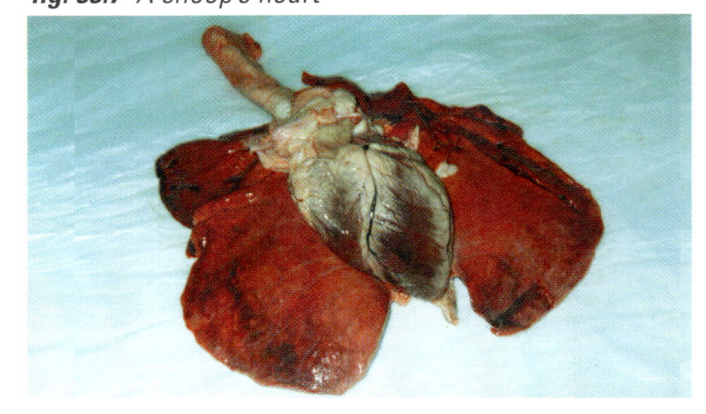

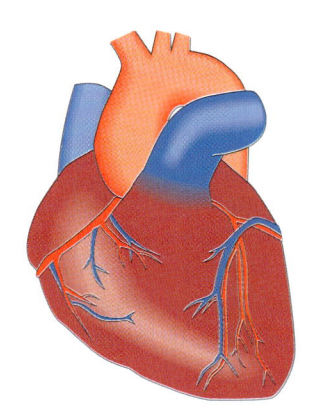

fig. 33.8 The human heart

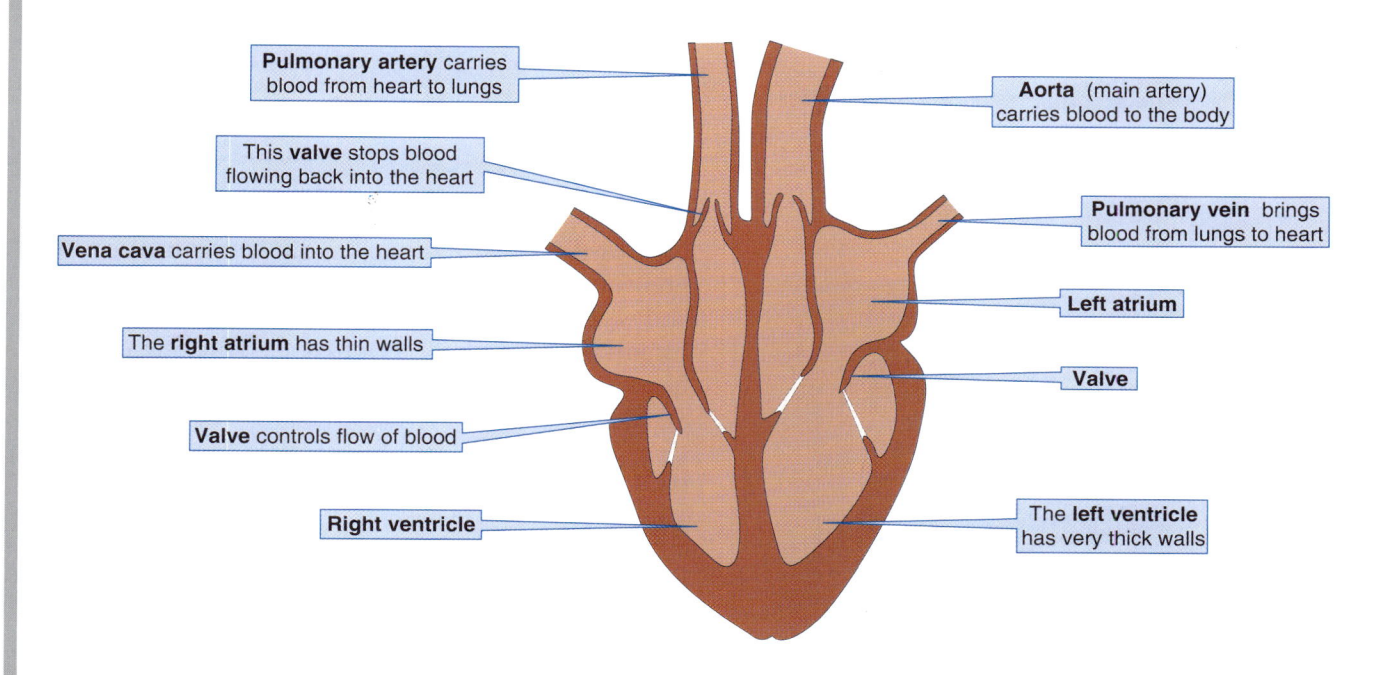

fig. 33.9 Structure of the human heart

The human heart is made of a special type of muscle called **cardiac muscle**, and it works 24 hours a day, 365 days a year, until the person dies. The heart is divided into two by a wall called the **septum**. The right-hand side of the heart pumps blood from the heart to the lungs. The left-hand side of the heart pumps blood from the heart to the rest of the body. As the left side of the heart has to pump blood a longer distance, the muscular wall on the left-hand side is much thicker than that on the right-hand side. The distance that the blood has to be pumped from the right-hand side of the heart to the lungs is much shorter, so the muscular wall is thinner on this side.

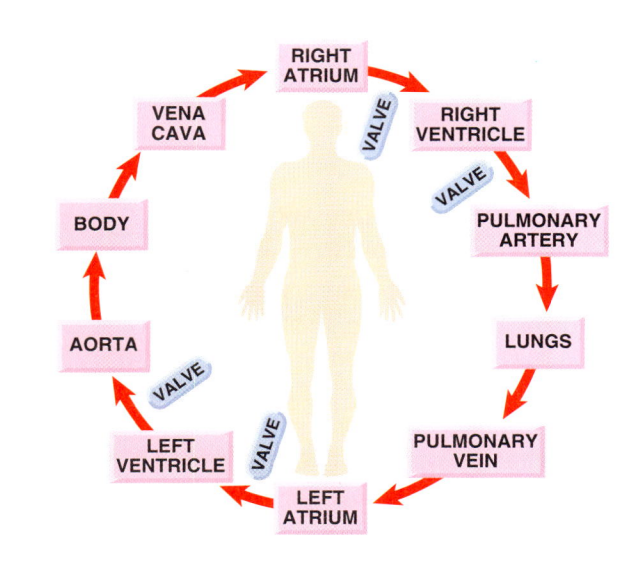

fig. 33.10 Blood flow in the body

Blood flow through the heart

The human heart has four chambers, **the left atrium, left ventricle, right atrium and right ventricle**. Blood enters the right atrium of the heart through the **vena cava**. When the right atrium is full of blood, it contracts, and the blood flows into the right ventricle through the valve. The right ventricle then pumps the blood through the **pulmonary artery** (the only artery to carry blood low in oxygen) to the lungs. The pressure of the blood causes the valve to close. In the lungs, the blood is transported in capillaries around the tiny **alveoli,** where it picks up oxygen and gets rid of carbon dioxide and water.

The blood which returns to the heart (from the lungs) is rich in oxygen. It travels to the heart through the **pulmonary vein** (the only vein to carry blood rich in oxygen). At the heart, it enters the left atrium, forces open a valve, and is pumped into the left ventricle. The left ventricle contracts, closing the valve and forcing the blood into the **aorta**.

The aorta branches off into many arteries, which transport blood to the arms, legs, head, stomach, liver, kidneys and all other parts of the body. Each artery branches into smaller and smaller vessels eventually becoming **capillaries**. The cells of the body use the oxygen brought to them by the blood and at the same time, the wastes produced in the cells pass back into the blood. The capillaries transport the blood from the cells back to the veins. The veins then bring blood back to the heart, entering it through the **vena cava**. The whole cycle continues again.

33 • Transport, Circulation and Excretion

The number of times the heart beats per minute is referred to as the pulse rate. Children have a higher pulse rate, while professional athletes have a lower-than-average rate. The pulse is a wave of pressure passing down the arteries, due to the action of the heart. The pulse can be felt where an artery is close to the surface of the skin, for example, at the wrist, temple and neck.

Experiment 33.4
To measure a pulse rate

To feel the human pulse, place two fingers on the wrist at the base of the thumb, and press gently. The pulse should then be felt; if not, move the fingers slightly until a steady pulse is detected. (Anyone with a heart or lung problem should not do this experiment.)

1. Work with a partner, and count the number of pulse beats per minute while he or she is at rest.
2. Repeat this measurement twice more, and then calculate the average rate.
3. Ask your partner to exercise for one minute. Suitable exercises include 'running' on the spot, or stepping up and down from a box 30 to 40 cm high.
4. When your partner sits down, count the number of pulses again in one minute. What do you notice about the pulse rate?
5. Measure the pulse rate every minute, until it returns to its original resting rate.
6. Repeat the procedure, reversing the roles.

A HEALTHY HEART

The heart and circulation system have to work very hard throughout each person's life, and it is important that this job is not made more difficult by the lifestyle of that person. Millions of people die every year from heart disease.

Like other muscles in the body, the heart muscle needs its own supply of both food and oxygen, that is, it needs its own blood supply. Without a good supply of oxygen it cannot work properly. Most people have had a muscle cramp such as a stitch in the side at some time – which is the result of the muscle not getting enough blood. If this happens to the heart muscle, it is extremely serious, as the heart may then stop pumping altogether; this is referred to as a heart attack.

There are many factors that can contribute to a person developing heart disease; they include:

- lack of exercise
- smoking
- eating too much fat, especially from animal foods
- having a stressful lifestyle
- an inherited family trait

In some people, a fatty substance called **cholesterol**, builds up on the inside of the blood vessels supplying the heart. Eventually this may causes a blockage that prevents blood from reaching part of the heart muscle, and without a good supply of blood, the heart muscle cannot work properly. In order to reduce the risk of heart disease you should eat less fat, exercise regularly, avoid smoking and try to reduce stress in your life.

QUESTIONS

Q. 33.1

Copy out the following paragraph and fill in the missing words.

The three types of cell found in blood are __ corpuscles, __ cells and __ . The __ cells help to fight disease, the __ corpuscles transport oxygen, and the __ help to form a clot when a blood vessel is cut. The blood cells are suspended in a liquid called __ . Other substances dissolved in the plasma include __ , __ and __ .

Q. 33.2

Copy out the following paragraph and fill in the missing words.

Blood is __ around the body in blood vessels. The __ carry blood away from the heart, these vessels have __ walls and the blood is under __ pressure. The __ carry blood towards the heart; the walls of these are __ and they have __ to help control the blood flow. The __ link the two types of blood vessel and the walls of these are only __ cell thick. They allow __ to reach the cells and remove __ and other wastes.

Q. 33.3

Copy out the following paragraph and fill in the missing words.

The __ is the pump that controls the flow of blood. It is made of a special type of muscle called __ __. This is very strong and needs a good supply of __. The heart has __ chambers, and it is divided in two by a wall called the __. Blood enters the __ side of the heart and is pumped to the __ where it collects __ . Blood leaves the left side of the heart through the __. As the left side of the heart pumps blood around the body the muscle here is much __ than the muscle on the __-hand side.

Q. 33.4

Write out correct statements by matching the names of each of the parts of the blood system (list A) with what it does (list B).

A The heart, Arteries, Veins, Capillaries, The lungs, Valves, The aorta

B are blood vessels leaving the heart.
is a pump to keep the blood moving.
link larger blood vessels.
is the main artery leaving the heart.
return blood to the heart.
controls the flow of blood through the heart.
allow gas exchange with the blood.

Q. 33.5

(a) State the function of the heart.
(b) Name the parts labelled A, B, C, D and E in the diagram of the heart (Figure 33.11).
(c) Give three ways in which the risk of heart disease may be reduced.

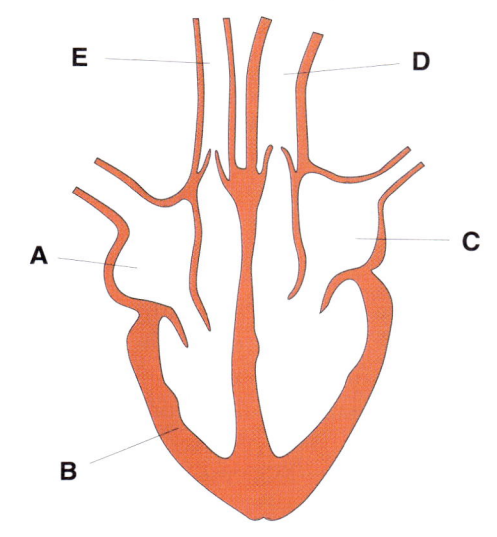

fig. 33.11

Q. 33.6

Copy out and complete the following table.

Blood vessel	Carries blood from	to	State of blood
Aorta	?	Body	Oxygenated
Pulmonary artery	Heart	?	?
?	Lungs	Heart	?
Vena cava	?	?	Deoxygenated

Q. 33.7

(a) Name the chemical found in red blood corpuscles which give them their red colour.
(b) State the function of valves in veins.
(c) What is unusual about the pulmonary artery and the pulmonary vein?

Q. 33.8

Write a paragraph explaining how a person's lifestyle can contribute to heart problems.

Q. 33.9

(a) Name the main blood vessels which enter the heart and those which leave the heart.
(b) Give the names of the four chambers in the heart.
(c) Describe the journey the blood takes through the heart starting with the right atrium.
(d) Draw a diagram to show the main differences between the structures of a vein, artery and capillary.

Q. 33.10

Figure 33.12 shows transverse sections through both an artery and a vein.

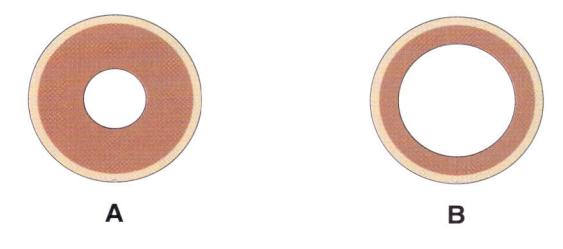

fig. 33.12

(a) Which diagram represents an artery and which represents a vein?
(b) Give two reasons to explain your chioce for each diagram.
(b) Name the type of blood vessels which connect an artery and vein.
(c) Name the structures in veins which help to control the flow of blood.

EXCRETION

A large number of chemical reactions takes place inside the human body in order to keep it alive and working well. The waste products of some of these reactions could be dangerous if they were allowed to accumulate, so they must be removed from the body.

The substances that are excreted are formed as by-products of the reactions that happen in the body.

33 • Transport, Circulation and Excretion

The organs from which excretion occurs are known as **excretory organs**. These organs are the lungs, kidneys and skin.

Excretion is the removal of the waste products of the body's chemical reactions.

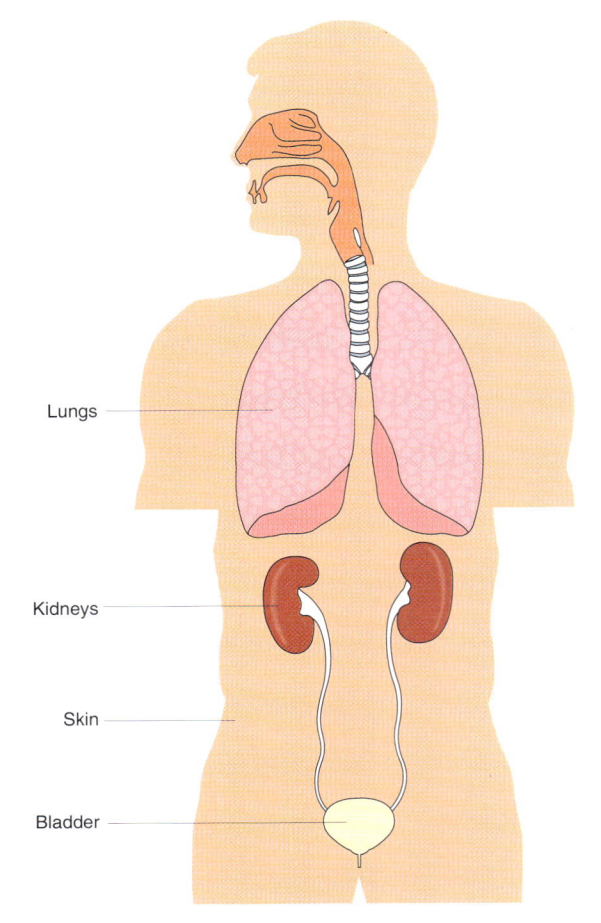

fig. 33.13

Excretory Organ	Waste product	How waste product is formed
Kidneys	urea and water	breakdown of protein in the liver
Lungs	carbon dioxide and water vapour	respiration in all body cells
Skin	water and salts	respiration and the breakdown of food

KIDNEYS

Renal artery brings blood into kidneys; blood contains urea

Renal vein carries the clean blood back to the heart

Kidneys filter blood and remove urea; the urea is mixed with water to form urine

Ureter carries urine to the bladder

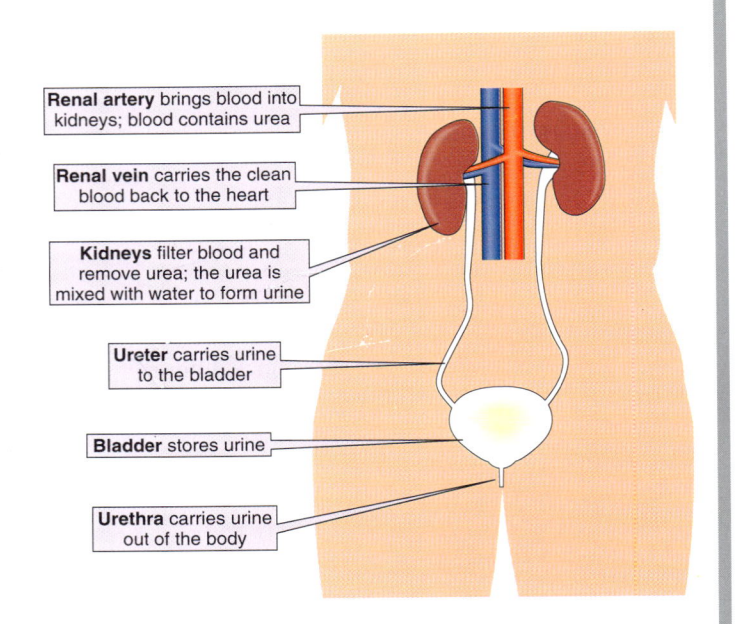

Bladder stores urine

Urethra carries urine out of the body

fig. 33.14

Urea

A balanced diet must include protein. The body cannot store protein, and unused protein is broken down in the liver to form a chemical compound called **urea**. If this compound were allowed to build up in the body, it would be toxic, and so it must be removed.

The kidneys carry out a very important function. They filter the blood and remove the urea and other waste products and, as a result, form urine. The urinary system contains a pair of kidneys, one at each side of the body. The renal arteries bring blood which is rich in oxygen and dissolved substances to the kidneys. Blood is brought away from the kidneys in the two **renal veins**. The kidneys remove the urea and other wastes, and the urine which is formed is transported to the **bladder** in a thin tube called the **ureter**. The urine is stored in the bladder until it is released from the body, through a tube called the **urethra**. A muscle called the **sphincter muscle** controls the opening of the bladder.

LUNGS

As described in Chapter 32, the function of the lungs is to exchange gases. Air breathed into the body travels down the **trachea**, into each **bronchus** and the **bronchioles**. The air then reaches the **alveoli**, the structures in which the exchange of gases takes place. Carbon dioxide and water vapour from the blood move from the capillaries into the alveoli.

These are excreted when we exhale. Experiments 32.1 and 32.2 show that the lungs give out carbon dioxide and water.

SKIN

The skin allows the body to get rid of excess water and salt from the blood. Sweat glands in the skin release water and salts which come to the surface through tiny openings called **pores**.

The skin also helps to control body temperature. When a person exercises and gets hotter, the heart rate and the blood flow increase. The capillaries near the surface of the skin get slightly wider, and as the blood flows through these, heat is lost. Also, sweat glands excrete sweat onto the surface of the skin, and the evaporation of this causes cooling (see Experiment 10.4). If the temperature drops, sweat production stops, the body shivers and the muscular movement in shivering creates heat. The skin also acts as a barrier to micro-organisms.

SUMMARY

- **Blood** is a fluid made up of **red blood corpuscles**, **white blood cells**, and **platelets**, suspended in a liquid called plasma. The blood is transported through arteries, veins and capillaries. **Arteries** carry blood away from the heart and **veins** carry blood towards the heart. **Capillaries** link the arteries and the veins, and oxygen travels from the capillaries to the body cells.

- The main functions of the blood are transport of substances around the body, defence against disease, and keeping the body temperature constant.

- The **heart** pumps blood around the body and it has four chambers. The right-hand side of the heart pumps blood to the lungs, and the left-hand side of the heart pumps blood to the rest of the body.

- Risk of heart disease is reduced by exercising, having a healthy diet and by not smoking.

- **Excretion** means getting rid of the waste products produced by the body. Humans excrete water, carbon dioxide, salts and urea. The main excretory organs in humans are the kidneys, skin and lungs. The **kidneys** remove urea from the blood and form urine; the **skin** excretes water and salts, and the **lungs** excrete carbon dioxide and water vapour.

QUESTIONS

Q. 33.11

Copy out the following paragraph, completing the blanks.

Excretion means the removal of __ from the body. The organs from which excretion take place are called the __ organs. The lungs excrete __ and __ __, the ___ excrete urea and the skin excretes __ and __. Urea comes from the breakdown of __ in the __ . The __ artery carries blood to the kidneys and the __ __ carries blood away. The ureter transports __ to the bladder where it is stored. The urine is transported to the outside of the body in a tube called the __ .

Q. 33.12

(a) Give the names of each of the parts shown on the diagram of the urinary system (Figure 33.15).

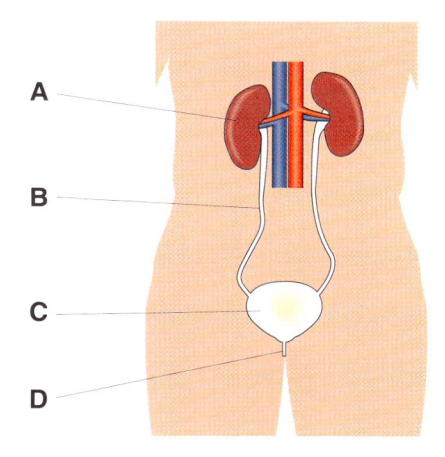

fig. 33.15

(b) Explain how urine is formed.
(c) Explain why must urea be removed from the body?
(d) What is the function of part A?

Q. 33.13

(a) Explain what is meant by the term excretion.
(b) Draw an outline diagram of the human body labelling the excretory organs.
(c) Name the substances excreted by each of these organs.

SUPPORT, MOVEMENT AND SENSITIVITY

Humans need skeletons to support their bodies. The **skeleton** is a framework of bones, cartilage and ligaments that work together to serve a number of important functions. The skeleton: (i) supports the body, (ii) provides protection for internal organs such as the heart and lungs, and (iii) with the aid of muscles, it makes movement possible. Without a skeleton the body would resemble a lump of jelly.

fig. 34.1 *What a human body would be like without a skeleton*

The human skeleton is made up of 206 bones. The largest of these is the thigh bone and the smallest are the bones in the ear. Children have a greater number of bones than adults, because as children grow, some of their bones fuse together to become one. Bone contains bone cells which, like all other cells, are living. These cells need a supply of food and oxygen, and also have to be able to get rid of waste. The blood transports food and wastes to and from the bone cells. Bone cells also need minerals and other nutrients, such as calcium and vitamin D, to enable them to form strong bones. The bones of some elderly people may lose some of their strength or become brittle, which means they are more likely to break. To help prevent this happening, foods containing calcium and vitamin D should be eaten regularly. Dairy products are a good source of calcium, and fish, liver and eggs are good sources of vitamin D.

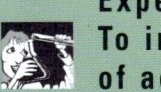

Experiment 34.1
To investigate the effect of acid on bone

In order to support the body, bones need to be strong. The following experiment shows how bone strength can be removed.

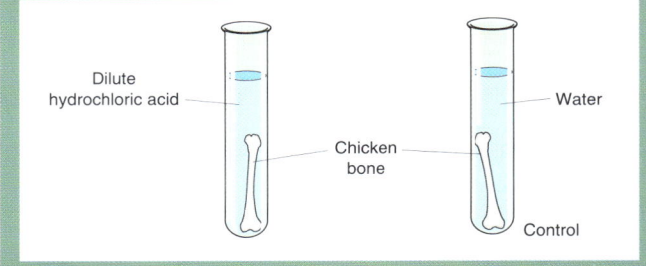

fig. 34.3

1. Set up apparatus as shown in Figure 34.3.
2. Leave it in position for 24 hours.
3. Carefully remove the bones and rinse them under a tap.
4. Test the strength of each bone by trying to bend them.

Do you notice that the bone which was placed in acid is not as strong as that which was placed in water. The mineral calcium gives bone its strength. When bone is placed in acid, the acid reacts with the calcium in the bone and so takes away the strength of the bone.

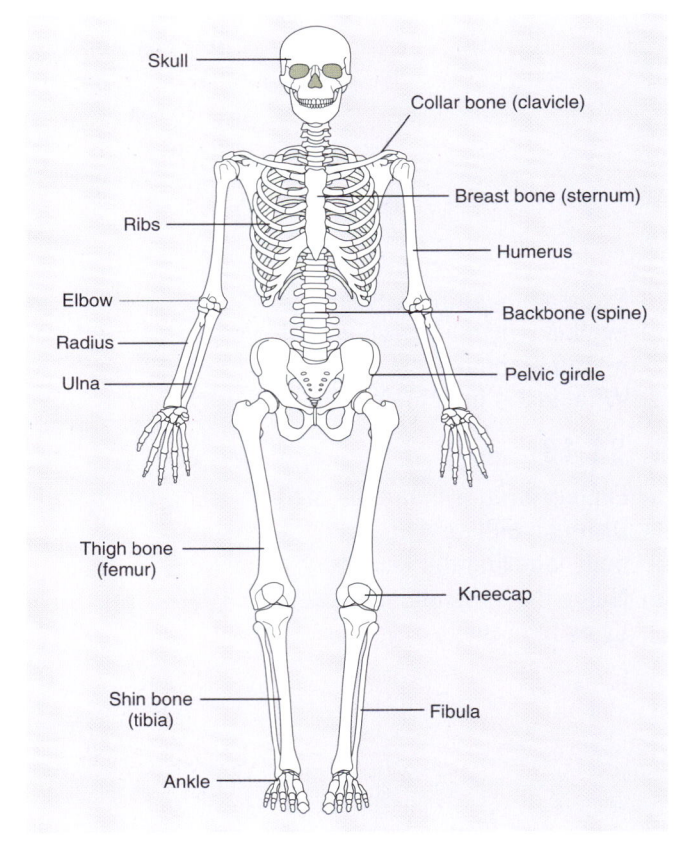

fig. 34.2 *The human skeleton*

JOINTS

Try walking without bending your knees. It is difficult, isn't it? Bones can move because of the action of joints, which make movement possible.

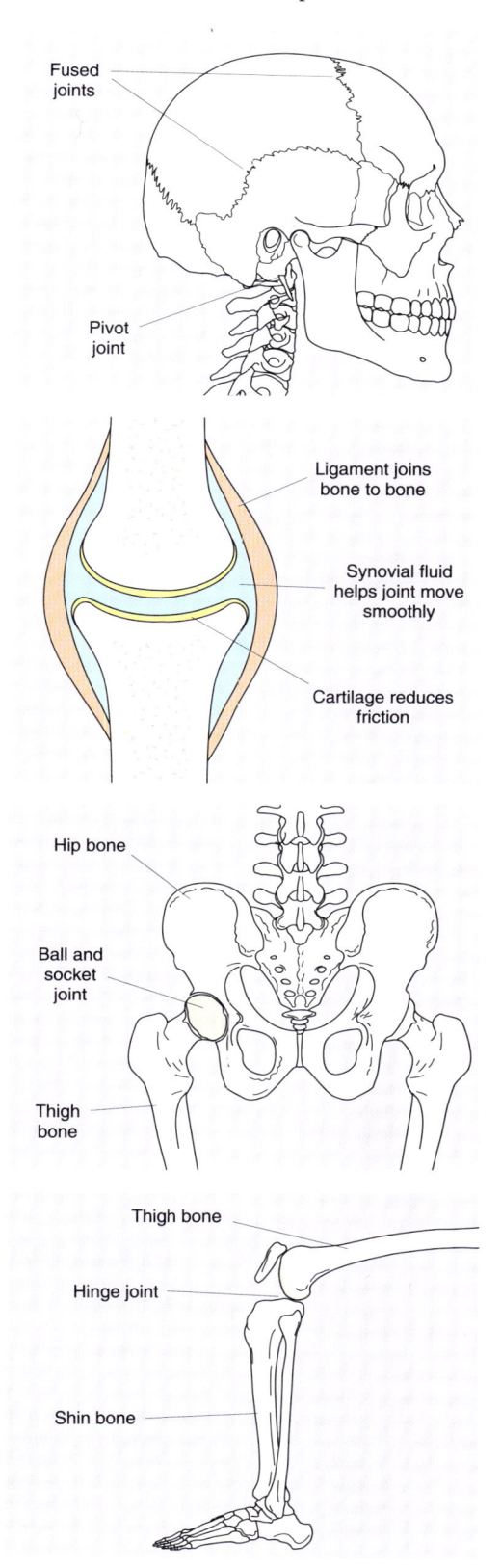

There are two main types of joint that you need to know about: fixed joints and synovial joints.

Fixed joints: In these, there is no movement between the bones. The skull contains fixed joints.

Synovial joints: These are joints at which there is movement. The surfaces of the bones in normal healthy joints do not touch (see diagram) as they are covered with tissue called **cartilage**, which helps to reduce friction. There is also a liquid called **synovial fluid** which lubricates the joints. There are several types of synovial joint:

(i) **Ball and socket** joints allow for movement in several directions; examples of these are the hip and shoulder joints.

(ii) **Hinge joints** are ones which can only bend in one direction. There are hinge joints at the knee and elbow.

(iii) **Gliding joints**: At these joints the bones glide over each other. There are gliding joints at the wrist and ankle.

(iv) **Pivot joint**: The pivot joint at the base of the skull allows you to nod and shake your head.

LIGAMENTS

The bones forming the joints are held in place by tough bands of fibrous tissue called **ligaments**. Ligaments hold the bones in position but allow movement between them; they help to prevent over stretching. Figure 34.4 shows the arrangement of ligaments and bones.

MUSCLES

Muscles provide the force needed to move bones. The muscles are attached to bones by elastic fibres called **tendons**. In animals, some bones work like levers; examples of these are the bones in the forearm and those in the jaw.

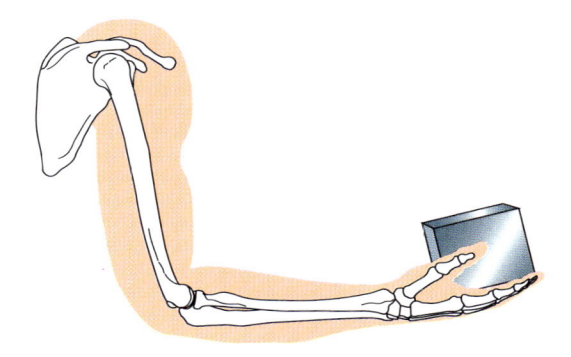

fig. 34.4

fig. 34.5

34 • Support, Movement and Sensitivity

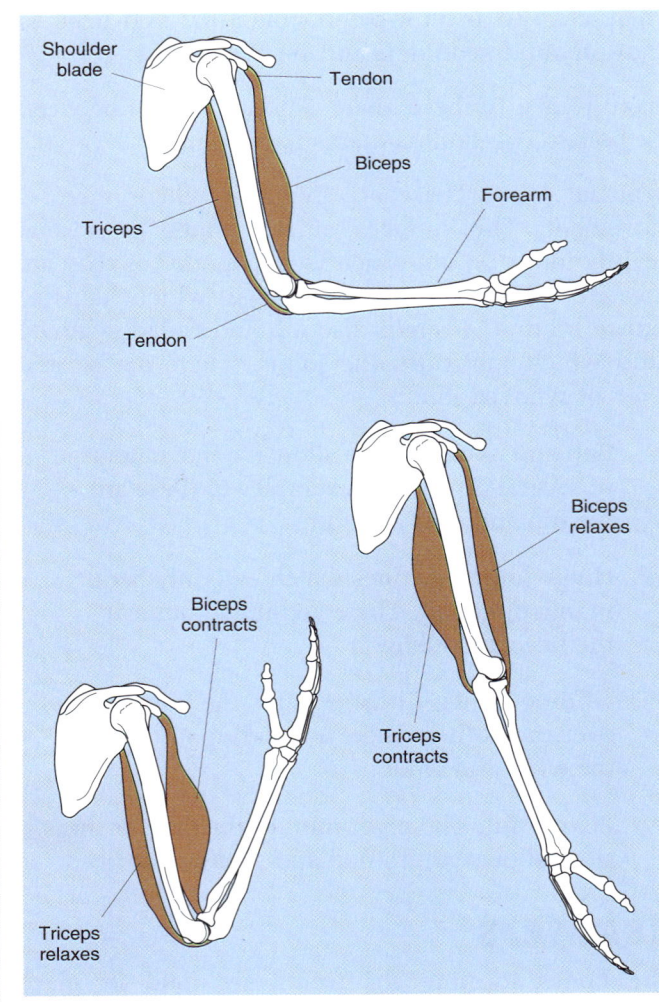

fig. 34.6 Antagonistic muscles in the arm

Figure 34.6 shows that there are two large muscles in the upper arm. These muscles are called the **biceps** muscle and the **triceps** muscle. Push against the underside of a bench with the back of your hand. What do you notice happening to your biceps muscle? It contracts and becomes shorter and fatter. Now push down with the back of your hand against the surface of the bench. Your triceps muscle contracts.

When you lift an object by raising your lower arm, the biceps contracts, and pulls the bones of your lower arm upwards. When you lower your arm, the biceps relaxes, and the triceps contracts, moving the arm downwards. Muscles that work alternately like this are called **antagonistic muscles**.

QUESTIONS

Q. 34.1
Rewrite the following paragraph, and complete the spaces.

The skeleton __ the body and helps to maintain its shape. The __ in the skeleton protect many important __ in the body, for example, the __. Connected bones move at __ . The elbow is an example of a __ joint and at the shoulder there is an example of a __ and __ joint.

Q. 34.2
Rewrite the following paragraph, and complete the spaces.

Your __ provide the force to move __ at joints. When a muscle contracts it gets __ and fatter. When a muscle is not contracting it is described as being __ .

Q. 34.3
Rewrite the following paragraph, and complete the spaces

Bones are moved by __. The joints at which bones move are called __ joints. At these joints, tough __ hold the bones together. At the ends of each bone there is a layer of __ which reduces friction and acts as a shock absorber. A liquid called __ fluid also helps to prevent wear and tear.

Q. 34.4
(a) State the function of
 (i) ligaments (ii) tendons.
(b) Describe how the movement of the forearm is controlled by the muscles which are shown in Figure 34.7.

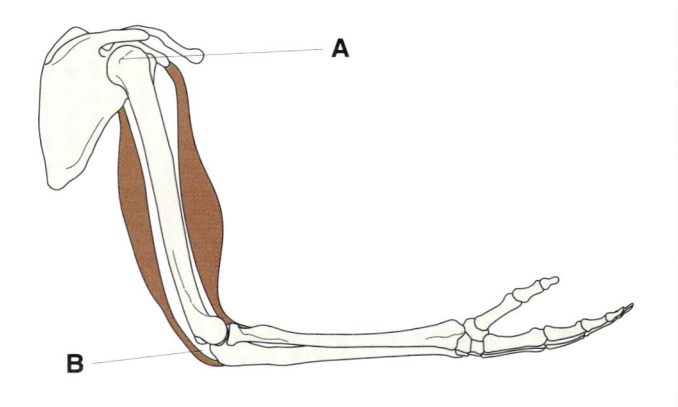

fig. 34.7

(c) Name the joints A and B.
(d) State one other location in the skeleton where a joint similar to A may be found.

Q. 34.5
The biceps and triceps are antagonistic muscles Explain, using a diagram, what this means.

Q. 34.6

(a) What name is given to the structures that join muscles to bones.
(b) Name the substance that is found at the end of bones which helps to reduce friction.
(c) What is the function of synovial fluid?
(d) Give an example of (i) a hinge joint and (ii) a ball and socket joint.
(e) Why is it important to have calcium in the diet?

Q. 34.7

Copy this table and complete the blanks, naming the type of joint found at each of the following parts of the skeleton.

Joint	Type of joint
knee	
base of skull	
elbow	
hip	
shoulder	
knuckle	

Q. 34.8

Name the vitamin and the mineral needed for healthy bones. Give the names of two foods containing these nutrients.

SENSITIVITY AND COORDINATION

In humans there are two systems for sending messages and for coordinating any actions needed as a result of messages received. The two systems are (i) **the nervous system** which sends messages in the form of electrical impulses, and (ii) **the endocrine (or hormonal) system** which sends chemical messages.

Our senses make us aware of changes in the world around us and enables us to respond. The nervous system acts quickly; nerve messages can produce an almost immediate response. Changes brought about by the chemical messages from the endocrine system act much more slowly.

THE NERVOUS SYSTEM

Animals can react very quickly to environmental changes, but plants respond more slowly. A change which results in an action is called a **stimulus** (plural **stimuli**) and the result is called the **response**. For example, if you accidentally place your hand on a hot cooker ring, your immediate reaction is to remove it from danger. The heat is the stimulus and the response is the hand being moved away.

To get information about what is going on around them, humans use one or more of their five sense organs. These are:

Sense organ	Sense
Eye	sight
Ear	hearing
Nose	smell
Tongue	taste
Skin	touch

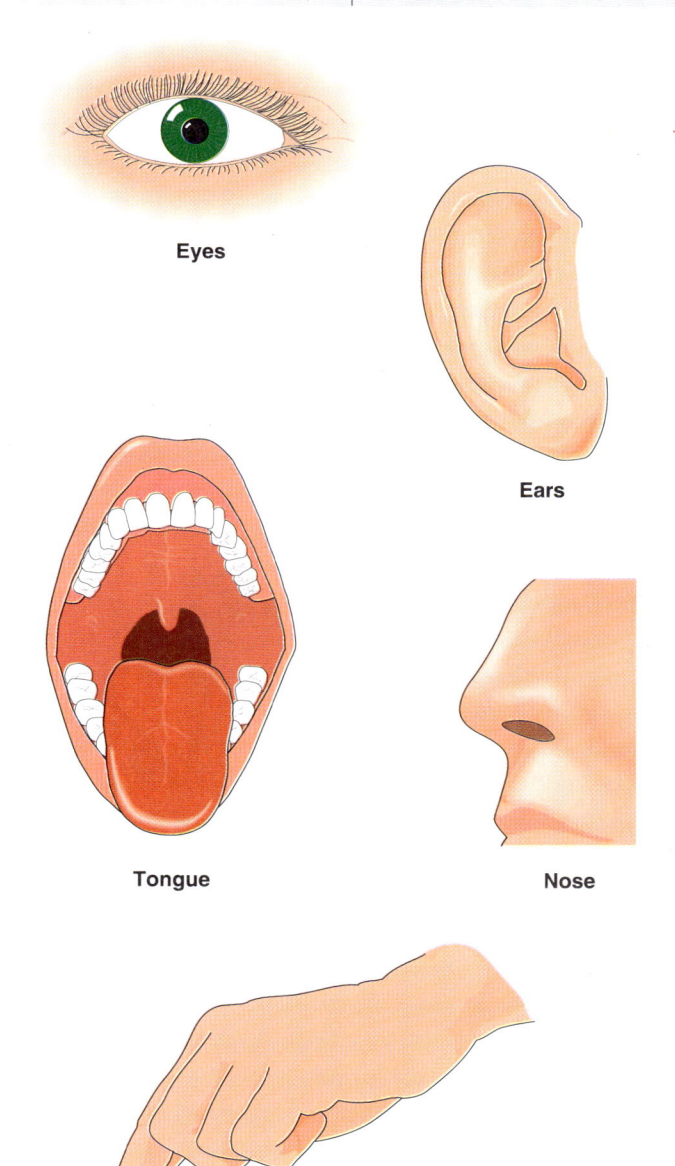

fig. 34.8 *The sense organs*

■ 34 • Support, Movement and Sensitivity

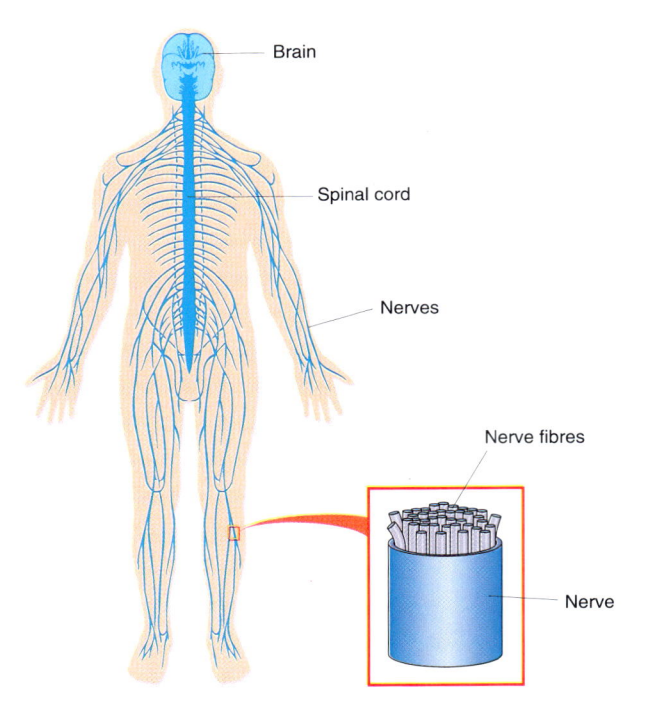

fig. 34.9 *The nervous system*

The nervous system enables the body to react to the information received by the sense organs, and it consists of the brain, spinal cord and nerves. Since the sense organs receive information, they are also referred to as **receptors**. When information is received by a sense organ, it is carried to the brain by nerves. Nerves consist of bundles of nerve cells called **neurons**. A nerve that brings information from a sense organ to the brain or spinal cord is called a **sensory**

> *Sensory* neurons carry messages *to* the brain. *Motor* neurons carry messages *away* from the brain.

nerve or **sensory neuron**. The brain receives and interprets the message and then reacts by sending another message back to a muscle. These messages travel in special nerves called **motor nerves** or **motor neurons**.

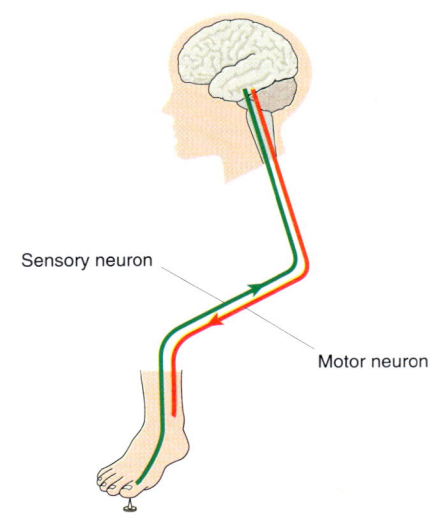

fig. 34.10 *Senses allow the body to react quickly*

The eye

In the nervous system, messages are transferred very quickly. A good example is provided by the optic

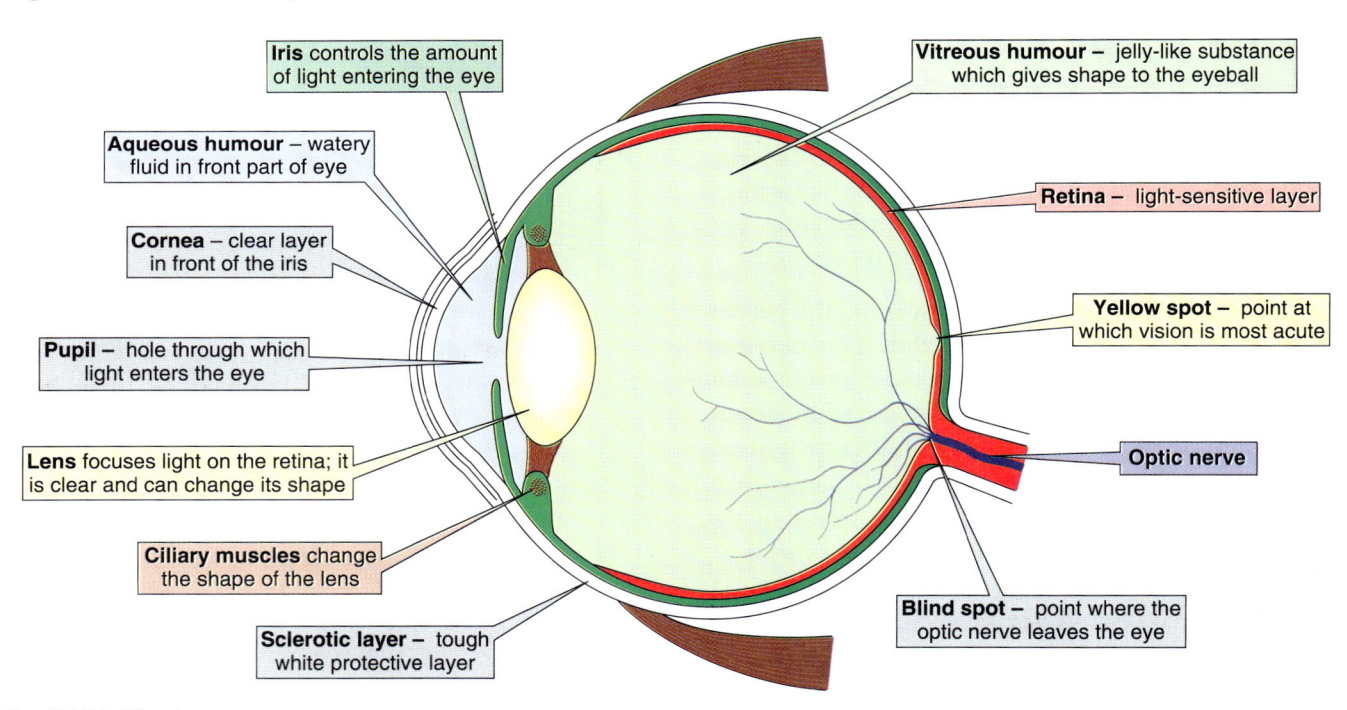

fig. 34.11 *The human eye*

system. Light enters the eye through the pupil, and is focused by the lens on the **retina** (the light sensitive layer). The light is changed into electrical impulses which are then transferred to the brain, via the **optic nerve**. The brain interprets the message and if the light, for example, is too bright, the brain sends a message to decrease the size of the pupil. This is controlled by changing the size of the iris. This whole process takes place very quickly.

THE ENDOCRINE SYSTEM

Some activities in the body are not easy to control with nervous impulses. Growth, for example, takes a lot of time, and involves changes in many cells. Chemical messages are sent by the endocrine system to bring about more gradual but longer-lasting changes. The chemicals in the endocrine system are called **hormones**, and they are secreted by glands in the body. The hormones are carried around the body in the blood, and each hormone acts on particular tissues and organs. The changes that take place in puberty for example, are controlled by hormones, and these changes affect many parts of the body.

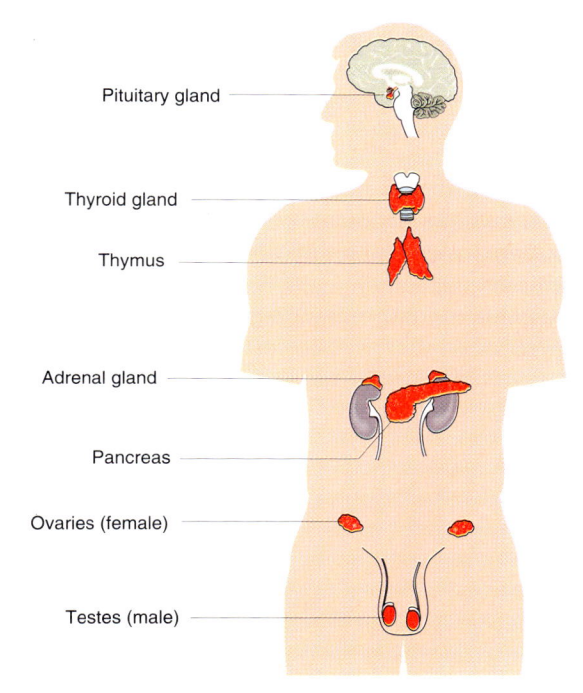

fig. 34.12 *The endocrine glands*

Insulin is a hormone which is made in the pancreas. It allows the body to control the level of sugar in the blood. It is especially important after a meal has been consumed as the level of sugar in the blood then rises. If too little insulin is produced, the level of sugar in the blood increases causing a condition called **diabetes**. People affected by this condition often need to take insulin and follow special diets.

SUMMARY

- The **skeleton** supports the body and gives it shape, protects vital organs, and enables it to move with the aid of muscles. Bones are made of minerals such as calcium. Soaking a bone in acid causes it to lose strength.

- **Joints** enable movement to take place between bones. The two types of joint are **fixed joints** and **synovial joints**. Fixed joints are found in the skull. There are several types of synovial joint: ball and socket joints (shoulder), hinge joints (knee), gliding joints (wrist) and pivot joints (base of the skull).

- **Muscles** contract and relax to bring about the movement of bones. Muscles which work alternately are called antagonistic muscles, e.g. biceps and triceps. Tendons join muscle to bone, and ligaments join bone to bone.

- The nervous system and the endocrine system work together to coordinate the activities in the body.

- The **nervous system** consists of the brain, spinal cord and nerves. **Sensory neurons** carry messages to the brain and **motor neurons** carry messages away from the brain. Sense organs receive information.

- The **endocrine system** consists of glands which produce chemical messages called **hormones**. Hormones are transported in the blood, and they bring about gradual changes in the body, for example, the changes at puberty are caused by hormones.

QUESTIONS

Q. 34.9

Copy the following paragraph, filling in the blanks.
The nervous system consists of the __ and __ __. The sense organs are also known as __ since they receive information. Information from the sense organs travels in __ neurons to the brain. The brain sends messages in __ neurons to bring about a response. The nervous system uses __ impulses to send messages and these last for only a __ time.

Q. 34.10

Copy the following paragraph, filling in the blanks.

The eye responds to __. The __ is a transparent layer which protects the eye and allows light through.

The __ __ humour is a watery layer in front of the lens. The __ is the coloured part of the eye. Light reaches the ___ through the ___ which is a hole in the iris. The __ focuses the light on the __ – which is the light sensitive layer. The __ __ is a clear, jelly like substance which gives shape to the eyeball. The light is converted into __ impulses. The __ nerve transfers the impulses to the __ .

Q. 34.11

Copy the following paragraph, filling in the blanks.

The endocrine system produces __ messages called __. These __ are transported around the body in the blood. They act __ but their effects last a __ time. The __ are produced by __ . The changes that take place in boys and girls during __ are brought about by __. Another important hormone is __ which helps control the level of sugar in the blood.

Q. 34.12

Name the five sense organs, and state what each of them responds to.

Q. 34.13

(a) What are hormones?
(b) Where are they produced in the body?
(c) How do hormonal responses differ from nervous responses?
(d) Give one example of a hormone and state why it is needed.

Part of the eye	Function
Lens	
Cornea	
Retina	
Pupil	
Optic nerve	
Blind spot	

Q. 34.14

Copy out and complete the following table, which is about the eye.

Q. 34.15

(a) Name the parts labelled A, B, C and X in Figure 34.13.

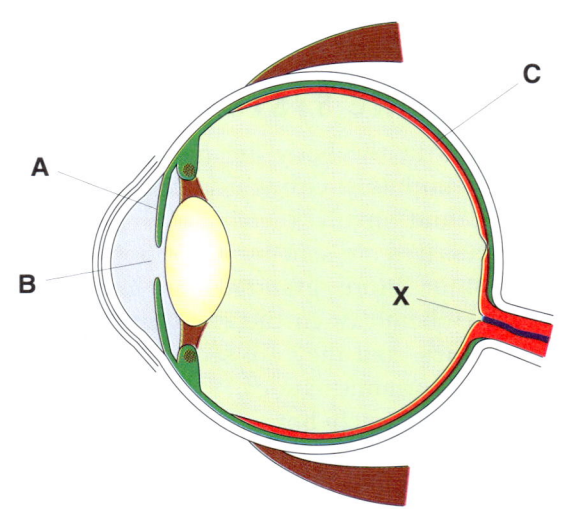

fig. 34.13

(b) State the function of parts A, B, C and X.

Q. 34.15

Which system, the nervous system or the endocrine system, is more involved when:

(a) a cat catches a mouse
(b) a kitten grows into a cat
(c) a person cycles a bicycle
(d) a tadpole changes into a frog

35

HUMAN REPRODUCTION AND INHERITANCE

Reproduction is the production of new individuals. These are needed to replace those individuals who die. They may also increase the size of the population.

Most animals reproduce sexually. This means that the nucleus of the male sex cell (**sperm**) joins with the nucleus of the female sex cell (**egg** or **ovum**). Another name for sex cells is **gametes**. The single cell that results is called the zygote. The **zygote** grows into a new individual.

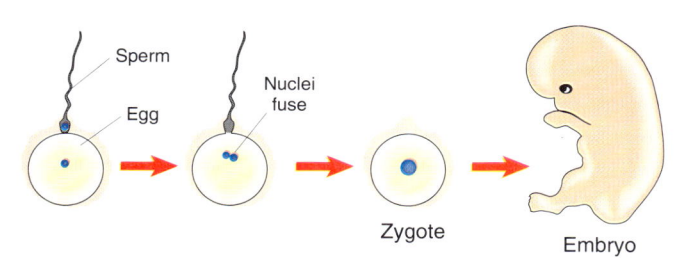

fig. 35.1 Sexual reproduction

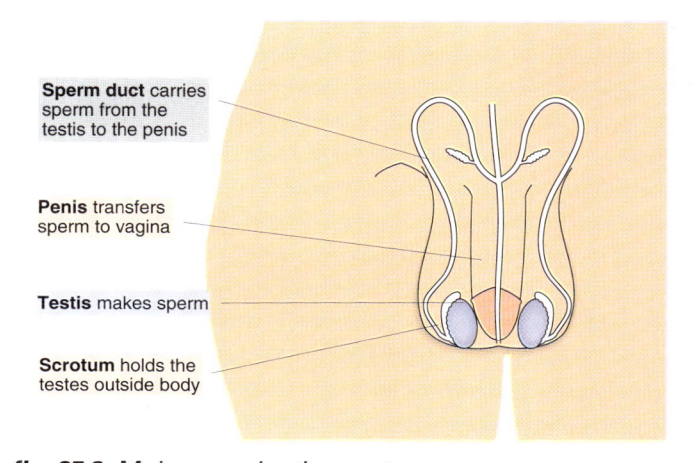

Female reproductive system

The reproductive system of a young girl undergoes certain changes between the ages of about 10 and 14. These changes are caused by hormones and are called **puberty**. The two main changes are (a) the ovaries start to ripen and release eggs (ova) and (b) the womb prepares to carry a baby. Other changes include the breasts enlarging, the hips widening and hair growing in the pubic and underarm areas.

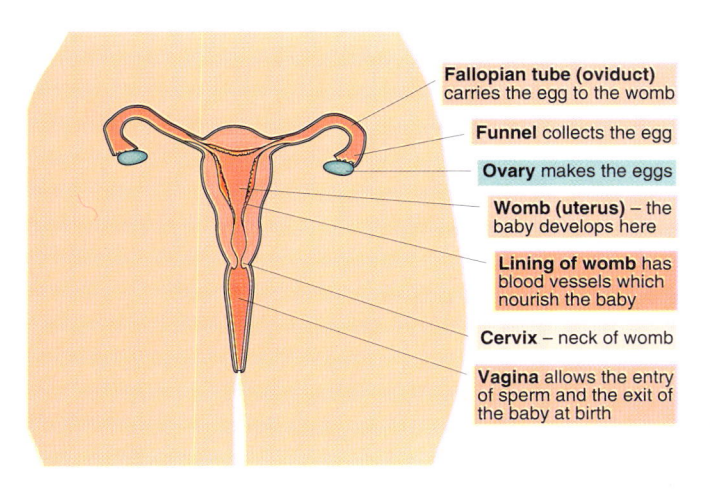

fig. 35.2 Female reproductive system

Male reproductive system

The start of sexual maturity (puberty) in boys is around 11 to 13 years of age. The main change is that the testes start to produce sperm cells. Other changes include the enlargement of the penis, the deepening (breaking) of the voice, the growth of hair (pubic, facial and around the body) and the enlargement of muscles.

fig. 35.3 Male reproductive system

Menstrual cycle

The menstrual cycle is a series of events that take place in the female body. These events usually occur every 28 days (i.e. once a month). The menstrual cycle starts at puberty and continues until the woman is in her fifties. When the menstrual cycle stops the woman is said to go through the 'change of life' or **menopause**.

The main events in the menstrual cycle are outlined below. Note that the timings differ from female to female and from month to month. The figures given below represent the average timings.

(a) **Days 1-5**. The lining of the **womb** or **uterus** (which had built up during the previous menstrual cycle) breaks down and is shed from the body through the vagina. This loss of blood is called **menstruation** (or having a period).

(b) **Days 6-13**. A new lining starts to form along the walls of the womb. This lining will be rich in blood vessels which will nourish a developing baby if the female becomes pregnant.

241

35 • Human Reproduction and Inheritance

(c) **Day 14**. An egg is released from the ovary. This is called **ovulation**. The egg will only live about one day. If there are no sperm in the female system, the egg will die.

(d) **Days 15 to 28**. The lining of the womb remains in place. A new cycle starts when the lining begins to be shed again, on day 28.

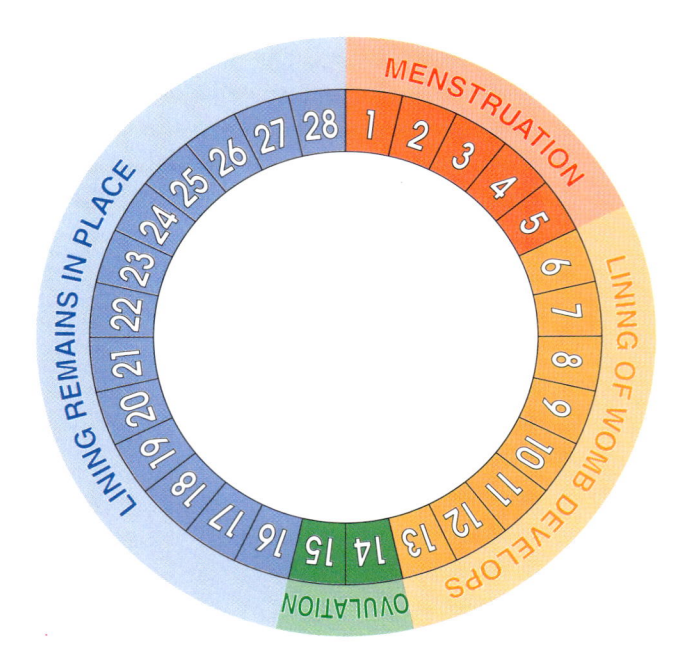

fig. 35.4 Menstrual cycle

Human sexual reproduction

Intercourse (also called copulation) is the placing of the penis into the vagina. It allows sperm to pass into the female body. The release of sperm from the penis (as a liquid called semen) is called ejaculation. The placing of sperm in the vagina is called insemination.

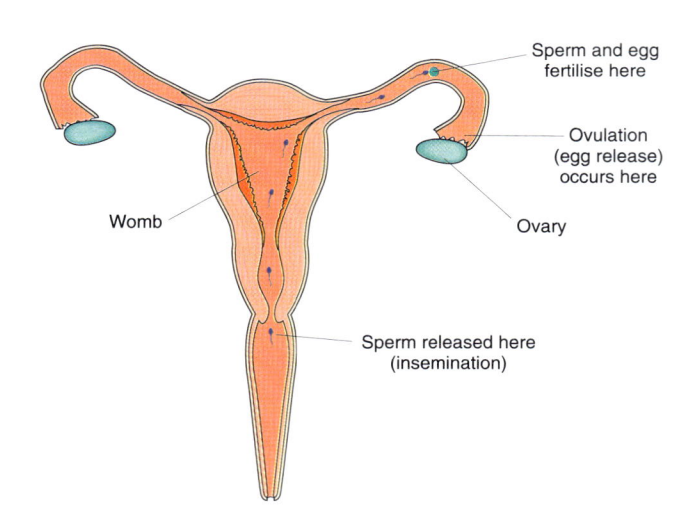

fig. 35.5 Path of sperm

Usually over 100 million sperm cells are released into the vagina. These sperm swim into the womb, along the lining of the womb and up into the Fallopian tubes. If there is no egg present, the sperm die. Sperm can survive for up to 72 hours.

If an egg is present (i.e. if ovulation has just taken place) sperm will swim to the egg, attracted by a chemical released by the egg. The nucleus of one sperm will join with the nucleus of the egg to form the zygote. This process is called **fertilisation** and it takes place in the Fallopian tube. The woman is now said to be pregnant (i.e. to have a new individual inside her).

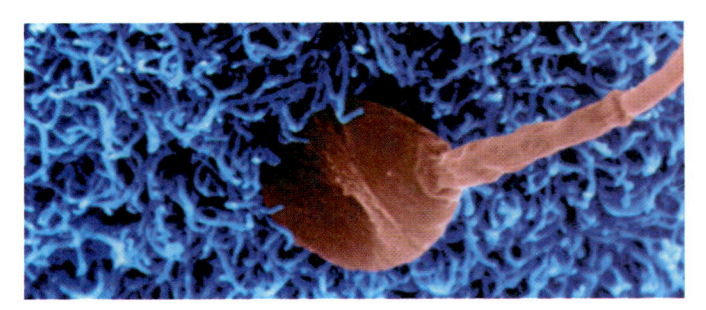

fig. 35.6 A sperm cell and egg at fertilisation

The **fertile period** is that time in the menstrual cycle when intercourse could lead to pregnancy. It starts at approximately day 12 and ends at day 17 (by which time the egg will be dead).

The zygote grows to become a young baby or **embryo**. As the zygote grows it is pushed down the Fallopian tube and into the womb. It attaches to the lining of the womb, a process called implantation. In order to allow it to develop, menstruation stops during pregnancy.

A tube (the umbilical cord) grows from the embryo (at the navel) and attaches to the lining of the womb at the placenta. The embryo becomes surrounded by a bag of liquid. The liquid is called **amniotic fluid** and the bag is the **amnion**.

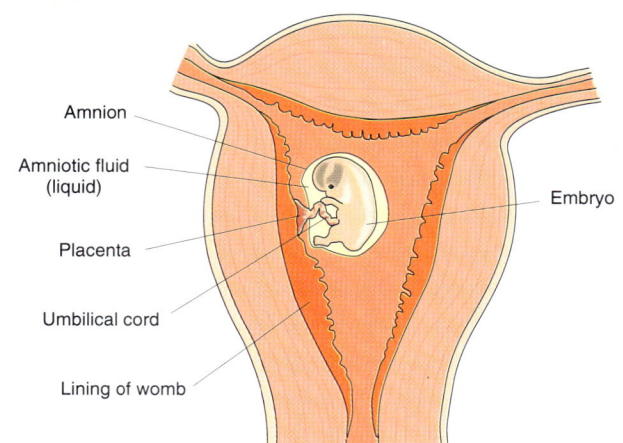

fig. 35.7 Embryo in the womb

The blood of the mother and her baby do not mix. Instead the placenta allows substances to pass in both directions between the mother and baby. The passage of most of these substances is useful (e.g. oxygen and food pass to the baby, carbon dioxide and wastes pass to the mother). However, harmful substances can also pass across the placenta from the mother into the baby (e.g. alcohol, drugs, nicotine from cigarettes).

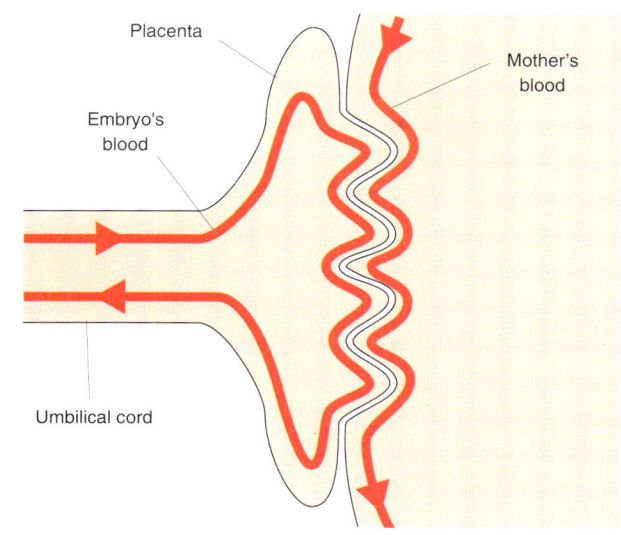

fig. 35.8 Structure of the placenta

About 8 weeks after fertilisation, the embryo will have formed all the organs present in an adult. It now looks like a human and is called a **foetus**.

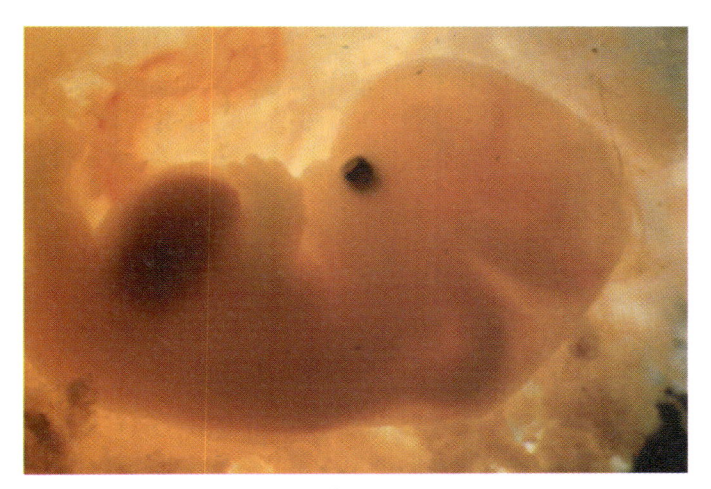

fig. 35.9 Embryo at 8 weeks

Birth takes place about 9 months after fertilisation. By this time the foetus will have turned so that its head is pointing down towards the cervix. The muscles of the womb contract. These contractions are called labour pains. The contractions cause the bag of fluid to burst and flow out through the vagina. This is called the 'breaking of the waters'. The baby is born soon after, usually head first.

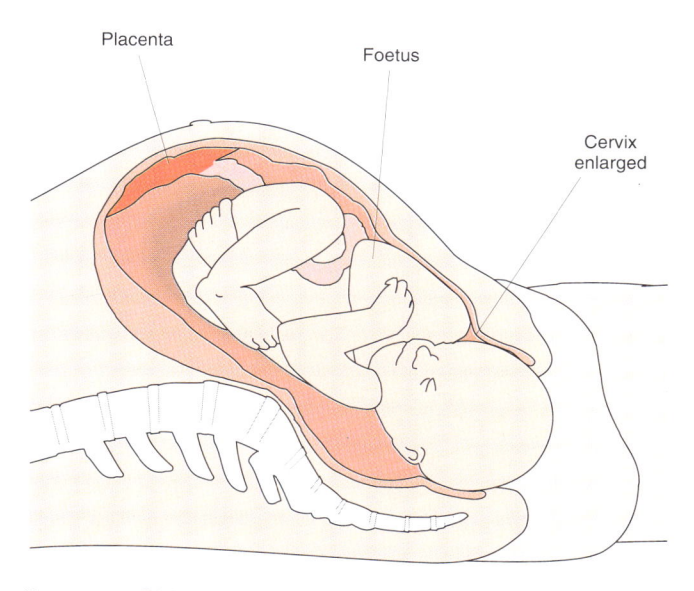

fig. 35.10 Childbirth

The umbilical cord is cut and the baby takes its first breath (and cries!). About 15 minutes after the baby is born, the continuing contractions of the womb cause the placenta and remaining umbilical cord to pass out of the mother. This material is called the **afterbirth**.

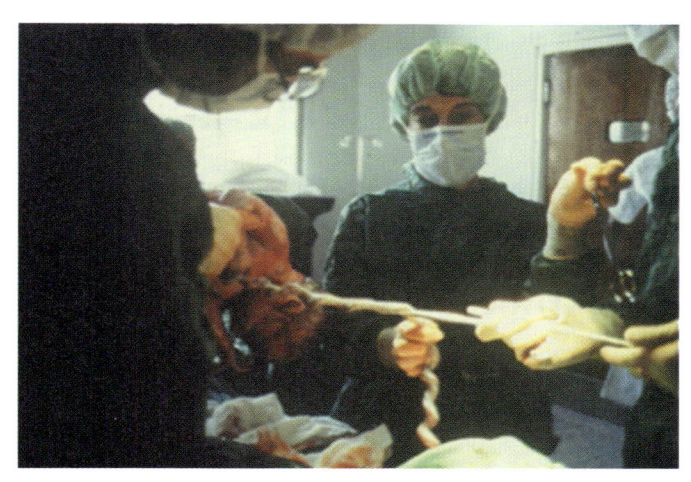

fig. 35.11 A new-born baby as the umbilical cord is cut

Contraception (family planning)

Contraception means that fertilisation is prevented (i.e. sperm are prevented from reaching the egg or no egg is released). Couples use contraception to prevent them having too many children or to prevent children being born too soon after each other.

Natural methods of contraception are those that do not involve the use of man-made materials. These methods centre around the couple avoiding intercourse around the time of ovulation. The time of ovulation can be predicted in one of three ways.

1. The woman records her temperature every day. Her temperature rises around the time of ovulation.
2. The woman checks for the presence of a special mucous at the cervix. This mucous indicates ovulation.
3. The woman predicts when she will ovulate, based on her previous cycles. This is called the rhythm method.

Artificial contraception involves using man-made materials. Examples of these methods include:

The pill method. The pill is a hormone tablet that a woman takes to prevent an egg being formed and released. As a result intercourse can take place without pregnancy occurring. The pill may have side effects such as an increased risk of cancer and blood clots.

Barrier methods. Various barriers are used to prevent the sperm and egg from fusing. The most common of these is the condom. This is a thin rubber sheath that is placed over the penis just before intercourse. It acts as a barrier to the sperm entering the vagina.

Sterilisation. Sterilisation means the Fallopian tubes of the female or the sperm duct of the male are cut and tied. These operations cannot be reversed easily and sterilisation is usually permanent.

No method of contraception is fully effective. Also, some religions and cultures do not allow the use of some forms of contraception.

INHERITANCE

Inheritable and non-inheritable characteristics

A normal baby has two arms, two legs, saliva in the mouth and many other features (also called characteristics or traits) similar to its parents. These traits are said to be inheritable (i.e. to be capable of being passed on from the parents to the offspring at birth). Inheritance or genetics is the study of how traits such as these are inherited.

Other inheritable characteristics include eye colour, hair colour and the shape of the mouth, face and body.

Some characteristics are not inherited at birth. These include such characteristics as the ability to speak a language, add and subtract, ride a bicycle, knit or use a computer. These characteristics are acquired (or learned) during life.

Chromosomes

The nucleus of most cells contains a number of long, thin strands called chromosomes. These are made of a material called DNA. Each chromosome has many regions called genes. These genes are arranged along the chromosomes like stations along a railway track.

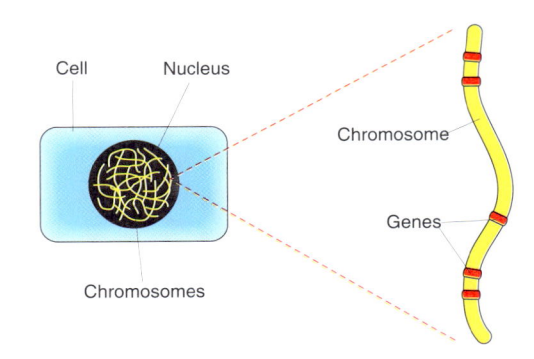

fig. 35.12 Chromosomes and genes

Each gene controls an inheritable characteristic. For example, there are genes to control eye colour, skin colour, height and production of acid in the stomach. Every inheritable characteristic is controlled by two genes in each cell. One gene (called the dominant) is stronger, while the other gene (the recessive) is weaker.

Recall that gametes are sex cells (i.e. sperm and eggs). Only one gene from each pair will be present in each gamete.

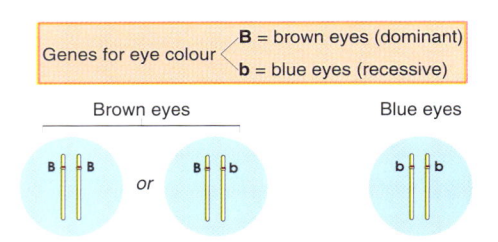

fig. 35.13 Genes for eye colour

For example, eye colour in humans is controlled by a pair of genes. The dominant gene (B) gives brown eyes, the recessive gene (b) gives blue eyes. This means that a brown-eyed person could be BB or Bb, because the dominant gene is present. A blue eyed person must be bb.

A person with the genes BB will produce gametes that all contain the B gene.

A person with the genes Bb will produce gametes with either B or b.

A person with the genes bb will produce gametes that all contain the gene b.

The following crosses show how eye colour may be inherited.

Show why a brown-eyed parent with the genes BB and a blue-eyed parent will always have brown-eyed children.

Cross 1

Parents: Brown eyes (BB) × Blue eyes (bb)
Gametes: B and b
Offspring (children): Bb — Brown eyes

Show how a brown-eyed father and a blue-eyed mother could have a blue-eyed child.

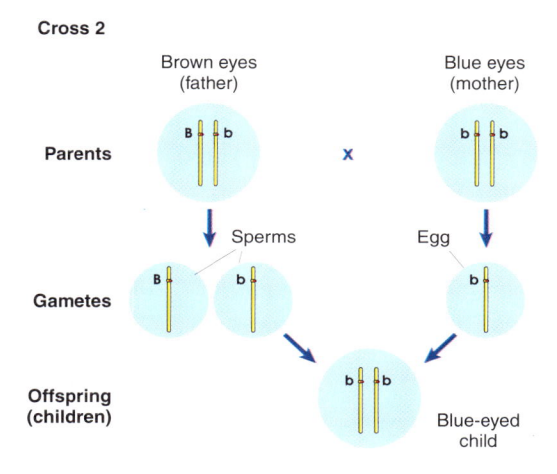

Cross 2

Parents: Brown eyes (father) (Bb) × Blue eyes (mother) (bb)
Gametes: Sperms B and b; Egg b
Offspring (children): bb — Blue-eyed child

Show how this couple could have a brown-eyed child.

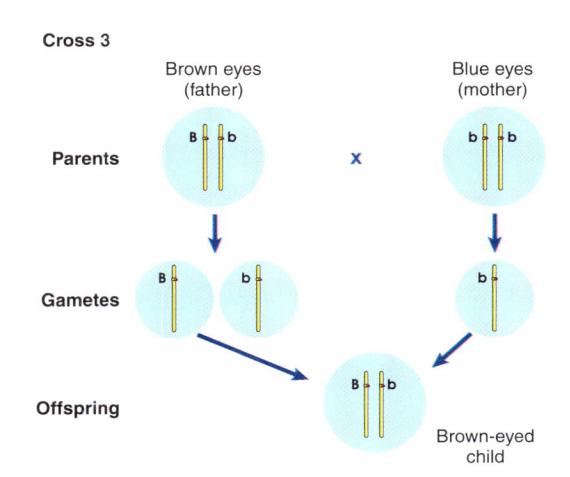

Cross 3

Parents: Brown eyes (father) (Bb) × Blue eyes (mother) (bb)
Gametes: B and b; b
Offspring: Bb — Brown-eyed child

fig. 35.14

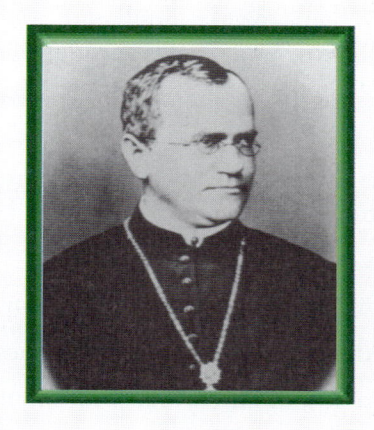

fig. 35.15 Gregor Mendel (1822–1884)

Gregor Mendel was an Austrian monk who discovered the basic laws of inheritance. He did most of his research with pea plants and published his results in 1856. Strangely his work was ignored until the early 1900s. He is now known as the 'father of genetics'.

SUMMARY

- Sexual reproduction means the union of a sperm and an egg.
- Gametes are sex cells – sperm in the male and eggs (ova) in the female.
- The menstrual cycle takes place in a woman's body every 28 days when she is not pregnant:
  - the lining of the womb builds up (days 6 to 13)
  - an egg is released from the ovary (ovulation on day 14)
  - the womb lining stays in place (days 15 to 28)
  - the lining of the womb is released from the body (days 1 to 5 of the next cycle)
- This cycle begins at puberty and continues to the menopause.
- Sexual intercourse is the placing of sperm from the penis into the vagina.
- Fertilisation is the joining of a sperm with an egg in the Fallopian tube. It results in pregnancy.
- Implantation is the attachment of the embryo to the lining of the womb.
- The developing embryo is surrounded by amniotic fluid and a sac called the amnion. *(continued)*

35 • Human Reproduction and Inheritance

> - The baby gets oxygen and food and gets rid of carbon dioxide and wastes through the placenta.
> - After 9 months in the womb, the baby is born, through the vagina.
> - Contraception means the prevention of fertilisation (or pregnancy).
> - Genetics is the study of inheritance.
> - Some traits are inherited, some are non-inheritable.
> - Inherited traits are controlled by genes.
> - Genes are found on chromosomes that are located in the nucleus of the cell.
> - Each trait is controlled by two genes, one inherited from the father and the other from the mother.

QUESTIONS

Q. 35.1
Explain what is meant by:
(a) reproduction
(b) gamete
(c) puberty
(d) zygote
(e) ovum

Q. 35.2
Draw large labelled diagrams of the
(a) female and
(b) male reproductive systems
Below each diagram list the functions of each part labelled.

Q. 35.3
Answer the following with regard to the menstrual cycle.
(a) At what age does it normally begin and finish?
(b) How many days does it usually last?
(c) What is menstruation?
(d) What is ovulation?
(e) On what days do menstruation and ovulation usually occur?

Q. 35.4
Write out the following paragraphs and fill in the blanks.
(a) Eggs are produced in the ____. The release of an egg is called ____. The placing of sperm in the vagina is called ____. The sperm swim up through the ____ and meet the egg in the ____. The joining of sperm and egg is called ____ and the first cell formed is called the ____.
(b) Implantation is the attachment of the ____ to the lining of the ____. The embryo is surrounded by a liquid called ____ ____, which is held in place by a sac called the ____. The tube emerging from the navel of the embryo is the ____ ____. It connects the embryo to the ____.
(c) The baby spends about ____ months developing in the ____. Birth is caused by contractions of the ____, which force the baby out ____ first. The release of fluids just before birth is called the ____ of the ____. Once the baby is born its ____ ____ is cut.

Q. 35.5
Suggest a reason for the following:
(a) A woman normally becomes pregnant around the middle of her menstrual cycle.
(b) If a mother smokes her baby may be smaller.
(c) A pregnant woman does not have periods.
(d) The baby in the womb gets oxygen even though it is surrounded by liquid.
(e) Sperm have tails.
(f) Very young children cannot have children.
(g) Pregnancy cannot take place unless fertilisation happens.

Q. 35.6
Draw a diagram of the female reproductive system and label on it the places where the following occur:
(a) ovulation
(b) fertilisation
(c) implantation
(d) insemination
(e) placenta attachment
(f) birth

Q. 35.7
(a) What is contraception?
(b) What is the difference between natural and artificial methods of contraception?
(c) Explain why sterilisation is a permanent method of contraception.

Q. 35.8
Name the changes in the (i) male and (ii) female body at puberty. State the cause of puberty.

Q. 35.9

(a) Name two substances that pass from the foetus to the mother.
(b) Name two useful substances that pass from the mother to the foetus. Name two harmful substances that could also be passed to the foetus.
(c) Name the structure through which these materials pass.

Q. 35.10

(a) What is genetics?
(b) Who was the 'father of genetics'?

Q. 35.11

(a) What is the difference between an inheritable and a non-inheritable trait?
(b) Give three examples of each type of trait.
(c) Say whether the following are inheritable or non-inheritable traits: speaking French, colour of hair, shape of face, writing, reading, number of ears, skating on roller blades, production of hormones.

Q. 35.12

Write out and complete the following:

(a) Chromosomes are found in the ____ of the cell. They are made of a chemical called ____. Each chromosome contains many ____ each of which controls an ____ characteristic.
(b) Cells have ____ genes for each trait. The stronger gene is called the ____ and the weaker is the ____. Only one of each gene will be carried in each ____.
(c) In rats, the gene B is responsible for black coat and the gene for white coat is b. A black rat can have the genes ____ or ____. A white rat must have the genes ____. The gametes of a black rat might have the gene ____ or ____, while ____ rats can only have gametes with the gene ____.

Q. 35.13

In pea plants, the gene for tall plant is T and the gene for small plant is t. Tallness is dominant over smallness.

(a) State the dominant and recessive genes.
(b) Show by diagrams why a tall plant (TT) and a small plant (tt) will always produce tall plants.
(c) Show by diagrams how a tall plant and a small plant could produce small plants.

36

PHOTOSYNTHESIS AND TRANSPORT IN PLANTS

The importance and uses of plants are described in Chapter 29. This chapter looks at plants in more detail – the parts of plants, how they get their food, and how substances are transported in them. One of the most important things about plants is that they make their own food. Often this food is used by humans, when they eat the various edible parts of plants.

PLANT STRUCTURE

Many different species of plant exist, but they have many features in common. A typical flowering plant consists of roots, stem, leaves and flowers.

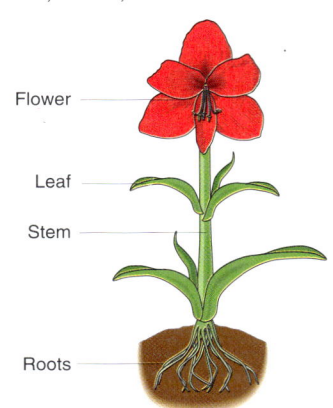

fig. 36.1 A typical flowering plant

PHOTOSYNTHESIS

Plants are referred to as **producers** because they make their own food. The process by which they do this is called **photosynthesis** and it takes place in the leaves and other green parts of the plant.

Plants manufacture their food – a simple sugar called glucose – from carbon dioxide (which they take from the air) and water (which they obtain from the soil). The energy needed for the chemical reaction to occur is provided by sunlight, which is trapped in the leaves of the plant by a green compound called **chlorophyll**. As a result of the reaction, oxygen is produced as a by-product, and is released into the air. This is the source of the oxygen that humans and other living organisms must have to live.

The equation for this photosynthesis reaction (both in words and chemical symbols) is:

$$\text{carbon dioxide} + \text{water} \xrightarrow[\text{chlorophyll}]{\text{light}} \text{glucose} + \text{oxygen}$$

$$6CO_2 + 6H_2O \xrightarrow[\text{chlorophyll}]{\text{light}} C_6H_{12}O_6 + 6O_2$$

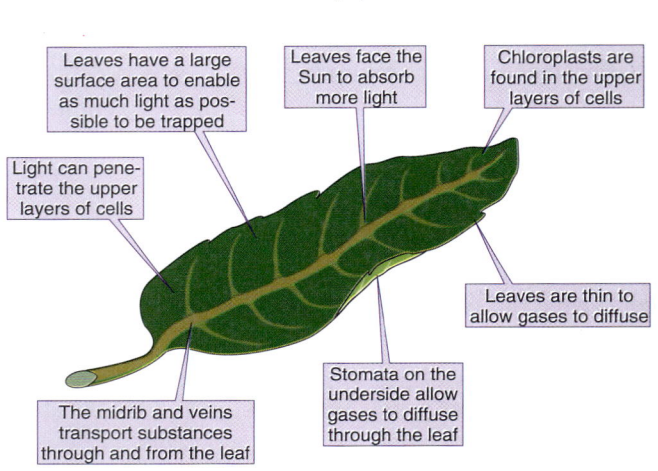

fig. 36.2 The structure of a leaf

Plant part	Functions
Roots	anchor the plant in the ground, absorb water and nutrients from the soil, act as food stores in some plants (e.g. carrots, parsnips, turnips).
Leaves	release water from the plant (this helps to cool the plant in hot weather), take in carbon dioxide for the plant, and give out the oxygen formed, make food by photosynthesis, act as food stores in some plants (e.g. lettuce, spinach, cabbage).
Stem	supports the parts of the plant above the ground, transports water and minerals from the roots to the leaves, transports food from the leaves to other parts of the plant, act as food stores in some plants (e.g. celery, rhubarb, leeks).
Flowers	produce seeds, so that the plant can reproduce.

Leaves are specially adapted to allow photosynthesis to take place. They have tiny holes (called **stomata**) on their undersides, through which the carbon dioxide passes in and the oxygen passes out. The holes also allow the escape of any excess water in the leaf. Also, leaves are very thin and so the carbon dioxide can easily reach the cells.

GLUCOSE USE BY PLANTS

The glucose that plants produce is used in many ways, for example:

- it provides energy for parts of the plant (such as the roots) that do not photosynthesise
- it is used to make the cellulose wall of the plant cells
- it is one of the compounds needed in the process by which plants manufacture protein
- it is converted to starch, which is stored in the roots, stem and leaves of the plant, and changed back into glucose when needed (see below)

STARCH

Starch is a compound consisting of long chains of glucose molecules combined together. When a plant photosynthesises, some of the glucose that is produced is converted to starch. Some of this starch is then stored in the plant leaves – to be converted back to glucose when it is needed. Therefore, if a plant has been photosynthesising, there will be starch present in its leaves.

EXPERIMENTS ON PHOTOSYNTHESIS

Photosynthesis, as explained above, consumes carbon dioxide and water, and generates glucose and oxygen. The following experiments describe how plants can be tested to show what is used during photosynthesis, and what is produced in the reaction. The plants for experiments 36.2 to 36.4 must be placed in darkness for 48 hours before use. This is to ensure that any starch made by the plant will have been used up before you carry out the experiment. A plant treated in this way is called a **destarched** plant.

Experiment 36.1
To test a leaf for starch

fig. 36.3

1. Set up a boiling water bath as shown.
2. Drop a leaf into the boiling water and leave it there for about half a minute. This kills the leaf and also softens it, so that iodine solution can enter the cells more easily.
3. Using forceps, remove the leaf from the boiling water. Turn off the bunsen burner.
4. Place the leaf in a test tube which is about half full of alcohol. (Chlorophyll is insoluble in water but soluble in alcohol.)
5. Stand the test tube in the beaker of hot water.
6. After about ten minutes, the alcohol will appear green in colour, as the chlorophyll has dissolved into the alcohol.
7. Remove the leaf from the alcohol and dip it into the warm water to make it soft again. Do not pour the alcohol down the sink.
8. Spread the leaf on a clean white tile, and cover it with iodine solution.

Did you notice that iodine solution turns blue-black? This means that starch is present and so the leaf has been photosynthesising. (Remember: iodine solution, which is brown, turns blue-black in the presence of starch.)

Experiment 36.2
To show that carbon dioxide is necessary for photosynthesis

The apparatus consists of two destarched plants, each covered by a plastic bag. Inside the bag surrounding plant A is a dish of soda-lime. This substance absorbs carbon dioxide from the air, and so plant A is lacking carbon dioxide. Plant B is exposed to normal atmospheric air.

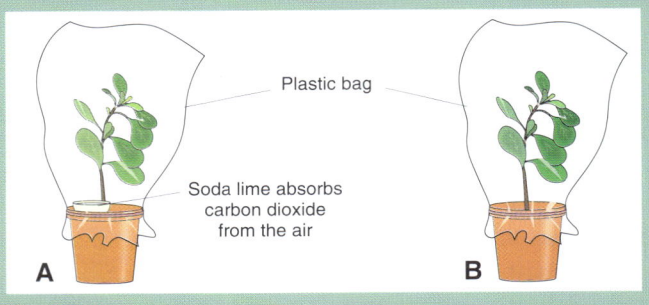

fig. 36.4

1. Destarch two similar plants by leaving them in the dark for 48 hours.
2. Arrange the plants as shown in Figure 36.4; make sure they are well watered.
3. Leave the plants in strong light for about six hours.
4. Remove the plastic bags and pick a leaf from each of the plants.
5. Test each leaf for starch (as described in Experiment 36.1).
6. Record your results, and suggest the reason for them.

Result: The iodine solution applied to the leaf from plant B turns blue-black. This shows that starch is present, and therefore plant B must have been photosynthesising. Iodine solution when applied to the leaf from plant A shows no change. Therefore starch is absent and so photosynthesis was not taking place – because plant A had no supply of carbon dioxide.

Conclusion: Plants need carbon dioxide for photosynthesis.

Experiment 36.3
To show that light is necessary for photosynthesis

1. Destarch a plant by leaving it in the dark for 48 hours.
2. Partly cover one of the plant leaves with paper to prevent light reaching it.
3. Draw a sketch of the leaf showing the area covered.
4. Place the plant in strong light for about 6 hours.
5. Remove the partially covered leaf and carry out a starch test (Experiment 36.1) in two places (i) on a part of which received light and (ii) on a part which had been covered and did not receive light.
6. Record the result.

fig. 36.5

Result: The iodine does not change colour on the part of the leaf which had been covered. This means that no starch has been formed – which means that photosynthesis has not occurred. The exposed part of the leaf turns blue-black, which means means that photosynthesis has ocurred.

Conclusion: Plants need light for photosynthesis.

Experiment 36.4
To show that chlorophyll is necessary for photosynthesis

fig. 36.6

1. Destarch a plant with variegated leaves. (Variegated leaves are ones which have only patches or stripes of green, the rest of the leaf being cream in colour.)
2. Draw a sketch of the leaf to show which areas are green.
3. Place the plant in strong light for about 6 hours.
4. Remove a leaf from the plant and carry out a starch test.

Result: Only the areas of the leaf which were green (i.e. containing chlorophyll) turn the starch blue-black; the cream areas do not.

Conclusion: Chlorophyll is necessary for photosynthesis.

Experiment 36.5
To show that oxygen is given off during photosynthesis

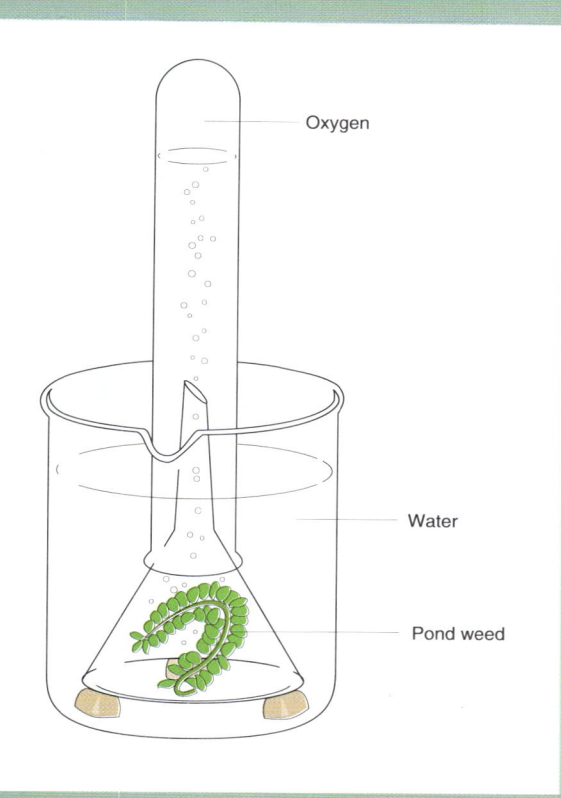

fig. 36.7

1. Set up the apparatus as shown in Figure 36.7.
2. Leave the apparatus in strong light for one week – by which time a gas should have formed in the top of the test-tube.
3. Test this gas with a glowing splint.

Result:
The glowing splint relights when placed in the gas; this means that oxygen is present.

Conclusion:
Plants produce oxygen gas during photosynthesis.

MINERAL NUTRITION IN PLANTS

When plants make food by photosynthesis, they consume carbon dioxide and water, but they also need certain minerals for the process – which must be available to them in the soil. To allow plants to grow fast and as strong as possible, farmers and gardeners often provide these minerals as fertilisers. The minerals may be added as artificial (man-made) fertilisers, or as natural fertilisers such as manure from cattle or pigs. The most important minerals needed by plants are **nitrogen**, **phosphorus**, and **potassium**. If plants lack any of these minerals they do not grow properly. Plants use the nitrogen to make protein and leaves, the phosphorus to make cell membranes and form strong roots, and the potassium to help form flowers and fruit.

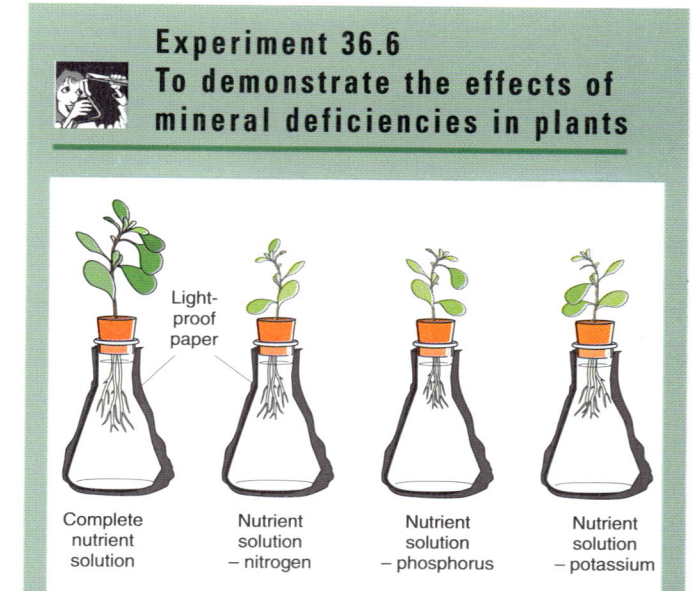

Experiment 36.6
To demonstrate the effects of mineral deficiencies in plants

fig. 36.8

In this experiment, four seedlings are placed in four different flasks, each flask containing a different nutrient solution. The solution in flask A is a mixture of the three required nutrients (nitrogen, phosphorus, potassium), the solution in B lacks nitrogen, C lacks phosphorus and flask D is lacking potassium.

1. Set up the apparatus as shown in Figure 36.8.
2. Fill the flasks with the different solutions, as described above.
3. Place light-proof paper around each flask to prevent algae growing.
4. Leave the seedlings for about two weeks, making sure they all receive equal amounts of light.
5. After the two weeks, compare the growth of the seedlings under the headings of:
   (i) length, (ii) number of leaves and
   (iii) colour of leaves.

Results and conclusion: The plant growing in the complete nutrient solution does best. Lack of nitrogen causes the plant to produce yellow leaves and with a weak stem. Lack of potassium produces poor flower and fruit growth, while lack of phosphorus causes poorly developed roots.

36 • Photosynthesis and Transport in Plants

QUESTIONS

Q. 36.1

Copy the following paragraph and complete the blanks.

Photosynthesis is the way in which plants make __. Plants need __ , __, __, and chlorophyll in order to carry out photosynthesis. During the process, __ and __ are produced. Photosynthesis in plants only takes place when __ is present but __ occurs all the time.

Q. 36.2

Copy the following paragraph and complete the blanks.

The main parts of the plant are the __, stem and __. Roots are needed to __ the plant in the ground and to absorb __ and __ from the soil. Leaves produce food, release __ from the __ on their surfaces and allow for the exchange of the __ carbon dioxide and oxygen.

Q. 36.3

Copy the following paragraph and complete the blanks.

When a leaf is to be tested for starch, it is first placed in boiling water to __ it. Next the leaf is placed in __ which dissolves the __. The leaf is again placed in hot water to __ it and finally it is placed on a white tile and covered with __ __. This solution turns from yellow-brown to __ - __ if starch is present.

Q. 36.4

Copy the following paragraph and complete the blanks.

In many photosynthesis experiments a __ plant is used, this means that the plant is left in darkness for about __ hours before the experiment. To show chlorophyll is necessary for photosynthesis a __ leaf is used. The areas which were green change to __-__ with the iodine solution, while the cream areas of the leaf do not change. To show that carbon dioxide is necessary for photosynthesis, two plants are used; one plant is enclosed with the chemical __ __ which removes __ __ from the air, while the other is enclosed with normal air. Without __ __ the plant cannot photosynthesise.

Q. 36.5

(a) What is photosynthesis?
(b) Name the green chemical necessary for photosynthesis.
(c) Name the gas produced in photosynthesis.
(d) Give the word equation for photosynthesis.

Q. 36.6

(a) What chemical is used to test for starch?
(b) When do plants carry out photosynthesis?
(c) When do plants carry out respiration?
(d) Which parts of plants do not photosynthesise?

Q. 36.7

(a) Name the three main nutrients needed by plants.
(b) Give the function of each of these nutrients.
(c) Describe an experiment to investigate how plants grow when these nutrients are not available.

Q. 36.8

(a) Write an account of an experiment to show that carbon dioxide is necessary for photosynthesis.
(b) Why is photosynthesis important to (i) plants, (ii) humans, (iii) other animals?

Q. 36.9

(a) Give the chemical equation for photosynthesis.
(b) State the conditions necessary for photosynthesis to occur.
(c) Describe a laboratory experiment to demonstrate one of the conditions necessary for photosynthesis.
(d) Figure 36.9 shows an experiment that was carried out in the laboratory. What is the purpose of this experiment?

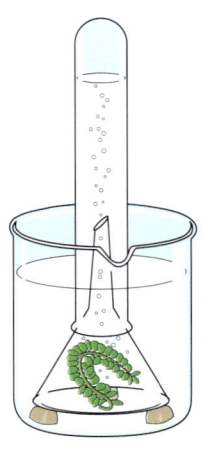

fig. 36.9

(e) Describe with the aid of a labelled diagram, how you would show in the laboratory that nitrogen is necessary for healthy plant growth. Name one other substance also necessary for healthy growth.

TRANSPORT IN PLANTS

Plant cells, like all other cells, must be supplied with food, and must have their waste products removed. This means that plants, like animals, must also have a transport system. In humans, the circulation system provides for the flow of substances around the body.

The transport system in plants is simpler; there is a flow of water and minerals from the roots up to the leaves, and there is a flow of the food made in the leaves to all other parts of the plant. In plants there are two types of transport vessel; **xylem** and **phloem**. Xylem carries water and minerals from the roots to the leaves, while phloem carries the food made in the leaves to other parts of the plant.

Absorption of water

The water that is needed by the plant is absorbed by the roots from the soil. The water travels up the plant stem through the xylem to the leaves, to be used in photosynthesis. A little water is also lost by evaporation from the surface of the leaves. Water therefore has to be replaced, and so it is continually travelling up the stem of the plant. The flow of water from the roots to the leaves is called the **transpiration stream**.

Experiment 36.7
To show the absorption of water by roots

The apparatus consists of two test tubes, each about half full of water, and with a seedling placed in one of them. Covering the water in each test tube is a thin layer of oil – to prevent the water from evaporating.

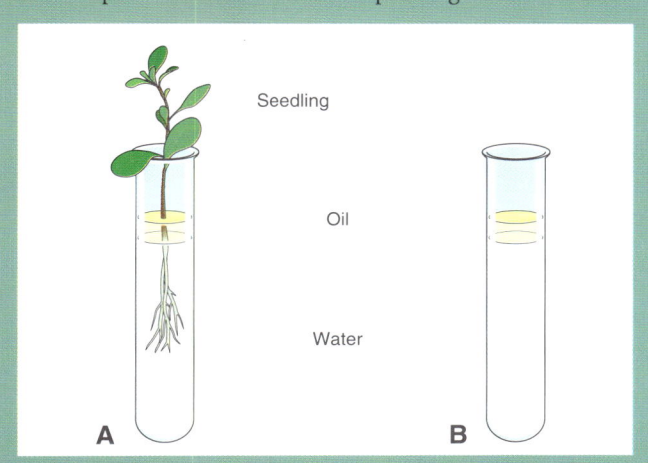

fig. 36.10

1. Set up the apparatus as shown in Figure 36.10.
2. Mark the levels of water in both test tubes.
3. Leave the tubes for one week.
4. After that time, mark the water levels in each tube again.

Result: The water level in test tube A has dropped but in B it has remained where it was.

Conclusion: The plant has absorbed the water.

Experiment 36.8
To show the movement of water in a plant

fig. 36.11

1. Set up the apparatus as shown in Figure 36.11.
2. Leave it where it will be undisturbed for a few days.
3. Remove the celery from the water and rinse the ink from the roots.
4. Observe the leaves and the stem of the plant.
5. Cut the stem and the root and examine them using a hand lens.

Result: The ink has travelled from the roots to the stem and leaves.

Conclusion: This shows that water moves upwards through the plant.

TRANSPIRATION

The loss of water vapour from the surface of a plant is known as **transpiration**. The loss of water by transpiration takes place through tiny pores called **stomata** in the leaves of the plant. As a result of transpiration:

(i) water is carried to the leaves for photosynthesis
(ii) minerals are carried up from the roots to the rest of the plant and
(iii) the plant is cooled

Factors affecting transpiration

The rate of transpiration is affected by a number of factors. These factors include sunlight, humidity, air movements, and amount of water in the soil. For example, if there is a high level of sunlight, the transpiration rate will be higher but if there is a high level of humidity the transpiration rate will be lower. The transpiration rate will be highest on a day where there is sun, wind and low humidity, and it will be lowest on a dull, calm day with high humidity.

Experiment 36.9
To show transpiration in a plant

1. Set up the apparatus as shown in Figure 36.12.
2. Water the plant well and then cover it with a plastic bag.
3. Leave the plant in a warm place for a few hours.
4. Observe that a liquid has condensed on the inside of the plastic bag.
5. Test the liquid using cobalt chloride paper.

Result: The cobalt chloride paper turns from blue to pink showing that the liquid is water.

fig. 36.12

- **Transpiration** is the loss of water from the surface of a plant. Water enters a plant through the roots and moves towards the leaves in a **transpiration stream**. The factors that affect transpiration are sunlight, humidity, air movements, and the amount of water in the soil.
- Water is transported in **xylem** and food is transported in **phloem**.

QUESTIONS

Q. 36.10
(a) What is meant by transpiration?
(b) Describe an experiment to demonstrate transpiration.
(c) State two factors which affect the rate of transpiration of a plant.

Q. 36.11
Figure 36.13 shows a rooted cutting of busy lizzie (impatiens), which has been placed in red ink for an hour. The red colour can be seen in the stem and leaves.

fig. 36.13

(a) Explain how the red ink is carried to the leaves.
(b) What process, taking place in the leaves, causes this to happen?
(c) Name the type of cell which is involved in this process.
(d) In what part of the plant is food made?
(e) Where in the plant is food usually stored?
(f) Name the types of cell involved in transporting food in plants.

Q. 36.12
(a) Describe an experiment to show that water is taken up by the roots of a plant.
(b) Name the type of plant tissue which carries water.

Q. 36.13
(a) List the factors that affect the rate of transpiration.
(b) Where can stomata be found?

SUMMARY

- Plants make their own food by a process called **photosynthesis**. In this process, carbon dioxide and water react in the presence of light and chlorophyll to produce glucose and oxygen:

$$\text{carbon dioxide} + \text{water} \xrightarrow[\text{chlorophyll}]{\text{light}} \text{glucose to oxygen}$$

$$6CO_2 + 6H_2O \xrightarrow[\text{chlorophyll}]{\text{light}} C_6H_{12}O_6 + 6O_2$$

- The **glucose** produced in photosynthesis is used to provide the energy for the plant, including those parts of it which do not photosynthesise. Glucose is used to form starch, cellulose and protein.
- For healthy growth, plants need certain nutrients or minerals, which they absorb from the soil. The main minerals required are **nitrogen**, **phosphorus** and **potassium**. A lack of any one of these will retard the growth of the plant.

37
PLANT RESPONSES

All living organisms are sensitive to changes in their environments. Animals respond quickly to changes but plants respond much more slowly. In humans, the sense organs act as receptors and allow us to respond to our surroundings. Something which triggers a receptor is known as a **stimulus** (plural **stimuli**). Plants also react in response to stimuli. The way in which a plant grows in response to a stimulus is called a **tropism**. Plants respond to light, water and gravity. A tropism is the growth of a plant in response to a stimulus.

PHOTOTROPISM

Phototropism is the growth response of a plant to light. The leaves of a plant will tend to turn to face the strongest source of light available, to allow them to get as much light as possible for photosynthesis. The stem will bend towards light. The roots of a plant, however, always grow away from light.

> **Shoots are called positively phototropic as they grow towards light.**

> **Roots are called negatively phototropic as they grow away from light.**

fig. 37.2 Plants growing towards the light

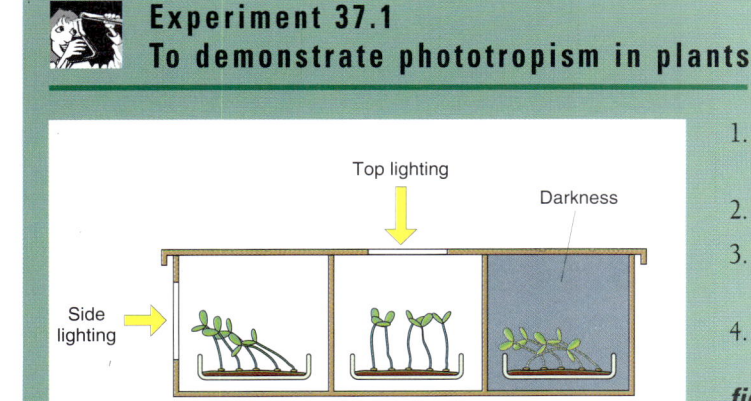

Experiment 37.1
To demonstrate phototropism in plants

1. Divide a cardboard box, such as a shoe box, into three sections, as shown in Figure 37.1.
2. Label three petri dishes A, B and C.
3. Place wet cotton wool in each of the three petri dishes.
4. Sprinkle cress seeds on the cotton wool.

fig. 37.1 Plant seedlings grow toward a light source; this is called phototropism

5. Place one dish in each section of the box.
6. Leave the box near a window for one week. If necessary, add some water to the cotton wool to keep it wet.

Results:
(i) The seedlings in dish A are exposed to light from one side and they grow towards that light.
(ii) The seedlings in B grow straight up as the light is coming from the top.
(iii) The seedlings in C have very stunted and straggly growth as they received no light.

Conclusion:
Plants grow towards a light source.

GEOTROPISM

The growth response of a plant to gravity is known as **geotropism**. Roots grow downwards in response to gravity, while shoots grow upwards away from gravity. When a seed is planted in the ground and starts to germinate, it sends its roots downwards in order to absorb water and minerals, and the shoot goes upwards so that leaves can form and photosynthesis will take place.

fig. 37.3 Roots grow downwards in response to gravity; this is called geotropism

Roots are called positively geotropic as they grow downwards in response to gravity.

Shoots are called negatively geotropic as they grow upwards against the force of gravity.

Experiment 37.2
To demonstrate geotropism in plants

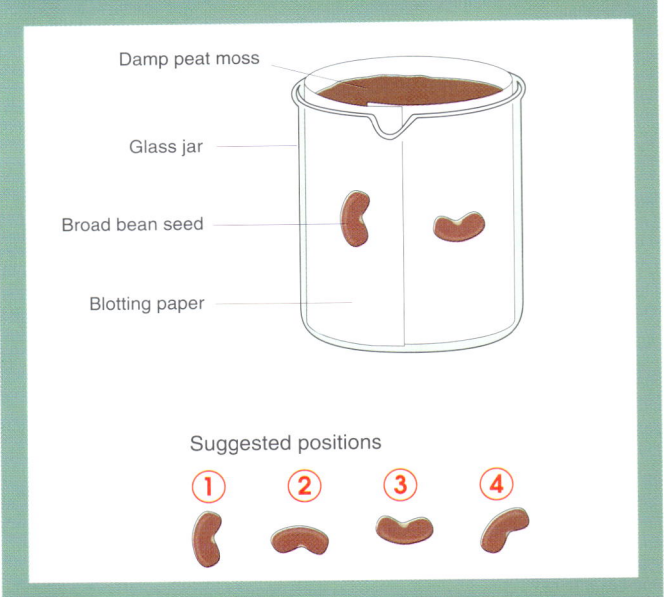

fig. 37.4

1. Line a large glass jar with blotting paper.
2. Fill the jar with peat moss and water it well.
3. Place three broad bean seeds between the glass and the paper around the jar, using a different position for each one.
4. Allow them to germinate in the dark for one week. Check the peat moss regularly and water it if necessary.

Result:
In each case the roots grow downwards, and the shoots go upwards even though the seeds were placed in different positions.

Conclusion:
Roots grow downwards in response to the force of gravity and shoots grow upwards away from the force of gravity.

SUMMARY

- Plants respond slowly to changes in their surroundings. The growth response of a plant is called a **tropism**. Plants grow in response to light, gravity, and water.
- The growth response of a plant to light is called **phototropism**. Shoots grow towards light and roots grow away from light.
- The growth response of a plant to gravity is called **geotropism**.

QUESTIONS

Q. 37.1

Copy out the following paragraph and complete the gaps.

Plants respond __ to changes in their environment. Stimuli such as __, __ and __ cause growth responses. The growth response of a plant to a stimulus is called a __. The growth response of a plant to light is called __ and the response to gravity is known as __. Shoots grow __ light but roots grow __ from light. When a seed germinates, the __ grow downwards in response to __, while the shoots grow __.

Q. 37.2

(a) Describe an experiment to demonstrate phototropism.
(b) Explain why is it necessary to occasionally turn house plants placed on a window sill.

Q. 37.3

Describe an experiment to demonstrate geotropism.

Q. 37.4

As living organisms both plants and animals are sensitive to changes in their environments. List the ways in which sensitivity in plants and animals differs.

PLANT REPRODUCTION

Sexual and asexual reproduction

Sexual reproduction involves the fusion of two sex cells or gametes. This fusion is called **fertilisation**. As a result, the offspring have characteristics of both the male and female parents. Most animals only reproduce sexually. Plants reproduce sexually and asexually.

Asexual reproduction involves only one parent. There are no gametes and therefore fertilisation does not occur. The offspring are identical to the parents. Examples of asexual reproduction are when the spores of a mushroom blow away and grow to produce a new mushroom or when daffodils or tulips are grown from bulbs.

Sexual reproduction in plants

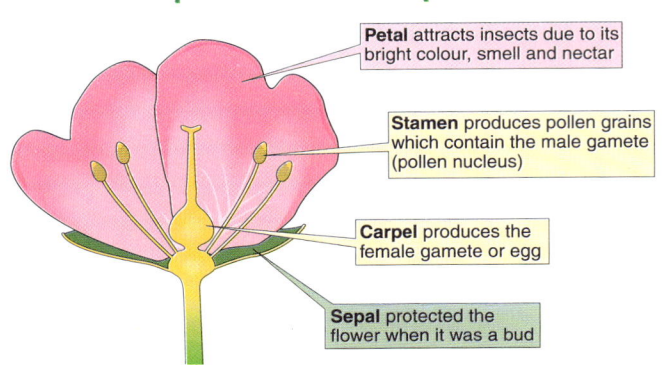

fig. 38.1 Structure of a flower

- **Petal** attracts insects due to its bright colour, smell and nectar
- **Stamen** produces pollen grains which contain the male gamete (pollen nucleus)
- **Carpel** produces the female gamete or egg
- **Sepal** protected the flower when it was a bud

The function of the flower is reproduction. This happens when the nucleus of the pollen grain joins with the egg nucleus to produce a seed. Pollen contains the male sex cell.

Structure of stamen and carpel

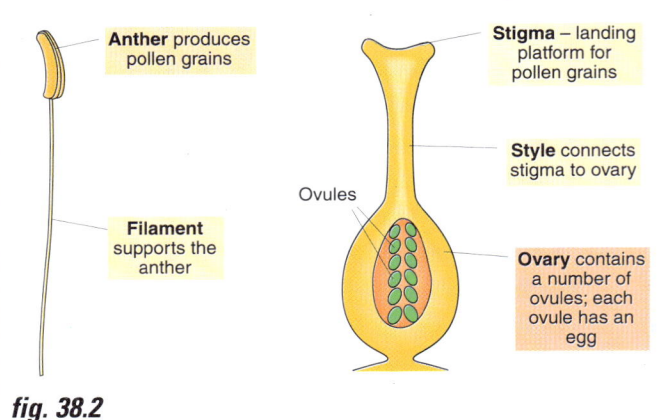

- **Anther** produces pollen grains
- **Filament** supports the anther
- **Stigma** – landing platform for pollen grains
- **Style** connects stigma to ovary
- **Ovary** contains a number of ovules; each ovule has an egg
- Ovules

fig. 38.2

Pollination is the transfer of pollen from the anther to the stigma. Plants use wind or insects (such as bees, wasps and butterflies) to carry out pollination.

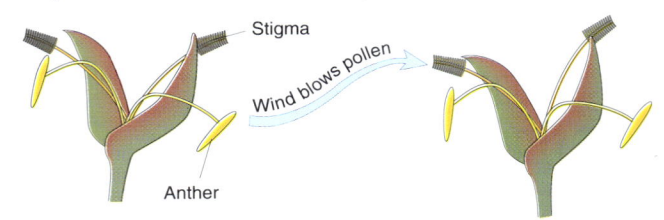

fig. 38.3 Wind pollination

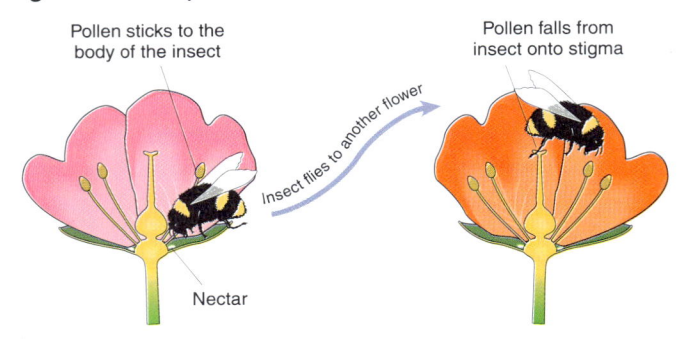

fig. 38.4 Insect pollination

The differences between wind and insect pollinated flowers are outlined in the table on the next page.

Once the pollen has landed on the stigma, it produces a pollen tube. This grows down through the style to the ovary. The nucleus of the pollen (the male gamete) moves down through the tube.

Fertilisation is when the pollen nucleus joins with the egg nucleus (female gamete) in the ovule. The fertilised ovule now becomes the seed. The surrounding ovary swells with food to become the fruit. The petals and sepals usually die and fall away from the fruit.

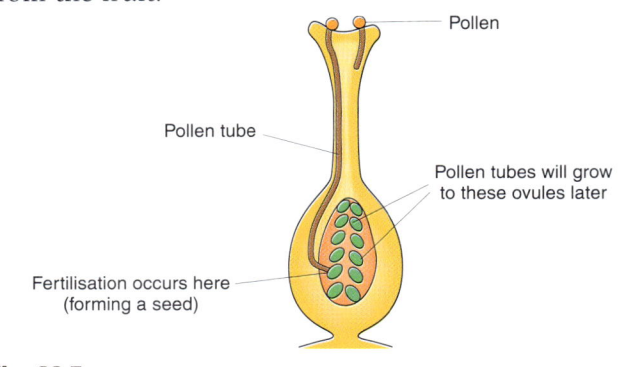

- Pollen
- Pollen tube
- Pollen tubes will grow to these ovules later
- Fertilisation occurs here (forming a seed)

fig. 38.5

Wind pollinated flowers	Insect pollinated flowers
1 Petals are small and green coloured	Petals are large and brightly coloured
2 Have no scent or nectar	Have scent and nectar (sugar water)
3 Large anthers, located outside the petals	Small anthers located inside the petals
4 Large feathery stigmas, outside petals	Small stigmas, inside petals
Examples are grasses and oak trees	Examples are buttercups, roses and primroses

Seed dispersal is the carrying of the seed (which is contained inside the fruit) as far as possible from the parent plant. This means that the young seedling will not have to compete with the parent for space, light, water and minerals.

The four methods that plants use for dispersal are wind, animal, self and water.

Wind dispersal

Wind-dispersed seeds are often small and light so they are easily carried away (e.g. orchids).

Larger seeds need help if they are to be dispersed. Dandelion and thistle seeds have hairy tufts which act like parachutes. Sycamore and ash have winged seeds which allow them to spiral to the ground like helicopters.

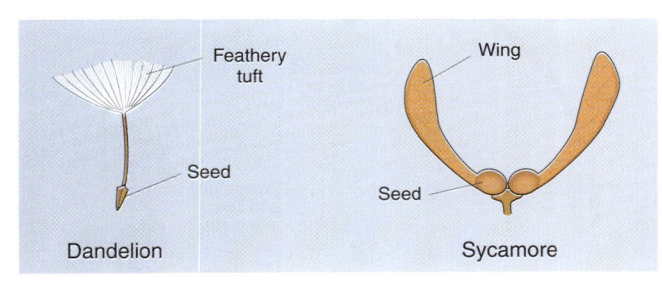

fig. 38.6 Wind-dispersed seeds

fig. 38.7 A dandelion spreads its seeds using the wind

Animal dispersal

This can involve the seeds being (a) eaten or (b) sticking to the animal. Edible fruits include blackberries, raspberries and strawberries. The animal eats and digests the fruit but the seeds (pips) pass out in the faeces or droppings.

fig. 38.8 Blackberry and strawberry seeds are dispersed by animals

Sticky fruits include burdock and 'stickybacks'. These attach to the animal but fall off at a later stage.

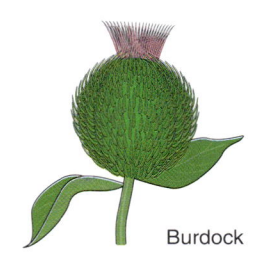

fig. 38.9 Burdock seeds

Self dispersal

This involves the fruit exploding when it dries out. In this way the seeds are flung away from the plant. Examples are the bursting of pea, bean and gorse pods.

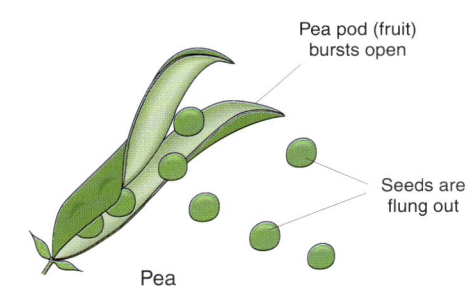

fig. 38.10 Self dispersal

Water dispersal

Some seeds or fruits are able to float. This allows them to be carried in streams, rivers or by ocean currents. Examples include alders, water lilies and coconuts.

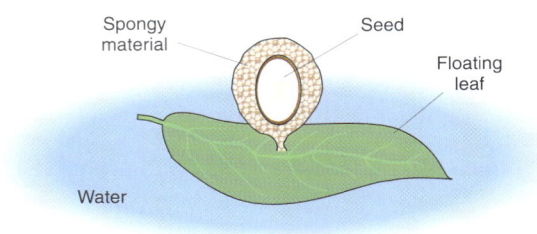

fig. 38.11 Water dispersal

Germination

Germination is the growth of the seed into a new plant. Very often seeds that are produced in the summer months remain in the soil during winter without growing. They are said to be dormant (resting). They will germinate when conditions are suitable.

The conditions necessary for germination are:
- water
- oxygen
- a suitable temperature (i.e. warmth)

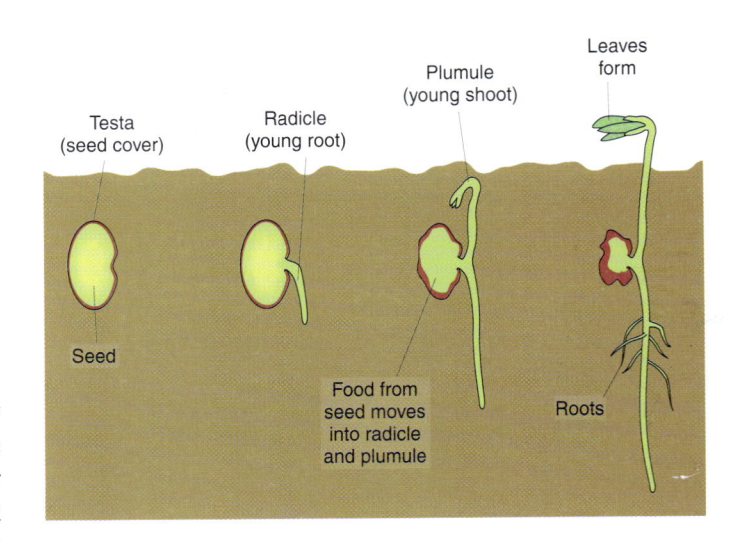

fig. 38.13 Germination

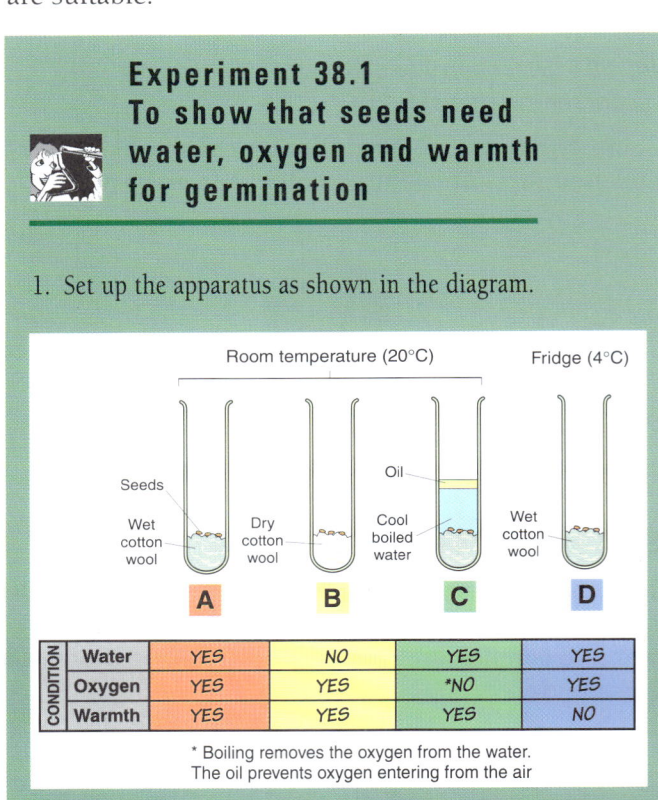

Experiment 38.1
To show that seeds need water, oxygen and warmth for germination

1. Set up the apparatus as shown in the diagram.

CONDITION	A	B	C	D
Water	YES	NO	YES	YES
Oxygen	YES	YES	*NO	YES
Warmth	YES	YES	YES	NO

* Boiling removes the oxygen from the water. The oil prevents oxygen entering from the air

fig. 38.12

2. The result is that the seeds in test tube A germinate after a few days, while those in tubes B, C and D do not.
3. This shows that water, oxygen and warmth are needed for germination.

Life cycle of a sunflower

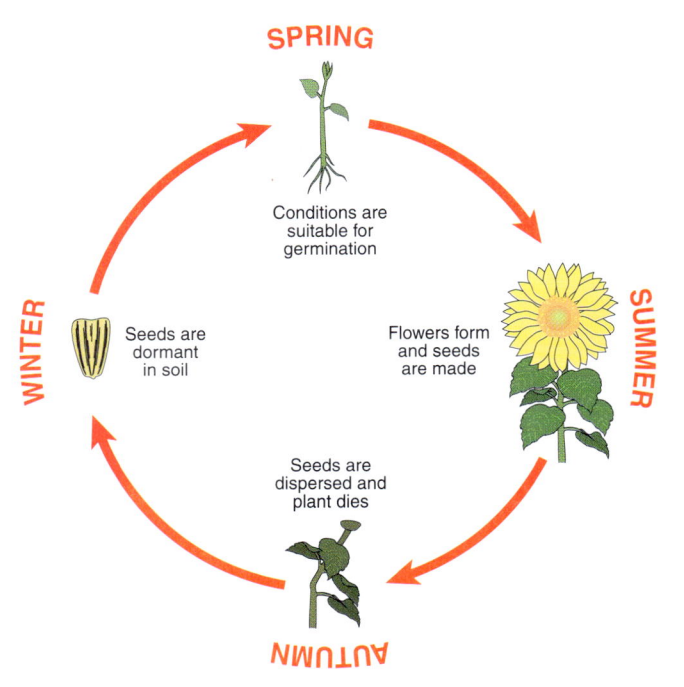

fig. 38.14 Life cycle of a sunflower

SUMMARY

- Sexual reproduction is the joining of two sex cells (i.e. two parents are involved).
- Asexual reproduction does not involve fertilisation (i.e. only one parent is involved).

- The function of the flower is reproduction:
  - sepals protect the flower when in bud
  - petals attract insects
  - stamens produce pollen
  - carpels produce eggs
- Pollination is the transfer of pollen from the anther to the stigma.
- The methods of pollination are (a) wind, (b) insect.
- Fertilisation occurs when the nucleus of the pollen fuses with the egg nucleus in the ovule.
- As a result of fertilisation:
  - the ovule becomes the seed
  - the ovary becomes the fruit
- Dispersal is the carrying of the seed (or fruit) away from the parent plant.
- The methods of dispersal are:
  - wind
  - animal
  - self
  - water
- Germination is the growth of the seed into a new plant.
- The conditions for germination are:
  - water
  - oxygen
  - suitable temperature

QUESTIONS

Q. 38.1
(a) Name the two types of reproduction.
(b) Explain clearly the difference between them.
(c) Which method is carried out by
   (i) animals, (ii) plants.

Q. 38.2
Give the functions of the following:
(a) a flower
(b) sepals
(c) petals
(d) stamens
(e) carpels

Q. 38.3
Say whether the following are male or female structures: anther, egg, ovule, filament, pollen, stamen, ovary, stigma, carpel, style.

Q. 38.4
(a) What is pollination?
(b) Name the methods of pollination.
(c) Draw a large, labelled diagram of a carpel after it has been pollinated, but before fertilisation occurs.

Q. 38.5
Suggest a reason for each of the following:
(a) Petals may be brightly coloured but sepals are not.
(b) Wind pollinated plants produce much more pollen than insect pollinated plants.
(c) Grasses do not have bright, obvious flowers.
(d) The stigma of some plants is feathery.
(e) Some plants produce nectar.

Q. 38.6
Copy out and complete the table below. (Note: adaptation means any feature that helps the seed to be dispersed.)

Q. 38.7
(a) What is meant by dispersal?
(b) Why is it necessary?

Plant	Dispersal method	Diagram of seed/fruit	Adaptation
Burdock			
Dandelion			
Coconut			
Strawberry			
Pea			
Orange			

38 • Plant Reproduction

(c) Name the methods of dispersal and, in each case, name one plant which uses that method.

Q. 38.8

Suggest a reason for each of the following:
(a) Seeds start to grow in spring.
(b) Many seeds will not germinate in summer.
(c) Alder seeds are very light.
(d) Dandelion plants are often found growing a long way from other dandelions, but sycamore trees usually grow close together.
(e) Grass seed should be lightly watered after sowing.
(f) Grass seeds are not heavily watered.
(g) Some plants (eg. mushrooms) do not produce flowers and yet they can reproduce.

Q. 38.9

(a) Draw a diagram of a germinating seed.
(b) Why do germinating seeds shrivel up during the process?
(c) What are the plumule, radicle and testa?

Q. 38.10

Describe the main events that take place in a plant during each of the four seasons.

Q. 38.11

(a) Name the parts A, B, C and D shown on the diagram.
(b) Name the type of cells produced by B and C.

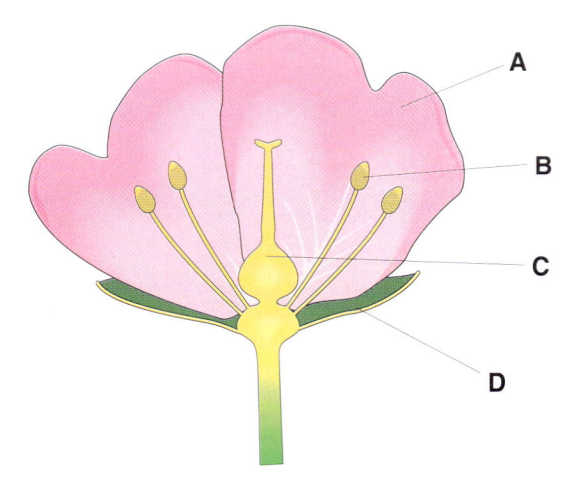

fig. 38.15

Q. 38.12

(a) Name the parts A to G on the diagram.
(b) State the method of pollination used by the flower in Question 38.11. Give two reasons for your answer.

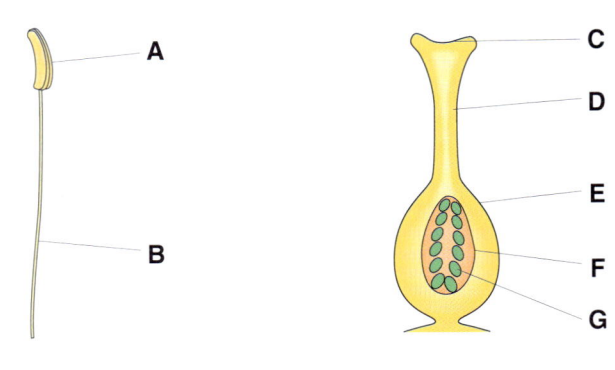

fig. 38.16

39
ECOLOGY 1

The word ecology is taken from the Greek word *oikos* which means a home. Ecology is the study of the 'homes' of living things. However, living things do not exist in isolation. They depend on each other and their surroundings for such things as light, food and shelter. This means that the study of ecology is broader than just the study of homes.

Ecology is the study of the relationships between plants, animals and their environment (or surroundings).

It would be too complex to study all plants and animals in the world. To simplify matters, the living world is divided into broadly similar areas such as deserts, tropical rainforests, grassland and bogland. Large areas such as these are called **ecosystems**.

Habitats

Ecosystems are still too big to study. Instead, a small, local area called a habitat is studied. A habitat is the area in which a plant or animal lives. There are a wide variety of habitats that you can study, e.g. a grassy field, a pond, a woodland, a rotting log or a local park. This chapter will deal with two sample habitats, a rocky seashore and a hedgerow, although you are only required to study one of these.

All the plants and animals that live in a habitat are called a **community**. All the animals on a local seashore, or the plants in a local hedgerow, are examples of communities.

fig. 39.1 *A rocky seashore*

39 • Ecology 1

Inter-relationships

One of the main lessons of ecology is that all living things (organisms) are dependent on each other and on their environment. If any one part of a habitat is altered, it will often have an effect on many other aspects of the habitat. The main ways in which organisms are interdependent are for food and shelter. This can be shown by a study of food chains.

Food chains

A food chain is a list of organisms in which each organism provides food for the next one.

Food chains must start with a producer. A **producer** is a plant that makes food (by the process of photosynthesis). In this way, producers convert the energy in sunlight into food. Examples of producers are blackberry bushes, bladder wrack (a common seaweed found on rocks at the seashore), cabbage and wheat.

Consumers are organisms that cannot make food. Instead, they feed on plants and animals. Examples of consumers are earthworms (feeding on dead plant material called humus), starfish (feeding on mussels and periwinkles), dolphins and eagles.

Herbivores are animals that eat only plants, e.g. slugs and limpets. They are called the primary consumers.

fig. 39.3 Limpets

Carnivores are animals that eat only meat, i.e. other animals. They can be secondary or tertiary consumers, e.g. sparrow hawks and crabs.

fig. 39.4 A velvet crab

Omnivores are animals that eat both plants and animals, e.g. humans, badgers and blackbirds. Sample food chains are shown in the table below.

fig. 39.2 Earthworm

Habitat	Producer	Primary consumer	Secondary consumer	Tertiary consumer
Hedgerow	Blackberry→ Dock leaves→	Caterpillar→ Slug→	Thrush→ Badger	Sparrow hawk
Rocky Seashore	Algae→ Plankton→	Limpet→ Mussels→	Whelk→ Starfish	Gull

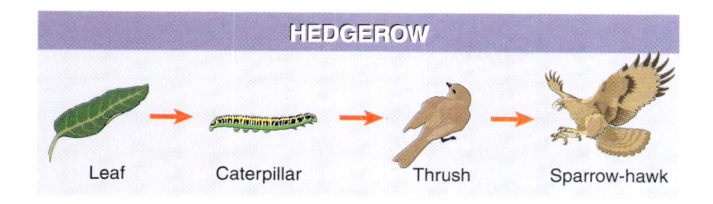

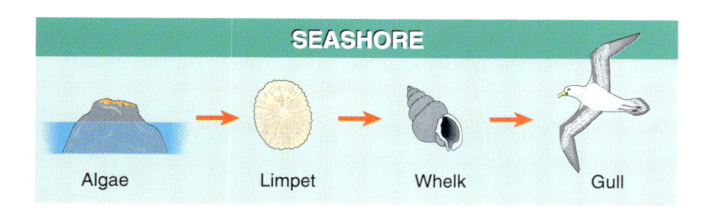

fig. 39.5 A food chain

Energy flow

The energy needed to maintain living things comes from the Sun. Producers trap this energy and convert it to the chemical energy of food. The energy then passes along the food chain as each organism eats the one before it.

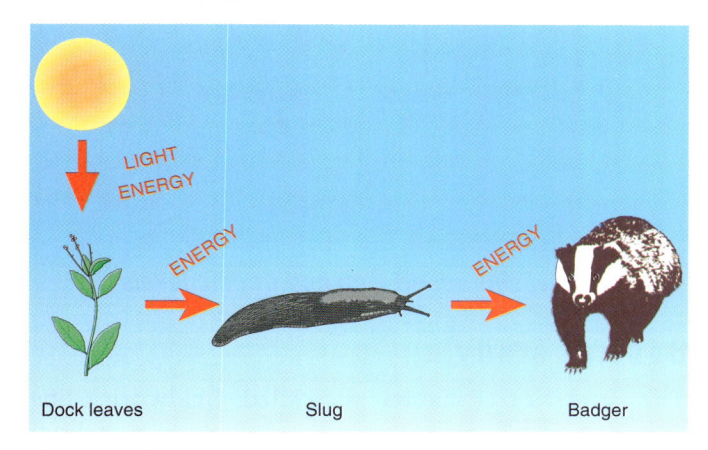

fig. 39.6 Energy transfer

Each organism uses some energy to move, grow and reproduce. A great deal of energy is lost from each organism in the form of heat. When the organisms die (or excrete waste) the energy is released by the process of decay.

Decay is caused by decomposers. These are small living things (micro-organisms) such as bacteria and fungi.

Decomposers play a vital role in habitats as they release the minerals (such as calcium or magnesium) from dead organisms into the soil. As a result minerals are taken up by the roots of other plants. This transfer of minerals from dead organisms to new ones is called **recycling**.

fig. 39.7 Bracket fungi on a rotting tree

Competition

Competition occurs when two or more organisms demand something that is in short supply. Plants compete for resources such as space, light, water and minerals from the soil. Animals compete for food, shelter, territory and mates.

Competition can take place between the same types (species) of plants and animals. For example, primroses compete with each other for space and light and crabs compete with each other for food.

Competition also takes place between different species of organism. For example, thrushes and blackbirds compete for food, caterpillars and greenfly both feed on the dog rose, different seaweeds compete for space on rocks, barnacles and seaweeds compete for space to attach to rocks.

Adaptations

Adaptations are structures or habits that enable organisms to survive in their habitat. Adaptations allow organisms to reduce competiton.

Examples of adaptations are shown in the table on the top of the next page.

Interdependence

Interdependence means that plants and animals need, or depend on, each other in order to survive. This dependence can be for food, gases, shelter, carrying pollen or seeds and even for clothing or medicines.

39 • Ecology 1

Habitat	Organism	Adaptation	Benefit
Hedgerow	Primrose	Grows and flowers in early spring	Gets plenty of light as other plants have not yet formed leaves
	Thrush	Can eat animal food	Avoids competing with blackbirds for seeds or fruits
	Caterpillar	Strong jaws	Chews leaves
	Greenfly	Hollow, tubular mouth parts	Sucks sap from leaves
Rocky seashore	Limpet	Shell	Protection from drying out or being eaten
	Bladder wrack	Bladders	Enables it to float and absorb more light
	Barnacles	Feathery feet	Stick out and trap plankton in the water
	Seaweeds	Holdfasts	Enables them to attach to rocks

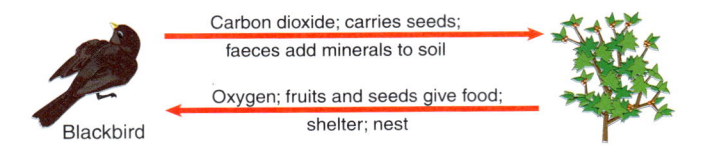

fig. 39.8 Examples of interdependence

Food web

A food web consists of two or more interconnected food chains. Food webs provide a more complete picture of the real feeding relationships in a habitat than food chains alone. Normally each organism feeds on more than one source of food, while food chains would indicate that they depend on only one.

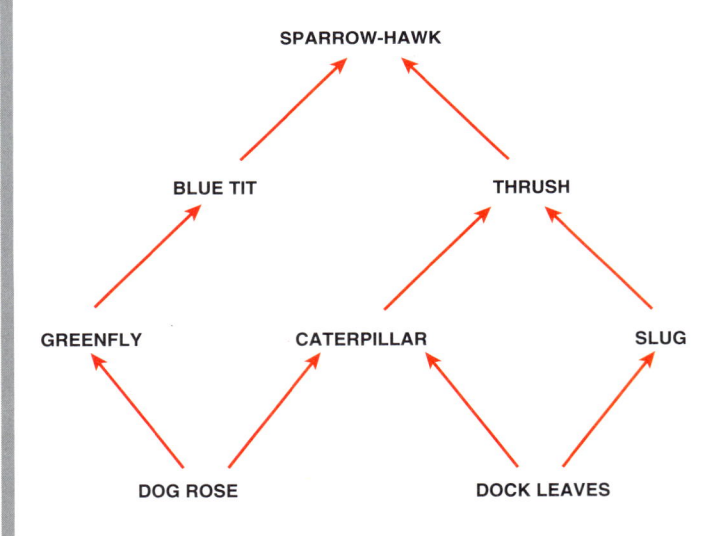

fig. 39.9 Hedgerow food web

Each feeding stage within a food chain or food web is called a **trophic level**. The producers form the first trophic level, the primary consumers are the second trophic level and so on.

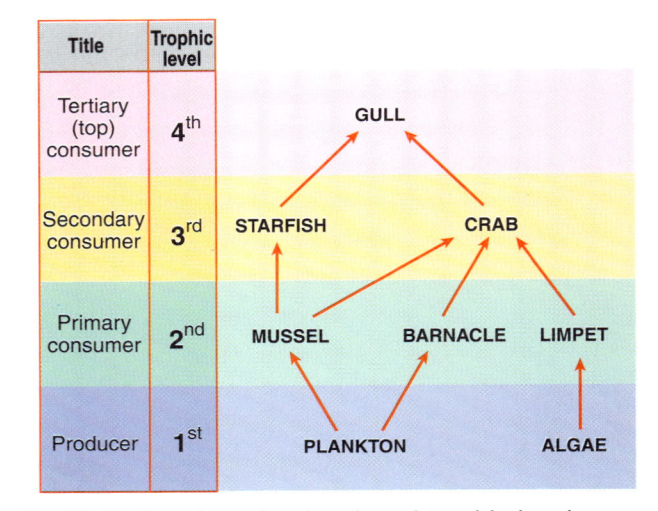

fig. 39.10 Seashore food web and trophic levels

Habitat study

The study of a habitat is called fieldwork. The presence and distribution of organisms in a habitat depends on a number of factors. These factors can be summarised as:

Non-living factors such as:

(a) soil type, water and air content, mineral and humus content and pH;

(b) physical (or climatic) factors such as temperature, rainfall, light, slope of ground, exposure to wind or waves.

Living factors such as food supply, building materials and the presence of competitors.

A habitat study consists of the following steps:

1. Draw a simple map of the habitat.
2. Measure and record the physical and soil factors.

3. Identify the plants and animals present.
4. Collect samples of those organisms that cannot be identified in the habitat.
5. Estimate the numbers of each organism in the habitat.

Drawing a map

Draw a simple map to show the main features of the habitat. Include a compass reading to show where north, south, east and west lie. In addition, photographs of the habitat can be taken.

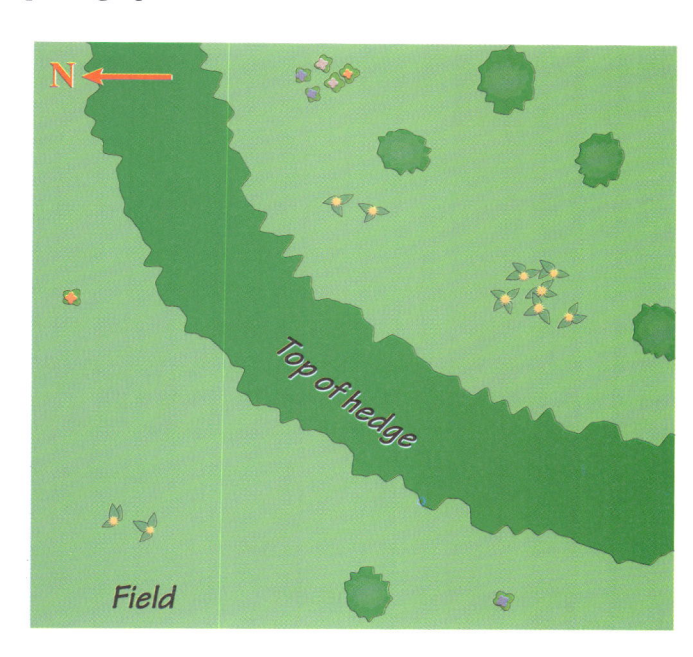

fig. 39.11 Sample hedgerow habitat map

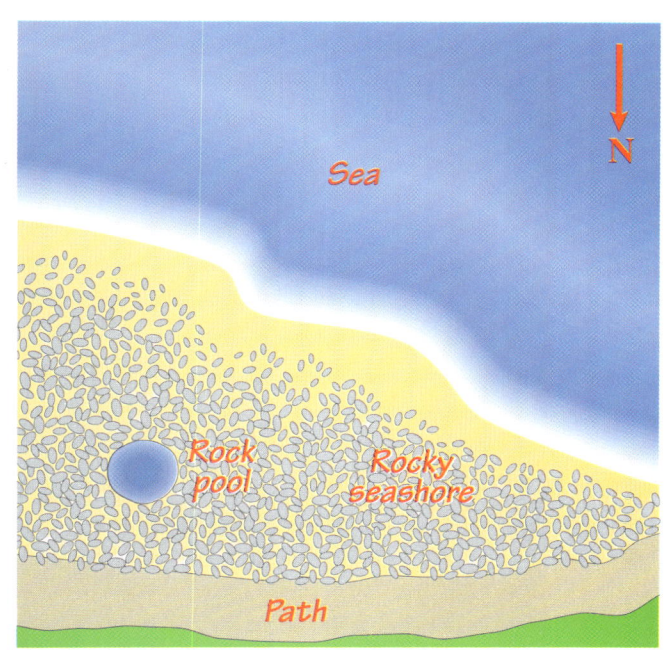

fig. 39.12 Sample seashore habitat map

Measuring non-living factors

Soil factors can be measured as shown in Chapter 40. Air, water and soil temperatures are taken with a thermometer. Light intensity can be recorded with a light meter (this is especially important in studying hedgerows, i.e. record the light in the field, at the base of the hedge and within the hedge).

Identification

This can be carried out by asking expert opinion, or by comparing the organism with labelled diagrams or photographs.

If identification is still difficult, a simple key can be used. These are available for each type of organism. Two sample organisms and a key are given below.

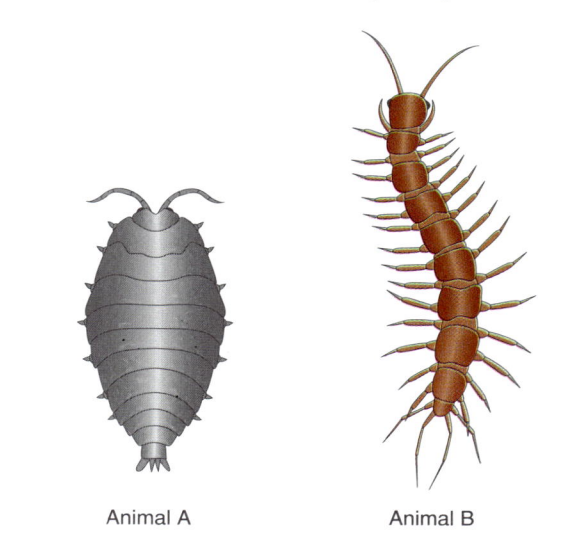

Animal A   Animal B

fig. 39.13 A simple key

1. Segmented legs present — 2
   Legs absent — worms
2. Three pairs of legs — insects
   Four or more pairs of legs — 3
3. Four pairs of legs — spiders
   More than four pairs of legs — 4
4. Wide body, seven pairs of legs, body enclosed in plates of armour — woodlouse
   Long and narrow body, many pairs of legs — centipede or millipede

From this key it is evident that animal A is a woodlouse and animal B is a centipede (millipedes have even more legs).

39 • Ecology 1

Collecting plants and animals

Organisms are only collected in order to identify them at a later stage.

Special apparatus is needed to collect fast moving animals. Some of the most commonly used methods are outlined in Figure 39.14.

Animals that do not move (e.g. barnacles, mussels) or move slowly (e.g. slugs, earthworms, limpets, periwinkles) can be collected directly. Animals are best stored in screwtop bottles.

Plants can be collected directly using a penknife or small trowel. Only one sample of each plant is

APPARATUS	DIAGRAM	USED	COLLECTS
Pooter	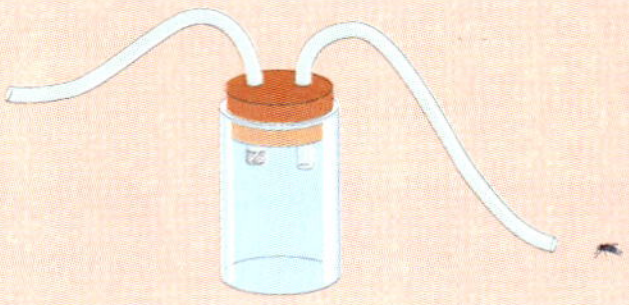	Suck the organism into the jar	Insects, spiders
Beating tray (or upturned umbrella or sheet)		Placed under bush which is shaken	Insects, caterpillars
Pitfall trap		Placed in soil, overnight if possible	Crawling animals e.g. snails, slugs, periwinkles
Sweep net		Swept through long grass or hedges	Insects
Plankton net	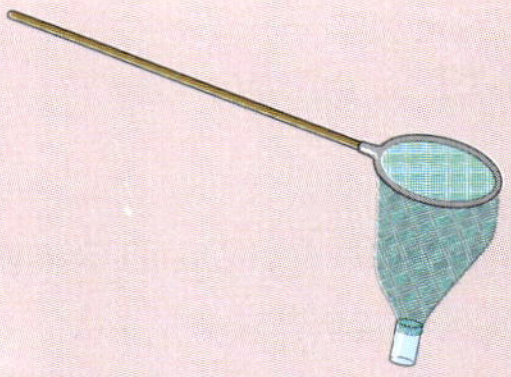	Drawn through the water	Plankton (in the jar)
Tullgren funnel		Heat from the bulb causes small organisms to move down	Small organisms from soil or leaf litter
Sieve	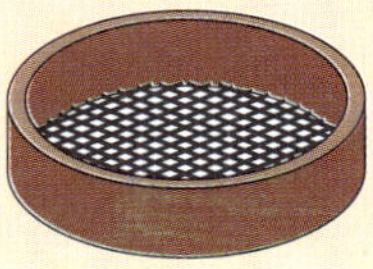	To separate soil from animals	Insects, snails, slugs

fig. 39.14

collected; rare plants should never be taken. The plants are best stored in plastic bags (labelled with information as to where they were found).

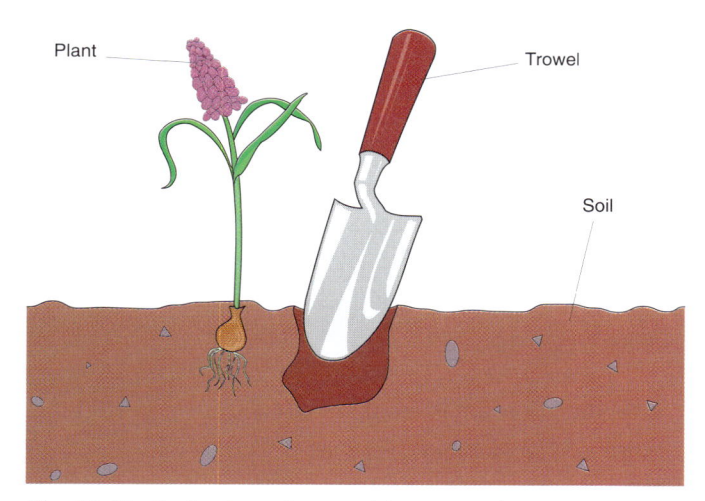

fig. 39.15 *Gathering plants with a trowel*

Estimating the numbers of organisms

A **quadrat** is a square frame which is thrown over your shoulder into the habitat. The most common quadrats are 1 metre square or 0.5 metre square. The names of each type of plant (and stationary or non-moving animals) inside the quadrat are recorded.

This is repeated for at least ten different throws of the quadrat. The information collected might look like that in the table below.

A **line index transect** is a length of string or rope marked with knots or tape at regular intervals. The intervals used can be 10 cm, 0.5 m or 1 m depending on the habitat being studied.

The transect is usually laid across the ground and fixed to the ground at each end. The name of each plant (or animal) touching the transect in each interval is recorded.

Transects are especially useful in showing the changes in plants (or some animals) from one part of the habitat to another. For example, they show the changes from the high rocks down to the waters edge or from the edge of a hedge out into the adjoining field.

Transects can also be taken at different heights to show how plants change the higher up you move (e.g. on an old wall or in a hedge).

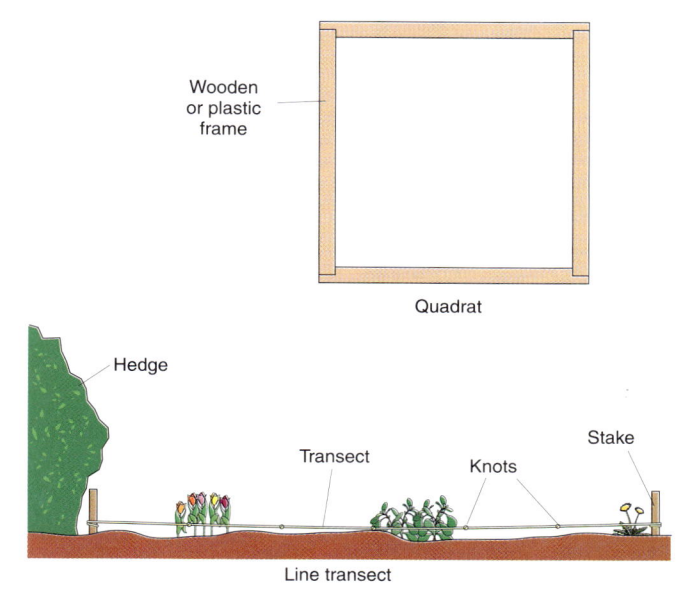

fig. 39.16 *A quadrat and line transect*

SAMPLE HABITAT

While two sample habitats are given, pupils are only required to investigate one local habitat.

Hedgerow

Hedgerows are strips of woodland. Many of these were planted about two hundred years ago to denote the ownership of land. Hedgerows are similar to the edge of a woodland. They show large changes based on light intensity. The outside edge has most light while the inside of the hedge is darker.

Plant	Quadrat number										Total
	1	2	3	4	5	6	7	8	9	10	
Dandelion	✓	✓	-	-	-	✓	✓	-	✓	-	5 (50%)
Dock leaves	-	-	-	✓	-	✓	-	-	-	-	2 (20%)
Clover	✓	✓	-	✓	✓	✓	✓	✓	-	✓	8 (80%)
Grass	✓	✓	✓	✓	✓	✓	✓	✓	-	✓	9 (90%)

39 • Ecology 1

Hedgerow sample habitat

Common plants	Adaptation
Ash trees	Grow tall to get more light
Blackberry bushes	Thorns prevent them being eaten by large animals
Ivy	Can tolerate low light
Primrose	Flower in early spring before other plants have formed leaves

Common animals	Feeding style	Adaptations
Rabbits	Herbivores	Large incisor teeth for nibbling plants
Caterpillars	Herbivores	Green colour to avoid detection
Snails	Herbivores	Shell prevents damage or drying out
Hedgehogs	Carnivore	Spikes prevent them being eaten
Ladybird	Carnivore	Bright colours warn others it is inedible (very acidic)
Badger	Omnivore	By coming out at night they avoid detection

Rocky seashore

The rocky seashore differs from other habitats by having no soil and being exposed to regular wave action. This habitat is divided into four zones based on tidal movements.

The **splash zone** is on high ground and is only covered by sea spray. The **upper shore** is not covered by normal tides but is covered at very high tides. The **middle shore** is between normal high and low tides. The **lower shore** is only exposed by very low tides.

Seashore sample habitat

Zone	Organism		Adaptation
Splash	Plants	Sea pink Lichens	Can tolerate salty soil Can attach to rocks
	Animals	Periwinkle (black) Shore crab	Have lungs to breathe air Flat body to shelter under rocks
Upper	Plant	Channel wrack	Groove in fronds (leaves) to hold water
	Animal	Barnacles	Feathery feet to filter plankton
Middle	Plant	Bladder wrack	Covered in mucilage to reduce water loss
	Animal	Limpets Whelks	Sharp tongue to scrape algae off rocks Make acid to dissolve through shells
Lower	Plant	Oarweed Corallina	Can cling to rocks Red pigments allow it to absorb very dim light
	Animal	Sponges Anemones	Can filter plankton out of water Have tentacles that sting small fish and shrimps

SUMMARY

- Ecology is the study of the relationships between plants, animals and their environment.
- A habitat is the area in which a plant or animal lives.
- Producers (plants) make their own food.
- Consumers (animals and micro-organisms) cannot make food. They take in food.
  - Herbivores feed on plants.
  - Carnivores feed on animals (meat).
  - Omnivores feed on plants and animals.
- A food chain is a list of organisms where each one feeds on the one before it. It must start with a producer.

Producer	Leaves
↓	↓
Primary consumer	Greenfly
↓	↓
Secondary consumer	Ladybird

- Energy from the Sun is changed to food. This energy is passed along the food chain as organisms are eaten. This is called energy flow.
- Competition means organisms seek scarce resources.
- Adaptations are special features that allow the organism to survive in its habitat.
- A food web is a number of interconnected food chains.
- A trophic level is a feeding stage in a food chain.

1st trophic level	Grass
↓	↓
2nd trophic level	Rabbits
↓	↓
3rd trophic level	Fox

- A habitat study involves drawing a map, recording physical factors, identifying organisms, collecting organisms and estimating the numbers of organisms.
- Apparatus for collecting animals include a pooter (sucks up insects), beating tray (collects insects from bushes), pitfall trap (collects walking animals), nets (catching flying insects) and a tullgren funnel (separates small animals from soil).
- To estimate the numbers of organisms a quadrat (square frame) or transect (rope with regularly spaced knots) is used.

QUESTIONS

Q. 39.1
Describe what is meant by
(a) ecology
(b) ecosystem
(c) habitat
(d) interdependence
(e) food chain

Q. 39.2
(a) Name the habitat you have studied.
(b) Define the following words, giving one example in each case from your habitat:
   (i) producer
   (ii) consumer
   (iii) secondary consumer
   (iv) carnivore
   (v) herbivore
   (vi) decomposer

Q. 39.3
(a) Name two animals from the same habitat and say how each one is adapted to life in this habitat.
(b) Name two plants and outline some ways they have adapted to their environment.

Q. 39.4
Suggest a reason for each of the following:
(a) All food chains start with a producer.
(b) An increase in the number of rabbits will cause an increase in the number of foxes.
(c) The rotting of leaves is beneficial to the soil.
(d) Limpets have shells.
(e) There is a limit to the number of hedgehogs living in one area.
(f) Plants depend on animals.
(g) Animals depend on plants.
(h) Bringing a knife on a habitat study.
(i) Studying a habitat and not an ecosystem.

Q. 39.5
Draw a labelled diagram and give the use for a
(a) pitfall trap
(b) tullgren funnel
(c) pooter
(d) quadrat
(e) transect

Q. 39.6

Describe how you would use each of the following

(a) pooter
(b) quadrat
(c) sweep net
(d) transect

Q. 39.7

Using the organisms thrush, cabbage and caterpillar:

(a) Draw a food chain.
(b) Name the producer, herbivore and carnivore in the food chain.

Q. 39.8

The diagram shows the results of a habitat study.

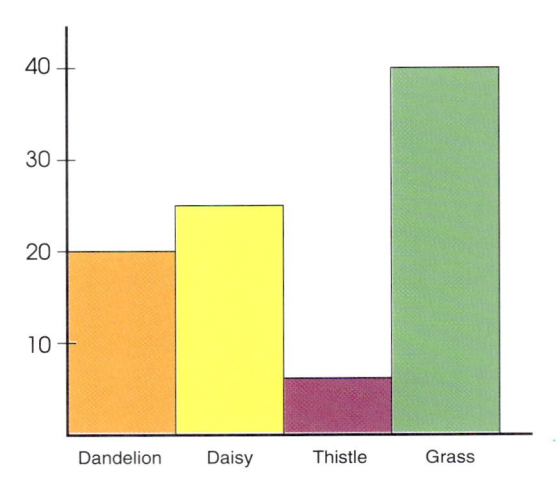

fig. 39.17

(a) What is the number of thistles in the habitat?
(b) What is the total number of plants in the study?
(c) Name the apparatus you would use to carry out such a study.
(d) What plant was found most often in the habitat?
(e) Name any three animals that might be found in this habitat.

Q. 39.9

(a) Name a habitat you have studied.
(b) Draw a simple map of this habitat.
(c) Name three plants and three animals from this habitat.
(d) State two examples of adaptations found in the study.
(e) Give two examples of competition from the habitat.
(f) Draw two separate food chains from the habitat.

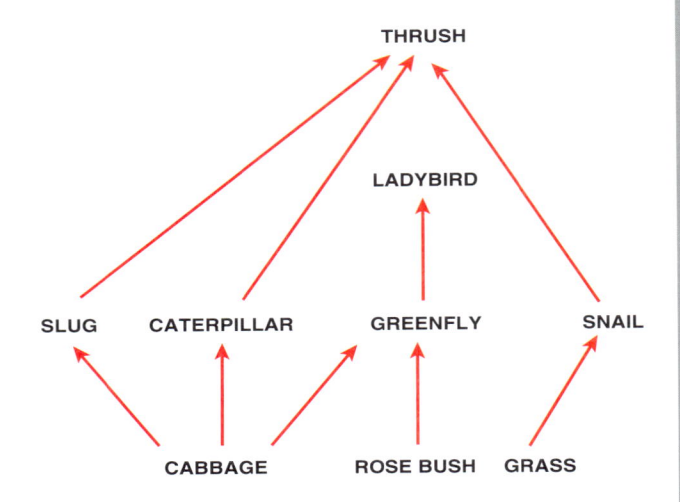

Q. 39.10

fig. 39.18

Based on the food web shown above,

(a) Name three different food chains.
(b) Name two organisms at the third trophic level.
(c) Name two carnivores.
(d) Name two primary consumers.
(e) Name two top consumers.
(f) What trophic level is occupied by the greenfly.

Q. 39.11

The following numbers of plants were recorded at different distances from the base of a hedge.

Distance from tree / m	0	2	4	6	8	10
Number of plants / unit area	0	12	23	42	82	105

fig. 39.19

(a) Suggest an apparatus you could use to obtain these results.
(b) Explain how you would use this apparatus.
(c) How many plants would you expect to find at a distance of (i) 14 metres and (ii) 9 metres from the hedge?
(d) Suggest a reason for the variation in plant numbers obtained.

Q. 39.12

Using the following organisms, oak, ash tree, caterpillar, spider, ladybird, greenfly (aphids), thrush and hawk:

(a) Construct two food chains.
(b) Name the organisms at the second trophic level of each food chain.
(c) Construct a food web using all the organisms.

CONSERVATION AND POLLUTION

Conservation is the wise management of the world's natural resources so that they are preserved for the future. It has been said that we borrow our environment from our parents and should pass it on safely to our children. It is not ours to damage or destroy.

Modern humans exploit nature in order to live in the way that they do. For example, on a worldwide scale we take large numbers of fish from the sea, grow huge areas of crops in places they would not normally grow, remove timber from forests for building and fuel, and alter the environment for houses, roads, industry and recreation.

Before humans first arrived in Ireland, the country was covered in oak, elm and ash woods. These have been cut down to such an extent that we now have less woodland than anywhere else in Europe. Many of the woodlands that are now being planted contain only one type of tree and do not support wildlife as well as the old woods did.

fig. 39.20 *Conifer woods*

fig. 39.21 *Broadleaved woods*

In addition, almost all of our native boglands have been drained, and over 90% are now destroyed. Grasslands which have developed over hundreds of years so that they contain many wild plants and animals are being replaced with a single type of grass or cereal.

THE NEED FOR CONSERVATION

At present many plants and animals are being wiped out (becoming extinct) due to the destruction of their habitats. It is estimated that, worldwide, one species of plant or animal is wiped out every day.

You have learned in ecology that all the organisms in a habitat are dependent on each other. This means that the loss of a single organism will have a series of effects on the other organisms in the food web. In addition, once a species is extinct there is no way to get it back. This means that any possible benefit they might have had for future generations is lost.

One of the main targets of conservationists is to preserve a wide variety of habitats. This will ensure a wide variety of different plants and animals.

DESERTIFICATION

This is the gradual enlargement of deserts so that they take over adjoining lands. It can be caused by climatic factors such as lack of rainfall or by poor conservation. For example, if grasslands are grazed by too many animals, or if too many plants are grown, the soil will become exposed and dry. This causes the vegetation to die and desert to form.

DEFORESTATION

This is the destruction of all the trees in an area. It causes huge losses in plant and animal life. In addition the remaining soil is more easily washed away by rain, or blown away by wind. This means it can no longer support plants.

Deforestation mostly occurs in the tropical rainforests of countries such as Brazil, Indonesia, Zaire and Malaysia. It is mainly caused by (a) local people burning forests to clear land for agriculture, (b) removing trees for export, (c) cutting trees to provide grassland for cattle ranches.

POLLUTION

Pollution is any undesirable change in the environment, and is mainly caused by human activity.

Pollutants are the substances that cause the pollution. The most common forms of pollution are air and water pollution.

fig. 39.22 Deforestation

Air pollution

The main source of air pollution is the burning of fossil fuels. These fuels include coal, gas, turf, oil and petrol. The pollutants produced cause damage to the environment and to health as outlined below.

Problem	Pollutant	Effect
Smog	Particles in air	Harmful to lungs, kills lichens
Acid rain	Sulphur and nitrogen oxides dissolved in rainwater	Burns leaves on trees, kills plants and fish. Dissolves marble, limestone and metal
Lead	'Leaded' petrol	Harmful to the brains of young children
Greenhouse gases	Increased levels of carbon dioxide (and other gases)	Causes the Earth to warm up, resulting in floods and weather changes
Dirt	Smoke and soot	Harmful to the lungs, blackens buildings
Less ozone	Chemicals called CFCs (chloro-fluorocarbons) found in aerosols and refrigerators	They destroy ozone (a form of oxygen) in the upper atmosphere, which lets in more ultra-violet radiation from the Sun causing more skin cancers

Water pollution

The main sources of water pollution are poorly treated sewage, domestic, agricultural and industrial wastes and oil spills.

If nutrients are added to water in a stream, river, pond, lake (or even the sea) they cause the growth of algae. This is called an algal bloom. When the algae die, they are decayed by bacteria which use up all the oxygen in the water. This causes the death of all the plants and animals in the water.

Nutrients can be added to water as sewage, slurry, excess fertiliser or leaks from silage pits. See the table at the bottom of the page.

fig. 39.24 Oil spill on sea birds

Pollution control

Pollution can be prevented by a number of methods. While these may be costly in the short term, they have long term benefits to our environment.

Some common pollution control measures are listed in the table on the following page.

fig. 39.23 A forest killed by acid rain

Water pollution

Problem	Pollutant	Effect
Untreated sewage	Micro-organisms Nutrients	Cause diseases Remove oxygen
Excess slurry, fertiliser or silage leaks	Nutrients	Remove oxygen
Industrial waste	Poisonous chemicals Nuclear waste	Harmful to health May cause mutations or cancer
Oil spills	Oil	Kills birds and fish, destroys beaches

Pollution control methods

Method	Benefit
Burning smokeless fuel	Less particles and sulphur oxides
Catalytic converters on cars	Less sulphur and nitrogen oxides from car exhausts
Lead-free petrol	Less lead released into the air
Reduced use of CFCs	Ozone layer can build up
Improved sewage treatment	Less untreated sewage in water
Better control of slurry, fertiliser and silage pits	Less nutrients in water
Organised tipheads for household and industrial wastes	Less waste dumped carelessly

SUMMARY

- Conservation is the wise management of the Earth's natural resources.
- Conservation is needed to pass on as many habitats, plants and animals as exist at present.
- Examples of poor conservation are:
  - desertification, which is the way deserts slowly expand to take over nearby lands;
  - deforestation, which is the cutting down of tropical rainforests.
- Pollution is any undesirable change in the environment caused by human activities.
- Air pollution is mostly caused by the burning of fossil fuels.
- Water pollution can be due to sewage, agricultural or industrial wastes and oil spills.

QUESTIONS

Q. 39.1
What is meant by
(a) conservation, (b) pollution, (c) pollutant?

Q. 39.2
(a) Name three types of habitats in Ireland that have been damaged by human activity.
(b) Describe how each of the named habitats was damaged.
(c) Suggest why habitat destruction is a harmful process.

Q. 39.3
(a) Explain the terms desertification and deforestation.
(b) Give two causes for each process.
(c) Explain how one of these processes took place in Ireland in ancient times.

Q. 39.4
Give a reason for each of the following:
(a) The growing use of lead-free petrol.
(b) The increased levels of carbon dioxide in the air since about 1850.
(c) The need for sewage treatment.
(d) Buildings in cities become blackened.
(e) The destruction of the Amazonian forests.
(f) The use of CFC-free sprays.
(g) The need for catalytic converters on cars.

Q. 39.5
State the environmental cause of
(a) acid rain, (b) brain damage to children,
(c) the warming of the planet, (d) smog.

Q. 39.6
Explain why the overuse of fertilisers can lead to fish kills in rivers.

Q. 39.7
(a) Name the main living creature causing pollution.
(b) Name three ways in which pollution can be reduced.
(c) What are the likely results of a failure to control pollution.

Q. 39.8
(a) State the main cause of air pollution.
(b) Name three fossil fuels.
(c) Name three pollutants produced when fossil fuels are burned.

Q. 39.9
(a) What is ozone?
(b) Where is it mostly found?
(c) Suggest a benefit of ozone.
(d) Name a substance that destroys ozone.

40
ECOLOGY 2

SOIL AND MICROBIOLOGY

The word soil refers to the layer of material that is found on top of the Earth's rocky crust. Soil is formed by the weathering of rock over long periods of time. The most fertile type of soil is called loam. It contains sand, silt and clay particles, each of which are increasingly small particles

Importance of soil

1. Soil provides anchorage for plants.
2. Soil provides water, minerals and air for plant roots.
3. Soil provides a habitat for soil organisms.

The content of soil

1. Soil particles

These range from large stones to sand, silt and clay (which is composed of the smallest sized particles).

2. Humus

This consists of decaying plant and animal remains. It returns valuable minerals to the soil. It also holds soil particles together, helping to form loam.

3. Water

Water is needed by plants for transpiration and photosynthesis. It also allows the plant to absorb and transport minerals from the soil.

4. Minerals

Minerals such as nitrogen (N), phosphorus (P) and potassium (K) are dissolved in soil water in the form of mineral salts.

5. Air

Air is found between soil particles. Oxygen in the air is needed by roots and other organisms.

6. Living organisms

Living organisms in soil include earthworms, centipedes, millipedes, insects and micro-organisms. Earthworms are of particular benefit to the soil. Their burrowing activity helps to let air pass into the soil and allows water to pass out (i.e. aeration and drainage). In addition they bring humus down into the soil, and they help to mix the different soil particles.

Experiment 40.1
To show the humus and minerals content of a soil sample

1. Place the soil sample in a tall container such as a graduated cylinder.
2. Add water so that the container is two thirds full.
3. Place your palm over the open end and shake vigorously for about a minute.
4. Leave to settle for at least an hour.
5. The result will be as shown in the diagram, with the heaviest particles being at the bottom.

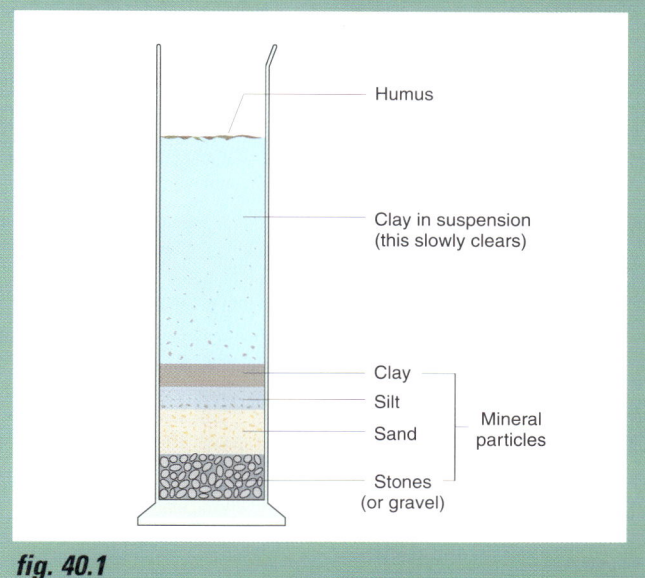

fig. 40.1

SOIL pH

The pH of a soil depends to a large extent on the type of rock from which it was formed. Most garden and agricultural soils are slightly acidic (pH between 6 and 7), and this suits most plants and animals.

Very acid soils are often found over granite rock, e.g. in bogs and mountain areas. Plants suited to these conditions are bogmoss, heather and rhododendrons.

Lime (from limestone) is sometimes added to soil to reduce its acidity (i.e. to raise the pH of the soil).

Water

Water is essential to plant life. However, if too much water is retained in the soil, waterlogging can result. This means the soil will have no air, and roots and organisms will die.

Experiment 40.2
To find the pH of a soil

1. Shake up a little soil with distilled water in a test tube.
2. Leave it to settle (or filter the shaken sample) to obtain a clear liquid.
3. Test the clear liquid with universal indicator.
4. Compare the colour obtained with the colour chart provided with the indicator to find the exact pH. See the universal indicator chart in Chapter 24.

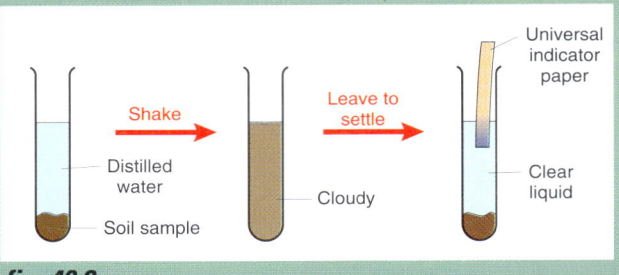

fig. 40.2

Experiment 40.4
To compare drainage rates in two different soils

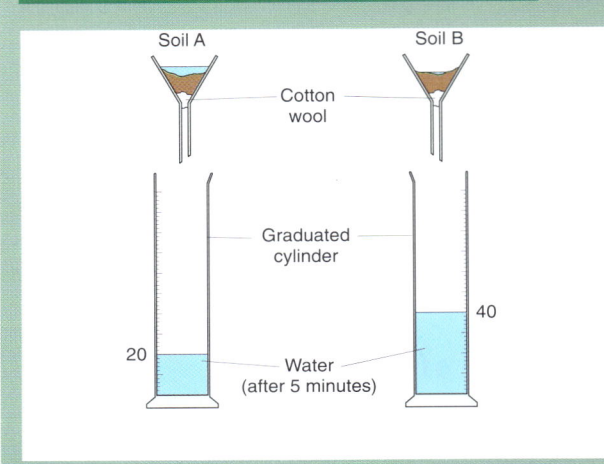

fig. 40.4

1. Set up the apparatus as shown, putting the same volume of each kind of soil in each funnel.
2. Pour 50 cm^3 of water into each funnel
3. Record the volume of water in each cylinder after 5 minutes.
4. The results shown in the diagram indicate that soil B has better drainage than soil A.

Experiment 40.3
To find the water content of a soil

fig. 40.3

1. Find the mass of a clean, dry evaporating dish.
2. Add some soil (about a large 'spoonful') to the basin.
3. Find the mass of the basin and soil, and then calculate the mass of the soil.
4. Place the basin of soil in an oven at 100°C for about 30 minutes. This removes any water present.
5. Remove the dish, allow it to cool, and find its mass again.
6. Repeat steps 4 and 5 until there is no further change in mass. This means that all of the water has been removed from the soil.
7. Record the final mass, and calculate the mass of water removed.
8. Calculate the percentage of water, as shown in the worked example.

Specimen results and calculation

Mass of clean, dry evaporating basin	50 g
Mass of basin and soil	200 g
Mass of soil (200 g – 50 g)	150 g
Mass of basin and soil after first heating	175 g
Mass of basin and soil after several heatings	170 g
Mass of water (loss of mass) (200 g – 170 g)	30 g

percentage of water $= \dfrac{30 \times 100}{150} = 20\%$

If too much water flows through soil, without enough being held the soil can become too dry. In addition, minerals can be washed out of the soil. This is called **leaching**.

Experiment 40.5
To find the air content of a soil

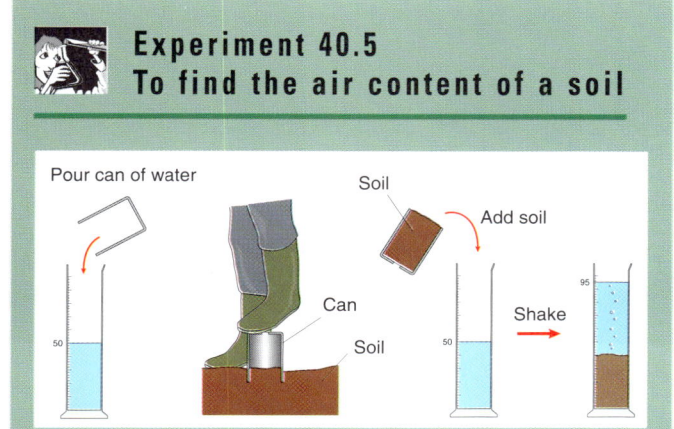

fig. 40.5

1. Fill a small can with water. Pour this water into a graduated cylinder and take the reading (for example 50 cm³). This gives the volume of the can.
2. Put a hole in the end of the can and fill it with soil as shown.
3. Pour all the soil into a large graduated cylinder containing 50 cm³ of water and shake to allow air bubbles to rise. Now record the final water level in the cylinder (for example 95 cm³).
4. If the soil had no air, the final water level would have been 100 cm³. The volume of air is given by the difference between 100 cm³ and the final level (100 – 95 = 5 cm³).
5. Calculate the % air as follows:

$$\% \text{ air} = \frac{\text{volume of air} \times 100}{\text{volume of soil}}$$

$$= \frac{5 \times 100}{50} = 10\%$$

Soil nutrients

Plants make their own food. In doing this, they need certain minerals (called nutrients), and they must absorb these from the soil in which they grow. These minerals enter the soil from the decay of dead plants and animals, or they may be added to the soil as fertilisers.

Soil pollution

Soil or land pollution is linked to water pollution (see Chapter 39). Leaching is the washing of nutrients and dissolved materials down through the soil by water. This lowers the mineral content of the soil. In addition pollutants are leached out of the soil and often end up in nearby rivers and lakes. The main causes of soil pollution are the dumping of wastes such as slurry, acid rain, and the misuse of chemical sprays.

MICRO-ORGANISMS

Micro-organisms are small living things. The three main types of micro-organism are viruses, bacteria and fungi. Micro-organisms are found in air, water, soil, and on human and animal skin and bodies. They are found in huge numbers, especially where they have a good food supply, e.g. where they cause decay. For example, one gram of soil can contain over 100 million bacteria, while 1 cm³ of fresh milk can have over 3000 million bacteria.

Viruses

A virus is the smallest micro-organism. Up to one million viruses can fit across the thickness of a thumbnail (1 mm). They can only reproduce by taking over the cells of another organism. They cause the other organism (the host) to produce new copies of the virus. Because they cannot reproduce by themselves, it is sometimes argued that they should not be called 'living things'.

In humans; viruses cause diseases such as measles, mumps, chicken pox, colds, influenza (flu), cold sores and AIDS. In other animals they cause rabies (in dogs, but can also affect humans) and foot and mouth disease (in cattle).

Some viruses also cause disease to plants.

The human body fights off viruses by producing antibodies that destroy the virus. Antibiotics have no effect on viruses. AIDS (acquired immune deficiency syndrome) is a condition caused by a virus called HIV (human immune virus). This virus enters the body in body fluids (e.g. through sexual intercourse with an infected partner, shared or dirty needles, blood transfusions where blood is contaminated).

Nutrients	Compound containing it	Function
nitrogen (N)	nitrates, urea	to form healthy leaves
phosphorus (P)	phosphates	to make healthy roots
potassium (K)	potash	to form flowers and fruits

HIV enters white blood cells and prevents them making antibodies. As a result the victim may die of other infections such as pneumonia.

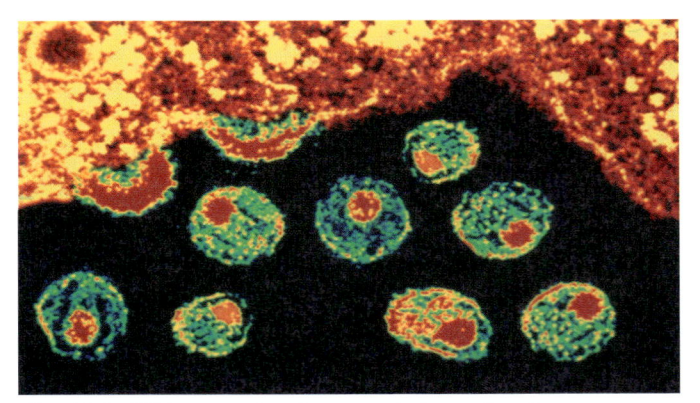

fig. 40.6 HIV emerging from an infected cell

Bacteria

Bacteria are very small. For example, about one thousand bacteria would fit across the thickness of a thumbnail. However, bacteria are much larger than viruses.

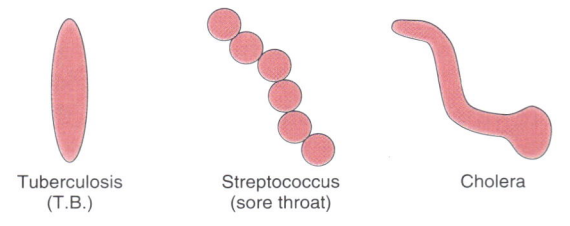

Tuberculosis (T.B.)   Streptococcus (sore throat)   Cholera

fig. 40.7 Shapes of micro-organisms

The three main types of bacteria are rod-shaped, round, and spiral. In order to grow, they require a suitable temperature, food and water. Bacteria that need oxygen are called **aerobic**; those capable of living without oxygen are called **anaerobic**. Most bacteria prefer a pH of 7 or higher.

Under ideal conditions they can grow (reproduce) very fast. In some cases they can double their numbers every twenty minutes. Antibiotics are chemicals, made by bacteria or fungi, that kill other bacteria. The first antibiotic, penicillin, was discovered by Sir Alexander Fleming in 1928.

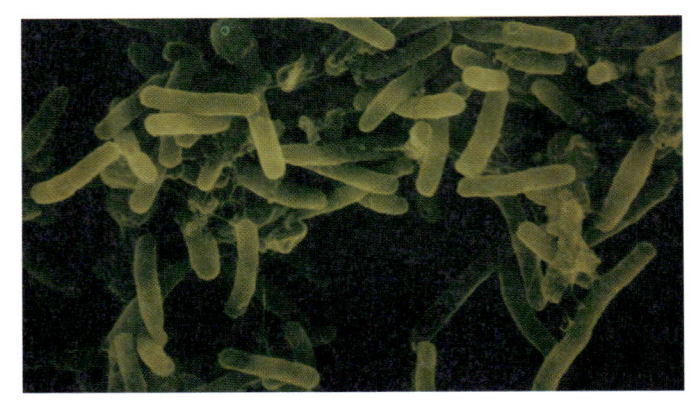

fig. 40.8 Rod bacteria

fig. 40.9 Sir Alexander Fleming (1881–1955)

Born in Scotland he first discovered penicillin in 1928. He was awarded the Nobel prize in 1945 for his work. Fleming's discovery is a good example of observation. He left a dish of bacteria open by mistake. A fungus grew on the dish. He noticed that there were no bacteria growing around the area of the fungus. He later isolated the antibiotic penicillin from the fungus.

Effects of bacteria

Useful	Harmful
1. Improve the soil by causing decay which forms humus and releases minerals back into circulation	Cause diseases such as tetanus (lock-jaw), TB, pneumonia, sore throats, boils, tooth decay
2. Produce cheese, butter and yoghurt	Destroy foods, e.g. cause milk to go sour
3. Make a range of products such as antibiotics, insulin, drugs and foods	Destroy crops

Experiment 40.6
To show that there are micro-organisms in soil

1. Obtain two sterile petri dishes containing nutrient agar. Sterile means there is nothing living in the dishes. Agar is made from seaweed and is used as a material on which to grow micro-organisms. Nutrient agar has extra foodstuffs to help micro-organisms to grow.
2. Barely open one petri dish and sprinkle a little fresh soil over the surface of the agar using a sterile spatula.
3. Do not open the second dish. This is the control.
4. Seal both dishes with tape, label them and place them in an oven (or incubator or warm place) at 20°C for a week.
5. Examine both dishes without opening them.
6. The result is that the dish with the soil has shiny patches (colonies) of bacteria and patches of fungus growth that resemble cotton wool. The control dish shows no growth.
7. This shows that soil contains bacteria and fungi.

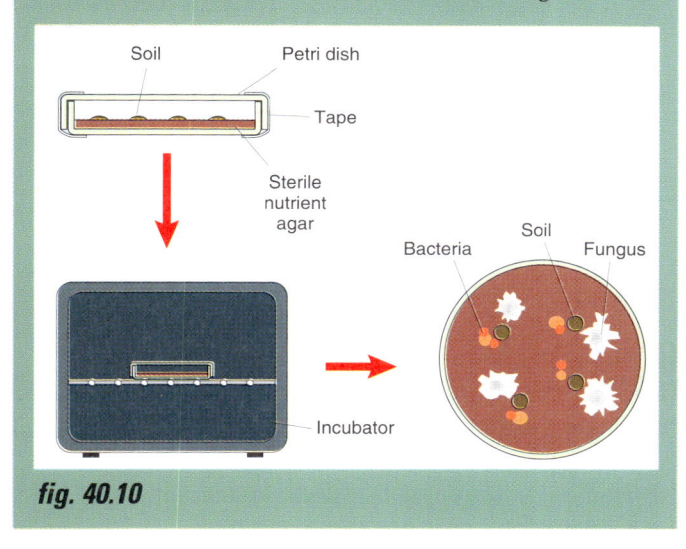

fig. 40.10

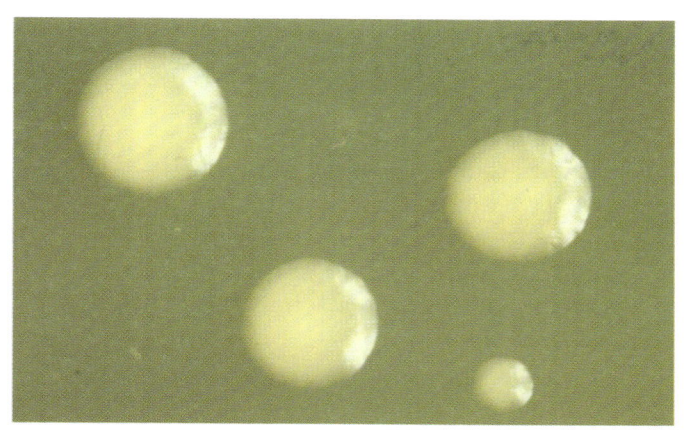

fig. 40.11 Bacteria colonies on a petri dish

Fungi

Fungi (singular, fungus) are micro-organisms that do not contain chlorophyll. As a result they do not make their own food. Some fungi obtain their food from living organisms. They are described as parasites. Other fungi get their food from dead sources and are called saprophytes.

Some fungi (e.g. yeasts) are composed of single cells. Other are made of tiny tubes called hyphae (e.g. a mushroom is made of thousands of tiny hyphae pressed together).

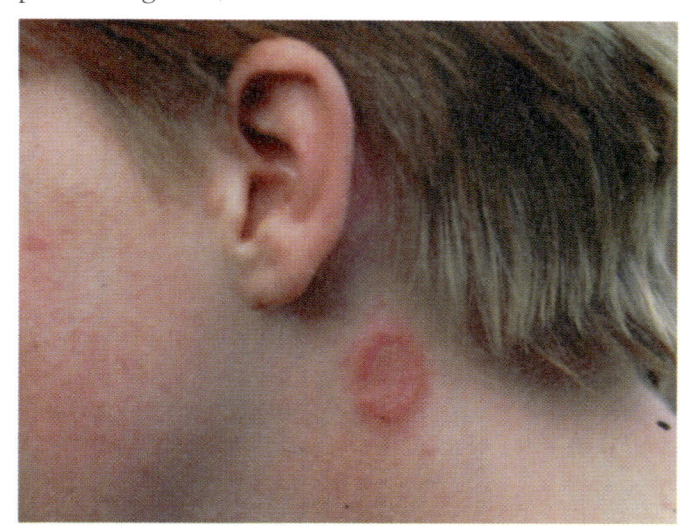

fig. 40.12 Ringworm infection

Effects of fungi

Useful	Harmful
1. Cause decay that enriches the soil	Cause human disease such as ringworm and athlete's foot
2. Some are edible, e.g. mushrooms	Cause plant diseases such as potato blight
3. Make products such as antibiotics, alcohol, drugs, flavour for cheese	Some are poisonous

SUMMARY

- Soil is made when rocks are weathered.
- Good soil contains:
  - particles (gravel (largest), sand, silt and clay (smallest)
  - humus (decaying organic matter)
  - water
  - minerals (nitrogen, phosphorus and potassium)
  - air
  - organisms
- Earthworms benefit soil by aeration, drainage, mixing and adding humus.
- Most plants prefer slightly acidic soils (pH 6 or 7).
- Leaching is the washing of minerals down through the soil.
- Nitrogen is needed for leaves, phosphorus for roots and potassium for flowers and fruits.
- Soil is polluted by dumping of wastes, acid rain and sprays.
- Micro-organisms can only be seen under a microscope.
- Viruses are the smallest micro-organisms.
- Diseases caused by viruses include colds, flu, mumps, measles and AIDS.
- Bacteria are larger than viruses.
- Uses of bacteria include improving soil, making cheese, yoghurt, antibiotics and insulin.
- Disadvantages of bacteria are diseases and decay of food and crops.
- Fungi include yeast and mushrooms.
- Benefits of fungi are their role in decay (recycle minerals), some are edible and others are used to manufacture antibiotics and drugs.
- Disadvantages of fungi are the causing of disease and that some are poisonous.

QUESTIONS

Q. 40.1
(a) What is soil?
(b) How is soil formed?
(c) Give three functions of soil.

Q. 40.2
(a) Name three living and three non-living things that are found in soil.
(b) Give the benefits of one of the living and one of the non-living things you have listed.

Q. 40.3
What is meant by:
(a) weathering
(b) humus
(c) loam
(d) soil nutrients

Q. 40.4
A sample of soil was shaken in water and allowed to stand for some time. The result was as shown.

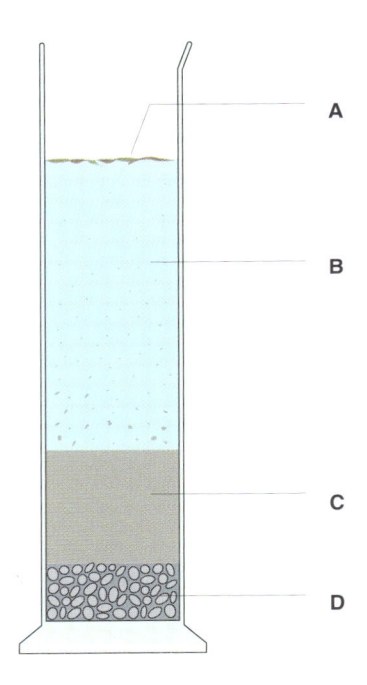

fig. 40.12

(a) Name the materials at A and D.
(b) Describe the appearance of layer B.
(c) Name the material that causes the appearance of B.
(d) Name the three types of particle found in C.
(e) Which of the previous three particles is closest to layer D? Give a reason for your answer.

Q. 40.5
Suggest a reason for each of the following.

(a) Lime is often added to soils.
(b) Soil should not be waterlogged.
(c) Earthworms are very beneficial to the soil.
(d) Heather will not grow well in many garden soils.
(e) Lawns need lots of fertiliser.
(f) Bacteria and fungi are vital in soils.

Q. 40.6

In an experiment the mass of a dish was found to be 60 g. The mass of the dish and some fresh soil was found to be 100 g. The dish of soil was placed in an oven for an hour. When its mass was measured again, it was found to be 95 g. These procedures were repeated until the mass of the dish remained constant at 90 g.

(a) What was the mass of the fresh soil?
(b) What was the mass of the soil at the end of the experiment?
(c) Why were the procedures repeated?
(d) Suggest a suitable temperature for the oven.
(e) Find the percentage water content of the fresh soil.
(f) Explain how you would find the pH of the fresh soil.

Q. 40.7

Equal volumes of water (100 cm^3) were poured onto two soil samples. After five minutes the results were as shown.

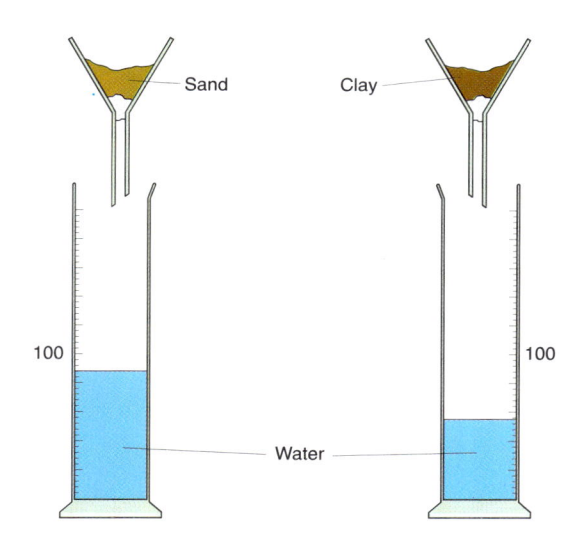

fig. 40.13

(a) Which soil had the greatest drainage?
(b) Explain these results in terms of particle sizes.
(c) Which soil would be most likely to be waterlogged?
(d) Explain why sandy soil often needs lots of added fertiliser.

Q. 40.8

50 cm^3 of soil was placed in a graduated cylinder and 50 cm^3 of water was added. The result is shown in the diagram.

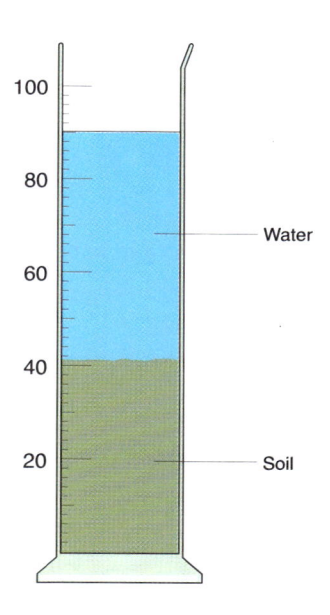

fig. 40.14

(a) What is the final volume in the cylinder?
(b) Why did the volume not rise to 100 cm^3?
(c) Calculate the percentage of air in the soil sample.

Q. 40.9

(a) What are micro-organisms?
(b) Name three types of micro-organism.
(c) Name the smallest type of micro-organism.

Q. 40.10

(a) How do viruses reproduce?
(b) Name five diseases caused by viruses.
(c) How does the body fight off viral diseases?
(d) Name the virus that causes AIDS. Explain how this virus (i) enters the body, (ii) affects the body, (iii) can be prevented from entering the body.

Q. 40.11

Suggest a reason for the following

(a) Viruses can pass through some sieves, while bacteria cannot.
(b) Antibiotics are not effective against the common cold.
(c) Bacteria and fungi are good for the soil.
(d) Fungi do not carry out photosynthesis.
(e) Instruments used in operating theatres must be sterile.
(f) It is dangerous to eat wild fungi.
(g) Bacteria are killed in the stomach.
(h) Dead plants and animals in bogs do not decay.
(i) Milk stays fresh longer in cold places.

Q. 40.12
Give six benefits and six disadvantages of micro-organisms.

Q. 40.13
An experiment was carried out to show the presence of bacteria in soil.
(a) Name the type of container used to grow the bacteria.
(b) Why is nutrient agar used.
(c) Why should you wash your hands before and after the experiment?
(d) Why should the container only be opened a small distance when adding the soil?
(e) Why are the containers sealed with tape?
(f) What is the reason for placing them in a warm place?
(g) If there was growth on the control what would you conclude?

Q. 40.14
(a) What are the functions of nitrogen, phosphorus and potassium in plants?
(b) Why would cabbage be given a high nitrogen fertiliser while strawberries are given potash (potassium)?

Q. 40.15
After applying fertiliser it is important that there should be slight rainfall, but not too much rain.
(a) Why is some rain beneficial?
(b) What is the name given to the problem caused by heavy rain when fertilizers have been spread on land?
(c) What type of soil suffers most from this problem?
(d) Explain how this problem can lead to soil pollution.

41
EARTH SCIENCE 1: ASTRONOMY

fig. 41.1 *The Milky Way galaxy*

OUR PLACE IN THE UNIVERSE

The Universe contains everything that exists. No one knows how big it is, or even if there is a limit to it. The Earth is just a very, very tiny part of the Universe. It is just one of nine planets orbiting a star which is called the Sun. The Sun is just one star in a group of millions of others which make up an enormous cluster of stars called the Milky Way galaxy. The Milky Way and the millions of other galaxies which exist make up the Universe. Astronomy is the study of the Universe.

Galaxies are very far apart. The nearest galaxy to the Milky Way is one called Andromeda which is two million light years away. This means that light from Andromeda takes two million years to reach us (travelling at the speed of 300 000 kilometres per second!). We are seeing Andromeda as it was two million years ago – before there were humans on Earth.

THE MOON

The Moon is a satellite of the Earth. A satellite is a body which travels around another body – in a path called an orbit. The diameter of the Moon is about one quarter of the Earth's diameter and its distance from Earth is about 410 000 kilometres. It revolves around the Earth every 28 days (approximately). It has no atmosphere and its force of gravity is about one sixth of that of the Earth. The Moon was first visited from Earth by an unmanned spacecraft in 1966 and by humans in 1969.

Phases of the Moon

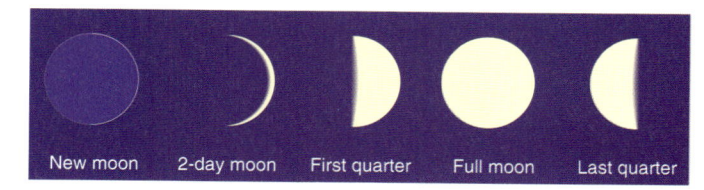

fig. 41.2 *Phases of the Moon*

When the Moon is viewed from Earth, its shape appears to change from night-to-night during the course of a month. Its different shapes as seen from Earth are called the **phases** of the Moon, which vary according to the relative position of the Moon and the Earth. The Moon only reflects the light of the Sun that falls on it, and at different times of the month, different amounts of the sunlit portion of the Moon are visible from Earth.

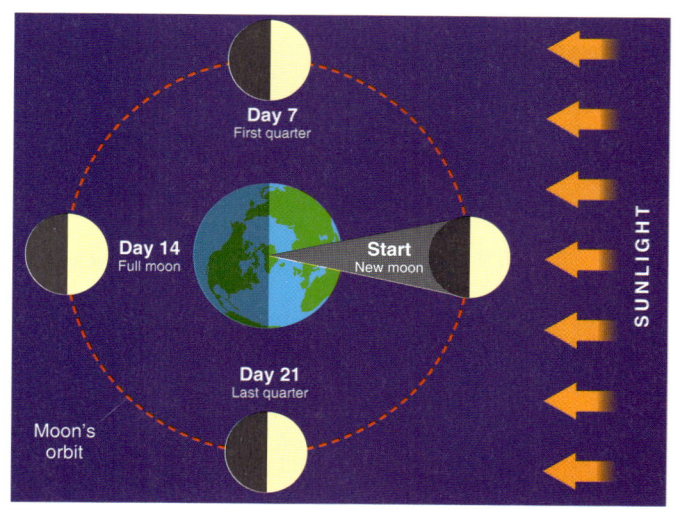

fig. 41.3 *The phases of the Moon are caused by the rotation of the Moon around the Earth*

When the Earth is in such a position that all of the illuminated part of the Moon can be seen, the Moon is described as being full. It then appears to be a bright round circle.

When the Earth is in such a position that the dark side of the Moon faces Earth, then little or none of the sunlight falling on it can be seen from Earth, and it is described as being **new**. The only light to be seen may be a small amount appearing around one side, making it look crescent-shaped.

Eclipses of the Moon

When you stand in front of a light you cast a shadow on whatever is behind you. The Earth and the Moon also cast shadows if there is something behind them. This is what happens during eclipses. The name **eclipse** refers to one body getting in the way of another.

An eclipse of the Moon, or **lunar eclipse**, occurs when the Moon passes into the Earth's shadow and the Earth blocks light from the Sun reaching it. A shadow of the Earth is then cast on the Moon. When this happens, the shape of the Earth's curved surface is seen on the Moon.

fig. 41.4 A lunar eclipse

Lunar eclipses are fairly common. On average, there are one or two every year. The dates of the next few are: 16 July 1997, 28 July 1999, 21 January 2000, 16 July 2000.

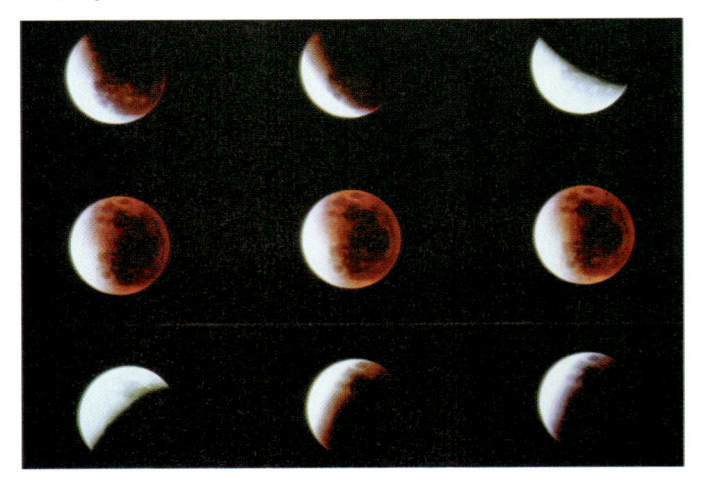

fig. 41.5 A series of nine photographs of the Moon taken during a lunar eclipse

Eclipses of the Sun

In an eclipse of the Sun, or **solar eclipse**, the shadow of the Moon falls on the Earth. The Moon then blocks out, for a while, the light from the Sun which should be reaching the Earth. Darkness occurs in the middle of the day, the stars can be seen, the temperature falls and the birds stop singing!

fig. 41.6 A solar eclipse

fig. 41.7 A series of five photographs of the Sun taken during a solar eclipse

Tides

People that live near the coast will be very familiar with the way that the level of the sea, or of a coastal river, rises and falls during the course of a day. High water level is described as the tide being in, and low water as the tide being out.

The tides are caused by the waters of the Earth being attracted to the Moon, and (to a smaller extent) the Sun. The attraction causes the water on the Earth to 'bulge' outwards towards the Moon, giving a region of high tide. (For reasons that don't matter here, there is also another high tide bulge on the opposite side of the Earth.) Because the Earth rotates once every 24 hours, every place has two high tides per day.

Applied Science • 41

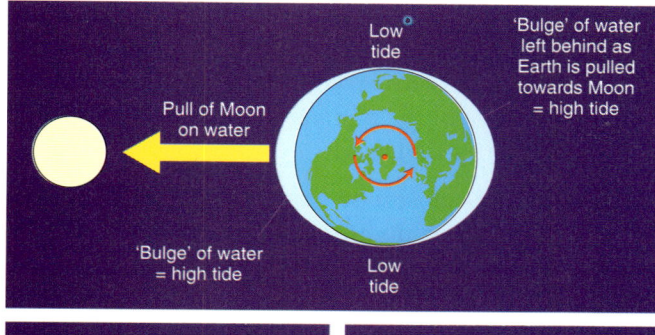

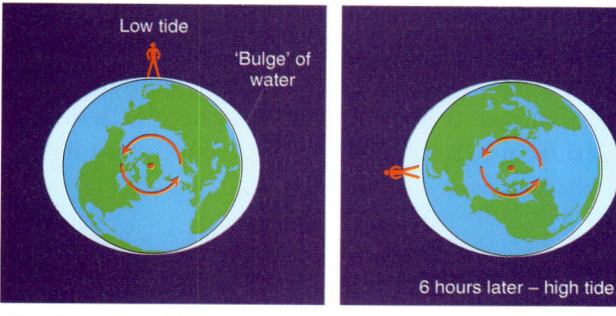

fig. 41.8 *The Moon causes the tides*

Spring and neap tides

The pull of the Sun on the waters of the Earth has also an effect. When both the Moon and the Sun are attracting the water in the same direction, a very high tide – a **spring tide** – occurs (Figure 41.9(a)). At other times, the Moon and the Sun are pulling at right angles to each other and the Sun therefore reduces the effect of the Moon. At such times, the high tide is much lower than normal and this is described as a **neap tide** (Figure 41.9(b)).

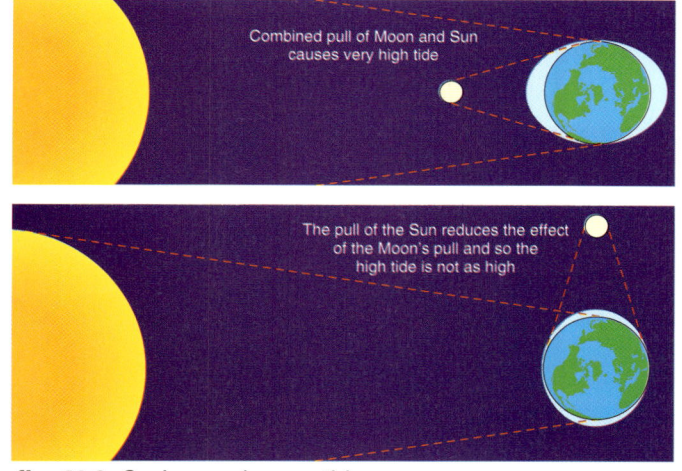

fig. 41.9 *Spring and neap tides*

THE SUN

The Sun is a star of medium size. It is composed of gases, and it produces heat and light from nuclear reactions which take place in its core. The temperature of the surface of the Sun is about 6000°C.

Day and night

Each day the Sun rises in the east, moves across the sky, and sets in the west – or so it seems. However, this is not so; the Sun does not move. It is the Earth spinning, or rotating on its axis, that causes day and night. On the side of the Earth facing the Sun and hence receiving light, it is daytime, whilst on the side away from the Sun where the light cannot reach, it is night-time. A day is 24 hours long because this is the time that the Earth takes to rotate once on its axis.

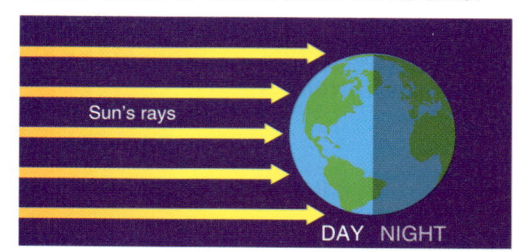

fig. 41.10 *America is in sunlight (it is daytime) while Europe and Africa are not (it is night-time)*

The seasons

The Earth revolves around the Sun every 365¼ days. As it does this, its north-south axis is slightly tilted (at 23½°), and this tilt is the cause of summer and winter.

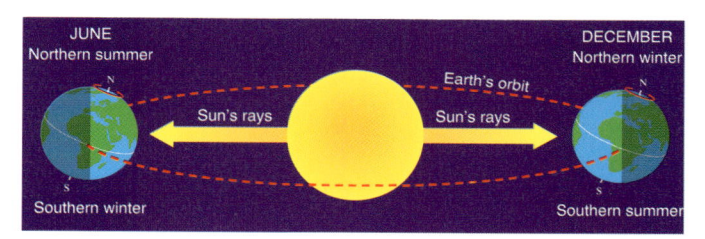

fig. 41.11 *Movement of the Earth around the Sun causes the seasons*

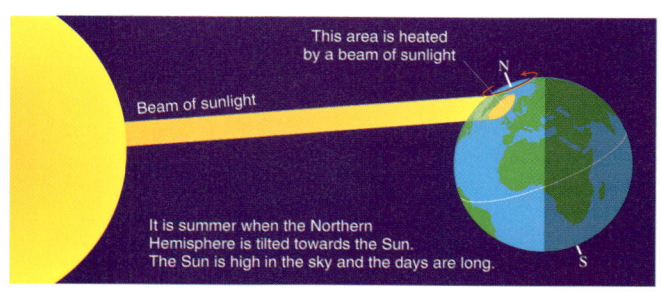

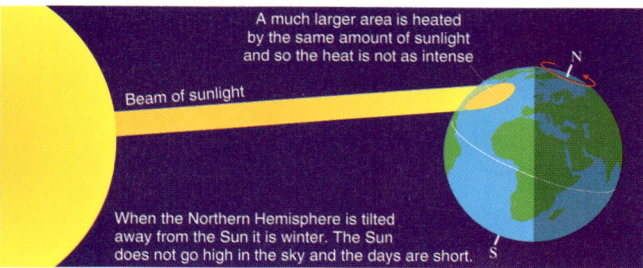

fig. 41.12

THE SOLAR SYSTEM

The Earth is just one of a series of planets which revolve around the Sun. The Solar System consists of the Sun and its nine planets (some of which have moons). Planets may look like stars but they are very different. They are much smaller than stars and do not shine by their own light. Like the Moon, they can be seen only because they reflect the light of the Sun that falls on them. The planets are all at different distances from the Sun, and they differ in diameter, gravity, atmosphere and temperature. The planets, in outwards order from the Sun are: **Mercury**, **Venus**, **Earth**, **Mars**, **Jupiter**, **Saturn**, **Uranus**, **Neptune** and **Pluto**.

The planets were noticed in ancient times. Early star-watchers picked them out because they moved against the background of ordinary 'fixed' stars. They discovered the first five of the planets or *wandering stars* and named them after their gods.

The two planets closest to the Sun are Mercury and Venus. **Mercury** has no atmosphere and is covered in craters. During the day it is baking hot; lead would melt on its surface. It travels quickly around the Sun, taking only 88 days to complete one orbit. **Venus**, sometimes called the evening star is next and can often be seen low in the sky at night, looking like a very bright star. It has a thick atmosphere with clouds of hot sulphuric acid. Nothing could survive on its hot poisonous surface.

Venus, Earth and Mars compared

Feature	Venus	Earth	Mars
Distance from Sun (compared with Earth's distance)	0.7	1	1.5
Diameter (compared to Earth's diameter)	0.95	1	0.53
Gravity (compared with Earth's gravity)	0.9	1	0.4
Time to orbit the Sun	225 days	1 year	nearly 2 years
Average temperature	450°C	20°C	−25°C
Atmosphere (main constituents)	CO_2, nitrogen, argon	oxygen, nitrogen	CO_2
Number of moons	0	1	2

Table of Comparisons

Planet	Diameter (Earth = 1)	Distance from Sun (Earth = 1)	Time to rotate once on axis	Time to orbit Sun ('year' length)	Mass (Earth = 1)	Surface gravity (Earth = 1)	Surface temp. (°C) (on sunny side)	Number of moons	Atmosphere
Mercury	0.4	0.4	59 days	88 days	0.1	0.4	350	0	None
Venus	0.95	0.7	243 days	225 days	0.8	0.9	480	0	CO_2, N_2,
Earth	1	1	24 hours	365 days	1.0	1.0	20	1	O_2, N_2, Ar
Mars	0.5	1.5	24 hours	2 years	0.1	0.4	−25	2	CO_2,
Jupiter	11	5	10 hours	12 years	320	2.6	−150	16	H_2, He
Saturn	9	9.5	10 hours	29 years	95	1.1	−180	about 20	H_2, He
Uranus	4	19	16 hours	84 years	15	0.9	−210	15	H_2, He
Neptune	4	30	19 hours	164 years	17	1.2	−220	8	H_2, He
Pluto	0.2	39	6 days	248 years	0.002	0.2	−230	1	None

Next past the Earth is Mars, often called the red planet because of the red rocks on its surface. It is much colder than Earth because it is further away from the Sun. It has large polar icecaps that can be seen through telescopes. **Jupiter** is an enormous planet. More than 1000 Earths could fit into its volume. When the Voyager 1 spacecraft flew by in 1979, it photographed active volcanoes. **Saturn** is best known for its rings, which are probably made up of fine rocks and ice particles. **Uranus** and **Neptune** come next. They are both big – about four times the size of Earth. The outermost planet and the smallest of them all is **Pluto**. Not that much is known about it. Its orbit is not quite circular like the others, and as well, its orbit overlaps, in places, the orbit of Neptune.

As far as is known, the Earth is the only planet capable of supporting life as we know it. The main reasons for this are that (i) it has an atmosphere containing oxygen, (ii) it has water, (iii) in most places, it has a suitable temperature.

THE LIFE OF A STAR

A star is not something that was always there and always will be. A star is 'born', has a life span, and eventually 'dies'. There are different types of star in the sky – young stars, stable period stars, red giants, white dwarfs and black dwarfs. From a study of these, astronomers have been able to work out what happens during the different stages of a star's life.

Stage 1. Formation

Space is not completely empty. There are particles of dust and tiny amounts of hydrogen and other gases floating about. A star, such as the Sun, is born out of a cloud of dust and gas, which, over millions of years have collected together. As gravity pulls the particles towards each other, the star starts to form, and the potential energy of all the particles changes to heat. The temperature rises, and eventually it gets so hot that nuclear reactions begin, and the hydrogen starts to 'fuse' into helium. The star has then been born and has started to shine.

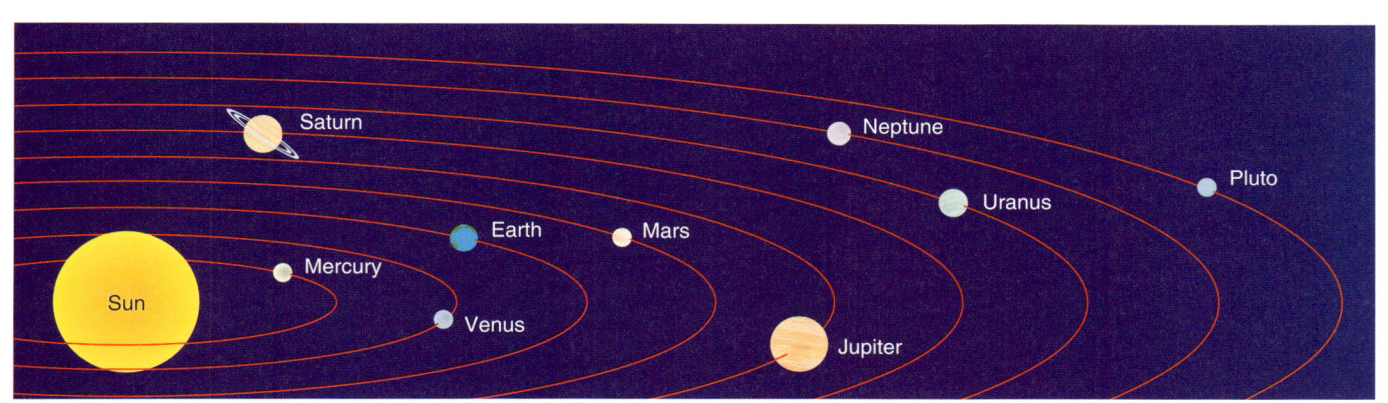

fig. 41.13 The solar system

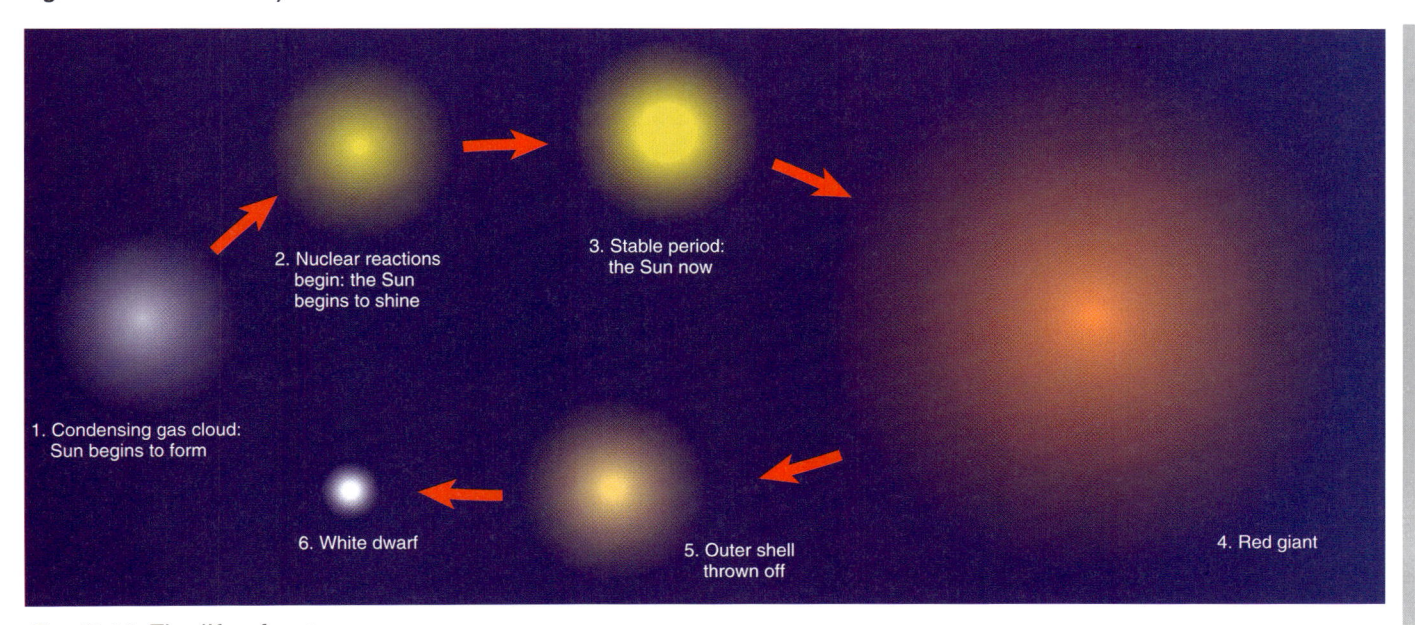

fig. 41.14 The life of a star

■ 41 • Earth Science 1: Astronomy

Stage 2. Stable period
Our Sun, which is a medium sized star, was formed in this way about 5000 million years ago, and it is estimated that it is about half way through its stable life.

Stage 3. Red giant
After millions of years, the hydrogen in the core gets used up, and the nuclear reactions spread outwards, releasing more heat, and causing the star to expand. It now becomes a huge star called a **red giant**. When this happens to the Sun, it will spread outwards and engulf the Earth. The oceans will evaporate and all living things on the planet will be burnt up.

Stage 4. White dwarf
The outer layers will use up their energy first and will be thrown off, to drift into outer space. Left behind will be the small dense core called a **white dwarf** – a star about the size of the Earth, but having a mass of about that of the present Sun. A cupful of such matter would weigh several tonnes.

SUMMARY

- The **Earth** is one of the nine planets that orbit the Sun. The **Sun** is just one star amongst millions of other stars which make up the **Milky Way** galaxy. The Milky Way is just one galaxy amongst millions of others which make up the **Universe**.

- The Earth spins on its axis every 24 hours, causing day and night.

- The **Moon** is a satellite of the Earth and orbits it every 28 days. It is about one quarter the size of the Earth and is about 400 000 kilometres distant. The Moon can be seen because it reflects light from the Sun which falls on it. During the course of a month, different amounts of the illuminated face of the Moon are visible from Earth; it therefore appears different and its different appearances are called the **phases of the Moon**.

- The Moon is the main cause of the tides – which are caused by the waters of the Earth being attracted towards it. The Sun also has an effect on the tides.

- An eclipse is the result of one body getting in the way of another. A **lunar eclipse** occurs when the Earth gets in between the Sun and the Moon (and casts a shadow on the Moon). A **solar eclipse** occurs when the Moon gets in between the Sun and the Earth and blocks sunlight from reaching the Earth.

(continued)

- The Sun, like other stars, does not move. Planets move around the Sun. The nine planets in the Solar System are **Mercury, Venus, Earth, Mars, Jupiter, Saturn, Uranus, Neptune** and **Pluto**.

QUESTIONS

Q. 41.1
Rewrite the following sentences and fill in the missing words.
(a) The Universe is grouped into clusters of ____ called ____ .
(b) The Solar System consists of ____ planets which ____ around the ____ .
(c) The two planets nearest the Earth are ____ and ____ .
(d) The Solar System is part of a galaxy called the __ __.

Q. 41.2
Copy out and complete the following paragraphs.
(a) The Earth rotates on its axis once every __ __ . This motion causes __ and __ . It is __ time on the side of the Earth facing the __ and __ time on the opposite side. As well as rotating on its axis, the Earth orbits the __ and the time it takes to make one revolution is __ __ . The __ result from the fact that the Earth's axis is tilted. When it is __ time, the axis is tilted towards the __ and in the __ the axis tilts away from the __ .
(b) The __ is a body which rotates around the Earth and it does so every __ days. This body has no light of its own; it can be seen only because of the light from the __ being reflected from it. The Moon's appearance changes from night to night and the different appearances are called the __ of the __. When all of the illuminated side can be seen from __ , the Moon is described as being __ and when only a small amount of light coming around the edge is visible, it is described as a __ __ . The two stages in between are called the first __ and the __ __ .
(c) The __ is a satellite of the Earth; this means that it __ around the Earth. Its distance from Earth is about __ miles. There is no air there and spacemen who went to it had to bring __ with them. They were able to jump about quite easily because the force of __ there is much __ than on Earth.

Q. 41.3
Explain with the aid of a diagram how day and night occur.

Q. 41.4
Explain why:
(a) A day is 24 hours long.
(b) There is one full moon every 28 days.
(c) A year is $365\frac{1}{4}$ days in length.
(d) Venus's year is much shorter than Earth's year
(e) Mars's year is longer than Earth's year.
(f) The Sun rises in the East.
(g) A spring tide occurs once each month.
(h) The north pole has constant darkness for 6 months of the year.

Q. 41.5
In the form of a table, compare the Earth, the Moon and Mars with regard to:
(i) distance from the Sun, (ii) diameter, (iii) gravity, (iv) surface temperature, (v) atmosphere, (vi) number of moons.

Q. 41.6
(a) What must the phase of the Moon be when (i) a lunar eclipse, (ii) a solar eclipse, occurs?
(b) What type of high tide occurs when the Moon is (i) full, (ii) new, (iii) last quarter?

Q. 41.7
Which planet:
(a) is the largest?
(b) is the smallest?
(c) is closest to the Sun?
(d) is furthest from the Sun?
(e) has the shortest day?
(f) moves around the Sun in the shortest time?
(g) has the shortest year?
(h) is the hottest?
(i) has the greatest number of moons?
(j) is nearest the Earth?

Q. 41.8
Explain with the aid of a diagram how the seasons are caused.

Q. 41.9
Draw diagrams to explain what causes (i) an eclipse of the Sun, (ii) an eclipse of the Moon. What would be observed during each of these eclipses?

Q. 41.10
(a) In what direction: (i) does the Sun rise? (ii) is the Sun at midday? (iii) does the Sun set?
(b) Which of these differ if you are living in Australia in the southern hemisphere?

Q. 41.11
Why is the Earth suitable for supporting life? Explain why is life not possible on:
(i) the Moon, (ii) Venus, (iii) Mars, (iv) Jupiter.

Q. 41.12
(a) What are the four main stages of a star's life?
(b) At which stage is the Sun at present?
(c) Towards the end of its life, a star becomes fainter and fainter and eventually dies. Why does this happen?

Q. 41.13
List two differences between stars and planets. Name any star and any planet and say where each is found.

EARTH SCIENCE 2: THE ATMOSPHERE

MOISTURE IN THE ATMOSPHERE

There is always moisture in the air. Even on a hot dry day there is a small amount present. Evaporation of water from seas, rivers and lakes is constantly occurring and this puts water vapour into the air. The water cycle has been described in Chapter 22 (page 156) and you should make sure that you understand it and know why it is called a cycle. Evaporation of water is an essential part of the cycle.

Evaporation is the changing of a liquid to a vapour. Heat and wind speed up evaporation. Clothes on a line dry best on warm, dry, windy days.

Condensation is the changing of a vapour to a liquid. It happens most easily in cold and moist conditions. It is a common observation that moisture condenses on a cold bathroom mirror after you have had a shower. In winter when you breathe into cold air your breath becomes visible. This is because the water vapour (invisible) that is present in breath condenses into tiny droplets of water – which can be seen.

The **hygrometer** (described on page 297) is an instrument that measures the amount of water vapour in the air.

CLOUDS, FOG AND FROST

Air can only hold a certain amount of water vapour. When it is holding as much as it is able, it is said to be **saturated**. Warm air can hold more water vapour than cold air. When air is cooled sufficiently, the water vapour present condenses, to form dew or frost, clouds, fog or mist.

Dew and frost

When water vapour in the atmosphere comes into contact with cold ground (e.g. during a cold night), it condenses and forms **dew**. You see dew on the ground, and on cars and roofs on autumn mornings after the temperature has been low at night. If the temperature is below freezing point, the vapour condenses directly to a solid and **frost** is the result.

Experiment 42.1
To investigate the best conditions for evaporation

Part 1

Wet a sheet of filter paper by spreading (from a dropper) 2 cm³ of water over its surface. Weigh the filter paper. Hang it up where it is not in a draught. After one minute, remove it and then reweigh it. Calculate its loss in mass, i.e. the mass of water which evaporated from it.

Part 2

Repeat the procedure of part 1, but when the paper is hanging up, blow cold air over it from a hair dryer. As before, find its loss in mass.

Part 3

Again repeat the procedure of part 1, but this time blow hot air over the paper when it is hanging up. Find its loss in mass.

Part 4

This time, fold the paper about three times before hanging it up. Blow cold air over it as before, and find its loss in mass.

What can you conclude about the effect of:
(i) temperature, (ii) wind, (iii) surface area, on evaporation?

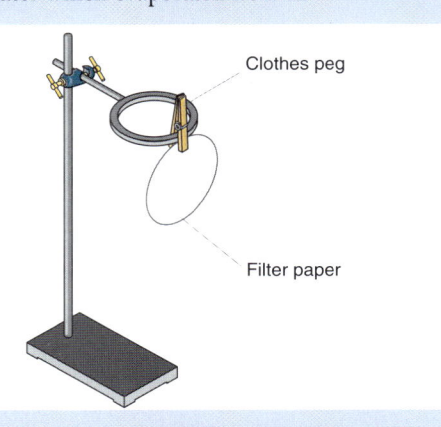

fig. 42.1

Applied Science • 42

Fog

When air is cooled, the water vapour present will often condense on the particles of dust that are always present. If this happens near the ground, the condensation is called **fog**.

Clouds and rain

When water vapour rises high into the atmosphere, it becomes cooled due to the altitude. The water vapour then condenses to become clouds. The vapour forms into tiny droplets of water that are so light they float about in the air. These droplets come together and form clouds. When the droplets in the cloud become large enough, they fall to the earth as rain.

Types of cloud

The main types of cloud are cirrus, cumulus, stratus and nimbus.

Cirrus

Cumulus

Stratus

fig. 42.2

Nimbus

Cirrus clouds are the thin and wispy or featherlike ones. They are very high (16 km or higher) and are composed of ice crystals.

Cumulus clouds are the puffy or 'piled up' clouds, rather like cotton wool.

Stratus clouds are sheetlike and consist of layers of cloud. Stratus clouds frequently cover the Irish countryside.

Nimbus clouds are rain bearing. They are low (usually under 2 km) and are dark coloured.

Alto means 'high' so, for instance, altocumulus are high cumulus clouds.

Experiment 42.2
To show cloud formation

In this experiment, air is compressed (this causes it to heat slightly), cooled back to room temperature and then allowed to suddenly expand. Expansion causes cooling, and as this happens, the water vapour which is present in the air condenses and forms a cloud.

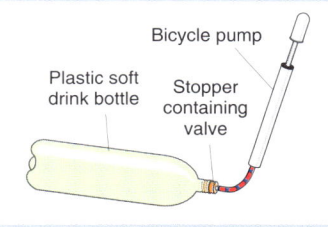

fig. 42.3

Arrange the apparatus as shown. Make sure that the stopper is really tight. Pump about 30 to 40 pumpfuls of air into the bottle and then remove the pump (but not the stopper containing the valve). Then run cold water over the bottle to cool it. Place the bottle in front of a black surface and suddenly pull out the stopper; as the air expands, it cools and a cloud is formed in the bottle. The cloud evaporates quickly so watch carefully as the stopper is being removed

42 • Earth Science 2: The Atmosphere

PROPERTIES OF GASES

In previous chapters (10, 12 and 17) several properties of gases were described; important properties of gases are:

- gases do not have fixed volumes; they fill any space into which they are put
- gases expand when heated and contract when cooled
- increasing the pressure of a gas reduces its volume (this is called compressing it)

The volume of a gas therefore depends on its temperature and pressure. Robert Boyle, a famous Irish scientist who lived in the 17th century, investigated how the volume of a gas depends on pressure, and in the next century, a famous Frenchman, Professor Jacques Charles, investigated how its volume depends on temperature.

Experiment 42.3
To investigate how volume depends on pressure

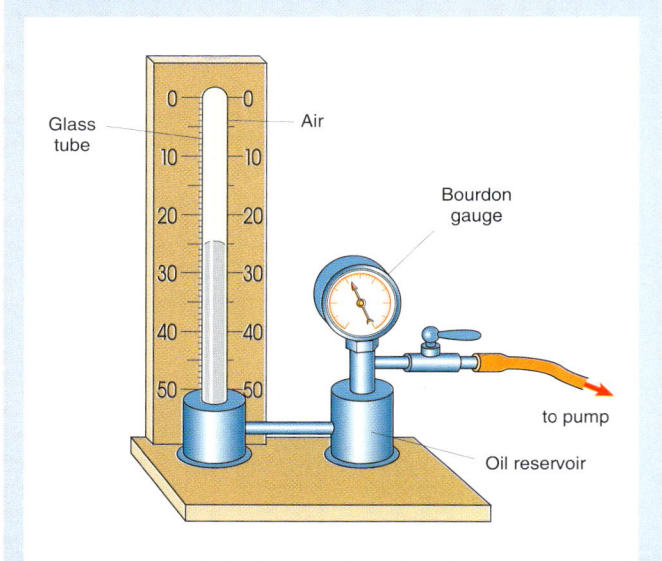

fig. 42.4

The apparatus used for this investigation is shown above. A fixed amount of air is trapped inside the glass tube. The pressure of the air inside the apparatus is changed by compressing it with a pump, and the value of that air pressure is read on the pressure gauge. Every time the pressure is changed, the volume of the air is read on the scale which is alongside it. In this way, six or more pairs of readings of pressure and volume are taken.

The following is a specimen set of readings:

Pressure (kPa)	40	60	80	100	120	140	160	180
Volume (cm³)	60	40	30	24	20	17.1	15	13.3

The best method of finding how one variable depends on another is to plot a graph of them, and so a graph is plotted of the volume of the air against its pressure. When this is done, the result is like that shown below. You can see that as the pressure gets greater, the volume gets smaller. This sort of relationship is described as 'inversely proportional'.

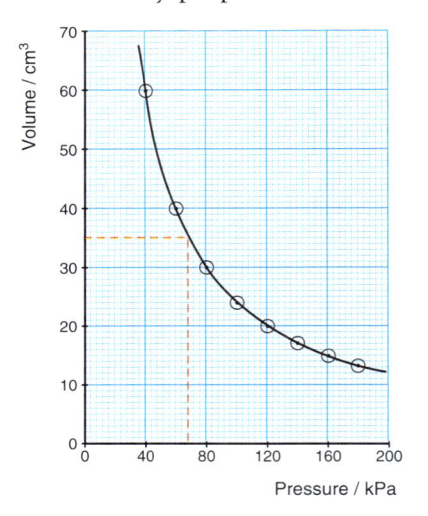

fig. 42.5

You should now, from your own graph, select any three points on it (preferably spaced some distance apart. From each of the three points, read off (i) the volume, and (ii) the pressure. Then multiply these two values together. How to do this is shown on the graph in Figure 42.5.

If you have worked accurately, you should have discovered that pressure multiplied by volume gives the same answer every time. This is what Boyle discovered 300 years ago, and it is known as **Boyle's law**. It states:

> **When a fixed mass of gas is kept at constant temperature, its volume multiplied by its pressure is constant.**

Mathematically the law can be expressed as pV is constant, but a more useful form of it is:

$$p_1V_1 = p_2V_2$$

Knowing the relationship between the two quantities, you can work out problems like this: if the pressure of a gas changes from 100 kPa to 200 kPa, what happens its volume? If you decided that the volume was halved, you were correct. Boyle's law calculations are done as follows:

Worked example

Q. At a pressure of 100 kPa, some gas occupies a pressure of 600 cm^3. What volume will it have when the pressure is 96 kPa?

A. The formula that relates pressure and volume is $p_1V_1 = p_2V_2$. Since three of the values in the equation are given in the question, the remaining one can be calculated:

$$100 \times 600 = 96 \times x, \text{ therefore}$$

$$x = \frac{100 \times 600}{96}$$

$$= 625 \text{ cm}^3$$

QUESTIONS

Q. 42.1
Some gas occupies a volume of 400 cm^3 when the pressure is 2400 Pa. What will be its volume when the pressure is reduced to 2000 Pa?

Q. 42.2
The volume of a gas is 60 cm^3 when the pressure is 100 kPa.
(a) What will the volume be when the pressure changes to (i) 50 kPa, (ii) 300 kPa, (iii) 120 kPa?
(b) At what pressure will the volume be (i) 30 cm^3, (ii) 40 cm^3, (iii) 80 cm^3?

fig. 42.6

Robert Boyle (1627–1691) was born in Lismore Castle in Co. Waterford. He was the first person to realise that most substances are combinations of a number of simple substances or *elements*. He became known as the 'Father of Chemistry'. He investigated the nature of air and discovered that if air is pumped out of a vessel, a candle will not burn in it and that sound will not pass through it. His best known investigation was on the 'spring of the air' and he discovered that the volume of a given amount of air depends on the pressure. Other discoveries were that there are two types of electric charges, that water expands when it freezes, and that increased pressure raises the boiling point of a liquid.

Experiment 42.4
To investigate how volume depends on temperature

The apparatus for this investigation is shown in Figure 42.7. The temperature of the air inside the glass tube is changed by immersing it in a cylinder of water, which is then heated up in stages. The temperature is read on the thermometer, which is part of the apparatus. For each value of the temperature used, the volume of the gas is read on the scale which is alongside the tube of air. In this way, six or more pairs of readings of volume and temperature are taken.

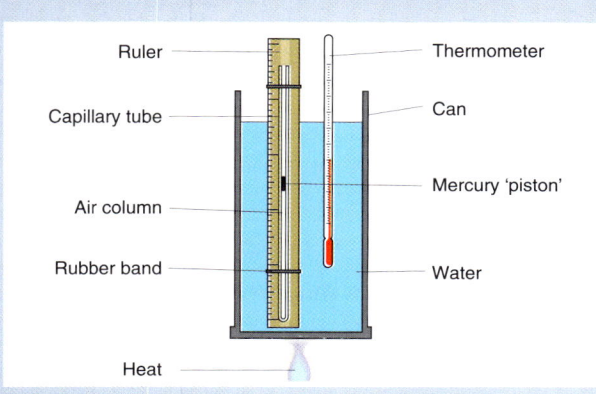

fig. 42.7

42 • Earth Science 2: The Atmosphere

The following is a specimen set of readings:

Temperature (°C)	10	20	30	40	50	60	70	80	90
Volume (cm³)	20.7	21.4	22.1	22.8	23.5	24.2	24.9	25.6	26.3

A graph is now drawn to show how the volume of the gas depends on the temperature, and when this is done, the result is like that shown below. You can see that as temperature gets greater, the volume also gets greater. The two variables (volume and temperature) are said to be proportional to each other.

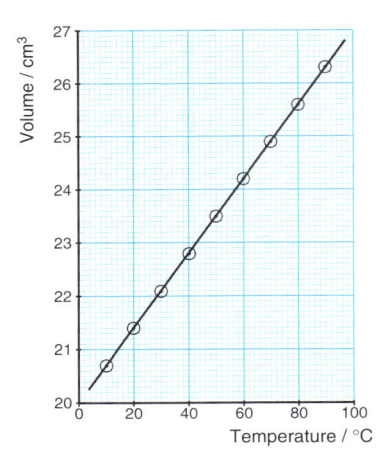

fig. 42.8

However, the graph does not pass through the origin. This means that although volume is proportional to temperature, it is not proportional to the **Celsius** temperature. If the graph is produced backwards, it cuts the temperature axis at −273°C, or put another way, the volume would be zero at a temperature of −273°C. A Scottish scientist, Lord Kelvin, proposed a scale with its zero at this point. This scale is called the Kelvin scale of temperature. Using the Kelvin scale, the volume of a gas is directly proportional to the temperature. This relationship was discovered by a French scientist, Professor Charles, and is called **Charles' law**. It states:

> **When a fixed mass of gas is kept at a constant temperature, its volume is directly proportional to the temperature on the Kelvin scale.**

LAND AND SEA BREEZES

Have you ever wondered why there always appears to be a breeze at the seaside? Coastal breezes result from natural convection currents which are set up by the Sun. During the day the temperature of the land increases more than that of the sea. The hot air above the land rises and is then replaced by colder air blowing in from the sea.

At night the opposite happens. The sea remains at an almost constant temperature while the land cools considerably. The sea is thus warmer than the land and the air above the sea rises. To replace that air, a breeze blows out from the land towards the sea.

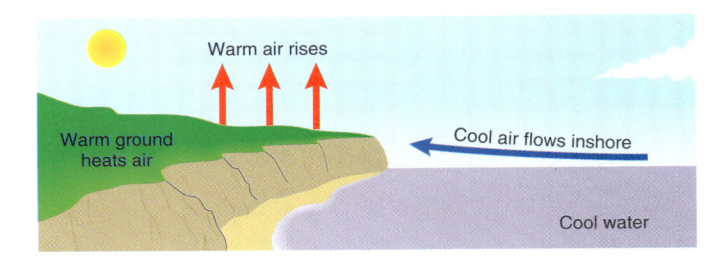

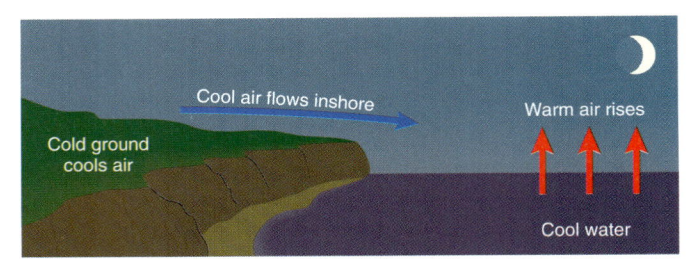

fig. 42.9

ATMOSPHERIC PRESSURE

This topic is explained in Chapter 12 and you should revise it. Things to be remembered are:

- Atmospheric pressure is measured with a barometer. A barometer works like a see-saw; atmospheric pressure is balanced by the weight of a column of mercury. The height of the column changes as the atmospheric pressure changes (description on page 82).

- Pressure can be expressed in:
    (i) millimetres of mercury (the height of the mercury in the barometer),
    (ii) pascals (these are the scientific pressure units – N/m^2),
    (iii) millibars or hectopascals, the units used by meteorologists or 'weathermen'.

- Normal atmospheric pressure is 760 mmHg or 100 kilopascals or 1000 millibars.

- Isobars are lines on a map drawn through places of equal atmospheric pressure.

- Atmospheric pressure decreases with altitude. At the top of Mount Everest for instance, the pressure is only about one quarter of what it is at sea-level.

WEATHER AND CLIMATE

Everyone takes an interest in the weather, particularly in places like Ireland where the weather often changes from day to day, or even from hour to hour. Weather is the state of the atmosphere at any given time or place, whereas the climate of an area is the average of its weather conditions over a long period of time.

How do meteorologists predict the weather, and why do they sometimes get it wrong? Weather forecasters use many instruments including:

- **barometers**, which give the value of atmospheric pressure
- **thermometers**, which show the atmospheric temperature
- **hygrometers**, which measure the amount of water vapour in the atmosphere
- **anemometers**, which measure wind speed
- **wind vanes**, which show the wind direction

Meteorologists also make use of weather satellites that take infra-red photographs of the Earth beneath them. These show up clouds and regions of warmer and/or cooler air. Clouds give very good clues about the type of weather that can be expected, and the various cloud types have been described on page 293.

WEATHER MEASURING INSTRUMENTS

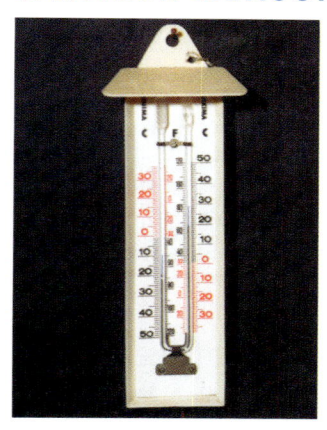

(a) A **maximum and minimum thermometer** shows the highest and the lowest temperatures that occurred since it was last set.

(b) A **hygrometer** measures humidity. The simple type consists of two thermometers, one normal, and the other with its bulb kept wet. Evaporation of the moisture on the wet bulb causes cooling, so it shows a lower temperature than that shown by the dry bulb. The difference in the temperatures shown by the two thermometers is related to the amount of moisture in the air.

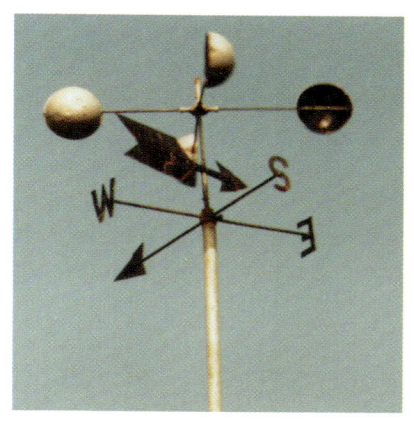

(c) An **anemometer** measures wind speed and a **weather** vane shows its direction. The photograph shows the two devices on the one mast.

(d) A **rain gauge** measures the amount of rain that has fallen since the gauge was last read and reset. When you hear on the radio that '1 cm of rain' fell, it means that if the rain were allowed to pile up, it would be 1 cm in depth. A simple rain gauge is shown in the diagram. It is used by being left out in the open (well away from buildings), and reading the height of the water in the cylinder after rain has fallen.

(e) Thermometers will give a false reading if the bulbs are in direct sunlight and to prevent this happening at a weather station, they are enclosed in a **Stevenson screen.** This is a box which is mounted above the ground, and has louvered sides so that air can circulate freely through it.

fig. 42.10

ENERGY FROM THE SUN, THE GREENHOUSE EFFECT AND GLOBAL WARMING

The Earth receives its energy from the Sun. Only about 50% of the energy that comes to the planet actually reaches its surface – the other 50% is absorbed by the atmosphere or reflected back into space. The 50% that does reach the Earth's surface is retained because of a property of the atmosphere called the **greenhouse effect**.

The greenhouse – a trap for heat

The glass of a greenhouse lets through the short wavelength radiation that comes from the Sun. Inside the greenhouse, these rays are absorbed by the plants and the soil, to produce heat. The soil, when it becomes warmed, gives off heat or infra-red rays. However, because the soil is not very hot (compared to the Sun), these rays have much longer wavelengths, and such rays cannot get out through the glass. So, energy can get in but not out, and therefore the temperature rises. (In time, heat escapes by conduction through the glass.)

The same effect keeps the Earth warm – at a comfortable 20°C or so, on average. The difference is that where a greenhouse is covered by a layer of glass, the Earth is covered by a layer of gases called the atmosphere. And in this atmosphere is carbon dioxide which acts like the glass of a greenhouse.

A problem that has arisen in the twentieth century is that the amount of carbon dioxide in the atmosphere is increasing. This is due to the increasing amounts of fossil fuels that have been burnt in the last fifty years or so. There is more traffic on the roads, more aircraft in the sky, more ships on the seas, and more coal and oil-burning power stations – all releasing enormous amounts of CO_2 into the atmosphere. And it is being released at a greater rate than it can be removed by photosynthesis.

This extra CO_2 has resulted in the Earth's temperature increasing – a problem called **global warming**. Scientists are concerned that in time the effect could have serious consequences, like the melting of polar ice, which would lead to a rise in sea level. This could cause the flooding of low-lying countries like Holland and Bangladesh.

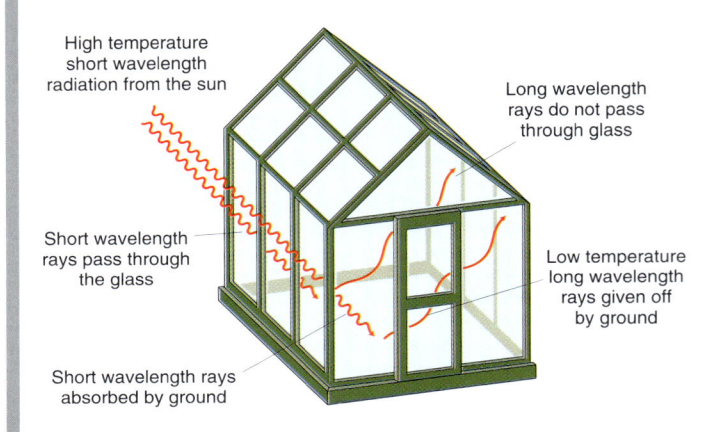

fig. 42.11 How a greenhouse traps heat

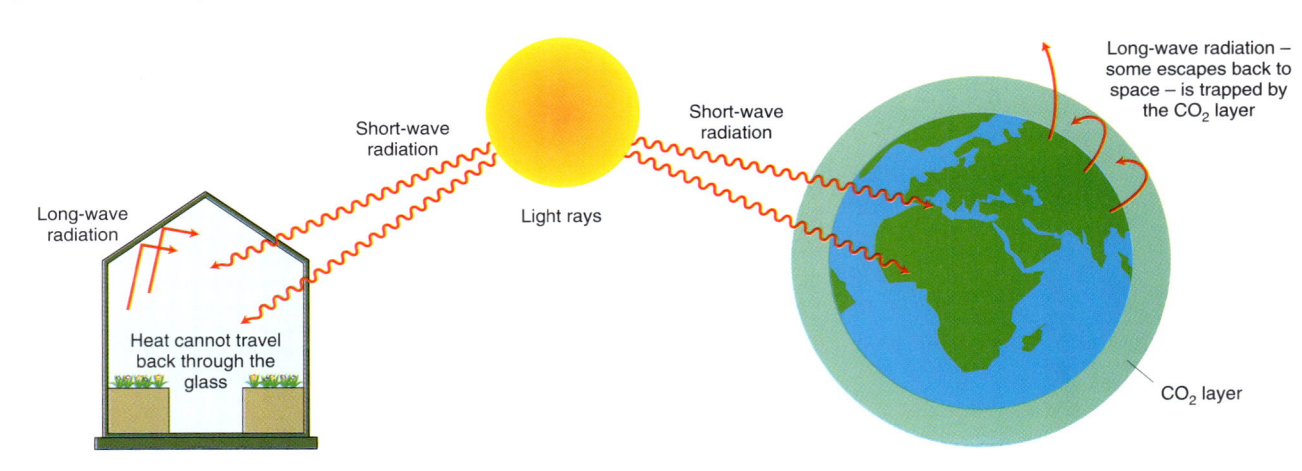

fig. 42.12 The greenhouse effect

SUMMARY

- There is always moisture in the atmosphere, caused by evaporation of water from the Earth. Heat and wind speed up evaporation. Condensation is the changing of vapour to liquid. Clouds, fog, dew and frost are caused by water vapour from the atmosphere condensing.
- The four main types of cloud are **cirrus**, **cumulus**, **stratus** and **nimbus**. The formation of cloud can be shown by allowing cold compressed air to expand suddenly – when it cools the water vapour condenses.

(continued)

- The volume of a gas depends on its pressure and its temperature. **Boyle's law** relates volume and pressure, and **Charles' law** relates volume and temperature.
- Land and sea breezes are caused by convection currents.
- Instruments used in meteorology (weather forecasting) include: **barometers** (to measure atmospheric pressure), **thermometers** (measure temperature), **hygrometers** (measure humidity), **anemometers** (measure wind speed), wind **vanes** (show wind direction).
- The Earth's atmosphere acts like a greenhouse; solar radiation can easily pass through it, but heat radiation from the Earth cannot so easily escape. This effect (called the greenhouse effect) is responsible for keeping the Earth at a comfortable temperature. The amount of carbon dioxide in the atmosphere is increasing and causing a temperature rise on Earth. In time, this could have serious ill effects.

QUESTIONS

Q. 42.3
Which of the following conditions would be the most suitable for drying clothes outside?
(a) a dry day or a moist day
(b) a hot or a cold day
(c) a windy or a still day
(d) to spread the clothes out or to fold them

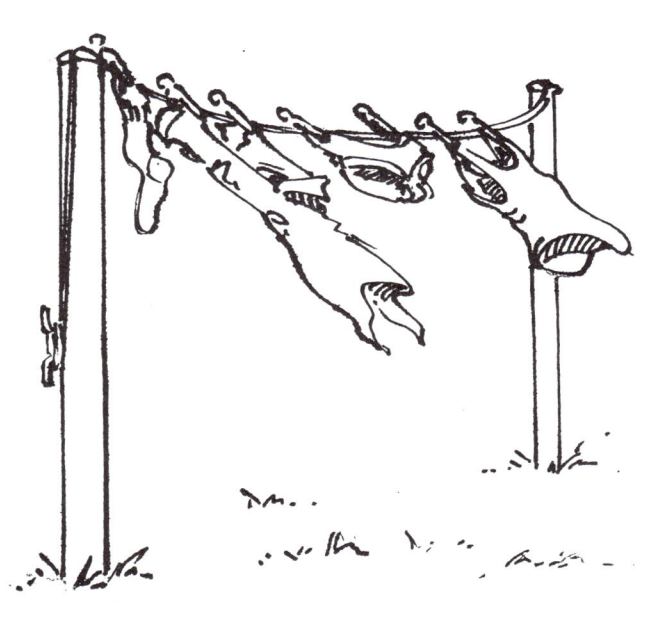

fig. 42.13

Q. 42.4
What is meant by condensation? Explain what each of the following consists of, and how it is formed: frost, fog, dew, clouds.

Q. 42.5
Describe an experiment to show cloud formation. How and why does this change occur in nature?

Q. 42.6
Describe the following types of cloud, and explain how they differ from each other: cirrus, cumulus, nimbus.

Q. 42.7
What is measured by each of the following?
(a) barometer
(b) thermometer
(c) hygrometer
(d) anemometer
(e) rain gauge
Draw a diagram of each instrument.

Q. 42.8
Name three measurements made of the atmosphere which are used in forecasting the weather. Describe how each of these is obtained.

Q. 42.9
Describe how you would set about keeping a record of the rainfall at a place over a period of time.

Q. 42.10
What is the greenhouse effect, and why are the peoples of the world dependent on it?

Q. 42.11
What is Boyle's law? Describe a laboratory experiment to demonstrate it.

Q. 42.12
Explain why:
(a) A beach ball may burst if left in the sun.
(b) There is no weather on the Moon.
(c) Co. Kerry is the wettest area of Ireland.
(d) Frost is unusual in summer.
(e) It never rains on the top of Mount Everest.
(f) Condensation forms on the surface of a mirror if you breathe on it.

HORTICULTURE 1

Horticulture is the study of how to grow plants. It includes the growing of indoor plants, gardening (lawns, shrubs and flowers, vegetables, fruits), commercial growing (nurseries for trees, bushes, flowers or farmers growing cereal or vegetable crops) and amenity horticulture (growing plants for enjoyment and leisure, e.g. parks, playing pitches, golf courses).

Growing medium

Plants need a material (**medium**) in which to grow. The growth material should provide (a) water, (b) nutrients, (c) air, (d) support. Examples of growth media are soil, compost and water.

The roots of a plant absorb water and dissolved minerals from the growing medium. This water passes up through the stem and into the leaves. The loss of water from the leaves is called **transpiration**. The flow of water from the roots, to the stem and out of the leaves is called the **transpiration stream**. Transpiration provides the plant (especially the leaves) with water for photosynthesis, and minerals for growth. It also helps to cool the plant in summer.

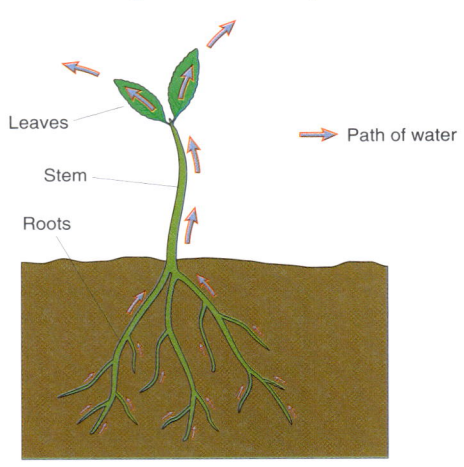

fig. 43.1 *Transpiration stream*

Air is needed in the growing medium so that the roots can respire. Roots use the energy from respiration for growth and to absorb minerals. If the roots have no air they (and the plant) will die.

The normal growth medium for a plant is soil. Many aspects of soil are dealt with in Chapter 40, which should be studied at the same time as this chapter.

Soil can be described as sandy, clay or loam. Sand particles are quite large. This provides large spaces between the soil particles. As a result these soils are light, easy to dig, aerated, well drained and easy for roots to penetrate. However they can dry out too quickly and suffer from a lack of minerals.

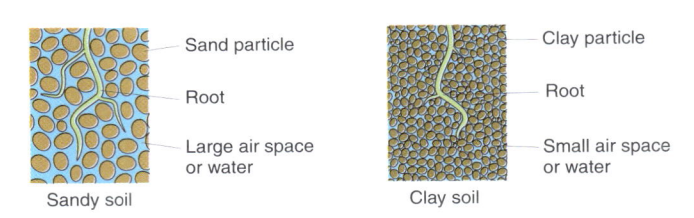

fig. 43.2 *Clay and sandy soil*

Clay particles are small and as a result, clay soils are compact, heavy, hard to dig, low in air, easily waterlogged and hard for roots to penetrate. They retain moisture and minerals.

Loam is a mixture of sand, silt and clay bound together with humus. It is the best soil for plants, having most of the advantages and none of the disadvantages listed above. Loam should be crumbly when broken between the fingers (i.e. it should have a good crumb structure, like bread).

Composts

Other growing media can be used apart from soil. These man-made media are called composts. Natural compost is made by mixing soft plant parts such as cut grass, dead flowers and hedge clippings with soil in a damp, but well aerated, container. When the material rots it forms natural compost.

fig. 43.3 *Compost heaps*

Artificial composts are often used because they are sterile. This means that they have been treated to kill micro-organisms and pests. Natural compost may contain micro-organisms and pests that can cause disease.

Peat is the basis of most composts. It is sterile and holds water and air very well. However it contains few nutrients and will not absorb water easily if it dries out.

Other materials are often mixed with peat. These include nutrients, sand (to improve drainage), perlite (white/grey granules of volcanic rock which also improve drainage) and vermiculite (a brown rock which absorbs large amounts of water and air). Different composts contain varying amounts of these materials and are used for different functions, e.g. rooting compost (equal amounts of peat and sand), compost for germinating seeds and general growing compost.

fig. 43.4 *Cuttings being planted in rooting compost*

Hydroponics

Hydroponics is the growing of plants without soil. Instead of soil, nutrient-rich water is used. Often the plant is supported by an inert (non-living) material such as vermiculite or sand. Hydroponic vegetables and flowers are grown in glasshouses.

Hydroponics allows plants to be grown without the danger of disease and pests, and under ideal conditions of light, temperature and humidity. Also, the plants can be grown near the area of use, saving on transport costs. Plants are often grown hydroponically in areas of poor soil.

The main disadvantage is cost. A hydroponic system is expensive to set up and to maintain the necessary levels of light, heat and aeration in the water.

Plant nutrients

The main plant nutrients are nitrogen (for leaves), phosphorus (for roots) and potassium (potash, for fruits and flowers). Other mineral nutrients needed by plants include sulphur, calcium, magnesium, iron, copper, zinc, manganese and boron. These are normally found in nutrient-rich soils. A lack of any of these nutrients causes the plant to turn yellow and have stunted growth. See Experiment 36.6, page 251.

Mulches

A mulch is a layer of material spread on top of the soil to prevent light from reaching the soil. It is used to stop weeds growing in the soil. Very often weeds grow faster than cultivated plants, so weed control is essential. Mulches also help to retain moisture in the soil.

In the past mulches were made from leaves, bark, grass cuttings, sawdust, peat or gravel. In all cases the mulch itself must be free of weeds and their seeds. Some of these mulches are too light and blow away easily. Nowadays black polythene is often used. The polythene is covered with a thin layer of compost or gravel to improve the appearance.

Growth medium	Advantages	Disadvantages
Soil	Cheap, may have nutrients	May not have correct composition. Soils can be very different
Natural compost	Definite composition. Rich in nutrients	May have diseases, pests or weeds. More costly than soil
Sterile compost	Definite composition. Sterile (nothing living)	Costly. Need to select the correct type
Water	Sterile. Total control of growing conditions	Costly. Complicated to set up

Mulch	Advantage	Disadvantage
Leaves	Prevent weed growth Form humus	Can cause fungus growth May shelter pests
Bark	Prevents weed growth Retains water in soil	May be blown away May be source of disease or pests
Plastic	Blocks out all light Long lasting	Unsightly More difficult to put down

Mulches result in the improved growth of cultivated plants, due to lack of weeds, and the presence of extra water in the soil under the mulch. They also reduce the time needed for hand weeding or hoeing.

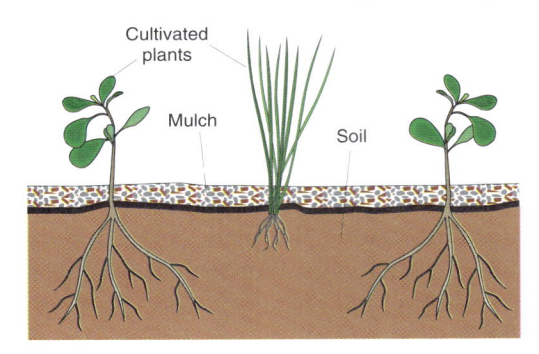

fig. 43.5

Plant diseases and pests

Plants are affected by a large number of diseases. These can be caused by fungi (mostly), bacteria and/or viruses. Root diseases are more difficult to detect and control. Diseases of the aerial parts are easier to detect and control, but can still be very damaging to the growth and appearance of the plant.(Aerial parts are the parts of the plant above ground.)

Plant pests include aphids, caterpillars, earwigs, slugs and snails. Aphids are insects and can be white, orange, grey, green (greenfly) or black. They have hollow, needle-like mouthparts which suck liquid sap from plants. They excrete a sticky, sugary liquid called honeydew onto leaves. Many fungi grow on this material, causing further problems. Aphids are especially troublesome in spring and summer when they attack young, soft growth.

LIFE CYCLE OF THE CABBAGE WHITE BUTTERFLY

There are four stages in the life cycle of the cabbage white butterfly.

Adult (or imago)

Adults first emerge in late spring and continue to emerge throughout the summer. They live for about three weeks and feed by sucking nectar from flowers. They mate and the female lays her eggs.

fig. 43.6 Adult cabbage white butterfly

Eggs

The female lays between 6 and 100 yellow eggs underneath cabbage leaves (or the leaves of other suitable plants). Eggs are laid twice a year. After about a week, tiny caterpillars emerge from the eggs.

Disease organism	Plant affected	Result
Potato blight fungus	Potatoes	The plant and the potatoes rot
Mildew fungi	Most trees or flowers	White 'powder' on leaves
Damping-off fungi	Roots and stems of young seedlings	Stem rots at ground level and falls over

Caterpillar (or larva)

This is the feeding stage. Caterpillars feed by chewing leaves. They live for about a month and can destroy the leaves as they feed almost continuously. In addition, the damaged leaves are more exposed to the risks of disease.

The caterpillars moult (shed their outer skin and grow rapidly) four times to reach full size.

When they are mature; they leave the plant and crawl to a dry, sheltered spot, e.g. under the branch of a tree or in a gap in a wall. Here they spin a web of silk and form the pupa.

Pupa (or chrysalis)

The pupa is the resting stage. The pupa has a hard, grey case (cocoon) which hangs from a silk pad. While in this cocoon, the caterpillar changes to become an adult butterfly, which emerges in time.

In summer the pupa lives for three weeks. However, if the pupa forms late in the year, the adult will not emerge until the following spring. Butterflies survive winter as pupae.

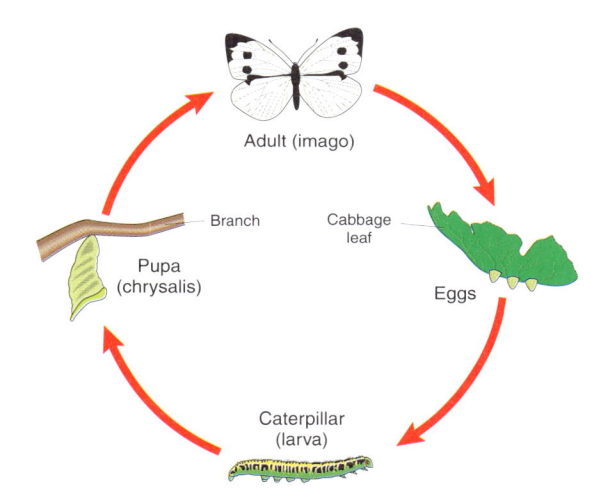

fig. 43.7 Life cycle of cabbage white butterfly

Host plants

Adults take nectar from many different flowers but do not cause damage to them. The caterpillars feed on the leaves of a group of plants called Brassica. Examples of these plants are cabbage, cauliflower, brussels sprouts, turnips, nasturtiums and other wild brassicas.

PROTECTION FROM DISEASES AND PESTS

Control of diseases and pests is achieved by carrying out good horticultural techniques. These include not overcrowding plants, supplying enough water and nutrients, ensuring good drainage and prompt removal of dead parts.

Fungal diseases are treated by spraying with chemicals that kill fungi (fungicides). Pests are killed by pesticide sprays. Slugs and snails are killed by using poison pellets in the soil. Larger pests can be removed by hand or they may be eaten by birds.

fig. 43.8 Pesticide being sprayed

Disadvantages of spraying

Sprays have a number of disadvantages. Some are poisonous and could cause ill health to the person spraying or to anything (or anyone) that eats the plant.

Pesticides kill useful organisms along with the pests. For example, bees and other insects may be killed and this may reduce the yields of fruit as there is less pollination. In addition, the toxic effect may be passed on along the food chain so that birds (especially birds of prey such as hawks) can be killed.

Finally, organisms can become resistant to sprays so that the chemical no longer affects them.

Biological control

This is the use of one living thing (the predator) to control a second living thing (the pest or prey). The advantages are that (a) only the pest is killed and there is no harm to other living things, (b) there is no build-up of poisonous material in the environment or in the food chain, (c) the pest does not develop a resistance.

The caterpillar of the cabbage white butterfly is killed by bacteria which are spread in commercial powders such as *Dipel*, *Thuricide* or *Bactospeine*. Caterpillars are also killed by the larva of ichneumon flies. In addition, caterpillars are eaten by birds such as thrush, robin and blue tits.

Biological control can also be achieved by hand picking the caterpillars to remove them from the environment.

Aphids can be controlled by the introduction of ladybirds (a type of beetle) which feed on them.

Chemical control

Caterpillars are killed by spraying chemicals such as *Ambush*, *Decis* or *Cyperkill*. Aphids are sprayed with malathion, derris or *Aphox*.

Integrated control

This means that a combination of biological and chemical control is used. In this system the predators are encouraged, and pesticides are only used in severe cases of infestation. The sprays are carefully selected so that they do not harm the predators and that they break down rapidly in the soil.

SUMMARY

- Horticulture is the study of how to grow plants.
- Growth media include soil, composts, nutrient rich water (hydroponics).
- A compost is an artificially prepared medium to replace soil.
- The growth media supplies water, nutrients, air and support.
- Plants need nitrogen, phosphorus and potassium, along with other nutrients, for healthy growth.
- Lack of any nutrient results in plants being yellow and showing weak growth.
- A mulch is a layer of material placed on top of the soil. They reduce weed growth (block out light) and hold water in the soil.
- Plant diseases are caused by fungi, bacteria and viruses.
- Plant pests include caterpillars, aphids, slugs and snails.
- Plants are protected from diseases and pests by:
  – observing proper growing methods
  – spraying with chemicals (fungicides for fungi, pesticides for pests)

(continued)

   – some pests are removed by hand or may be eaten by birds.
- Chemical sprays may poison (a) people, (b) other animals besides the pest, (c) animals that eat the pest. Pests often become resistant to chemicals.
- The life cycle of the cabbage white butterfly has four stages: adult (imago), eggs, caterpillar (larva), pupa (chrysalis).
- Caterpillars feed on brassica plants (cabbage, cauliflower, turnip).
- Biological control is the use of one living thing to limit the numbers of another. Examples of this control for caterpillars are:
  – spreading powder which contains a bacterium that kills caterpillars
  – encouraging thrushes, robins and blue tits.
  – picking them off leaves.
- Chemical control means spraying with toxic chemicals.
- Integrated control is a combination of biological and chemical control.

QUESTIONS

Q. 43.1
(a) What is horticulture?
(b) Give three examples of horticulture in everyday life.

Q. 43.2
(a) Name a growing medium which is
    (i) natural,
    (ii) artificial and
    (iii) contains no soil.
(b) Give one advantage and one disadvantage of each medium.

Q. 43.3
(a) What is the difference between natural and artificial composts?
(b) What is the main ingredient in most man-made composts?
(c) Give one reason in each case why the following might be added to the compost: (i) nutrients, (ii) sand, (iii) vermiculite or perlite.

Q. 43.4
(a) What is hydroponics?
(b) Why are plants grown by this method?
(c) Why is this method not used more widely?

Q. 43.5
(a) Name and give the main function of the three main plant nutrients.
(b) Name three other plant nutrients.
(c) How are plants affected by the lack of any nutrient?

Q. 43.6
(a) What is a mulch?
(b) Name four materials that can be used to make mulches.
(c) Give two benefits and two disadvantages of mulches.

Q. 43.7
Write out the following paragraphs and fill in the missing words.

(a) Plant diseases can be caused by ____, ____ or ____. Aphids are plant pests that ____ up liquid ____ through ____ mouth parts. Other examples of pests are ____, ____ and ____.
(b) The stages in the life cycle of the cabbage white butterfly are the adult, ____, ____ and ____. The only one of these that survives during winter is the ____. The stage that causes greatest harm is the ____ as it eats the ____ of plants such as ____, ____ or ____. The adult causes no harm as it drinks ____ which it gets from ____.
(c) The three methods of pest control are ____, ____ and ____. The method that causes the least pollution is ____. ____ control of caterpillars is carried out by collecting them by hand or by ____ or ____. Sprays used for caterpillars are ____ and ____.

Q. 43.8
Give a reason for each of the following.
(a) Sand is added to rooting compost.
(b) Plants in waterlogged soil often die.
(c) Household plants are not grown in soil.
(d) Rain or watering is needed after applying lawn fertilisers.
(e) Humus is needed in soil.
(f) Plants do not grow well in pure peat.
(g) In hydroponically grown plants the water must be well aerated.
(h) Earthworms are the soil's best friend.
(i) Butterflies do not harm roses.

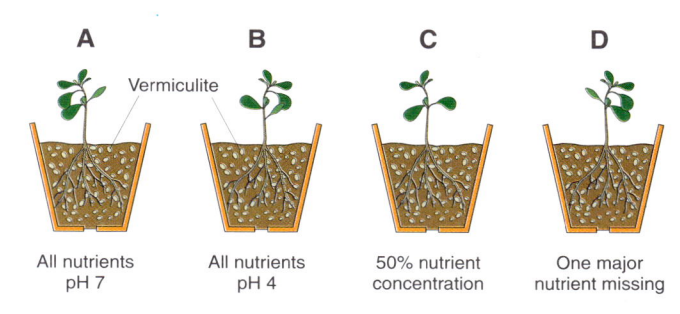

Q. 43.9

A — All nutrients pH 7
B — All nutrients pH 4
C — 50% nutrient concentration
D — One major nutrient missing

fig. 43.9

An experiment was set up as shown in the diagram.
(a) Why was vermiculite added to the pots?
(b) Which plant would you expect to show normal growth. Explain the results you would expect in the other plants.
(c) Name five minerals that should be in pots A and B.
(d) How would you test the pH of the nutrient solutions?
(e) What nutrients could be left out of pot D.

Q. 43.10
(a) Name a plant pest.
(b) Give an account of its life cycle, include diagrams in your answer.
(c) Based on your account say how, or if, each stage (i) feeds, (ii) moves, (iii) causes damage.
(d) At what time(s) of the year would you expect each stage to be present?

Q. 43.11
(a) Name three categories of pest control.
(b) Give one example of the use of each type of control, naming the material used and the pest affected in each case.
(c) Give one benefit and one disadvantage of each form of control.

44

HORTICULTURE 2

GROWING PLANTS

Plant life cycles

Plants are often arranged into categories according to the lengths of their life cycles.

Annuals are plants that germinate, grow, flower, form seeds and then die all within one growing season (spring to autumn). These include cereal crops such as wheat and barley, along with vegetables such as lettuce, peas and beans.

Annual flowers can be sub-divided into **hardy annuals** (which can tolerate frost and grow out of doors, e.g. sweet pea and nasturtium), and **half-hardy annuals** (not tolerant of even mild frost, so are sown indoors and planted out later in the year, e.g. busy lizzie and marigolds).

Biennials are plants that take two years to complete their life cycles. In the first year they germinate and grow, but do not flower, seed and die until the second year. They include sugar beet, cabbage, carrot, turnip, ornamental daisies and wallflowers.

fig. 44.1 Cabbage grown as a crop

fig. 44.2 Ornamental cabbages

Perennials live for many years and produce flowers and seed each year. **Herbaceous perennials** lose their aerial (above ground) parts at the end of each year. They survive underground during winter, e.g. potatoes, rhubarb, onions, daffodils, tulips. **Woody perennials** retain their aerial parts and have woody stems, e.g. trees and hedges such as privet.

Propagation

Propagation means the production of new living things (i.e. reproduction). Plants can be propagated by sexual or asexual methods.

Sexual reproduction occurs when the pollen and egg nuclei join to form a seed. In most plants the seed is enclosed in a fruit. **Asexual reproduction** is explained on page 258.

In order to avoid competition, the seeds are carried away (dispersed) from the parent plant. This is achieved by (a) small, light seeds blowing in the wind, (b) special structures to help carry the seed on the wind (e.g. the parachutes of dandelions and the wings of sycamore and ash), (c) seeds or fruit sticking to animals, and (d) animals eating fruits and expelling the seeds later.

Applied Science • 44

fig. 44.3 Strawberries

Germination is the growth of a seed into a new plant. The main conditions needed for germination are (a) the presence of water, (b) oxygen, and (c) a suitable temperature.

In general seeds and fruits form in the summer and are dispersed in late summer or early autumn. The seeds remain in the soil during winter and germination takes place the following spring.

Sowing seed

The basic rules for sowing seeds are as follows:

1. Use a seed tray or pot that has drainage holes.
2. Wash the seed tray if it has been used before.
3. Use damp seed compost (75% peat, 25% sand).
4. Sow the seeds at a depth of about twice their diameter.
5. Sprinkle a dusting of compost over small seeds.
6. Do not sow seeds too close together.
7. Cover the container with a sheet of dark paper.
8. A plastic bag or sheet of glass on top of the paper, or the use of a propagator will speed up germination.
9. Keep the compost damp, but do not overwater.
10. Once germination begins, remove the paper and open the glass or propagator slightly.

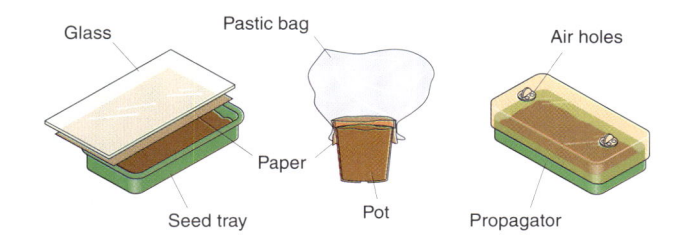

fig. 44.4

Experiment 44.1
To grow lettuce seed to maturity

1. Sow lettuce seed in damp seed compost, as described in the basic rules or on the seed packet.
2. When the first leaves develop, gently lift the seedlings out and transplant them into larger seed boxes. This is called pricking out and will give them the space to grow.
3. The seedlings are hardened off by slowly moving them to cooler (indoor) locations. This prepares them for outdoor conditions.
4. Prepare the soil outdoors (soil beds) by digging, breaking up the large lumps, removing stones and adding fertiliser. The sowing area is marked out with pegs and twine.
5. The seedlings (or in some cases the seed) are sown at the correct depth and spacing when all danger of frost is gone.
6. Protect the seedlings from pests (using string and aluminium foil to scare off birds and, perhaps, sprays for insects, or pellets for slugs).
7. Make sure the soil is kept moist and weed free.
8. It may be necessary to thin out the crop (i.e. remove the weaker plants to allow space for those remaining).

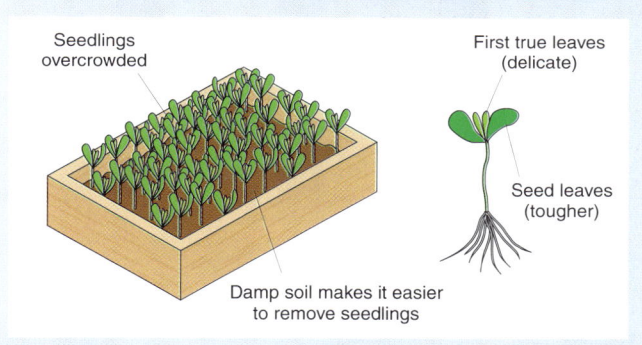

fig. 44.5

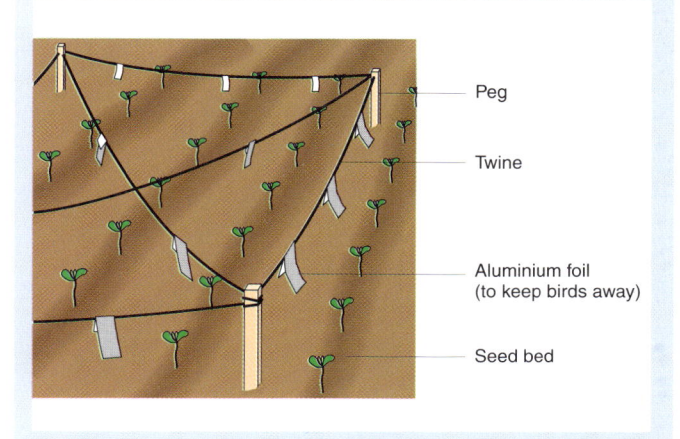

fig. 44.6 Seedlings growing

44 • Horticulture 2

Experiment 44.2

Part (a) To investigate the germination of seeds under different sowing conditions

1. Prepare the containers and smooth down the compost gently with a piece of wood.
2. Sow more of the same type of seeds (lettuce, cress, grass, marigold, sunflower or nasturtium) in container A as instructed on the label.
3. Sow more of the same type of seeds more densely in container B and deeper in container C.
4. Observe the containers every day for a few weeks.
5. The results expected are:

   Container A shows normal, healthy seedlings.

   Container B has some tall, weak seedlings. Some of these seedlings rot at the base of the stem and fall over. This is called **damping off** and is due to a fungal disease.

   Container C may show fewer germinated seedlings and those that are growing will be weak. This is because most of the food in the seed was used to allow the seed to grow the longer distance to the surface. As a result the stems are weak.

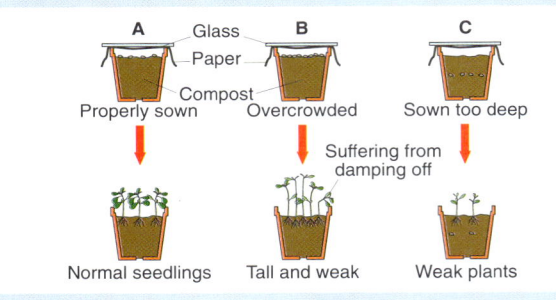

fig. 44.7

Part (b) To calculate the rate of germination

1. Place some damp germinating compost or seed compost in the base of a seed tray and smooth it down lightly.
2. Cut out a square of absorbent paper (e.g. blotting or filter paper) 10 cm × 10 cm. Mark it out in 1 cm^2 squares.
3. Place the paper on the compost.
4. Place one seed in each of the 100 squares and push them through the paper.
5. Cover the tray with dark paper and a sheet of glass.
6. Leave the tray in a warm place.
7. Count the number of germinated seeds at the end of the first, and again at the end of the second week.
8. Calculate the results as follows

   % germination = $\dfrac{\text{number of germinated seeds} \times 100}{\text{number of seeds sown (100)}}$

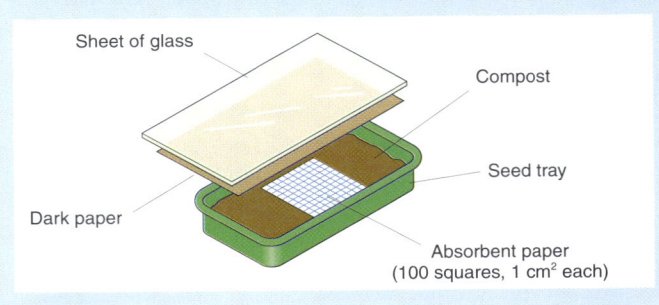

fig. 44.8

Part (c) To grow spring bedding plants

1. Bedding plants are plants that are germinated indoors and planted out when they are well developed. Spring bedding plants are often biennials that are grown indoors and planted outside the following spring, e.g. wallflowers, forget-me-nots, sweet william and ornamental daisies.

   (Summer bedding plants are usually annuals, e.g. marigolds and sweet peas)

2. The flower bed should be designed with the following factors in mind:
   - the size of the plants (i.e. tall plants at the back)
   - the colours of the flowers should be different, yet matching
   - the time of flowering should allow colour for most of the year
   - planting distances and conditions must be correct

3. The soil is prepared by digging, raking, weeding and mixing in fertiliser.
4. Place the bedding plants into the soil, firm them in and water them, especially in dry weather.
5. The flower bed should be kept free of weeds and pests. This may involve hand weeding, hoeing and a suitable form of pest control.
6. Dead flowers should be removed from the plant. This is called deadheading. It prevents the formation of seeds and encourages the formation of new flowers.

fig. 44.9 Bedding plants

DORMANCY

Dormancy is a period of time during which a seed will not germinate, even if all the external conditions are suitable. The dormant (or resting) condition can be due to chemicals in the seed or the fact that the seed coat (testa) is too tough.

Dormancy can be prevented by collecting seeds early so that the seed coat or the chemicals responsible for dormancy have not formed. These chemicals may be broken down by frost, i.e. during winter. Sometimes seeds are placed in bags of damp compost and left in a refrigerator to break the dormancy (i.e. destroy the chemicals). In other cases the chemicals are washed out of the seed by water during winter, especially when the seed coat decays. This can be copied by scraping the seeds and soaking them in water.

GROWING CONDITIONS FOR PLANTS

To grow properly, plants need water, nutrients, air in the soil, carbon dioxide, a suitable temperature and space. In addition they need protection from diseases, pests and bad weather. Any factor which, in short supply, reduces the plant's ability to grow properly, is called a limiting factor.

Limiting factors

Light is needed for healthy growth and colour of leaves and flowers. Plants have different requirements for light, e.g. bluebells and ivy prefer shade, while most flowering plants are suited to bright light (however many indoor plants do not like full sunlight).

Plants also need light for over 12 hours a day if they are to grow actively.

Experiment 44.3
To investigate dormancy in ash or sycamore seeds

1. These seeds are green when freshly collected in September or October but they turn brown by the following spring when they have dried out.
2. Soak some green seeds overnight in warm water and sow them in germinating compost.
3. Leave them in a warm place and count the number that germinate after three weeks.
4. Leave the remainder of the seeds in a dry place until the following April. Sow them as before and note how many germinate.
5. Result: Most of the green seeds germinate, none of the brown seeds germinate. This is because the green seeds have not developed the chemicals responsible for dormancy whereas the brown seeds have.

Note

If the brown seeds are placed in damp compost in a refrigerator for a few weeks and then sown most of them will germinate.

fig. 44.10

Dormancy in sycamore and ash

Advantage	Disadvantage
1. Allows the plant to avoid the harsh conditions of winter	Some seeds may not survive, i.e. may rot or be eaten
2. By germinating in spring, the seedlings have a long season of good weather to get established	Some seeds never germinate, i.e. dormancy is never broken

In glasshouses, the panes of glass should be kept clean by regular washing. In some cases a white, reflective material is used on the ground to increase natural light. Some commercial glasshouses use artificial light to produce flowers out of season.

Water is needed by plants for photosynthesis and support. The amount of water needed depends on the type of plant, the time of year and the size of the plant. In general, the soil should be kept moist, but not saturated, when plants are actively growing. Less water is needed when the plant is dormant.

Too much water is damaging to plants. Waterlogging causes the air content of the soil to be reduced and encourages the growth of disease causing fungi. Most pot plants are killed by kindness, i.e. overwatering. The compost from the top to a depth of 1 cm should be left to dry between each watering.

In dry conditions gardeners supply water to the soil by **irrigation** methods. This may involve growing plants on a bed of sand which supplies the water to the plants by capillary action or watering the plants with hosepipes or sprinklers.

Waterlogging is prevented by ensuring good **drainage**. This can involve growing on a layer of sand, or by digging drainage channels.

Temperature. A suitable temperature is needed for plants to grow actively. The higher the temperature (up to about 35°C), the better the plant will grow.

Plants can be germinated and grown indoors and planted out later in the year when it is warmer. Plants grown in this way are called bedding plants. Glasshouses can be heated in cold weather to allow growth all year round. However if the temperature is above about 35°C the plants may be damaged.

Space is needed for the aerial parts to absorb light, and for the roots to absorb water and nutrients. When seeds germinate, the seedlings are often overcrowded. To give each plant the space it needs, the weaker seedlings are removed. This process is called **thinning out**. Larger plants need more space than smaller plants.

Carbon dioxide is needed for photosynthesis. In glasshouses, the concentration of carbon dioxide can be increased by **ventilation** (i.e. opening windows) or by lighting a gas burner. The extra carbon dioxide can greatly increase the yield of flowers, fruit and vegetables.

Nutrients are needed in the soil to supply the needs of the growing plant. Plants with lots of leaves (e.g. lettuce, cabbage, grass) need a good supply of nitrogen. Root vegetables (e.g. carrots, turnips) require phosphorus, while fruits and flowers require potassium (potash).

These nutrients may be found in the soil, or can be added in the form of fertilisers, natural compost or farmyard manure.

Asexual reproduction (also called vegetative propagation) is the production of new plants from only one parent. This does not involve the fusion of sex cells or gametes. Vegetative reproduction happens naturally when plants produce bulbs, corms, tubers, runners or rhizomes. It can be carried out artificially by taking cuttings or grafting.

There are two main benefits of asexual reproduction.

1. The new plant will be an exact copy of the parent.
2. It is a simpler process than sowing seeds and the young plants become established faster in the soil.

CUTTINGS

A cutting is a piece of a plant (root, stem or leaf) that is grown into a new identical plant.

The most common type of cutting is a stem cutting. **Softwood cuttings** are taken from soft, non-woody stems. They are often taken in spring and allowed to root indoors. **Hardwood cuttings** are taken from woody stems in autumn after the leaves have fallen. They are usually planted outdoors.

Experiment 44.4
To root a softwood cutting

1. Cuttings are best taken early in the morning and should be planted as quickly as possible.
2. Cut a number of Busy lizzie stems about 10 cm long. These cuttings can be taken at any time of the year. Make the cut just below a leaf node.
3. Remove the leaves from the lower half of the cutting. This reduces water loss from the cutting.
4. Dip 2 cm of the cutting into rooting hormone powder. This stimulates faster root formation.

(continued)

5. Make holes in the rooting compost with a pencil and place a cutting in each of the holes.
6. Gently press the compost down around the base of the cutting.
7. Water the cuttings with a fine mist.
8. Cover the pot with a plastic bag to ensure the air is kept humid.
9. Leave the pot in a warm place and out of direct sunlight. Roots generally form in about six weeks.

(Note Geranium (pelargonium) cuttings are best taken as close to summer as possible. They do not need rooting hormone and the leaves should not be misted).

fig. 44.11 The growth of cuttings

Experiment 44.5
To grow a plant in a pot

1. Select a suitable growing container. Plastic containers have a greater variety of colours, but clay pots are less likely to be waterlogged. All containers should have drainage holes in the base.
2. Fill the pot with potting compost. Do not fill the pot to the top. Space is needed for watering.
3. Take cuttings of busy lizzie or geranium, as described in the previous experiment and plant them in the compost.
4. When the cutting starts making new growth, remove the tips of the main shoot (and larger side shoots if necessary) by pinching them out. This is called **stopping**, and it encourages bushy growth and flower development.

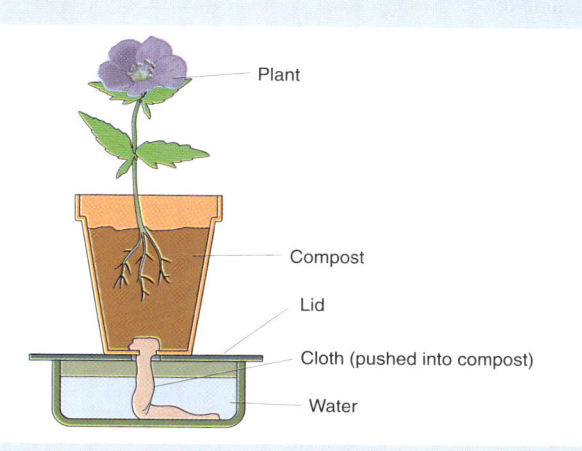

fig. 44.13 The wick system of self watering

7. The plant can be trained to grow along a support such as canes pushed well down into the compost. The stems should not be tied too tightly to the support.

fig. 44.12 Stopping a plant

5. Water the plant as needed. The water should contain a few drops of liquid plant feed to supply nutrients.
6. If the plant is left unattended for some time it can be watered using the wick method. This involves pushing a piece of cloth (e.g. an old pair of nylon tights) into the compost with the other end in water. The water moves along the cloth by capillary action.

fig. 44.14 Geranium

■ 44 • Horticulture 2

Experiment 44.6
To root a hardwood cutting

1. Take 25 cm cuttings from healthy blackcurrant, privet, escallonia or willow in autumn (October or November).
2. Remove the leaves from most of the lower end of the cutting.
3. Plant the cuttings out of doors, in a trench, with sand at the base.
4. Firm down the soil and keep it free of weeds.
5. The cuttings can be left to grow in this position or they can be moved to their final growing positions in March of the following year when their roots have formed.

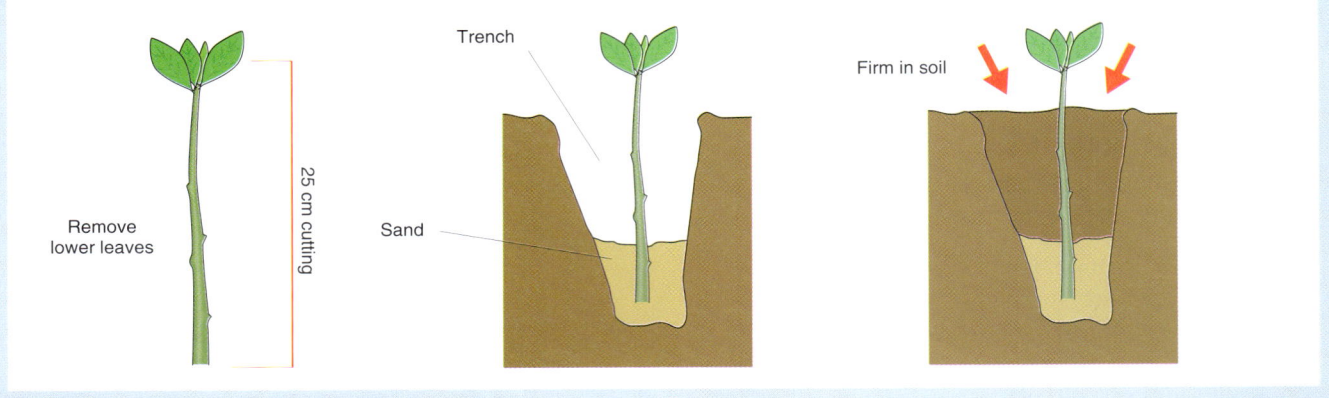

fig. 44.15 *Rooting hardwood cutting*

GRAFTING

This is the process of joining two parts of different plants together so that they grow as one plant. Generally the stem or bud of one plant (called the scion) is attached to the root or stem of another (called the stock plant).

Cambium is a layer of growth cells located just inside the bark of woody plants. The cambium produces new xylem (water transport) and phloem (food transport) tissues. In a graft it is important for the cambium of the scion and the stock to meet as closely as possible so that they can join together as one. For this reason grafting is often carried out in spring. Grafting is only successful between closely related plants.

For successful grafting the cuts must be sharp and the junction should be sealed as quickly as possible. The junction is wrapped with polythene and sealed with wax to ensure there is no water loss. Sometimes the graft is wrapped with raffia (a type of twine) to support it.

Grafts can often be seen on the stems of cherry, apple or weeping ash trees.

fig. 44.16 *A graft on an apple tree*

Advantages of grafting

1. To grow plants that will not grow easily from seeds or cuttings.
2. To grow stems (scions) that are resistant to pests and diseases.
3. To grow dwarf fruit trees (e.g. apple scions are grafted onto dwarf rootstocks to form miniature apple trees for gardens).
4. It gives extra vigour to some plants, e.g. roses.
5. Plants can be grown in soil conditions that they would not normally tolerate.

CUTTING AND CARE OF FLOWERS

In order to prolong the life of cut flowers it is important that (a) their water content remains high, i.e. they remain firm and do not wilt, (b) they do not lose more water than they can absorb, (c) there are no air bubbles in the stems and (d) their water supply remains fresh.

These factors are ensured in the following ways:

1. Flowers in bud are cut early in the morning when they are full of moisture.
2. The stem should be cut as long as possible using a scissors or secateurs. The lower leaves are removed to reduce water loss (by transpiration).
3. Place the stems in luke warm water and cut off their ends. Cutting underwater prevents air bubbles entering the stem.
4. The end of the stem is crushed (or cut at a slant) to allow more surface area for water absorption.
5. Keep the cut flowers in water in a cool place.
6. Chemicals can be added to the water to supply nutrients and to prevent the growth of micro-organisms. Both of these result in longer life for cut flowers.

Experiment 44.7
To graft a plant

1. Clean the rootstock and scion of the plants to be grafted, e.g. apple, weeping ash or birch trees.
2. Cut the stock and scion with a sharp knife, as shown in the diagrams.
3. Insert the scion inside the flap on the stock and seal the cut surfaces with polythene and grafting wax.
4. Plant out of direct sunlight and keep the soil well watered.
5. Gradually new cells (called a callus) form at the cut surfaces. When these turn brown the graft is complete.
6. Any growth that emerges from the rootstock must be cut away, as this growth (called suckers) will eventually take over the plant.

(Note: Different shaped cuts can be used in grafting, as shown below).

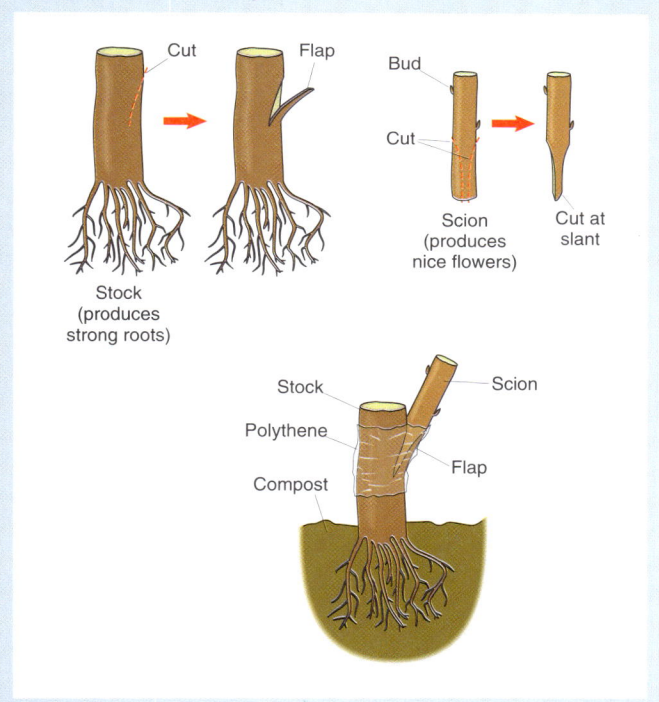

fig. 44.17 Grafting technique

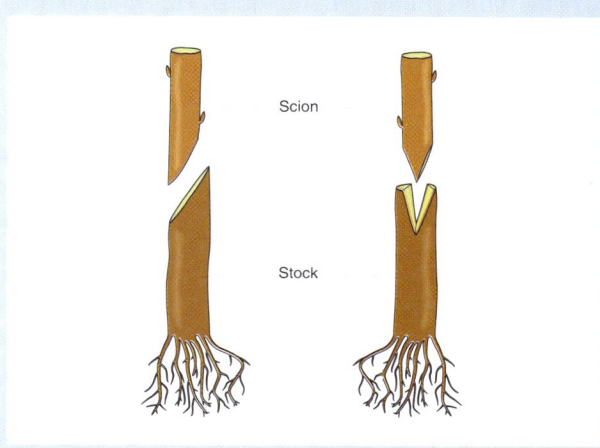

fig. 44.18 Alternative forms of grafting

Experiment 44.8
To investigate the conditions that affect the freshness of cut flowers

1. Cut some daffodils or tulips and set up as shown in the diagram. The procedures mentioned on the previous page are followed unless otherwise stated.

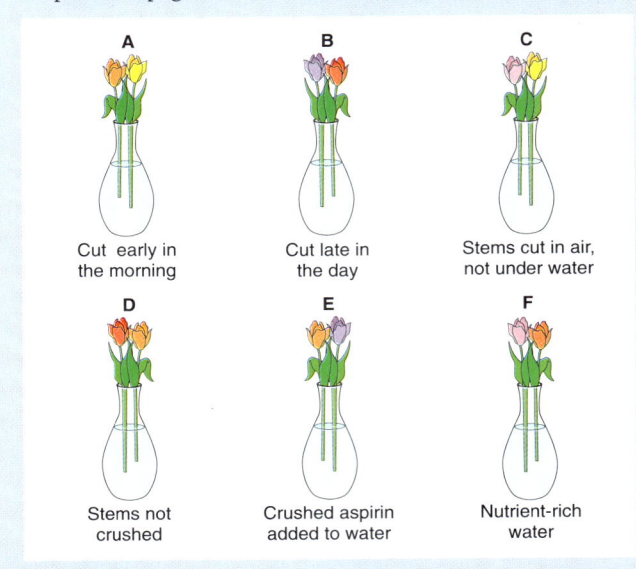

A — Cut early in the morning
B — Cut late in the day
C — Stems cut in air, not under water
D — Stems not crushed
E — Crushed aspirin added to water
F — Nutrient-rich water

fig. 44.19

2. Label the containers and leave in a cool place. Observe daily and note the condition of the flowers.
3. Results:
   The flowers in A survive well, but not as well as those in E and F. The flowers in B, C and D do not survive for very long.

GRASSES

There is a wide variety of different grasses throughout the world. The climate in Ireland is especially suited to the growth of grass. Grass is grown for different reasons, e.g. lawns, sports fields or to feed animals.

Many different grasses can be sown. Each variety has its own characteristics and advantages. See the table below.

The grass sown in most amenity areas is a mixture of those grasses below, and other grasses. The finer and more delicate areas such as lawns and golf greens use browntop, bent and chewing's or creeping red fescue. For more rugged areas the seed mix contains greater amounts of ryegrasses.

Experiment 44.9
To investigate the growth of grasses

1. Sow bent, fescue and ryegrass seeds in compost in three different deep seed trays.

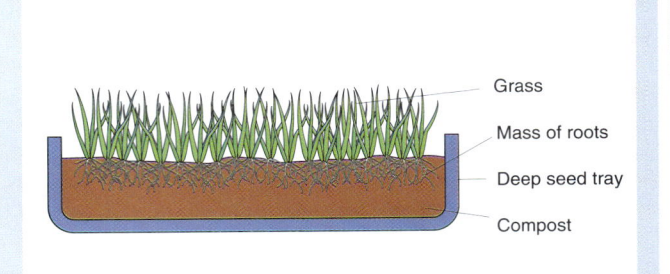

Labels: Grass, Mass of roots, Deep seed tray, Compost

fig. 44.20

2. When the grasses have matured the roots will form a mat or carpet with the compost.
3. Transplant these mats into a prepared area of soil.
4. Observe the appearance, texture and growth of each grass.

Natural meadowland

Lawns and grass fields are not natural habitats. This is because cutting, grazing or adding fertilisers encourages grass growth but reduces the number of other flowering plants.

Grass type	Uses	Advantages	Identification
Bent	Luxury lawns, bowling and golf greens	Delicate leaves look nice, slow growing	Fine velvety leaves, rhizomes (underground) and stolons (creep along ground)
Fescue	Normal lawn, sheep pasture	Tolerates mowing, looks well	Rhizomes, fine leaves
Dwarf Ryegrass	Sports fields Animal pasture	Hard-wearing Fast-growing	Broad leaves Tough stems

If grassland is left uncut for a few years many wild flowers usually develop. This results in a complex and beautiful natural meadowland. Such a habitat is rich in natural flowers and can support a wide range of wildlife. It is said to be species rich and to show great **biodiversity** (i.e. many living things).

Natural meadowland can be sown by hand using packets of wild seed and by leaving the grass uncut. Farmers are now encouraged to cut their grassland later in the year and to cut it from the inside out to the edges. This allows animals such as the corncrake to raise their young and to escape from the cutting machines.

fig. 44.21 Natural meadowland

SUMMARY

- Annuals complete their life cycle in one year, biennials grow for two years and perennials live many years.
- Plants can be propagated by sexual means (seed) or by asexual methods (bulbs, corms, cuttings and grafting).
- Seed germination requires air, water and warmth.
- Bedding plants are germinated indoors and planted outdoors when partly grown.
- Dormancy is a resting period during which seeds do not germinate.
- Dormancy allows seedlings to avoid growing in winter and to have a long growing season by germinating in spring.
- Limiting factors reduce the growth of plants if they are in short supply. They include light, temperature, space, carbon dioxide and nutrients.
- Cuttings are pieces of plants that grow into new plants.
- Softwood cuttings are taken in spring from woody trees or bushes.
- Grafting means that parts of two different plants are joined so that they grow as one plant.
- Cut flowers remain fresh longer if their water content is kept high, air is prevented from entering the stems, nutrients are added to their water, and their water is kept fresh.
- Lawn grasses include bent grass (thin leaves and delicate), fescue and ryegrass (broad leaves and tough).
- Natural meadows contain a variety of flowering plants.

QUESTIONS

Q. 44.1
Write out the following and fill in the gaps.

(a) Plants that are grown indoors and planted out later are called _____ plants. Examples of spring bedding plants are _____ and _____ . In designing a flower bed _____ plants should be placed at the _____ , the _____ of the flowers should be considered along with _____ the flowers are formed. Once placed in the soil the plants should be well _____ . The removal of dead flowers from the stems is called _____ . This helps the growth of new _____ and stops the production of _____ .

(b) The conditions needed for germination are _____ , _____ and _____ . If all these conditions are present and the seed still will not germinate it said to be _____ . Seeds often remain _____ during the winter in order for the young seedling to avoid _____ weather. By germinating in _____ the seedling gets a _____ growing _____ to establish itself.

(c) Plants grown asexually are _____ to the parent plant. Cuttings should be taken in the _____ and the cut should be just _____ a leaf node. The _____ should be removed from the end of the cutting, which may be dipped in _____ hormone. The cutting is placed in the _____ and covered with a _____ plastic bag. This _____ water loss from the _____ .

Q. 44.2
Explain and give one example of: (i) annuals, (ii) hardy annuals, (iii) half-hardy annuals, (iv) biennials, (v) perennials, (vi) herbaceous perennials, (vii) woody perennials.

Q. 44.3
(a) What is meant by propagation?
(b) What is the difference between sexual and asexual propagation?
(c) Give one example of each type of propagation.
(d) What are the benefits of asexual propagation?

Q. 44.4
(a) Name a vegetable you have grown.
(b) In the case of the named vegetable describe how you: (i) sowed the seed, (ii) grew the plant to maturity, (iii) looked after the plant as it matured.

Q. 44.5
Suggest a reason for each of the following:
(a) A sandy compost is used for growing seeds.
(b) Cabbage plants are rarely seen to flower.
(c) Seeds should not be sown too close together.
(d) The growth tip is sometimes removed from a plant.
(e) Twine with aluminium foil is often placed over seed beds.
(f) Seedlings are pricked out.
(g) Plants are thinned out.

Q. 44.6
(a) Name a plant from which softwood cuttings can be taken.
(b) A cutting was treated as shown in the diagram. Give a reason for each of the following. (i) The use of the plastic bag. (ii) Not removing the upper leaves. (iii) The compost contains sand. (iv) The plastic bag must be transparent. (v) As soon as new growth is visible the plant is stopped.

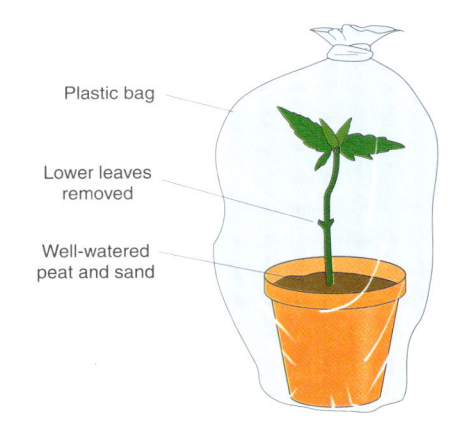

fig. 44.22

Q. 44.7
Explain, with the help of a diagram, how a pot plant can be watered when left unattended for a long time in summer.

Q. 44.8
(a) When are (i) softwood, (ii) hardwood cuttings normally taken?
(b) Name a plant suitable for taking hardwood cuttings and describe how the procedure is carried out.

Q. 44.9
(a) What is meant by limiting factors?
(b) Name the limiting factors and give two ways by which each one can be eliminated in glasshouses.

Q. 44.10
Explain the following terms and give one advantage for each.
(a) Irrigation
(b) drainage
(c) pinching out
(d) pricking out
(e) propagator
(f) dormancy
(g) deadheading
(h) cuttings
(i) hoeing
(j) training a plant

Q. 44.11
(a) What is grafting?
(b) Give two benefits of grafting.
(c) Name two plants that can be grafted.
(d) When is grafting best carried out?

Q. 44.12
In terms of grafting explain the following:
(a) scion   (b) stock
(c) cambium   (d) callus
(e) suckers

Q. 44.13
(a) Describe, with the help of a diagram, how you carried out a graft on a named plant.
(b) Give a reason for each of the following: (i) the use of polythene and wax, (ii) using raffia, (iii) removing suckers.

Q. 44.14
(a) Name three types of grass.
(b) Which type is most suitable for (i) football pitches, (ii) golf greens?
(c) State one way you could identify each type of grass.
(d) State one advantage of each type of grass.

Q. 44.15

(a) Give one reason why natural meadows have more flowering plants than most lawns.
(b) Give a biological advantage of natural meadows.

Q. 44.16

(a) List four ways by which cut flowers can be kept fresh longer.
(b) Describe an experiment to show that sugar promotes the life of cut flowers. Outline the results you would expect.

45

MATERIALS

A great number of different materials are in use every day. Some have been used for thousands of years and are found naturally on, or under, the Earth's surface – materials like stone, timber, copper, iron, and wool. Other materials, and these include most of those in use today, are manufactured or 'man-made' from naturally occurring substances. Materials that are man-made are called **synthetic**.

fig. 45.1 In this kitchen you should be able to see lots of synthetic materials, as well as some natural ones. Can you select six of each kind?

A material is selected for a particular purpose because it has one or more properties which make it especially suitable for that purpose. For example, a knife is made of metal because metal is strong and can be sharpened, a tea cosy is made of wool because wool is a good heat insulator, and a margarine box is made of plastic because plastic is cheap, can be moulded and is non toxic.

CLASSIFYING MATERIALS

Scientists are always sorting things into groups or 'classifying' them. There are many different ways of classifying materials. Listed below are five groups into which materials can be classified.

Hydrocarbons

These are chemical compounds consisting of hydrogen and carbon only. Hydrocarbons are used as fuels. The fossil fuels (coal, oil, gas) are all hydrocarbons. Their origin is described on page 20 in Chapter 3.

Plastics

Plastic is not a single substance. Just as there are many different metals, there are many different plastics. A plastic is a substance that can be softened by heat. Common plastics include polythene, polystyrene, PVC (polyvinyl chloride), polyurethane.

Textiles

A textile or cloth is a material that is made from woven fibres. There are both natural fibres, like cotton, wool, linen and silk, and also synthetic ones, such as nylon, polyester and Lycra.

Metals

There are hundreds of different metals. About ninety of them are elements and the rest are alloys (mixtures of metals). Iron and steel, copper, lead, zinc, brass, and aluminium are metals in common everyday use.

Others

This group is for the 'leftovers' or the substances which don't belong to any of the above four groups, i.e. substances such as glass, wood, concrete, rubber, paper, leather, ceramics, etc.

USES OF MATERIALS

A great number of today's materials are versatile – which means that they can be put to many different uses. On the other hand, many different materials can often be used for the same purpose. The two charts give some examples of what materials are used for.

Chart 1: Many uses of the same material	
steel	cars, railway lines, girders, gas pipes, pylons, tools, window frames
polystyrene	yogurt cartons, building insulation, packaging, flower pots, egg boxes
nylon	tights, socks, ropes, toothbrushes, carpets, bearings, parachutes
timber	furniture, electricity poles, pencils, floors, boxes, rulers, toys
aluminium	aircraft, window frames, drink cans, cooking foil

Chart 2: Many materials for the same use

window frames	steel, aluminium, timber, PVC
chairs	PVC, steel, timber
saucepans	steel, iron, copper, glass
sweaters	wool, cotton, polyester, acrylic
buildings	stone, concrete, timber, brick, aluminium

MIXED MATERIALS

Many of today's materials are mixtures. For example, brass and steel are mixtures of metals (alloys), and polyester cotton is a mixture of fibres. The properties of a mixture are similar to the properties of the materials from which it is made, but the mixture is often more useful or has better properties than the original materials. The usefulness of alloys has already been explained (page 189).

Polyester cotton is a good example of the advantages of a mixed fibre. Polyester, a synthetic fibre, is hard-wearing and crease-resistant, but does not absorb moisture (it can therefore make you feel 'sweaty' in hot weather). Cotton absorbs moisture, but is not hard wearing. Polyester cotton is a mixture of the two fibres and has the advantages of both; it is hard wearing, doesn't crease easily and absorbs moisture. A mixture of 70% cotton and 30% polyester is often used for shirts and blouses, and for bed linen.

QUESTIONS

Q. 45.1
Classify the following list of objects and materials into

(a) hydrocarbons
(b) plastics
(c) textiles
(d) metals, and
(e) others

cotton shirt, a £1 coin, yogurt carton, nylon tights, bottled gas, pair of scissors, a candle, glass, a brick, petrol, a supermarket bag, coal, a 'Coke' can, a sweater, a biro case, sugar, a brass screw, a cork

Q. 45.2
Select ten items that can be seen in the photograph of the kitchen (Fig. 45.1), say what material each item is made of, and give two reasons why that material is used.

Q. 45.3
Select, from the picture of the kitchen (Fig. 45.1), two metals, two plastics, two textiles, two hydrocarbons and two other materials.

Q. 45.4
For each of the materials listed in Chart 1, (page 318) select one use, and say why the material is suitable for that use.

DIFFERENT TYPES OF MATERIALS AND THEIR PROPERTIES

In this section of the course, candidates taking ordinary level have to study the properties of ONE of plastics, metals, textiles, or timber.

Candidates taking higher level have to study TWO of the above.

MATERIAL 1 – PLASTICS

Hundreds of everyday items are made from plastic. However, there is no single substance called 'plastic'. Like metals, there are many different plastics, each with its own characteristic properties that distinguish it from other plastics. Plastics are a large family of materials which have several features in common, the most important being:

(i) they soften and can be moulded by heat and pressure, and

(ii) they consist of **polymers** – giant molecules made up of thousands of smaller molecules (called **monomers**), combined together to form a repeating structure.

Crude oil provides the raw materials for the manufacture of plastics (and also for many synthetic fibres). The compound ethene, C_2H_4, is an example of a substance which comes from crude oil. When this compound is polymerised (made into a polymer) the product is polyethene or polythene. Ethene is thus the monomer for the manufacture of polyethene. Other common plastics are polystyrene, PVC (polyvinyl chloride), Teflon and polyurethane.

PROPERTIES OF PLASTICS

The properties of different plastics vary slightly, but in general, plastics are flexible, soft and scratch easily, waterproof, good heat insulators, and excellent electrical insulators. When burnt, many plastics produce suffocating and toxic fumes.

45 • Materials

EXPERIMENTS

Experiment 45.1
To compare densities of plastics

Details of how to measure densities are given on page 43. Use this method to measure the densities of various plastics

Experiment 45.2
To compare the flexibility of plastics

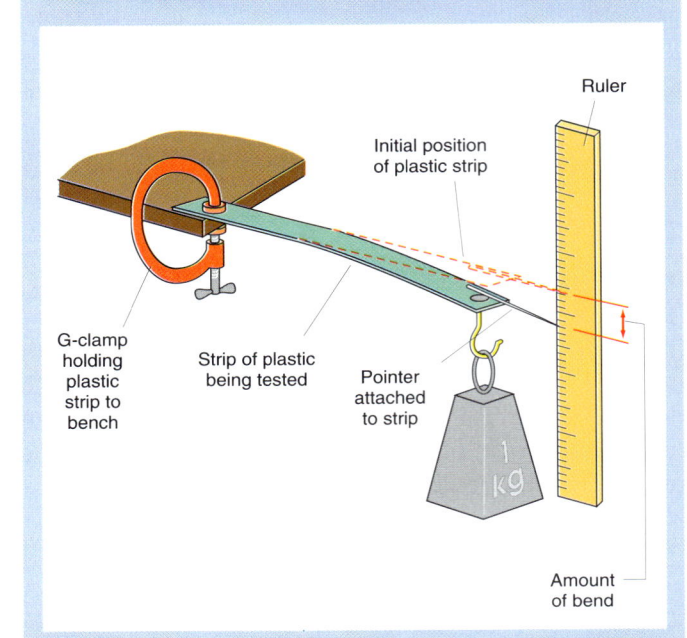

fig. 45.2

The diagram shows a simple way of testing materials for flexibility. A weight of 2 to 5 newtons (200 to 500 g) is hung from the end of the piece of plastic under test, and the amount by which the plastic bends is read on the scale. The same test is then done with a piece of another plastic of the same dimensions.

DETERIORATION, PROTECTION AND CARE OF MATERIALS

All materials deteriorate (decay or decompose) to some extent. Some, like concrete, are very long-lasting, while others, like wood that has become wet, can decay very quickly. Causes of decay are the weather, pest infestation, corrosion, etc. Most plastics are long-lived, the main cause of deterioration being ultra-violet rays (from sunlight).

QUESTIONS

Q. 45.5
Name two common plastics, and mention an everyday item made out of each of them.

Q. 45.6
Describe, using a diagram, an experiment to compare the bending strengths of two different plastics.

Q. 45.7
Describe, using a diagram, an experiment to compare the densities of two different plastics.

Q. 45.8
Describe, using a diagram, an experiment to compare the heat insulating abilities of two different plastics.

Q. 45.9
With the aid of chemistry books from your school or local library, write an account of how plastic is manufactured from crude oil.

MATERIAL 2 – TEXTILES

Textiles are materials that are made from fibres by weaving. Fibres are filaments (tiny 'threads') that can be spun or made into continuous twisted strands called yarn, which is then made into fabrics. There are both natural fibres (which may be of animal or plant origin) and artificial ones (made by chemical reactions). The table (page 321) lists some commonly-used textiles, along with their sources and some of their common uses.

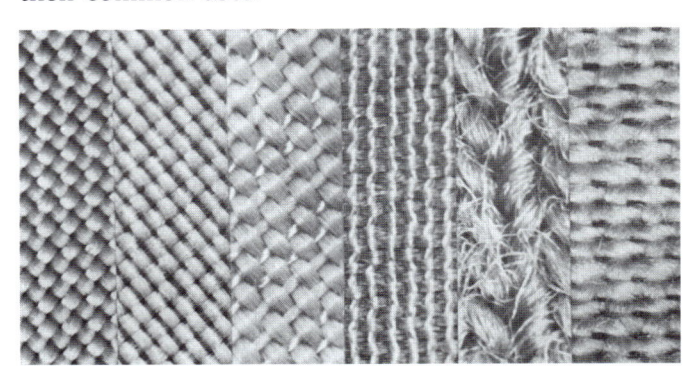

fig. 45.3 Close-up photographs of some artificial and some natural fibres – from left, rayon, nylon, terylene, cotton, wool and silk

FLAME PROOFING

All fabrics burn, some very well, and some only smoulder. Some give off choking or poisonous fumes. Flame proofing refers to the treatment of fabrics with special chemicals in order to reduce the risk of the

Textile	Natural or synthetic	Source or Chemical Composition	Uses
Cotton	natural	cotton plant	towels, underwear, T-shirts, sheets
Wool	natural	sheep and other animals	sweaters, carpets, blankets, coats
Linen	natural	flax plant	tablecloths, jackets, tea towels
Silk	natural	silkworms	underwear, blouses, ties, scarves
Nylon	synthetic	polyamide	swimsuits, umbrellas, tights, rainwear
Terylene	synthetic	polyester	net curtains, sewing thread, tablecloths
Lycra	synthetic	polyurethane	swimsuits, leotards, leggings
Acrylic	synthetic	polyacrylonitrile	sweaters, blankets, carpets

fabric burning. Items which are often flame proofed include seat upholstery, childrens' nightclothes, and firefighters' suits. Some fabrics are treated to make them waterproof or mothproof.

MANUFACTURER'S LABELS

Labels on clothing items give useful information about the care (particularly relating to washing and ironing) which should be taken with the item. Following these instructions will prolong the life of the item. Commonly found labels are given on the chart in Figure 45.5.

fig. 45.4 Some garment labels

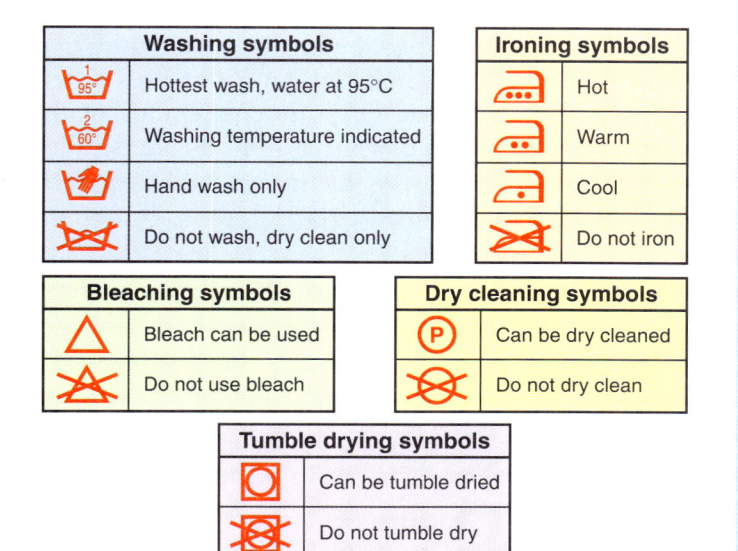

Washing symbols	
95°	Hottest wash, water at 95°C
60°	Washing temperature indicated
	Hand wash only
	Do not wash, dry clean only

Ironing symbols	
	Hot
	Warm
	Cool
	Do not iron

Bleaching symbols	
△	Bleach can be used
	Do not use bleach

Dry cleaning symbols	
P	Can be dry cleaned
	Do not dry clean

Tumble drying symbols	
	Can be tumble dried
	Do not tumble dry

fig. 45.5 Care labels

EXPERIMENTS

Experiment 45.3
To investigate resistance to wear of some textiles

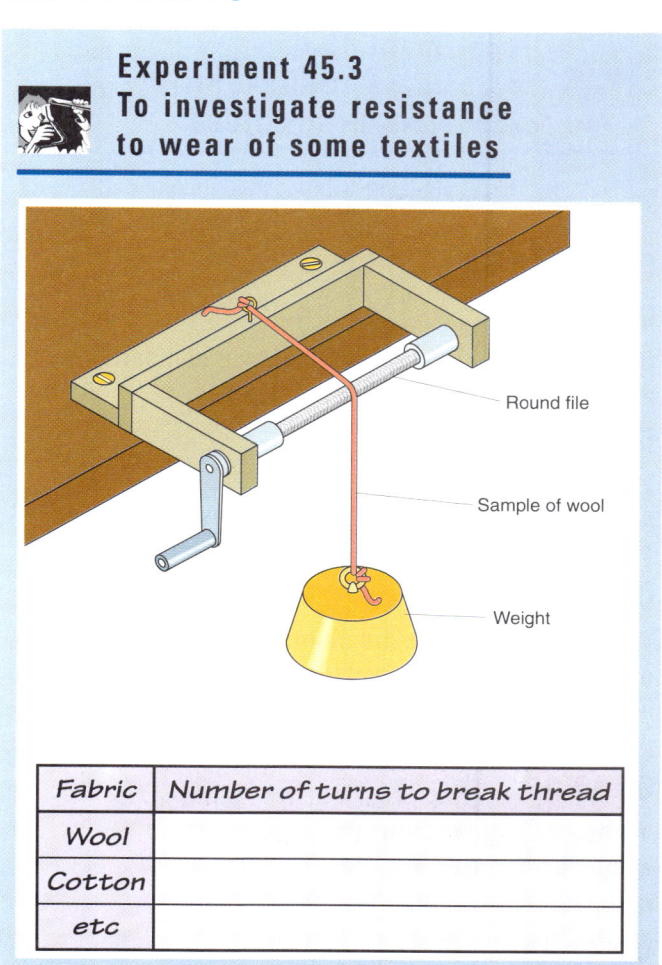

Round file
Sample of wool
Weight

Fabric	Number of turns to break thread
Wool	
Cotton	
etc	

fig. 45.6

The device shown is for testing the 'wear resistance' of fabrics or yarns. As the handle of the device is turned, the material being tested is rubbed by the file. The number of turns needed to wear the material to breaking point in measured. Similar sized pieces of other materials are tested in the same way, and the one that can withstand the greatest number of turns has the greatest resistance to wear.

Experiment 45.4
To compare absorbency of some textiles

For this test you need pieces of equal mass of the textiles being tested, a trough of water, and a tripod. Take the first textile piece and find its mass. Immerse the piece in water and squeeze it to make sure that there are no trapped air bubbles in it. Remove it from the water, and hang it over one of the legs of an inverted tripod.

Leave it there until it stops dripping, then remove it and find its mass again. Calculate the increase in mass – which is the mass of water absorbed by it. Repeat this procedure for each of the textiles being tested.

Experiment 45.5
To compare the insulating properties of textiles

Details for this experiment will be found on page 31.

QUESTIONS

Q. 45.10
Describe an experiment in which you compared the absorbency of two different textiles.

Q. 45.11
What is meant by the term textile? Name two natural textiles and two synthetic ones. Mention an everyday item commonly made from each material.

Q. 45.12
With the aid of books (home economics texts or encyclopaedias) from your school or local library, write an account of how a textile is produced from a raw material.

Q. 45.13
What is meant by a mixed textile? Give two examples of these. Explain why items of clothing are often made of such materials.

Q. 45.14
The measurements in the following table are the results of an experiment to compare the absorbency of some textiles (as described in the text).

(a) For each textile, calculate the mass of water absorbed by it.
(b) List the textiles in order of decreasing absorbency (the best absorber first).
(c) Which textile would dry most quickly?
(d) Which would be best for towel material?

Textile	Dry mass/g	Wet mass/g
Cotton	12.2	17.0
Nylon	12.0	13.0
Acrylic	11.9	14.9
Wool	12.1	16.3
Polyester	12.0	13.8

DETERIORATION, PROTECTION AND CARE OF MATERIALS

All materials deteriorate (decay or decompose) to some extent. Some like concrete, are very long lasting while others, like wood which has become wet, can decay very quickly. Causes of decay are the weather, pest infestation, corrosion, etc. Some protection methods for prolonging the life of textiles are shown below.

Material	Cause of decay	Effect of decay	Protection methods
Textiles	Incorrect care, moths, age	Shrinkage	Follow manufacturer's instructions
		Holes, becomes weak	Moth repellents

MATERIAL 3 – METALS

Two thousand years ago about ten different metals were known. Today there are about five thousand metals and alloys in use. Each one has a special property which makes it very suitable for doing its job. Metals are found in the Earth's crust. The few unreactive metals like gold and silver are found 'free' (this means in the uncombined state), but most metals occur as ores in rocks. Ores are compounds of the metal. The extraction of a metal from its ore is called smelting. The chart lists some metals with their ores, and where they are mined.

Metal	Ore	Where mined
Iron	Haematite	USSR, Australia
Copper	Malachite	USA
Lead	Galena	Navan, Co. Meath Galmoy, Co. Kilkenny
Zinc	Zinc Blende	Navan, Co. Meath Galmoy, Co. Kilkenny
Aluminium	Bauxite	Australia

Mining in Ireland

In the past, there have been a number of mines around the country extracting lead, zinc, silver and copper ores from under the ground, but at present there are only two of significance. Both companies export zinc and lead concentrates to Europe for smelting.

Tara Mines at Navan, Co. Meath is the largest producer of zinc in Europe. It exports about 170 000 tonnes of zinc and 46 000 tonnes of lead per year.

Arcon Mines at Galmoy, Co. Kilkenny recently developed the first major new metal mine in Ireland since Tara was established in the early 1970s. At full production, the Galmoy mine will yield 120 000 tonnes per year of zinc, and a smaller amount of lead. This material is exported to Europe for smelting.

fig. 45.7 Inside a mine

METAL ORES

Metals occur in nature as ores, which are compounds of the metal. Many metal ores consist of the oxide of the metal, and so the process of extracting the metal from it is a reduction reaction (removal of oxygen).

Experiment 45.6
To extract a metal from a metal ore

One of the ores of copper is called malachite, which is a substance that contains copper carbonate. The copper can be extracted from it as follows.

1. If the malachite is lumpy, grind it into a fine powder with a pestle and mortar.
2. Put some of the powder to a depth of about 2 cm in a **dry** test tube. Heat it, gently at first, and then more strongly, until **all** of it has been converted to black copper oxide.
3. Take about 15 cm^3 of dilute sulphuric acid in a beaker and add the black copper oxide to it.
4. Gently heat the beaker for a few minutes (do not let the liquid boil).
5. Filter the mixture into a second beaker. Discard the residue in the filter paper. The filtrate is a solution of copper sulphate.
6. Place a clear iron nail in the blue solution for about one minute. Lift it out (use tongs) and observe that it has been covered with copper. This is the copper which was originally in the malachite ore.

PROPERTIES OF METALS

Metals are described in Chapter 27. Refer to:
- the list of the properties of metals (page 188)
- the table of alloys (page 190)
- metal ores (below)
- corrosion and its prevention (page 191)

EXPERIMENTS

Experiment 45.7
To compare densities of metals

Details of how to measure densities are given on page 43.

Experiment 45.8
To compare heat conductivities of metals

Details of this experiment are given on page 30.

Experiment 45.9
To compare reactivities of metals

The order of reactivities of metals (in decreasing order) is called the activity series. How metals are arranged in this order is described on page 190.

QUESTIONS

Q. 45.15
(a) What is meant by a metal ore?
(b) Name two metals that are mined in Ireland.
(c) Name two everyday use of each of these metals.

Q. 45.16

Describe the experiment (Experiment 45.6) in which you extracted copper from a copper ore. In your account, use diagrams to illustrate your answers. Also write out and complete the equations (in words or using symbols) for the three reactions that occurred:

(i) Copper carbonate → copper oxide + ___
    $CuCO_3$ → CuO + ___

(ii) Copper oxide + sulphuric acid →
                                copper sulphate + ___
    $CuO + H_2SO_4$ → $CuSO_4$ + ___

(iii) Iron + copper sulphate → copper + ___
    $Fe + CuSO_4$ → Cu + ___

Q. 45.17

Rewrite the following paragraph but with the blanks completed.

Malachite is an example of a metal compound which occurs in __; it is known as a metal __. When malchite (which is __ in colour) is heated, it gives off the gas __ which turns limewater __. The substance which remains is __ in colour. When this substance is added to sulphuric acid it forms a __ solution of the compound __ __. When an iron nail is dipped into this solution, it becomes covered with a __ coloured layer of the metal __. This is the metal that was originally in the malchite. Malachite is therefore an ___ of the metal __.

Q. 45.18

Describe an experiment in which you compared the densities of two different metals.

DETERIORATION, PROTECTION AND CARE OF MATERIALS

All materials deteriorate (decay or decompose) to some extent. Some like concrete, are very long lasting while others, like wood which has become wet, can decay very quickly. Causes of decay are the weather, pest infestation, corrosion, etc. Some protection methods for prolonging the life of metals are shown below.

Material	Cause of decay	Effect of decay	Protection methods
Iron and steel	Moisture and oxygen	Rust	Painting, galvanising, electroplating, alloying

MATERIAL 4 – TIMBER AND MANUFACTURED BOARDS

Wood, or timber, comes from trees. Wood is a natural material and is a renewable resource, because after trees have been felled, new ones can be planted in their place. There are two main types of wood: hardwood and softwood.

Hardwoods come from deciduous trees, i.e. broad-leaf trees that lose their leaves in winter. Examples are beech, oak, ash, teak, mahogany. Hardwood is used in making furniture, doors and window frames.

Softwoods come from coniferous trees, i.e. cone-bearing trees that have thin or needle-shaped leaves. Examples of these are pine, redwood, larch, spruce. Softwoods are much used in building, for making floor and roof joists, floorboards and door frames. Other items made from softwoods are fencing, telegraph poles, pallets and shelving.

Hardwoods in general are harder and more dense than softwoods, but there are exceptions. Balsa is a hardwood (because it is derived from a deciduous tree) but is very soft and light (it is used for model aeroplanes). Yew is a softwood (because the tree is coniferous) but yew wood is much harder than many hardwoods.

MANUFACTURED BOARDS

There are a number of 'man-made' boards in use today, the most common ones being hardboard, plywood, blockboard and chipboard. They consist of timber, but are manufactured in the sense that the timber has been processed or assembled differently. Manufactured boards often make use of parts of the timber that would otherwise go to waste.

Hardboard   Plywood

Blockboard   Chipboard

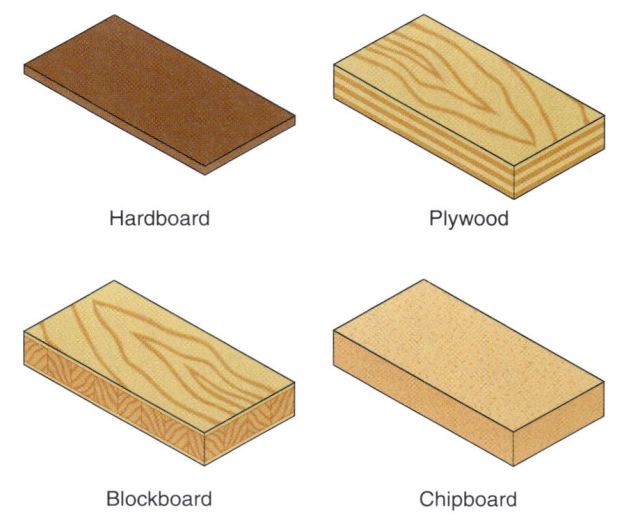

fig. 45.8 *Some manufactured boards*

Hardboard is made from wood chips that have come from either small branches or waste material. The chips are made into pulp, mixed with hardening agents and then compressed into sheets. Sheets vary in thickness from 3 mm to 9 mm, with one surface smoothly polished. Hardboard is used for purposes like the backs of cupboards and the bottoms of drawers. 'MDF' (medium density fibreboard) is a modern type of hardboard which can be machined (planed and polished, etc.) to a high standard, and is sometimes used for furniture.

Plywood is made from thin sheets of wood glued together, the grain of alternate sheets being at right angles to each other. This gives the plywood extra strength. Plywood is available in various thicknesses. Some plywoods are veneered (covered with a thin layer) with a better wood, plastic or metal. Plywood is strong, and is used for furniture, panelling and tea-chests.

Blockboard is made from strips of wood, glued together, and covered on both sides with a thick veneer. Blockboard is strong and is often used for flooring.

Chipboard is made from wood chips and sawdust set in glue and compressed into sheets. It is a low-cost board. It is often covered ('veneered') with better wood for use in furniture, or with formica, for use as kitchen counters.

PROPERTIES OF TIMBER

The properties of the different timbers vary considerably. Some are very hard (e.g. teak, oak) and others soft (balsa, pine). The strength of a piece of timber depends on grain direction. Along the grain it is strong, but across the grain is it much weaker.

Most woods float in water (have a density less than 1 g/cm³) but ebony is one that sinks. Some resist water well (mainly the hardwoods); others rot in time. Moisture makes most woods expand – which is why wooden window frames often stick in damp weather. Wood should be 'seasoned' (fully dried out) before being used. Manufactured boards have minimal resistance to moisture; some quickly fall apart after they have been soaked with water.

FORESTRY IN IRELAND

Forestry is an important industry and a valuable resource in Ireland. About 570 000 hectares (1.4 million acres) or 8% of the land is forested. Most of the forests are state owned. Forestry offers many benefits:

- it provides employment for about 16 000 people
- poor land such as bogs and mountain sides can be used
- it provides habitats for many animals and birds
- timber is a much-needed resource in the country
- softwood trees grow quickly in this country because of the climate
- state forests are open to the public for hiking and walking and some have nature trails laid out

fig. 45.9 A state forest

EXPERIMENTS

Experiment 45.10 (a)
To compare the bending strengths of different timbers

This can be done in the same manner as described for plastics (page 320).

Experiment 45.10 (b)
To investigate the effect of grain on timber strength

The same apparatus is used for this investigation. Two similar strips of the same timber are tested, one which has the grain running along the strip, and the other with the grain across the strip.

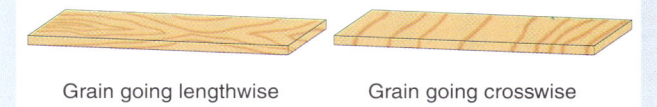

Grain going lengthwise | Grain going crosswise

fig. 45.10 Strips of timber

Experiment 45.11
To measure the moisture content of a sample of timber

1. Take a sample of the timber being tested and find its mass.
2. Place it in a warm oven (between 50 and 70°C) and leave it there for 24 hours.
3. Find the new mass of the timber; subtract the two values to find the loss in mass (mass of moisture lost).
4. Calculate this as a percentage of the original mass of the timber.

DETERIORATION, PROTECTION AND CARE OF MATERIALS

All materials deteriorate (decay or decompose) to some extent. Some like concrete, are very long lasting while others, like wood which has become wet, can decay very quickly. Causes of decay are the weather, pest infestation, corrosion, etc. Some protection methods for prolonging the life of timber are shown below.

QUESTIONS

Q. 45.19
(a) What is the difference between hardwoods and softwoods?
(b) Give two examples of each.
(c) Name a common use of each type of wood.
(d) State a property of each type which makes it suitable for the use you have named.

Q. 45.20
Describe, with the aid of a diagram, an experiment in which you compared the bending strengths of two different pieces of timber.

Q. 45.21
With the aid of books (wood technology texts or encyclopaedias) from your school or local library, write an account of how any named manufactured board is produced.

Q. 45.22
Name two ways in which timber can deteriorate. How would you recognise each. What can be done to prevent each of these happening?

Material	Cause of decay	Effect of decay	Protection methods
Timber	Wet rot	Softens, loses strength disintegrates	Varnishing, painting, oiling preservatives (e.g. creosote)
	Dry rot	Turns into a powder	Preservatives, good ventilation
	Woodworm	Infested with holes	Chemical treatment

46

FOOD TYPES, FOOD PROCESSING, FOOD PRESERVATION

All living things need food. Plants make their own food during the process of **photosynthesis**. Animals are not able to make their own food so they must eat plants and/or other animals. Plants and animals use food:

- to provide themselves with energy
- to allow for the growth and repair of cells
- to stay in good health

fig. 46.1 Samples of food from the main nutrient groups

NUTRIENT GROUPS

The main nutrient groups are: carbohydrates, fats, protein, vitamins and minerals. In order for a person to be healthy, sufficient of each of these is necessary in the person's diet. In addition water is essential.

Carbohydrates

The main sources of carbohydrates are sugary and starchy foods. Foods that are rich in sugars include sweets, jams, cakes, biscuits and sweet fruits. Starch is found in potatoes, flour, pasta, and rice. The function of carbohydrates is to provide energy, and during respiration every gram of carbohydrate releases about 17 kJ of energy. Carbohydrates are compounds consisting of carbon, hydrogen and oxygen. **Glucose**, the simplest carbohydrate, is a simple sugar. In **sucrose** (table sugar), each molecule is made up of two simple sugars chemically combined together. **Starch** is made up of a chain of simple sugar molecules. When foods containing starch are being digested, the starch molecules are broken down into simple sugar molecules. The chemical energy stored in simple sugars is released by cells during respiration.

fig. 46.2 Examples of carbohydrates

One way in which plant cells differ from animal cells is that plant cells have cell walls in addition to cell membranes (see Chapter 30). The cell wall is formed mainly from a substance called cellulose, which is a carbohydrate. Some animals such as cows and sheep have the ability to digest this cellulose, but humans are not able to do so. **Fibre** or roughage is the commonly used term for cellulose. When we eat food products that come from plants, such as grains, fruit, and vegetables, we are provided with fibre. Fibre is not broken down by the digestive system but it is needed to aid the movement of food through the gut, and this helps to prevent constipation.

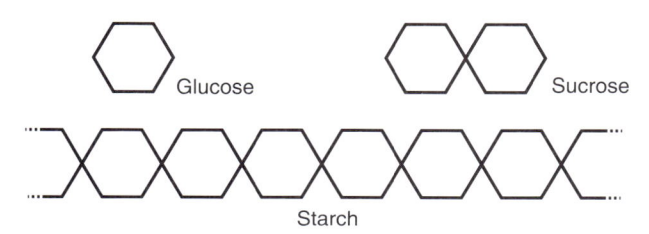

fig. 46.3 Glucose, sucrose and starch molecules

46 • Food Types, Food Processing, Food Preservation

> **Experiment 46.1**
> **To test foods for starch**
>
> 1. Place a spatula full of the food to be tested in a test tube.
> 2. Using a dropper, add 2 to 3 drops of **iodine solution**.
> 3. Note any colour change.
> 4. Record your result.
>
> *Result:* If starch is present in the food, the iodine solution will turn from yellow/brown to blue/black in colour. 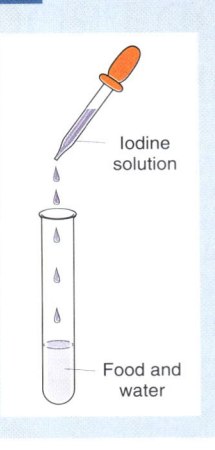
>
> **fig. 46.4**

> **Experiment 46.2**
> **To test for reducing sugar** 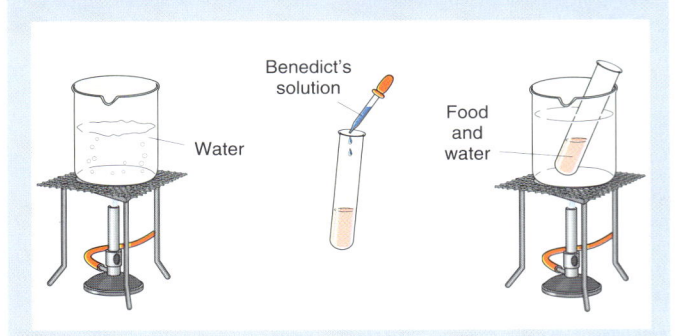
>
> **fig. 46.5**
>
> 1. Set up a boiling water bath as shown in the diagram.
> 2. Place some glucose solution into a test tube to a depth of about 2 cm. If solid glucose is supplied, then place a spatula full in the test tube and dissolve it in about 5 cm³ of water.
> 3. Pour some **Benedict's solution** into another test tube to a depth of 2 cm.
> 4. Add the Benedict's solution to the glucose solution. Make a note of the colour that is produced.
> 5. Place the test tube in the boiling water bath and leve it there for about three minutes.
> 6. Carefully remove the test tube and note if any colour change occurs.
> 7. Record your result.
> 8. Repeat the test, using each of the other food substances provided.
>
> *Result:* If the solution turns a red/orange colour, glucose is present in it.

Fats

fig. 46.6 Foods that are good sources of fats and proteins

Examples of foods in this group are butter, margarine, fish oils, vegetable oils, and fats from meat and meat products. A certain amount of fat is needed by the body and this should come from both plant and animal sources. Too much animal fat in one's diet may contribute to the build-up of fat deposits in arteries.

The function of fats is to provide energy. Every gram of fat releases about 38 kJ of energy during respiration. Fats also help to insulate the body. Fats, which contain the elements carbon, hydrogen and oxygen are broken down (during digestion) into compounds called fatty acids and glycerol.

Fat molecule   Fatty acid and glycerol

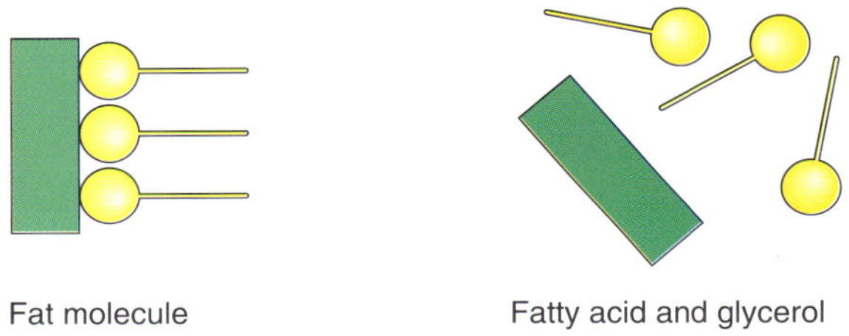

fig. 46.7 Fats are broken down into fatty acids and glycerol

Protein

Protein is found in lean meat, fish, egg white, peas, beans, lentils, nuts, cheese and milk. The main function of protein is to enable the growth and repair of body cells. Protein is also used to produce the enzymes that aid digestion, and the antibodies that help the body to fight disease. As protein is essential for growth, it is necessary to eat foods containing it daily. Proteins are made from long chains of compounds called **amino acids**, which contain the elements carbon, hydrogen, oxygen and nitrogen (and some also contain sulphur). There are 20 different amino acids. In order to allow the formation of different types of proteins the amino acids arrange themselves in a variety of sequences.

Experiment 46.3
To test for fats in foodstuffs

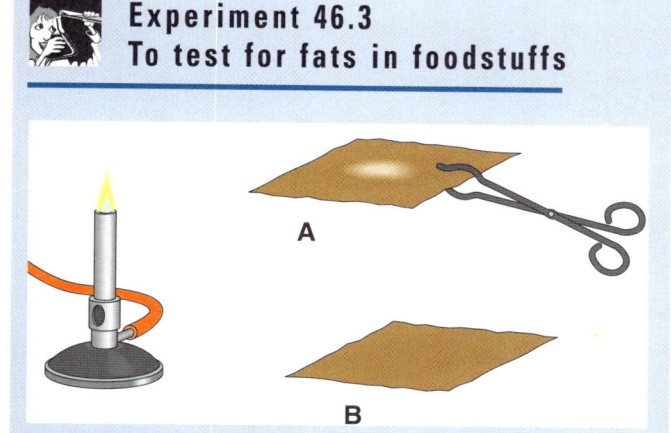

fig. 46.8

1. Rub the piece of food on a piece of brown paper; label this piece of paper A.
2. Add a drop of water to another piece of brown paper and label this B.
3. Warm both pieces of paper gently in a bunsen flame until the water dries.
4. Hold them up to the light and make a note of any difference between them.

Result:

If fat is present in the food, a translucent (partially 'see-through') spot will be seen, whereas the water on B will dry, leaving no mark.

fig. 46.9 *A selection of healthy vegetarian foods containing fats, carbohydrates and proteins*

Different amino acids

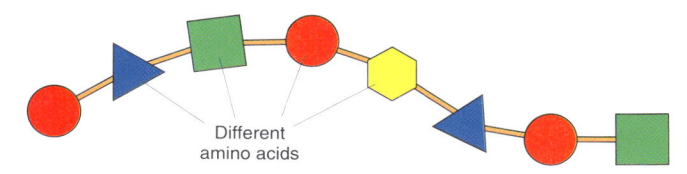

fig. 46.10 *Proteins are made up of chains of amino acids*

Vitamins

Vitamins are chemicals that the body needs in order to keep it working well. Vitamins are only required in tiny amounts, and a good balanced diet usually provides all the necessary vitamins.

Experiment 46.4
To test for protein (the Biuret test)

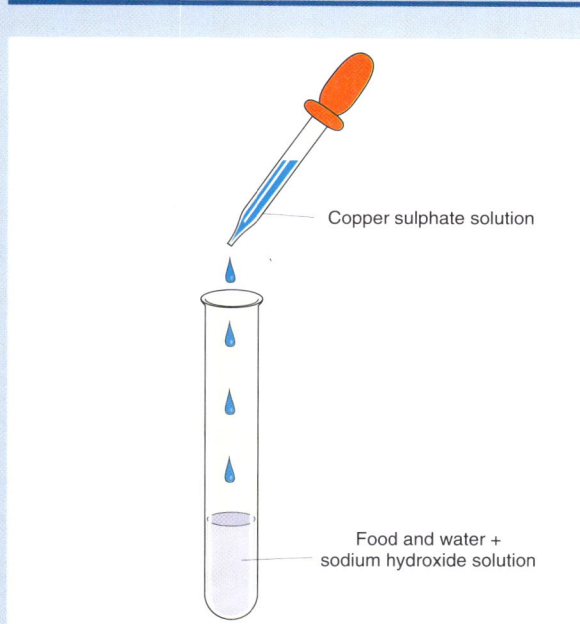

safety glasses needed

Caution: Sodium hydroxide is corrosive, so handle it with care.

1. Put a dropper full of the food sample being tested into a test tube. Add a dropper full of water. (If the substance is solid, mix it with a little water to form a paste and then transfer it to the test tube. Add dropper full of water.)
2. Add an equal volume of 10% sodium hydroxide solution and mix it with the food.
3. Add three drops of 1% copper sulphate solution, and shake gently to mix this also.

Result:

If protein is present, a violet colour appears.

Copper sulphate solution

Food and water + sodium hydroxide solution

fig. 46.11

Vitamin	Source	Function	Deficiency disease
A	Carrots, green vegetables, cheese, butter, milk, eggs	Helps to form pigments in the retina of the eye	Poor night vision
B group	Whole cereals, peas, beans, yeast	Helps to develop the nervous system	Beriberi
C	Oranges, lemons, grapefruit, tomatoes, fresh green vegetables, potatoes	Necessary for healthy gums and skin	Scurvy
D	Butter, cheese, egg-yolk, liver, fish-liver oil	Helps in the formation of strong bones	Rickets

Minerals

Like vitamins, minerals have no energy value, but they are needed for good health. Most of the necessary minerals are supplied in a balanced diet.

Mineral	Source	Function
Iron	Liver, meat, spinach, cabbage	Helps to form haemoglobin (the pigment in blood that carries oxygen)
Calcium	Milk, cheese and other dairy products	Helps to strengthen bones
Iodine	Sea fish, shellfish and some vegetables	Necessary for the thyroid gland in order to make the hormone **thyroxine**

WATER

Water forms almost 70% of body tissues. Water is also the main substance in body fluids such as blood, urine and sweat. Digested food, salts and vitamins are carried around the body in an aqueous (watery) solution in the blood. Water is important for two reasons: (i) as a solvent, and (ii) as a transport fluid in the body. The body loses water in several ways (sweating, producing urine, and respiration), so it is necessary to replace this lost water by including it in the diet.

QUESTIONS

Q. 46.1

(a) List two reasons why food is needed by the body.
(b) What are the main nutrient groups?
(c) Give three examples of foods in each group.

Q. 46.2

(a) State the function of each of the main nutrient groups.
(b) What other substances are needed in order to provide a balanced diet?
(c) State the function of fibre in the diet. Give two examples of foods rich in fibre.

Q. 46.3

Glucose is a simple carbohydrate.
(a) Describe how you would test food for simple sugars.
(b) Describe a simple experiment to test for the presence of starch.

Q. 46.4

(a) What elements are found in fats? Name the chemical compounds that result from the breakdown of fats.
(b) Describe a simple experiment to test for the presence of fats.

Q. 46.5

(a) What are the main functions of protein in the diet?
(b) List the elements found in protein.
(c) Describe how foodstuffs can be tested for protein.

Q. 46.6
Explain why water is needed in your diet.

Q. 46.7
Cheese is a good source of calcium in the diet. Why is calcium needed in the diet? Name another food that is rich in calcium.

Q. 46.8
(a) State the function of vitamin D in the human body.
(b) Give one source of this vitamin.
(c) Why is vitamin A needed in the diet?
(d) Name two minerals that are needed in our diet.
(e) Name a food that is rich in one of these minerals.

Q. 46.9
From the following list, pick out two foods that are good sources of protein: cheese, bread, fish, butter, carrots.

A BALANCED DIET

A balanced diet is one that contains all the substances that the body needs, and in the correct amounts. A diet that consists of too much or too little of any one food group leads to poor nutrition. Eating a balanced diet does not mean a person cannot eat snack foods and sweets, but these should form only a small part of the overall diet. If a person takes in more food than they use up, the body stores this as fat, and it leads to an increase in body mass (body 'weight'). If this builds up, the person becomes overweight and this can lead to health problems, such as heart disease, later in life.

You can avoid putting on too much weight by controlling your diet. This does not necessarily mean eating less, but eating differently. Avoid too much sugar and processed food with a high sugar content, such as cakes, sweets, and biscuits, and include more vegetables, fruit and wholemeal bread in your diet. Your teeth, waistline, intestines and health in general will benefit. For any person who is unsure of how to plan a safe weight loss programme, it is a good idea to consult a doctor or dietitian for advice, to make sure the diet you have chosen is suitable for your age and lifestyle.

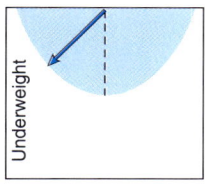

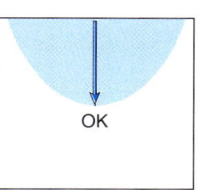

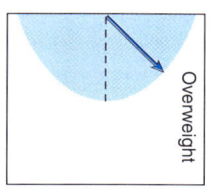

Underweight	OK	Overweight
When the amount of food taken in is less than the body needs.	'Weight' stays the same as food intake balances activity.	When the amount of food taken in is greater than the body needs.

fig. 46.12 It is important to maintain a healthy weight

ENERGY VALUES OF FOODS

Energy used for a range of activities:

Activity	kJ/hr
sitting	400
walking slowly	600–700
running	3000–4000
bicycling	2000
swimming	3000–3700

People need to take in different amounts of energy in their diet depending on their age, lifestyle and occupation.

Individual	Energy requirement kJ (per day)
Child aged 1	3250
Child aged 8	8500
Boy aged 15	11 400
Active woman aged 25	11 000
Breast feeding woman	11 700
Active man aged 50	12 000
Sedentary woman aged 70	8200

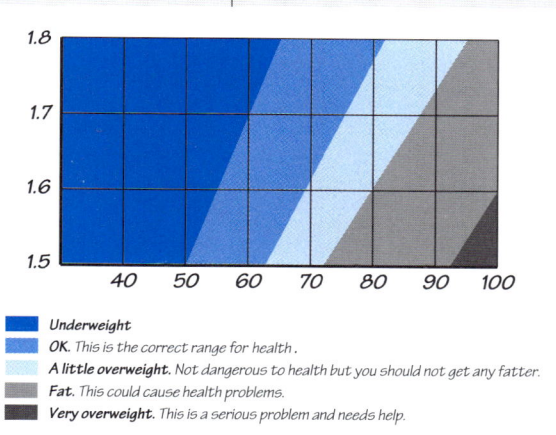

- **Underweight**
- **OK.** This is the correct range for health.
- **A little overweight.** Not dangerous to health but you should not get any fatter.
- **Fat.** This could cause health problems.
- **Very overweight.** This is a serious problem and needs help.

fig. 46.13 Height-weight chart

PROBLEMS OF WORLD FOOD SUPPLY

We live in a world where millions starve, while many nations have a surplus of food. In Western countries that produce more food than is needed, there are 'food mountains'. A food mountain refers to an over-supply of a food product such as meat, milk powder or grain. In such a situation in Europe, the EU pays to have these products held in cold storage for long periods of time, so that the market price of the products does not drop due to too much being available.

Famine occurs when food shortages are so great that they affect a whole region or country. The main causes of famine are:

- Crop failure caused by drought, floods or pests. When a crop fails for several years in a row, the results are disastrous.

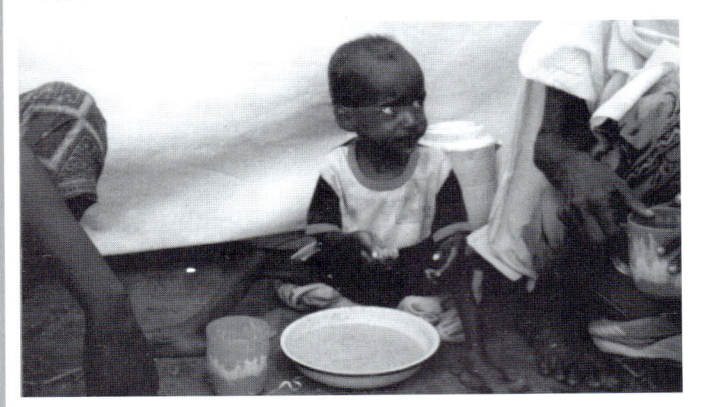

fig. 46.14 *Famine affects many countries*

- Poor farming techniques, which remove nutrients from the ground and lead to erosion, where the rich upper layer of the soil is removed. This can eventually lead to desertification (this means the changing of fertile land into desert).

fig. 46.15

- In many Third World countries, some farmers may grow only one type of crop, which is exported to rich countries. Such crops (called cash crops) are those that the farmer sells to earn money. When the farmer continues to grow the same crop in an area without applying fertilisers, the nutrient supply becomes exhausted. Food for the people has then to be imported.
- Also, in some Third World countries, unstable political situations can cause civil wars. The countries' governments then increase the spending on weapons, and reduce the amount of money spent on improving farming.
- Malnutrition occurs when a person's diet is very unbalanced. In famine conditions malnutrition leads to serious health problems. People are unable to fight off infections, the growth of children is stunted and in many cases people die of starvation.

FOOD ADDITIVES

Food additives are substances added to food to improve colour, flavour, and texture, and also to kill bacteria. Many people believe that if a food label has an E number on it, it means the food may be harmful. This is not so; the **E number** is a code assigned by the European Union for a substance that has been passed as being safe for adding to food. Many E numbers are codes for substances that are found naturally in foods.

Types of food additives

Food Colourings (E100–180)

These begin with the number 1.
They are added to foods to replace the colour that may be lost during cooking.

Preservatives (E200–297)

These begin with the number 2.
Preservatives slow down or kill the bacteria that spoil food.

Antioxidants (E300–385)

These begin with the number 3.
Antioxidants stop fats and oils from decaying, and they help to prevent the discolouring of canned meats and fruits. Vitamin C (E 300) is an example of an antioxidant used in canned fruit.

Emulsifiers and stabilisers (E400–495)

These begin with the number 4.
Emulsifiers help oil and water mix together. Stabilisers prevent them from separating again.

Advantages of food additives

- preserve food
- prevent disease
- improve the appearance and taste of food

Disadvantages of food additives

- some cause allergies
- certain additives destroy vitamins in food

READING LABELS

Current regulations state that food labels must show the following:

- the name of the food
- the net mass ('weight') or volume
- a date mark or 'best before date'
- the name and address of the manufacturer
- a list of all ingredients including food additives, in decreasing order of mass present

In addition, many products give information about the nutritional content, for example, the number of grams of carbohydrate, fats, proteins etc. per 100 g of the food. It is a helpful exercise to examine a variety of food labels and compare the nutritional information on them.

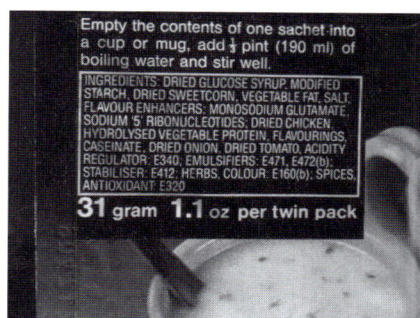

fig. 46.16 Food labels provide information about the contents of food products

QUESTIONS

Q. 46.10
(a) What is meant by a balanced diet?
(b) Why is it necessary to eat a balanced diet?

Q. 46.11
(a) Explain why a person may eat a lot of food and yet suffer from a lack of nutrients.
(b) Give an example of a lunch that (i) would provide a balance of nutrients and (ii) would provide poor nutrition.

Q. 46.12
What steps should people take if they wish to reduce their weight?

Q. 46.13
While some countries have an oversupply of food, others are experiencing famine conditions. Describe the main causes of famine in Third World countries.

Q. 46.14
Give two advantages and two disadvantages of food additives.

Q. 46.15
What information does an E number on a food packet give? Name four types of food additives. E 104 is a food additive.
(a) Which type of food additive is it?
(b) Why is it used?
(c) Give a disadvantage of using this type of additive?

Q. 46.16
(a) Why are stabilisers added to food?
(b) What types of additives prevent fats and oils from decaying? Give an example of one such additive.
(a) Why are preservatives added to food?
(b) Why are colourings added to food?

Q. 46.17
(a) What information should a food label include?
(b) Why is it useful to include details on the wrapper of the nutrients in foods.

FOOD PRESERVATION

Micro-organisms spoil food by changing its taste and/or its appearance. Preserving food prevents the growth of bacteria, which may cause disease. Preservation also prolongs the shelf life of food products.

Method	Procedure	Function
Refrigeration	Food is stored below 4°C. Any fresh food such as raw meats, milk and cheese.	Preserves food longer by slowing down the growth of bacteria.
Pasteurisation	Milk is heated to 72°C for 15 seconds and then cooled to below 10°C. Milk and fruit juices are pasteurised.	Kills bacteria.
Freezing	Food is stored below −18°C.	Prevents growth of bacteria.
Canning	Bacteria are killed by adding chemicals; food is stored in airtight containers. Examples are fruit, vegetables, soups and meats.	Prevents contamination.

(continued)

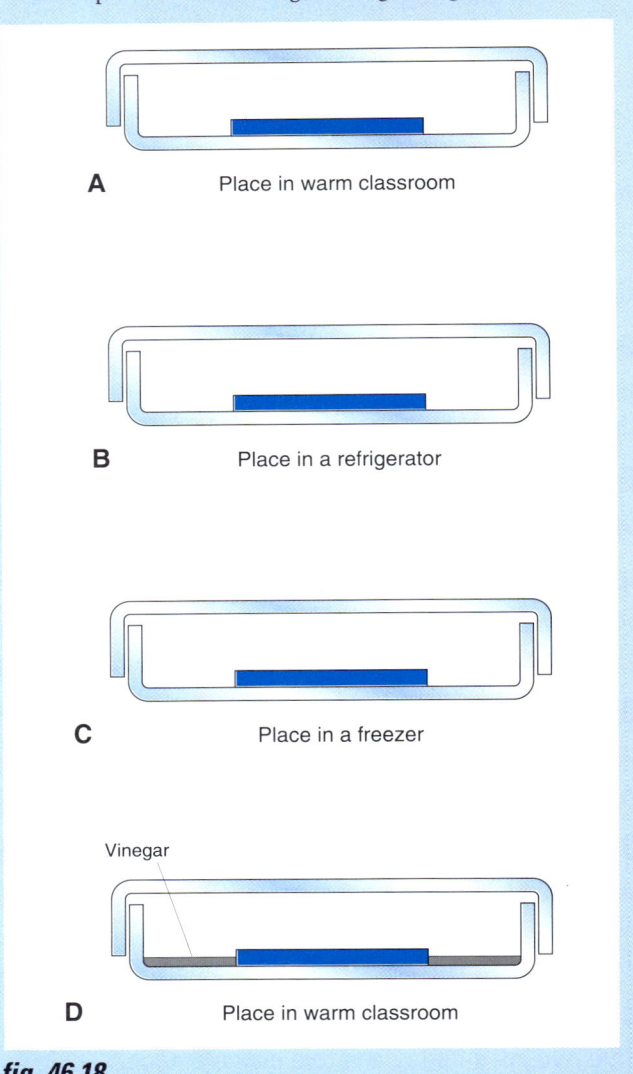

46 • Food Types, Food Processing, Food Preservation

Dehydration	Food is freeze dried, for example, vegetables and fruit.	Bacteria cannot multiply without water.
Irradiation	Food is sterilised by exposing it to gamma radiation. Used on soft fruit.	Stops bacterial cells from multiplying.
Chemical additives	Salt, sugar, vinegar or spices are added to food. Examples are jams, fruit in syrup, salted fish and pickled onions.	Bacteria cannot multiply as the sugar, salt or vinegar make conditions unsuitable for them to reproduce.

Experiment 46.6
To investigate some preserving methods

1. Label four petri dishes A, B, C and D.
2. Place one slice of fresh beetroot in each.
3. Treat the dishes as follows.
   Cover dish A with cling film, and place it in a warm place in the laboratory. Cover dish B with cling film, and place it in a refrigerator. Cover dish C with cling film, and place it in a freezer. Soak the beetroot in vinegar, cover dish D with cling film and leave it in a warm place in the laboratory.
4. Examine each dish after one week, and make a note of changes that have occurred.

Did you notice micro-organisms growing on the beetroot in dish A. The temperature of dishes B and C was too low to allow the growth of micro-organisms and the low pH in dish D prevented micro-organisms growing there.

A — Place in warm classroom

B — Place in a refrigerator

C — Place in a freezer

D (Vinegar) — Place in warm classroom

fig. 46.18

Experiment 46.5
To demonstrate the presence of micro-organisms in the air

Plate A — Exposed to the air for 30 minutes

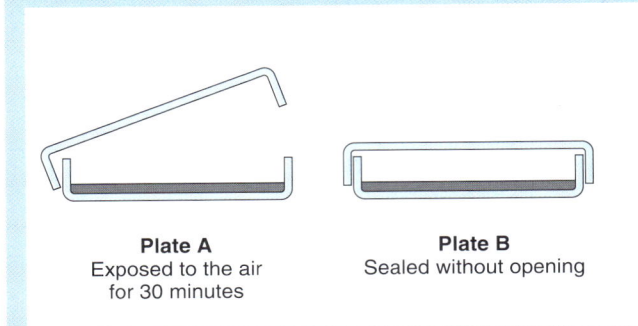

Plate B — Sealed without opening

fig. 46.17

1. Label two nutrient agar plates A and B.
2. Open plate A to the air and leave it exposed for 30 minutes.
3. Replace the cover and seal the plate securely with tape.
4. Seal plate B without opening it. This is called the control.
5. Place the two plates in an incubator for a couple of days. (This provides the ideal temperature for the micro-organisms to grow)
6. Examine the nutrient agar plates without opening them, and note any differences between them.

Result: Do you notice that the agar plate that was exposed to the air had clusters of micro-organisms growing on it? Where did they come from? What do you notice about the agar plate labelled B.

Applied Science • 47

fig. 46.19 Canning is one method of food preservation

Experiment 46.7
To examine the effect of sugar on rhubarb stem cells

1. Place a thin piece of red rhubarb stem on a glass slide, add a drop of water and place a cover slip over it.
2. Observe the cells under a microscope, at both low and medium powers.
3. Draw a diagram of what you observe.
4. Set up another slide but in this case use sugar solution instead of water.
5. Repeat step 2 and 3.
6. Make a note of the differences between the cells.

Result: Did you notice that the cells of the rhubarb stem placed in the sugar solution look different? This is because the water moves from the cells into the sugar solution, causing the cytoplasm to shrink. When bacterial cells are placed in a sugar solution, the same process takes place, and the cells cannot survive due to the removal of water.

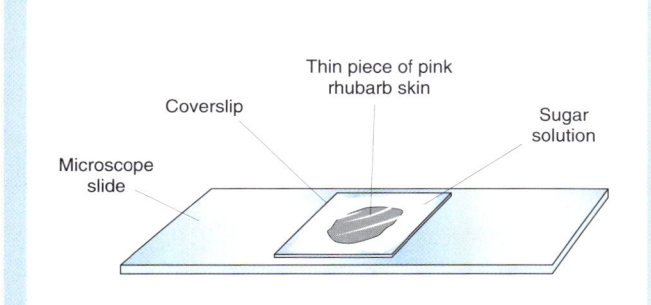

fig. 46.20

QUESTIONS

Q. 46.18

(a) Why is it necessary to preserve food?
(b) List four methods of food preservation.

Q. 46.19

Some foods are preserved by storing them in vinegar. Name one food that is preserved in this way and explain how the vinegar preserves the food.

Q. 46.20

Describe an experiment to investigate methods of preserving beetroot.

Q. 46.21

Micro-organisms are present in the air and are also found on food. Describe an experiment to show that a food contains micro-organisms.

Q. 46.22

What is pasteurisation? Why is milk normally pasteurised?

FOOD PROCESSING

The dairy industry

Milk is not only a rich source of protein for humans, but it also provides ideal conditions for the growth of bacteria and other micro-organisms. While some of these micro-organisms cause diseases, many of them are useful in making dairy products such as cheese and yoghurt.

■ 46 • Food Types, Food Processing, Food Preservation

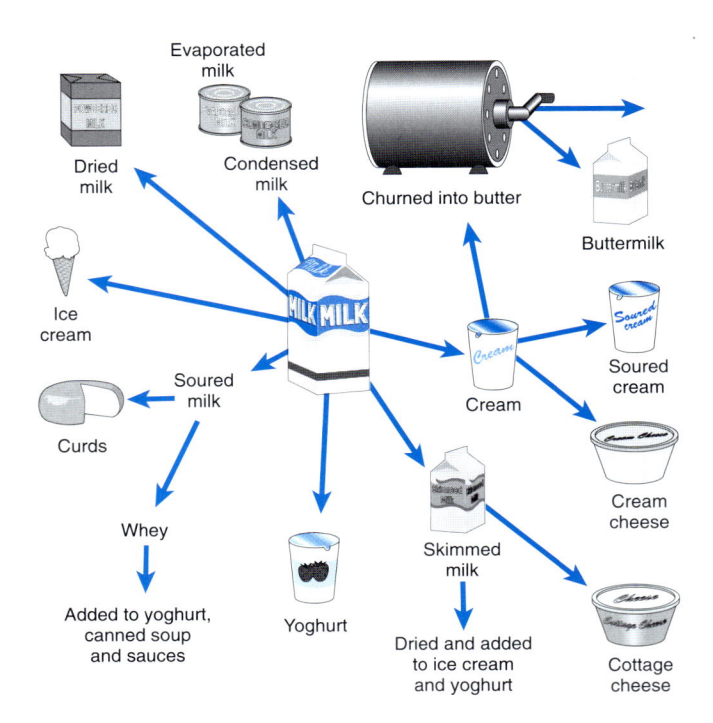

fig. 46.21 *Milk is used in many different ways*

Pasteurisation

Pasteurisation is a process used to kill microorganisms, without affecting the taste and appearance of food. The process was developed by a French scientist called Louis Pasteur in the 1860s, to preserve wine and beer.

Milk is pasteurised by heating it to 72°C for at least 15 seconds and then rapidly cooling it to below 10°C. The milk is then put into either bottles or cartons for distribution. Pasteurised milk should be stored in a refrigerator, below 5°C. Refrigeration slows down the growth of the bacteria, but it does not stop it completely. This is why milk, even when stored in the refrigerator, will go sour after a number of days.

Cheese production

Milk is used in the production of cheese.

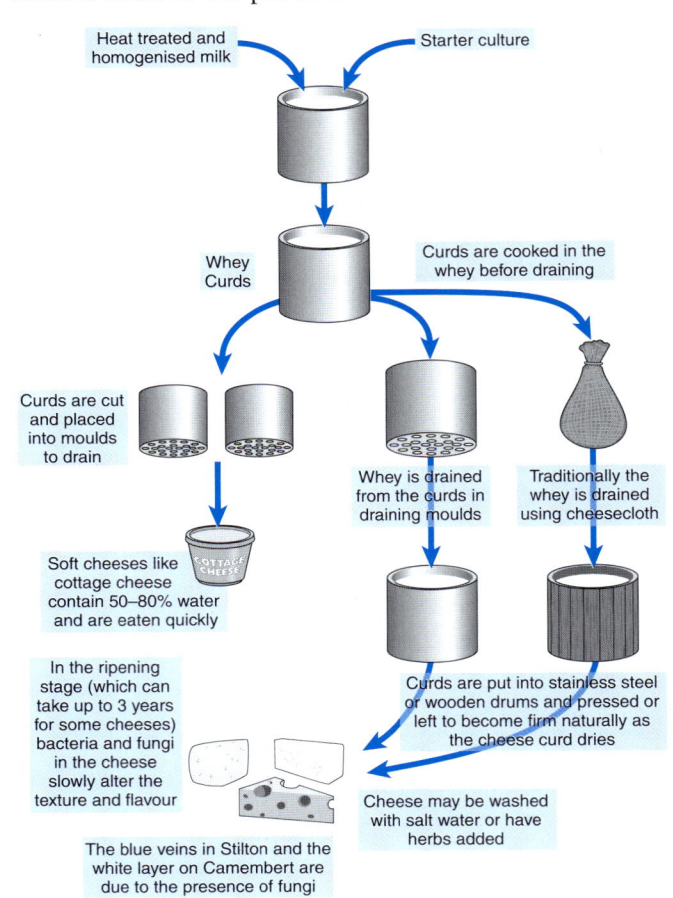

fig. 46.22 *Cheese production*

Making cheese

Fresh milk is pasteurised to kill bacteria. Special bacteria are then added to sour the milk. A substance called rennet is added to clot the milk – this makes solids in the milk clump together. (Rennet is prepared from the linings of calves' stomachs.) Whey (the watery

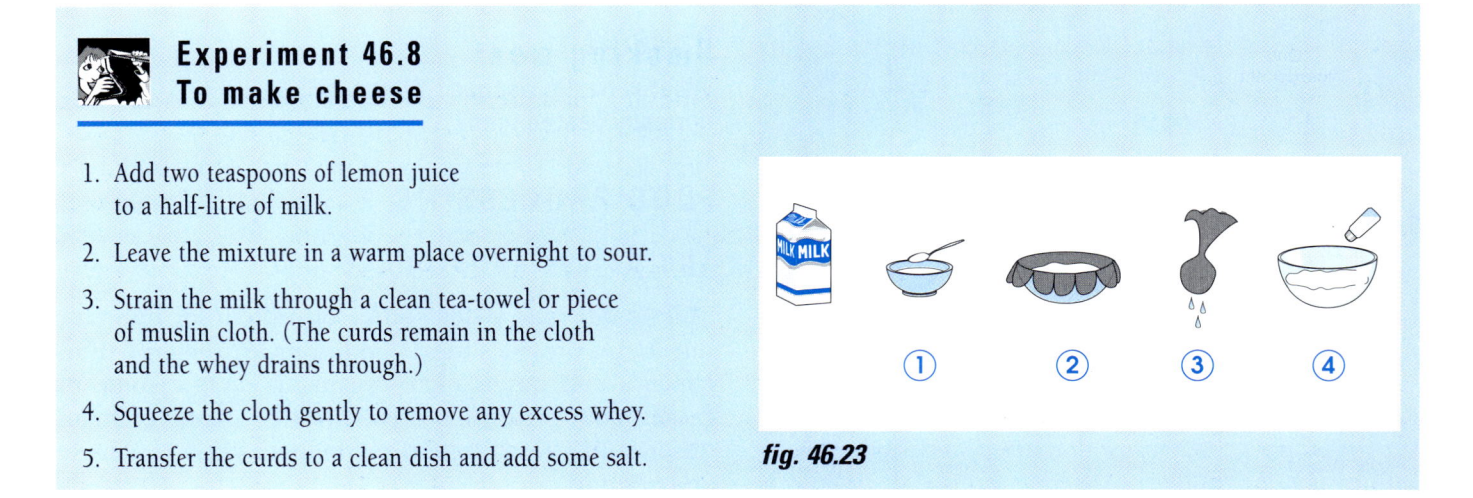

Experiment 46.8
To make cheese

1. Add two teaspoons of lemon juice to a half-litre of milk.
2. Leave the mixture in a warm place overnight to sour.
3. Strain the milk through a clean tea-towel or piece of muslin cloth. (The curds remain in the cloth and the whey drains through.)
4. Squeeze the cloth gently to remove any excess whey.
5. Transfer the curds to a clean dish and add some salt.

fig. 46.23

liquid that is formed) is removed from the curd. The curd (formed when the solids in the milk clump together) is salted, and then pressed into slabs and allowed to mature.

Experiment 46.9
To make yoghurt

Caution: This experiment should be carried out in a kitchen, rather than in a laboratory.

You will need: a glass container, a plastic cup, a plastic spoon, a heating pan, 50 cm³ of milk, a thermometer and cling film.

1. Sterilise the equipment by soaking it in Milton (one bottle cap per two litres) in a basin for one minute. Then rinse each item carefully in cold water.
2. Put 50 cm³ of milk in the pan.
3. Pasteurise the milk by heating to 72°C for 15 seconds. Then quickly cool to 37°C by standing the pan in a basin of cold water. This is the most suitable temperature for the bacteria to work.
4. Transfer the mixture to a plastic cup and stir in one teaspoonful of natural yoghurt.
5. Cover the top of the cup with cling film.
6. Leave it in a warm place for 6–8 hours.
7. Place it in refrigerator overnight, and inspect and taste it the next day.

Result: Did you notice that the sample in the cup has a creamy texture. The teaspoon of natural yoghurt contains the bacteria that converted the milk to yoghurt.

fig. 46.24

MAKING BUTTER

Cream is churned up (in the home this could be done using a food mixer). This causes the separation of the cream into a sour watery liquid (buttermilk and a solid material (butter). After the liquid buttermilk is drained off, salt is added to and mixed with the butter to improve its taste.

fig. 46.25 *Butter making*

Making yoghurt

Yoghurt is made from milk by adding special bacteria to it. The bacteria causes the milk to become thick and creamy and slightly sour. This mixture is yoghurt and is a good source of calcium. There are many varieties of yoghurt such as natural (plain) yoghurt, and those flavoured with fruit or containing nuts.

MEAT PRODUCTS

Meat products are a good source of protein in the diet. Many different methods are used to preserve meat, but the main ones are smoking and curing.

Curing pork

One of the methods used to preserve pork is to salt it; on doing this, the pork becomes ham or bacon. Bacteria are living organisms, so they require water in order to survive. When salt is added to the pork, the salt causes the bacteria to lose water, and so kills them. The meat then lasts for a longer period of time. Salting is also used in the preservation of some types of fish.

Smoking meat

Smoking food preserves it and also adds to its flavour. To smoke food, it is hung over the smoke from a wood fire. The chemicals in the smoke coat the food and are absorbed into it, killing the bacterial cells. Smoking is used in the preservation of pork, fish, cheese and sausages. In some cases, other forms of preservation, such as refrigeration, are used in addition to smoking.

Antibiotics in meat

Modern farming is very intensive and animals are often kept in confined conditions. This can lead to animals developing infections and illnesses. In order

46 • *Food Types, Food Processing, Food Preservation*

to cure the animals, antibiotics (chemicals that fight infection) are given to them. This a necessary process, but problems can arise if eggs, milk or meat from the animal are eaten while the antibiotic is still in the animal's system. In some cases in the past, antibiotics were added to animal feed to prevent infections, rather than waiting until they developed. Scientific research has since shown that this is not a good idea.

The food products from the animal may contain traces of the antibiotic. If the antibiotic is present in large amounts, traces of the antibiotic can be passed to humans when they eat the food products. Some of the bacteria that the antibiotics fight can develop a resistance to the antibiotic and this can cause problems for humans. For example if a doctor prescribes the same antibiotic to a patient, the antibiotic will be less effective as the bacteria may be resistant to it.

Growth hormones

In the past some farmers used growth hormones to produce leaner cattle and improve milk yields. The EU has now banned the use of growth hormones, due to concern that they could build up in humans, and possibly cause health problems at a later stage. Fortunately, both consumers and farmers are becoming more aware of the problems that can arise when natural growth processes are artificially speeded up.

FERMENTATION (alcohol production)

Micro-organisms have been used in methods of food preservation for many centuries. One of the oldest of these methods is **fermentation**. Fermentation is a chemical reaction brought about by enzymes or by micro-organisms. It is used to make alcohol from carbohydrates like starch, cereals or sugar. The micro-organism used is a fungus called yeast. During fermentation, sugar is converted into alcohol and carbon dioxide by the action of yeast. This reaction takes place in the absence of oxygen. Fermentation is used in the production of alcoholic drinks such as beer, wine, and spirits. Yeast is also used in baking. Bread is made to rise by the carbon dioxide that is produced by the action of yeast on carbohydrates, such as flour.

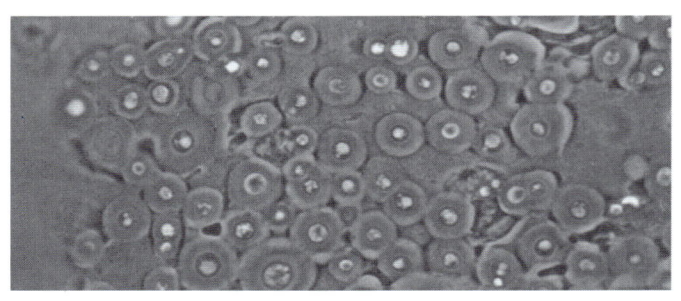

fig. 46.26 *Yeast cells as seen under a microscope*

Brewing

Beer, lager and stout are brewed from barley or other cereal crops. In the presence of yeast and water, the barley ferments, and beer is formed. This process, called brewing, is explained in figure 46.27.

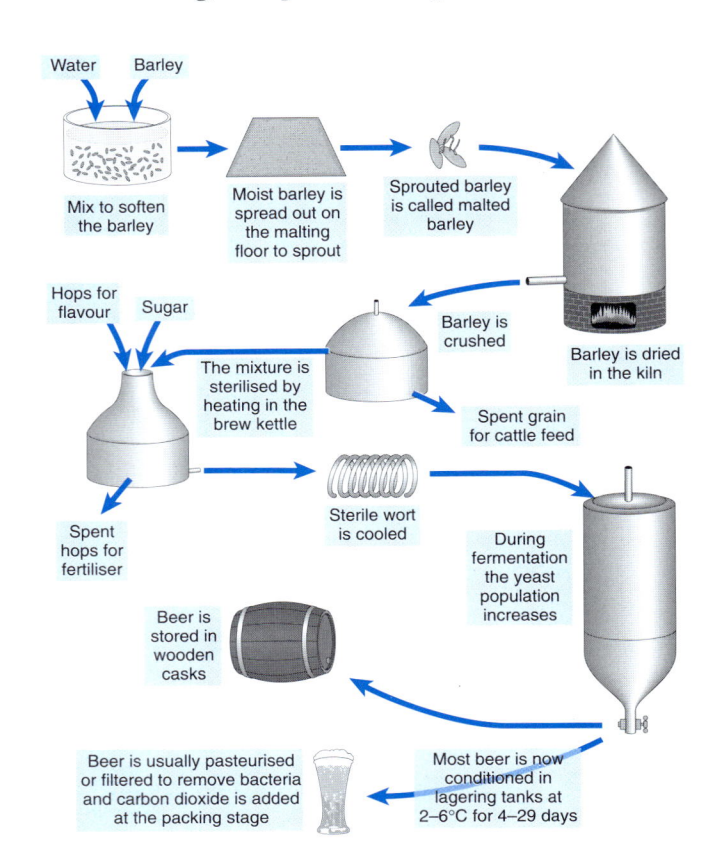

fig. 46.27 *The brewing process*

Wine making

Yeasts are found naturally on the skin of grapes. When the grapes are crushed, the yeasts and natural sugars in the grapes ferment and alcohol is produced.

Distilling

Distillation is the process of boiling a liquid and then condensing the vapour that is formed. When wine is distilled the alcohol content is increased and the product formed is called brandy. The process of distillation is explained in Chapter 18.

SILAGE

Silage is preserved grass that is used as feed for animals in winter when the natural growth of grass is low. In making silage, the grass is cut, chopped into small pieces and packed into an airtight silo or silage pit. In some cases, the silage is wrapped in large sheets of plastic to form individual bales.

Experiment 46.10
To make alcohol from sugar and yeast

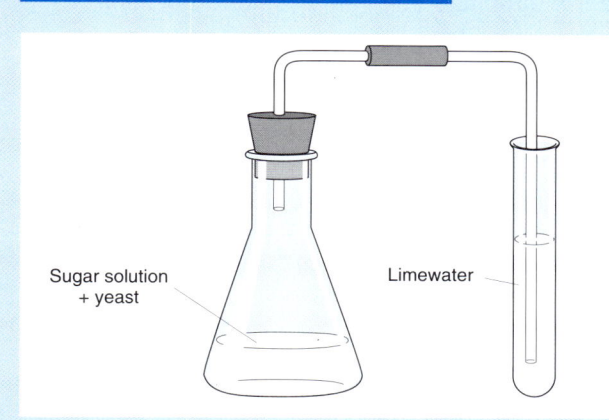

fig. 46.28

1. Set up the apparatus as shown in the diagram.
2. Place the apparatus in a warm place for a couple of days.
3. Note the smell from the flask and observe any changes in the limewater.

Result: Did you notice that the limewater turns cloudy. This shows that carbon dioxide has been produced. The sweet smell is due to the alcohol that has formed.

Experiment 46.11
To make silage

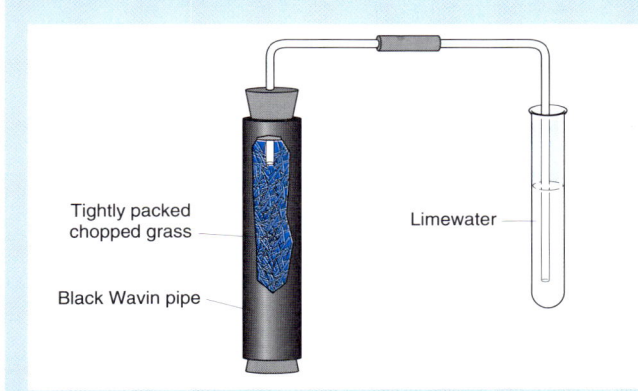

fig. 46.30

1. Freshly cut grass is packed into a suitable container as shown in figure 46.30.
2. The container is sealed and left for two weeks.

Result: The bacteria present on the grass converts the sugar in the grass to lactic acid. The lactic acid preserves the grass. Carbon dioxide is produced and the limewater turns milky.

Micro-organisms grow on the grass and when this occurs, the sugars in the grass ferment and form lactic acid, which preserves the grass. Molasses (a thick, brown, uncrystallised bitter sugar which is a byproduct of sugar refining) and formic acid are added. Molasses contains sugar, which provides an energy source for the micro-organisms that are working to convert the grass into silage. The formic acid prevents the growth of micro-organisms that would cause the silage to decay.

The micro-organisms involved in this process only work when oxygen is absent. For this reason, and also to prevent other micro-organisms from entering and decaying the silage, the storage area must be kept airtight.

Care must be taken to hold the liquid that runs off the silage, as it is very acidic and could pollute streams and rivers. The silage is removed from the storage area as it is needed during the winter months.

fig. 46.29 Silage is stored to provide food for animals in winter

BIOTECHNOLOGY

Biotechnology is the name given to the use of biological organisms, such as plants, animals and micro-organisms, to produce or process materials that are needed in today's world. Biotechnology has been used for thousands of years, in brewing, in the making of dairy products, and in bread making. Modern biotechnology makes use of micro-organisms for new purposes, such as producing antibiotics, medicines, food and biological washing powders. In the future micro-organisms may be used to improve our immunity to diseases or to decompose plastics.

46 • Food Types, Food Processing, Food Preservation

SUMMARY

- The main nutrient groups are carbohydrates, proteins, fats, vitamins, minerals. Water is also necessary in the diet.

- Carbohydrates provide energy, and examples are glucose, sucrose and starch. Fibre is also a carbohydrate and it is needed to help prevent constipation.

- Fats are necessary to provide energy.

- Proteins are needed for growth and repair of cells and body tissues. They are made up of compounds called amino acids, which contain the elements carbon, hydrogen, oxygen and nitrogen.

- Vitamins and minerals are needed in small amounts and a diet lacking in these can cause a deficiency disease.

- A balanced diet is one that contains all the required nutrients in the required amounts.

- The main causes of famine are crop failure, poor farming techniques, countries relying on one cash crop, and wars.

- E numbers are substances added to food to improve its colour, flavour, texture, and to preserve it. These include and E1— colourings, E2— preservatives, E3— antioxidants, and E400 emulsifiers and stabilisers.

- Food preservation prevents disease and prolongs the shelf life of food.

- The dairy industry processes milk to butter, yoghurt and cheese. Micro-organisms are necessary for this to occur.

- Some food products are preserved by curing (adding salt) or smoking.

- Fermentation is the conversion of sugars into alcohol and carbon dioxide, using yeast. It happens in the absence of oxygen.

$$\text{Sugar} \xrightarrow{\text{yeast}} \text{alcohol} + \text{carbon dioxide}$$

- Yeast is used in brewing, wine making, and bread making.

- Silage is preserved grass, which is fed to cattle during the winter.

- Biotechnology is the use of biological organisms, such as plants, animals or micro-organisms, to produce or process materials that are needed in today's world.

QUESTIONS

Q. 46.23

Milk can be processed to provide many foodstuffs. List three products that can be made from milk.

Q. 46.24

Describe a simple experiment to prepare yoghurt.

Q. 46.25

While some micro-organisms cause disease, others are used in the food processing industry. Describe two food industries that use micro-organisms, and say what each produces.

Q. 46.26

Describe an experiment to make cheese.

Q. 46.27

(a) What is fermentation? Name the micro-organism used in fermentation.
(b) Give examples of three foods or drinks that are produced using yeasts.

Q. 46.28

(a) What is silage?
(b) Describe an experiment to prepare silage in the laboratory.
(c) Explain why (i) acid and (ii) molasses are added to the silage.
(d) What precautions must be taken when silage is being stored?

Q. 46.29

What is biotechnology?
Give one example of its use.

47

ELECTRONICS

fig. 47.1 *This is part of the electronics of a small portable radio. It contains resistors, capacitors, diodes, coils, switches, transformers and potentiometers, all soldered on to a printed circuit of copper, on the reverse side of the base.*

You live in a world of electronics. You are constantly surrounded by electronic gadgets and devices – radios, TVs, videos, CD players, computers, calculators, digital watches, telephones, security lights, tape decks, 'Walkmans', bar-code readers, automatic teller machines, musical doorbells, synthesisers, and the list could go on. **Electronics is all about devices which control the movement of electrons.**

SIMPLE CIRCUITS

In order to learn about electronics, it is essential that basic work on electric circuits is properly understood. So, the starting point for a study of electronics is Chapter 9. You must make sure you know about electric circuits, voltage, current, resistance (and their units), series and parallel arrangements, and most important, the symbols for the various electrical devices (shown on page 54).

SWITCHES

There are many types of switches, but they all do essentially the same job: they complete a circuit when switched on, and they break a circuit when switched off. A circuit may contain more than one switch, and some circuits with two or more switches are illustrated in Figures 47.2, 47.3 and 47.4.

1. Switches in series

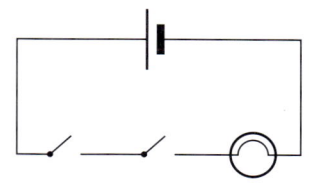

fig. 47.2

When two switches are connected in series with each other, both switches must be on to complete the circuit. An arrangement like this is called an **AND gate**. There is an AND gate in a washing machine. It is there to ensure that the machine will operate only when (i) it is switched on, **and** (ii) when the door is closed.

2. Switches in parallel

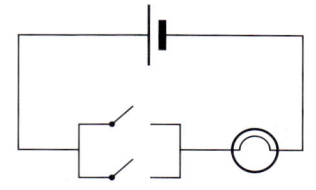

fig. 47.3

When two switches are connected in parallel, switching either of them on will complete the circuit. Such an arrangement is called an **OR gate**. There is an OR gate in a burglar alarm circuit. The alarm will ring when either a door, **or** a window is forced open.

3. Two-way switches

Two-way switches are used in places such as light switches near stairs. They enable the lights to be switched on or off, at the bottom of the stairs or at the top. The circuit is as shown in Figure 47.4.

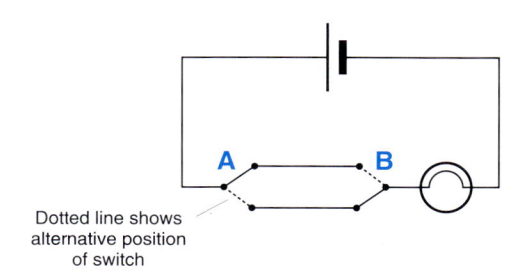

Dotted line shows alternative position of switch

fig. 47.4

47 • Electronics

The circuit as drawn is incomplete. Switching either A or B will complete the circuit, making the light go on. And when it is on, switching either A or B will make it go off again.

RESISTANCE AND RESISTORS

Resistance is the property of a material that opposes the flow of electric current. A component that is constructed to do this is called a **resistor**. Resistors keep currents and voltages at the correct values for other components in circuits to work properly. As the resistance of a circuit increases, the current that flows in it decreases.

A **variable resistor** or **rheostat** can be used in two ways: (i) to vary the current flowing in a circuit, and (ii) to vary the voltage obtainable from a battery or other voltage source. The use of the variable resistor to vary current is explained in Chapter 9 (page 57). How it is used to vary voltage is a little more complicated.

Potential dividers

Consider the circuit shown in Figure 47.5.

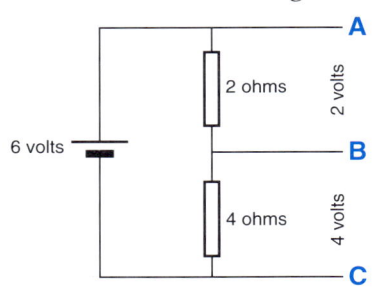

fig. 47.5

Two resistors are connected across the battery, so that each is getting a share of the 6 volts from the battery. The resistors divide the voltage in proportion to their resistances, so there is a voltage or potential difference of 2 volts between points A and B, and 4 volts between B and C. This arrangement is called a **potential divider**. By changing the ratio of the two resistors, any desired voltage (up to 6 volts) may be obtained.

Potentiometers

Using the same principle, a variable resistor can be used to continuously vary the available voltage from a battery. In the circuit shown in Figure 47.6, a variable resistor is connected across the battery, and as it is shown, the sliding contact is two thirds of the way up the resistance coil. So the arrangement is similar to that shown in (Figure 47.5). Thus, a voltage or potential difference of 4 volts is available between points B and C, (and 2 volts from points A and B).

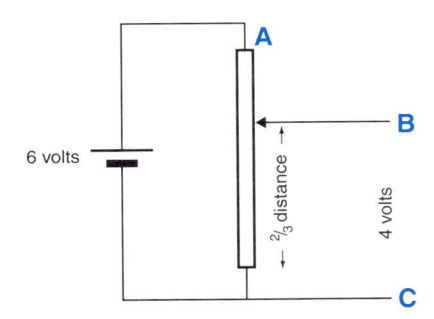

fig. 47.6

Now imagine the slide of the variable resistor being moved down to the half way position. The 6 volts will then be equally divided, and there will be 3 volts available between B and C. Conversely, if the slide is moved upwards to, say, $5/6$ of the total distance, then there will be 5 volts between B and C. So, the voltage can be varied between zero (slide fully down) and the full battery voltage (slide fully up). When it is used like this, a variable resistor is called a **potentiometer**. The volume and tone controls of radios, and the brightness and contrast controls of TVs and computer screens are potentiometers.

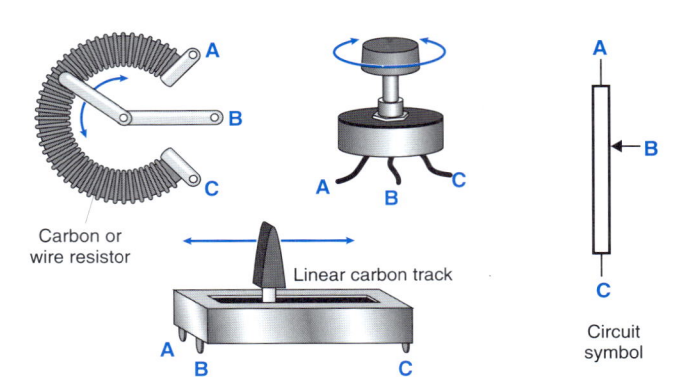

fig. 47.7 Some variable resistors

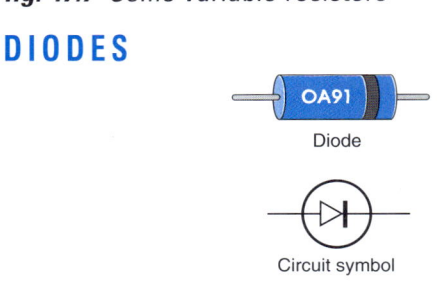

DIODES

fig. 47.8

Diodes are devices that allow current to flow in one direction only. The following two circuits show what happens. In circuit A, the diode is connected the 'right way round'. This means that the negative terminal of the battery is connected to the negative end (the cathode) of the diode. It conducts electricity and so the bulb lights. Connected like this, it is said to be **forward biassed**.

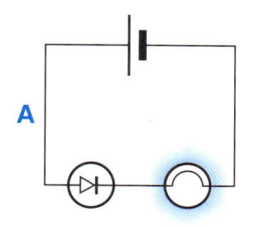

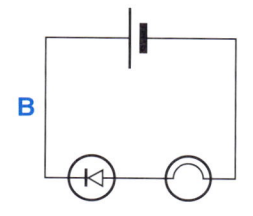

fig. 47.9 Diodes in circuits;
(A) forward biassed, (B) reverse biassed

In circuit B, the positive terminal of the battery is connected to the negative end of the diode. The diode then 'blocks' the current so no current flows When connected like this, it is said to be **reverse biassed**.

The band near one end of the diode indicates the cathode end, and the arrow on the symbol shows the direction in which the current can flow.

Use of diodes

Like other electronic components such as resistors and transistors, the diode is found in practically every piece of electronic equipment. One of its important uses is in changing alternating current to direct current – a process called **rectifying**. Alternating current (a.c.) is current which is 'surging' back and forth, as distinct from the direct current (d.c.) from batteries, which is flowing in one direction only. Most electronic circuits work on direct current and in order to operate them from the mains electricity (which is alternating current), it is necessary to rectify it. 'Mains adapters', which covert a.c. to d.c., allow things like radios and tape recorders to be plugged in to the mains.

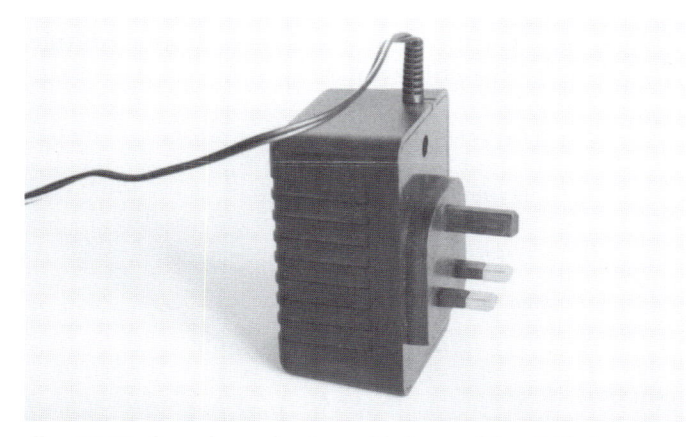

fig. 47.10 A mains adapter which provides 6 V, d.c.

When there is a diode in a circuit that is being supplied with alternating current, the diode lets through the forwards part of the alternating current, but blocks the backwards part. So the current that actually flows in the circuit is direct. (It is however, not a steady current, but can easily be made so.)

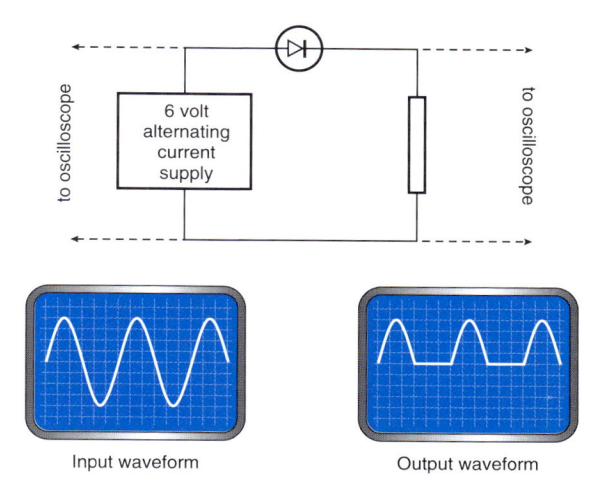

fig. 47.11 A rectifying circuit. Although the circuit is powered by an alternating current supply, a direct current flows. If an oscilloscope is connected where shown, it will display the input voltage (at the left-hand end) and the output voltage (at the right-hand end).

The diagram also shows the waveform of the input, and the output of the circuit, as would be displayed on a cathode ray oscilloscope.

Light-emitting diodes (LEDs)

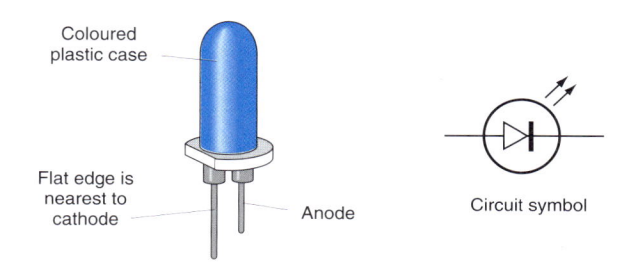

fig. 47.12

A light emitting diode (LED) is a diode that gives out light when current flows through it. Like all diodes, it only allows current to flow when it is forward biassed. An LED cannot carry a large current and in use, a resistor must be connected in series to limit the current passing through it. LEDs are used as indicators on radios, videos and many other electronic devices. LEDs can be used to display numbers. Seven LEDs, arranged as shown and lighting up in different combinations, can display any number from 0 to 9.

fig. 47.13 LED digits

47 • Electronics

LEDs are available in several different colours. The circuit shown below can be used to find out which terminal of a battery is positive and which is negative.

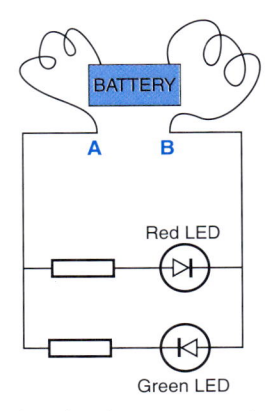

fig. 47.14 *Investigating battery terminals*

The battery is connected. If the red LED lights, it is the positive terminal of the battery that is connected to A, whereas if the green LED lights, the negative terminal of the battery is at A.

A simple water-level detector (1)

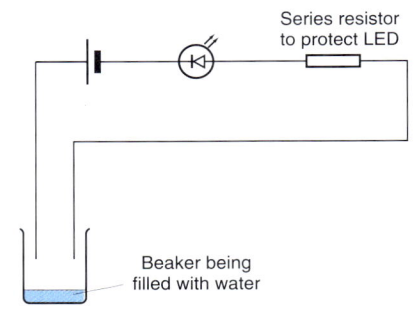

fig. 47.15

The circuit shown in Figure 47.5 is incomplete because there is a gap between the two wires in the beaker. If water is poured into the beaker, the LED lights up when the water reaches the level of the bottom of the wires. However, water is not a very good conductor of electricity, and the current that flows may not be enough to light the LED properly. The detector can be made more reliable by introducing a transistor into the circuit (see Figure 47.20).

The light-dependent resistor

fig. 47.16 *LDR; actual appearance (left) symbol (right)*

The light-dependent resistor (LDR) is a device whose resistance depends on the intensity of the light falling on it. In darkness it has an extremely high resistance (e.g. 1 MΩ) but in bright light the resistance can be as low as about 500 Ω. If an LDR is connected into a circuit with an ohm-meter (an instrument for measuring resistance), and the light intensity varied, it will be noticed that the resistance of the LDR changes: bright light $\Rightarrow$ low resistance, and dim or no light $\Rightarrow$ high resistance. Photographic light meters (for measuring light intensities) make use of LDRs.

LDRs are used along with transistors (next section), in circuits that control street lights, making them automatically switch on at dusk and off at dawn.

The thermistor

The thermistor is another frequently-used component in electronics. Its resistance changes with temperature, becoming low when the temperature is high, and high when the temperature is low. It is used in fire warning and frost warning circuits, or for sensing if the temperature in a freezer is rising, indicating a possible fault.

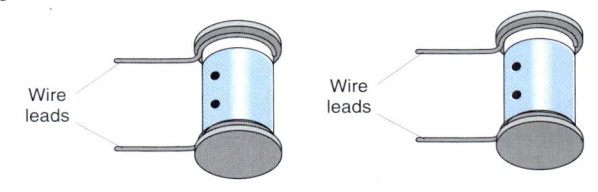

fig. 47.17 *A thermistor*

TRANSISTORS

The transistor is essentially a current-controlled switch. A transistor has three terminals, the **emitter**, the **base**, and the **collector**.

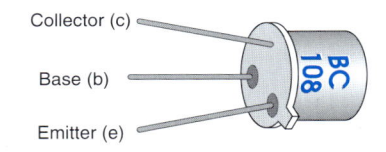

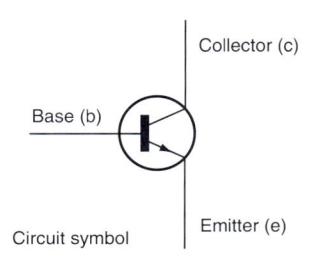

fig. 47.18 *npn transistor; actual appearance (top) symbol (bottom)*

There are two current paths through a transistor. The path for the main current is from collector to emitter* and this current is called the **collector current**. Collector current only flows when there is a small current, called the **base current**, flowing into the base. If there is no base current, the transistor does not conduct.

* For the npn type, which is the more common type of transistor.

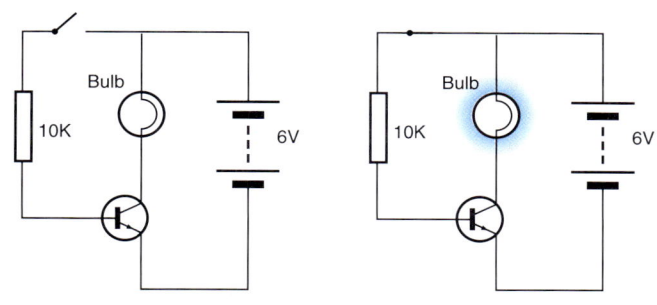

fig. 47.19 Transistor circuit

In other words, the main current flow through the transistor is controlled by the base current. A very small base current can cause a large collector current to flow. The diagram shows one type of transistor, but there are many different shapes and sizes.

A water-level detector (2)

Using a transistor, the simple water-level detector, described earlier, can be made more reliable. The circuit is as shown in Figure 47.20.

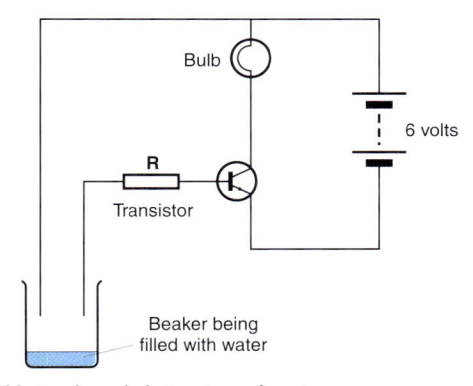

fig. 47.20 Water level detector circut

The difference is due to the amplifying properties of the transistor. A very tiny base current can produce a collector current large enough to light an LED, or to work a buzzer. When the circuit is completed by the water level reaching the wires, the circuit ABCD is completed: base current (even though very small) flows into the transistor, and the transistor 'switches on'. This means that a collector current flows and operates the bulb, buzzer or whatever else is in its circuit.

Such a circuit could be used for detecting the level of water in a storage tank. When the water level drops, the circuit could switch on a pump to refill the tank.

Light-operated switch

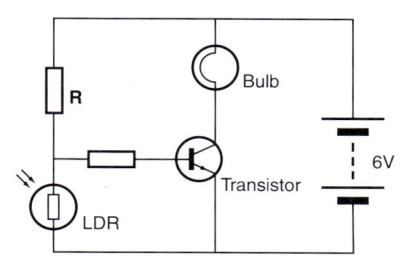

fig. 47.21 Light-operated switch

In darkness, the resistance of the light-dependent resistor (LDR) is very high. So the current flowing from R goes into the base of the transistor rather than through the LDR. The transistor is therefore switched on, and the bulb or LED in the collector circuit lights up. When the LDR is illuminated, its resistance drops, and the current from R flows through the LDR rather than into the base of the transistor. The transistor is therefore switched off; current in the collector circuit ceases, and the bulb goes out. The circuit could be used as an intruder alarm; when the intruder walked through an invisible beam of light, the circuit could activate a bell.

Temperature-operated switch

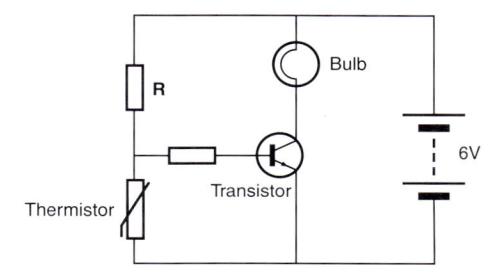

fig. 47.22 Temperature-operated switch

A circuit that could be used for frost-warning is shown in Figure 47.22. Its operation is similar to that of the the circuit containing the LDR. When the temperature becomes very low, the resistance of the thermistor becomes high, and the current from R goes into the base of the transistor rather than through the thermistor. The transistor is therefore switched on, and the LED, bulb or buzzer in the collector circuit operates. When the thermistor's temperature increases, its resistance drops, and the current from R flows through it rather than into the base of the transistor. The transistor is therefore switched off and the current in the collector circuit ceases. The circuit could be made to switch on a greenhouse heater if the

47 • Electronics

weather became very cold. It could also be altered slightly and turned into a fire alarm, so that it detects heat rather than cold.

TRANSDUCERS

These are devices that convert energy from one form to another. Some of them are described in the Chapter 3. The following are some common transducers.

Device	Changes	To
bulb	electrical energy	light energy
solar cell	light energy	electrical energy
bell	electrical energy	sound energy
dynamo	kinetic energy	electrical energy
loudspeaker	electrical energy	sound energy
microphone	sound energy	electrical energy
photocell	light energy	electrical energy
thermistor	heat energy	electrical energy
LED	electrical energy	light energy

SUMMARY

- As well as the following, refer to the summary of Chapter 9.
- A **diode** is a device that allows current to flow in one direction only. When the diode is connected so that it conducts, it is described as being **forward biassed**; when it is connected so that it blocks the current, it is **reverse biassed**. A diode can be used to rectify alternating current (this means converting it to direct current).
- A **light emitting diode** (LED) is a diode that gives out light when current flows through it. Like other diodes, it only conducts when it is forward biassed. LEDs are used as indicator lamps on electronic equipment.
- A **variable resistor** can be used to control current (it is then called a **rheostat**), or to control voltage (used for this it is called a **potentiometer**).
- A **light-dependent resistor** (LDR) is a resistor whose resistance depends on the intensity of the light falling on it – the more light, the lower is its resistance.
- A **thermistor** is a resistor whose resistance depends on its temperature – the higher the temperature, the lower its resistance.

- A **transistor** is a current-controlled switch. It has three terminals, the **emitter**, the **base** and the **collector**. There are two current paths through a transistor; the main current path is from the collector to the emitter, and this can only flow when there is a small current flowing into the base (and from there to the emitter). A very small base current can cause a large collector current to flow.

QUESTIONS

Q. 47.1

Write out the following paragraphs and complete the spaces in it.

(a) A diode allows current to flow through it in __ direction only. If the diode is connected the wrong way round, __ current can flow. A __ __ __ is often referred to as an LED. This device gives out __ when current flows through it, and a common use of this is as an __ in electronic equipment.

(b) The full name of an LDR is a __ __ __, and the resistance of this device depends on the amount of __ falling on it. Its resistance is high when the amount of __ is __, and the resistance is low when the __ is __.

(c) A transducer is a device that converts __ from one form to another. When a battery is in use, the __ energy in the battery is being converted to __ __, and if the battery is connected to a light bulb, the __ energy is then converted to __ and __.

Q. 47.2

For each of the following circuits, say what is the effect on the bulbs (A, B, etc.) of closing the 'starred' switches.

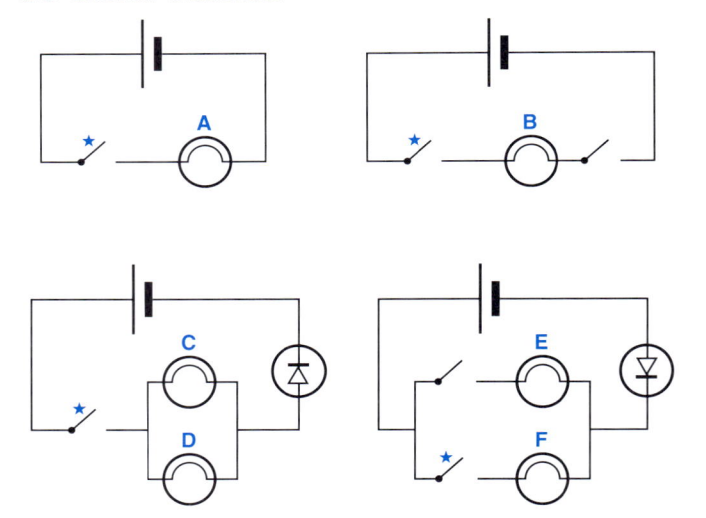

fig. 47.23

Q. 47.3
Refer to the circuit shown.

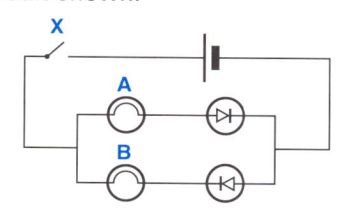

fig. 47.24

(a) If switch X is closed, which bulb will light?
(b) Explain why it can light.
(c) Explain why the other bulb does not light.

Q. 47.4
Refer to the circuit shown.

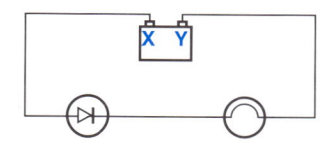

fig. 47.25

X and Y are the terminals of a battery connected in series with a bulb and diode. If both the battery and the bulb are in working order and the bulb fails to light, which terminal is positive and which is negative? Redraw the circuit and include the battery – connected so that the bulb does light.

Q. 47.5
Name the components shown in the diagram. Identify the lettered terminals.

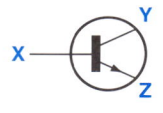

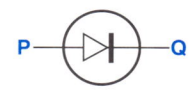

fig. 47.26

Q. 47.6
In which of the following circuits does the bulb light? Explain why it does not light in the other circuits.

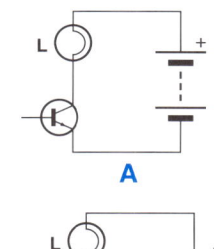

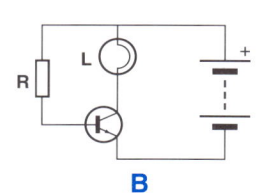

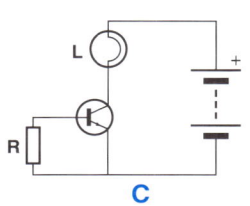

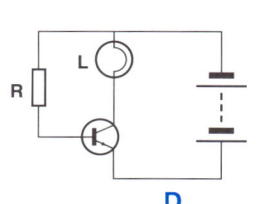

fig. 47.27

Q. 47.7
Refer to the circuit in Figure 47.28. Which path is taken by (i) the base current, (ii) the collector current?

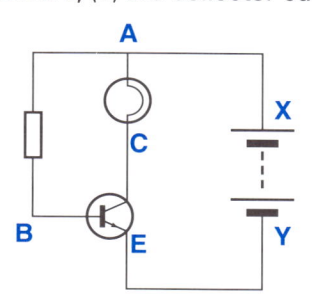

fig. 47.28

Q. 47.8
The diagram shows a transistor circuit.

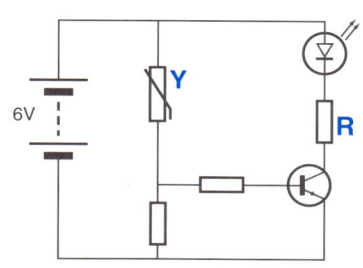

fig. 47.29

(a) Name the device labelled Y.
(b) State what happens to the resistance of Y when it is heated.
(c) Why is the resistor R placed in series with the LED?
(d) Suggest a use for this circuit.

Q. 47.9
The diagram shows a circuit which controls a lamp E.

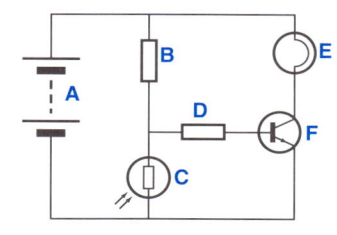

fig. 47.30

(a) Name the components A, B, C, D, E and F.
(b) What happens to C when light is shone on it?
(c) The lamp in the circuit could be replaced by an LED with a resistor in series with it. What is the function of the resistor?

Q. 47.10
What is the purpose of an electrical transducer? Name two electrical transducers. In each case state the function of the transducers you have named.

48

ENERGY CONVERSIONS

ENERGY CONVERSIONS 1

fig. 48.1 *In this steam train, the chemical energy in coal is converted to the heat energy of hot steam and then to the kinetic energy of the moving train*

At this stage, you should know quite a lot about energy. It was introduced in Chapter 3, and more about it is to be found in Chapters 11, 14, 15, 16, 21 and 28. So you see, it is a very important topic. To understand this chapter, it is particularly important to have a good understanding of Chapter 3. Important things to recall from earlier chapters are:

- energy is the ability to do work
- the Sun is the Earth's principal source of energy
- there are many different forms of energy
- potential energy is one form of stored energy
- kinetic energy is the energy possessed by a moving body
- energy can be converted from one form to another
- most of the machines found in homes, schools and factories convert energy from one form to another.

STORED ENERGY

Energy can be stored in two main forms: potential energy and chemical energy. **Potential energy** is the energy that a body has because of its position. The wound-up weights of a cuckoo clock (page 16) have potential energy because in falling down, they keep the hands of the clock moving. The wound up spring in the clockwork dinosaur (page 16) has potential energy because, as the spring unwinds, it makes the dinosaur move. The water stored behind a dam has potential energy because of its height above the ground in front of the dam wall (page 17).

Energy can also be stored as **chemical energy**. Fuels are stores of chemical energy because as the fuel burns, heat and light are produced. Batteries are stores of chemical energy because as the battery is being used, it produces electrical energy – which, in turn, is then converted to other forms of energy. Foods are stores of chemical energy, because, in your body, the food combines with oxygen and makes you warm (releases heat energy), enables you to move (kinetic energy), and talk (sound energy). The process of energy release from food is called respiration and it happens in the cells of the body.

Nuclear energy is also a store of energy, contained in the nuclei of atoms of some heavy elements like uranium and plutonium. Nuclear energy is explained on page 164.

Experiment 48.1
To show the release of heat energy from food

1. Half fill a test tube with water. Measure its temperature.
2. Support the test tube in a clamp attached to a stand.
3. Take a peanut on a needle or hold it in a pair of tongs.
4. Ignite the peanut in a bunsen flame and then remove it from the flame.
5. Hold the peanut under the test tube of water until it has burned away.
6. Note the new temperature of the water.
7. (a) Did the water get hot?
   (b) Where did the heat come from?
   (c) In what form was the energy stored at the start of the experiment?
   (d) In what form is the energy at the end of the experiment?

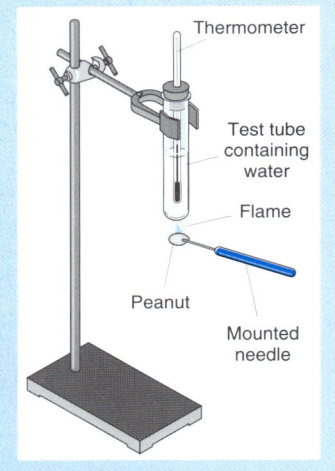

fig. 48.2

ENERGY CHANGES

Energy changes are happening all the time. In most of the activities you do, you are changing energy from one form to another. The table summarises some common changes.

From	To	Example
kinetic	heat	rub your hands together, file a piece of metal and then feel the file (do anything involving friction)
kinetic	sound	bang a drum, strike a tuning fork
kinetic	electrical	ride your bike with the dynamo working
chemical	heat	strike a match, light a bunsen, burn a fuel
chemical	electrical	use a battery
electrical	light	switch on a light
electrical	heat	plug in an electric fire
electrical	kinetic	use anything containing an electric motor
light	electrical	use a solar-powered calculator

Many everyday activities and/or machines involve several energy changes at the same time.

fig. 48.3 When you use a torch, chemical energy in the battery is converted to electrical energy which is then converted to light energy in the bulb

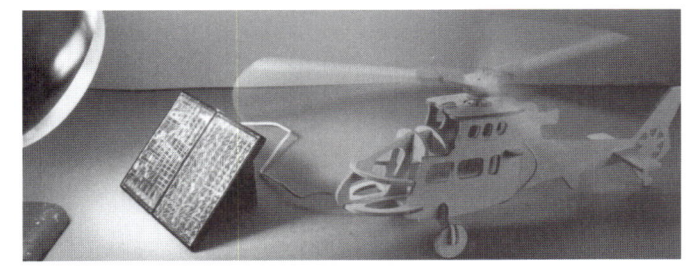

fig. 48.4 In this toy helicopter, light energy that falls on the solar cell is converted to electrical energy which is then converted to kinetic energy in the motor

Experiment 48.2
The 'cornflour bomb'

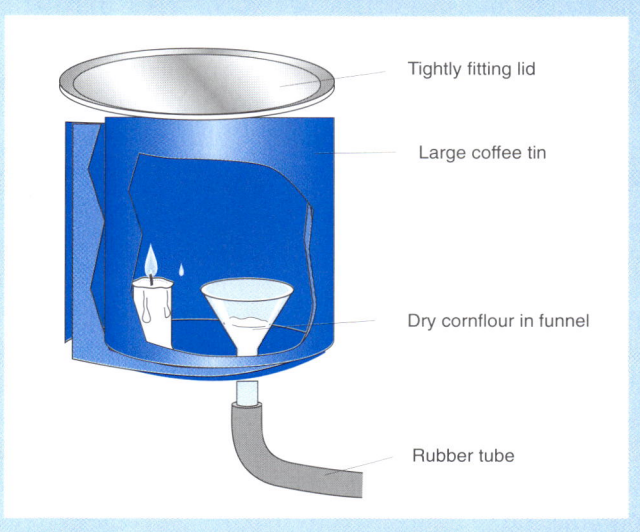

fig. 48.5

This piece of apparatus can demonstrate in a dramatic way the chemical energy of flour being converted to heat, light and kinetic energy. The apparatus is shown. To carry out the demonstration, the candle is lit, the lid placed tightly on, and the tube is sharply blown into. This distributes the cornflour as fine powder throughout the tin and in this state it instantly catches fire and burns – creating pressure, which blows the lid off the tin!

fig. 48.6

ENERGY CONVERSIONS 2 – ELECTROMAGNETISM

Electricity and magnetism are very closely related to each other. Electricity can cause magnetism, and magnetism can cause electricity. Electricity causing magnetism is used in electromagnets, electric motors and transformers, and magnetism causing electricity is used in dynamos, generators (large dynamos) and transformers.

ELECTROMAGNETS

An electromagnet consists of a coil of wire wound on an iron core. When a current flows through the coil, the core becomes a magnet. Electromagnets have an advantage over permanent magnets in that they can be switched on and off. They are used in places like scrap yards for moving scrap iron about. There is photograph of a large electromagnet on page 91.

Experiment 48.3
To construct an electromagnet

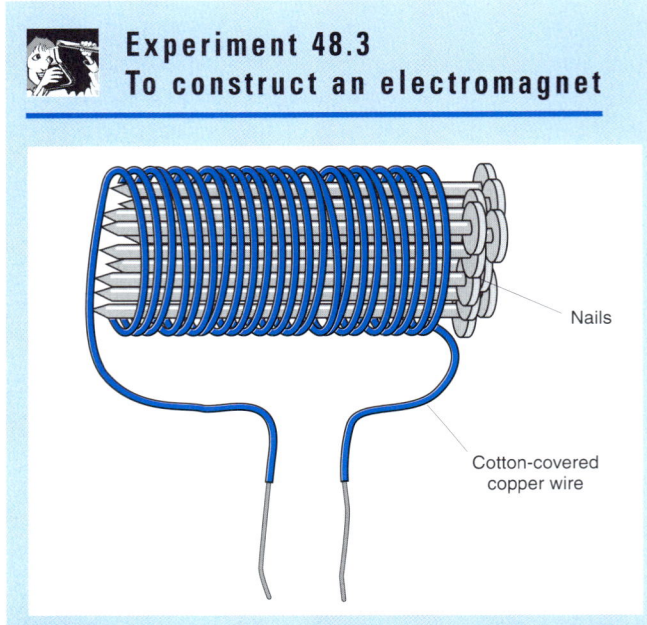

fig. 48.7

For this experiment you need a about 20 iron nails ('2 or 3 inch ovals' are about the right size) and about 5 metres of thin insulated copper wire (wire with thin insulation, such as cotton covered wire, is best). Gather the nails into a bundle and secure them with some sellotape; (this is the iron core for the magnet). Leaving about 30 cm of wire free, start winding the wire around the core – tightly and in layers and making sure that it doesn't slip over the ends of the core. When there are only about 30 cm of wire left unwound, bind the coil with more sellotape so that it can't unwind. Connect the two free ends of the wire to a battery and see how many paper clips or pins can be picked up. What then happens when the battery is disconnected?

The electric bell

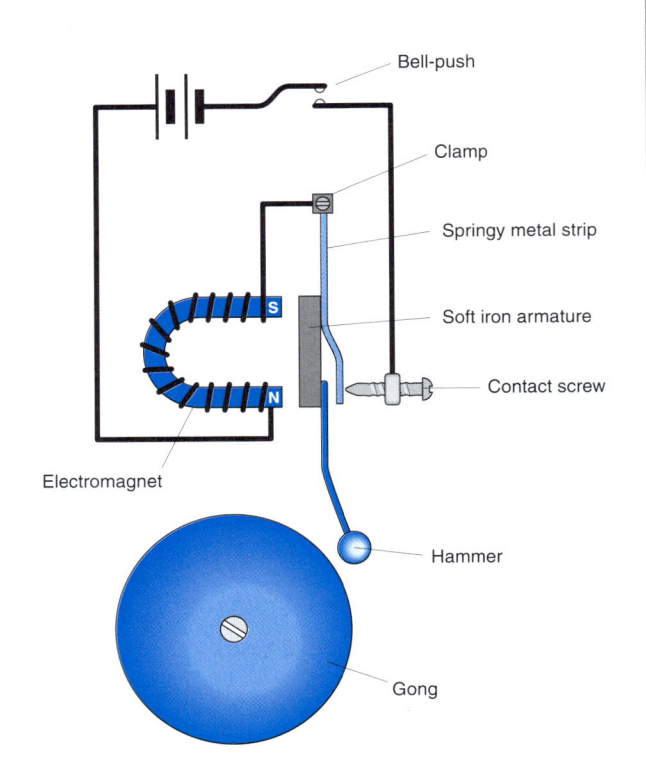

fig. 48.8

Small electromagnets are an essential part of many electrical devices like loudspeakers, remote-controlled door locks, electric bells. A diagram of a simple bell is shown. It works as follows. Pressing the switch (the bell push on the door) completes the circuit. Current flows and the electromagnet becomes magnetic. The movable iron armature is then attracted to the electromagnet, causing the hammer to hit the gong which then sounds. The other result of the armature moving is that the electrical contacts are separated and the circuit is broken. The electromagnet ceases to be magnetic, and the iron armature springs back. This means that the contacts close, the circuit is completed, current flows, and the whole cycle is rapidly repeated – as long as the switch is held closed.

The electric motor

Electric motors form the heart of hundreds of electrical devices ranging from household gadgets like juice extractors to huge industrial machines like cranes. An electric motor converts electrical energy to kinetic energy. It works because of an important property of an electric current. **When a wire carrying a current is placed in a magnetic field** (between the poles of a magnet), **there is a force on the wire** and the wire will move (if it is free enough to do so). This effect is easily demonstrated.

Applied Science • 48

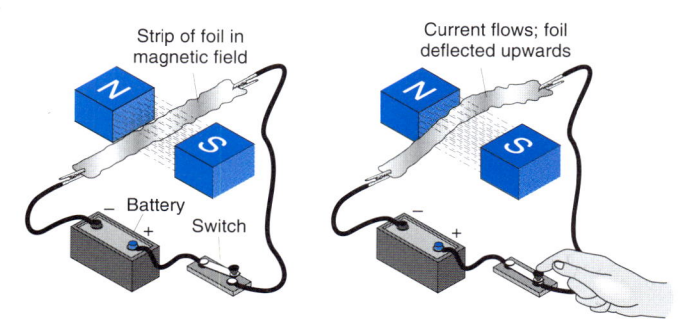

fig. 48.9 Method of showing the force exerted on a conductor in a magnetic field

Arrange the apparatus as shown in Figure 48.9. Aluminium tape is used as wire on account of its lightness. Switch on the current. The aluminium tape jumps either out of, or into, the magnetic field, depending on which way the current is flowing. Now reverse the direction of the current (reverse the connections to the battery). The wire jumps the other way. Electric motors work because of the force acting on current-carrying conductors in a magnetic field.

Experiment 48.4
To construct a simple electric motor

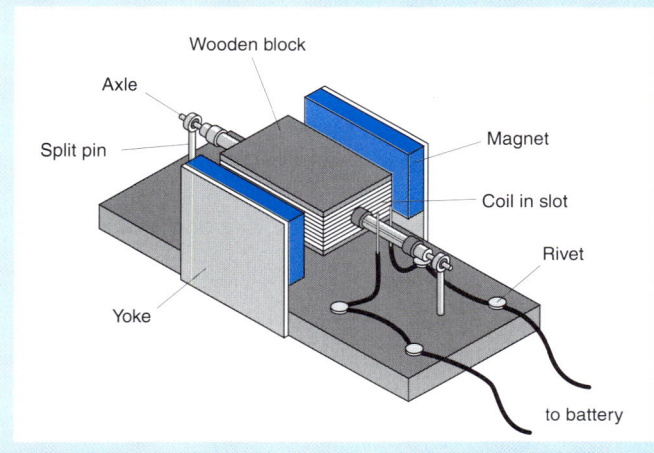

fig. 48.10

The motor described here is made from a kit of parts available for the purpose, and is assembled as follows:

1. Wind a layer of sellotape around the long end of the metal tube which passes through the wooden block (if the kit has been used before, this may have already been done).
2. Cut two small rings off a piece of rubber tubing and slip them onto the sellotaped end of the metal tube.
3. Remove about 4 cm of insulation from one end of the insulated wire, and fix this end under both of the rubber rings (see note below). The bare wire should be held tightly against the sellotape. This piece of wire is one side of the commutator.
4. Wind 10 turns of wire around the wooden block, in the slot provided. It should be wound neatly and fairly tightly. Now cut the wire, leaving enough to finish the other side of the commutator.
5. Bare the end of the wire, and fix the end underneath the rubber bands, in the same way as the start of the wire. However, the end of the wire must be on the opposite side of the metal tube from the start of the wire. This piece of wire is the other side of the commutator. The whole assembly (coil and metal tube with commutator on it) is the rotor (the turning part) of the motor.
6. Push the axle through the hole in one of the split pins, then through the metal tube of the rotor, and finally through the hole in the other split pin.
7. Arrange two $1/2$ metre lengths of wire to act as brushes (see diagram) and also as connecting wires to the battery.
8. Adjust the positions of the two commutator wires on the metal tube, so that when the coil is horizontal, they touch the brushes (which must be vertical). **This step is most important.**

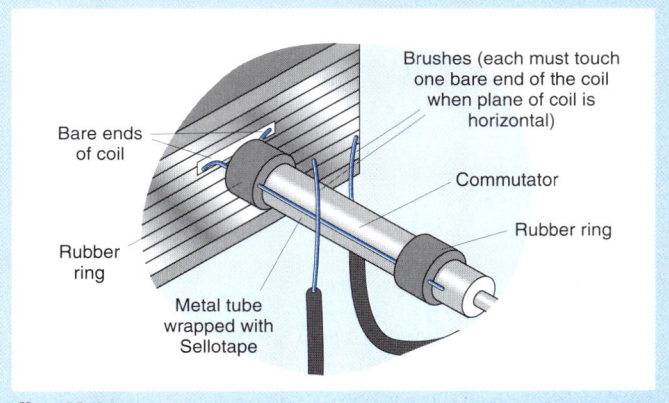

fig. 48.11

9. Attach the magnets, with **opposite poles facing each other**.
10. Connect to a 3 volt battery (or low voltage d.c. supply) and a slight push should start the rotor spinning.

Note that if, instead of using a single wire as the commutator, a doubled back wire is used, the motor will spin better. The doubled back wire enables contact with the brushes to be maintained over a greater part of a revolution, with a consequent increase in power.

48 • Energy Conversions

fig. 48.12 Inside an electric drill

The dynamo

You have just seen that electricity can cause movement. The reverse is also true: movement can cause electricity, and this property is used in dynamos and generators. In a dynamo, kinetic energy ('movement' energy) is converted to electrical energy. The dynamo principle is easily demonstrated.

fig. 48.13 Demonstrating the dynamo effect

The apparatus consists of a coil of wire connected to an electrical meter. When a magnet is moved into the coil, the meter shows that a current is produced. When the magnet is moved out of the coil, the meter also shows a reading (but in the opposite direction). When the magnet is stationary in the coil, the meter shows a zero reading. Conclusion: a magnet moving in a coil of wire causes a current to flow.

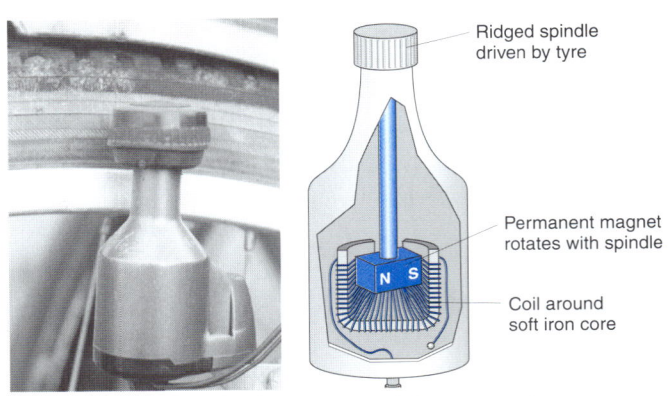

fig. 48.14 A bicycle dynamo contains a moving magnet inside a coil of wire

THE TRANSFORMER

A transformer is a device for changing an a.c. voltage from one value to another – which can be either greater or smaller. It consists of two separate coils of wire, a primary coil (the input) and a secondary coil (the output). The coils are electrically insulated from each other, but they have a common iron core. Magnetism in the core links the two coils together.

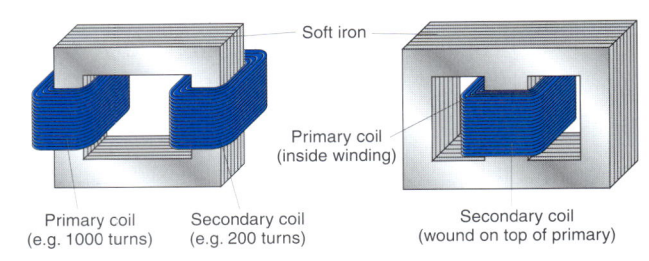

fig. 48.15 Two methods of transformer layout

The transformer formula

The output voltage from a transformer depends on the ratio of the number of turns of wire on the primary and on the secondary coils.

$$\frac{\text{secondary voltage}}{\text{primary voltage}} = \frac{\text{secondary turns}}{\text{primary turns}}$$

If the secondary coil has more turns than the primary coil, then the secondary or output voltage is greater than the primary or input voltage. Such a transformer is called a step-up transformer, and there is one of these in every television set – to provide the 16 000 volts that the picture tube needs (remember: the supply voltage to your house is 230 volts).

Conversely, if the secondary has a smaller number of turns than the primary, then the output voltage is less than the input voltage. This type is called a step-down transformer, and ones like this are used to power doorbells, model railways and are contained in mains adapters for devices like portable radios.

Worked example

Q. The primary coil of a transformer has 500 turns of wire, and the secondary has 20 turns. If the primary is connected to a 250 volt supply, what voltage is produced in the secondary coil?

A. Use the transformer formula:

$$\frac{\text{secondary voltage}}{\text{primary voltage}} = \frac{\text{secondary turns}}{\text{primary turns}} \Rightarrow \frac{V}{250} = \frac{20}{500}$$

Cross multiply:

$$500 \times V = 20 \times 250,$$
$$\Rightarrow V = \frac{20 \times 250}{500} = 10 \text{ volts}$$

fig. 48.16 *A transformer at an electricity distribution centre*

SUMMARY

- See summary of Chapter 3.
- Energy can be stored as potential, chemical and nuclear energy.
- The chemical energy in food can be converted to heat energy, kinetic energy, and sound energy.
- Electricity can cause magnetism; this effect is used in electromagnets, electric motors and transformers.
- Magnetism can cause electricity; this effect is used in dynamos, generators and transformers.
- The transformer formula is:

$$\frac{\text{secondary voltage}}{\text{primary voltage}} = \frac{\text{secondary turns}}{\text{primary turns}}$$

QUESTIONS

Q. 48.1
Name the three types of stored energy. What kind of energy is stored in food? Describe an experiment to show that the energy in food can be converted to heat.

Q. 48.2
State two energy conversions that take place in each of the following:
- **(a)** a ringing electric bell
- **(b)** a battery-operated torch in use
- **(c)** a hair dryer being used
- **(d)** a life or escalator which is ascending
- **(e)** a hydroelectric power station

Q. 48.3
Name an electrical device in which:
- **(a)** electrical energy is converted to kinetic energy
- **(b)** kinetic energy is converted to electrical energy

Name an everyday use of each of these devices.

Q. 48.4
For what purpose is a transformer used? Name two everyday devices that make use of a transformer.

Q. 48.5
You are asked to carry out an experiment to find out how the lifting power of an electromagnet depends on the current passing through it. Devise an experiment, and describe how you would do it. Use a diagram to illustrate your answer.

Q. 48.7
Draw a diagram of an electromagnet, and write an account of an experiment in which you constructed one. Describe how you tested the magnet.

Q. 48.6
The table below is about transformers. Copy it out, and fill in the missing values.

Primary turns	Secondary turns	Primary voltage	Secondary voltage	Step-up or step-down?
200	20	230		
400	8000	230		
500		125	5	
25 000	1000		500	

GLOSSARY

Note: Words in *italics* have their own entries. Consult these for more information.

Absorption The movement of food from the intestines into the bloodstream.

a.c. See *alternating current*.

Acceleration Increase in velocity per unit time.

Acid *Compound* containing hydrogen which can be replaced by a metal forming a salt.

Activity series A list of metals in decreasing order of reactivity.

Adaptation The way in which living things adjust to their surroundings so they can survive and reproduce better.

Aerobic Needing oxygen.

Alkali Substance that reacts with an acid forming a *salt* and water only.

Alkali metals The elements of Group 1 of the Periodic Table. They are lithium, sodium, potassium, rubidium and caesium.

Alloy A mixture of metals.

Alternating current Electric current which is constantly changing direction at regular intervals. (See also *direct current*.)

Alveolus Air sac in the lungs where gas exchange takes place.

Amino acid Chemical compound that forms the building blocks of protein molecules.

Amnion The membrane surrounding a developing *embryo*.

Ampere ('amp') The unit of electric current.

Amplitude The maximum displacement of any part of a wave from its mean (average) position.

Anaerobic Oxygen is not needed.

Anemometer Instrument for measuring wind speed.

Anhydrous Not containing combined water.

Anode Positive electrode (that which is connected to the positive terminal of a battery).

Anther The part of a flower that produces pollen.

Antibody Protein substance produced in the body that fights infection.

Antioxidant Chemical added to foods to stop fats and oils from decaying.

Aorta Main artery leaving the heart.

Antibiotic A chemical that kills off bacterial or fungal infections.

Artery Blood vessel that transports blood from the heart.

Asexual reproduction Reproduction that does not involve the union of sex cells.

Assimilation The conversion of nutrients into complex chemicals in an organism.

Atom Smallest part of an element that can exist.

Atomic mass The average mass of an atom of an element.

Atomic number The number of *protons* in an atom of an element.

Bacteria Single celled micro-organisms. Some cause disease but others are useful in food processing and decaying dead plants and animals.

Base A substance which neutralises an *acid* to produce *salt* and water only.

Bimetallic strip A device consisting of two different metals welded together; when heated, it bends into a curved shape.

Biomass energy Energy extracted from biological material (e.g. burning timber).

Biotechnology The use of biological organisms, such as plants, animals or micro-organisms to produce or process materials that are needed in today's world.

Bladder Part of the urinary system which stores urine before it is excreted.

Boiling The changing of a liquid to a vapour at a fixed temperature.

Boiling point The temperature at which a liquid changes to a gas or vapour.

Bond Force of attraction that holds atoms together.

Bronchiole A branch of the *bronchus* ending in the alveoli.

Bronchus One of the main branches of the *trachea* leading to the lungs.

Brownian movement (or motion) The movement of very small particles in a gas or liquid, caused by them being bombarded by the molecules of the gas or liquid.

Burning (see *combustion*)

Capillary Narrow thin-walled blood vessel linking arteries and veins.

Carbohydrate Nutrient needed in the diet whose main function is to provide energy.

Cardiac muscle The special muscle from which the heart is made.

Carnivore Animal that only eats meat.

Carpel The female part of the flowering plant.

Cartilage Tissue covering the ends of bones, which helps to reduce friction.

Catalyst Substance that speeds up a chemical reaction but without being consumed.

Cathode Negative electrode (that which is connected to the negative terminal of a battery).

Cell (1) Basic unit of all living material. (2) A single unit battery.

Cellulose Carbohydrate present in plants that is necessary for the formation of plant cell walls.

Cell wall Structure made of *cellulose* present in plant cells which gives strength to the cell.

Centre of gravity The point in an object where all its whole weight acts, or appears to be concentrated.

Chemical change A change in which a new substance is formed.

Chemical digestion The breakdown of food using enzymes.

Chlorination The addition of chlorine to water for the purpose of sterilising it.

Chlorophyll Green pigment in plants required for photosynthesis.

Chloroplast A structure in plant cells which contains *chlorophyll*.

Chromosome Strands of a chemical called DNA in the nucleus of a cell. Each chromosome contains *genes*.

Combustion (burning) Chemical reaction in which a substance combines with oxygen, and which is accompanied by light and heat.

Competition Where two or more organisms require scarce resources.

Complementary colours Two colours, which, when mixed, produce white.

Compound Substance composed of two or more elements chemically combined together.

Concentrated A solution in which a lot of the solute is dissolved (see also *dilute*).

Condenser Apparatus for converting a vapour into a liquid during distillation.

Condensing The changing of a gas or vapour to a liquid.

Condensation Water that has been condensed from water vapour.

Conduction (1) The process by which heat travels through solids. (2) The process by which electricity travels through metals.

Conductor, electrical A material through which electric current can flow.

Conservation The wise use of natural resources.

Conservation of energy, law of Energy can neither be created nor destroyed, but can be changed from one form to another.

Constant A quantity that does not vary (see *variable*).

Consumer An organism that takes in food.

Corrosion An undesirable process in which a metal slowly changes to an oxide or other compound of the metal.

Covalent bond A chemical *bond* consisting of a pair of electrons shared by two atoms.

Convection The transfer of heat through a *fluid*, by the upwards movement of the fluid itself.

Convection current The upwards movement of a heated fluid.

Crest The top of a *wave*.

Crystal A substance that has a regular arrangement of particles and therefore has a regular geometrical shape.

Current A flow of electric charge.

Cytoplasm Name given to everything inside the cell membrane except the nucleus.

Decay (decomposition) The breakdown of dead *organisms* by *bacteria* and *fungi*.

Decanting Method of separating a solid and a liquid by just pouring off the liquid.

Decomposer An organism that causes the breakdown (rotting) of dead matter into simple compounds.

Dehydration The removal of water from a substance.

Density The mass per unit volume of a substance; normally expressed in g/cm^3.

Diaphragm A sheet of muscle which separates the chest from the lower body and is involved in breathing.

Diffusion The spreading out of gases and liquids throughout any space into which they are put.

Digestion The breakdown of nutrients to make them soluble and allow them to be absorbed by the body.

Dilute A solution in which only a small amount of the solute is dissolved (see also *concentrated*).

Direct current Electric current that is flowing in one direction only. (See also *alternating current*.)

Dispersion The splitting up of light into its component colours.

Distillation A process in which a liquid is boiled and the vapour from it is condensed. (see also *fractional distillation*).

Echo A reflection of sound.

Ecology The study of the relationships between plants, animals and their *environment*.

Ecosystem A well-defined group of animals, plants and their environment, all interacting together.

Egestion The process of getting rid of undigested material from the intestines.

Electrode Conductors by which electric current enters and leaves a liquid.

Electrolyte A substance which, when dissolved in water or when molten, conducts electricity.

Electrolysis The decomposing of a compound by passing an electric current through it.

Electromagnet A *solenoid* with an iron core; it becomes a magnet when a current flows through the wire.

Electromagnetic spectrum The large band of rays or waves similar to light, and containing *infra-red, ultra-violet,* radio waves, etc.

Electron Negatively charged sub-atomic particle, of mass $1/1840$, and orbiting the *nucleus*.

Electroplating Process in which one metal is covered with a thin layer of another, for protection and/or improved appearance.

Electrostatics The study of static electricity (electricity at rest).

Element A substance that cannot be split up into simpler substances by chemical means.

Embryo A baby up to 8 weeks old in the uterus (see also *foetus*).

Emulsifier Used in food processing to help oil and water mix together.

Endothermic reaction A reaction that requires heat for it to occur.

Endocrine system The system of the body which is responsible for the secretion of hormones.

Energy The ability to do work; measured in joules.

E number A code assigned by the European Union for a substance that has been passed as safe for adding to food.

Environment A term to describe the surroundings in which an organism lives.

Enzyme A protein made by living things to speed up a reaction. Often referred to as a *biological catalyst*.

Epiglottis A flap of tissue that prevents food entering the trachea.

Equilibrium Term used to describe an object that is standing or suspended in such as way that it stays as it is. Equilibrium may be stable, unstable, or neutral.

Evaporation The changing of a liquid to a vapour (see also *boiling*).

Excretion The removal of waste products from the body.

Exothermic reaction A reaction in which heat is liberated.

Fatty acid A chemical compound formed as a result of the breakdown of fats in the diet.

Fat Nutrient necessary in the diet to provide energy.

Fermentation A chemical reaction brought about by enzymes or micro-organisms. It is used to make alcohol from carbohydrates and also releases carbon dioxide.

Fertile period The time during the menstrual cycle when intercourse is most likely to lead to *pregnancy*.

Fertilisation The joining together of a male and female gamete to form a fertilised cell (zygote).

Filtration Method of separating a solid and a liquid. The mixture is poured into a filter paper, which allows the liquid to pass through, but holds back the solid.

Fibre See *Cellulose*

Flammable (often referred to as 'inflammable') Describes a substance which is easily set on fire. The opposite term is non-flammable.

Fluid A substance which can flow, i.e. a liquid or a gas.

Fluoridation The addition of a fluorine compound to water supplies, for the purpose of teeth protection.

Foetus The developing baby in the uterus after 8 weeks.

Food chain A way of showing the feeding relationships between organisms.

Food web One or more interlinked food chains.

Force A push or a pull; measured in units called newtons.

Fractional distillation A form of distillation used to separate a mixture of liquids; it makes use of the fact that different liquids have different boiling points.

Freezing The changing of a liquid to a solid.

Frequency The number of vibrations or the number of waves occurring per second.

Friction The force that exists between surfaces that are rubbing together, and which tends to slow down their movement.

Fuel A substance that burns easily in air to produce heat energy.

Fulcrum The point about which a lever rotates.

Fuse A safety device in an electric circuit; it consists of a piece of thin wire which melts if the current flowing through it becomes too great.

Gamete A sex cell.

Gene A piece of DNA that carries instructions to allow the cell to form a product.

Genetics The study of inheritance.

Gland An organ that produces and secretes a chemical compound e.g. a *hormone*.

Glycerol A chemical compound formed as a result of the breakdown of fat in the diet.

Habitat Area where plants and animals live.

Haemoglobin The chemical that enables red blood corpuscles to carry oxygen to other cells of the body.

Halogens The elements of Group 7 of the Periodic Table. They are fluorine, chlorine, bromine and iodine.

Hard water Water that needs a lot of soap to produce a lather.

Herbivore Animal that only eats plants.

Hertz Unit of *frequency*, equal to one vibration or one wave per second.

Hormone A chemical 'messenger' that has a specific function; hormones are produced by a gland of the endocrine system.

Humus The decaying remains of plants and animals.

Hydrated Containing combined water.

Hydrocarbon Chemical compound consisting of hydrogen and carbon only.

Hydroelectricity Electricity that has been generated by falling water.

Hydrometer Instrument for measuring densities of liquids.

Hygrometer Instrument for measuring humidity.

Immiscible Does not mix with.

Implantation The attachment of a fertilised egg to the lining of the uterus.

Indicator A substance which shows, by means of a colour change, whether a substance is acidic or alkaline.

Induced magnetism Temporary magnetism in a piece of iron owing to it being in contact with or near to another magnet.

Inert Unreactive.

Inflammable See *flammable*

Infra-red rays *Electromagnetic* rays or waves of longer *wavelength* than light.

Insoluble Does not dissolve in a solvent.

Insulator (1) a material through which electric current cannot flow. (2) a material that is a poor conductor of heat.

Insulin A hormone secreted by the pancreas, which allows the body to control the level of sugar in the blood.

Interdependence The way in which plants and animals need each other for survival.

Invertebrate The term used to describe animals that do not have a back bone.

Irradiation The sterilising of food by exposing it to gamma radiation.

Ion An atom that has either lost or gained *electrons* and so has become either positively or negatively charged.

Ionic bond Electrical force of attraction between oppositely charged *ions*.

Isobars Lines drawn through places at equal atmospheric pressure.

Isotopes Elements having the same atomic number but different mass numbers, owing to different numbers of neutrons present.

Joule Unit of energy.

Kilowatt hour The unit in which electricity is bought. It is the amount of electricity supplied when one kilowatt is used for one hour.

Kinetic energy The energy possessed by a body because of its motion.

Latent heat The heat needed to change the state of a substance.

Latent heat of ice The heat needed to change ice to water at 0°C.

Latent heat of steam The heat needed to change water at 100°C to steam.

Lever A rigid body that can rotate about a fixed point called the fulcrum.

Ligament A tough band of fibrous tissue that attaches bone to bone.

Limewater Solution used to test for the presence of carbon dioxide.

Linear In a straight line.

Litmus A purple compound extracted from certain lichens and used as an *indicator*.

Luminous Term which means the giving out of light.

Lunar Relating to the Moon.

Magnification The number of times larger which an object appears to be when viewed through a microscope.

Mariculture The growing and harvesting of organisms that live in water.

Mass The quantity of *matter* in an object; measured in grams and kilograms.

Mass number The number of *protons* and *neutrons* in an atom of an element.

Matter Anything that has mass and occupies space.

Meniscus The curved shape of the surface of a liquid.

Menopause The age at which the *menstrual cycle* stops occurring in females.

Menstrual cycle A series of changes in the female body occurring about every 28 days.

Menstruation The loss of the blood-rich lining of the uterus in each *menstrual cycle*.

Micro-organism Organism that is too small to be viewed with the naked eye; examples are *bacteria,* some *fungi* and *viruses*.

Mineral Chemical substance needed in minute amounts in the diet; minerals form a vital part of plant and animal tissue.

Mixture Substance consisting of two or more different substances together, and with no chemical bonding between them.

Molecule Particle made up of two or more *atoms* combined together.

Molten Melted.

Moment The product of a force and the distance between it and the *fulcrum*.

Momentum The product of the mass of a body and its velocity.

Mucus A sticky substance produced by the lining of the breathing system.

Nerve A tissue through which impulses pass to and from the nervous system.

Neuron A nerve cell. A sensory neuron takes messages to the brain; a motor neuron takes messages from the brain.

Neutral (1) Neither acidic nor alkaline. (2) The wire in a 3-wire circuit that is connected to earth.

Neutron Uncharged sub-atomic particle, of mass 1 and occurring in the *nucleus*.

Neutralisation Reaction between an *acid* and an *alkali,* in which the properties of each disappear, and in which a *salt* and water are formed.

Newton The unit of force.

Noble gases The elements of Group 0 of the Periodic Table; they are helium, neon, argon, krypton and xenon.

Nuclear energy Energy which is stored in the nuclei of certain atoms and which is released when these atoms are split into smaller ones.

Nuclear fission The splitting up of unstable atomic nuclei with the release of enormous quantities of energy. (See *radioactivity*)

Nucleus (1) The 'core' or central part of the atom, containing *protons* and *neutrons*. (2) A region in cells that contains chromosomes enclosed in a membrane. The nucleus controls the cell.

Nutrient A substance serving as or providing food.

Nutrition The intake and use of food in animals.

Octet Arrangement of eight electrons in the outer shell of an atom.

Oesophagus The tube that transports food from the mouth to the stomach.

Ohm Unit of electrical resistance.

Omnivore An animal that eats both plants and animals.

Organ Part of an animal or plant that performs a particular function. Made up of groups of tissues.

Organism Term used in biology to refer to all living things.

Ovary The structure in plants and vertebrates, in which the female gamete (egg) is produced.

Ovulation The release of an egg from the *ovary*.

Oxidation The combining of a substance with oxygen or the loss of electrons from a substance.

Oxide Compound containing oxygen combined with one other element.

Parasite An organism that feeds on living plant or animal material.

Periodic Table Table of elements in increasing order of atomic number, and arranged in columns (called groups) and horizontal rows (called periods); devised by Mendeleev.

Peristalsis The forcing of food through the intestines by muscular action.

pH A scale of numbers from 0 to 14, on which acidity is expressed.

Phases of the Moon The apparent changes in the shape of the Moon as viewed from Earth, owing to the amount of sunlight falling on it.

Phloem The tissue in plants that carries food.

Photosynthesis The process in which plants produce their own food.

Physical change A change in which no new substance is formed.

Pigment A substance that provides colour in plants and animals, e.g. chlorophyll in plants.

Pitch The quality of a sound which depends on the *frequency* of the vibration causing it.

Placenta The structure linking the foetus to the lining of the womb.

Plasma The liquid part of the blood. It is mostly water but has many substances dissolved in it.

Plating The covering of one metal with another, usually for protection and/or improved appearance.

Platelet Cell fragment whose main function is to clot the blood.

Pollination The transfer of pollen from the male to the female part of a plant.

Pollution The presence of any unwanted materials in the environment.

Potential difference (or voltage) Electrical 'pressure', a measure of the strength of a battery, in units called volts.

Potential energy The energy possessed by a body because of its position.

Precipitate A solid that is formed in a chemical reaction and which settles to the bottom of the container.

Pregnancy The time during which a woman has an embryo or foetus developing in her uterus.

Pressure Force acting on unit area; can be expressed in N/cm^2 or N/m^2.

Primary colour One of the three colours which when mixed together produce white. The three primary colours are red, green and blue.

Producer An organism that can make its own food.

Proportional Describes quantities which are so related that if one doubles, the other doubles, or if one is halved, the other is halved, etc.

Protein A nutrient needed in the diet for growth and repair of body tissues.

Proton Positively charged sub-atomic particle, of mass 1 and occurring in the *nucleus*.

Puberty The stage in boys' and girls' lives when their reproductive organs begin to work.

Pulmonary Relating to the lungs.

Radiation The transfer of heat by means of invisible rays which travel outwards from a hot source.

Radioactivity The spontaneous breaking apart of unstable atomic nuclei accompanied by the release of radiation.

Reactant One of the substances taking part in a chemical reaction.

Red blood corpuscle A blood cell that contains haemoglobin and carries oxygen to other cells of the body.

Reduction A reaction in which a substance has oxygen removed from it, or in which a substance gains electrons.

Reflection The 'bouncing off' of light from an object.

Refraction The 'bending' of light when it passes from one medium into another.

Resistance The property of a material that opposes the flow of electricity; measured in units called *ohms*.

Respiration The process in which chemical energy is released by means of a series of chemical reactions in the body.

Response A reaction of a living organism to a stimulus.

Rheostat A resistor whose *resistance* can be varied.

Rickets Deficiency disease caused by a lack of vitamin D.

Roughage See *Fibre*.

Rust A brown oxide of iron.

Salt Compound formed when a metal replaces the hydrogen in an *acid*.

Saturated solution A solution that is holding as much of the solute as will dissolve.

Scurvy A deficiency disease resulting from a lack of vitamin C.

Secondary colour Colour produced when two of the *primary colours* are mixed together. The three secondary colours are cyan, yellow and magenta.

Sensitivity The ability of living organisms to react to what is happening around them.

Sexual reproduction The fusion of two sex cells to produce a new offspring.

Short circuit A connection, usually made accidentally, in which two points in an electric *circuit* are connected together, resulting in the *current* bypassing a device through which it should flow.

Silage Preserved grass used as feed for animals in winter.

Soft water Water that needs little soap to produce a lather.

Solar Relating to the Sun.

Solenoid A long, open coil of insulated wire, usually circular in cross section.

Solute The solid which is dissolved in a solution.

Solution (1) The answer to a problem. (2) A uniform mixture of (usually) a solid and a liquid.

Solvent The liquid in which a solid is dissolved in a solution.

Species The smallest natural group of organisms.

Spectrum The band of colours produced when light is *dispersed*.

Sphincter muscle Muscle which controls the opening from the bladder to the urethra.

Stamen The male part of a flower, made of the anther and filament.

Starch A carbohydrate produced by plants from a chain of glucose molecules.

Static electricity ('static') A build-up of electric charge on an insulator.

Stomata The tiny holes on the undersides of the leaves of plants, through which gas exchange occurs.

Stabiliser Substance which prevents water and oil from separating in processed foods.

Sterile Contains nothing living.

Stimulus A change in the surroundings of an organism that produces a response.

Sublimation The changing of a solid directly into a gas.

Sucrose A carbohydrate that results from the combining of two simple sugar molecules.

Surface tension A force in a liquid that pulls surface molecules inwards.

Suspension A mixture of a liquid and an finely-divided insoluble solid, which is evenly distributed throughout the liquid.

Synovial joint A joint at which there is movement.

System A group of organs of the body working together.

Temperature A measure of how hot or hot cold something is; its units are degrees.

Tendon An elastic fibre which attaches muscle to bone.

Testis (plural testes) The part of the male reproductive system that produces sperm.

Tissue A group of similar *cells* specialised for a particular function.

Thermometer Instrument for measuring *temperature*.

Thyroid gland A gland in the neck that secretes *thyroxine*.

Thyroxine A hormone produced by the thyroid gland which increases the rate of food breakdown.

Tog value A number indicating the heat insulating value of a material.

Trachea The tube (the 'windpipe') leading from the throat to the bronchi.

Transformer Electrical device for changing an *a.c.* voltage from one value to another.

Transpiration The loss of water vapour from the surface of a plant.

Transpiration stream The flow of water from plant roots to the leaves.

Tropism The growth *response* of a plant to a *stimulus*.

Trough (1) A basin-like vessel used in the laboratory for holding water. (2) The bottom part of a *wave*.

Turbine A device in which the flow of a liquid or gas produces rotation. (A turbine is often connected to a generator of electricity.)

Ultra-violet rays *Electromagnetic rays* or waves of shorter *wavelength* than light.

Upthrust The upwards force exerted on a body when placed in a liquid.

Urea Waste product of the breakdown of protein in the liver.

Urine The liquid stored in the bladder and excreted from the kidneys.

Uterus The part of the female reproductive system in which the *foetus* develops during pregnancy.

Ureter Tubes that transport urine from the kidneys to the bladder.

Urethra Tube through which urine is released from the body.

Vacuole A fluid-filled space within a plant cell.

Vacuum A space from which all matter has been removed.

Valency A measure of the combining power of an element, equal to the number of electrons that an atom of that element must lose or gain to become stable.

Variable A quantity which changes, e.g. the temperature of a room (see *constant*).

Vein A blood vessel that transports blood to the heart.

Velocity Distance travelled per unit time, in a particular direction.

Vena cava Main vein carrying blood to the right-hand side of the heart.

Vertebrate An animal with a backbone.

Virus A tiny organism that can only reproduce inside other living cells.

Vitamin Diet constituent needed in small amounts for good health.

Volatile Easily evaporated because of having a low boiling point.

Voltage See *potential difference*.

Volume The amount of space occupied by something (do not confuse with *mass*).

Wave A method of energy transfer through a medium by the vibrations of the medium but without any net movement of it.

Wavelength The distance between two successive *crests* (or troughs) in a wave motion.

Weight The downwards force exerted on an object by the Earth (or other body such as the Moon). Measured in newtons.

Welding The joining together of two metals by melting them together.

Womb See *uterus*.

Work What is done when a force moves something; measured in joules.

Xylem The tissue in plants that carries water.

Zygote The cell formed by the fusion of two sex cells.

INDEX

A

absorbency, 322
absorption, stage in nutrition, 214
acceleration, 71
acid rain, 173
acids, 168, 172
    acetic acid, 173
    citric acid, 173
    lactic acid, 173
    nitric acid, 174
    phosphoric acid, 173
    tartaric acid, 173
activity series, 190
adaptations to habitat, 265
aeroboard, 31
agar, 281
agriculture, 201, 202
AIDS, 279
air, 140, 142
alkalis, 168, 172
alkali metals, 159, 189
alloy, 125, 189
Alnico, 38, 190
alternating current, 97
altimeter, 82
altitude, 82
aluminium, 318
amino acids, 328
ammeter, 54
ammonia, 173
amperes, 53
amplitude, 112, 114
amylase, 215
Andromeda, 285
anemometer, 297
aneroid barometer, 82
animals
    importance of, 201
    recognising, 205
animal cells, 207
annuals, 306
    half-hardy annuals, 306
    hardy annuals, 306
antagonistic muscles, 236
antibiotics, 280
    in meat, 337
antibodies, 227
antioxidants (E300-385), 332
aorta, 229
Arcon mines, 323
argon, 162
arteries, 227, 228
assimilation, 214
astronomy, 2, 285
atmosphere, 140, 292
atmospheric pressure, 80, 296
atomic number, 161
atomic structure, 159
atoms, 123
atrium, right, 229
atrium, left, 229

B

bacteria, 280
barometer, 81
bases, 168, 172
battery, 54
beating tray, 268
bedding plants, 308
biceps, 236
biennials, 306
bimetallic strip, 63
biology, 2, 200

biomass, 21
biotechnology, 339
birth, 243
bladder, 232
blind spot, 238
blockboard, 325
blood
    blood flow through heart, 229
    components of, 227
    deoxygenated, 228
    functions of, 227
    oxygenated, 228
blood vessels, 227
Bohr, Niels, 161
boiling, 119
    boiling point, 67, 84
bonding, 177
botany, 2
bottled gas, 148
Boyle, Robert, 294
Boyle's law, 294
brass, 126, 190
breathing, 143, 219
breathing system, structure, 220
bromine, 164
bronchioles, 220
bronchus, 220
bronze, 190
Brownian motion, 122
bulb, 54
bunsen burner, 4
burette, 10
burning, 140, 143
butter, making, 337

C

cabbage white butterfly, 302
calcium, 234
callipers, 8
cambium, 312
canines, 214
capillaries, 221, 227, 229
capillarity, 155
capillary action, 155
carbohydrates, 212, 327
carbon dioxide, 141, 146
cardiac muscle, 229
carnivores, 204, 264
carpel, 258
cartilage, 235
catalyst, 141
caterpillar, 303
cathode ray tube, 160
caustic soda, 173
cell (battery), 54
cells, animal and plant, 207
    cell membrane, 207
cellulose, 327
Celsius scale, 67, 296
centre of gravity, 50
CFCs, 274
Chadwick, James, 160
characteristics of living things, 200
charcoal, 149
Charles' law, 296
cheese, making, 336
chemical, 136
chemical changes, 136
chemical bonds, 177
chemical symbols, 125
chemistry, 2
chipboard, 325
chlorination, 157
chlorine, 164
chlorophyll, 207

chloroplasts, 207
chromosomes, 244
circuits
    parallel, 55
    series, 55
    short, 88
circuit breakers, 88
climate, 297
clouds, 293
coal, 148
cobalt chloride paper, 155, 219
colour, 106
    complementary colours, 106
    primary colours, 106
    secondary colours, 106
combustion, 143
commerce, 202
compass, 39
competition amongst species, 265
composts, 300
compounds, 123, 125
concave lens, 105
concentrate, 130
condensation, 292
condenser, 132
condensing, 119
conduction, 29
conductors, 55
conservation, 202, 273
consumers, 204, 264
contraception (family planning), 243
convection, 29, 32
    convection current, 32
convex lens, 105
copper sulphate, 155, 173
cornea, 238
cornflour bomb, 349
corrosion, 191
covalent bonding, 179
cupro-nickel, 190
current
    potential, 53
    difference, 53
curved lines, 8
cut flowers, 313
cuttings, 310
cytoplasm, 207

D

dairy industry, 335
Dalton, John, 160
day and night, 287
deadheading flowers, 308
decanting, 132
decay, 265
decomposers, 265
deforestation, 274
density, 42
desertification, 274
destarched plant, 249
dew, 292
diaphragm, 220
diet, balanced, 213, 331
diffusion, 121
digestion, 212, 214, 215
dilute, 130
diodes, 342
direct current, 97
disclosing tablets, 214
dispersal of seeds, 259
dispersion of light, 105
distance/time graphs, 73
distillation, 132
    fractional distillation, 133
dormancy in seeds, 309
double glazing, 31

dry cell, 195
dry ice, 146
dynamo, 352

E

E numbers, 332
Earth, 288
earthing, 89, 98
echo, 110
eclipse
    lunar, 102
    solar, 102
ecology, 263
ecosystems, 263
egestion, 214
ejaculation, 242
electricity, 93, 194
    electric bell, 350
    electric charges, 53, 58
    electric circuits, 53
    electric current, effects of 87
    electric motor, 350
    electrical power, 94
electrochemistry, 179
electrolysis, 153, 195, 196
electromagnetic spectrum, 107
electromagnetism, 89, 350
electromagnets, 90, 350
electronics, 341
electrons, 60, 160
    structures, 161
electroplating, 196
electrostatic force, 24
element, 87, 123
emulsifiers (E400–E495), 332
endocrine system, 237, 239
endothermic reactions, 138
energy, 15, 75, 101
    alternative sources, 20
    chemical energy, 15
    changes, 349
    conversions, 348
    flow, 265
    heat energy, 15
    kinetic energy, 15
    nuclear energy, 18, 164, 348
    potential energy, 15, 348
    renewable sources of, 20
    stored energy, 348
    wave energy, 21
    wind energy, 21
enzymes, 215
equations, chemical, 181
equilibrium, 50
evaporation, 119, 292
excretion, 201, 231
excretory organs, 232
exothermic reactions, 138
expansion
    of gases, 64
    of liquids, 64
    of solids, 63
    of water, 66
eye, 238
fat, 212

F

fermentation, 338
fertile period, 242
fertilisation, 242
fibre, 327
fieldwork, 266
filtration, 131
fire, 148
    fire triangle, 149
    fire extinguishers, 150

flame proofing, 320
Fleming, Sir Alexander, 280
floating, 44
flower, 248, 258
fluoridation, 157
fluorine, 164
foetus, 243
fog, 293
food, 212
    food energy values, 331
    food labels, 333
    food preservation, 333
    food processing, 335
food additives, 332
    advantages of, 332
    disadvantages of, 332
    food colourings, 332
food chain, 204, 264
food supply, world, 331
food web, 266
force, 23
forestry, 325
formulae, chemical, 181
fossil fuels, 19
fractional distillation, 133
Franklin, Benjamin, 59
freezing, 119
    freezing point, 67
frequency, 3, 112
friction, 24, 25
frost, 292
fruit, 258
fuels, 148
fulcrum, 46
fungi, 281
fuses, 54, 88, 98

G

gaseous exchange
    in humans, 221
    in other organisms, 222
gases, 117, 122, 294
gene, 244
genetics, 244
geotropism, 256
germination, 260
global warming, 298
glucose, 327
    use by plants, 249
grafting, 312
graphs, 72
grasses, 314
gravity, 23, 27
    centre of gravity, 50
greenhouse effect, 298
group number, 164
growth hormones, 338

H

habitats, 200, 263
    habitat key, 267
haemoglobin, 227
halogens, 160, 164
hard water, 184
hardboard, 325
hardness, 184
    permanent, 184
    temporary, 184
hardwoods, 324
hardwood cuttings, 310
Harvey, William, 226
heart, human, 228
    healthy heart, 230
heat, 29
heat radiation, 34

heating effect, 87
hedgerow, 269
helium, 145, 162
herbaceous, 306
herbivores, 204, 254
HIV, 279
Hofmann's voltameter, 153, 196
Hooke, Robert, 210
hormones, 239
horticulture, 300
humus, 277
hydrocarbons, 20, 318
hydrochloric acid (HCl), 171
hydrogen peroxide, 141
hydroponics, 301
hygrometer, 297
hyphae, 281

I

implantation, 242
incisors, 214
infra-red, 107
ingestion, 214
inheritance, 244
insemination, 242
insulators, 30, 31, 55
intercourse, 242
iodine, 164
    iodine solution, 210
ion exchangers, 186
ionic bond, 177
ions, 177
iris, 238
irrigation, 310
isobars, 83

J

joints
    ball and socket, 235
    fixed, 235
    gliding, 235
    hinge, 235
    pivot, 235
    synovial, 235
Jupiter, 288

K

kelvin scale, 296
key, to habitat, 267
kidneys, 232
kilowatt hour, 95
kinetic theory, 121

L

laser beams, 101
latent heat, 69
    of ice, 69
    of steam, 69
LDR, 344
leaching, 279
leaf, structure of, 248
leaves, 248
Leewenhoek, Anton van, 209
leisure, 202, 203
lenses, 104, 238
levers, 46
liebig condenser, 132
life of a star, 289
ligaments, 235
light, 101
light-dependent resistor, 344
light-emitting diodes (LEDs), 343
lightning, 59, 60
limewater, 141, 146

liquids, 117, 122
lithium, 159, 189
litmus, 168
litre, 10
loam, 300
loudness, 113
luminous, 4
lunar eclipse, 286
lungs, 221

M

Magdeburg hemispheres, 81
magnetism, 38
    Earth's, 40
    magnetic effect, 89
    magnetic fields, 39
maltase, 215
manganese dioxide, 141
mariculture, 201
Mars, 288
mass, 27
mass number, 162
materials, 318
matter, 117, 120
medowland, natural, 314
measuring, 7
meat products, 337
    antibiotics in, 337
medicine, 202, 203
melting, 119
    melting point, 84
Mendel, Gregor, 245
Mendeleev, Dimitri, 163
meniscus, 10
menopause, 241
menstrual cycle, 241
menstruation, 241
Mercury (planet), 288
mercury barometer, 81
metal ores, 323
metals, 188, 318, 322
methane, 21
micro-organisms, 279
microbiology, 277
microscope, 209
    magnification, 209
Milk of Magnesia, 173
Milky Way, 285
mineral nutrition, 251
minerals, 212, 330
mining, 323
mixtures, 125, 129
moisture in atmosphere, 292
molars, 214
molecules, 125
moment, 47
momentum, 75
Moon, 27, 285
    eclipses of, 286
    phases of, 285
motion, 71
    motion graphs, 72
motor, electric, 54
motor neurons, 238
mulch, 301
muscles, 235

N

natural gas, 148
neon, 145, 162
Neptune, 288
nervous system, 237
neutralisation, 171
neutrons, 160, 162
Newton, Sir Isaac, 23, 105

Newton's disc, 106
newtons, 23
nitric acid (HNO_3), 171
nitrogen, 145
nitrogen dioxide, 174
nitrous acid (HNO_2), 174
noble gases, 162
nuclear fission, 165
nucleus, of atom, 160
nucleus, of cell, 207
nutrient groups, 327
nutrition, 212
nylon, 318

O

octet rule, 177
omnivores, 204, 264
opisometer, 8
optic nerve, 238
organisms, 200
organs, 207, 208
oscilloscope, 112
ovulation, 242
oxidation, 191
oxides, 142
oxygen, 140, 143
ozone, 274

P

Pascal's vases, 79
pasteurisation, 336
peat, 148, 301
perennials, 306
period number, 164
Periodic Table, 163
perspex, 61
pesticide, 303
petrol, 149
petroleum, 149
pH scale, 169
phloem, 253
photosynthesis, 204, 207, 247
phototropism, 255
physical changes, 136
physics, 2
pipette, 10
pitch, 113
pitfall trap, 268
placenta, 243
plankton net, 268
plants
    absorption of water, 253
    cells, 207
    diseases, 302
    growth, 309
    importance of, 202
    pests, 302
    structure, 248
    recognising, 204
    responses, 255
    in plants, 252
plant growth, limiting factors, 309
plants, disease and pest protection
    biological control, 303
    chemical control, 304
    integrated control, 304
plasma, 226
plastics, 318
platelets, 226, 227
Pluto, 288
plywood, 325
pollination, 258
pollutants, 274
pollution, 173, 274
polystyrene, 318

polythene, 61
pooter, 268
pork, curing, 337
potassium, 159, 189
potentiometers, 342
power ratings, 95
premolars, 214
preservatives (E200-297), 332
pressure, 77
Priestly, Joseph, 147
prism, 105
producers, 204, 264
propagation, 306
proteins, 212, 328
protons, 160
puberty, 241
pulmonary vein, 229
pulmonary artery, 229
pupa, 303
pupil, 238

Q

quadrat, 269

R

radiation, 29, 34
radicals, 180
radioactivity, 164
radiometer, 17, 18, 101
rain, 293
rain gauge, 297
rectifying a.c., 343
recycling, 265
red cabbage indicator, 170
red giant, 290
red blood corpuscles, 226, 227
reduction, 191
reflection, 102
refraction, 103
reproduction, 200
reproduction, human, 241
    female reproductive system, 241
    male reproductive system, 241
reproduction, plant 258
    asexual, 258
    sexual 258
resistance, 55, 56, 94
resistors, 54
respiration, 201, 219, 222
response, to stimulus, 237
retina, 238
rheostats, 55, 56, 324
rocky seashore, 270
roots, 248
rusting, 191
Rutherford, Ernest, 160

S

salts, 170
sand filters, 157
saprophytes, 281
satellite, 285
saturated solution, 130
Saturn, 288
scale, 185
scion, 312
seasons, 287
sedimentation, 156
seed, 258
sensitivity, 200
    and coordination, 237
sensory nerve, 238
sensory neuron, 238

separating funnel, 133
septum, 229
short circuit, 88
sieve, 268
silage, 338
skeleton, 234
skin, 233
slinky spring, 111
smoking, 221
soap, 184
sodium, 159, 189
sodium chloride, 173, 178
softening water, 186
softwoods, 324
softwood cuttings, 310
soil, 277
solar system, 288
solar eclipse, 286
solar cell, 18
solder, 190
solenoids, 90
solids, 117, 122
solute, 130
solutions, 129
solvent, 130
sound, 109
sowing seed, 307
spectrum, 105
speed, 71
stabilisers (E400–495), 332
stamen, 258
star, life of, 289
starch, 249, 327
states of matter, 117
static electricity, 58
steel, 190, 318
stem, 248
sterile, 281
Stevenson screen, 297
stimulus, 237, 255
stock, 312
stomata, 249, 253
stopping, 311
sub-atomic particles, 160
sublimation, 119
substances, 117
sucrose, 327
sulphuric acid (H_2SO_4), 171
sun, 287
sundial, 102
surface tension, 154
suspensions, 133
sweep net, 268
switches, 54, 341
symbols, chemical 125
synovial fluid, 235
systems, in organisms 207, 208

T

Tara mines, 323
teeth, 214
    decay, 214
temperature, 12
tendons, 235
textiles, 320, 318
thermistor, 344
thermometers, 67
    maximum and minimum, 297
Thermos flask, 35
thinning out seedlings, 310
tides, 286
timber, 324, 325, 318
tissue, 207
tog value, 31
tone of sound, 113
tooth decay, 214

trachea, 220
transducers, 346
transect, 269
transformer, 352
transistors, 344
transpiration, 253
    transpiration stream, 253
triceps, 236
trophic level, 266
tropism, 255
troposphere, 83
trundle wheel, 8
Tullgren funnel, 268
tuning fork, 110

U

ultra-violet, 107
universe, 285
upthrust, 24
Uranus, 288
urea, 226, 232
ureter, 232
urethra, 232

V

vacuoles, 207
valency, 180
Van de Graaff Generator, 59
variable resistor, 54, 342
veins, 227, 228
veins, renal, 232
velocity, 71, 112
velocity/time graphs, 73
ventilation, 310
ventricle, right, 229
ventricle, left, 229
Venus, 288
viruses, 279
vitamin D, 234
vitamins, 212, 329
Volta, Alessandro, 54, 194
voltameter (Hofmann's), 153, 196
voltmeter, 54
volts, 53
volume, 9

W

water, 152, 330
    water cycle, 156
    water purification, 156
    water vapour, 141
    water supply. 79
waterlogging of soil, 310
watts, 94
waves, 111
    waveform, 114
    wavelength, 111
weather, 83, 297
weather vane, 297
weight, 27
white blood cells, 226, 227
white dwarf, 290
woody perennials, 306
work, 75

X

xenon, 145
xylem, 253

Y

yoghurt, making, 337

Z

zoology, 2